Jenneke van der Wal and Larry M. Hyman (Eds.)
The Conjoint/Disjoint Alternation in Bantu

Trends in Linguistics
Studies and Monographs

Editor
Volker Gast

Editorial Board
Walter Bisang
Jan Terje Faarlund
Hans Henrich Hock
Natalia Levshina
Heiko Narrog
Matthias Schlesewsky
Amir Zeldes
Niina Ning Zhang

Editors responsible for this volume
Walter Bisang und Volker Gast

Volume 301

The Conjoint/Disjoint Alternation in Bantu

Edited by
Jenneke van der Wal and Larry M. Hyman

DE GRUYTER
MOUTON

ISBN 978-3-11-063499-0
e-ISBN (PDF) 978-3-11-049083-1
e-ISBN (EPUB) 978-3-11-048842-5
ISSN 1861-4302

Library of Congress Cataloging-in-Publication Data
A CIP catalog record for this book has been applied for at the Library of Congress.

Bibliographic information published by the Deutsche Nationalbibliothek
The Deutsche Nationalbibliothek lists this publication in the Deutsche Nationalbibliografie; detailed bibliographic data are available on the Internet at http://dnb.dnb.de.

© 2018 Walter de Gruyter GmbH, Berlin/Boston
This volume is text- and page-identical with the hardback published in 2016.
Typesetting: Integra Software Services Pvt. Ltd.
Printing and binding: CPI books GmbH, Leck

♾ Printed on acid-free paper
Printed in Germany

www.degruyter.com

Preface

In the Spring of 2013 the two editors discovered that we had both perceived the need for a synthesis of the widespread Bantu phenomenon of what Meeussen (1959) had first identified as the conjoint/disjoint (CJ/DJ) alternation. Although other studies following Meeussen pointed out similar distinctions in other Bantu languages, often using different terms, we both noted that the reported cases could vary quite a bit from one language to another. We had independently written overview statements (which appear in revised form as Chapters 2 and 4 of the present volume) which told only part of the story. Van der Wal's was mostly concerned with the nature of the CJ/DJ distinction itself, how it varies across Bantu languages, and how it should be analyzed, e.g. whether as a manifestation of differences in information structure ("focus") or constituency. Hyman was more concerned with determining the origins of the contrast, its relation to other Bantu phenomena involving the verb, and the immediate after verb (IAV) constituent. It was (and remains) clear to us that the CJ/DJ distinction has broad implications both for Bantu and general linguistics. Given the richness and variation in the realization of the CJ/DJ alternation, we agreed that the time had come to assemble the considerable knowledge and data that had amassed over the past decades and attempt to establish a reference point for subsequent research.

At the 5th International Conference on Bantu Languages in Paris (June 12-15, 2013) we agreed that it would be beneficial to the field if we collaborated in a published work that could provide such a reference point. With the goal of assembling a group of papers that would deal with the intricacies of the CJ-DJ phenomenon in different Bantu languages, we contacted a number of colleagues to see if they would be interested in participating. After a smooth though extended writing and reviewing period, and a joint editorial week in Berkeley, the first editor supported in part by Darwin College Cambridge, the result is the present volume.

We would like to thank all the authors for their careful work in writing their own and reviewing other chapters, and for their patience throughout the process. We are also very grateful to the anonymous external reviewer of the whole volume, and the external reviewers of the chapters: Thomas Bearth, Leston Buell, Brent Henderson, Michael Marlo, Maarten Mous, Fidèle Mpiranya, Peter Muriungi, Malin Petzell, Gérard Philippson, and John Watters.

Jenneke van der Wal
Larry M. Hyman

Table of contents

Contributors —— ix

Jenneke van der Wal and Larry M. Hyman
1 Introduction —— 1

Jenneke van der Wal
2 What is the conjoint/disjoint alternation? Parameters of crosslinguistic variation —— 14

Hannah Gibson, Andriana Koumbarou, Lutz Marten and Jenneke van der Wal
3 Locating the Bantu conjoint/disjoint alternation in a typology of focus marking —— 61

Larry M. Hyman
4 Disentangling conjoint, disjoint, metatony, tone cases, augments, prosody, and focus in Bantu —— 100

Maud Devos
5 Shangaji paired tenses: Emergence of a CJ/DJ system? —— 122

Yukiko Morimoto
6 The Kikuyu focus marker *nĩ*: Formal and functional similarities to the conjoint/disjoint alternation —— 147

Ines Fiedler
7 Conjoint and disjoint verb forms in Gur? Evidence from Yom —— 175

Denis Creissels
8 The conjoint/disjoint distinction in the tonal morphology of Tswana —— 200

Sophie Manus
9 The conjoint/disjoint alternation in Símákonde —— 239

Nancy C. Kula
10 The conjoint/disjoint alternation and phonological phrasing in Bemba —— 258

Jochen Zeller, Sabine Zerbian and Toni Cook
11 Prosodic evidence for syntactic phrasing in Zulu —— 295

Claire Halpert
12 Prosody/syntax mismatches in the Zulu conjoint/disjoint alternation —— 329

Jean Paul Ngoboka and Jochen Zeller
13 The conjoint/disjoint alternation in Kinyarwanda —— 350

Ernest Nshemezimana and Koen Bostoen
14 The conjoint/disjoint alternation in Kirundi (JD62): A case for its abolition —— 390

Nobuko Yoneda
15 Conjoint/disjoint distinction and focus in Matengo (N13) —— 426

Language Index —— 453

Subject Index —— 456

Contributors

Koen Bostoen
BantUGent - UGent Centre for Bantu Studies
Ghent University
E-Mail: koen.bostoen@ugent.be

Toni Cook
University of KwaZulu-Natal, Durban
E-Mail: tonicook@gmail.com

Denis Creissels
Université Lyon 2
E-Mail: denis.creissels@univ-lyon2.fr

Maud Devos
Royal Museum for Central Africa
E-Mail: maud.devos@africamuseum.be

Ines Fiedler
Humboldt University Berlin
E-Mail: ines.fiedler@staff.hu-berlin.de

Hannah Gibson
SOAS, University of London
E-Mail: hg6@soas.ac.uk

Claire Halpert
University of Minnesota
E-Mail: halpert@umn.edu

Larry M. Hyman
University of California, Berkeley
E-Mail: hyman@berkeley.edu

Andriana Koumbarou
SOAS, University of London
E-Mail: 258539@soas.ac.uk

Nancy C. Kula
University of Essex
E-Mail: nckula@essex.ac.uk

Sophie Manus
Laboratoire Dynamique du Langage (CNRS) & Université Lumière Lyon 2
E-Mail: sophie.manus@univ-lyon2.fr

Lutz Marten
SOAS, University of London
E-Mail: lm5@soas.ac.uk

Yukiko Morimoto
Humboldt University of Berlin
E-Mail: mokochanluv@yahoo.com

Jean Paul Ngoboka
University of KwaZulu-Natal Durban
E-Mail: jeanngoboka@gmail.com

Ernest Nshemezimana
Ghent University
E-Mail: ernesto7620@gmail.com

Jenneke van der Wal
University of Cambridge
E-Mail: jennekevanderwal@gmail.com

Nobuko Yoneda
Osaka University
E-Mail: yonedanb@lang.osaka-u.ac.jp

Jochen Zeller
University of KwaZulu-Natal
Durban
E-Mail: zeller@ukzn.ac.za

Sabine Zerbian
University of Stuttgart
E-Mail: sabine.zerbian@ifla.uni-stuttgart.de

Jenneke van der Wal and Larry M. Hyman
1 Introduction

In this introduction we highlight some of the recurring issues with respect to the conjoint/disjoint (CJ/DJ) alternation and the results that can be drawn from the current volume. In Section 2 we group these issues into five themes. However, to fully appreciate the contributions of the following chapters it will be helpful to mention some of the salient features of Bantu grammar, which is the goal of Section 1.

1 Bantu basics and the CJ/DJ alternation

Most of the languages discussed in this volume have SVO as a basic word order. In addition, they all distinguish up to 20 noun classes, as visible in the nominal morphology and the agreement and concord patterns in the phrase and clause. More relevant to the CJ/DJ alternation is the verbal inflectional morphology. As summarized below, based on Meeussen (1967), a Bantu verb root can be extended and inflected by multiple prefixes and suffixes:

1	2	3	4	5	6	7	8	9
Pre-initial	Subject	Negation	Tense	Aspect	Object	Root	Extensions	Final Vowel	Post-Final

These slots are illustrated in the Luganda verb in (1):

Luganda
(1) à-   bá-   tà-   lì-   tù-   yìimb -ír   -á   =kô
    AUG- 2SM- NEG- F$_2$- 1PL.OM- sing -APPL -FV =17LOC
    1   2   3   4   6   R   7   8   9
    'they who will not sing for us a little'

As will become clear from the chapters in this volume, languages that display the CJ/DJ alternation inflect their verbs not just for TAM and polarity, but also for 'junctivity', that is, whether the verb takes a conjoint or disjoint form. This marking often interacts with the TAM segmental prefixes, suffixes and tones.

As an initial characterization, the Bantu CJ/DJ distinction refers to certain verb tenses which are marked with different allomorphs. These potentially correlate with differences in focus, constituent structure, and/or phonological phrasing. The terms "conjoint" and "disjoint" were first used by Meeussen (1959) in his description of Kirundi. He noticed that some conjugations form pairs and described them as expressing a difference in the relation of the verb with the element following it. Hence the term *conjoint* (< French, 'linked') for a sequence of verb and postverbal element that is very close, and the term *disjoint* ('separated, loose') for a structure in which the verb does not have such a close relation with a following element – if one in fact follows the verb. Meeussen (1959) gives the examples in (2) as an illustration of the alternation.

Kirundi (Meeussen 1959: 216)
(2)   a. CJ *Imuúngu*   *zi-rya*   *i-gĭti.*
              10.woodworms 10SM-eat 7.wood
              '(The) woodworms eat wood (and nothing but wood).'

   b. DJ *Imuúngu*   *zi-ra-ryá*   *uruugi.*
              10.woodworms 10SM-PRES.DJ-eat 11.door
              '(The) woodworms eat through the door.'

These conjoint and disjoint verb forms in Kirundi differ in various respects. For example, the disjoint form is marked by an extra prefix -*ra*- in (2b) and the tone on the verb differs. The conjoint verb form cannot appear finally in a main clause, whereas the disjoint form can (but does not need to). The interpretation is also different for the two verb forms: The conjoint verb form "highlights the following word" and the disjoint form "does not have a special relation with a possible following word" (Meeussen 1959: 106).[1]

The morphological marking in prefixes and suffixes is clearly illustrated in Manus' coverage of Símákonde, where she points out the following differential marking in the P2 remote past tense:

Símákonde (Manus this volume)
(3) CJ *tú-Ø-súm-ílé*   *sí-lóongo*
          1PL-P2-buy-FV   7-pot
          'We bought a pot.'

     DJ *tú-ndí-suûm-a*   (*sí-lóongo*)
          1PL-P2-buy-FV   7-pot
          'We bought (a pot).'

As seen, the CJ lacks a prefix, but is marked by the final suffix -*ílé*, while the corresponding DJ is marked by a -*ndí*- prefix and the final suffix -*a*. As also observed in the above examples, the CJ verb + object constitutes a single phonological

---

[1] In the original French, conjoint: "forme mettant en évidence le mot suivant" vs. disjoint: "forme sans rapport spécial avec un mot suivant éventuel".

phrase whose penultimate vowel undergoes lengthening. If the DJ form is followed by another constituent, the verb is typically phrased separately from this constituent.

One of the issues that arise throughout this volume is whether the CJ category should be identified only in cases where it contrasts with a DJ form, or wherever the CJ allomorph occurs. Thus, there is a difference in the definition of the CJ and DJ verb forms. The conjoint can be defined either by form (= Hyman and Watters 1984) or by contrast with the disjoint form (= van der Wal 2009). The difference can be seen in the relative and negative: Although the CJ/DJ contrast is typically restricted to the main clause affirmative (MCA), TAM marking in the corresponding relative clause affirmative typically resembles the MCA CJ form. TAM marking in negative clauses also often resembles the CJ form of MCAs. It should be noted that when an author states that CJ forms may not occur at the end of a sentence or utterance, what is meant is that the CJ form cannot occur finally *in a MCA*. Thus, although the Símákonde CJ verb form cannot occur at the end of a MCA meaning 'we bought', it can occur finally in a sentence ending with the relative clause 'the pot that we bought'.

With this background, we can turn to a discussion of the chapters in this volume and the linguistics issues to which they each contribute.

2 The broader issues addressed in this volume

Over the last decade it has become more and more apparent that cross-Bantu variation is found not only in the morphology that marks the CJ/DJ alternation (compare (2) and (3)), but also in the phonology, syntax and information structure. The descriptions and analyses gathered in the present volume clearly attest to this variation, and jointly provide the basis for a better understanding of the phenomenon. There are five areas in which we feel substantial progress has been made: (1) the description and methodology in studying individual languages, (2) the comparative perspective, (3) prosodic phrasing, (4) the interface between morphosyntax and information structure, and (5) the diachronic development of the CJ/DJ alternation. We take up each of these, in turn.

2.1 Individual languages

All of the chapters in this volume provide additional data in support of the analysis of the alternations in each language. This is particularly clear in the four chapters that provide a first description of (what looks like) the CJ/DJ alternation in

Símákonde (Manus), Shangaji (Devos), Matengo (Yoneda), and the Gur language Yom (Fiedler). These new data are crucial in understanding how the CJ/DJ alternation functions within the grammar of each language, as well as establishing the scope of cross-linguistic variation.

Further descriptive progress has been made by achieving more in-depth and systematic knowledge of the alternation in the remaining individual languages as well. Even if a basic description of the alternation was available before, much more fine-grained data and theoretically informed analyses are now available, especially for Kinyarwanda (Ngoboka and Zeller), Bemba (Kula), Kirundi (Nshemezimana and Bostoen), and Tswana (Creissels).

A third point to be mentioned here are the advances in methodology to which the chapters in this volume amply attest. Nshemezimana and Bostoen draw on data from a corpus of spoken and written Kirundi data, which is still quite rare in the field of Bantu linguistics. Particularly in the area of information structure, however, this method can provide invaluable insights into language function and language use. For Zulu, Zeller et al. use an experimental approach to study the interaction between syntax and prosody and test their hypotheses on more than just speaker judgements. Furthermore, in various other chapters a number of tests are brought together and are used to diagnose the influence of constituency (Halpert) and the logical independence of phonological phrasal marking from the CJ/DJ alternation, with which there is sometimes only partial overlap (Kula, Zeller et al., Creissels).

2.2 Comparative perspective

With more and more data and analyses for Bantu languages becoming available, Henderson (2011: 23) notes that "this descriptive and theoretical base makes formal micro-parametric work possible in ways that it simply was not 20 years ago. We now know it is not the case that once you have seen one Bantu language, you have seen them all". Typological Bantu research is a growing area, and the current volume adds to this in two ways: first, charting the variation in the CJ/DJ alternation Bantu-internally (Van der Wal) and with respect to other morphosyntactic focus-marking strategies (Gibson et al.), and second, comparing the CJ/DJ alternation to phenomena that are reminiscent of the alternation.

These latter phenomena discussed by Hyman include metatony, tone cases, predicative lowering and the presence/absence of the augment. These all concern the relation between the verb and a following element, just like the CJ/DJ alternation, but with crucial differences. First, whereas the verb is marked in the CJ/DJ alternation, it is the focused term that is marked in predicative lowering and tone cases. Second, the choice between the different forms is related to information structure and constituency for the CJ/DJ alternation, but seems to be automatic for most tone cases and for metatony. Furthermore, the phenomena analysed by Hyman all concern the element immediately after the verb, whereas the CJ/DJ alternation is shown by Gibson et al. to be in principle independent of the immediate after verb (IAV) position (cf. Creissels for Tswana).

On the basis of the lack of a sentence-final restriction, Devos argues that despite the similarities with the CJ/DJ alternation, the system of paired tenses in Shangaji is not the same, nor does it seem to be developing towards a typical CJ/DJ alternation. Morimoto and Fiedler, however, show for Kikuyu and Yom, respectively, that the alternating verb forms do display a sentence-final restriction and also correlate with focus. Especially when looking beyond Bantu languages, three points of interest emerge from this cross-linguistic perspective: third verb forms in addition to the CJ/DJ forms, multiple marking, and the relation between finality and marking.

The first concerns the existence of conjugations that seem to partly overlap or interact with the verb forms in the CJ/DJ alternation. These are for example the 'background form' in Yom (Fiedler) and the so-called 'exclusive form' in Changana (Sitoe 2001). Determining the precise environments in which these forms occur can help us determine the distribution and function of the CJ/DJ forms, e.g. establishing that the CJ/DJ alternation is determined by constituency, whereas the exclusive form is focus-related.

The second point is briefly brought up by Gibson et al., where the "double" marking of focus by both morphology and word order "triggers the question of whether either topological or morphological marking can be said to be the 'real' or primary focus marker". A clear example of multiple focus marking is found in Makhuwa, where focus on the object is apparent in the dedicated IAV focus position, the CJ form of the verb, as well as tonal lowering on the object itself. If economy plays any role in the structure of language, its acquisition and/or processing, then the point of departure should be either that each marking expresses a distinct property, or that one type of marking is dependent on another, but not that both express the same. It is therefore important to assess the exact relation between the various markings and the syntactic and information-structural factors (see also below on the independence of phonological phrasing). Furthermore, if it turns out that there is indeed multiple marking of a single function, it may not be an accident that it concerns focus: this is the highlighted part of the sentence, which should therefore be easily discernible for the listener and hence more clearly marked. With respect to the syntax/information structure interface, the broader question arises of how head vs. dependent marking of syntactic relations compares to, and potentially correlates, with term vs. verb marking for focus relations.

The third point of interest from the comparative typological view is the recurring set of consistent properties across these systems: 1) there is a finality restriction; 2) the verb form allowed in final position is the formally more marked one; 3) predicate-centred focus (verum, verb, and/or TAM focus) is associated with this final verb form, whereas term focus is associated with the other form; 4) this alternation is restricted to a subset of tenses; 5) this restriction is mostly restricted to main clauses. These co-occurring and jointly recurring properties require an explanation, which could at least partly be found in hypothesized diachronic developments (see Section 2.5), but a structural or functional explanation would be welcome in further research.

2.3 Prosodic effects

One of the most striking properties of the CJ/DJ contrast is how often it co-occurs with a contrast in prosodic marking. While this most commonly involves different tonal effects, the widespread phenomenon of Bantu penultimate vowel lengthening may also be implicated. Concerning tone, care must be taken to distinguish between morphological tones which may be assigned differently in CJ vs. DJ verb forms and tonal effects that are realized at the phrase level. A common pattern is for the CJ verb to join the following IAV element within a single prosodic domain, while the DJ verb form and the IAV element are phrased separately. Thus, one approach to the Kirundi examples seen above in (2) would be to provide different phonological phrasings, as in (4).

(4) a. CJ $(Imuúngu)_\varphi$ $(zi$-rya i-$gĩti)_\varphi$
        10.woodworms 10SM-eat 7.wood
        '(The) woodworms eat wood (and nothing but wood).'

   b. DJ $(Imuúngu)_\varphi$ $(zi$-ra-$ryá)_\varphi$ $(uruugi)_\varphi$
        10.woodworms 10SM-PRES.DJ-eat 11.door
        '(The) woodworms eat through the door.'

Meeussen (1959) proposes a rule deleting the verb root tone in CJ forms, which can apply in (4a), where the verb is not domain-final. In (4b) the DJ verb form is phonological phrase-final, and its high tone is not deleted. (In both examples the subject is phrased separately as in Bantu in general.)

Such prosodic effects are not limited to tone. Although penultimate vowel lengthening has significantly different phrasal manifestations in various Bantu languages (Hyman 2013), both Devos and Manus discuss cases where its presence vs. absence intersects with the CJ/DJ distinction. Thus, the Símákonde examples seen above in (3) exhibit the following differences in phonological phrasing:

(5)   CJ   (tú-Ø-súm-ílé   sí-lóongo)$_\varphi$ (one prosodic domain)
           1PL-P2-buy-FV   7-pot
           'We bought a pot.'

       DJ   (tú-ndí-suûm-a)$_\varphi$ (sí-lóongo)$_\varphi$ (two prosodic domains)
           1PL-P2-buy-FV   7-pot
           'We bought (a pot).'

When the verb is in the CJ form, only the noun object undergoes penultimate lengthening, whereas in the DJ form both the verb and the object undergo penultimate lengthening.

Given such overlaps, it is tempting to view the morphological marking of CJ/DJ and the two types of phonological phrasing as isomorphic. However, Manus, Kula, Halpert, and Zeller, Zerbian & Cook all show that phrasing is not sufficient to identify the CJ/DJ distinction. First, as several chapters point out, there often are similar phrasings within the noun phrase. Second, Halpert shows that we can find phrase-final prosody on forms with a segmentally CJ form (rather than the expected DJ prosody) under special syntactic conditions that lead to a surface-final verb (where material in the vP is not pronounced). Third, the phrasing differences may extend to verbal constructions and TAMs that do not contrast distinct CJ/DJ forms. Since the prosodic effects are not probative, it is better to simply determine the ways in which the independently identified CJ/DJ forms interact with the more general properties of phonological phrasing in the various Bantu languages. In other words, the existence of a of CJ/DJ distinction must be defined in strictly morphological terms, either by segmental prefixes and suffixes, or by the tonal morphology, i.e. tone that is introduced via the inflection morphology. This latter should thus not be confused with phrase-level tonal distinctions which may be general, e.g. joining or separating postlexical constituents, or quite specific, even idiosyncratic (Creissels). As indicated above, and in several of the chapters, the postlexical phrasings or domains may sometimes correlate with the CJ/DJ distinction, but they may also follow from other principles.

The above only gives a general characterization of the wide range of tonal complications that are reported in the different chapters and which bear on several broader questions:

i.   Is there ever a prosodic effect that is limited to the CJ/DJ distinction? We do not think so. Instead, it appears that prosodic domains have a broader function which comes to overlap with the CJ/DJ distinction, often imperfectly. For this reason, while previous literature has emphasized the tonal correlates of the distinction in Bemba, Kula concludes that the CJ/DJ distinction is not tonally encoded.

ii. How does the CJ/DJ distinction figure into the interface between prosody and focus? Maud Devos (pers.comm.) points out for Makwe that the choice between forming a single phonological phrase or not is determined by exactly the same pragmatic factors involved in the choice between a CJ and DJ segmental verb form. This raises the question as to why this independent phonological marking never applies across all tenses (as far as we know), i.e. why there are tenses that are "DJ only"? In most cases both the CJ/DJ distinction and phrasing are at best only partially effective in marking one or another type of focus.

2.4 The relation with focus

Although the alternation is ultimately related to focus in all languages, the more we look into the exact interpretation and the syntactic conditions for each individual language, the clearer it becomes that there are two fundamentally different types of alternation (Van der Wal). One is directly focus-based, whereas the other is based on constituency, with an indirect relation to focus. The contrast comes out particularly clearly in the comparison between the closely related languages Kirundi and Kinyarwanda. For Kirundi, Nshemezimana and Bostoen argue that the alternation is directly determined by information structure. More specifically, they claim that the DJ form indicates predicate-centred focus (see Güldemann 2003 and 2009 for this term). For Kinyarwanda, on the other hand, Ngoboka and Zeller show that the alternation seems not to be primarily determined by information structure, but rather by constituency. The relation with focus is in these cases an indirect one: the CJ form is licensed only if some element follows the verb within the same constituent, which is taken to be the verb phrase. The domain of focus is that same verb phrase. Therefore, both the CJ form and the focus are tied to the verb phrase, but not directly to each other. This is illustrated in the different choice of verb form for the two languages in a number of environments, one of which is subject inversion. In Kinyarwanda, a non-topical postverbal subject requires the use of the CJ verb form, since the verb is not constituent-final cf. (6). Conversely, the use of the CJ form in Kirundi subject inversion is only licensed if the postverbal subject is the narrow focus of the sentence, as evident in the focus particle 'only' in (7).

Kinyarwanda (Ngoboka and Zeller this volume)
(6) CJ *Murí iyo miínsi híigaga abáana baké.*
murí iyo mi-nsi ha-á-íig-aga a-ba-áana ba-ké
18.LOC 4.DEM 4-day EXPL-REM-study-IPFV AUG-2-children 2-few
'In those days few children studied.'

Kirundi (Nshemezimana and Bostoen this volume)
(7) CJ *Haákomaanga abagabo gusa.*
　　　　ha-á-ø-kómaang-a　　　　　　　　　　[a-ba-gabo　gusa.]
　　　　IMPRS-REM.PST-CJ-beat.the.ground-IPFV　AUG-2-man　only
　　　　'Only men beat the ground.'

The diagnostics for establishing whether the alternation in a certain language is sensitive to constituency or to focus have become clearer and more extended. Building on Buell (2005, 2006), Halpert provides a number of tests to establish that the alternation in Zulu is determined by constituency, for example the correlation with object marking, and the position of postverbal elements with respect to adverbs, vocatives and second objects. Similarly, Yoneda exploits the special case of Matengo, where the alternating forms are not only restricted by syntax (sentence-finality) and focus, but also differ in tense-aspect semantics. This unique set of interacting constraints allows her to hierarchize these three conditions, by testing what the language does in cases of conflicting restrictions. One such conflict arises when a speaker wants to express an intransitive verb in the present tense, but the present tense only has a CJ form and hence needs a following element. The results show that the syntactic restrictions on sentence-finality are always observed, while focus can only influence the choice of the verb form if the other restrictions are satisfied.

　　Another interesting point that comes up in various chapters is the *type* of focus that the alternation is linked to. More specifically, this concerns term focus being expressed on some element following the CJ verb form, and/or predicate-centred focus being expressed by the DJ verb form. From the chapters in this volume it emerges that all analyses take one of the forms as the neutral/default form (the "elsewhere" case) while treating the other form as more restricted in syntactic and/or information-structural terms (though not in morphological terms, where the DJ form is usually the more marked one — see also Section 2.5).

　　These points bear on various broader issues concerning the interface between syntax and information structure, specifically:
i.　Is there indeed a default or neutral form, and how can we see to what extent contrasting verb forms should be interpreted as a CJ/DJ alternation in a given language? Nshemezimana and Bostoen pose the question for Kirundi whether this should be seen as an alternation between verb forms, or just a marking of predicate-centred focus by means of morphology on the verb.
ii.　With respect to the fluidity between syntax and information structure, to what extent does each influence the word order, morphology and prosody of a language?

iii. What do sentence-final restrictions tell us about verbs and constituency? Not much attention has been paid to syntactic and/or IS restrictions that prohibit certain inflected verb forms from occurring sentence-finally. For the CJ/DJ alternation, this seems to be key, and such sentence-final restrictions are attested in more and more languages (see e.g. Yom and Kikuyu).
iv. How can we detect whether focus is a formal feature in the grammar? The CJ/DJ alternation seems to be a good test case, since it can be focus-based directly influencing the morphosyntax or constituency-based, where the focus interpretation is indirect, i.e. potentially not formally present in the syntax.

2.5 Diachronic issues

As mentioned in various places, it is an open question how the CJ/DJ alternation has come into being. On the one hand, both Güldemann (2003) and Nurse (2008) suggest that the alternation could have been present in Proto-Bantu, and Meeussen (1967: 109) explicitly reconstructs *-da- as a Proto-Bantu morpheme for "disjunct". In a footnote, Güldemann (2003: 355) speculates that this could have been developed from a verb meaning 'take' in a grammaticalising auxiliary construction. On the other hand, as evident in the chapters in this volume, the variation in the formal marking of the alternation across Bantu languages as well as language-internally across tenses, suggests that this is not the sole origin of the marking used to express the alternation. Any diachronic proposal should also take into consideration that similar distinctions are found outside Bantu, e.g. Fiedler on Yom in this volume and other examples cited in Hyman and Watters (1984).

Van der Wal (2010, this volume) suggests that verb forms can be "recruited" to express the CJ/DJ alternation in the diachronic stage of renewal, when there are two "layered" forms expressing the same tense. As Hopper and Traugott (2003: 124) note: "Rather than replace a lost or almost lost distinction, newly innovated forms compete with older ones because they are felt to be more expressive than what was available before." We can imagine that the renewed periphrastic (and hence more marked) form expresses focus on the verb itself, and the original (less marked) form is kept either with a neutral interpretation or strengthened to express focus after the verb (exaptation). This accounts for the fact that the DJ form has more pre-stem material, since its origins lay in a combination of auxiliary plus infinitive verb. This in turn explains the predicate-centred focus associated with the DJ form: it was originally a focus on the infinitive following the 'CJ' form of the auxiliary. This is still visible in the Matuumbi, Ndengeleko and Shangaji DJ(-like) verb forms derived from the verb 'to go' with an infinitive

(Devos and van der Wal 2010). It also accounts for the fact that the alternation is only found in a subset of tenses. This subset always includes the basic tenses, which are more prone to renewal (Bybee et al. 1994). In this way they develop a second morphological form which becomes available to produce the CJ/DJ contrast. Finally, this diachronic scenario also explains why the alternation is mostly restricted to affirmative main clauses, since we know that these tend to be more innovative, whereas subordinate clauses are more conservative (Hooper and Thompson 1973, among others). The DJ segmental morphology would thus be an innovation rather than a retention, which throws a new light on Meeussen's original reconstruction. Nevertheless, it is plausible that some alternation must have been present in the language in order to recruit new linguistic material to encode it. This is also what allowed Mauritian Creole to develop a similar alternation (Van der Wal and Veenstra 2015).

A further diachronically interesting pathway is the development from the DJ or more marked form to progressive aspect, as observed and analysed by Hyman and Watters (1984) and Güldemann (2003). The in-depth descriptions of the alternating pairs in Shangaji (Devos), Kikuyu (Morimoto), and Kinyarwanda (Ngoboka and Zeller) again attest to this recurrent property.

With respect to the diachronic relation between the CJ/DJ alternation and related phenomena such as metatony and tone cases, Hyman is convinced that "all of the above have multiple historical sources and are at least potentially interrelated" (cf. van der Wal 2006; Kavari et al. 2012). There appears to be a historical relation with the augment, where nouns that did not have an augment 1) typically form a close relation with a preceding verb, and 2) have a focus interpretation. This can be seen in the complement tone case (Blanchon 1999), augmentless nouns licensed in IAV focus position (Hyman and Katamba 1993 for Luganda) and tonal lowering in IAV focus position (Devos for Shangaji, Schadeberg and Mucanheia 2000 for Ekoti, Guérois 2015 for Cuwabo, van der Wal 2006 for Makhuwa). The (historical or current) presence of the augment blocks a close relation with the verb, which is visible in separate phonological phrasing, without a necessary focus interpretation (Hyman and Katamba 1993 for Luganda, cf. Halpert 2012 for Zulu). As Hyman shows, morphemes such as the augment and the predicative marker *ní leave high tonal traces behind that take on a new life of their own, e.g. as so-called tonal cases, metatony, or reinforcement of independent CJ/DJ marking.

These considerations relate to wider questions in diachrony, such as
i. How does the influence of syntax and information structure (Section 2.4) change over time from 'syntax-configurational' to 'discourse-configurational' word order and morphology, and vice versa?
ii. What are the circumstances under which such an alternation can develop?

3 Conclusion

Partly along the lines of the topics discussed in this introduction, the rest of the volume has been organized into four subsections, looking at the conjoint/disjoint alternation from a comparative perspective (Chapters 2 and 3), from the point of view of similar phenomena (Chapters 4–7), interfaces with phonology (Chapters 8–12) and with syntax and focus (Chapters 13–15).

Various points for further research have been identified above, from which two main conclusions can be drawn. A first conclusion is that in the area of the CJ/DJ alternation, as for other linguistic phenomena, the microvariation in Bantu is a fascinating and rewarding treasure chest for any linguistic research. Given this extensive crosslinguistic variation, a second conclusion is how important it is to analyse the CJ/DJ alternation on a language-individual basis.

Finally, we strongly believe that combining systematic descriptions of new data with broader comparative and theoretical perspectives is the way forward in African and general linguistics, thereby allowing us to discover more about the nature of human language in general. We offer the current volume in hope that it is a step in that direction.

References

Blanchon, J. A. 1999. 'Tone cases' in Bantu group B.40. In J.A. Blanchon & Denis Creissels (eds.), *Issues in Bantu tonology*, 37–82. Cologne: Rüdiger Köppe Verlag.

Buell, Leston C. 2005. *Issues in Zulu morphosyntax*. Los Angeles: University of California PhD dissertation.

Buell, Leston C. 2006. The Zulu conjoint/disjoint verb alternation: Focus or constituency? *ZAS Papers in Linguistics* 43. 9–30.

Bybee, Joan, Revere Perkins & William Pagliuca. 1994. *The evolution of grammar*. Chicago and London: The University of Chicago Press.

Devos, Maud & Jenneke van der Wal. 2010. 'Go' on a rare grammaticalisation path to focus. In Jacqueline van Kampen & Rick Nouwen (eds.), *Linguistics in the Netherlands* 27, 45–58. Amsterdam: John Benjamins.

Guérois, Rozenn. 2015. *Le Cuwabo: description linguistique dans un cadre historique et comparatiste de langues du Nord-Est du Mozambique*. Lyon: Université Lumière Lyon 2 dissertation.

Güldemann, Tom. 2003. Present progressive vis-à-vis predication focus in Bantu: A verbal category between semantics and pragmatics. *Studies in Language* 27 (2). 323–360.

Güldemann, Tom. 2009. Predicate-centered focus types : A sample-based typological study in African languages. Application for project B7 in the CRC 632 Information structure.

Halpert, Claire. 2012. *Argument licensing and agreement in Zulu*. Cambridge, MA: MIT PhD dissertation.

Henderson, B., 2011a. African languages and syntactic theory: impacts and directions, in: Bokamba, E., Shosted, R.K., Ayalew, B.T. (Eds.), 40th Annual Conference on African Linguistics, 15-25. Cascadilla Proceedings Project.

Hooper, Joan & Thompson, Sandra A. 1973. On the applicability of root transformations. Linguistic Inquiry 4.4: 465–491.

Hopper, Paul & Elizabeth C. Traugott. 2003. *Grammaticalization*. Cambridge: Cambridge University Press.

Hyman, Larry M. & John Watters. 1984. Auxiliary focus. *Studies in African Linguistics* 15. 233–273.

Hyman, Larry M. & Francis X. Katamba. 1993. The augment in Luganda: Syntax or pragmatics? In Sam Mchombo (ed.), *Theoretical aspects of Bantu grammar*, 209–256. Stanford: CSLI.

Hyman, Larry M. 2013. Penultimate lengthening in Bantu. In Balthasar Bickel, Lenore A. Grenoble, David A. Peterson & Alan Timberlake (eds.), *Language typology and historical contingency: In honor of Johanna Nichols*, 309–330. Amsterdam: John Benjamins.

Kavari, Jekura U., Lutz Marten & Jenneke van der Wal. 2012. Tone cases in Otjiherero: Head-complement relations, linear order, and information structure. *Africana Linguistica* XVIII. 315–353.

Meeussen, A. E. 1959. *Essai de grammaire Rundi*. Tervuren: Musée Royal de l'Afrique Centrale.

Meeussen, A. E. 1967. Bantu grammatical reconstructions. *Annales du Musée Royal de l' Afrique Centrale* 61.

Nurse, Derek. 2008. *Tense and aspect in Bantu*. Oxford: Oxford University Press.

Sitoe, Bento. 2001. *Verbs of motion in Changana*. Leiden: CNWS Publications.

Van der Wal, Jenneke. 2006. Predicative tone lowering in Makhuwa. In Jeroen van de Weijer & Bettelou Los (eds.), *Linguistics in the Netherlands* 23, 224–236. Amsterdam: John Benjamins.

Van der Wal, Jenneke. 2009. *Word order and information structure in Makhuwa-Enahara*. Utrecht: LOT.

Van der Wal, Jenneke and Tonjes Veenstra. 2015. The long and short of verb alternations in Mauritian Creole and Bantu languages. Folia Linguistica 49(1), 85–116.

Jenneke van der Wal
2 What is the conjoint/disjoint alternation? Parameters of crosslinguistic variation

1 Introduction

As mentioned in the introduction to this volume, there has been a growing interest in recent years in the phenomenon referred to as the conjoint/disjoint alternation (Creissels 1996; Ndayiragije 1999; Buell 2006, 2009; Van der Wal 2006, 2009, 2011; Halpert 2012). The fact that the title of this book refers to *the* conjoint/disjoint alternation suggests that this is a unified phenomenon, but the literature mentioned and the other chapters of this book show considerable variation in how the alternation manifests itself. The aim of the current chapter is to chart this Bantu-internal variation. The research questions for this comparative overview are thus, first, which properties have been associated with the alternation, and second, how these properties vary across Bantu languages. A third, more specific question is whether the alternation is primarily determined by focus or by constituency, i.e. whether the relation with information structure is direct or indirect. Before exploring the comparative properties and their variation, the rest of this introduction first discusses a working definition of the alternation, the terms that have been used in referring to it, and its geographical spread.

The alternation can informally be characterised as (otherwise interchangeable) verbal conjugations that differ in their relation with what follows the verb. Thus, in the following example from Makhuwa, the conjoint form (1a) indicates a close relation between the verb and the following element, and the disjoint form (1b) indicates a looser relation.

The initial research for this paper was carried out at the Royal Museum for Central Africa as part of the research project 'Grammaticalization and (Inter)subjectification' (GRAMIS), funded by the Belgian Science Policy. Additional research took place as part of the ReCoS project, European Research Council Advanced Grant No. 269752 "Rethinking Comparative Syntax" at the University of Cambridge. I am indebted to Leston Buell, Lisa Cheng, Kristina Riedel, Laura Downing, Denis Creissels, Lutz Marten, Maarten Mous, Maud Devos, Jacky Maniacky, Tonjes Veenstra, Ernest Nshemezimana, Tom Güldemann, Larry Hyman, Nancy Kula, Sophie Manus for discussion and data, and particularly Thilo Schadeberg for many discussions on 'junctivity' over several years, as well as an anonymous reviewer for JALL and the audiences at Syntax of the World's Languages IV in Lyon (2010) and Syntax Lab at the University of Cambridge (2012) where previous versions were presented. Any errors and specific views expressed in this chapter remain my responsibility.

DOI 10.1515/9783110490831-002

Makhuwa (P31, van der Wal 2011: 1735)[1]

(1) a. CJ *Nthíyáná   o-c-aalé   nramá.*
       1.woman   1SM-eat-PERF.CJ   3.rice
       'The woman ate RICE.'

  b. DJ *Nthíyáná   o-hoó-cá   (nráma).*
       1.woman   1SM-PERF.DJ-eat   3.rice
       'The woman ate RICE.'

More precisely, and based on the comparative study in this chapter, I propose the following working definition for the alternation, which will be considered in greater detail in the final section, but can be kept in mind throughout the following discussion.

(2) The conjoint/disjoint alternation is an alternation between verb forms that are formally distinguishable, that are associated with an information-structural difference in the interpretation of verb and/or following element and of which one form is not allowed in sentence-final position.

These properties can to some extent be seen in (1): the conjoint form cannot appear sentence-finally and the element following the verb is (part of) the focus, whereas the DJ form appears elsewhere and is allowed sentence-finally.

While the terms "conjoint" and "disjoint" were coined by Meeussen (1959) in his description of Kirundi, the phenomenon had been known under different names in Southern Bantu languages for much longer, e.g., Endemann (1876) for Sotho, Doke (1927) for Zulu and Warmelo (1937) for Venda. The labels that are used to refer to the alternation vary widely in these descriptive grammars, but the numerous terms can be categorised into the following five groups (cf. Güldemann 2003).

I. The first group refers to the form of the verbs: "short" vs. "long" or "abbreviated form" for the conjoint form. These terms are frequent in grammatical descriptions of the Nguni and Sotho-Tswana languages.

II. A second group takes the relation with the following element as the basis for the names. Here we find "conjoint/disjoint" or "conjunctive/disjunctive", but also "strong-bond/weak-bond", "stable/unstable", "independent/dependent" (e.g. Sharman 1956 for Bemba). A potentially confusing aspect of these terms is that for some authors the term 'strong' refers to the disjoint form (because it is strong enough to stand by itself and does not need a complement), whereas

---

[1] The Bantu languages are conventionally classified by a letter and a number, the letters referring to geographical zones, according to Guthrie's (1948) classification updated by Maho (2009).

for others 'strong' refers to the conjoint form (because there is a strong linkage between the conjoint verb form and the following element).
III. Some grammatical descriptions analyse the conjoint/disjoint forms as tenses distinguished with respect to time or aspect, such as 'continuous/simple' or a label for the disjoint form as 'progressive', 'present-present' or 'completive' (e.g. Ziervogel 1959 for Ndebele).
IV. Some terms have been coined based on the interpretation of the verb and/or the following element, like 'emphatic/unemphatic', 'definite/indefinite' and 'verb-focal/noun-focal' (e.g. Odden 1996 for Kimatuumbi). However, the term 'focus' can also be confusing, referring sometimes to the disjoint form because focus on the verb is implied and sometimes to the conjoint form when focus on the following element is implied.
V. The final group uses neutral labels: 'II/I' or 'A/B' (e.g. Endemann 1876).

Although all of these labels have a motivation, at least within the grammar of the language for which they are used, none of them adequately reflect the full extent of the alternation within the Bantu languages that have the alternation. In fact, in most cases the labels cannot be taken to reflect the main properties of the alternation even within one language. In this chapter (and throughout this volume), the terms 'conjoint' (CJ) and 'disjoint' (DJ) are adopted simply because these seem to be the terms used in current research. Furthermore, the relatively neutral expression 'verb form' is used to refer to the alternating conjugated verbs. These can be seen as two forms occuring in the same tense that are in some way connected as a pair. That is, they form pairs in most languages, but see Section 5.2 for exceptions.[2]

With respect to the geographical spread, all the languages for which an alternation is reported are Eastern Bantu languages – see Hyman (this volume) for related phenomena that seem to be complementary in Western Bantu. The languages with a CJ/DJ alternation range from Haya (J20), Kirundi, Kinyarwanda, Ha (J60) in the north, and Sambaa (G23), Bemba (M40), Tonga (M60), Lozi (K21/S30), Matengo (N13), Ngindo, Ndengeleko, Kimatuumbi (P10), Makonde, Makwe (P20), Makhuwa and Chuwabo (P30) in the centre, down to Venda (S20), Tswana, Sotho (S30), Xhosa, Zulu, Swati, Ndebele (S40), Tshwa, Tsonga/Changana, Ronga (S50) and Chope (S60) in the south. These are coloured in the map in Figure 1.

---

[2] Alternatively one can view them as different tenses in the sense of the French *tiroir*. This means that the two related tenses belong to two paradigms which are restricted by different syntactic and interpretational properties (Schadeberg 2004).

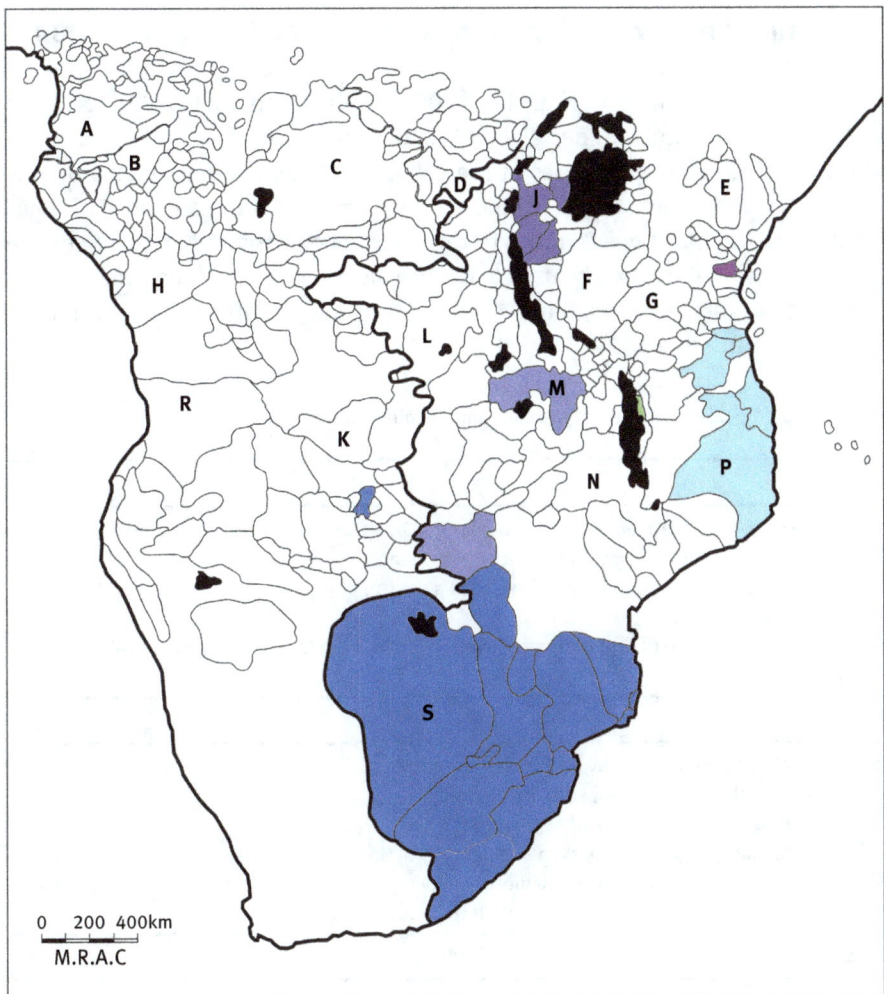

Figure 1: The geographical distribution of the CJ/DJ alternation

The remainder of this chapter is organised as follows. After setting out the parameters of variation in Section 2, each of the parameters is further discussed and illustrated in the subsequent sections: the distribution of the verb forms (Section 3), the formal properties of morphological and prosodic marking (Section 4), the tenses in which the alternation is found (Section 5) and the interpretational properties or association with focus on the verb and/or the element following it (Section 6). Section 7 mentions further extensions to the behaviour of the alternation for clausal complements and the nominal domain. Section 8 summarises and concludes.

2 Parameters of variation in the conjoint/disjoint alternation

In the same tradition as Marten et al. (2007), Marten and Kula (2012), Kavari et al. (2012), Marten and Van der Wal (2015), and further inspired by Güldemann's (2003: 328) recurrent properties of the CJ/DJ alternation, this chapter proposes 14 parameters that are relevant to the CJ/DJ alternation. These are mostly formulated as yes/no questions in order to register the constant and variable surface properties, which can then be used to deduce more fundamental parameters. The 14 parameters are subdivided into 4 areas: distribution, form, tenses, and interpretation, as in Table 1.

Table 1: Typological parameters of the conjoint/disjoint alternation.

Distribution
1. Is one form (CJ) restricted to non-sentence-final position in main affirmative clauses?
2. Is the other form (DJ) always final in its constituent?
2a. If object marking is non-doubling: does a post-DJ object obligatorily occur with an object marker?
2b. Is a post-DJ constituent obligatorily preceded by a prosodic break / pause?
2c. Do clitics take a CJ form?
Form
3. Is the alternation marked by segmental morphology?
3a. Is it marked by prefixes, suffixes, or both?
3b. Is only the DJ form marked segmentally?
3c. Is the alternation only marked segmentally in the present tense?
4. Is the alternation marked by tonal morphology?
5. Does phonological phrasing co-vary with the alternation?
Tenses
6. How many tenses participate in the alternation?
7. Do relative tenses have the alternation?
8. Do negative tenses have the alternation?
9. Is every CJ form paired with a DJ form in the same TAM?
Interpretation
10. Does focus require a particular verb form?
10a. Does predicate-centred focus require the DJ form?
10b. Do postverbal focused terms require the CJ form?
11. Does a particular verb form entail focus?
11a. Does the DJ form entail predicate-centred focus?
11b. Does the CJ form entail focus on an element following the verb?
12. Does the verb take the CJ form in thetic subject inversion?
13. Does the verb take the CJ form in VP focus?
14. Is there a dedicated postverbal focus position?

Table 2: Properties of 11 Bantu languages with the CJ/DJ alternation, where 1 = yes, 0 = no, and an empty cell represents a lack of (clear) data. A question mark indicates a strong suspicion but no clear confirmation.

	Kirundi	Kinyarwanda	Makhuwa	Matengo	Zulu	Tswana	Sotho	Bemba	Simákonde	Haya	Sambaa
1. One form restricted?	1	1	1	1	1	1	1	1	1	1	1
2. Other form always const-final?	0	1	0	?	1	1	1	0	1		0
2a. OM: post-V O in DJ dislocated?	0	1	n.a.	n.a.	1	1	1	n.a.	n.a.		n.a.
2b. Break: post-V O dislocated?	0	1	0	0	1	1	1	0	0		0
2c. Clitics take CJ form?	0	1	0		1						
3. Segmental morph?	1	1	1	1	1	1	1	1	1	1	1
3a. Pre/suffix?	prefix	prefix	both	both	both	prefix	prefix	both	both	prefix	both
3b. Only DJ marked?	1	1	0	0	0	1	1	0	0	1	0
3c. Only present tense?	0	0	0	0	0	1	1	0	0	1	0
4. Tonal morph?	1	1	0	0	0/1	1	1	1	1		
5. P-phrasing?	0	0	0	1	1	1	1	1	1	1	
6. How many tenses?	3 or 5	4+2	4	15	2+	1+12	1+12	10	3/4		3
7. Relatives?	0	0	0	0	1	0	0	0	0	0	0
8. Negatives?	0	0	1	0	1	1	1	0	0	0	0
9. CJ always paired in same TAM?	1	1	1	0	1	1	1	1	1	1	1
10a. DJ = V foc?	0	0	0	0	0	0	0	0			0
10b. Vfoc = DJ?	1	1	1	1	1	1	1	1	1		

(continued)

Table 2: Continued

	Kirundi	Kinyarwanda	Makhuwa	Matengo	Zulu	Tswana	Sotho	Bemba	Simakonde	Haya	Sambaa
11a. CJ = post-V foc?	1?	0	1	0	0	0		0	1		
11b. post-V foc = CJ?	1	1	1	0	1	1	1	1	1		0/1
12. VP focus = CJ?	0	1	1	1	1	1	1	0			0
13. Thetic VS = CJ?	0	1	0	0/1	1	1	1	1			0
14. Dedicated position?	final	final?	IAV	IAV	IAV	0	0	IAV	IAV?		

The parameter settings are primarily based on the following sources:

- Kirundi: Ndayiragije (1999), Nshemezimana & Bostoen (this volume), Ferdinand Mberamihigo p.c.
- Kinyarwanda: Kimenyi (1980), Ngoboka & Zeller (this volume)
- Makhuwa: own fieldwork
- Matengo: Yoneda (2009, this volume)
- Zulu: Buell (2005, 2006, 2009), Halpert (2012), Zeller (2012)
- Tswana: Creissels (1996, 2011, this volume)
- Northern Sotho: Zerbian (2006, p.c.)
- Bemba: Kula (this volume), Costa & Kula (2008), Sharman (1956)
- Simakonde: Manus (2007, this volume, p.c.)
- Haya: Hyman & Byarushengo (1984), Hyman (1999)
- Sambaa: Riedel (2009), Buell & Riedel (2008)

The first parameter – the finality restriction – turns out to be a defining and easily recognisable property.[3] For ease of reference, the other parameters refer to the form that is restricted to non-final position as 'conjoint' and the other form as 'disjoint', that is, conjoint and disjoint are for these parameters defined *only* with respect to their finality in order to avoid circularity in diagnosing the commonalities and variation in various languages that can be said to have the alternation.

These parameters are examined in 11 languages, the majority being examined in the other chapters of this volume, and additional languages that I had a reasonable amount of data for. Each parameter is discussed and illustrated in the following sections of this chapter, and the parameter settings for each of the 11 languages is summarised in Table 2.

3 Distribution

Parameters 1 and 2 refer to the distribution of the two forms, which is key to understanding the alternation. The first parameter establishes an opposition in sentence-finality between the alternating verb forms, and the second parameter diagnoses whether constituent-finality has an influence in the language.

3.1 Parameter 1: Sentence-finality

1. Is one form (CJ) restricted to non-sentence-final position in indicative non-relative clauses?

Between all the different languages with diverse conjugational systems, sentence-finality is a defining shared property: the CJ verb form can never occur sentence-finally in an affirmative main clause. This is the one property that holds for the CJ/DJ alternations in all languages under study. As discussed in the introduction to this volume, it is important to distinguish main from subordinate clauses, since the form of the relative or participial verb is in many languages isomorphic with the CJ form in main clauses. If there are no alternating relative verb forms, however, that particular form may of course occur sentence-finally in a relative clause. In this chapter, I define the CJ/DJ alternation *not* by the formal properties of the verb, but by their alternating verb forms. For clarity, in the first parameter I restrict the question to affirmative main clauses. Examples (3)-(6) illustrate the sentence-final restriction for a range of languages.

---

[3] See section 5 for the explicit mention of main affirmative clauses.

Sambaa (G23, Riedel 2009: 32)

(3) a. CJ *Ni-it-iye*   *kaya.*
         1SG.SM-go-PERF.CJ   16.home
         'I went home.'

     b. CJ * *Niitiye.*

     c. DJ *N-za-ita.*
         1SG.SM-PERF.DJ-go
         'I went.'

Ha (JD66, Harjula 2004: 167)

(4) a. CJ *Ba-rima*   *ibiharagi.*
         2SM-cultivate   8.beans
         'They cultivate beans.'

     b. CJ * *Barima.*

     c. DJ *Ba-ra-rima*   (*ibiharagi*).
         2SM-PRES.DJ-cultivate   8.beans
         'They cultivate/are cultivating (beans).'

Símákonde (P23, Manus 2007)

(5) a. CJ *Ngú-súmá*   *sílóólo.*
         1SG.SM-buy   7.mirror
         'I am buying a mirror.'

     b. CJ * *Ngúsúúmá.*

     c. DJ *Ni-nku-súúma*   *sílóólo.*
         1SG.SM-PRES.PROG-buy   7.mirror
         'I am buying/will buy a mirror.'

Xhosa (S41, Du Plessis and Visser 1992: 93)

(6) a. CJ *Umfazi*   *u-pheka*   *inyama.*
         1.woman   1SM-cook   9.meat
         'The woman is cooking meat.'

     b. CJ * *Umfazi upheka.*

     c. DJ *Umfazi*   *u-ya-pheka.*
         1.woman   1SM-PRES.DJ-cook
         'The woman is cooking.'

Whether the element following the CJ form is an argument or an adjunct is not of any influence, as long as some overt element follows the verb. This can for example be a manner adverb as in (7a), a locative nominal adjunct as in (7b) or a prepositional phrase as in (7c). If it is an argument, it can be a primary or secondary object as in the examples above, or in some languages a subject (8); see further under parameter 14.

Makhuwa (P31, Van der Wal 2014: 49)

(7) a. CJ *Eshímá   e-ruw-iy-é   tsiítsáale.*
         9.shima   9SM-stir-PASS-PERF.CJ   like.that
         '(the) Shima is cooked like that.'

   b. CJ *Ni-n-rúpá   wakhaámá-ni.*
         1PL.SM-PRES.CJ-sleep   16.bed-LOC
         'We sleep in a bed.'

   c. CJ *Ki-naan-alé   n'   iipulá.*
         1SG.SM-wet-PERF.CJ   with   9.rain
         'I got wet by the rain.' lit. 'I was wetted with rain.'

Kimatuumbi (P13, Odden 1984: 295)[4]

(8) CJ *Agonja   Mambóondo.*
       1SM.sleep   1.Mamboondo
       'Mamboondo is sleeping.'

Not only nominals but also following clauses can license a CJ verb form (see Section 7). Halpert (2012) shows for Zulu that complement clauses headed by the complementizer *ukuthi* can be preceded by the CJ form.

Zulu S42, Halpert 2012: 175)

(9) CJ *Ngi-cabanga   [ukuthi   uMlungisi   u-ya-bhukuda   manje].*
       1SG.SM-think   COMP   1.Mlungisi   1SM-PRES.DJ-swim   now
       'I think that Mlungisi is swimming now.'

For Makhuwa, I show in Van der Wal (2014) that complement clauses (11) as well as adverbial subordinate clauses (10) can license the use of a CJ verb form, although the two differ in their possible interpretations.

Makhuwa (Van der Wal 2014: 57, 60)

(10) CJ *Ákwáatú   a-n-réerá   [ya-khal'   oóríipa].*
        2.cats   2SM-PRES.CJ-be.good   2SM.SIT-stay   2.black
        'Cats are beautiful (only) if they're black.'

---

[4] The reverse, where the CJ form would be clause-final, is ungrammatical: * *Mamboondó agóonja* 'Mamboondo is sleeping' (Odden 1984: 295).

(11) CJ Ki-n-tsúwéla   [wiírá   etthépó   tsi-hááná   mpwína].
        1SG.SM-PRES.CJ-know   COMP   10.elephants 10SM-have   4.trunks
        'I know that elephants have trunks.'

In summary, the CJ verb form is restricted to a non-final position, but it seems that any following DP, PP or CP, whether argument or adjunct, is acceptable to make the verb non-final. It is interesting to note here that some lexical items display peculiar behaviour. More specifically, I found that in a number of different languages the adverb 'well' seems to be restricted to one verb form (which can be CJ or DJ, but there is never a choice), apparently independent of other properties of the language or the particular discourse situation. In Tswana, Kinyarwanda, Zulu (12) and Bemba it is reported as always following the CJ form, whereas in Makhuwa (13) and Sambaa it must be preceded by the DJ form. This remains as a puzzle for further research.

Zulu (S42, Leston Buell p.c.)
(12) a. CJ [Ngi-cul-a   kahle.]
            1SG.SM-sing-FV   well

     b. DJ *[Ngi-ya-cul-a]   kahle.
            1SG.SM-PRES.DJ-sing-FV well
            'I sing well.'

Makhuwa (P31, Van der Wal 2009: 222)
(13) a. CJ O-n-tthává   tsayi?
            1SM-PRES.CJ-plait how
            'How does she plait?'

     b. CJ * O-n-tthává   saána.
            1SM-PRES.CJ-plait well

     c. DJ O-náá-tthává   saána.
            1SM-PRES.DJ-plait well
            'She plaits well'

The second parameter regarding the distribution of the two verb forms concerns the non-restricted verb form, coined 'disjoint'.

3.2 Parameter 2: Constituent-finality

2. Is the other form (DJ) always final in its constituent?

This parameter aims to establish whether the distribution of the two forms is mainly determined by syntactic constraints, the alternative being a focus-based alternation (see Section 6). Van der Spuy (1993) and Buell (2006) convincingly argue for Zulu that the choice of the verb form depends on whether the verb is final in some constituent, which could be the IP (Buell 2006) or the vP (Adams 2010; Cheng and Downing 2012; Halpert 2012; Zeller 2012). When the verb is not final, i.e. when some element follows within the same constituent, the verb takes a CJ form, and when it is final, it takes a DJ form (14). Note that some element may still *linearly* follow the DJ verb form (like *izitshudeni* in 14b), but this element is *structurally* not in the right constituent (vP) to license a CJ verb form.

Zulu (S42, Van der Spuy 1993: 348, adapted)
(14) a. CJ [*Si-bon-e*   *izitshude:ni.*]$_{vP}$
           1PL.SM-see-PERF.CJ   students
           'We saw the students.'

      b. DJ [*Si-zi-bon-i:le*]$_{vP}$ *izitshude:ni.*
           1PL.SM-10OM-see-PERF.DJ   10.students
           'We saw them, the students.'

However, in order to know whether an object is dislocated, and whether the verb is thus final in its constituent,[5] some independent diagnostics are needed (see also Buell 2008). Two properties that are relatively easy to test concern object-marking and pauses:

2a. If object marking is non-doubling: does a post-DJ object obligatorily occur with an object marker?
2b. Is a post-DJ object obligatorily preceded by a prosodic break / pause?

---

[5] This diagnostic only takes V O sequences into account. It is, of course, possible to have a CJ form if another element still follows the verb within the right constituent (e.g. VOO). In (i), the benefactive *ubaba* 'father' is dislocated (and object marked on the verb), but since the theme *kudla kuni* 'what food' is still within the vP, the CJ form is used.

Zulu (S42, Buell 2009:168)
(i) CJ *U-m-phek-ela* t_i *kudla*   *kuni*   *ubaba*$_i$?
      2SG.SM-1OM-cook-APPL   15.food   15.what.kind   1.father
      'What kind of food are you cooking Father?'

These questions diagnose whether an object following the DJ verb form is outside of the relevant constituent, that is, whether it is (right) dislocated. In a language where object markers on the verb function as pronouns, the object marker is in complementary distribution with the coreferring DP (see Bresnan and Mchombo 1987 and much following work). If in a given language the object marker cannot 'double' a postverbal DP in the same domain, then the presence of the object marker signals that the following DP is dislocated. This in turn means that the verb is final and hence must take a DJ form. For several languages this bidirectional relation has been noticed between the form of the verb and the presence of the object marker: if a postverbal object is object-marked on the verb, the verb must take its DJ form, and reversely, if an object follows a DJ verb form, an object marker must be present on the verb (15b,d). The element following the verb can then never be object-marked on a CJ verb form (15a,c).

Tswana (S31, Creissels 1996: 112, 113)
(15) a. CJ *Re-thúsá   Kítso.*
              1PL.SM-help   1.Kitso
              'We help Kitso.'

      b. DJ *Re-a-**mo**-thúsá   Kítso.*
              1PL.SM-DJ-1OM-help   1.Kitso
              'We help him, Kitso.'

      c. CJ * *Re-**mo**-thúsá Kítso.*

      d. DJ * *Re-a-thúsá Kítso.*

This correlation has been described for the Nguni languages, Sotho, Tswana, and Kirundi, since object marking in these languages is 'non-doubling'. The strict correlation between object marking and the DJ verb form (via dislocation) thus argues for an analysis of the alternation being based on the position of the verb in the constituent. In a language that does allow object marking of in situ objects, the test cannot be applied, since objects will be marked regardless of their position in a constituent, and hence nothing can be deduced about the position of the verb either. Two examples where object marking has a different function are Kimatuumbi and Makhuwa. In Kimatuumbi, the presence of an object marker referring to the full object after the verb indicates definiteness of that object (16).

Kimatuumbi (P13, Odden 2003: 544, glosses added)
(16) a. CJ *Ni-nolya   baandu   yiímbe.*
              1SG.SM-sharpen 2.people knives
              'I'm sharpening knives for people'

b. CJ *Ni-**ba**-nólya*   *baandu*   *yiímbe.*
       1SG.SM-2OM-sharpen 2.people   knives
       'I'm sharpening knives for **the** people'

In Makhuwa, object marking does not have any obvious function: there are object markers only for 1st and 2nd person and for classes 1 and 2, which are obligatorily used when the object is in that class, independent of syntactic position, definiteness or animacy (17). In both of these languages, object marking is allowed with both CJ and DJ verb forms and there is no relation with dislocation or the alternation.

Makhuwa (P31, van der Wal 2009: 244)
(17) CJ *Ki-ni-ḿ-wéha*   *Hamísi /*   *namarokoló /* *nancoólo.*
         1SG.SM-PRES.CJ-1OM-look 1.Hamisi /   1.hare /   1.fish.hook
         'I see Hamisi / (a/the) hare / (a/the) fish hook'

     DJ *Ki-ná-ḿ-wéha*   *Hamísi /*   *namárókoló /* *nańcóólo.*
         1SG.SM-PRES.CJ-1OM-look 1.Hamisi /   1.hare /   1.fish.hook
         'I see Hamisi / (a/the) hare / (a/the) fish hook'

Similarly, parameter 2b diagnoses dislocation of the following object by testing whether the object DP needs to be separated from the verb by a pause. This is illustrated for Kinyarwanda, where an object following a DJ verb form must be preceded by a pause (and object-marked on the verb).

Kinyarwanda (JE61, Ngoboka & Zeller this volume)
(18) DJ *Abáana*   *baára*(ya)nyóoye*   **(,)* *amatá*
         a-ba-áana   ba-á-ra-ya-nyo-ye   a-ma-tá
         AUG-2-child 2SM-REM-DJ-6.OM-drink-PERF   AUG-6-milk
         'The children drank it, the milk.'

In summary, a strict correlation between the DJ verb form and dislocation (as diagnosed by non-doubling object marking and a necessary pause) suggests that the DJ verb form is always constituent-final, even if it is linearly followed by some argument or adverb. If the DJ verb form is always associated with being constituent-final (sentence-final necessarily being constituent-final), this forms a strong argument for a constituency-based analysis of the alternation. If the alternation is *not* determined by constituency, however, the question is what controls the choice for the one or the other verb form. In Section 6 we will see that the alternative is a focus-based analysis. This is also where parameter 2c (clitics following a CJ form) will be discussed. First, however, the crosslinguistic variation is presented with respect to the formal marking of the two alternating verb forms (Table 3).

Table 3: Distributional CJ/DJ parameters.

	Kirundi	Kinyarwanda	Makhuwa	Matengo	Zulu	Tswana	Sotho	Bemba	Simakonde	Haya	Sambaa
1. One form restricted?	1	1	1	1	1	1	1	1	1	1	1
2. Other form always const-final?	0	1	0	?	1	1	1	0	1		0
2a. OM: post-V O in DJ dislocated?	0	1	n.a.	n.a.	1	1	1	n.a.	n.a.		n.a.
2b. Break: post-V O dislocated?	0	1	0	0	1	1		0			0

4 Formal properties

The languages with a CJ/DJ alternation must all somehow make the alternation apparent, but the linguistic means to mark the alternating verb forms vary between and even within languages.[6] Since most Bantu languages use tone to make lexical and grammatical distinctions, tone can be analysed as a morpheme, that is, a minimal conventional association of a tonal pattern and an interpretation. It is not surprising, then, that the CJ/DJ alternation may be marked by segmental and/or tonal morphology, where the segmental marking can surface as a prefix or suffix. This section discusses the presence and shape of affixes, tonal alternations and phonological marking of phrase boundaries, which can all be related to the CJ/DJ alternation.

4.1 Parameter 3: segmental morphology

3. Is the alternation marked by segmental morphology?

Despite this being a fairly easy question, which can in most cases be answered on the basis of even superficial knowledge of the language, there are three factors that make it difficult to describe what marks the alternation. The first is that the morphological marking is always combined or fused with the tense-aspect morphology (pre- and suffixal), and therefore it is hard to indicate and demarcate one

---

[6] By 'marking' or 'marked' is meant that a verb form has some formal sign on it, not that it is a non-default counterpart of 'unmarked'.

specific morpheme that encodes the CJ or DJ nature of the verb form. A second point of potential confusion is that the DJ-marking morphology can be multifunctional, as Ngoboka and Zeller (this volume) demonstrate for the Kinyarwanda prefix -ra-, which is also used in progressive/future tenses. Finally, a third factor that blurs the picture is the fact that the marking varies from one pair of verb forms to the next; there is generally not one morpheme that marks the DJ form in both the present tense and the past perfective, for example. This is the reason for including three subquestions:

3a. Is the alternation marked by prefixes, suffixes, or both?
3b. Is only the DJ form marked segmentally?
3c. Is the alternation only marked segmentally in the present tense?

The variation in segmental marking across tenses is shown for Swati in (19): in the present tense the CJ form is not marked or has a zero morpheme and the DJ form has the prefix -ya- (19a,b), while in the perfective the CJ and DJ form differ in the suffix on the verb stem -e vs. -ile (19c,d).[7]

Swati (S43, Ziervogel and Mabuza 1976: 97,98)
(19) a. CJ *Ngi-natsa...*
             1SG.SM-drink
             'I drink...'

      b. DJ *Ngi-ya-natsa.*
             1SG.SM-PRES.DJ-drink
             'I am drinking.'

      c. CJ *Ngi-nats-é...*
             1SG.SM-drink-PERF.CJ
             'I have drunk...'

      d. DJ *Ngi-nats-ile.*
             1SG.SM-drink-PERF.DJ
             'I have drunk.'

There appears to be a general pattern that the DJ form is always marked in some way, whereas the CJ form may be unmarked (Nshemezimana & Bostoen this volume, cf. Morimoto, this volume). This can be related to the hypothesised origin of the alternation where the DJ form originates in a periphrasis, as briefly discussed

---

[7] Larry Hyman (p.c.) expresses doubt as to whether the -e/-ile alternation should be treated as the same as the Ø/-ya- alternation, considering that it may also surface in relative clauses, for example (see parameter 7).

in Section 5.1. It is also why for the southern Bantu languages the DJ form has been called 'long' as opposed to the 'short' CJ form.

Furthermore, if the CJ form is marked, then the alternation has suffixes, and if the language marks any other tense than the present tense, it also has suffixal marking. These implicational relations are visible in table 5 further below.

Parameter 3c is relevant for languages such as Tswana, Sotho, Haya, and Bemba, where only the present tense shows the alternation in the segmental morphology – other tenses may mark it by tonal differences (see the next Section 4.2 and references mentioned there).

4.2 Parameter 4: tonal morphology

4. Is the alternation marked by tonal morphology?

In all languages under discussion there is at least one tense where the distinction is marked on the verb by segmental morphology, as shown in the examples above. In Tswana the alternation is also marked by a segmental morpheme -*a*-, but only in the present tense, as in (20a, b). However, Creissels (1996) shows that it is not only the present tense that distinguishes CJ and DJ forms. Although other tenses are not marked by a special affix, they do show a difference in the tonal pattern on the verb. The tonal pattern of the perfect CJ form in (20c) differs from that of the perfect DJ form in (20d). In other tenses, like the future, only the tone on the last syllable differs: in the CJ form in (20e) the verb stem ends in HL, whereas the DJ form in (20d) ends in HH.

Tswana (S31, Creissels 1996: 109, glosses added)
(20) a. CJ Dikgomó dí-fúla   kwa nokeng.
             10.cows   10SM-graze   at   river
             'The cows graze/are grazing at the river.'

   b. DJ Dikgomó dí-á-fúla.
          10.cows   10SM-PRES.DJ-graze
          'The cows are grazing.'

   c. CJ Bá$_i$-tsamá-íle lé   boné$_k$.
          2SM-go-PERF with 2.PRO
          'They have gone with them.'

   d. DJ Bá$_i$-tsáma-ile lé   boné$_{i.}$
          2SM-go-PERF with 2.PRO
          'They too have gone.'

e. CJ *Ke-tlaa-bína*   lé   ené.
       1SG.SM-FUT-dance with   1.PRO
       'I shall dance with him/her.'

f. DJ *Ke-tlaa-bíná*   lé   nná.
       1SG.SM-FUT-dance with   1SG.PRO
       'I too shall dance.', 'I shall dance, me too.'

A further illustration of tonal morphology as a marker of CJ/DJ is found in Haya (Hyman and Byarushengo 1984; Hyman 1999). Hyman (1999) provides the following overview of tenses in Haya, where only the today past shows a segmental marking (*-a-* vs *-áa-* in (21)) and in other tenses the alternating forms are only distinguished by their tonal pattern, as shown in Table 4.

Haya (JE22, Hyman 1999: 160)

(21) a. CJ *Y-a-kom-a*   *Káto.*
            1SM-PAST1-tie   1.Kato
            'He tied Kato.'

     b. DJ *Y-áá-mu-kôm-a.*
            1SM-PAST1.DJ-1OM-tie
            'He tied him.'

It is important to keep in mind that the tonal behaviour must be established per alternating tense, that is, the precise tonal patterns may vary between two tenses (say, the present CJ & DJ forms vs. the present perfective CJ & DJ). It can be particularly puzzling, as Creissels (this volume) notes for Tswana, 'that the tonal melodies that in some tenses characterize the DJ form may be very similar to those characterizing the CJ form in other tenses, and vice-versa'.

Furthermore, it must be established whether the tonal alternations are indeed part of the alternation as such, or if they can be derived from general phonological rules, as Kula (this volume), Zeller et al. (this volume) and Creissels (1996), this volume) examine. For Bemba, Kula (this volume) concludes 'that the CJ-DJ alternation is not tonally encoded', contrasting this with systems where tone is indeed a morphological marking of the alternation: 'In this sense Tswana fundamentally differs from Bemba in that the surface tonology of all verbs in Bemba can be predicted directly from the general tone rules of the language, whereas this is not the case in Tswana where an independent tone pattern must be specified to apply in particular TAMs and therefore treated as encoding the CJ-DJ alternation'. Interestingly, Zeller et al. (this volume) propose that Zulu has an H-toned morpheme, marking the CJ form optionally in some tenses. A question is whether this tonal marking is independent from phonological phrasing, as discussed in the next section.

Table 4: Tonal reduction in Haya cj/dj tenses.

	DJ 'they tie'	CJ 'they tie Kato'
present habitual	ba-kóm-a	ba-kom-a káto
past 1	bá-á-kôm-a	ba-a-kom-a káto
past 2	ba-kom-íle	ba-kom-ile káto
past habitual	ba-a-kóm-ag-a	ba-a-kom-ag-a káto
future 1	ba-laa-kôm-a	ba-laa-kom-a káto
future 2	ba-li-kóm-a	ba-li-kom-a káto

4.3 Parameter 5: phonological phrasing

5. Does phonological phrasing co-vary with the alternation?

The closer (CJ) or looser (DJ) relation between the verb and what follows is often reflected in the phonological phrasing. Where phonological phrases are discernable, the CJ form is always phrased together with the following element, whereas the DJ form is in a phonological phrase by itself. The boundaries of these phonological phrases –or typically just the right boundary– are marked in the prosody, by lengthening and/or tonal alternations. However, not all languages indicate phonological phrase boundaries, and the languages that do mark them differ in the phonological processes involved. For example, right boundaries in Makonde are marked by lengthening of the penultimate syllable. In example (22) the right boundaries of phonological phrases are indicated by a vertical line. Only the verb in its DJ form appears at the right edge of a phonological phrase, and hence the penultimate syllable of the verb is lengthened (as indicated by the double vowel) in the DJ form in (22c), but not in the CJ form in (22a), where only the object is lengthened.

Makonde (P23, Kraal 2005: 235, glosses added)
(22) a. CJ *Tu-va-yangata vayéeni|.*
1PL.SM-2OM-help 2.guests
'We help *the guests*.'

b. DJ *Tu-na-va-yangaáta| vayeéni|.*
1PL.SM-PRES.DJ-2OM-help 2.guests
'We help the guests.'

Two issues are related to the prosodic marking of the CJ/DJ alternation and phonological phrases. The first is whether phonological phrasing is an independent strategy to mark the CJ/DJ alternation, as discussed in the introduction to this volume.

Table 5: Formal CJ/DJ parameters.

	Kirundi	Kinyarwanda	Makhuwa	Matengo	Zulu	Tswana	Sotho	Bemba	Símákonde	Haya	Sambaa
3. Segmental morph?	1	1	1	1	1	1	1	1	1	1	1
3a. Pre/suffix?	prefix	prefix	both	both	both	prefix	prefix	both	both	prefix	both
3b. Only DJ marked?	1	1	0	0	0	1	1	0	0	1	0
3c. Only present tense?	0	0	0	0	0	1	1	0	0	1	0
4. Tonal morph?	1	1	0	0	0/1	1	1	1			
5. P-phrasing?	0	0	0	1	1	1	1	1	1	1	

If no morphological marking (tonal or segmental) were present in any tense, this would presumably just be seen as different phonological phrasing, rather than an alternation related to focus and/or constituency. Therefore, as seen in the working definition in (2), phrasing alone is not considered to be indicative of the alternation, although the alternation can be *reflected* in the phrasing. The same conclusion is also reached for Bemba (Kula this volume) and Zulu (Zeller et al. this volume).

The second issue is the mapping between phonological phrases and syntactic phrases. Cheng and Downing (2009) have shown that in Zulu, phonological phrase boundaries coincide with syntactic phrases. Hence, the phonological phrasing can for Zulu be used as a diagnostic to determine the position of the verb and the following elements, which is relevant to the discussion of whether the alternation is based on constituency or focus (see also Sections 3.2 and 6.7). The phonological phrasing can thus be hypothesised to be 'read off' the syntactic phrasing, just like the CJ/DJ alternation is in this constituency-based system (though see Halpert (this volume) on the mismatches between syntax and prosody). The settings for the parameters of formal marking are summarised in Table 5.

5 Tenses in which the alternation is found

In none of the languages do all tenses form CJ/DJ pairs; there is always a restriction on the occurrence of the alternation to a smaller number of tenses. If a language has CJ and DJ verb forms, they will be present in the affirmative indicative tenses, most often in the present tense. Languages thus differ in the number of tenses displaying the alternation, but also in the presence of the alternation in the negative and relative tenses and in other moods (although this is rare). Finally, not all languages have neat pairs where each CJ form alternates with a corresponding DJ form. The parameters relating to tenses thus consist of the following questions:

6. How many tenses participate in the alternation?

7. Do relative tenses have the alternation?
8. Do negative tenses have the alternation?
9. Is every CJ form paired with a DJ form in the same TAM?

5.1 Parameters 6–8: which tenses?

The number of tenses involved in the alternation is a point of much variation across the Bantu languages. In Venda, for example, the alternation is reported for the present tense only (Poulos 1990),[8] whereas Makhuwa has four CJ/DJ pairs in segmentally marked tenses. In Sotho, like in Tswana, only the present CJ and DJ tenses are marked segmentally, but 12 other CJ/DJ pairs are marked tonally in Southern Sotho (Letsh'eng 1995). While this variation can in itself already form interesting information, it is possibly even more revealing *which* tenses show the alternation.

An implicational hierarchy appears to emerge here: if a language displays the alternation in the 'marked' tenses (relative, participial, optative, negative tenses), it is also present in 'unmarked' affirmative indicative tenses. In the languages of zone P (Kimatuumbi, Makonde, Makwe, Makhuwa) the alternation is not present in the relative tenses, whereas the Nguni languages (S40) do distinguish CJ and DJ verb forms in the relative perfect (23).

Zulu (S42, Buell 2006: 20)
(23) a. CJ *Yi-mali*   *engi-m-nik-e*   *yona.*
                COP.AUG-9.money   REL.1SG.SM-1OM-give-PERF.CJ   9.PRO

      b. DJ *Yi-mali*   *engi-m-nik-ile-yo.*
                COP.AUG-9.money   REL.1SG.SM-1OM-give-PERF.DJ-REL
             'It's the money that I gave him.'

In the same way, the distinction is restricted to affirmative tenses in most languages, but also available in some negative tenses in Zulu (Buell 2011) and Southern Sotho (24), where the distinction is marked tonally on the last syllable of the verb (also depending on the lexical tone of the verb).

Southern Sotho (S33, Letsh'eng 1995: 57, glosses added)
(24) a. CJ *Ha-kí-ja-búá*   *ahólo.*
                NEG-1SG.SM-PERF-talk   much
             'I haven't talked much.'

---

[8] A thorough tonal analysis of Venda verb forms would be welcome, though.

b. DJ *Ha-kí-ja-búa.*
   NEG-1SG.SM-PERF-talk
   'I haven't talked.'

In Makhuwa there are two negative paradigms for the alternating tenses, of which the CJ form is not used often – the DJ form is the regular negative form. The present tense forms are illustrated in (25). Note that the CJ form is not analysable as a pseudocleft ('what he doesn't buy is what'), since the subject marker on the verb would then be in class 9.

Makhuwa (P31, Van der Wal 2009: 219)
(25) a. CJ *O-hi-ń-thúma*   *esheeni?*
         1SM-NEG-PRES-buy.CJ   9.what
         'What doesn't he buy?'

   b. DJ *Kha-ń-thúma.*
         NEG.1SM-PRES-buy.DJ
         'He doesn't buy (it).'

The restriction to the 'basic' or less marked tenses (affirmative, non-special mood) requires some explanation. Three functional suggestions have been made with respect to the apparent incompatibility of CJ/DJ and non-basic TAM categories. The first is proposed by Hyman and Watters (1984) (see also Hyman 1999 and this volume), who state that negation and some TAM categories are inherently focal. For example, negation expresses focus on the polarity of the verb, and a progressive aspect focuses on the ongoing action (cf. Güldemann 2003). If the CJ/DJ alternation is also involved in focus marking (see Section 6), the inherently focal tenses or 'marked tenses' (Hyman 1999) cannot combine with the CJ/DJ alternation. A second suggestion (Thilo Schadeberg, p.c.) is that tenses are restricted in their semantic load, or in other words that each verb form 'can only express so much'. Some forms express temporal and aspectual meaning, some combine aspect and modality, and some conjugational categories contain temporal reference and information on the status of the discourse interpretation of a following element – but expressing all three would be 'too much'. Third and related is Givón's (1975) hypothesis that relatives and negatives represent a 'narrowing of focus' such that the object rather than the verb is always in focus and hence requiring the CJ form, which according to Givón represents 'complement focus' (see the discussion on formal or alternating definitions of the alternation in Section 1).

In addition, and possibly independent of these motivations, the diachronic development of the alternation has probably had an influence on the restriction in the number and sort of tenses that display the alternation (Van der Wal 2010 and the introduction to this volume). That is, if tenses are 'recruited' for use in the CJ/DJ alternation in the stage of renewal (when there are two forms to express the same tense (layering)), the number and types of tenses that show the alternation depends on which tenses tend to renew. As the affirmative and basic tenses are known to be more prone to renewal, it stands to reason that these are the tenses that are marked segmentally and participate in the CJ/DJ alternation.[9] This, however, is only one possible analysis, and the diachronic considerations of the alternation deserve more attention.

5.2 Parameter 9: is every CJ form paired with a DJ counterpart?

Since CJ verb forms are more restricted in their distribution in the sentence, they are typically expected to be paired with a less restricted DJ form. While this is the canonical situation, and all languages have at least one pair in the same TAM category, in some languages the pairs are not as straightforward.

For Makwe, Devos (2004) describes a tripartite conjugational system. Some tenses in Makwe belong to a pair (being CJ or DJ), some only occur as DJ and some are CJ/DJ (neutral), being morphologically identical but occurring in contexts that are typical for the CJ form as well as sentence-finally like the DJ form. An overview is given in Table 6.

Example (26) illustrates the past imperfective CJ and its DJ counterpart (paired tense) and (27) shows the present progressive, which is a neutral tense (Devos 2004). The neutral CJ/DJ tenses *optionally* form a phonological phrase with the following word, depending on whether they are used 'as CJ' or 'as DJ'.

Makwe (G402, Devos 2004: 217)
(26) a. CJ *A-yúmá vítáabu.|*
 1SM-buy 8.books
 'She was buying books.'

 b. DJ *Á-ná-yúúma.|*
 1SM-PRES.DJ-buy
 'She was buying.'

---

9 This also accounts for 1. the DJ form having more pre-stem material, since it would have been derived from a grammaticalised periphrastic construction (see the complex forms in Ndengeleko (Ström 2013) and Shangaji (Devos, this volume)), and 2. the variation in marking across different tenses.

Table 6: Makwe conjugational system.

paired CJ/DJ	Present Imperfective, Present Perfective, Past Imperfective, Past Perfective, Counterfactual Conditional 2
neutral	Infinitive, Resumptive, Present Progressive, Imperative (without OM), Optative (without OM), Rel. Past Imperfective
disjoint only	Purposive Infinitive, Suppositional/Subsecutive, Counterfactual Conditional 1, Situative Progressive, Imperative (with OM), Optative (with OM), Subsecutive, all negative tenses; all relative tenses (except Rel. Past Imperfective)

(27) a. CJ   *A-nku-yúmá   vitáabu.|*
           1SM-PROG-buy 8.books
           'She is buying books.'

   b. DJ   *A-nku-yúúma| vitáabu.|*
           1SM-PROG-buy 8.books
           'She is buying books.'

However, Zeller et al. (this volume) rightly pose the question of 'whether any of the phonological properties we observe [...] should be interpreted as grammatical markers of the CJ/DJ alternation, or whether they simply follow from general phonological principles of the language' (see Section 4.3, also Kula this volume and Creissels 1996, this volume on this issue). It is thus debatable whether in Makwe the 'neutral' tenses should be seen as participating in the alternation, or whether their phonological phrasing can be explained by independent principles at the interface between syntax and phonology. The same question holds for Símákonde, see Manus (this volume). In favour of treating p-phrasing as an inherent part of the alternation, Maud Devos (p.c.) points out for Makwe that the choice between forming a single phrase or not is determined by exactly the same factors as the choice between a CJ and the corresponding DJ tense. One of the questions would indeed be why the independent phonological marking would not hold across all tenses, that is, why there are 'DJ only' tenses at all.

A particularly interesting case under this parameter is Matengo. So far, Matengo seems to be the only language that has 'CJ only' tenses, without an equivalent DJ counterpart, as shown in the overview in Table 7.

Table 7: Matengo conjugational system, indicative mood (Yoneda 2009).

CJ		DJ	
simple far past	SM-a-VB-aje		
		perfect past	SM-a-VB-iti
simple today past	SM-VB(-it)-áje		
		perfect present	SM-VB-ití
simple present	SM-VB-a		
simple future	SM-í-VB-aje	confirm future	SM-í-VB-a
simple go-future	SM-aká-VB-aje	confirm go-future	SM-aká-VB-a

The simple present tense in Matengo occurs only in the CJ form: it cannot appear sentence-finally, as shown in (28b) and (29b). In order to use this tense with an intransitive verb, one has to employ either a 'dummy object' after the verb, such as the cognate object *lihengu* 'work' in (28a), or a 'dummy verb' - *tenda* 'do' followed by the infinitive of the actual verb, as in (29a).

Matengo (N13, Yoneda 2009, and this volume)
(28) a. CJ *Ju-henga   lihengu.*
              1SM-work   5.work
              'He works (work).'

      b. CJ **Ju-henga.*
              1SM-work

(29) a. CJ *Maria   ju-tenda   ku-pomulela.*
              1.Maria 1SM-do   15-rest
              'Maria is resting.'

      b. CJ **Maria   ju-pomulela.*
              1.Maria 1SM-rest

To sum up, although languages differ with respect to the number of tenses that display the alternation and the sort of tenses that alternate, an implicational relation seems to hold that if a language has the alternation in a non-basic tense, it also has it in one or more of the basic tenses. An additional point of variation is found in the crumbling system of Matengo CJ/DJ, where it is not even the case that CJ and DJ forms are always paired. This sparks further research questions on transitivity alternations in general and on the relative priority of TAM semantics, sentence-finality restrictions and interpretation (which are not addressed in this chapter, but see Yoneda this volume for some discussion). The settings for the tense parameters are summarised in Table 8.

Table 8: Tense CJ/DJ parameters, where '1+12' means 1 tense is marked segmentally and 12 tonally.

	Kirundi	Kinyarwanda	Makhuwa	Matengo	Zulu	Tswana	Sotho	Bemba	Simákonde	Haya	Sambaa
6. How many tenses?	3 or 5	4+2	4	15	2 +	1+12	1+12	10	3 or 4	1	3
7. Relatives?	0	0	0	0	1	0	0	0	0	0	0
8. Negatives?	0	0	1	0	1	1	1	0	0	0	0
9. CJ always paired in same TAM?	1	1	1	0	1	1	1	1	1	1	1

6 Interpretational properties

In general, it is very difficult to establish the precise difference in semantic or discursive interpretation between the CJ and the DJ verb form. This becomes apparent in the various grammar books of the languages that show the distinction. In some grammatical descriptions it is not even detected, in some it is treated as a mere variation, and sometimes one can find remarks like the following:

> Cole (1955: 444, on Tswana S31)
> "...different shades of significance, the long form being slightly more definite or emphatic, or expressive of continuous action."

> O'Neil (1969: 18, on Ndebele S44)
> "The student is advised to use the [DJ form] whenever in doubt as to which of the two forms is more correct. To define wherein the precise distinction between the two forms of the present tense consists, is almost impossible."

> Meeussen (1959: 216, on Kirundi JD62)
> "L'emploi et le sens des formes de conjoint et de disjoint devront être étudiés de plus près, de préférence par un grammairien du Burundi même, vu le caractère délicat de cette distinction." [The use and meaning of the conjoint and disjoint form should be studied more closely, preferably by a Burundian grammarian, considering the subtle character of this distinction.]

Indeed, the meaning and inferences conveyed and the proper contexts for use are complicated and hence difficult to describe and establish. Moreover, these also vary from language to language, as is shown in this section.

6.1 Tense-aspect semantics

In Matengo it is clear that the CJ/DJ forms may differ in TAM semantics (see Table 7). However, even in languages where the CJ and DJ verb forms function as pairs, in traditional grammar descriptions the difference is often described in terms of tense-aspect semantics. Such a difference is usually mentioned for the present tense, where the CJ form tends to be felt as more habitual or neutral, and the DJ form variously as a near future, immediate present, progressive or continuous, as is visible in the following citation and example (30).

> Hurel (1951: 137/139, on Kinyarwanda JD61)
> 'Présent de durée' [disjoint] "indique une action qui a lieu actuellement, mais avec une idée implicite de prolongation dans la suite.[...] Cependant cette forme est encore employée pour un futur très prochain..."
> 'Présent habituel' [conjoint] "indique une action qui se fait habituellement"
>
> [The disjoint form "refers to an action that currently takes places but with the implicit idea of continuation. [...] Yet this form is still used for an immediate future." The conjoint form "refers to an action that is habitually carried out."]

Ndebele (S44, Ziervogel 1959: 87)
(30) a. CJ ń-khámbha   'I walk' ("simple aspect")
     b. DJ ndí-yá-khámbha 'I am walking' ("continuous aspect")

Furthermore, there is a diachronic relation between the forms in the alternation and the development to progressive aspect (Hyman and Watters 1984; Odden 1996; Güldemann 2003, cf. Morimoto this volume, Devos this volume, Odden 1996). Nevertheless, it is my impression that in most cases, these tense-aspect differences are not essential to the CJ/DJ distinction, but that they are used in the description simply because we are used to describe differences between tenses in temporal or aspectual terms. The tense-aspect differences reported for the CJ and DJ forms remain vague and ambivalent, and they tend to 'disappear' when used in contexts that are typical for the one or the other verb form. Question-answer combinations are one such case. Congruence is expected in temporal reference (and very often aspect) between the question and the answer, but whereas the question in (31) necessarily uses a CJ form, the answer can only be DJ.

Makhuwa (P31, Van der Wal 2009: 224)
(31) a. CJ Ashínúni   yiir-ál'   ésheeni?
            2.DIM.birds   2.SM.PAST.do-PERF.CJ 9.what
            'What did the birds do?'

b. DJ *Ashínúní   yaahí-váva.*
   2.DIM.birds   2SM.PAST.PERF.DJ-fly
   'The birds flew.'

Furthermore, it is often the case that CJ and DJ correspond to one form in negation. This suggests that the CJ and DJ form are in the same temporal-aspectual category. Buell (2005: 145) also argues against a tense-aspect difference between the CJ and DJ forms in Zulu, and Kosch (1988) does the same for Northern Sotho. If in general the CJ/DJ alternation does not encode a difference in tense-aspect semantics, and assuming that variation in morphosyntax is never completely functionless, there must be some other difference in interpretation between the CJ and the DJ verb form.

6.2 Parameter 10: does focus require a particular verb form?

The alternation has often been described in terms of old/new information, focus, expressiveness etc., as seen in the following descriptions of the interpretation of the two forms.

> Van Eeden (1956: 245, on Zulu)
> (about DJ form) "wanneer die klem op die handeling, en net op die handeling val; vandaar dat dit 'n emfatiese of sterk tijdvorm genoem kan word" [The disjoint form is used "when the emphasis/stress falls on the action and just on the action; hence this can be called an emphatic or strong tense".]
>
> Bagein (1951, on Kirundi)
> (about the DJ form) "On retranche souvent la particule -*ra*- pour donner plus de vicacité." [One often omits the particle -*ra*- to give more liveliness.]

The various descriptions and analyses of the alternation suggest a relation between on the one hand the DJ verb form and predicate-centred focus (i.e. focus on the lexical value of the verb, on the TAM or the truth value), and on the other hand the CJ verb form and focus on a postverbal element (cf. Buell's 2006 Verb Focus Hypothesis and Postverbal Term Focus Hypothesis). The questions for each individual language are whether these relations are direct or indirect, and whether they are bidirectional (i.e. focus requiring a certain form vs. a certain form always triggering a focus). Parameter 10 tests one direction:

10a.   Does predicate-centred focus require the DJ form?
10b.   Do postverbal focused terms require the CJ form?

Perhaps surprisingly, both these correlations hold in all languages, with the exception of Matengo. As Yoneda (this volume) shows, expressing the correct tense-aspect semantics takes precedence over choosing the most appropriate form in terms of focus, leading to the use of the DJ form with a postverbal focused element in some circumstances. In all other languages there is a clear (at least unidirectional) relation between term focus and a CJ verb form, as seen in answers to wh questions and terms modified by the focus particle 'only'. Many grammatical descriptions also note a restriction on the occurrence of inherently focused wh-elements, which are only allowed after a CJ verb form and ungrammatical after a DJ form, as illustrated in (32).

Swati (S43, Ziervogel and Mabuza 1976: 175, adapted)
(32) a. CJ *Ba-bona-ni?*
2SM-see-what
'What do they see?'

b. DJ ** Ba-ya-bona-ni*
2SM-PRES.DJ-see-what

Similarly, when the verb lexeme or the TAM are contrasted (what Güldemann 2009 refers to as state-of-affairs focus and operator focus), the DJ form is chosen consistently.

The fact that a focused element takes a certain verb form does not show conclusively that the alternating verb forms inherently express or mark that focus (cf. Devos, this volume). The reverse correlation does not hold in all languages, and this is where the difference between a focus-based analysis versus a constituency-based analysis will become clear. The next three parameters address exactly that difference.

6.3 Parameter 11: does a particular verb form entail focus?

The other half of the relation with focus are the unidirectional questions for both verb forms as to whether they encode focus, specifically:

11a. Does the DJ form entail predicate-centred focus?
11b. Does the CJ form entail focus on an element following the verb?

Odden (1996) describes a combination of these two for Kimatuumbi. He calls the CJ form 'noun-focal', expressing focus on the element following the CJ verb form (33a), and the DJ form 'verb-focal', expressing focus on the verb (33b).

Kimatuumbi (P13, Odden 1996: 60, 61, glosses added)

(33) a. CJ *Ni-kata   kaámba.*
    1SG.SM-cut rope
    'I am cutting ROPE (not something else).'

   b. DJ *Eendá-kaatá.*
    1SG.SM.PROG.DJ-cut
    'He is cutting.'

   c. DJ *Eendá-kaatá   kaámba.*
    1SG.SM.PROG.DJ-cut rope
    'He is CUTTING rope (not doing something else to it).'

The two subparameters 11a and 11b can be studied separately, however. The correlation in 11a, DJ encoding predicate focus, has been mentioned for Zulu by several authors and is claimed for Kirundi by Nshemezimana & Bostoen (this volume), cf. Devos and van der Wal (2010) and Devos (this volume) for Shangaji. Güldemann (2003) suggests that the DJ form encodes predication focus in a large part of the southern CJ/DJ Bantu languages, where 'predication focus' can refer to a contrast on the lexical value of the verb, the tense/aspect or the truth/polarity. The DJ form in (34b) could thus not only be translated as 'he *reads* the letter' (implying that he does not write or burn it), but also as 'he does read the letter' (contrasting a possible earlier statement that he did not). The CJ form is said to not have a special interpretation and is analysed as the unmarked form by Güldemann.

Zulu (S42, Van Eeden 1956: 251, glosses added)

(34) a. CJ *U-funda le   ncwadi.*
    1SM-read 9.DEM 9.letter
    'He reads this letter.'

   b. DJ *U-ya-yi-funda   le   ncwadi.*
    1SM-PRES.DJ-9OM-read 9.DEM 9.letter
    'He READS this letter.'

However, it does not seem to be the case that within a single language all instances of the DJ verb form are in focus, nor is it the case that crosslinguistically the DJ form clearly expresses focus on the verb. Considering the language-internal picture, Buell (2006) shows that a DJ form is sometimes required when the verb is clearly not in focus, as illustrated in (35) and (36).[10]

---

[10] Note, though, that the CJ form in this example may be required by the adverb 'well', as noted in Section 3.1.

Zulu (S42, Buell 2006: 20)

(35)　DJ　A-ngi-dans-i　　　　kahle, kodwa　ngi-cul-a　　kahle.
　　　　　NEG-1SG.SM-dance-FV　well　but　　1SG.SM-sing-FV　well
　　　　　'I don't dance well, but I sing well.'

(Buell 2011: 808–809)

(36)　a.　DJ　A-wu-gqok-ile　　　ngani?
　　　　　　　NEG-2S-wear-PERF.DJ　why

　　　b.　CJ　*A-wu-gqok-e　　　ngani?
　　　　　　　NEG-2S-wear-PERF.CJ　why
　　　　　　　'Why aren't you dressed?'

Considering the crosslinguistic validity of 11a, Stucky (1985: 56) notes for Makhuwa-Imithupi that the DJ form 'is simply used to indicate that the action took place'. In fact, in at least Matengo, Makwe and Kirundi, the DJ form is also used when the element following the verb, rather than the verb itself, forms the new information, for example in a thetic verb-subject sentence (37). Thetic sentences present the whole clause as new or non-topical, including the postverbal subject. Preceding this detopicalised subject, in Makwe a DJ verb form is used (37).

Makwe (G402, Devos 2004: 316)

(37)　DJ　Aniúuma　　　　　　　nakádíimu.
　　　　　1SM.PRES.PERF.come.out　1.giant
　　　　　'And so, Nakadimu leaves.'

This implies that while a focused verb needs to take a DJ form (parameter 10a), the reverse in parameter 11a shows variation: not all instances of the DJ form encode focus on the verb.[11]

The same variation is found with respect to the other half of parameter 11, as in 11b: while focus on a postverbal element triggers the CJ form, it is not always the case that the CJ form encodes focus on an element following the verb. There is language-internal as well as crosslinguistic variation. A language that shows a consistent mapping between the CJ form and a focus interpretation is Makhuwa. Various tests show that the element following a CJ verb form is always (part of) the focus, and moreover, this is an exclusive type of focus (van der Wal 2011). This can be illustrated for the object *ntthu* 'person', which can receive an indefinite

---

11 In this respect I disagree with Nshemezimana & Bostoen's (this volume) conclusion that the DJ morpheme in Kirundi is a marker of predicate focus.

non-specific interpretation ('someone') when preceded by a DJ verb form (38a), but not when preceded by a CJ verb form (38b). The CJ form in Makhuwa places the postverbal element in exclusive focus: at least some of the alternative object referents must be excluded. Since this is impossible for an indefinite non-specific DP ('anyone' cannot exclude referents), 'person' can only be interpreted as a generic, as in (38c).

Makhuwa (P31, Van der Wal 2011: 1740)
(38) a. DJ *Ko-ḿ-wéha*   *ńtthu.*
              1SG.SM.PERF.DJ-1OM-look 1.person
              'I saw someone.'

      b. CJ * *Ki-m-weh-alé*   *ntthú.*
              1SG.SM-1OM-look-PERF.CJ 1.person
              int: 'I saw someone.'

      c. CJ *Ki-m-weh-alé*   *ntthú,*   *nki-weh-álé*   *enáma.*
              1SG.SM-1OM-look-PERF.CJ 1.person NEG.1SG-look-PERF 9.animal
              'I saw a person/human being, not an animal.'

Turning again to Zulu, Buell (2006) shows that the CJ form does not necessarily trigger focus on a postverbal term, as it is also used when the verb is followed by a resumptive pronoun, which cannot be focused (39).

Zulu (S42, Buell 2006: 18)
(39) CJ *Indawo lapho* [*ngi-cul-e*   *khona.*]
          9.place there   1SG.SM-sing-PERF.CJ there
          'The place where I sang.'

If even non-focusable clitics can satisfy the non-finality restriction of the CJ form (parameter 2c), then we can deduce that the alternation is sensitive to constituency, rather than focus (see also Halpert this volume on clitics in Zulu). This is the case in Kinyarwanda (40), but strikingly not in its neighbour Kirundi, where the CJ form requires a following element even if there is a clitic (41).

Kinyarwanda (JE61, Ngoboka & Zeller this volume)
(40) CJ *Twaányuzeyó.*
          Tu-á-nyúr-ye-yó.
          1PL.SM-REM-pass-PERF-LOC19
          'We passed there.'

Kirundi (JE62, Ernest Nshemezimana, p.c.)
(41)   a.   DJ   *Tw-a-a-c-íiye-yó.*
                1PL.SM-PR-DJ-come-PERF-LOC
                'We passed there.'

       b.   CJ   *Tw-aa-c-iiye-yó*   *(mw'ijoro).*
                1PL.SM-PR-come-PERF-LOC   18.night
                'We passed there in the night.'

The evidence for parameter 10 suggests that there is a relation with focus, but the data bearing on parameter 11 suggest that there are two types of languages: one in which there is a direct correlation between focus and the form of the verb; and one in which the relation is indirect, and the form of the verb is determined by the syntax. This I refer to as a 'focus-based' vs. a 'constituency-based' alternation (see also Section 3.2). Further evidence for this distinction can be found in subject inversion and VP focus.

6.4 Parameter 12: subject inversion

12. Does the verb take a CJ form in thetic subject inversion?

If the alternation is determined by constituency, any element within the right constituent is expected to trigger the CJ verb form, regardless of whether it has a specific focused interpretation or not. This is the case in Sotho, where the element following the CJ form is not necessarily interpreted as narrow or contrastive focus. Example (42a) is a thetic sentence, presenting both the verb and the postverbal subject as one piece of (new) information. The subject is not topical, but it need not be narrowly focused either –although it can be, as in (42b).

Northern Sotho (S32, Zerbian 2006: 48, 60)
(42)   a.   CJ   *Go-bina*   *basadi.*
                17SM-dance   2.women
                'There are women dancing.'

       b.   CJ   *Go-binne*   *basadi   fela.*
                17SM-dance.PAST 2.women   only
                'Only women danced.'

In contrast, in focus-based languages the CJ form is expected to always trigger a narrow focus reading, not an underspecified 'non-topical' interpretation. Hence, in thetic sentences the DJ form is used in Makwe, as illustrated in (37) above.

A CJ form would be inappropriate in an out-of-the-blue context, as it would trigger focus on the postverbal subject only.

6.5 Parameter 13: VP focus

13. Does the verb take a CJ form in VP focus?

As expected under the hypothesis of focus-based vs. constituency-based variation, languages differ in whether they employ the CJ or DJ form when the whole verb phrase is in focus. In an answer to a wh question regarding the verb phrase ('what did he do?'), it is not just the object but the combination of object and verb that is focused. These answers often require a CJ form (43), but some languages use a DJ form (44).

Makhuwa (P31, Van der Wal 2011: 1743)
(43) a. CJ *O-n-iír'   ésheeni?*
              1SM-PRES.CJ-do   9.what
              'What is she doing?'

      b. CJ *O-n-lép'   epapheló.*
              1SM-PRES.CJ-write 9.letter
              'She is writing a letter.'

      c. DJ *# O-náá-lépá   epaphélo.*
              1SM-PRES.DJ-write 9.letter

Bemba (M42, Kula this volume)
(44) a. CJ *Bushe baChocho bá-ˈcít-à   inshi?*
              Q   2.Chocho 2SM-do-FV   what
              'What does Chocho do?'

      b. DJ *Bá-lá-sáámbílíl-á.*
              2SM-HAB.DJ-learn-FV
              'She studies/goes to school.'

      c. DJ *Bá-lá-sáámbílíl-á   palicisano na   pacibelushi.*
              2SM-HAB.DJ-learn-FV   16.Friday   CONJ 16.Saturday
              'She studies on Friday and Saturday.'

If the alternation in a certain language is hypothesised to be constituent-based, then only the CJ form is expected for a transitive predicate in this environment, since the verb is not constituent-final. If, on the other hand, the alternation is thought to be focus-based, the parameter can be interpreted in either of two ways:

we can reason that the object is still part of the VP focus, and therefore the CJ form should be used; or that it is no longer the postverbal element itself that is in focus, and that therefore the DJ form is used. This property thus only works unidirectionally: if the DJ form is used in transitive VP focus, the alternation is determined by focus, but if the CJ form is used, it can be focus-based or constituency-based.

6.6 Parameter 14: focus position

14. Is there a dedicated postverbal focus position?

The CJ/DJ alternation has interfaces not just with morphology and prosody, but also with word order. As explored in more detail by Gibson et al. (this volume), some Bantu languages have a dedicated postverbal position for focus, specifically the position Immediately After the Verb (IAV) or the clause-final position. This IAV focus position was first described (and named) by Watters (1979) for Aghem and in recent years has been described as such for other languages as well (e.g., Van der Wal 2009 for Makhuwa, Buell 2009 for Zulu, Yoneda 2011 for Matengo). In addition to the constraint that focused elements appear after a CJ verb form, the focused element appears immediately after the verb (45) and nothing may intervene between the verb and the focused element (which is the question word *esheeni* in (46)).

Bemba (M42, Costa and Kula 2008: 315)
(45) a. CJ Tù-kà-byáálà   ínyànjè| mwííbàlà   màílò.|
            1PL.SM-FUT-plant 9.maize   16.garden tomorrow
            'We will plant MAIZE in the garden tomorrow.'

     b. CJ Tù-kà-byáálà   mwííbàlà| ínyànjé   màílò.|
            1PL.SM-FUT-plant 16.garden 9.maize   tomorrow
            'We will plant maize IN THE GARDEN tomorrow.'

Makhuwa (P31, Van der Wal 2009: 225)
(46) a. CJ O-n-koh-al'   éshéeni   Apákhári?
            2SG.SM-1OM-ask-PERF.CJ   9.what   1.Apakhari
            'What did you ask Apakhari?'

     b. CJ * O-n-koh-alé   Apákhári   eshéeni?
            2SG.SM-1OM-ask-PERF.CJ   1.Apakhari 9.what
            int. 'What did you ask Apakhari?'

However, Buell (2011) finds that in Zulu the question word *ngani* 'why' appears in IAV position but nevertheless follows a DJ verb form (see (36) above). Moreover,

Sotho and Tswana do not appear to have a dedicated focus position (Zerbian 2006; Creissels this volume), and in Kirundi the focus position is sentence-final (Ndayiragije 1999, and see Ngoboka & Zeller this volume for similar data from Kinyarwanda), as illustrated in (47).

Kirundi (JD62, Sabimana 1986: 91)
(47) a. DJ *Mudúga,*   *y-a-hâye*   *a-b-âna*   *i-gi-tabo.*
            Muduga   1SM-F.PAST-give   AUG-2-child   AUG-7-book
            'Muduga, he gave the children A BOOK.'

      b. CJ *Mudúga,*   *y-a-hâye*   *i-gi-tabo*   *a-b-âna.*
            Muduga   1SM-F.PAST-give   AUG-7-book   AUG-2-child
            'Muduga, he gave THE CHILDREN a book.'

Although the CJ/DJ alternation is linked to postverbal focus, and the IAV position is linked to postverbal focus as well, the CJ/DJ alternation is not necessarily conditioned by a focused IAV or other dedicated position, as Sotho and Tswana already show.

     The indirect relation is also shown in Zulu. If focused elements should occur in IAV position, they could just move there, possibly deviating from the canonical word order. However, Buell (2006, 2009) finds that there is a 'no-crossing' constraint: focused elements cannot cross over an intervening element to appear in IAV position. Instead, the intervening element must be dislocated. This is illustrated in (50). In the canonical word order the recipient object *ubaba* 'father' is in IAV (50a). When the theme object is questioned and hence focused, it should appear in IAV, but instead of simply switching the two objects (50b), the non-focal object *ubaba* must be dislocated and the object marker *-m-* referring to the dislocated object must be present on the verb (50c). In this way the focused theme remains in the right domain for a non-topical interpretation.

Zulu (S42, Buell 2009: 168, and p.c.)
(48) a. CJ *U-phek-ela*   *ubaba*   *inyama.*
            2SG.SM-cook-APPL   1.father   9.meat
            'You are cooking Father some meat.'

      b. CJ ** U-phek-el-a*   *kudla*   *kuni*]$_i$ *ubaba t$_i$?*]
            2SG.SM-cook-APPL   15.food   15.what.kind   1.father
            int. 'What kind of food are you cooking Father?'

      c. CJ *U-m-phek-ela*   *t$_i$*   *kudla*   *kuni*]   *ubaba$_i$?*
            2SG.SM-1OM-cook-APPL   15.food   15.what.kind   1.father
            'What kind of food are you cooking Father?'

An open question is to what extent word order and the CJ/DJ alternation influence and/or determine each other, and to what extent they are independent focus-marking strategies (cf. Gibson et al. this volume).

6.7 Focus-based or constituency-based

An important question concerning the interpretation is whether the association between (one or both forms of) the CJ/DJ alternation and a focus interpretation is direct or indirect. There are two points to be made here.

First, the fact that the CJ form often goes together with a focus interpretation of the following element does not mean that the CJ form *encodes* that interpretation; it could also be an inference or an indirect effect of the sentence construction (see Matić and Wedgwood 2013). The question is whether the interpretation is the main factor determining the distribution and use of the CJ and DJ verb forms or whether there is something else, which allows an indirect link to information structure. This is the second point, as already mentioned at various points above: the occurrence of the CJ and DJ verb forms can be directly determined by focus, or indirectly, instead having a correlation with constituency.

Especially for the Southern CJ/DJ Bantu languages, it has often been observed that the CJ and DJ verb form 'may in certain contexts differ in meaning but for the most part are used in different syntactical positions' (Ziervogel and Mabuza 1976: 174 on Swati). As mentioned in Section 3.2, Van der Spuy (1993) and others after him analyse the CJ/DJ alternation as determined purely by constituency: when the verb is final in the vP constituent, it takes the DJ form; when it is not final, i.e. some element follows within the vP, the verb takes a CJ form. This is visible in the right dislocation of elements following the DJ verb form (as diagnosed by the object marker and phonological phrasing), the use of the CJ verb form before non-focusable elements like resumptive pronouns and clitics, and the use of the CJ form in VP focus and in thetic VS order. The CJ/DJ alternation in Zulu is thus concluded to be constituent-based (as also confirmed by Halpert, this volume).

Quite the opposite is Makhuwa, where the alternation is focus-based: the element following the CJ form is (part of) exclusive focus, and the DJ form is used elsewhere. There is no evidence of dislocation of elements following the DJ form, and the DJ form is used with clitics in thetic VS order. Also, the ungrammaticality of non-exclusive elements in post-CJ position in Makhuwa (as in (38b) above and (49) below) remains unexplained in an analysis where constituency is the main factor in determining the form of the verb. See Van der Wal (2011) for details.

An interesting parallel example with 'even' further illustrates the difference between Zulu and Makhuwa as constituency-based vs. focus-based. The element

Table 9: Constituency-based (Zulu) and focus-based (Makhuwa) alternations.

	2a	2b	2c	10a	10b	11a	11b	12	13
Zulu	1	1	1	0	1	0	1	1	1
Makhuwa	n.a.	0	0	0	1	1	1	0	1

following the CJ verb form is interpreted as exclusive in Makhuwa and hence the particle 'even', which entails that nothing is excluded, cannot be used after a CJ form. In Zulu this is perfectly fine, because the CJ verb form is not final in the vP constituent.

Makhuwa (P31, Van der Wal 2009: 236)
(49) a. CJ *Ki-n-thotol-alé   hatá   Láúra.
              1SG.SM-1OM-visit-PERF.CJ even   1.Laura
              int. 'I visited even Laura.'
      b. DJ Ko-ń-thótólá   hatá   Láúra.
              1SG.SM.PERF.DJ-1OM-visit even   1.Laura
              'I visited even Laura.'

Zulu (S42, Buell 2008: 45)
(50) a. CJ [Ngi-bon-e   ngisho n-oSipho.]
              1SG.SM-see-PERF   even   and-1.Sipho

      b. DJ [Ngi-m-bon-ile]   ngisho n-oSipho.
              1SG.SM-1.OM-see-PERF even   and-1.Sipho
              'I even saw Sipho.'

The differences between these systems can be summarised as in Table 9.

From the data available for the 11 languages under study, it appears that there are 5 constituency-based languages (Zulu, Sotho, Tswana, Kinyarwanda,[12] Matengo), 4 focus-based languages (Makhuwa, Bemba, Kirundi and Sambaa) and 2 languages that cannot (yet) be diagnosed as one or the other type (Símákonde, Haya).

If the form of the verb is determined by the syntactic environment, that is, being positioned constituent-final or not, we can see the indirect relation with

---

[12] The parameter settings of Kinyarwanda as discussed here are more in line with the alternation being constituency-driven, although Ngoboka & Zeller (this volume) point out problematic aspects for both a constituency-based and a focus-based analysis.

information structure. The non-topical interpretation is linked to the post-verbal domain (as proposed in Buell 2006, cf. Diesing 1992), and more specifically to the constituent containing the verb. This constituent is in turn linked to the form of the verb. Taken together, this means that both the CJ form and the focus interpretation are linked to the constituent containing the verb, and it also entails that when this constituent does not have any other material, the verb forms the information peak and can be interpreted as the focus of the sentence. In contrast, the use of the CJ form is directly linked to a focus interpretation in Makhuwa.

Concluding this section on the interpretational variation, there may be a slight temporal-aspectual difference between the verb forms, but the alternation is in all languages (also) linked to a difference in information structure. The (non-)topical or (non-)focal interpretation of the verb and/or the following element differ per language; similarly, having a dedicated position for focus in IAV or sentence-final position also varies cross-linguistically. This results in an overall variation in the direct or indirect relation between the use of the verb forms and the interpretation: in some languages the alternation is demonstrably dependent on constituency, rather than semantic-discursive meaning, whereas in others there are strong arguments to assume a direct relation between focus and the alternation.

	Kirundi	Kinyarwanda	Makhuwa	Matengo	Zulu	Tswana	Sotho	Bemba	Símákonde	Haya	Sambaa
10a. DJ = V foc?	0	0	0	0	0	0		0			0
10b. Vfoc = DJ?	1	1	1	1	1	1	1	1	1		
11a. CJ = post-V foc?	1?	0	1	0	0	0		0			
11b. post-V foc = CJ?	1	1	1	0	1	1	1	1	1		0/1
12. VP focus = CJ?	0	1	1	1	1	1		0			0
13. Thetic VS = CJ?	0	1	0	0/1	1	1	1	1			
14. Dedicated position?	final	final?	IAV	IAV	IAV	0	0	IAV	IAV?		0

7 Extensions

There are at least two possible parameters that could also be included in the typological overview of the CJ/DJ alternation: which form is used preceding a clause, and whether the alternation also occurs in the nominal domain. These were not included for full discussion in this chapter, because for the majority of languages the data are simply lacking. Hence they are mentioned here only as extensions that should be included in further research.

7.1 Preceding a clause

The parameters for the CJ/DJ alternation have so far been illustrated for nominal phrases, be they arguments or adjuncts. However, as mentioned in Section 3.1, verbs can obviously also be followed by a clause, and when in the right tense, they need to take either the CJ or the DJ form. The initial questions that should be answered for this parameter are the following:

Parameter X: How does the alternation behave preceding a clause?
Xa. Which form is used before a complement clause?
Xb. Which form is used before an adverbial clause?
Xc. If both forms can be used, what is the difference in interpretation?

In Makhuwa, adverbial clauses form part of the information structure of the main clause, whereas the information-structural interpretation of complement clauses is unclear, whether they are preceded by a CJ or DJ form (van der Wal 2014).

Variation is also to be expected in different types of complement clauses, as Halpert (2012) shows for Zulu: a clause introduced by the complementiser *ukuthi* can be preceded by either form of the verb (depending on whether the CP is dislocated or not), whereas a clause introduced by the complementiser *sengathi* requires a CJ form (see also Halpert and Zeller 2015).

Zulu (S42, Halpert 2012: 178, 179)
(51) a. CJ uMandla   u-bona   [ukuthi   ngi-ya-m-thanda.]
             1.Mandla 1SM-see that   1SG.SM-PRES.DJ-1OM-like
             'Mandla sees that I like him.'

     b. DJ uMandla   u-ya-bona   [ukuthi   ngi-ya-m-thanda.]
             1.Mandla 1SM-PRES.DJ-see that   1SG.SM-PRES.DJ-1OM-like
             'Mandla sees that I like him.'

(52) a. CJ uMandla   u-bona   [sengathi ngi-ya-m-thanda.]
             1.Mandla 1SM-see as.if   1SG.SM-PRES.DJ-1OM-like
             'Mandla is of the opinion that I like him.' (implies that I don't)

b. DJ   *uMandla   u-ya-bona   [sengathi   ngi-ya-m-thanda.]
         1.Mandla   1SM-PRES.DJ-see   as.if   1SG.SM-PRES.DJ-1OM-like

For Kirundi and Kinyarwanda, Nshemezimana & Bostoen (this volume) and Ngoboka & Zeller (this volume) indicate a difference between subordinate clauses introduced by *ko* (which allow only the CJ form) and quotative clauses introduced by *ngo* (which can take either form). This could be a difference in true subordination vs. parataxis, since the quotative *ngo* introduces reported speech. See also Güldemann (1996) for further discussion on subordinate clauses in Bantu.

7.2 The nominal domain

For Makonde (Kraal 2005; Manus 2007) and Makwe (Devos 2004) a CJ/DJ alternation is proposed to exist in the nominal domain as well (see also Creissels 2009 on Tswana). In both languages the right boundary of a phonological phrase is indicated by lengthening of the penultimate syllable, and this p-phrasing patterns with the CJ/DJ alternation. Just like the verb can be phrased either together with the following object (conjoint) or separately (disjoint), the noun can also be phrased with a following modifier, or not. In Símákonde, demonstratives are obligatorily phrased with the noun (53), adjectives cannot phrase with the noun (53b) and for possessives the phrasing is optional (53c,d).

Símákonde (P23, Manus 2007 and p.c.)
(53) a. *sîlóló   asiilá|*
          mirror   that
          'that mirror'

      b. *lyoônga| líkúmeêne|*
          arrow   big
          'a big arrow'

      c. *muuko | wáangu |*
          bag   my

      d. *mukó   waángu |*
          bag   my
          'my bag'

For Makwe, Devos (2004) describes a different pattern, but whether noun and modifier phrase together or not is still 'to a large extent lexically determined' by the modifier. However, there is a link with focus: the CJ modifiers, that are obligatorily phrased together with the noun, all have some selective function, thereby indicating contrastive focus. Examples of CJ modifiers are 'only', 'which' and possessives. Only demonstratives have a choice to be phrased with the noun or not, and 'whether a p-phrase is formed or not depends on the way the speaker wants to present the information' (p.311). With the CJ phrasing in (54) the demonstrative induces an exclusive reading, which would be absent with a DJ phrasing.

Makwe (G402, Devos 2004: 311)
(54) Ni-lembela   kítábúucí. |
       1SG.SM-want   7.book:7.DEM.I
       'I want this book (not another one).'

While the differences with the verbal CJ/DJ alternation are evident, the similarities are striking. The same is true for Bemba, where p-phrasing in the noun phrase is also variable. Although Sharman and Meeussen (1955) argue that this is the same alternation as found in the verbal domain, Kula (this volume) shows that 'the patterning of nominals can be easily explained by the same tone rules/p-phrasing without postulating that the CJ/DJ alternation is also encoded in nominals'.

8 Conclusion

There is a large amount of crosslinguistic variation for the conjoint/disjoint alternation, which has been charted in 14 parameters, mentioning 2 possible extra parameters. The parametric settings found for 11 languages show that there are at least three constant factors: (i) all languages have a sentence-final restriction on one form (parameter 1); (ii) there is a correlation between focal elements requiring one or the other form (parameter 10); (iii) all languages have some morphological marking to make the alternation apparent. This is what motivates the working definition of the alternation, repeated below:

(55) The conjoint/disjoint alternation is an alternation between verb forms that are formally distinguishable, that are associated with an information-structural difference in the interpretation of verb and/or following element and of which one form is not allowed in sentence-final position.

Further research should reveal in which other languages we find a similar alternation, candidates being Yom (Fiedler this volume), Kikuyu (Morimoto this volume), Shangaji (Devos this volume), Aghem (Watters 1979; Hyman and Polinsky 2009; Hyman 2010), Majang (Joswig 2015), Doyayo (Elders 2006), Wolof (Creissels and Robert 1998; Robert 2000, 2010), Mauritian Creole (Van der Wal and Veenstra 2015), Igbo (and other Benue-Kwa languages, Manfredi 2005), Sinhala (Herring and

Paolillo 1995; Slade 2011), and Nigerian Benue-Congo languages such as Efik (Cook 2002), Gwari and Ejagam (Watters where distinct verb forms are used to indicate argument vs. verb phrase focus (Hyman and Watters 1984, cf. Gibson et al. this volume). It would be highly interesting to see the parameter settings for these and other languages, checking their patterns against the proposed definition.

Some of the parameters were shown to be useful as diagnostics distinguishing constituency-based systems from focus-based systems, which seems to be a general choice languages make. In the constituency-based languages, focus is indirectly associated with the alternation, and possibly with a dedicated focus position (although this is not necessary). This can further inform theories on the interface between syntax and information structure. Furthermore, the variation in mapping between syntax and prosody will also shed light on the interface between these two areas. Both are left for further research, but a possible way in may be to examine how the various focus and constituency marking strategies cooperate, and whether one has a more primary task in marking focus (see also the discussion in Yoneda this volume and Gibson et al. this volume).

Another interesting topic for further research is the diachronic development of the alternation (cf. Hyman this volume). Both Güldemann (2003) and Nurse (2008) suggest that the alternation could have been present in Proto-Bantu, since it would be unexpected for several languages to develop a system that is so much alike. Meeussen (1967: 109) also reconstructs *-da- as a Proto-Bantu morpheme for 'disjunct'. Güldemann (2003) proposes a development for the marker -a- or -ya- (and maybe -ra- is also related) from a disjoint focus marker to a progressive marker to a present tense morpheme. However, we have seen that the alternation is not marked by one morpheme across languages and across tenses. It is not just one verb form, but rather a system or a conjugational parameter (like aspect and evidentiality are). As such, it is difficult to establish the grammaticalisation path of the forms indicating the alternation and the development of the alternation itself, but comparative syntactic research may further elucidate the issue.

Abbreviations and symbols

High tones are indicated by an acute accent, low tones are unmarked. Numbers refer to noun classes, or to persons when followed by SG or PL.

|	right boundary phonological phrase	APPL	applicative
*	ungrammatical	AUG	augment
#	infelicitous	CJ	conjoint verb form
		CONN	connective

COP	copula	PASS	passive
DEM	demonstrative	PERF	perfective
DIM	diminutive	PL	plural
DJ	disjoint verb form	POSS	possessive
FM	focus marker	PR	recent past
F.PAST	far past	PRES	present tense
FUT	future tense	PRO	pronoun
FV	final vowel	PROG	progressive
HAB	habitual	REL	relative
LOC	locative	REM	remote past tense
NEG	negation	SM	subject marker
OM	object marker		

References

Adams, Nikki B. 2010. *The Zulu ditransitive verb phrase*. Chicago: University of Chicago dissertation.

Bresnan, Joan & Sam Mchombo. 1987. Topic, pronoun, and agreement in Chichewa. *Language* 63. 741–782.

Buell, Leston C. 2006. The Zulu conjoint/disjoint verb alternation: Focus or constituency? *ZAS Papers in Linguistics* 43. 9–30.

Buell, Leston. 2005. *Issues in Zulu morphosyntax*. Ph. D. dissertation, University of California, Los Angeles.

Buell, Leston C. 2008. VP-internal DPs and right-dislocation in Zulu. In Marjo van Koppen & Bert Botma (eds.), *Linguistics in the Netherlands* 25, 37–49. Amsterdam: John Benjamins.

Buell, Leston C. 2009. Evaluating the immediate postverbal position as a focus position in Zulu. In Masangu Matondo, Fiona Mc Laughlin & Eric Potsdam (eds.), *Selected Proceedings of the 38th Annual Conference on African Linguistics: Linguistic Theory and African Language Documentation*, 166–172. Somerville, MA: Cascadilla Proceedings Project.

Buell, Leston C. 2011. Zulu ngani 'why': postverbal and yet in CP. *Lingua* 121 (5). 805–821.

Cheng, Lisa Lai-Shen & Laura J. Downing. 2009. Where's the topic in Zulu? *The Linguistic Review* 26 (2–3). 207–238.

Cheng, Lisa Lai-Shen & Laura J. Downing. 2012. Against FocusP: Arguments from Zulu. In Ivona Kucerova & Ad Neeleman (eds.), *Information structure. Contrasts and positions*, 247–267. Cambridge: Cambridge University Press.

Cole, Desmond T. 1955. *An introduction to Tswana*. Capetown: Longman.

Cook, Thomas. 2002. Focus in Efik. *Journal of African Languages and Linguistics* 23 (2). 113–152.

Costa, João & Nancy C. Kula. 2008. Focus at the interface: Evidence form Romance and Bantu. In Cécile De Cat & Katherine Demuth (eds.), *The Bantu-Romance Connection*. Amsterdam: John Benjamins. 293–322.

Creissels, Denis. 1996. Conjunctive and disjunctive verb forms in Setswana. *South African Journal of African Languages* 16 (4). 109–115.

Creissels, Denis & Stéphane Robert. 1998. Morphologie verbale et organisation discursive de l'énoncé: l'exemple du Tswana et du Wolof. In Suzy Platiel & Raphaël Kabore (eds.), *Faits de Langues = Revue de Linguistique*, 161–178.

Creissels, Denis. 2009. Construct forms of nouns in African languages. In Peter K. Austin, Oliver Bond, Monik Charette, David Nathan & Peter Sells (eds.), Proceedings of Language Documentation and Linguistic Theory 2, 73–82. London: SOAS.

Devos, Maud. 2004. *A grammar of Makwe*. University of Leiden dissertation.

Devos, Maud & Jenneke van der Wal. 2010. 'Go' on a rare grammaticalisation path to focus. In Jacqueline van Kampen & Rick Nouwen (eds.), *Linguistics in the Netherlands*, 45–58. Amsterdam: John Benjamins.

Diesing, Molly. 1992. *Indefinites*. Cambridge, MA: MIT Press.

Doke, Clement M. 1927. *Text-book of Zulu grammar*. Johannesburg: University of the Witwatersrand.

Du Plessis, Jan A. & Marianna Visser. 1992. *Xhosa syntax*. Pretoria: Via Afrika.

Elders, Stefan. 2006. Conjoint and disjoint in Doyayo: Bantu-like verb forms in an Adamawa language. Paper presented at Workshop on focus in African languages, Berlin.

Endemann, Karl. 1876 (reprinted 1964). *Versuch einer Grammatik des Sotho*. Ridgewood, NJ: The Gregg Press.

Givón, Talmy. 1975. Focus and the scope of assertion: Some Bantu evidence. *Studies in African Linguistics* 6 (2). 185–205.

Güldemann, Tom. 1996. Verbalmorphologie und Nebenprädikation im Bantu. Bochum: Universitätsverlag Dr. N. Brockmeyer.

Güldemann, Tom. 2003. Present progressive vis-à-vis predication focus in Bantu: A verbal category between semantics and pragmatics. *Studies in Language* 27 (2). 323–360.

Guthrie, Malcolm. 1948. *The classification of the Bantu languages*. London: Oxford University Press.

Halpert, Claire. 2012. *Argument licensing and agreement in Zulu*. Cambridge, MA: MIT dissertation.

Halpert, Claire & Jochen Zeller. 2015. Right-disocation and raising-to-object in Zulu. *The Linguistic Review* 32(3). 475–513.

Harjula, Lotta. 2004. *The Ha Language of Tanzania: Grammar, text and vocabulary*. Cologne: Rüdiger Köppe Verlag.

Herring, Susan & John C. Paolillo. 1995. Focus position in SOV languages. In Pamela Downing & Michael Noonan (eds.), *Word order in discourse*, 163–198. Amsterdam: John Benjamins.

Hurel, Eugène. 1951. *Grammaire Kinyarwanda*. Ruanda: Imprimerie de Kabgayi.

Hyman, Larry M. & Ernest R. Byarushengo. 1984. A model of Haya tonology. In George N. Clements & John A. Goldsmith (eds.), *Autosegmetal Studies in Bantu Tone*, 53–103. Dordrecht: Foris.

Hyman, Larry M. & John Watters. 1984. Auxiliary focus. *Studies in African Linguistics* 15. 233–273.

Hyman, Larry M. 1999. The interaction between focus and tone in Bantu. In Georges Rebuschi & Laurie Tuller (eds.), *The grammar of focus*, 151–177. Amsterdam: John Benjamins.

Hyman, Larry M. & Maria Polinsky. 2009. Focus in Aghem. In Caroline Féry & Malte Zimmermann (eds.), *Information structure. Theoretical, typological and experimental perspectives*, 206–233. Oxford: Oxford University Press.

Hyman, Larry M. 2010. Focus marking in Aghem: syntax or semantics? In Ines Fiedler & Anne Schwarz (eds.), *The expression of information structure: a documentation of its diversity across Africa*, 95–116. Amsterdam: John Benjamins.

Joswig, Andreas. 2015. Syntactic sensitivity and preferred clause structure in Majang. In Angelika Mietzner & Anne Storch (eds.), *Nilo-Saharan: Models and descriptions*, 169–176. Cologne: Rüdiger Köppe Verlag.
Kavari, Jekura U., Lutz Marten & Jenneke van der Wal. 2012. Tone cases in Otjiherero: head-complement relations, linear order, and information structure. *Africana Linguistica* XVIII. 315–353.
Kosch, Ingeborg M. 1988. 'Imperfect tense –a' of Northern Sotho revisited. *South African Journal of African Languages* 8 (1). 1–6.
Kraal, Peter. 2005. *A grammar of Makonde*. Leiden: Leiden University dissertation.
Maho, Jouni. 2009. NUGL online: the online version of the New Updated Guthrie List, a referential classification of the Bantu languages. Available online at glocalnet.net/mahopapers/nuglonline.pdf
Manfredi, Victor. 2005. Conjoint/disjoint in western Benue-Kwa. Paper presented at Humboldt Universität Berlin, and LUCL Leiden.
Manus, Sophie. 2007. Phrasal tone & the conjoint/disjoint distinction in Símákonde. Paper presented at ZAS Berlin.
Marten, Lutz, Nancy C. Kula & Nhlanhla Thwala. 2007. Parameters of morpho-syntactic variation in Bantu. *Transactions of the Philological Society* 105 (3). 253–338.
Marten, Lutz & Nancy C. Kula. 2012. Object marking and morphosyntactic variation in Bantu. *South African Journal of African Languages* 30 (2). 237–253.
Marten, Lutz & Jenneke van der Wal. 2015. A typology of Bantu inversion constructions. *Linguistic Variation* 14 (2). 318–368.
Matić, Dejan & Daniel Wedgwood. 2013. The meanings of focus: The significance of an interpretation-based category in a cross-linguistic perspective. *Journal of Linguistics* 49 (1). 1–37.
Meeussen, A. E. 1955. Tonunterschiede als Reflexe von Quantitätsunterschieden im Shambala. In Afrikanistische studien, ed. J. Lukas. Berlin: Akademie Verlag.
Meeussen, A. E. 1959. *Essai de grammaire Rundi*. Tervuren: Musée Royale de l'Afrique Central.
Meeussen, A. E. 1967. Bantu grammatical reconstruction. Annales du Musée Royal de l'Afrique Centrale Tervuren 8. 80–121.
Ndayiragije, Juvénal. 1999. Checking economy. *Linguistic Inquiry* 30. 399–444.
Nurse, Derek. 2008. *Tense and aspect in Bantu*. Oxford: Oxford University Press.
O'Neil, rev. J. 1969. *A grammar of the Sindebele dialect of Zulu*. Ellis Allen.
Odden, David. 1984. Formal correlates of focusing in Kimatuumbi. *Studies in African Linguistics* 15 (3). 275–299.
Odden, David. 1996. *The phonology and morphology of Kimatuumbi*. Oxford: Clarendon Press.
Odden, David. 2003. Rufiji-Ruvuma (N10, P10-20). In Derek Nurse & Gérard Philippson (eds.), *The Bantu languages*, 529–545. London: Routledge.
Poulos, George. 1990. *A linguistic analysis of Venda*. Pretoria: Via Afrika.
Riedel, Kristina. 2009. *The syntax of object marking in Sambaa: A comparative perspective*. Utrecht: LOT.
Robert, Stéphane. 2000. Le verbe wolof ou la grammaticalisation du focus. In Bernard Caron (ed.), *Topicalisation et focalisation dans les langues africaines*, 229–267. Louvain: Peeters.
Robert, Stéphane. 2010. Focus in Atlantic languages. In Ines Fiedler & Anne Schwarz (eds.), *The expression of information structure. A documentation of its diversity across Africa*, 233–260. Amsterdam: John Benjamins.
Sabimana, Firmard. 1986. *The relational structure of the Kirundi verb*. Bloomington: Indiana University dissertation.

Schadeberg, Thilo C. 2004. Conjoint & disjoint; grammaticalized information structure in Bantu. Paper presented at Universiteit van Amsterdam.

Sharman, J. C. 1956. The tabulation of tenses in a Bantu language (Bemba: Northern Rhodesia). *Africa* 16. 29–46.

Slade, Benjamin Martin. 2011. *Formal and philological inquiries into the nature of interrogatives, indefinites, disjunction, and focus in Sinhala and other languages*. Urbana-Champaign: University of Illinois dissertation.

Ström, Eva-Marie. 2013. *The Ndengeleko language of Tanzania*. Gothenburg: University of Gothenburg.

Stucky, Susan. 1985. *Order in Makua syntax*. New York: Garland Publishing.

Letsh'eng, 'Makhauta C. 1995. Les tiroirs verbaux du Sesotho. Mémoire, Université Stendhal (Grenoble III).

van der Spuy, Andrew. 1993. Dislocated noun phrases in Nguni. *Lingua* 90. 335–355.

van der Wal, Jenneke. 2006. The disjoint verb form and an empty Immediate After Verb position. *ZAS Papers in Linguistics* 43. 233–256.

van der Wal, Jenneke. 2009. *Word order and information structure in Makhuwa-Enahara*. Utrecht: LOT.

van der Wal, Jenneke. 2010. Grammaticalisation and pragmatic strengthening of conjugations in southern and eastern Bantu languages – a diachronic perspective on conjoint and disjoint verb forms. Paper presented at Annual Conference on African Linguistics 41, Toronto.

van der Wal, Jenneke. 2011. Focus excluding alternatives: Conjoint/disjoint marking in Makhuwa. *Lingua* 212 (11). 1734–1750.

van der Wal, Jenneke. 2014. Subordinate clauses and exclusive focus in Makhuwa. In Rik van Gijn, Jeremy Hammond, Dejan Matic, Saskia van Putten & Ana Vilacy Galucio (eds.), *Information structure and reference tracking in complex sentences*, 45–70. Amsterdam: John Benjamins.

van der Wal, Jenneke & Tonjes Veenstra. 2015. The long and short of verb alternations in Mauritian Creole and Bantu languages. *Folia Linguistica* 49 (1). 85–116.

Van Eeden, B. I. C. 1956. *Zoeloe-grammatika*. Stellenbosch/Grahamstad: De Universiteit-suitgewers en -boekhandelaars.

van Warmelo, N. J. 1937. *Tshivenda-English dictionary*. Pretoria: Government Printer.

Watters, John. 1979. Focus in Aghem. In Larry M. Hyman (ed.), *Aghem grammatical structure*. Los Angeles: University of Southern California.

Yoneda, Nobuko. 2011. Word order in Matengo (N13): Topicality and informational roles. *Lingua* 121(5). 754–771.

Zeller, Jochen. 2012. Object marking in isiZulu. *Southern African Linguistics and Applied Language Studies* 30 (2). 219–235.

Zerbian, Sabine. 2006. *Expression of information structure in Northern Sotho*. Berlin: Humboldt University dissertation.

Ziervogel, Dirk. 1959. *A grammar of Northern Transvaal Ndebele*. Pretoria: J.L. van Schaik.

Ziervogel, Dirk & Enos J. Mabuza. 1976. *A grammar of the Swati language*. Pretoria: J.L. van Schaik.

Hannah Gibson, Andriana Koumbarou, Lutz Marten
and Jenneke van der Wal
3 Locating the Bantu conjoint/disjoint alternation in a typology of focus marking

1 Introduction

The Bantu conjoint/disjoint (CJ/DJ) alternation has attracted considerable attention in the recent (African) linguistics literature. The conjoint/disjoint alternation is found, for example, in Bemba (1) and Tswana (2), where the conjoint form cannot appear sentence-finally in main clauses, in contrast with the disjoint form, which can appear in a sentence-final position:

(1) Bemba

    a. *Tù-lòòndòlòl-à   lyòònsé.* (CJ)
       1PL.SM-explain-FV always
       'We explain all the time.'

    b. *Tù-là-lòòndòlòl-à.* (DJ)
       1PL.SM-DJ-explain-FV
       'We (usually) explain.' (Kula this volume)

(2) Tswana

    a. *Kè-tlàà-bín-à   lé   èné.* (CJ)
       1SG.SM-FUT-dance-FV with him/her
       'I shall dance with him/her.'

    b. *Kè-tlàà-bín-á.* (DJ)
       1SG.SM-FUT-dance-FV
       'I shall dance.' (adapted from Creissels 1996: 110)

In Bemba, the alternation is indicated segmentally – the disjoint form in (1b) is marked by the marker *-la-*. In Tswana, whilst the alternation is marked segmentally in some tenses, in other tenses the marking is tonal (2). Several key

---

Jenneke van der Wal's part of this work is funded by the European Research Council Advanced Grant No. 269752 'Rethinking Comparative Syntax'. We would like to acknowledge our gratitude to Tim Bazalgette, Nancy Kula, and Thilo Schadeberg for discussion of some of the issues raised in this chapter.

aspects of the alternation have been shown to pose a challenge for a comprehensive analysis (see e.g. Hyman and by Van der Wal in this volume). These include the formal marking of the alternation and the relation with other prosodic markers of constituency, the restriction to specific tense-aspect paradigms, and the role of syntax and/or information structure in the distribution of the forms. In addition, there exists a high degree of micro-variation of conjoint/disjoint marking within Bantu, giving rise to typological and comparative-historical challenges.

Conjoint/disjoint systems have not been documented as such outside of Niger-Congo, and appear to be mostly found in Bantu languages, making the alternation geographically and typologically highly restricted.[1] The aim of the present chapter is to locate the alternation within a wider typology of focus marking. This will enrich the broader research on focus by allowing it to draw on evidence from Bantu, as well as helping us to better understand the conjoint/disjoint alternation through observed cross-linguistic parallels. It may also contribute to wider familiarity with the construction, and in doing so help to find instances of conjoint/disjoint systems outside of Niger-Congo.

For the purpose of the present study, we restrict our empirical scope to the expression of term focus, leaving aside for the time being focus on the verb or truth value (see discussion in Section 3). This allows us to establish the relevant typological space of our comparison through the use of two parameters: syntactic position and morphological marking. Syntactic position (or topology) has the four values left-peripheral, right-peripheral, immediately-before-the-verb (IBV) and immediately-after-the-verb (IAV), while morphological marking has the two values 'marking on the focused term' or 'marking on the verb' (while still marking term focus). Within this typology, typical Bantu conjoint/disjoint systems are characterised by combining focus marking on the verb and the use of the IAV position, while the systems of some other Bantu languages have only one of these two values: For example, Kinyarwanda shows focus on the verb but not IAV

---

[1] Conjoint/disjoint alternations in Bantu languages such as Bemba (Sharman 1956; Costa and Kula 2008), Kirundi (Meeussen 1959) and Tswana (Creissels 1996) have been the most well-documented cases; Kavari et al. (2012) note the similarity between conjoint/disjoint systems and 'tone cases' in Otjiherero – see also Hyman (this volume) on the comparison with tone cases, the augment and metatony. Non-Bantu languages for which conjoint/disjoint distinctions have been reported include Doyayo (Adamawa; Elders 2006), Igbo (and other Benue-Kwa languages) (Manfredi 2005), Majang (Nilo-Saharan; Joswig 2015), and Yom (Gur; Fiedler this volume). Although not explicitly referred to as conjoint/disjoint systems, comparable distinctions are also found in Bantoid (Aghem, Ejagham) and Nigerian Benue-Congo languages such as Efik and Gwari, where distinct verb forms are used to indicate argument vs. verb phrase focus (Hyman and Watters 1984).

(focus is clause-final), and Aghem shows IAV, but (term) focus is marked on the term rather than on the verb. We extend the account to non-Bantu languages with the goal of interrogating whether additional patterns can be identified through the application of these parameters.

Based on a small convenience sample of sixteen Bantu languages and nine non-Bantu languages, we examine construction types in which focus is encoded through a combination of a dedicated focus position and the use of morphological marking, hence double marking. At present we do not include the third main focus coding strategy – prosody – since inclusion of prosody would make the study more complex than current space allows, and since we do not have sufficient information on prosodic marking for many of the languages included in our study. We do, however, include prosodic morphemes (such as grammatical tone marking the conjoint/disjoint distinction), as these fall within morphological marking. In terms of empirical scope, we adopt an inclusive approach to focus and focus marking, including data described as relating to focus in the literature, and including Bantu conjoint/disjoint systems from a variety of different languages. There is considerable variation between Bantu languages with respect to the function of conjoint/disjoint systems – some clearly relating to identificational focus, others clearly related to constituency, and some possibly performing a function which lies in between these two. A future study may well distinguish these different systems, as well as different kinds of focus more generally. However, for the present study, we include a wide selection of languages, based on formal criteria of morphological and syntactic marking, and develop a typology based on these.[2] Overall, we show 1) that all eight logically possible combinations of topology and morphological marking are found in our sample, 2) that Bantu and non-Bantu languages occupy largely exclusive areas in the typological space, and 3) that, although this difference results to a large extent from the strong head-marking tendency in Bantu languages, the difference between Bantu and non-Bantu cannot be reduced to a single parameter.

The chapter is organised as follows. In Section 2, we introduce our typology of focus marking along with the parameters of syntactic position and morphological marking. In Section 3, we discuss methodological issues and the empirical limitations of the study, and provide a more detailed explication of the notion of focus we adopt. Section 4 presents a summary of our findings, based on our sample of 25 languages, discussing first non-Bantu languages and then Bantu languages, showing how the conjoint/disjoint alternation fits into this typological space. In Section 5, we present a summary of the discussion, draw a number of conclusions and identify possible directions for further research.

---

[2] We provide a more detailed discussion of our working definitions and methodology in Section 3.

2 A typology of morphosyntactic focus marking

A cross-linguistic comparison of how focus is expressed reveals a great deal of variation (see e.g. Foley 1994; Van Valin 1999; Drubig and Schaffar 2001; Büring 2010; Smit 2010). Generally speaking, focus can be expressed linguistically in prosody, morphology and/or syntax. Assuming that there is a unified conceptual notion of focus (cf. Molnár 2002; Neeleman et al. 2009; Zimmermann and Onea 2011), we examine a typology of focus marking along two parameters: syntactic position (or topology) and morphological marking. The former refers to focus marking through a dedicated syntactic position, and the latter to the use of dedicated morphological focus markers. The purpose of the current section is to present the parameters and illustrate their possible values in turn; further discussion on the definition and identification of focus follows in Section 3.

2.1 Topology

Many languages make use of a dedicated position for the expression of focus. A cross-linguistic comparison of the syntactic expression of focus reveals four possibilities for such a position: initial, immediately before the verb (IBV), immediately after the verb (IAV) and final. These are identified with respect to adjacency to the verb (IBV and IAV) or sentential edges (initial and final).

A sentence-initial focus position is illustrated in (3) with data from Hausa, an SVO language. Example (3a) shows an instance of basic word order with a neutral information structure. In (3b) *teelà* 'tailor' is in focus and placed in a sentence-initial position.[3]

(3) Hausa
    a. *Bintà zaa tà biyaa teelà.*
        B. FUT 3SG.F pay tailor
        'Binta will pay the tailor.'

    b. *Teelà (nee) Bintà zaa tà biyaa.*
        tailor FOC B. FUT 3SG.F pay
        'Binta will pay the TAILOR.' (Hartmann and Zimmermann 2007: 99)

Ostyak (Uralic, SOV) has an IBV focus position as shown in (4). Example (4a) shows that a wh-question word corresponding to the passive agent adjunct must

---

3 In example (3b) the term in focus can optionally be followed by the masculine focus marker *nee*.

occur in the IBV position. In (4b) the same is shown for a wh-question word corresponding to the indirect object, while (4c) shows that the focused element in the answer to (4b) also obligatorily occurs in the IBV position:

(4) Ostyak
    a. (*Xoj-na) tam a:n xoj-na tu:-s-a?
        who-LOC this cup who-LOC take.away-PAST-3SG.PASS
        'Who took away this cup?'

    b. (*Xoj e:lti) tăm a:n xoj e:lti ma-s-e:n?
        who to this cup who to give-PAST-2SG.OM2
        'To whom did you give this cup?'

    c. (*Juwan-a) tam a:n Juwan-a ma-s-e:m.
        John-LAT this cup John-LAT give-PAST-1SG.OM2
        'I gave this cup to John.' (Nikolaeva 2001: 18)

The use of the IAV focus position can be seen in Aghem (Grassfields Bantu, Cameroon). In examples (5a) and (5b) the focused term, án˅sóm and áfɨn respectively, is placed immediately after the verb.[4] Since the canonical word order in Aghem is S(Aux)VOX, the non-canonical position of the adverbial and the subject show that IAV is a dedicated focus position.

(5) Aghem
    a. Fíl á mɔ̀ zɨ́ án˅sóm bé-˅kɔ́.
        friends SM PAST₂ ate LOC-farm fufu-CL
        'The friends ate fufu in the FARM.'

    b. À mɔ̀ zɨ́ á-fɨn bé-˅kɔ́ án˅sóm.
        ES PAST₂ ate friends fufu-CL LOC-farm
        'The FRIENDS ate fufu in the farm.' (Watters 1979: 144, 147)

Final focus position can be seen in Tangale (Chadic, Nigeria, SVO) with focused subjects. Example (6a) shows a wh-question word and (6b) shows a focused subject appearing in the clause-final position.

---

[4] The term IAV was first used by Watters (1979). In addition to this focus position, Aghem also uses verbal and auxiliary marking to express focus. This is discussed in further detail below. Watters (1979: 148–152) also identifies an immediately before the verb (IBV) position in Aghem which may host presupposed material.

(6) Tangale
    a. *Pàd-gò   tàabéè   nóŋ?*
       buy-PERF   tobacco   who
       'Who bought tobacco?'

    b. *Pàd-gò   tàabéè   kài.*
       buy-PERF   tobacco   Kai
       'KAI bought tobacco.' (Kidda 1993: 131 via Zimmermann 2011: 1173)

This gives us Table 1, which illustrates our first parameter and contains languages in which one of the four focus positions can be identified:

Table 1: Topology parameter and its values.

Topology	Initial	IBV	IAV	Final
	Hausa	Ostyak	Aghem	Tangale

2.2 Morphological focus marking

Some languages make use of morphological markers for the expression of focus. Morphological focus marking can involve the attachment of a focus marker on the focused term itself, or on the verb, either of which can express a focused interpretation of a term, i.e. an argument or adverb but not the predicate.[5,6]

The following data from Sri Lankan Malay illustrate morphological focus marking on the term. In (7) an enclitic *-jo* is suffixed to participants which appear in their canonical position:

(7) Sri Lankan Malay
    a. (So, [while] the king was planning to make a fool out of Andare)
       Raja=jo   su-jaadi   enco.
       king=FOC   PST-become   fool
       'The KING (himself) became a fool.'

---

[5] Marking on the term could be considered analogous to dependent-marking while marking on the verb could be considered as head-marking. However, these terms typically refer to syntactic relations in the clause, rather than to information structural properties and the relation between terms and the wider discourse structure, and so we chose not to employ this terminology here.

[6] It is logically possible, although appears to be rare, to have morphological marking on both the term and the verb. This can be seen in the optional term marking in the Colloquial Sinhala examples in (8), in Aghem (Hyman and Polinsky 2009), Yom ('background tense', Fiedler this volume) and Baynunk (Robert 2010).

b. (Now that we've done all this)
   ...*Siini=jo   ara-duuduk.*
   here=FOC   PRS-stay
   '... here we stay.' (Smit 2010: 242, who refers to Nordhoff p.c.)

Verb-marking term focus is encountered in Colloquial Sinhala. In a neutral context the final vowel of the verb is -*a* (8a), but when a pre- or post-verbal term is in focus, the verb ends in the vowel -*e*, as in (8b) and (8c). The focused term can have additional marking, but this is said to be optional, whereas the marking on the verb is obligatory (Slade 2011: 61).

(8) Colloquial Sinhala

    a. *Mamə   gamətə   yann-a.*
       1SG.NOM village-DAT go.PRES-NFOC
       'I go to the village.'

    b. *Mamə   gamətə(-y)   yann-e.*
       1SG.NOM village-DAT(-EMPH) go.PRES-FOC
       'It is to the village I go.'

    c. *Mamə   yann-e   gamətə(-y).*
       1SG.NOM go.PRES-FOC village-DAT(-EMPH)
       'It is to the village I go.' (Slade 2011: 63, 64, adapted)

Our second parameter, morphological marking (of term focus), can thus be set as 'on the focused term' or 'on the verb' as indicated in Table 2.

Table 2: Morphological focus-marking parameter.

Morphological focus marking	On focused term	On verb
	Sri Lankan Malay	Sinhala

2.3 Combination of syntactic and morphological focus marking

So far we have looked at syntactic and morphological strategies as logically independent means of focus marking. We have discussed them separately showing a single focus-marking mechanism (topological or morphological) per language. With the conjoint/disjoint systems in mind, however, we are interested in the combination of syntactic and morphological means for the expression of focus.

Table 3: Parametric settings for the expression of focus.

Morphology \ Topology	Initial	IBV	IAV	Final
On term				
On verb				

If we merge the two previously shown tables (Tables 1 and 2), we obtain eight possible ways in which syntactic and morphological strategies can be combined as shown in Table 3.

Table 3 is to be filled with languages which show a focus-marking strategy involving the simultaneous use (optional or obligatory) of syntactic and morphological means for marking term focus. Note that we do not claim that the constructions we are discussing are the only strategies for the realisation of focus in a given language, rather we aim to show a cross-section of strategies in different languages without implying an exhaustive description.

Having introduced the typological parameters established for the purpose of this study, we turn now to our methodology (Section 3) before proceeding to our findings and outlining the typological context within which the conjoint/disjoint systems will be discussed (Section 4).

3 Methodology, empirical focus and scope of the study

Some of the methodological issues that need to be addressed concern definitions, sample choices, the inclusion and exclusion of different kinds of data, and possible limitations of the study. In particular, we will discuss our empirical concentration on term focus (rather than predicate-centred focus), and on morphological and syntactic encoding of focus (rather than prosodic encoding), as well as the particular kinds of focus constructions we have included. It is also worth noting that our sample of languages is a convenience sample, without any claims of balance or exhaustiveness. In selecting languages, we were mainly guided by previous comparative, descriptive or theoretical studies, and our primary aim was to establish a typological space within which to locate conjoint/disjoint systems, without taking into account the frequency or representativeness of different constructions (although this would obviously be an interesting point for further research).

3.1 Term focus vs. predicate-centred focus

As shown by the data discussed in the preceding section, we are comparing the Bantu conjoint/disjoint alternation with cross-linguistic variation in marking of term focus, as opposed to verb or predicate-centred focus (including polarity, TAM and verb focus, and other forms of focus related to the predicate or the clause; Güldemann 2009, also Morimoto this volume). In some sense, this is only half the relevant context, as conjoint/disjoint systems have often been related to both term focus (i.e. marking a following constituent as being in focus) and predicate focus (i.e. marking the predicate itself as being [included in] the focus) (cf. Hyman and Watters 1984; Güldemann 1996, 2003; Nshemezimana & Bostoen this volume; Voeltz 2004). Nevertheless, there is a clear correlation between the use of the conjoint verb form and a term being (part of the) focus, whereas it is not the case that each occurrence of the disjoint verb form results in predicate-centred focus (but see Nshemezimana & Bostoen this volume). This is one motivation for first examining the expression of term focus. Secondly, there is more readily available literature on term focus, and so it is easier to establish the typological background and variation of term focus. In contrast, typological variation of predicate-centred focus is more restricted – or possibly less well described – with the major patterns being marking of the predicate by stress, or some form of reduplication (cf. e.g. Aboh 2004; Güldemann et al. 2014), neither of which is directly relevant for attested conjoint/disjoint systems. So, while a more detailed study of variation in predicate-centred focus marking, and its relation to conjoint/disjoint systems would be worthwhile undertaking in the future, for the purposes of the present chapter, we restrict our investigation to term focus and the way(s) in which this is expressed morphologically or syntactically across different languages.

3.2 Morphological/syntactic vs. prosodic encoding of focus

A second restriction of our sample is that we are only looking at morphological and syntactic marking of focus, disregarding prosodic marking. As with the concentration on term focus, this decision is partly driven by operational reasons: Morphological and syntactic marking of focus are better described overall. We also wish to exclude from the study languages in which focus is marked solely through prosody. We therefore concentrate on languages which mark focus morphologically, while making no claims that these languages do not also employ prosodic mechanisms for information structure purposes.

The relation between focus and prosody is well established in languages like English and Italian, where the difference between the two languages is often analysed as a difference between fixed word order and variable prosodic prominence in the sentence in English as opposed to prosodic prominence, fixed stress and variable word order in Italian (see Zubizarreta 1998; Lambrecht 1994; Vallduví 1992; Van Valin 1999; Samek-Lodovici 2005; Büring 2010; among others). However, in many Bantu – and indeed African – languages, stress or corresponding forms of prosodic prominence such as vowel lengthening do not play a direct role in focus marking (cf. Hyman 1999; Zerbian 2007; Downing 2013, see also other Chapters in this volume, especially by Kula, by Halpert, and by Zeller, Zerbian & Cook).

To illustrate, in Chichewa, prosodic prominence (penultimate lengthening) is assigned to the penultimate syllable preceding an intonation phrase boundary. It typically occurs clause-finally, but may also occur, for example, on preverbal topics, and so prosodic prominence can be assigned to several constituents in the clause. Furthermore, no word order change needs to occur in Chichewa to express focus: Both prominence and word order can remain invariant, and so focus can remain unmarked. Penultimate lengthening in (9) can be seen with the topic *mwaáná* 'child', which is (optionally) phrased as extra-clausal, and with the final constituent *mwáálá* 'rock'. Crucially, there is no prosodic marking (stress or lengthening) on the focused constituent *nyumbá* 'house', indicating that penultimate lengthening is not directly related to focus.

(9) Chichewa
 Mw-aáná á-naa-ménya nyumbá ndí mwáálá.
 1-child 1SM-TAM-hit 9.house with 3.rock
 'The child hit THE HOUSE with a rock.'
 (Answer to 'What did the child hit with the rock?')
 (Downing and Pompino-Marshall 2013: 661)

Since Chichewa, unlike other Bantu languages, also does not have a syntactic IAV position or conjoint/disjoint verb forms, focus is not marked in this example.

Furthermore, Cheng and Downing (2009) argue that even in Bantu languages which exhibit a focus-related word order change – such as the use of the IAV position in Zulu – underlyingly, word order change is not directly related to prosodic prominence, although the focused constituent may attract prosodic marking by virtue of being phrase-final. In (10), the focused phrase is VP-final, and the following NP *ínkukhu* 'chicken' is right-dislocated, as indicated by the co-referential object marker on the verb form.

(10) Zulu
 a. (Ú-si:pho) (ú-yí-phékéla ba:ni) (ín-ku:khu).
    1-Sipho 1SM-9OM-cook.for 1.who 9-chicken
    'Who is Sipho cooking the chicken for?'

 b. (Ú-síph' ú-yí-phékél' ízí-vakâ:sh') (ín-ku:khu).
    1-Sipho 1SM-9OM-cook.for 8-visitor 9-chicken
    'Sipho is cooking the chicken for the visitors.' (Downing 2013: 34)

The absence of a direct relation between focus and prosodic marking has, in part, informed our decision to set prosodic marking to one side, and to concentrate on morphological and syntactic expression of focus for the present study.[7] Research building on this initial typology could involve prosodic marking of focus.

3.3 Focus

In comparing the variation in the expression of term focus, we must define what we mean by 'focus' and how we establish whether a certain linguistic strategy expresses focus. We adopt a broad definition of focus, including both 'new information' and contrastive or identificational focus (compatible with Dik's 1997 focus and subtypes, see also Lambrecht 1994; É. Kiss 1998; Krifka 2007). Although many of the examples below have a clear contrastive or identificational interpretation, in other cases we have to rely on secondary sources where 'focus' is underspecified. It may thus be the case that we can or should employ a more narrow definition of focus, but for now we need to keep it broad. Furthermore, even though it may turn out in more detailed research that 'contrast' should be taken as a separate notion (Molnár 2002, Neeleman et al. 2009), for this comparative overview we do not examine it separately.

In Section 2 we saw examples of a dedicated focus position and of focus-marking morphology. The question arises as to how we can determine whether a certain position or morphological marking actually indicates focus. As Matić and Wedgwood (2012) point out, it may be that the relevant strategy does not actually encode focus, and that focus interpretation is a side-effect of some other mechanism (i.e. a pragmatic implicature).

---

[7] It has to be kept in mind here that conjoint/disjoint marking is often tonal, i.e. often involves assignment of different verb tones, but that in that case, the marking is morphological (through tonal morphemes) rather than attributable to phrasal prosodies.

While keeping this in mind, and in part having to rely on the authors' description of a phenomenon as 'marking focus', we have three well-established diagnostics to check for focus: question-answer pairs, wh-words, and focus particles (see Van der Wal 2016 for further focus diagnostics and for detailed references). These are the contexts and tests that we will see in the examples in Section 4, when discussing focus positions and morphology in the various languages. In the current section, the tests are discussed in turn and illustrated for Makhuwa, which has an IAV focus position (topology) and the conjoint/disjoint alternation (morphological marking on the verb).

A well-known and widely accepted diagnostic for focus is question-answer pairs. Essentially, a wh-question always asks for new information. If focus is defined as the new information in a sentence, then it follows that in the answer to a wh-phrase – the phrase that replaces the wh-element – is in focus:

(11) Q-A test (Kasimir 2005: 12)
 If a question asks for some X (X being a syntactic category), in a direct answer to this question, the constituent which corresponds to X is focused.

If the NP that forms the answer to a wh-question must be located in a specific position and is ungrammatical elsewhere, this can be taken as evidence that the position is a dedicated focus position. In Makhuwa, answers to non-subject wh-questions must occur in the IAV position, possibly resulting in topical elements being moved to the preverbal domain:[8]

(12) Makhuwa
 a. O-n-thum-el-alé   páni   ekúwo?
    1SG.SM-1OM-buy-APPL-PFV.CJ 1.who 9.cloth
    'Who did you buy a cloth for?'

 b. (Ekúwó) ki-n-thum-el-alé   Ańsha.
    9.cloth 1SG.SM-1OM-buy-APPL-PFV.CJ 1.Ansha
    'The cloth, I bought for Ansha.' (database Van der Wal)

In the same way, morphological marking can also be tested: If a focused reading is only possible with a particular morphology, then this morphology can be said to encode focus. This is shown in (13), where the verb in the answer necessarily appears in the conjoint form in order to be appropriate:[9]

---

8 Note that Makhuwa has as a neutral order theme > benefactive, which is unusual for Bantu languages. See also Van der Wal (2009).
9 The conjoint or disjoint form of the verb is indicated in the gloss and before the example.

(13) Makhuwa

    a. CJ   *O-lomw'*   *éshéeni?*
           1SM-fish.PFV.CJ 9.what
           'What did he catch?'

    b. CJ   *O-lomwé*   *ehopá.*
           1SM-fish.PFV.CJ 9.fish
           'He caught fish.'

    c. DJ   # *Oo-lówá*   *ehópa.*
           1SM.PFV.DJ-fish 9.fish
           'He caught fish.' (Van der Wal 2009: 232)

A second diagnostic are the wh-words themselves. Wh-words very often pattern with focus, and hence if wh-words are restricted in their occurrence to a certain position or must occur with a certain morphology, this forms evidence for a dedicated focus position and dedicated focus morphology, respectively. In Makhuwa, non-subject wh-words must occur in the IAV position, as shown in (14) and they must occur with the conjoint verb form (15):

(14) Makhuwa

    a. CJ   *O-n-rúw-áka*   *tsayi* *eshíma?*
           2SG.SM-PRES.CJ-stir-DUR how   9.shima
           'How do you make shima?'

    b. CJ   **O-n-rúw-áka eshímá tsayí?*
           (Van der Wal 2009: 225)

(15) Makhuwa

    a. CJ   *O-n-c'*   *éshéeni?*
           2SG.SM-PRES.CJ-eat 9.what
           'What are you eating?'

    b. DJ   **O-náá-ca eshéeni?*
           (Van der Wal 2009: 231)

A difficulty here is that interrogatives do not pattern with focus in every language. In our sample, Kirundi shows a final focus position (16) but wh-words can appear in situ rather than in the final position (17). This does not invalidate interrogatives as a heuristic for focus, but does bring a warning that it is not a conclusive test and more than one diagnostic should be applied (cf. Aboh 2007).

(16) Kirundi
    a. DJ *Mudúga, y-a-hâye   a-b-âna   i-gi-tabo.*
           Muduga   1SM-F.PAST-give   AUG-2-child   AUG-7-book
           'Muduga, he gave the children A BOOK.'

    b. CJ *Mudúga, y-a-hâye   i-gi-tabo   a-b-âna.*
           Muduga   1SM-F.PAST-give   AUG-7-book   AUG-2-child
           'Muduga, he gave THE CHILDREN a book.' (Sabimana 1986: 91)

(17) Kirundi
    CJ *Y-a-zan-i-ye   ndé   u-mu-pira?*
        1SM-R.PAST-bring-APPL-ASP   who   AUG-3-ball
        'For whom did she bring a ball?' (Sabimana 1986: 193)

A third diagnostic are so-called focus particles or focus-sensitive operators. These trigger a focused reading on the element they modify, or associate with the focus of the sentence. Common focus particles include scalar 'even', additive 'also', and exclusive 'only' (see Van der Wal 2014 for further discussion of this diagnostic). If an element modified by such a particle is distributionally restricted to a certain position, or must occur with a certain morphology, this again shows that there is a dedicated focus position or dedicated focus morphology. The Makhuwa data show that an NP with the exclusive particle *paáhí* 'only' must appear in IAV position (compare (18a) and (18b)), and it must follow a conjoint form, not a disjoint form (18c).

(18) Makhuwa
    a. CJ   Maríyá   o-m-vah-alé   [ekamitsa paáhí]   [Apútáála].
              1.Maria   1SM-1OM-give-PFV.CJ   9.shirt   only   1.Abdallah
              'Maria gave Abdallah only a shirt.'

    b. CJ   ?? Maríyá   o-m-vah-alé   [Apútáálá]   [ekamitsa paáhi].
              1.Maria   1SM-1OM-give-PFV.CJ   1.Abdallah   9.shirt   only
              'Maria gave Abdallah only a shirt.'

    c. DJ   * Maríyá   o-ḿ-váhá   [ekamitsa paáhí]   [Apútáála].
              1.Maria   1SM.PFV.DJ-1OM-give   9.shirt   only   1.Abdallah
              'Maria gave Abdallah only a shirt.' (Van der Wal 2009: 226)

There is a crucial difference between these focus *particles*, which carry some semantic value (scalar, additive, exclusive) and what we call focus *markers*, which are purely functional morphological markers of focus. This latter type is illustrated by data from Gungbe, where the marker wὲ marks focus on the preceding element, cf. (19b) and (19c). The particle and the marker can actually co-occur, as shown in (19d).

(19) Gungbe
    a. *Sɛ́ná xìá wémà.*
       Sena read.PERF book
       'Sena read a book.'

    b. *Sɛ́ná #(wɛ̀) xìá wémà.*
       Sena FOC read.PERF book
       'SENA read a book.'

    c. *Wémà *(wɛ̀) Sɛ́ná xìá.*
       book FOC Sena read.PERF
       'Sena read a BOOK.'

    d. *Wémà lɔ́ co *(wɛ̀) Sɛ́ná xìá.*
       book DET only FOC Sena read.PERF
       'Sena read only the book.' (Aboh 2004 and personal correspondence)

Two issues arise with respect to establishing what constitutes a focus-marking strategy, whether topological or morphological. The first concerns the strictness of the focus marking. For topology, it is hardly ever the case that *all* focused NPs can appear in the focus position. For example, the IAV position in Makhuwa can only express focus on objects and adverbs; subjects are ungrammatical in the position directly following a conjoint verb form (Van der Wal 2009). Subjects in Makhuwa can only be focused in a cleft sentence. Another example of a non-strict focus position is when elements other than the focused one seem to have priority. In Turkish, for example, which has been characterised as a language with an IBV focus position (Butt and King 1996),[10] indefinite nouns also need to occur in the IBV position and they apparently take priority over (focused) wh-words, as illustrated in the examples in (20) below.

(20) Turkish
    a. *Kim para al-dı?*
       who money steal-PAST
       'Who stole (some) money?'

    b. **Para kim čal-dı?*
       money who steal-PAST
       'Who stole (some) money?'

---

[10] See also Göksel and Özsoy (2000), who argue that focused constituents can appear in any preverbal position.

c. *Para-yi   kim   čal-di?*
money-ACC who steal-PAST
'Who stole the money?' (Kim 1988: 158)

It remains an open and perhaps unanswerable question as to how much 'leaking' a particular position is allowed and can yet still be characterised as a focus position. For the current discussion, we rely on claims in the literature for a certain dedicated position, while being aware of critical counterexamples (Drubig and Schaffar 2001; King 2004; Yip 2004). These counterexamples can lead us to reject a claim of a language having a dedicated focus position. Eastern Armenian, for example, has been characterised as requiring the focus to be adjacent to the auxiliary, much like an IBV focus position (Tamrazian 1991). However, new information can occur in non-IBV position, negation can intervene between focus and the auxiliary, and indefinite nominals need to be adjacent to the auxiliary too, like in Turkish (Comrie 1984). It seems that, rather than having a dedicated focus position, Eastern Armenian has a mobile auxiliary clitic that marks focus (Megerdoomian 2011), and thus should not be considered as a language with an IBV focus position.

What we thus mean when referring to a focus position is a position that various tests show to be in an unambiguous relation with focus, while leaving room for minor consistent exceptions. An initial position is a position where it is clear that other elements (typically or exclusively) follow the focused element, and a final position is one where other elements precede the focused element, excluding possible hanging topics in the left periphery that are outside the core clause ('fish, I like cod') and afterthoughts or marginalised elements in the right periphery ('I like it, the fish that is'). For example, when an SVO language expresses object focus by the order OSV, this shows that focus is not expressed in its canonical position and also that the focus position is not immediately before the verb, but rather it is initial.

A second issue concerns the structure of a sentence containing term focus as a biclausal cleft structure or a monoclausal focus strategy. The biclausal cleft consists of a predicative nominal ('it is the stick') and a relative clause ('that the children broke'), which together result in a focus reading:

(21)   Lubukusu
Lw-á-bá   lú-u-saala   ní-lwó   bá-bá-ana   bá-a-lu-funa.
11SM-PST-be AUG-11-stick COMP-11 AUG-2-child 2SM-PST-11OM-break
'It was the stick that the children broke.' (Diercks 2011: 708)

This construction is known to frequently develop into a monoclausal focus marking strategy (Heine and Reh 1984; Harris and Campbell 1995), where in various steps the clauses undergo fusion and often one of the morphemes in the original cleft, such as the copula or the relative marker, becomes a morphological focus marker:

(22) [copula NP] - [relative clause] > [NP$_{focus}$ verb]
It is Maud - (the person/one) who made pancakes > MAUD (FOC) made pancakes

This is presumably what has happened in Kikuyu, where the copula in an original cleft ('it **is** water') has grammaticalised to become a focus marker in a simple clause:

(23) Kikuyu
 a. *Abdul ne morutani.*
  Abdul COP teacher
  'Abdul is a teacher.'

 b. *Ne mae abdul a-ra-nuy-irɛ.*
  COP/FOC 6.water Abdul SM1-T-drink-PERF
  'Abdul drank WATER.' (Schwarz 2007: 140,141, adapted)

However, it is often difficult to establish where a construction in a given language is in the grammaticalisation process. Grammaticalisation proceeds via small changes, such as the ones in (24). As they may show conflicting properties, some being evidence of biclausality and others of monoclausality, it is not always possible to establish whether the underlying structure is a cleft or a simple focus construction.

(24) Changes biclausal > monoclausal (Harris and Campbell 1995: 166, 167)
– changing the case of the focused constituent
– changing the form of the focus marker to look less like the copula or relativiser
– dropping the copula or relativiser altogether
– ceasing to use a special verb form
– (re)introducing agreement according to monoclausal structure
– reordering of constituents

This is relevant to our research, as it is concerned with the expression of focus in dedicated positions *within* the clause. As such, biclausal clefts are different from monoclausal focus constructions and therefore should not to be taken into account in our comparative overview. We have taken this into consideration when looking at the various focus strategies in our sample, but again have to rely in part on what the authors describe. Yucatec Maya is an example of a language for which inclusion in the sample is debatable. Term focus in this VSO language is expressed in the position immediately before the verb, as shown in the OVS order in (25). When the agent is focused, a special form of the verb needs to be used, as seen in the difference between the neutral example in (25b) and subject focus in (25c).

(25) Yucatec Maya
    a. *Òon   t=u   hàant-ah   Pèedróoh.*
       avocado PFV=PMA.3 eat:TRR-CMPL(PMB.3.SG) Pedro
       'It was (an) avocado that Pedro ate.'

    b. *T=u   hàant-ah   òon   Pèedróoh.*
       PFV=PMA.3 eat:TRR-CMPL(PMB.3.SG) avocado Pedro
       'Pedro ate avocado.'

    c. *Pèedróoh hàant   òon.*
       Pedro eat:TRR(SUBJ)(PMB.3.SG) avocado
       'It was Pedro who ate (an) avocado.' (Verhoeven and Skopeteas 2015: 3,4)

Yucatec Maya could thus be seen as a language with IBV focus position and morphological marking on the verb (i.e. in the same category as the Bantu languages Mbuun and Kikongo, discussed below). Indeed, a monoclausal analysis has been proposed by Gutiérrez Bravo and Monforte (2009) and Verhoeven and Skopeteas (2015). However, it has also been shown that the verbal morphology is present not just in the case of subject focus, but in extraction in general (Stiebels 2006). Furthermore, since nominal predication is not marked (i.e. no copula is required), the focus construction can also be analysed as a bare cleft, as argued for by Bricker (1979), Bohnemeyer (2002, 2008), Tonhauser (2003), and Vapnarsky (2013). Since the status of the construction as monoclausal or biclausal is unclear, we have not included it in our study.

Having discussed the definitional and methodological preliminaries to our study, in the next section we turn to the results of our research into the typology of focus-expressing strategies in morphology and word order, and especially the combination of the two.

4 The focus-marking landscape

As described in Section 2, we propose a typology of focus marking defined along two parameters: syntactic position and morphological marking. The current section presents the results of our cross-linguistic study of topological and morphological focus marking.

Table 4: Distribution of languages with simultaneous syntactic and morphological marking of focus.

Morphology \ Topology	Initial	IBV	IAV	Final
On term	Gungbe, Jamaican Creole, *Kikuyu*, *Kituba*, *Lingala*	Hindi, Selayar	*Aghem*, *Noni*, *Tunen*	Ngizim
On verb	Gâbunke Fula, Karitiâna, Sereer	*Mbuun*, *Kikongo*	*Bemba*, *Haya*, *Makhuwa*, *Matengo*, *Naki*, Podoko, *Zulu*	*Kinyarwanda*, *Kirundi*

In Section 2 we established four settings for our topology parameter: initial, immediately before the verb (IBV), immediately after the verb (IAV) and final. With four possible structural positions, each of which is defined binarily for marking on the term itself or marking on the verb, the findings of our study are presented in Table 4. As can be seen in the table, there are eight possible combinations for morphological and topological marking of focus, all of which are encountered. Bantoid/Bantu languages in the table are in italics.[11]

An examination of the table reveals that the heart of the conjoint/disjoint alternation is found in the combination of an IAV focus position and morphological marking on the verb. Other Bantu languages also use one of these values, combining IAV with morphological marking on the term, or combining marking on the verb with a final position. The post-verbal (IAV and final) positions seem to be preferred in Bantu. With respect to the non-Bantu languages in our sample, they are distributed across five of the eight possible combinations, generally preferring pre-verbal positions.

The subsequent sections of this chapter illustrate the focus-marking strategies employed by the non-Bantu languages and the Bantu languages of our sample, fitting these within the wider cross-linguistic typology. Observations resulting from this exploration will constitute conclusions presented in Section 5.

4.1 Non-Bantu languages: the wider typology

As Table 5 shows, the non-Bantu languages of our sample occupy five of the cells in the table: Focus can be marked topologically in every position (initial/final,

---

[11] We group Aghem (Grassfields Bantu), Naki and Noni (non-Bantu Bantoid) together with the Bantu languages of our sample in a (strictly speaking) Bantoid/Bantu group, although in what follows we will refer to the group simply as Bantu.

Table 5: The non-Bantu languages.

Morphology \ Topology	Initial	IBV	IAV	Final
On term	Gungbe, Jamaican Creole	Hindi, Selayar		Ngizim
On verb	Gâbunke Fula, Karitiâna, Sereer		Podoko	

IBV/IAV) but there are restrictions on the morphological marking, which appears on the term only when the focus position is not IAV, and on the verb when the focus position is initial or IAV. In other words, it is only the initial focus position in which both morphological marking on the term and on the verb are found, while the three other positions go with one or the other of the morphological marking options.

The first combination of values is illustrated by Gungbe (Aboh 2007) and Jamaican Creole (Durrleman-Tame 2008), which employ the clause-initial position and morphologically mark focus on the term. Gungbe (Kwa, Benin) is an SVO language in which focused constituents are positioned in the sentence-initial position.[12] Thus in the examples in (26) below, the focused nominal expressions *Sèsínú* and *Àsíàbá* are placed clause-initially. These nominal elements are also obligatorily followed by the morphological focus marker *wè*.

(26) Gungbe
    a. *Sèsínú wè dà Àsíàbá.*
       Sessinou FOC marry Asiaba
       'SESSINIOU married Asiaba.'

    b. *Àsíàbá wè Sèsínú dà.*
       Asiaba FOC Sessinou marry
       'Sessinou married ASIABA.' (Aboh 2007: 289)

An initial focus position is found in a number of Atlantic languages (Robert 2010), represented by Gâbunke Fula (Atlantic, Senegal) and Sereer (Atlantic, Senegal) in the table, as well as in Karitiâna (Tupi, Brazil), all of which exhibit SVO constituent order. However, in these languages the morphological marking of focus is located on the verb. We illustrate this for Karitiâna, where the object-focus prefix *ti-* is attached to the verb to mark focus on the object. At the same time, the focused object occurs in a non-canonical initial position, as seen by the subject intervening between the focused object and the verb (resulting in OSV order):

---

[12] Disregarding possibly preceding topics, as mentioned in Section 3.

(27) Karitiâna
    a. *Mõrãmõn a-ti-hĩrã?*
       what   2SG.ABS-OF-smell
       'What did you smell?'

    b. *Eposi:d ĩn ti-hĩrã̞ -t.*
       flower   1SG   OF-smell-NFUT
       'I smelled a flower.'

(28)   *Mõrãmõn sopãm ti-m?a-tĩnã-t   (hĩ)?*
       what/who Sopãm OF-make-PROG-NFUT Q
       'What is Sopãm making?' (Everett 2006: 325, via Van Valin 2009)

Hindi and Selayar (Austronesian, Indonesia) in Table 5 are languages which show an IBV focus position and also employ a morphological strategy for the expression of focus (see Butt and King (1996), Kidwai (1999) for this in Hindi and Finer (1994) and Frascarelli (1999) for this in Selayar). Combining IBV focus position with a focus marker on the term is illustrated here with data from Hindi.

While Hindi has a dominant SOV order, a sentence with a subject, verb and object can have all six possible constituent orders (Butt and King 1996). When there is more than one preverbal element, the first is typically interpreted as the topic and the immediately preverbal one as the focused constituent. IBV in Hindi is illustrated in (29), where the subject *Raam* is in focus:

(29)   Hindi
       Kitaab Raam laayegaa, (siitaa nahii).
       book   Ram   bring.FUT   Sita   not
       'RAM will bring the book, not Sita.' (Kidwai 1999: 228)

Hindi also makes use of the morphological focus marker *hii*, which marks narrow focus (Kidwai 1999; in Sharma 2003 *hii* marks exclusive contrastive focus) and can follow the focused constituent in the IBV position:

(30)   Hindi
       Kitaab Raam-hii laayegaa (siitaa nahii).
       book   Ram-FOC   bring.FUT   Sita   not
       'RAM will bring the book, not Sita.' (Kidwai 1999: 223, adapted)

The focus marker *hii*, however, can be used independently of the IBV focus position as can be seen in (31) and (32), where the focused subjects appear in their canonical position:

(31) Hindi
Maya=ne hii anu=ko kitaab dii.
Maya=ERG FOC anu=DAT book.NOM give.PERF.F.SG
'MAYA only gave Anu a book.' (Sharma 2003: 63)

(32) Hindi
Raam-hii kitaab laayegaa, (siitaa nahii).
Ram-FOC book bring.FUT Sita not
'RAM will bring the book, not Sita.' (Kidwai 1999: 228, adapted)

The two strategies (topological and morphological focus marking) can thus be used simultaneously or independently in Hindi. In our typology we are concerned with co-occurring syntactic and morphological focus-marking strategies, which seems to be the case in (30), where the focused subject *Raam* is not in its canonical position and is followed by *hii*. The independence of syntactic and morphological marking is further discussed in our conclusion in Section 5.

The use of the IAV position with focus marked on the verb is found in Podoko (Chadic, Cameroon). Podoko has a basic VSO word order with possible focused elements intervening between the verb and the subject (Jarvis 1991). For example, in (33b) *á dzangə* 'on the mountain' is placed immediately following the verb, which is preceded by *a*. In contrast, in (33a) no expression intervenes between the verb and the subject, which is now marked with a high tone *údzəra* 'child' (or in the case of some pronouns it will carry the prefix *m-*). Also, the verb is not preceded by *a*.[13]

(33) Podoko
 a. Gələ údzəra.
    PRF.grow NFOC.child
    'The child grew up.'

 b. A gə́lə á dzangə udzəra.
    FOC PRF.grow on mountain child
    'It was on the mountain that the child grew up.'
    (Jarvis 1991: 216, adapted glosses)

Our study identified one language which employs the sentence final position for topological marking of focus and morphological marking on the term. Ngizim (West Chadic, Nigeria) is an SVO language which employs an inversion construction, resulting in a focused subject. In these constructions, the basic 'neutral' word order is deviated from and the focused subject appears in the final position

---

13 See Jarvis (1991) for more information on the additional role of aspect in Podoko.

preceded by a focus particle *n* (Zimmermann 2011). This is illustrated in (34) with a question-answer pair where both the wh-word and the term in focus are realised in a final position.

(34) Ngizim
    a. ɗaurəw   Nyabe   n   tai?
       call.PFV   Nyabe   FOC   who
       'Who called Nyabe?'

    b. ɗaurəw   Nyabe   n   Anja.
       call.PFV   Nyabe   FOC   Anja
       'Anja called Nyabe.'

    c. *ɗaurəw   Nyabe   Anja.
       call.PFV   Nyabe   Anja
       Intended: 'Anja called Nyabe.' (Grubic 2010: 21–22)

In sum, the non-Bantu languages of our sample predominantly mark focus morphologically on the term, and topologically in initial, IBV or final position. Ngizim is the only language in our sample which combines focus marking on the term with a final focus position, while Podoko is the only non-Bantu language in our sample which combines the IAV position with term focus morphologically marked on the verb. In contrast, several languages employ an initial focus position, and a combination of both marking on the verb and on the term. As we will show in the next section, the typological space occupied by the Bantu languages of our sample is in largely complementary distribution with the space occupied by the non-Bantu languages.

4.2 The Bantu languages

As outlined at the beginning of this section, Bantu languages occupy five of the cells in our table. Kikuyu, Kituba and Lingala occupy the initial/on term cell; Mbuun and Kikongo occupy the IBV/on verb cell; and the closely related Kirundi and Kinyarwanda occupy the final/on verb cell. The remainder of the Bantu languages in our sample are concentrated in the IAV position. The IAV/on term languages are Aghem, Noni and Tunen, while the languages which employ the IAV position and mark focus morphologically on the verb are Bemba, Haya, Makhuwa, Matengo, Naki and Zulu. This is summarised in Table 6.

The first combination of parameters we discuss with respect to Bantu languages is focus marked on the term in the initial position. Kituba and Lingala

Table 6: Locating the Bantu languages within the broader typology.

Morphology \ Topology	Initial	IBV	IAV	Final
On term	Kikuyu, Kituba, Lingala		Aghem, Noni, Tunen	
On verb		Mbuun, Kikongo	Bemba, Haya, Makhuwa, Matengo, Naki, Zulu	Kinyarwanda, Kirundi

(Van der Wal and Maniacky 2015) as well as Kikuyu (Schwarz 2007; Morimoto this volume) employ this strategy. In Kikuyu (E51, Kenya), both question words and answers need to occupy the initial position and be preceded by the marker *ne*:

(35) Kikuyu

    a. *N-oo   o-ðom-ay-era   mwana   iβuku?*
        FOC-who   1SM-read-HAB-APPL   1.child   5.book
        'Who (usually) reads a/the book to the child?'

    b. *Ne   Abdule   o-ðom-ay-era   mwana   iβuku.*
        FOC   1.Abdul   1SM-read-HAB-APPL   1.child   5.book
        'It is Abdul who reads a/the book to the child.' (Schwarz 2003: 57)

A further combination of parameter settings is to have a dedicated focus position immediately before the verb (IBV) but indicate focus morphologically on the verb rather than the term itself. This is the case in Mbuun (Bantu B87, DRC) and Kikongo (H16, DRC). Bostoen and Mundeke (2012) show that in Mbuun the subject marker in class 1 varies depending on which element in the sentence is focused, as given in Table 7. This can be seen as a morphological marking of focus on the verb, even if it differs from the conjoint/disjoint marking as found in other Bantu languages, and also from non-Bantu focus morphology on the verb, where the morphology seems attached to TAM morphology. De Kind (2014) shows the same pattern for varieties of Kikongo.

Bostoen and Mundeke (2012) also show that focused elements are placed in the position immediately preceding the verb, as shown in (36a) and (36b): the

Table 7: Class 1 subject markers in Mbuun.

	Past/perfect	Other tenses
No argument focus	ká-	á-
Object focus	ká-	ká-
Non-object focus	á-	á-

basic word order is SVO, object focus SOV, and subject focus OSV. An exception is adjunct focus, which can be expressed in-situ (usually with SVO ordering).

(36) Mbuun

a. *Mpfúm   ná   ká-wó-ból?*   SOV
president who   1SM-PST-hit
'Who did the president hit?'

b. *Mpfúm   ná   á-wó-ból?*   OSV
president who   1SF.SM-PST-hit?
'Who hit the president?'

c. *Ampfúm   á-ker-loon   búl.*
president 1SF.SM-FUT-repair 14.country
'The president will rebuild the country.'

d. *Báná   ká-ker-bú-loonne?*
2.who   1SM-FUT-14OM-repair.APPL
'For whom will he rebuild it?'

e. *Ámpúr   ká-ker-bú-loonne.*
2.poor 1SM-FUT-14OM-repair.APPL
'He will rebuild it for the poor.'
(Bostoen and Mundeke 2012: 146, 147, adapted glosses)

Moving to the postverbal domain, Bantu languages that have an IAV focus position can morphologically mark the focus on either the term or the verb. The former combination is found in Aghem (Watters 1979; Hyman and Watters 1984; Hyman and Polinsky 2009), Noni (Hyman 1981; Kalinowski and Good 2014) and Tunen (Mous 1997). Aghem (Grassfields Bantu, Cameroon) has a dominant SVO order (37a). Despite this, variable constituent orders can be employed to convey considerations of information structure. Focus expressions and wh-words invariably appear in the IAV position. In fact, it was Aghem focus that was first analysed in detail as having an IAV focus position by Watters (1979). In (37b) the noun phrase *tíbvú tìbìghà* 'two dogs' appears in the IAV position resulting in a focus interpretation of the subject expression. This can also be seen in (37c), where *né* 'today' appears in the IAV position and is focused. The focused term may be an argument, e.g. a subject (37b), or an adjunct (37c).

(37) Aghem

a. *Tí-bvú   tì-bìghà   mɔ́   zì   kí-bɛ́   ↓né.*
dogs   two   PAST1   eat   DET-fufu today
'The two dogs ate fufu today.'

b. À mɔ̀ zɨ́ tɨ́-bvú tɨ̀-bìghà bé ⁺kɔ́ né.
   ES PAST1 eat dogs two fufu DET.OBL today
   'The TWO DOGS ate fufu today.'

c. Tɨ́-bvú tɨ̀-bìghà mɔ̀ zɨ́ né ⁺bé ⁺kɔ́.
   dogs two PAST1 eat today fufu DET.OBL
   'The two dogs ate fufu TODAY.' (Hyman and Polinsky 2009: 206/7)

The Aghem IAV position is associated with identificational focus. Wh-words also appear in the IAV position (38).

(38) Aghem

a. Bvú ⁺tɨ́ mɔ̀ zɨ́ kwɔ̀ né (à).
   dogs DET PAST2 eat what today QM
   'What did the dogs eat today?'

b. À mɔ̀ zɨ́ ndúghɔ́ ⁺bé ⁺kɔ́ né (à).
   ES PAST1 eat who fufu DET.OBL today QM
   'Who ate the fufu today?'

c. Tɨ́-bvú tɨ̀-bìghà mɔ̀ zɨ́ zín bé ⁺kɔ́ (á).
   dogs two PAST1 eat when fufu DET.OBL QM
   'When did the two dogs eat the fufu?' (Hyman and Polinsky 2009: 207/8)

Noun phrases in Aghem also exhibit an alternation in form according to their focal status, differing between so-called A and B forms such as *tɨ́bvú* 'dogs' (A form) and *bvú*⁺tó 'dogs' (B form) or *álɨ́m* 'yams' (A form) and *lɨ́m ghɔ́* 'yams' (B form). The A form is used when the noun is in focus or is expectedly out of focus (Watters 1979: 56), e.g. when it is an object and appears in the IAV position. In contrast, the B form is used when the noun is unexpectedly out of focus. The noun for 'fufu', for example, appears in the A form as *kɨ́bé* (comprised of the prefix *kɨ́-* and the nominal root *bé*) and when it is the object of an affirmative sentence (39a). However, it appears in the B form as *bé*⁺kó (with the root *bé* and the determiner *kɔ́*) when it is not focused, e.g. when it appears after a focused IAV element (39b) or in the IBV position (39c).[14]

(39) Aghem

a. Ǹ mɔ̀ zɨ́ kɨ́-bé ⁺né.
   I PAST₁ ate fufu today
   'I ate fufu today.'

---

14 In (39c) *bé*⁺kɔ́ appears as *bé*⁺kɨ́ due to a phonological rule which results in the allomorphic realization of *Cɨ* and *Cɔ*. This does not relate to focus in the same way as the distinction between *kɨ́bé/bé*⁺kɔ́.

b. M̀ mɔ́ zɨ̀ ⁺né bé-kɔ́.
   I PAST₁ ate today fufu
   'I ate fufu TODAY.' (Hyman 1979: 56, 59)

c. Ò mɔ́ bé ⁺kɨ́ zɨ̀ né.
   SM PAST1 fufu DET eat today
   'He ate fufu TODAY.' (Hyman 2010: 101, adapted)

The B form is also used in non-IAV post-verbal position (40a) (where the use of the A form would render the sentence ungrammatical) and after the focal auxiliary *maa* (40b), which renders focus on the truth value rather than the postverbal element. The B form is also required in relative clauses and with negatives and imperatives.[15]

(40) Aghem

a. Ò mɔ́ zɨ̀ né ⁺bé ⁺kɔ́. (*kɨ́-bê)
   SM PAST₁ eat today fufu DET
   'He ate fufu TODAY.'

b. Ò mâa zɨ̀ bé ⁺kɔ́ né.
   SM PAST₁-FOC eat fufu DET today
   'He did eat fufu today.' (Hyman 2010: 101/2, adapted)

In Aghem, a matrix clause cannot end in a bare verb. Rather, intransitive verbs and transitive verbs that appear without a postverbal object obligatorily have their IAV position filled. This results in an 'in situ' focus reading of the verb which has been analysed in similar terms as the conjoint/disjoint alternation (Hyman and Watters 1984; Creissels 1996; Güldemann 2003; Buell 2006). The obligatory placement of the particle *nò* after verbs without postverbal objects can be seen in (41).

(41) Aghem

a. Ò mɔ́ bvù *(nò).
   3SG PAST1 fall FM
   'He fell.'

b. Ò mɔ́ zɨ̀ *(nô).
   3SG PAST1 eat FM
   'He ate (it).'

c. Bvú ⁺tí mɔ́ bé ⁺kɨ́ zɨ́ *(nô).
   dogs DET PAST2 fufu DET eat FM
   'The dogs ATE the fufu.' (Hyman and Polinsky 2009: 207)

---

[15] The full picture is actually slightly more complicated than we present it here, and a comprehensive analysis of the facts remains outstanding. Cf. Hyman (1979, 1985, 2010) and Watters (1979) for discussion.

Like Aghem, Tunen marks focus in the IAV position. However, while Aghem is a basic SVO language, word-order in Tunen is more complex and it is one of the few Bantu languages in which the direct object typically precedes the verb (42a). When the object is (contrastively) focused, it follows the verb, and is in addition marked with a contrastive particle *á* (42b).

(42) Tunen
    a. Àná mòné índì.
       3s:PST money give
       'S/he gave money.'

    b. Àná índì á mòné.
       3s:PST give PRT money
       'S/he gave MONEY.' (Mous 1997: 126)

Our small typology thus shows that IAV focus is found with both SVO languages (Aghem, Noni, Bemba, Haya, Makhuwa, Matengo, Naki, Zulu) and SOV languages (Tunen). Conversely, the two Bantu languages with IBV focus – Mbuun and Kikongo – are otherwise SVO languages. There is thus no absolute correlation in our sample between basic word-order and focus position with respect to the verb (IBV/IAV), in contrast to wider cross-linguistic trends (cf. Herring 1990).

The other option for languages with an IAV focus position is to morphologically mark focus on the verb. The one non-Bantu language identified in our study which belongs to this system is Podoko, but the majority of the languages belonging to this type are Bantu languages, since this is the combination as instantiated in the canonical conjoint/disjoint system. Languages in our sample which fall into this category include Bemba (M42), Haya (E24), Matengo (N13), Makhuwa (P31), Naki and Zulu (S42). For example, Makhuwa makes use of an IAV position which is directly and unambiguously related to (exclusive) focus. This was illustrated in Section 3, where three tests were applied to both the topology and the morphology marking focus in Makhuwa. Naki, a SVO Bantoid language of Cameroon, also employs the IAV position for the marking of verbal focus. In some tenses this construction in Naki is also associated with a special tone marking. This can be seen in comparison of the examples (43) below, where the verb in example (43a) exhibits a High-Mid tone pattern while example (43b) shows High-High.[16]

---

16 Whilst Naki is not considered to have a conjoint/disjoint alternation in the true sense, Good (2010: 18) notes that the distinction between confluentive and disfluentive verb forms found in Naki (as exemplified in 43) is "clearly reminiscent of the opposition between conjoint and disjoint verb forms found in many (Narrow) Bantu languages...".

(43) Naki

    a. *Kúm   ájē   ūnā   wə̀*
       Kum eat.PST 5.fufu 5.the
       'Kum ate the fufu.'

    b. *Ūnā   wə̀   ájé   Kúm*
       5.fufu 5.the eat.PST.DSF   Kum
       'KUM ate the fufu.' (Good 2010: 47)

Finally, we identified only two Bantu languages which make use of the final position to mark focus, with focus morphologically marked on the verb. These are Kirundi and Kinyarwanda, two closely related languages spoken in Burundi and Rwanda respectively. It appears that these two languages reflect a minor variant of sorts, showing a geographically restricted distribution of the conjoint/disjoint form found in contiguous countries.

In Kirundi (D62), the disjoint form conveys focus on the verb (Sabimana 1986; Ndayiragije 1999; Nshemezimana & Bostoen this volume), while use of the conjoint verb form results in focus on the element in clause-final position. As such, we consider Kirundi to be an example of a language which employs a sentence-final dedicated focus position (but see Nshemezimana and Bostoen this volume for a different analysis). The use of this position can be seen in the examples below where (44a) shows the conjoint form resulting in clause-final focus while (44b) shows the disjoint form, resulting in focus on the verb.

(44) Kirundi

    a. CJ *Mariya a-Ø-kund-a   a-b-âna.*
          Mary   1SM-PRES-like-ASP   AUG-2-child
          'Mary likes CHILDREN.'

    b. DJ *Mariya a-Ø-ra-kûnd-a   a-b-âna.*
          Mary   1SM-PRES-DJ-like-ASP AUG-2-child
          'Mary LIKES children.' (Sabimana 1986: 237)

An attempt at using the disjoint form renders the sentence ungrammatical when some other NP in the clause is focused (cf. (45a) and (45b)) where the conjoint form must be used instead (45c).

(45) Kirundi

    a. DJ **H-ǎ-ra-sinziriye   Mudúga.*
          16SM-F.PAST-DJ-sleep   Muduga
          'It is Muduga who slept.'

b. DJ *Ha-Ø-ra-kund-a   a-b-âna   Mariyá.
         16SM-PRES-DJ-like-ASP AUG-2-child Mary
         'It is Mary who likes children.'

c. CJ Ha-Ø-kund-a   a-b-âna   Mariyá.
         16SM-PRES-like-ASP AUG-2-child Mary
         'It is Mary who likes children.' (Sabimana 1986: 62, 238)

The conjoint form is used in question-answer pairs for both objects and adverbs (46).

(46) Kirundi (Nshemezimana and Bostoen 2013)
   a. CJ A-ba-na   ba-nyu   ba-kund-a   i-bi-igwa   ki?
              AUG-2-child POSS-2PL 2SM-like-FV AUG-8-subject which
              'Which subjects do your children like?'

   b. CJ A-ba-iísuumbur-ye ba-Ø-kuund-a   i-bi-háryyri   u-wu-kí-ri
              AUG-2-be.big-PFV   2SM-CJ-like-FV AUG-8-maths   AUG-1-PERS-be
              mu-tó na wé   a-kuund-a   i-bi-gi-an-ye
              1-young and 3sg 1SM-Ø-like-FV AUG-8-go-ASS-PFV
              n'   i-n-domé.
              with AUG-10-literature
              'The older ones like maths, but the youngest like subjects related to literature.'

Where Kirundi is special as compared to other conjoint/disjoint languages is its final focus position. This can be seen in subject focus (47), which shows Verb-Goal-Patient-Subject order, and in double object constructions, where the relative order of the two objects is determined by considerations of focus, as in (48).

(47) Kirundi
      H-a:-zan-i-ye   a-b-âna   u-mu-pǐra   Maríya.
      16SM-R.PAST-bring-APPL-ASP AUG-2-child AUG-3-ball Mary
      'It is Mary who brought a ball for the children.' (Sabimana 1986: 191)

(48) Kirundi
   a. Mudúga, y-a-hâye   a-b-âna   i-gi-tabo.
      Muduga   1SM-F.PAST-give   AUG-2-child AUG-7-book
      'Muduga, he gave the children A BOOK.'

   b. Mudúga, y-a-hâye   i-gi-tabo   a-b-âna.
      Muduga   1SM-F.PAST-give   AUG-7-book   AUG-2-child
      'Muduga, he gave THE CHILDREN a book.' (Sabimana 1986: 91)

To summarise, this section has provided an overview of the findings of our study in relation to both the Bantu and non-Bantu languages. Employing the four syntactic parameters each defined for morphological marking on the term or on the verb, we have identified eight possible combinations of focus marking. Our study has shown that all cells in the table are filled, i.e. that all combinations of parameter settings are encountered. The non-Bantu languages occupy five of the cells of our table: morphological marking on the term plus initial, IBV or final position, and morphological marking on the verb in conjunction with an initial or an IAV focus position. The Bantu languages occupy five spaces identified by morphological marking on the verb with IBV, IAV or final position, and morphological marking of the term with initial or IAV position all attested. The next section identifies and discusses this distribution in more detail, and offers some conclusions that can be obtained from this observation and related findings.

5 Conclusions

The main contribution of our chapter has been to show how Bantu conjoint/disjoint systems relate to the wider typology of focus marking. We have restricted our attention to the interaction of syntactic and morphological marking of term focus, disregarding for the time being prosodic marking of focus and the expression of predicate-centred focus. We concentrated on languages with constructions which simultaneously employ syntactic and morphological means to mark focus and used a sample of 25 languages where these constructions can be found, including sixteen Bantu and nine non-Bantu languages. Adopting two dimensions of variation – syntactic focus position and marking on the term vs. marking on the verb – we created a typological space of eight logically possible value combinations for the two dimensions, which provided the basis for our classification, shown here again in Table 8.

The main findings of our study are as follows. Firstly, even based on our relatively small sample, we show that the entire typological space is exploited, and so that each possible value combination is attested by at least one language. Our typology thus models a cross-linguistically well-populated aspect of variation in focus marking. Secondly, the distribution of Bantu languages and non-Bantu languages in our sample is largely complementary, with only two cells 'overlapping'. Thirdly, the distribution of the Bantu languages in general, and of those Bantu languages with conjoint/disjoint systems, cannot be described by one dimension or a unique value combination.

The complementarity of Bantu and non-Bantu languages in our sample can be seen to result from two central aspects of Bantu focus marking: First, Bantu

Table 8: Distribution of 25 languages with simultaneous syntactic and morphological marking of focus.

Morphology \ Topology	Initial	IBV	IAV	Final
On term	Gungbe, Jamaican Creole, *Kikuyu*, *Kituba*, *Lingala*	Hindi, Selayar	*Aghem*, *Noni*, *Tunen*	Ngizim
On verb	Gâbunke Fula, Karitiâna, Sereer	*Mbuun*, *Kikongo*	*Bemba*, *Haya*, *Makhuwa*, *Matengo*, *Naki*, *Zulu*, Podoko	*Kinyarwanda*, *Kirundi*

languages show a general preference for focus to be post-verbal, whether in the IAV or final position. Second, morphological focus marking on the verb seems to be rare outside Bantu (although see the Atlantic languages). This may be due to the restriction that morphological marking of focus on the verb appears not to occur in languages which are generally dependent-marking (Van der Wal 2014), and the general head-marking nature of Bantu languages. This in turn triggers the question of whether a linguistic profile of rich verbal morphology is a precondition across the board for marking term focus on the verb (see also Kalinowski and Good 2014). In addition, one may ask whether areal influences play a role, for example in the Bantoid languages of the north-west, where Naki, Noni and Aghem all show the IAV effect (Good 2010).

With respect to the internal variation of focus marking in Bantu, it is interesting to note that the cases of an initial focus position with morphological marking on the term are all (relatively) transparent and recently derived from a cleft construction. The various morphological markings on the verb, in contrast, are all much older and (as a result) much less transparent. Further observations are the independence of IAV and conjoint/disjoint, as witnessed by the languages from the northwest of the Bantu area (only IAV) and Kirundi/Kinyarwanda (only conjoint/disjoint), as well as the presence of an IAV focus position in languages with basic SVO order such as Aghem or Bemba (as expected) and (less expectedly) in Tunen, which has SOV.

There are aspects of conjoint/disjoint systems, and focus marking more widely, which are not addressed by our study, inclusion of which would almost certainly make the situation more complex than can be seen from our findings. Firstly, with only 25 languages, our sample is small. The overall picture would be likely to change if more languages were included, either by identifying more languages with the relevant morphosyntactic profile (Southern Quechua, cf. Muysken 1995, and Yoruba, cf. Bisang and Sonaiya 2000, being possible candidates), or by inclusion of a wider range of constructions, for example constructions with only one strategy of focus marking, e.g. only a morphological marker on the term or only marking on the verb (see again Smit 2010; Kalinowski and Good 2014). An inclusion of prosodic marking and verb focus would also further diversify the picture.

In addition, even for the constructions which we did include, there remain aspects which have not been taken into account, in part because relevant information is often hard to find. Two main issues here are the exact interpretation of the focus, and optionality of focus marking strategies. With respect to the first, it would be interesting to see whether there is a consistent correlation between certain topological and morphological marking (and/or combinations thereof) and a certain type or scope of focus. For example, is it the case that an initial position always expresses identificational focus on the term, or that marking on the verb is new information focus? Could it be that the IBV and IAV positions are always underspecified for object and VP focus?

With respect to the second point, our investigation concentrated on languages in which a construction is present which involves the simultaneous use of topological and morphological focus marking. We found, however, that there are languages in which the two strategies may optionally be used together. For example, while Gungbe obligatorily combines the use of a focus marker with a dedicated focus position, in Hindi the two may be used simultaneously or independently of each other. Another relevant example here is Ngizim in which subjects have a special status when it comes to focus – focus on subjects is always 'doubly marked' (Zimmermann 2011: 1167) as opposed to focus on non-subjects. We thus find three types of languages: 1) Where the two types of markings have to co-occur, 2) Where either type of marking can occur independently, and 3) Where one marking type is dependent on the presence of the other.[17] This is a particularly interesting issue with respect to conjoint/disjoint systems as we know that the distinction is often restricted to only a subset of tense-aspect paradigms, and so the question arises whether syntactic marking is independent of the presence of head-marking. For example, in Zulu the conjoint/disjoint distinction is restricted to the present and perfect tenses, where IAV and morphological marking on the verb go hand-in-hand (Buell 2006). But is focus in, for example, the future tense in Zulu – which does not show morphological conjoint/disjoint marking (but see Zeller, Zerbian & Cook this volume) – still related to the IAV position? Questions such as these all remain as paths for

---

17 The distribution poses also an interesting question for language change and whether diachronic processes can be found resulting in the building up of double marking and its loss.

future enquiry. Furthermore, Hartmann and Zimmermann (2004: 217) note that "languages that mark focus by movement sometimes use morphological marking or a change of verbal aspect in addition. Their grammatical systems appear to be somewhat uneconomical with respect to focus marking." This triggers the question of whether either topological or morphological marking can be said to be the 'real' or primary focus marker.

In summary, we established a focus-marking typology based on syntactic position and morphological marking of term focus. Based on our sample of 25 languages we have shown Bantu languages to occupy positions which largely reflect the predominance of verbal marking for term focus and a syntactic IAV position in the language family. We make no claims of exhaustivity. However, we believe we have shown that it is profitable to embed the Bantu conjoint/disjoint systems within the wider typological context of cross-linguistic marking of focus, both from the point of view of comparative Bantu, and from the point of view of cross-linguistic investigations into variation in the expression of information structure.

Abbreviations

A	augment	F.PAST	far past
ABS	absolutive	FOC	focus
ACC	accusative case	FUT	future
APPL	applicative	FV	final vowel
ASP	aspect	LAT	lative
ASS	associative	LOC	locative
B	person marker	NFOC	non-focus
CJ	conjoint	NOM	nominative case
CL	clitic	OBL	oblique
CMPL	completive	OF	object focus
COMP	complementiser	OM	object marker
COP	copula	PASS	passive
DAT	dative	PAST1	recent past
DET	determiner	PAST2	distant past
DJ	disjoint	PERF	perfect
DSF	disfluentive	PERS	persistive
DUR	durative	PFV	perfective
EMPH	emphatic	PL	plural
ERG	ergative	PMA	person marker of set 'A'
ES	expletive subject	PMB	person marker of set 'B'
F	feminine	POSS	possessive
FM	focus marker	PRES	present

PRS	person	SG	singular
PRT	particle	SUBJ	subject
PST	past	SM	subject marker
Q	interrogative	T	tense
QM	question marker	TAM	tense-aspect-mood
R.PAST	recent past	TRR	transitivizer
SF	subject focus		

References

Aboh, Enoch O. 2004. *The morphosyntax of complement-head sequences: Clause structure and word order patterns in Kwa*. Oxford: Oxford University Press.

Aboh, Enoch O. 2007. Focused versus non-focused wh-phrases. In Enoch O. Aboh, Katharina Hartmann & Malte Zimmermann (eds.), *Focus strategies in African languages*, 287–314. Berlin: de Gruyter.

Bisang, Walter & Remi Sonaiya. 2000. Information structuring in Yoruba. *Linguistics* 38 (1). 169–197.

Bohnemeyer, Jürgen. 2002. *The grammar of time reference in Yukatek Maya*. Munich: LINCOM.

Bohnemeyer, Jürgen. 2008. Linking without grammatical relations in Yucatec. Alignment, extraction and control. In Johannes Helmbrecht, Yoko Nishina, Y.-M. Shin, Stavros Skopeteas & Elisabeth Verhoeven (eds.), *Form and function in language research*, 185–214. Berlin: De Gruyter.

Bostoen, Koen & Leon Mundeke. 2012. Subject marking, object-verb order and focus in Mbuun (Bantu, B87). *Southern African Linguistics and Applied Language Studies* 30 (2). 139–154.

Bricker, Victoria R. 1979. Wh-questions, relativization, and clefting in Yucatec Maya. In Laura Martin (ed.), *Papers in Mayan linguistics*, 109–138. Columbia, MO: Lucas Brothers.

Buell, Leston C. 2006. The Zulu conjoint/disjoint verb alternation: focus or constituency? *ZAS Papers in Linguistics* 43. 9–30.

Büring, Daniel. 2010. Towards a typology of focus realization. In Malte Zimmermann & Caronline Féry (eds.), *Information structure*, 177–205. Oxford: Oxford University Press.

Butt, Miriam & Tracy Holloway King. 1996. Structural topic and focus without movement. In Miriam Butt & Tracy Holloway King (eds.), *Proceedings of the First LFG Conference*. Stanford: CSLI Publications.

Cheng, Lisa Lai-Shen & Laura J. Downing. 2009. Where's the topic in Zulu? *The Linguistic Review* 26 (2–3). 207–238.

Comrie, Bernard. 1984. Some formal properties of focus in Modern Eastern Armenian. *Annual of Armenian Linguistics* 5. 1–21.

Costa, João & Nancy C. Kula. 2008. Focus at the interface: Evidence from Romance and Bantu. In Cécile De Cat & Katherine Demuth (eds.), *The Bantu-Romance Connection*, 293–322. Amsterdam: John Benjamins.

Creissels, Denis. 1996. Conjunctive and disjunctive verb forms in Setswana. *South African Journal of African Languages* 16 (4). 109–115.

de Kind, Jasper. 2014. Word order in Kikongo (H16): On the origins of a preverbal focus position and the pragmatic neutralization of SOV. Talk given at SynPhonIS, ZAS, Berlin.

Diercks, Michael. 2011. The morphosyntax of Lubukusu locative inversion and the parameterization of Agree. *Lingua* 121 (5). 702–720.
Dik, Simon C. 1997. *The theory of functional grammar*. Berlin, New York: Mouton de Gruyter.
Downing, Laura J. 2013. Issues in the phonology-syntax interface in African languages. In Olanike Ola Orie & Karen W. Sanders (eds.), *Selected Proceedings of the 43rd Annual Conference on African Linguistics*, 26–38. Somerville, MA: Cascadilla Proceedings Project.
Downing, Laura J. & Bernd Pompino-Marshall. 2013. The focus prosody of Chichewa and the Stress-Focus constraint: A response to Samek-Lodovici (2005). *Natural Language & Linguistic Theory* 31. 647–681.
Drubig, Hans Bernard & Wolfram Schaffar. 2001. Focus constructions. In Martin Haspelmath, Ekkehard König, Wulf Oesterreicher & Wolfgang Raible (eds.), *Language typology and language universals*, 1079–1104. Berlin: De Gruyter.
Durrleman-Tame, Stephanie. 2008. *The syntax of Jamaican Creole*. Amsterdam: John Benjamins.
É. Kiss, Katalin. 1998. Identificational focus versus information focus. *Language* 74 (2). 245–273.
Elders, Stefan. 2006. Conjoint and disjoint in Doyayo: Bantu-like verb forms in an Adamawa language. Talk given at Workshop on focus in African languages, Berlin.
Everett, Caleb. 2006. *Patterns in Karitiâna: Perception, articulation and grammar*. Houston: Rice University PhD thesis.
Fiedler, Ines. This volume. Conjoint and disjoint verb forms in Gur? Evidence from Yom.
Finer, Daniel L. 1994. On the nature of two A' positions in Selayarese. In Norbert Corver & Henk van Riemsdijk (eds.), *Studies on scrambling*, 153–184. Berlin: Mouton de Gruyter.
Foley, William A. 1994. Information structure. In Asher, R. E. (ed.), *The encyclopedia of language and linguistics*, 1678–1685. Pergamon Press.
Frascarelli, Mara. 1999. Subject, nominative case, agreement and focus. In Lunella Mereu (ed.), *Boundaries of morphology and syntax*, 195–217. Amsterdam: John Benjamins.
Göksel, Aslı & A. Sumru Özsoy. 2000. Is there a focus position in Turkish? In Aslı Göksel & Celia J. Kerslake (eds.), *Studies on Turkish and Turkic languages; Proceedings of the ninth International Conference on Turkish Linguistics*, 219–228. Wiesbaden: Harrassowitz.
Good, Jeff. 2010. Topic and focus fields in Naki. In Ines Fiedler & Anne Schwarz (eds.), *The expression of information structure. A documentation of its diversity across Africa*, 35–68. Amsterdam: John Benjamins.
Grubic, Mira. 2010. Ngizim fieldnotes. In Petrova, S. & M. Grubic (eds.), *Linguistic fieldnotes I: Information structure in African Languages. Working Papers of the SFB 632 (ISIS)*. 1–76.
Güldemann, Tom. 1996. *Verbalmorphologie und Nebenprädikation im Bantu*. Bochum: Universitätsverlag Dr. N. Brockmeyer.
Güldemann, Tom. 2003. Present progressive vis-à-vis predication focus in Bantu: A verbal category between semantics and pragmatics. *Studies in Language* 27 (2). 323–360.
Güldemann, Tom. 2009. Predicate-centered focus types: A sample-based typological study in African languages. Application for project B7 in the CRC 632 Information structure.
Güldemann, Tom, Ines Fiedler, and Yukiko Morimoto. 2014. The verb in the preverbal domain across Bantu: infinitive "fronting" and predicate-centered focus. Paper presented at the Workshop on preverbal domains. ZAS, Berlin.
Gutiérrez Bravo, Rodrigo & Jorge Monforte. 2009. Focus, agent focus, and relative clauses in Yucatec Maya. In Heriberto Avelino, Jessica Coon & Elisabeth Norcliffe (eds.), *New perspectives in Mayan linguistics*. MIT Working Papers in Linguistics.

Harris, Alice C. & Lyle Campbell. 1995. *Historical syntax in cross linguistic perspective*. Cambridge: Cambridge University Press.
Hartmann, Katharina & Malte Zimmermann. 2004. Focus strategies in Chadic: the case of Tangale revisited. In Shinichiro Ishihara, Michaela Schmitz & Anne Schwarz (eds.), *Interdisciplinary studies on information structure*, 247–243. Potsdam: Universitätsverlag Potsdam.
Hartmann, Katharina & Malte Zimmermann. 2007. Focus strategies in Chadic: The case of Tangale revisited. *Studia Linguistica* 61. 95–129.
Heine, Bernd & Mechtild Reh. 1984. *Grammaticalization and reanalysis in African languages*. Hamburg: Helmut Buske.
Herring, Susan. 1990. Information structure as a consequence of word order type. *Proceedings of the Sixteenth Annual Meeting of the Berkeley Linguistics Society*, 163–174.
Hyman, Larry M. 1979. Nouns: A-forms (in focus). In Larry M. Hyman (ed.), *Aghem grammatical structure*, 16–27. Los Angeles: UCLA.
Hyman, Larry M. 1981. Noni grammatical structure. With special reference to verb morphology. *California Occasional Papers in Linguistics 9*.
Hyman, Larry M. 1985. Dependency relations in Aghem syntax: the mysterious case of the empty determiner in Aghem. *Précis from the 15th Annual Conference on African Linguistics. Supplement 9 to Studies in African Linguistics*. 151–156.
Hyman, Larry M. 1999. The interaction between focus and tone in Bantu. In George Rebuschi & Laurice Tuller (eds.), *The Grammar of Focus*, 151–178. Amsterdam: John Benjamins.
Hyman, Larry M. 2010. Focus marking in Aghem: syntax or semantics? In Ines Fiedler & Anne Schwarz (eds.), *The expression of information structure: a documentation of its diversity across Africa*, 95–116. Amsterdam: John Benjamins.
Hyman, Larry M. & John Watters. 1984. Auxiliary focus. *Studies in African Linguistics* 15. 233–273.
Hyman, Larry M. & Maria Polinksy. 2009. Focus in Aghem. In Caroline Féry & Malte Zimmermann (eds.), *Information structure. Theoretical, typological and experimental perspectives*, 206–233. Oxford: Oxford University Press.
Jarvis, Elizabeth. 1991. Tense and aspect in Podoko narrative and procedural discourse. In Stephen C. Anderson & Bernard Comrie (eds.), *Tense and aspect in eight languages of Cameroon*, 213–237. Dallas: SIL and University of Texas at Arlington.
Joswig, Andreas. 2015. Syntactic sensitivity and preferred clause structure in Majang. In Angelika Mietzner & Anne Storch (eds.), *Nilo-Saharan: Models and descriptions*, 169–176. Cologne: Rüdiger Köppe Verlag.
Kalinowski, Cristin & Jeff Good. 2014. Non-canonical head-marking of information structure in African languages. Talk given at Workshop on information structure in head-marking languages, Nijmegen, MPI.
Kasimir, Elke. 2005. Question-Answer test and givenness: some question marks. *Working Papers of the SFB632, Interdisciplinary Studies on Information Structure* (*ISIS*) 3. 1–52.
Kavari, Jekura U., Lutz Marten & Jenneke van der Wal. 2012. Tone cases in Otjiherero: head-complement relations, linear order, and information structure. *Africana Linguistica* 18. 315–353.
Kidda, Mairo E. 1993. *Tangale phonology. A descriptive analysis*. Berlin: Reimer.
Kidwai, Ayesha. 1999. Word order and focus positions in universal grammar. In George Rebuschi & Laurice Tuller (eds.), *The grammar of focus*, 213–244. Amsterdam: John Benjamins.

Kim, Alan H.O. 1988. Preverbal focusing and type XXIII languages. In Michael Hammond, Edith A. Moravcsik & Jessica Wirth (eds.), *Studies in syntactic typology*, 147–169. Amsterdam: John Benjamins.

King, Deborah. 2004. Structural and pragmatic functions of Kuki-Chin verbal stem alternations. *Journal of the Southeast Asian Linguistics Society* 1. 141–157.

Krifka, Manfred. 2007. Basic notions of information structure. In Caroline Féry, Gisbert Fanselow & Manfred Krifka (eds.), *Working Papers of the SFB 632, Interdisciplinary Studies on Information Structure*, 13–55. Potsdam: Universitätsverlag Potsdam.

Lambrecht, Knud. 1994. *Information structure and sentence form*. Cambridge: Cambridge University Press.

Manfredi, Victor. 2005. Conjoint/disjoint in western Benue-Kwa. Talk given at Humboldt Universität, Berlin, and LUCL, Leiden.

Matić, Dejan & Daniel Wedgwood. 2013. The meanings of focus: the significance of an interpretation-based category in a cross-linguistic perspective. *Journal of Linguistics* 49 (1). 1–37.

Meeussen, A. E. 1959. *Essai de grammaire Rundi*. Tervuren: Musée Royale de l'Afrique Central.

Megerdoomian, Karine. 2011. Focus and the auxiliary in Eastern Armenian. Talk given at BLS 2011 – languages of the Causasus.

Molnár, Valeria. 2002. Contrast – from a contrastive perspective. In Hilde Hasselgård, Stig Johansson, Bergljot Behrens & Cathrine Fabricius-Hansen (eds.), *Information structure in a cross-linguistic perspective*, 147–162. Amsterdam: Rodopi.

Morimoto, Yukiko. This volume. This Kikuyu focus marker *nī*: formal and functional similarities to the conjoint/disjoint alternation.

Mous, Maarten. 1997. The position of the object in Tunen. In Rose-Marie Déchaine & Victor Manfredi (eds.), *Object positions in Benue-Kwa*, 123–137. Den Haag: Holland Academic Graphics.

Muysken, Pieter. 1995. Focus in Quechua. In Katalin É. Kiss (ed.), *Discourse configurational languages*, 375–393. New York, Oxford: Oxford University Press.

Ndayiragije, Juvénal. 1999. Checking economy. *Linguistic Inquiry* 30. 399–444.

Neeleman, Ad, Elena Titov, Hans van de Koot & Reiko Vermeulen. 2009. A syntactic typology of topic, focus and contrast. In Jeroen Van Craenenbroeck (ed.), *Alternatives to Cartography*, 15–52. Berlin: Mouton de Gruyter.

Nikolaeva, Irina. 2001. Secondary topic as a relation in information structure. *Linguistics* 39 (1). 1–49.

Nshemezimana, Ernest & Koen Bostoen. 2013. Alternance conjoint/disjoint en kirundi (JD62). Talk given at Workshop in information structure in Bantu, Berlin.

Nshemezimana, Ernest, & Koen Bostoen. This volume. The conjoint/disjoint alternation in Kirundi (JD62): A case for its abolition.

Robert, Stéphane. 2010. Focus in Atlantic languages. In Ines Fiedler & Anne Schwarz (eds.), *The expression of information structure. A documentation of its diversity across Africa*, 233–260. Amsterdam: John Benjamins.

Sabimana, Firmard. 1986. *The relational structure of the Kirundi verb*. Bloomington: Indiana University PhD thesis.

Samek-Lodovici, Vieri. 2005. Prosody-syntax interaction in the expression of focus. *Natural Language & Linguistic Theory* 23. 687–755.

Schwarz, Florian. 2003. Focus marking in Kikuyu. *ZAS Papers in Linguistics* 30. 41–118.

Schwarz, Florian. 2007. Ex-situ focus in Kikuyu. In Enoch O. Aboh, Katharina Hartmann & Malte Zimmermann (eds.), *Focus strategies in African languages: The interaction of focus and grammar in Niger-Congo and Afro-Asiatic*, 139–160. Berlin: Mouton de Gruyter.

Sharma, Devyani. 2003. Discourse clitics and constructive morphology in Hindi. In Miriam Butt & Tracy King (eds.), *Nominals: inside and out*, 59–84. Stanford, CA: SCLI.

Sharman, J. C. 1956. The tabulation of tenses in a Bantu language (Bemba: Northern Rhodesia). *Africa* 16. 29–46.

Slade, Benjamin Martin. 2011. *Formal and philological inquiries into the nature of interrogatives, indefinites, disjunction, and focus in Sinhala and other languages*. Urbana-Champaign: University of Illinois dissertation.

Smit, Niels. 2010. *FYI*. Amsterdam: University of Amsterdam PhD thesis.

Stiebels, Barbara. 2006. Agent focus in Mayan languages. *Natural Language & Linguistic Theory* 24. 501–570.

Tamrazian, Arminé. 1991. Focus and wh-movement in Armenian. *UCL Working Papers in Linguistics* 3. 101–121.

Tonhauser, Judith. 2003. F-constructions in Yucatec Maya. In J. Menéndez-Benito Andersen & Adam Werle (eds.), *Proceedings of semantics of under-represented languages in the Americas II*, 203–223. Amherst: UMASS.

Vallduví, Enric. 1992. *The informational component*. New York: Garland Publishing Inc.

Van der Wal, Jenneke. 2009. *Word order and information structure in Makhuwa-Enahara*. Utrecht: LOT.

Van der Wal, Jenneke. 2014. Morphological marking of term focus. Talk given at workshop Information structure in head-marking languages, Max Planck Institute, Nijmegen.

Van der Wal, Jenneke. 2016. Diagnosing focus. Studies in Language 40 (2). 259–301.

Van der Wal, Jenneke. To appear. Diagnosing focus. Studies in Language.

Van der Wal, Jenneke & Jacky Maniacky. 2015. How 'person' got into focus: grammaticalisation of clefts in Lingala and Kikongo areas. *Linguistics* 53 (1). 1–52.

Van Valin Jr., Robert D. 1999. A typology of the interaction of focus structure and syntax. In Raxilina, E. & J. Testelec (ed.), *Typology and the theory of language: From description to explanation*, 511–524. Moscow: Languages of Russian Culture.

Van Valin Jr., Robert D. 2009. Information structure in Banawá, Wari' and Karitiâna: an overview. Report to US National Science Foundation.

Vapnarsky, Valentina. 2013. Is Yucatec Maya an omnipredicative language? Predication, the copula and focus constructions. *Sprachtypologie und Universalienforschung* 66 (1). 40–86.

Verhoeven Elisabeth & Stavros Skopeteas. 2015. Licensing focus constructions in Yucatec Maya. *International Journal of American Linguistics* 81 (1). 1–40.

Voeltz, F.K.E. 2004. Long and short verb forms in Zulu. Ms., University of Cologne.

Watters, John. 1979. Focus in Aghem. In Larry M. Hyman (ed.), *Aghem grammatical structure*, 137–198. Los Angeles: University of Southern California.

Yip, Moira. 2004. Phonological markedness and allomorph selection in Zahao. *Language and linguistics* 5 (4). 969–1001.

Zerbian, Sabine. 2007. Phonological phrasing in Northern Sotho (Bantu). *The Linguistic Review* 24 (2-3). 233–262.

Zimmermann, Malte. 2011. The grammatical expression of focus in West Chadic: Variation and uniformity in and across languages. *Linguistics* 39 (5). 1163–1213.

Zimmermann, Malte & Edgar Onea. 2011. Focus marking and focus interpretation. *Lingua* 121 (11). 1651–1670.

Zubizarreta, Maria Luisa. 1998. *Prosody, focus, and word order*. Cambridge, MA: MIT Press.

Larry M. Hyman
4 Disentangling conjoint, disjoint, metatony, tone cases, augments, prosody, and focus in Bantu

1 Introduction

The purpose of this paper is to disentangle a number of overlapping concepts that have been invoked in Bantu studies to characterize the relation between a verb and what follows it. Starting with the conjoint/disjoint distinction, I will then consider its potential relation to "metatony", "tone cases", "augments", prosody, and focus in Bantu.

2 Conjoint/disjoint (CJ/DJ)

In many Bantu languages TAM and negative paradigms have been shown to exhibit suppletive allomorphy, as in the following oft-cited Bemba (M42) sentences, which illustrate a prefixal difference in marking present tense, corresponding with differences in focus (Sharman 1956: 30):

(1) a. *disjoint* -la- : bušé mu-<u>la</u>-peep-a 'do you (pl.) smoke'?
    b. *conjoint* -Ø- : ee tu-peep-a sekelééti 'yes, we smoke cigarettes'
    c. *disjoint* -la- : bámó bá-<u>la</u>-ly-á ínsoka 'some people actually eat snakes'

In (1a) the verb is final in its main clause and must therefore occur in the disjoint form, marked by the prefix *-la-*. In (1b), the answer to the question in (1a), the verb occurs in the conjoint form, which lacks the *-la-* prefix, since the verb is presupposed and 'cigarettes' is in focus. A table of Bemba conjoint/disjoint forms is provided from Hyman and Watters (1984: 251) in (2), drawing on Sharman and Meeussen (1955), Sharman (1956) and Givón (1972):

This paper was originally presented at the Workshop on Prosodic Constituents in Bantu languages: Metatony and Dislocations, Université de Paris 3, June 28–29, 2012. Several months after presenting this paper, I received two papers (now see Creissels and Van der Wal, this volume) which cover much more on the conjoint-disjoint distinction and overlaps with some of the discussion of further sections below. Following them, I will adopt the practice of referring to conjoint and disjoint as CJ and DJ. Thanks to Jenneke van der Wal and an anonymous reviewer for comments on an earlier version of this paper.

DOI 10.1515/9783110490831-004

(2)

		non-progressive					progressive		
		conjoint		disjoint					
Present/Hab.	:	-Ø-	-a	-la-	-a-	[±TS]	-lée-	-a	[±TS]
$Past_1$/Fut_1	:	-á-	-a	-áa-	-a	[±TS]			
$Past_2$	:	-ácí-	-a	(complex)			-ácíláa-		[±TS]
$Past_3$	:	-á-	-ile	-álii-	-a	[±TS]	-álée-		[±TS]
$Past_4$	:	-a-	-ile	-alí-	-ile	[+TS]	-alée-		[±TS]
PresLinger	:	-Ø-	-ile	náa-´	-á	[-TS]			
PastLinger	:	-a-	-á	-alí	-a	[+TS]			
$Future_2$	:	(-ka-	-a	-ka-	-a)	[+TS]	-kalée-		[±TS]

In the above table, the feature [TS] stands for 'tone spreading': Verb forms which are [+TS] spread their last underlying H tone to the end of the word (Sharman and Meeussen 1955: 395). All conjoint forms are [-TS]. The two sentences in (3) show the [±TS] of the P_1 correlating with the CJ/DJ distinction (Sharman 1956: 40):

(3) a. *conjoint* [-TS] : nga mw-aa-tób-a úmutóndó, twáákuláatápíla múnsupa
    'if you break the POT, we will have to use a calabash to draw water'
  b. *disjoint* [+TS] : nga mw-aa-tób-á úmutóndó, bálééisaafúlwá
    'if you BREAK THE POT, they will get angry'

As seen from the words that I have placed in small caps in the glosses, the information structure of the two if-clauses is different: the first places greater focus on the pot, while the second appears to treat the whole verb phrase as in focus. Some of the terminological history of the distinction is summarized in (4) (cf. Hyman and Watters 1984: 251; Güldemann 2003: 328):

(4) | Meeussen (1959) | Sharman (1956) | Givón (1972) | Givón (1975) | Southern Bantu |
|---|---|---|---|---|
| conjoint | strong link | [-action focus] | COMP focus | short form |
| disjoint | weak link | [+action focus] | VP focus | long form |
| | = *prosody* | = *information structure* | | = *morphology* |

As Meeussen was aware in introducing the terminology, the CJ/DJ distinction represents a package of potential differences in morphology, prosody (tone) and information structure (cf. Van der Wal, this volume). In (5) I list the canonical properties of the conjoint/disjoint distinction, not all of which will be present at one time:

(5) a. differences in inflectional prefix morphology on the verb
     b. differences in inflectional suffix morphology on the verb
     c. differences in prosodic cohesion with what follows the verb
     d. differences in information structure (focus)
     e. differences in distribution within the clause (final vs. non-final)
     f. differences in distribution across clause types (main vs. subordinate; root vs. non-root)

While both the CJ/DJ terminology and much of the current discussion has centered around Narrow Bantu, where the affixal differences mentioned in (5a,b) are often involved, CJ/DJ-like distinctions also exist beyond Narrow Bantu and even outside of Niger-Congo (Hyman and Watters 1984). Thus consider the following Hodiernal Past$_1$ examples from Aghem (Grassfields Bantu) (cf. Anderson 1979: 99), where /nò/ is a focus marker:

(6)   *conjoint* [-focus]   *disjoint* [+focus]
     a. ò mɔ̀ zɨ̀ kɨ́bɛ́   's/he ate fufu'   ò máà zɨ̀ bɛ́ ꜜkɔ́   's/he ate/did eat fufu'
     b. *ò mɔ̀ zɨ̀°   's/he ate'   ò máà zɨ̀°   's/he ate/did eat'
     c. ò mɔ̀ zɨ̀ nô   's/he ATE'   *ò máà zɨ̀ nô
     d. wɨ̀zɨ́n wɨ̀là ò mɔ̀ zɨ́   'the woman who ate'   *wɨ̀zɨ́n wɨ̀là ò <u>máà</u> zɨ́

Based on ungrammatical examples such as (6b), it is often stated that conjoint verb forms cannot occur at the end of a sentence:

> [Conjoint forms] ... throw emphasis (if any) on what follows the verb, or more precisely, are strongly linked to what follows (and formally therefore cannot stand at the end of the sentence ...). (Sharman 1956: 30)
> "The CJ form can never appear sentence-finally ... ; i.e., some object or adjunct has to follow .... The DJ form, on the other hand, may occur sentence-finally ..., but does not need to, i.e., something can still follow the DJ verb form ...." (Van der Wal 2009: 127)

However, the tense-aspect-mood (TAM) forms one gets in relative and other backgrounded (non-root) clauses are typically identical to the conjoint forms in main (root) clauses and in these cases the conjoint form can appear sentence-finally:[1]

> In most Bantu languages, important differences are noted in the marking of tense aspect in main vs. relative clauses. In some languages, such as KiRundi and ChiBemba, the forms

---

[1] The same is often true of negative forms, which may have inflectional marking identical to the conjoint forms of the respective TAMs.

> which occur in relative clauses (where there is no focus distinction) also occur in main clauses. (Hyman and Watters 1984: 249)
>
> ... there is no CJ/DJ alternation in the relative conjugations [in Makhuwa]. The relative verb forms, both in the affirmative and negative conjugations, are formally identical to the CJ verb form, the negative using the prefix -*hi*-. (Van der Wal 2009: 128)

At the same time, some Bantu (and non-Bantu) languages which have different TAM marking in main clause affirmative vs. relative and/or negative clauses do not have a CJ/DJ contrast in main clauses. Such contrasts can also exist without prosodic/phrasing differences:

> One such language studied by the second author is Ngie (Grassfields Bantu, Cameroon), where one set of tense markers is found in main clauses and another in relative clauses. This ... explains the widespread use of such terms as "main" vs. "relative" tenses in the literature. (Hyman and Watters 1984: 254)

As a result of this overlap, there are two ways to define "conjoint": (i) by form (= Hyman and Watters 1984); (ii) by contrast with disjoint (= Van der Wal 2009). If one goes strictly by form, the distributions are as in the following table from Hyman and Lionnet (2012: 13):

(7)

		final	non-final
conjoint	main clause	−	+
	relative clause	+	+
disjoint	main clause	+	+
	relative clause	−	−

As seen, CJ forms can occur at the end of a sentence, as long as the verb is in a relative (or other backgrounded) clause. For this reason I prefer to restate the restriction as "The CJ form cannot occur at the end of a main clause."

As can be seen from the Bemba table in (2) above, some TAMs do not distinguish CJ/DJ, e.g. Future$_2$, while others have only a [±TS] distinction, e.g. progressive forms. Recognizing the importance of specific TAMs in determining CJ vs. DJ marking, Hyman and Watters (1984) distinguish two types of "auxiliary focus", i.e. interactions between focus, TAMs, and polarity:

(8) a. Type 1: syntactic [±focus]   (= the above)
     b. Type 2: morphologized [±F]   (= the immediate following)

While we have been discussing Type 1, where CJ/DJ encodes differences in syntax and information structure, Type 2 has to do with the intrinsic focus of certain "marked" TAMs (and negation) which exhibit a prosodic break ("weak link") with what follows. This is seen in the following Haya (JE22) sentences in the today past tense (Hyman and Watters 1984: 260, based on Hyman and Byarushengo 1984):

(9) a. [-F] bá-á-kôm-a 'they tied' ba-a-kom-a Káto 'they tied Kato'
    b. [+F] ti-bá-á-kom-a 'they didn't tie' ti-bá-á-kom-a 'they didn't tie
                                                Káto   Kato'

In (9a) we see that when a constituent follows the affirmative verb, the H(igh) tones are deleted. This occurs whether focus is on *Káto* or on the entire verb phrase. In the corresponding negative sentence in (9b), the H tones are not deleted. The following table summarizes the major [±F] distinctions in Haya (cf. Hyman et al. 1987: 92–94 for similar facts from closely related Luganda):

(10) *Affirmative* [-F]   *Affirmative* [+F] + *All Negs* = [+F]   } marked polarity
      0   (present habitual)   PROG   (progressive)
      P_1 (today past tense)   PERF   (perfect 'to have already . . .') } marked tense-
      P_2 (yesterday past   EXP   (experiential 'to have done   } aspect
            tense)   before')
      PH   (past habitual)   PRST   (persistive 'still')
      F_1 (today future)   SJCT   (subjunctive)   } marked mood
      F_2 (general future)   IMPER (imperative)

The following summarizes the differences between intrinsic, morphologized [±F] TAMs/negation vs. CJ/DJ [±focus]:

(11) a. [±F] effects occur independently of semantics/pragmatics (focus) of the utterance
     b. [±F] contrasts are maintained in backgrounded (e.g. relative) clauses
     c. [±F] distinctions have prosodic effects, and sometimes also affect nominal marking (cf. (13, 14))

Intrinsic [±F] TAMs/negation are however reminiscent of CJ/DJ [±focus] in the following ways:

(12) a. [-F] forms, like conjoint, have a "strong link" with what follows; [+F] forms, like disjoint, have a "weak link" with what follows
     b. the "unmarked" [-F] TAMs are also the ones where CJ/DJ allomorphs arise
     c. both have to do with information structure/focus, although [±F] is morphologized

While we have been focusing on the morphology of the verb, Aghem distinguishes an A-form vs. B-form of NPs. As seen in (13), the appropriate form is determined by both [±focus] and [±F] on the auxiliary (Hyman and Watters 1984: 234, 243; Hyman 2010).² In the following, IAV = "Immediate After Verb":

(13) a. IAV: ò mɔ̀ zɨ̀ kɨ́-bɛ́ ↓nɛ́ 's/he ate fufu today'
 b. post-IAV: ò mɔ̀ zɨ̀ nɛ́ ↓ bɛ́ ↓kɔ́ 's/he ate fufu TODAY'
 c. post-[+focus]: ò máà zɨ́ bɛ́ ↓kɔ́ (nɛ́) 's/he did eat fufu (today)'
 d. post-[+F]: zɨ́ ↓ bɛ́ ↓kɔ́ (nô) 'eat fufu!' ('eat FUFU!')

In (13a) the direct object kɨ́-bɛ́ 'fufu' appears in A-form after a [-F] TAM such as the [-focus] form of the today past tense marked by mɔ̀. When the IAV is occupied by another element, e.g. the temporal nɛ́ 'today' in (13b), the post-IAV object bɛ́ ↓kɔ́ now appears in B-form. Although the object appears to be in the IAV position in (13c), the same B-form is observed when the auxiliary is the [+focus] máà form of the today past. The forms in (13a-c) might suggest that the A- vs. B- distinction is directly attributable to information structure: A-form = in focus, B-form = not in focus. However, (13d) shows that the B-form is required after the [+F] imperative, independent of focus: The "out-of-focus" B-form is required even if (13d) is a response to the question "What should I eat?". A second difference in NP marking concerns the Bantu augment, discussed in the next section.

3 The Bantu augment

In a number of Bantu languages, the "article-like" augment morpheme appears to be (or to have been) implicated in the prosodic realization of the CJ/DJ distinction. However, differences in nominal marking are potentially independent of whether the verb+complement form a prosodic domain or not. This is seen in Luganda (JE15) H tone plateauing, whereby H-L^n-H becomes all H within a tone group (TG) (Hyman et al. 1987, Hyman and Katamba 2010). As seen in (14a), the augment (here, e-) is present on an object that forms part of a wide focus, but is absent on an object occurring under IAV focus in (14b).

(14) a. affirmative [+Augment] = 2 TGs : y-a-láb-à e-bi-kópò 's/he saw cups'
   H L   H L
 b. affirmative [-Augment] = 1 TG : y-a-láb-á bí-kópò 's/he saw CUPS'
   H Ø   H L
 c. negative [-Augment] = 2 TGs : te-y-a-láb-à bi-kópò 's/he didn't see cups'
   H L   H L
 d. negative [+Augment] : *te-y-a-láb-à e-bi-kópò

---

2 In (13d), /nò/ is a focus marker.

As also seen, there is no H tone plateauing between the verb and the augmented noun object in (14a) as there is in (14b). While it is the case that the augment blocks formation of a TG, (14c) shows that [+F] TAMs, also block TG-formation. Negation was chosen to illustrate this in (14c), since as seen in (14d), the augment is disallowed after a negative verb.

The question which thus arises is whether the differences between Luganda (14a) and (14b) are related to the CJ/DJ distinction: the occurrence vs. non-occurrence of H tone plateauing? the presence vs. absence of the augment? As the table in (15) shows, the answer appears to be no: CJ is not isomorphic with [-F], the absence of the augment ([-A]), H tone plateauing (HTP), or [-IAV focus] (MC = main clause):

(15)

	[±F]	[±A]	[±HTP]	[±IAV focus]
MC Affirmative	+	+	−	−
MC Affirmative	−	+	−	−
MC Affirmative	+	−	−	+
MC Affirmative	−	−	+	+
MC Negative	+	−	−	−
	verbal	nominal	phrasing	information structure

The generalizations from the table in (15) are as follows (for fuller discussion see Hyman and Katamba 1990, 1993):

(16) a. if [+F] or [+A], then [-HTP], i.e. there are two blockers of H tone plateauing
b. if [+IAV focus], then [-A]; but note that [-A] does not imply [+focus]
c. if NEG, then [+F], [-A], [-HTP]; [-IAV focus] is at least preferred

It should be noted, however, that HTP will also apply between a [-F] verb and a prepositional phrase which, not being nominal, cannot take an augment.

While the match-up may not be perfect, the augment H tone can potentially contribute to the tonal marking of the CJ/DJ distinction in at least two (almost opposite) ways:[3]

(17) a. the augment (and/or its H) is absent after a conjoint verb, e.g. Makhuwa (P31) (cf. Luganda [-F])
b. the augment (and/or its H) is absent after a disjoint verb, e.g. Tonga

---

[3] It has been hypothesized that the Proto-Bantu augment had H tone in all but noun classes 1 and 9 (de Blois 1970), although the *H generalizes to all classes in all cases I know.

Termed predicative lowering by Schadeberg and Mucanheia (2000), Makhuwa deletes the first H of a nominal after a conjoint verb (cf. Stucky 1979: 191; Van der Wal 2006, 2009: 128; also Devos, this volume). Thus the H of the citation form of *maláshi* 'grass' is observed after the DJ verb in (18a), but is absent after the CJ verb in (18b).

(18) a. disjoint : enyómpé tsi-náá-khúúr-á maláshi 'the cows eat grass'
    b. conjoint : enyómpé tsi-n-khúúr-á mal<u>a</u>shi 'the cows eat GRASS'[4]

As Van der Wal (2009: 32) succinctly puts it:

> Only nouns and adjectives which had a pre-prefix or augment in some earlier stage of the language have the possibility to undergo P[redicate] L[owering] and have a different tone pattern.

It is thus clear that the deleted H of *maláshi* comes from the historical augment (cf. Van der Wal 2006), which would have been class 6 *á-* in the example. In this case, we identify absence of the augment and IAV focus with CJ.

In Luganda we saw that the absence of an augment allowed a [-F] verb to form a tight bond ("tone group") and undergo H tone plateauing with the IAV constituent. In Tonga (M64), nouns appear to assign a final H to a CJ verb, as in (19a), but not to a DJ verb (Goldsmith 1984: 24, based on Carter 1962):

(19) a. conjoint : 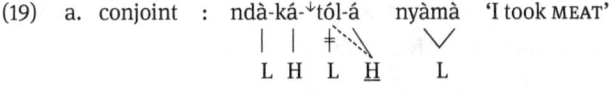 'I took MEAT'

    b. disjoint : 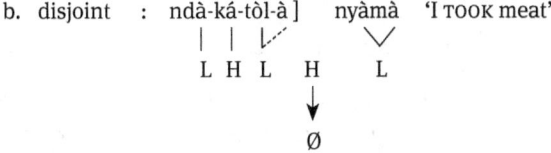 'I TOOK meat'

As schematized in (19a), the nominal H in question is from the historical augment which links onto the preceding CJ verb. In (19b), where the bond is less tight with a preceding DJ verb, the H of the augment is instead deleted as it is on the citation form of nouns. Again, this effect is expected only when the IAV constituent is nominal, hence capable of having taken an historical augment. However, the CJ/DJ distinction has never been limited to whether the following constituent is a NP, an object or something else.[5] Since the CJ/DJ distinction has ultimately to do with focus (whether directly or indirectly), the post-verbal element can be any

---

4 By a separate rule, all L *malashi* becomes *malashí* before pause.
5 Similarly, Luganda HTP not only occurs when a nominal is [-A] but also when a [-F] verb is followed by a prepositional phrase.

constituent (argument, adjunct) within the same clause. This naturally brings us to the issue of "metatony" discussed in the next section.

4 Metatony

The term "metatony" was originally introduced by Meeussen (1967: 111) to characterize the tone of the final vowel of the class 15 *ku-* infinitive: "The final element has to be set up as *-a* (low) or *-á* . . . (with metatony: high if an object follows, low otherwise)." Canonical examples are presented in (20) from Songye (L23) (Stappers 1964, cited by Dimmendaal 1995: 32 and Schadeberg 1995: 176):

(20) a.   ku-sep-a   'to laugh (at)'   (without metatony)
      b.   ku-sep-á mfumu   'to laugh at the chief' (with metatony)

Both Dimmendaal and Schadeberg point out that the "metatonic" final H is lacking when the infinitive is followed by a connective (genitive) NP:

(21)   ku-sep-a   kwǎ-mbwá   'the laughing of the dog'   (without metatony)
         to laugh   of-dog

Citing several cases, Hadermann (2005: 405) shows that metatony can also be observed in verb conjugations built historically on the *ku-* infinitive, e.g. the Lega (D25) progressive form in (22a) from Meeussen (1971):

(22) a.   be-ko-bolót-á ↓mózígi   'they are pulling the rope'   (with metatony)
      b.   be-ko-bolot-a tɔŋgɔ   'they are pulling also'   (without metatony)

As seen, the concept of metatony originally referred to constructions which involve (i) the *ku-* . . . *-a* infinitive and (ii) a following object NP. However, subsequent to Meeussen (1967), the term *metatony* has been extended to describe tonal alternations in certain conjugated verb forms which clearly do not involve the infinitive *ku-* prefix or require the following constituent to be an object. In synchronic analyses, the assumption appears to be that the final H is derived, as evident in the following quotations:

> In the languages concerned here [Duala (A24) and Basaa (A43)], a verb-final vowel becomes high when it is followed by a complement. (Costa and Kula 2008: 313)
> . . . metatony, whereby in certain T[ense]A[spect] forms a high tone replaces a low or falling tone on post-radical syllables . . . if and only if the verb is not phrase-final, that is, followed by other material such as an object or adverbial. (Nurse 2008: 48)

Both Dimmendaal (1995) and Schadeberg (1995) speculate that metatony derives from the *H augment. This is schematized in (23), where I have indicated a hypothetical augment *ú-:

(23) 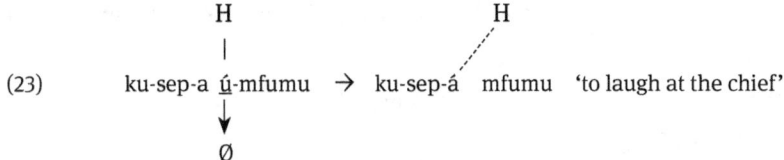 'to laugh at the chief'

As in the case of predicative lowering in Makhuwa, if this reconstruction is correct, there should originally have been no metatony before a nominal which lacked an augment in PB (e.g. kinship terms, names), although subsequent analogy is always possible. As far as I know, the lack of metatony under such conditions has not been shown.

Another speculation is that metatony is related to focus and the CJ/DJ distinction:

> [Metatony] is often described as just a tonal process, but it is striking that it has certain characteristics linking it to focus . . . . This suggests it has a syntactic-semantic function . . . . (Nurse 2008: 204)
>
> . . . in Duala and Basaa, where a tonal distinction with respect to a following complement can still be seen, we have [immediate after verb] focus as opposed to initial focus, pointing to the fact that the tonal effects . . . are the indicator of focus (via prosodic structure). (Costa and Kula 2008: 313)

In fact, it is not clear that metatony *sensu stricto* is ever related to focus. Abo (Bankon) (A42), a language closely related to Basaa, shows three verb tone patterns illustrated with the L tone verb *pɔ̀ŋɔ̀* 'make, create' (Hyman and Lionnet 2012):[6]

(24) | | suffix tone | TAM | pre-pause | + bìtámbé 'shoes' | |
| --- | --- | --- | --- | --- | --- |
| a. | -L ~ -H | present | ă pɔ̀ŋɔ̀ | ă pɔ̀ŋɔ́ bítámbé | 'he is making shoes' |
| | | past | à pɔ́ŋɔ́ | à pɔ́ˇŋɔ́ bítámbé | 'he made shoes' |
| | | perfect | à má pɔ́ŋɔ́ | à má pɔ̀ŋɔ́ bìtámbé | 'he has made shoes' |
| b. | -L | future | à káà pɔ̀ŋɔ̀ | à káà pɔ̀ŋɔ̀ bìtámbé | 'he will make shoes' |
| c. | -H | stative | à pòŋó | à pòŋó bìtámbé | 'he has made shoes'[7] |
| | | imperative | pɔ̀ŋɔ́ | pɔ̀ŋɔ́ bìtámbé | 'make shoes!' |
| | | subjunctive | sá pɔ́ˇŋɔ́ | sá pɔ́ˇŋɔ́ bìtámbé | 'let's make shoes!' |

While (24b,c) have a stable final -L and -H tone, respectively, the tenses in (24a) show an alternation between -L and -H. As seen in the representative examples in (25),

---

[6] Makasso (2012) treats similar phenomena in closely related Basaa.
[7] In this sentence the stative is used transitively as a resultative; the subjunctive is also used as a hortative.

the -L ~ -H alternation occurs before all parts of speech and all constituents within the clause:

(25) a. ǎ sɔ̀ŋsɛ̀ 'he is counting'
b. ǎ sɔ̀ŋsɛ́ mɔ́⁺ní 'he is counting money' __ noun
c. ǎ s sɔ̀ŋsɛ́ àmù mɔ̀ní 'he is counting this money' __ demonstrative
d. ǎ sɔ̀ŋsɛ́ mɔ́ 'he is counting it' __ pronoun
e. ǎ sɔ̀ŋsɛ́ látâlá 'he is counting now' __ adverb
f. ǎ sɔ̀ŋsɛ́ nì mìnnyɔ́ɔ́ myé 'he is counting with his fingers' __ prepositional phrase
g. ǎ sɔ̀ŋsɛ́ nì/tɔ̀ sák 'he counts and/or dances' __ conjoined verb

The sentences in (26) show that metatony occurs independently of where the focus is within the sentence (*ndí* is a focus marker):

(26) a. *"neutral" focus* măn ǎ sɔ̀ŋsɛ́ másɔ̌ŋ mé 'the child is counting his teeth'
b. *subject focus* măn ndì ǎ sɔ̀ŋsɛ́ másɔ̌ŋ mé 'the CHILD is counting his teeth'
c. *non-subject focus* măn ǎ sɔ̀ŋsɛ́ ndí másɔ̌ŋ mé 'the child is counting his TEETH'

The same three-way distinction in final tone is also observed in corresponding relative clauses, where focus marking is typically limited:

(27)   suffix tone   TAM   pre-pause   + bìtámbé 'shoes'
a.   -L ~ H   present   mùt nú pɔ̀ŋɔ̀   mùt nú pɔ̀ŋɔ́ bítámbé   'the person who is making shoes'
                    past   mùt nú pɔ́ŋɔ̀   mùt nú pɔ́⁺ŋɔ́ bítámbé   'the person who made shoes'
b.   -L   future   mùt nú káà pɔ̀ŋɔ̀   mùt nú káà pɔ̀ŋɔ̀ bítámbé   'the person who will make shoes'
c.   -H   stative   mùt nú pòŋó   mùt nú pòŋó bìtámbé   'the person who has made shoes'

To account for such alternations, Hyman and Lionnet (2012) propose that metatonic tenses such as those in (24a) end /-H/, which undergoes H → L pre-pausally, while the final H tenses in (24c) are /-HL/ (and therefore fail to undergo final lowering). The most direct evidence for this analysis can be observed by placing a /H/-initial constituent after the different tenses.[8]

---

8 This is quite hard to find in Abo, since most words begin L. As seen, the headless genitive construction, here *bí mán* 'the ones (cl.8) of the child/the child's' (e.g bìtámbé 'shoes'), provides a particularly clear case.

(28)   suffix tone   TAM   pre-pause   + bí mán 'the child's'
   a. /-H/   present   ă pɔ̀ŋɔ̀   ă pɔ̀ŋɔ́ bí mán   'he is making the
                                                                     child's'
                     past   à pɔ́ŋɔ̀   à pɔ́ˉŋɔ́ bí mán   'he made the child's'
                     perfect   à má   à má pɔ̀ŋɔ́ bí   'he has made the
                                  pɔ̀ŋɔ̀   mán   child's'
   b. /-L/   future   à káà   à káà pɔ̀ŋɔ̀ bí   'he will make the
                                  pɔ̀ŋɔ̀   mán   child's'
   c. /-HL/   stative   à pòŋó   à pòŋó ˉbí   'he has made the
                                                 mán   child's'
                     imperative   pɔ̀ŋɔ́   pɔ̀ŋɔ́ ˉbí mán   'make the child's!'
                     subjunctive sá pɔ́ˉŋɔ́   sá pɔ́ˉŋɔ́ ˉbí   'let's make the
                                                 mán   child's!'

From the above (and further evidence in Hyman and Lionnet 2012) we conclude that Abo metatony (i) is not likely derived from the *H of the augment; (ii) is analyzeable in terms of underlying suffix tones on the verb; (iii) does not insert a H; metatonic tenses undergo clause-final H → L; (iv) is not related to marking objects, focus, or the conjoint-disjoint distinction.

Despite the conclusion in (iv), it is rather striking that languages identified with metatony are in near-perfect geographic complementary distribution with those identified as having a "conjoint/disjoint". Thus, as seen in the table in (29), languages reported to have metatony tend to occur in the Northwest Bantu zones, while those exhibiting the CJ/DJ distinction are found in the Eastern and Southern zones:

(29) Metatony (Hyman and Lionnet 2012)   CJ/DJ (Nurse 2006: 193; Van der Wal 2009: 216; this volume)

A20	Bakweri, Duala	C30	Binza	DJ60	Rundi, Rwanda, Ha	P20	Makonde
A40	Abo, Basaa	C60	Mbole-Tooli	EJ20	Haya	P30	Makhuwa
A50	Bafia	D10	Mituku, Enya	G20	Shambala	S20	Venda
A70	Eton, Ewondo	D20	Lega, Binja-Sud	K20	Lozi	S30	Tswana, Sotho
B30	Pove	D30	Bodo	M40	Bemba	S40	Xhosa, Swati, Zulu
B40	Sango	D40	Nyanga	(M50)	Lamba?	S50	Tsonga
B70	Teke	D50	Bembe	M60	Tonga		
C20	Mboshi	L23	Songye				

It is hard to evaluate the alleged relationship between metatony and CJ/DJ, since we do not know if metatony represents a unified phenomenon. There are at least two possibilities: (i) If all cases of metatony are the same and all cases of CJ/DJ are the same, they may or may not have a common source (if yes, this has not been demonstrated); (ii) if not all cases are the same, then some cases of metatony may be the same as CJ/DJ. Unfortunately, the work has not yet been done, especially as concerns metatony: We need more detailed studies like Hyman & Lionnet on Abo to see if there is a general phenomenon that can be identified as the same metatony across Bantu languages. The same is true concerning tone cases, to which we now turn.

5 Tone cases

In addition to the augment and metatony, it has also been suggested that so-called "tone cases" may be related to the CJ/DJ distinction:

> The CJ/DJ distinction may diachronically, and possibly synchronically as well, also be linked to the so-called tone cases . . . (Schadeberg 1986). (Van der Wal 2009: 217)
> . . . the two systems – verbal conjoint-disjoint inflection and nominal tonal "case" inflection – are in fact quite similar. Apart from the marking of verbs as opposed to nouns, the two systems are broadly similar with respect to the use of prosodic means to express the distinctions, the relation of the marking to parts – but not the whole – of the tense-aspect paradigm, the absence of distinctions in relative clauses, and the relation of the systems to information structure and linear order/constituency. (Kavari et al. 2012: 1)

Let us first consider Otjiherero (R31), which distinguishes the following four tone cases (Kavari et al. 2012: 2):

(30) a. default   L-L : òtjì-hávérò tj-á ù   'the chair fell down'
      b. complement   L-H : vé múná òtjí-hávérò   'they usually see the chair'
      c. predicative H-L : ótjì-hávérò   'it's a chair'
      d. vocative   Ø-L : tjì-hávérò   'o chair!'

The default tone case (30a) is found on nouns in citation or subject position, while the complement tone case (30b) is found on object nouns in main clauses. The predicative (or "copulative") and vocative tone cases are illustrated in (30c,d). Whether an object will receive complement (C) or default (D) case depends on the TAM, polarity, and clause type (all objects receive D in relative clauses, for instance). The following table based on Kavari et al. (2012: 5) shows that complement case tends to appear after what would be [-F] TAMs in Haya, Luganda etc.:[9]

---

9 Coincidentally, the abbreviations C and D can serve as mnemonic for CJ and DJ, the verb marking to which the respective tone cases correspond.

(31)	TAMs assigning C	Aff.	Neg.	TAMs not assigning C	Aff.	Neg.
	Factive-Habitual	C	C~D	Present, Near Future	D	D
	Recent Past [-perf]	C	D	Indefinite Future	D	D
	Remote Past [-perf]	C	C	Imperative	D	D
	Recent Past [+perf]	C	D	Optative	D	D
	Remote Past [+perf]	C	C	Subjunctive	D	D
	Subsecutive (Narrative)	C	D		

Such nominal tone marking is found quite extensively in westerly Bantu languages from Gabon down to Namibia, with considerable variation and complexity. In Giphende (L11) there are five apparent tonal cases which have a rather odd distribution quite different from Otjiherero:[10]

(32)

	a.	b.	c.	d.	e.	f.	g.	h.
URs:	/L-L.L/	/L-L.L.L/	/L-L.H/	/L-L.H.L/	/L-H.L/	/L-H.H/	/L-H.H.L/	/L-H.H.H/
1.	L-L.L	L-L.L.L	L-L.H	L-L.H.L	L-H.L	L-H.H	L-H.H.L	L-H.H.H
2.	H-H.L	H-H.H.L	L-L.H	L-L.H.L	L-H.L	L-H.H	L-H.H.L	L-H.H.H
3.	H-H.L	H-H.H.L	H-L.H	H-L.H.L	L-H.L	L-H.H	L-H.H.L	L-H.H.H
4.	H-H.L	H-H.H.L	H-H.↓H.L	H-↓H.L	H-↓H.L	H-↓H.H	H-↓H.H.L	H-↓H.H.H
5.	H-H.L	H-H.H.L	H-L.H	H-L.H.L	H-H.L	H-H.H	H-H.H.L	H-H.H.H

1. citation, subject, object of a negative infinitive, left-dislocation
2. focused object
3. genitive, second object, object after a negative verb, subject after a relative verb
4. object after an affirmative verb or after *na* 'with'
5. predictative ('it's ...')

As seen, the bold line separates those forms which receive an initial H from those which do not. Giphende might be interpreted in terms of prefixal or proclitic H "co-phonologies" converting toneless prefixes to H- as follows:[11]

(33)   a.   case 1:   Ø- remains Ø- on all nouns

---

[10] In the table in (32), based on joint work with Mwatha Ngalasso in 1998, L- and H- represent the noun prefix, whereas stem syllables are separated by a dot. Underlyingly toneless (Ø) syllables receive L pitch by default. For other discussion of tone cases, see Daeleman (1983) for Kikongo [DRC] and Blanchon (1999a, 1999b) for a historical account with tones coming in cyclically from the left.
[11] Note that any H- prefix/proclitic will spread to the penult if the noun is completely toneless. As seen, when the noun has a /H/, the variation in (32b-e) concerns whether and how the prefix/proclitic H can appear with different resolutions of OCP(H).

b. case 2: ∅- → H- unless there is a H anywhere in the stem = a skeleton-insensitive OCP(H) restriction
c. case 3: ∅- → H- unless there is a H in the first syllable of the stem to avoid a local, skeleton-sensitive OCP(H) restriction
d. case 4: ∅- → H- in all nouns; the H spreads to the penult or up to a H, which is downstepped to avoid an OCP violation
e. case 5: ∅- → H- in all nouns; the H spreads to the penult if the stem is all L, otherwise is realized only on the prefix, without downstepping the following H, the OCP violation thus being tolerated

While Giphende has no augment, involvement of the augment with case marking is found in Umbundu (R11), which has only two nominal forms, but three cases (Schadeberg 1986: 431):[12]

(34)

	noun with augment	noun without augment	'bark'	'Doctor'
Common case (CC)	∅-	∅-	o-ci-peta	ci-mbanda
Object case (OC)	H-	∅-	ó-cí-péta	ci-mbanda
Predicative	H-	H-	ó-cí-péta	cí-mbánda

Examples of Umbundu nominals with and without the augment *o-* and a bisyllabic stem are seen in (35).

(35)

	'to meet'	'to read'	'vein'	'hippo'	(derived name)
	/-sang-a/	/-táng-a/	/-singá/	/-gevé/	/-gevé/
CC	o-ku-sang-a	o-ku-táng-á	o-lu-singá	o-n-gevé	n-gevé
OC	ó-kú-sáng-a	ó-kú-↓táng-á	ó-lú-sí↓ngá	ó-n-gé↓vé	n-gevé
Pred	ó-kú-sáng-a	ó-kú-↓táng-á	ó-lú-sí↓ngá	ó-n-gé↓vé	n-gé↓vé

Schadeberg (1986: 444–445) proposes the following stages in the development of the augmented common and object cases: (i) The high tone on the augment is generalized to all classes (including classes 1 and 9); (ii) the initial consonant of the augment is lost (cf. Lubukusu *ba-ba-ntu* vs. Luganda *a-ba-ntu*); (iii) the augment vowel *o-* is generalized at the expense of *e-* and *a-* to certain classes, e.g. class 7 *o-ci-*; (iv) the *o-* augment is generalized for all syntactically defined environments. As Schadeberg puts it:

---

[12] Schadeberg states that "the augment is retained in all syntactic environments", but that some nouns lack an augment, e.g. proper nouns, and there are morphological contexts where the augment does not occur (p.430).

Tonally, the old distinction was preserved; thus, UMbundu OC continues the PB presence of the augment, and CC continues its absence. Semantically, it seems problematic to start from De Blois' determinative function of the augment. If "determinative" may be interpreted as "making definite", it should have become a subject marker whereas in fact it has turned into an object marker . . . It therefore seems possible that the augment further weakened to an indefinite determiner . . . . Of course, no sharp line separates augment from case languages. Also, the tonal marking of focus that has been claimed for Makua (Stucky 1979) is very likely to be another derivative of the augment. (p.445)

The contexts where the Umbundu common vs. object cases occur are summarized as follows (Schadeberg 1986: 432–437):

(36) *Common Case (= default)*
  • subject, left- & right-dislocations
  • "second complement"
  • complement of negative verb form
  • complement of a progressive verb form
  • complement in a subordinated clause
  • before a numeral (some optionality)

Object (complement) case
  • "first complement of an affirmative, non-subordinated verb"
  • after *kwéndá* and *la-* 'and'; probably also after connective
  [+F] TAM/polarity
  [-focus] clause

The critical observation is that, quite consistently in such languages, the tone case is different on an immediately post-verbal nominal (e.g. object) vs. subsequent nominals. Thus compare the following sentences, where (37a,b) involve two different verbs 'to give' (Schadeberg 1986: 433–434):

(37) a. o-njalí yá⁺h̩á ó-⁺mál̩a e-pako   'the parent gave the children the fruit'
   b. o-njalí yá⁺cá é-páko k-o-mál̩a   'the parent gave the fruit to the children'
   c. ndalúmáníwa k-ó-mbwá   'I was bitten by a dog'[13]

As seen, in so-called object- or complement case the *H of the augment is preserved with a "strong link" between an appropriate verb and an IAV nominal, as in Tonga (recall (19a)).

Although the H tone which marks the first complement is clearly related to the augment, how do we account for its restriction to "first complement of an affirmative, non-subordinated verb"? While the non-H common case is as expected after negatives where objects lacked an augment, the H object case does not correlate with definiteness or specificity, as Schadeberg notes. This in fact appears to be the opposite of Luganda and Makhuwa, where it is the absence of the augment that correlates with IAV focus. Finally, if the H object case is like "strong link"

---

13 Note in (37c) that the verb need not end H.

conjoint marking, why isn't it found in relative clauses? The inevitable conclusion is that there has been considerable restructuring of the original situation (which we independently know because of the innovated distribution of the segmental augment *o-*).

6 Summary and conclusion

In the above discussion we have seen that the effects on the verb or IAV constituent can be several:

(38) a. verb morphology: prefix/suffix inflections, including tonal morphology
 b. noun morphology: presence vs. absence of the augment, tone cases
 c. phrasing: V + IAV functioning vs. not functioning as a prosodic domain, e.g. "tone group", or perhaps being final vs. non-final within a syntactic constituent (Van der Spuy 1993; Buell 2006)

There have been three intersecting issues concerning verb/IAV interactions:

(39) a. typology : what and how many different phenomena are there?
 b. terminology : what should we call these phenomena?
 c. history : where do these phenomena come from?

Concerning the first issue, typology, we have seen the following variations, where the clause-mate IAV constituent can be any of the following:

(40) a. anything : conjoint, Abo metatony, Haya tone reduction
 b. anything lacking an augment : Luganda H tone plateauing
 c. any nominal : complement tone case in Otjiherero, Umbundu
 d. any (historically) augmented nominal : predicative lowering in Makhuwa
 e. an object only : original Meeussen metatony, only with *ku*-infinitive

Despite the above differences, in all cases the TAM/polarity is implicated and usually the clause type as well. In no case is there an interaction which affects ALL combinations of verb + IAV constituent, e.g. no across-the-board conjoint/ disjoint verb morphology, "accusative" case, V + IAV co-phrasing, consistent tonal or focus marking etc.

While the above has dealt exclusively with the relation of a verb and what follows it, it is important to note that many of the same phenomena occur within the noun phrase (cf. Manus, this volume). However, although there can be comparable effects between the noun and a following modifier, I have found no case where the head noun is affected before any and all IAN ("immediate after noun") constitutents. Recall Haya (JE22) tone reduction in (9), where [-F] verbs lose their H tones when a constituent follows in the same clause. As seen in (41a), H tones are maintained on a noun when it occurs before a demonstrative or numeral, but are reduced before a possessive pronoun or nominal or an adjective, as in (41b).

(41) a. e-ki-kómbe kî-li   'that cup'   b. e-ki-kombe kyáitu   'our cup'
         e-ki-kómbe kî-mo   'one cup'   e-ki-kombe kyaa káto   'Kato's cup'
                                               e-ki-kombe ki-lúngi   'good cup'

Similarly, compare the following Luganda forms with the H tone plateauing (HTP) in (14b), which occurs between a [-F] verb and a [-A] nominal:

(42) a. e-bi-kópò bi-sátù   'three cups'
         e-bi-kópò bi-rî   'those cups'
         bi-kópò binénè   '(they are) big cups'
     b. e-bi-kópó byáá wálúsìmbi 'Walusimbi's cups'

In (42a) there is no HTP between a noun and a numeral, demonstrative or adjective. However, (42b) shows that HTP applies between a noun and a following connective, e.g. *byaa* 'cl. 8' (cf. *byaa= Walúsìmbi* '(they are) Walusimbi's'. Thus, while a verb + IAV constituent often constitutes a well-defined prosodic domain, a parallel domain typically exists within the noun phrase as well.

Turning to the second issue, terminology, the following can be noted:

(43) a. *conjoint/disjoint* seems fairly entrenched now in Bantu studies, referring to cases where the verb shows two forms in main clause affirmative clauses, different morphology and often different phrasing, as in Bemba, "long" vs. "short" verb forms in Sotho-Tswana (S30) and Nguni (S40), but also potentially involving only the tone of the final (Creissels 1996a, 1996b).
     b. *metatony* is considerably less clear; in its restricted sense, it refers to a -L ~ -H alternation on the final *-a* of the *ku-* infinitive, which can be conditioned only by an object; in its more general usage it refers to a -L ~ -H alternation with any TAM and followed by anything (but should it be used to refer to CJ/DJ final -L vs. -H in Tonga (M42) and Tswana (S31) (Creissels 1996a, 1996b)?).[14]

---

14 Jenneke van der Wal (pers.comm.) rightly points out that that metatony and the tonal marking of CJ/DJ differ in that metatony is automatic (in the appropriate TAMs etc.), whereas the same TAMs offer a CJ/DJ choice, a contrast in main clauses. In this sense metatony pairs with the [-F] TAMs, where the tonal effects are also obligatory.

c. *tone cases:* as seen from Giphende (L11), there is considerable variation; a key issue has been whether these are really "cases" and/or syntactically conditioned tonal alternations capturable in other ways; some are related to the tone of the augment or predication marker historically; it is probably good to keep the term, as we know what it refers to (vs. other more general terms such as *syntactic tone, tonal frames* etc.).
d. other terms that will doubtless be needed include *relative TAMs, negative TAMs, marked* or *[+F] TAMs*, which may be implicated, but should be distinguished from the above

Finally, there is the question of history: where do all of these markings come from? What motivates them, and how do they evolve over time? My own conclusions and suspicions are the following:

(44) a. All of the above have multiple historical sources and are at least potentially interrelated.
b. Disjoint marking of TAMs is generally innovated in the main clause affirmative, with the conjoint being more conservative (typically preserved in negative and in relative clauses).
c. The history of Meeussen's metatony is less clear, but the Abo case shows that there can be a strictly phonological origin.
d. Tone cases generally owe their existence to earlier prefixal and proclitic tones, as Blanchon (1999a, 1999b) has shown; these include the *H augment and predicative tones, which have very different distributions: the definite article-like augment is expected on subjects, while predicators/focus markers are expected on the IAV.
e. One should be careful not to equate metatony or any other final vs. non-final distinction on verbs to focus: as we have seen, verb + IAV effects can be quite varied, sometimes having to do with objecthood, sometimes with the position of the verb within the clause, the nature of the clause, or phonological phrasing.
f. The best strategy in getting it right is to describe and analyze individual cases as systematically and exhaustively as possible.

In all of the above it is especially important to pay attention to tone, which can be quite subtle. As Creissels (1996a: 115) puts it: "it is vital to pay more attention to the tonal variations of verb forms (and to tonal variations in general) in the description of Bantu languages."

Abbreviations

[±A]	feature designating the presence vs. absence of the augment	CJ	conjoint form of the verb
		COMP	complement focus
[±F]	feature designating whether a specific TAM has morphologized focus or not	DJ	disjoint form of the verb
		HTP	high tone plateauing
		IAV	immediate after verb position
[±TS]	feature designating whether there is tone spreading (of high tone) or not	MC	main clause
		NP	noun phrase
		TAM	tense, aspect, mood
CC	common case	VP	verb phrase

References

Anderson, Stephen C. 1979. Verb structure. In Larry M. Hyman (ed.), *Aghem grammatical structure*, 73–136. Southern Calfornia Occasional Paper in Linguistics 7. Los Angeles: University of Southern California.

Blanchon, Jean Alain. 1999a. Semantic/pragmatic conditions on the tonology of the Kongo noun-phrase: a diachronic hypothesis. In Larry M. Hyman & Charles W. Kisseberth (eds.), *Theoretical aspects of Bantu tone*, 1–32. Stanford: CSLI.

Blanchon, Jean. 1999b. 'Tone cases' in Bantu group B.40. In Jean A. Blanchon & Denis Creissels (eds.), *Issues in Bantu tonology*, 37–82. Köln: Rüdiger Köppe Verlag.

Buell, Leston. 2006. The Zulu conjoint/disjoint verb alternation: Focus or constituency? *ZAS Papers in Linguistics* 43.9–30.

Carter, Hazel. 1962. *Notes on the tonal system of Northern Rhodesian Plateau Tonga*. H.M. Stationery Off. London.

Costa, João & Nancy C. Kula. 2008. Focus at the interface: Evidence from Romance and Bantu. In Cécile de Cat & Katherine Demuth (eds.), *The Bantu-Romance connection*, 293–322. Amsterdam: John Benjamins.

Creissels, Denis. 1996a. Conjunctive and disjunctive verb forms in Setswana. *South African Journal of African Languages* 16. 109–115.

Creissels, Denis. 1996b. La tonalité des finales verbales et la distinction entre formes verbales conjointes et formes verbales disjointes en tswana. *Africana Linguistica* XI. 27–47. Tervuren: Musée Royal de l'Afrique Centrale.

Daeleman, Jan (1983). Tone-groups and tone-cases in a Bantu tone-language. *ITL: Review of Applied Linguistics* 60/61. 131–141.

De Blois, Kees. 1970. The augment in the Bantu languages. *Africana Linguistica* 4. 85–165.

Dimmendaal, Gerrit. 1995. Metatony in Benue-Congo: Some further evidence for an original augment. In E. 'Nolue Emenanjo & Ozo-mekuri Ndimele (eds.), *Issues in African languages and linguistics*, 30–38. Aba: NINLAN.

Givón, Talmy. 1972. Studies in ChiBemba and Bantu grammar. *Studies in African Linguistics*, Supplement 5.

Givón, Talmy. 1975. Focus and the scope of assertion: Some Bantu evidence. *Studies in African Linguistics* 6. 185–205.

Goldsmith, John. 1984. Tone and accent in Tonga. In George N. Clements & John Goldsmith (eds.), *Autosegmental studies in Bantu tone*, 19–51. Dordrecht: Foris.

Güldemann, Tom. 2003. Present progressive vis-à-vis predication focus in Bantu. *Studies in Language* 27.323–360.

Hadermann, Pascale. 2005. Eléments segmentaux et supra-segmentaux pour marquer la fonction 'object' dans quelques langues bantoues. In Koen Bostoen & Jacky Maniacky (eds.), *Studies in African comparative linguistics, with special focus on Bantu and Mande*, 397–410. Tervuren: Musée Royal de l'Afrique Centrale.

Hyman, Larry M. 2010. Focus marking in Aghem: Syntax or semantics? In Ines Fiedler & Anne Schwartz (eds.), *The expression of information structure: A documentation of its diversity across Africa*, 95–116. Amsterdam: John Benjamins.

Hyman, Larry M. & Ernest Rugwa Byarushengo. 1984. A model of Haya tonology. In George N. Clements & John Goldsmith (eds.), *Autosegmental studies in Bantu tone*, 53–103. Dordrecht: Foris.

Hyman, Larry M. & Francis X. Katamba. 1990. The augment in Luganda tonology. *Journal of African Languages and Linguistics* 12. 1–45.

Hyman, Larry M. & Francis X. Katamba. 1993. The augment in Luganda: Syntax or pragmatics? In Sam Mchombo (ed.), *Theoretical aspects of Bantu grammar*, 209–256. Stanford: C.S.L.I.

Hyman, Larry M. & Francis X. Katamba. 2010. Tone, syntax, and prosodic domains in Luganda. *ZAS Papers in Linguistics*, 53. 69–98.

Hyman, Larry M., Francis X. Katamba & Livingstone Walusimbi. 1987. Luganda and the strict layer hypothesis. *Phonology [Yearbook]* 4. 87–108.

Hyman, Larry M. & Florian Lionnet. 2012. Metatony in Abo (Bankon), A42. In Michael R. Marlo, Nikki B. Adams, Christopher R. Green, Michelle Morrison & Tristan M. Purvis (eds.), *Selected Proceedings of the 42nd Annual Conference on African Linguistics*, 1–14. Somerville, MA: Cascadilla Proceedings Project.

Hyman, Larry M. & John Robert Watters. 1984. Auxiliary focus. *Studies in African Linguistics* 15. 233–273.

Kavari, Jekura U., Lutz Marten & Jenneke van der Wal. 2012. Tone cases in Otjiherero: head-complement relations, linear order, and information structure. *Africana Linguistica* 18.315–353.

Makasso, Emmanuel-Moselly. 2012. Metatony in Basaa. In Michael R. Marlo, Nikki B. Adams, Christopher R. Green, Michelle Morrison & Tristan M. Purvis (eds), *Selected Proceedings of the 42nd Annual Conference on African Linguistics*, 15–22. Somerville, MA: Cascadilla Proceedings Project.

Meeussen, A.E. 1959. *Essai de grammaire rundi*. Tervuren: Musée Royal de l'Afrique Centrale.

Meeussen, A.E. 1967. Bantu grammatical reconstructions. Tervuren: Musée Royal de l'Afrique Centrale.

Meeussen, A.E. 1971. *Eléments de grammaire lega*. Tervuren: Musée Royal de l'Afrique Centrale.

Nurse, Derek. 2006. Focus in Bantu: Verbal morphology and function. *ZAS Papers in Linguistics* 43. 189–207.

Nurse, Derek. 2008. *Tense and aspect in Bantu*. Oxford University Press. Oxford; New York : Oxford University Press, 2008.

Schadeberg, Thilo C. 1986. Tone cases in Umbundu. *Africana Linguistica* X. 423–447.

Schadeberg, Thilo C. 1995. Object diagnostics in Bantu. In E. 'Nolue Emenanjo & Ozo-mekuri Ndimele (eds), *Issues in African languages and linguistics*, 173–180. Aba: National Institute for Nigerian Languages.

Schadeberg, Thilo C. & Francisco Ussene Mucanheia. 2000. *Ekoti: The Maka or Swahili language of Angoche*. Cologne: Rüdiger Köppe Verlag.

Sharman, John, C. & Achille E. Meeussen. 1955. The representation of structural tones, with special reference to the tonal behavior of the verb in Bemba, Northern Rhodesia. *Africa: Journal of the international African Institute* 25(4). 393–404.

Sharman, J. C. 1956. The tabulation of tenses in a Bantu language (Bemba: Northern Rhodesia). *Africa* 25. 393–404.

Stappers, Leo. 1964. *Morfologie van het Songye*. Tervuren: Musée Royal de l'Afrique Centrale.

Stucky, Susan U. 1979. The interaction of tone and focus in Makua. *Journal of African Languages and Linguistics* 1. 189–198.

van der Spuy, Andrew. 1993. Dislocated noun phrases in Nguni. *Lingua* 90. 335–355.

Van der Wal, Jenneke. 2006. Predictive lowering in Makhuwa. In Jeroen van de Weijer & Bettelou Los (eds.), *Linguistics in the Netherlands* 23, 224–236. Amsterdam: John Benjamins.

Van der Wal, Jenneke. 2009. *Word order and information structure in Makhuwa-Enahara*. Utrecht: LOT.

Maud Devos
5 Shangaji paired tenses: Emergence of a CJ/DJ system?

1 Introduction

Shangaji is an endangered variant of Makhuwa (P31), which during some time in its history was heavily influenced by Swahili. Like Makhuwa it has tenses that come in pairs. They are morphologically different but share the same TAM semantics. An example of such a pair is given in (1).

(1) a) *a-ttóo-thíimb-a*
    1SM-PRS$_F$-dig-FV
    'she digs / is digging'

  b) *a-tti-thímb-á*   *n-ttuupha*   (citation form: *nttúupha*)
    1SM-PRS-dig-FV   3-hole
    'she digs / is digging a hole'

The forms in (1a) and (1b) are reminiscent of the Makhuwa-Enaharra disjoint and conjoint forms in (2a) and (2b), respectively.

(2)   Makhuwa-Enaharra (Van der Wal 2009: 126)
  a) *o-náa-thíp-á*
     1SM-PRS.DJ-dig-FV
     'she is digging'

  b) *o-n-thíp-á*   *n-littí*   (citation form: *nlítti*)
     1SM-PRS.CJ-dig-FV   5-hole
     'she digs a hole'

The Shangaji and Makhuwa forms in (1a) and (2a) can occur pre-pausally, whereas the forms in (1b) and (2b) are immediately followed by a focused noun whose tonal pattern is lowered in both languages.[1] However, the Shangaji form in (1b) is also crucially different from Makhuwa conjoint verb forms. In fact, it does not share the most important property of all Bantu conjoint verbs in that it can occur in utterance-final position (cf. Van der Wal's working definition in this volume).

---

[1] When focus lowering results in an all-low noun in Makhuwa-Enaharra, a boundary H tone is added on the last syllable (hence, *nlittí* rather than *nlitti*) (Van der Wal 2009: 119).

The verb in (1b) is immediately followed by a lowered noun but it can also be followed by a noun with its regular, lexical tonal pattern, as in (3a), and, more importantly, it can also occur in phrase-final position (cf. (3b)).

(3)   a)   *ki-tti-thímbá n-ttúupha*   'I am digging a hole'

        b)   *ki-ttí-thiímb-a*   'I dig / am digging'

In this chapter I describe the Shangaji paired tenses and compare them to more canonical CJ/DJ pairs in related Bantu languages (Section 3). The similarities of the Shangaji alternating verb forms with CJ/DJ forms in Makhuwa but also more distantly related Kimatuumbi (P13) and Ndengeleko (P11) suggest a possible evolution towards a more canonical CJ/DJ system. Section 5 discusses whether there are synchronic indications for the emergence in Shangaji of a CJ/DJ alternation. The chapter sets out by giving a short description of phonological phrasing and its relation to focus in Shangaji (Section 2).

2 Penultimate lengthening and phonological phrasing in Shangaji

Phonological phrasing in Shangaji is marked by automatic penultimate lengthening (cf. Manus, this volume). Words that are uttered in isolation always have penultimate lengthening (PUL) applied to them (cf. (1a)).[2] Within a sentence words either group together or belong to different phonological phrases. In (4), for example, the verb forms a single phonological phrase with the following noun, whereas the subject phrases separately.

(4)   *hasáani*   *a-n-véng-él-e*   *papáa-w-e*
        Hasani   1SM-1OM-beg-APPL-PFV   1A father-1-POSS1
        'Hasani begged his father'

The same utterance can also have three separate phonological phrases, as seen in (5).

(5)   *hasáani anvéngéele papáawe*

While more research is needed to ascertain whether this depends solely on the speech rate or has a pragmatic effect, some combinations always occur in a single

---

2 There are three sources of surface vowel length in Shangaji: (1) automatic penultimate lengthening at the end of a phonological phrase, (2) compensatory lengthening after vowel coalescence with or without glide formation and (3) lexical vowel length. All long vowels are transcribed as double vowels. For more on the co-occurrence of contrastive vowel length and automatic penultimate lengthening in Shangaji, unusual from a Bantu-perspective, see Devos (2013).

phonological phrase, even in careful speech. Within the noun phrase, nouns and possessives always form a single phonological phrase, as in (6).

(6) n-zúrúkhu   w-áangu
    3-money   3-POSS1SG
    'my money'

A verb always phrases together with an element marked by focus lowering. The verb and the lowered noun in (1b) cannot occur in separate phonological phrases (cf. (7)).

(7) *kittíthiímba nttuupha
    'int. I dig / am digging a pit'

When the noun has its regular tonal pattern, as is the case in (3a), separate phonological phrases are possible (cf. (8)).

(8) kittíthiímba nttúupha
    'I dig / am digging a pit'

As will be argued further below, focus lowering typically expresses exclusive focus, as defined by van der Wal for Makhuwa-Enaharra (2009, 2011). Possessives likewise select a possessor to the exclusion of other possible possessors (as in 'my money, not yours'). In sum, the obligatory joining of more than one element in a single phrase in Shangaji appears to correlate with exclusive focus.

3 Shangaji paired tenses

As is typical for Bantu languages, Shangaji has rich verbal morphology. Up to 36 tenses (including negative and relative tenses) can be distinguished on morphological and / or prosodic grounds. Out of these 36 tenses, 16 main tenses are of special interest as they come in simple/complex pairs (cf. Table 1). The terms 'simple' and 'complex' are used because the complex tenses are probably all derived from a periphrastic construction containing the auxiliary -entta 'go (to)' (cf. Section 3.2). These pairs do not differ as to their temporal or aspectual semantics, rather the choice of one vs. the other of the pair is determined by information structure. If the verb is followed by a focused element, only simple forms can be used (cf. (9)). If focus is on the verb, the use of a complex form is obligatory (cf. (10)). In (9a) the element immediately following the verb has exclusive focus, which is marked by focus lowering. The use of the corresponding complex form is not allowed (cf. (9b)).

(9) a) *ki-tti-vénk-á*   n-zuruukhu (cf. *nzúrúukhu*)
 1SG.SM-PRS-beg-FV   3-money
 'I am begging for money [not something else]'

 b) **ki-ttóo-vénk-á*   n-zuruukhu
 1SG.SM-PRS$_F$-beg-FV   3-money
 int. 'I am begging for money [not something else]'

In (10a) the second verb is focused and cannot be replaced by the corresponding simple form (cf. (10b)).

(10) a) *o-tti-réntt-aá=ni?*   *ki-ttóo-fuúl-a*
 2SG.SM-PRS-do-FV=what   1SG.SM-PRS$_F$-wash-FV
 'what are you doing? I am washing'

 b) *o-tti-réntt-aá=ni?*   **ki-ttí-fuúl-a*
 2SG.SM-PRS-do-FV=what   1SG.SM-PRS-wash-FV
 int. 'what are you doing? I am washing'

In other contexts the choice between simple and complex forms is less clear-cut as will be discussed more fully in Sections 3.1 and 3.2.

The 8 pairs are listed in Table 1 together with their morphological and prosodic structure. The morphological structure of Shangaji verbs follows a recurring template in Bantu languages (for which see i.a. Schadeberg 2003: 151). The verbal stem (S) consists of the verbal base (including the root and derivational suffixes) and an inflectional final suffix. It is preceded by a combination of morphemes including the (obligatory) subject marker (SM) and the object marker (OM). Shangaji verb roots do not have lexical tone. Depending on the tense, melodic H tones are assigned to different positions within the (macro-) stem (the macro-stem being the stem with the preceding object marker).[3] These positions are given between square brackets for each tense (i.e., MS1 stands for melodic H on the first mora of the macro-stem, S3 for melodic H on the third mora of the stem, etc.). A hyphen indicates the absence of melodic H tones. If a pre-stem mora has a H tone assigned to it, it is marked on the pre-stem mora itself.

---

[3] Melodic H tones are not attributed to particular verbal morphemes. Instead, they are realized as H tones in specific positions in the verb stem in a particular inflection. (For more on melodic tone in Bantu see the various papers in *Africana Linguistica* 20, 2014.) In some tenses the type of subject marker or the presence vs. absence of the object marker has prosodic and/or (segmental) morphological consequences. This explains the different rows in the simple Present and Perfective tenses.

Table 1: Shangaji paired tenses.

		simple	complex
Present	1SG, 2SG, cl 1, 1PL, 2PL	SM-**tti**-(OM-)VB-**a** [MS1 S3]	SM-**ttó(o)**-(OM-)VB-**a** [S3]
	cl 2ff	SM-**ń**-(OM-)VB-**a** [S3]	SM-**ńtto**-(OM-)VB-**a** [S3]
Perfective	1SG, 2SG, cl 1	SM-VB-**V**[4] [-]	SM-**entt-e** Infinitive
	1SG, 2SG, cl 1	SM-OM-VB-**V** [S1]	
	1PL, 2PL, cl 2ff	SM-(OM-)VB-**V** [MS1]	
Past IPFV		SM-**a-o**-VB-**a** [S2]	SM-**a-nttó**-(OM-)VB-**a** [S3]
		SM-**a-o**-OM-VB-**a** [MS1 S3]	
Past PFV		SM-**a-ó**-(OM-)VB-**V** [-]	SM-**a-ńtto**-(OM-)VB-**a** [MS1 S3]
Neg Present		kha-SM-**ń**-(OM-)VB-**a** [S3]	kha-SM-**ńtto**-(OM-)VB-**a** [S3]
Neg. Perfective		kha-SM-(OM-)VB-**éni** [-]	kha-SM-**entt-éni** Infinitive SM-**entt-e** Negative Infinitive
Neg Past IPFV		kha-SM-**a-o**-VB-**a** [S2] kha-SM-**a-o**-OM-VB-**a** [MS1 S3]	kha-SM-**a-nttó**-(OM-)VB-**a** [S3]
Neg Past PFV		khá-SM-**a-o**-(OM-)VB-**é** [-]	SM-**a-ńtto-sí**-(OM-)VB-**a** [-]

The presence of the alternation in negative tenses is surprising (Hyman and Watters 1984), but see remarks on frequencies below. The absence of the alternation in relative tenses, on the other hand, is more in line with general expectations (see Hyman, this volume, Van der Wal, this volume). Relative tenses resemble simple tenses segmentally but have diverging tonal patterns. The Relative Present (SM-**ń**-(OM-)VB-**a-yó**) is a case in point. It is morphologically very similar to the Present in Table 1, the only difference being that the tense marker is always -ń- irrespective of the form of the subject marker. Prosodically, the Relative Present tense is unlike the (non-relative) Present in that it lacks melodic high tones.

---

[4] The symbol 'V' is used to represent the perfective final which in affirmative main tenses is a copy of the last vowel of the verbal base, except for verbs ending in a passive extension which always take final -**a**.

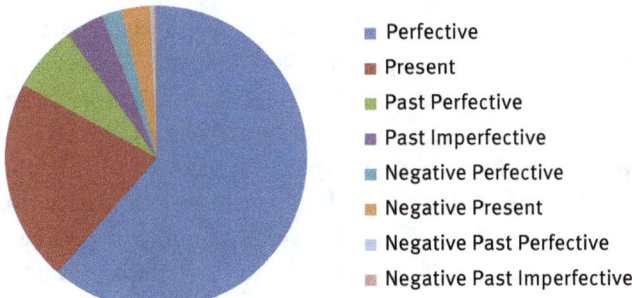

Figure 1: Relative frequency of paired tenses.

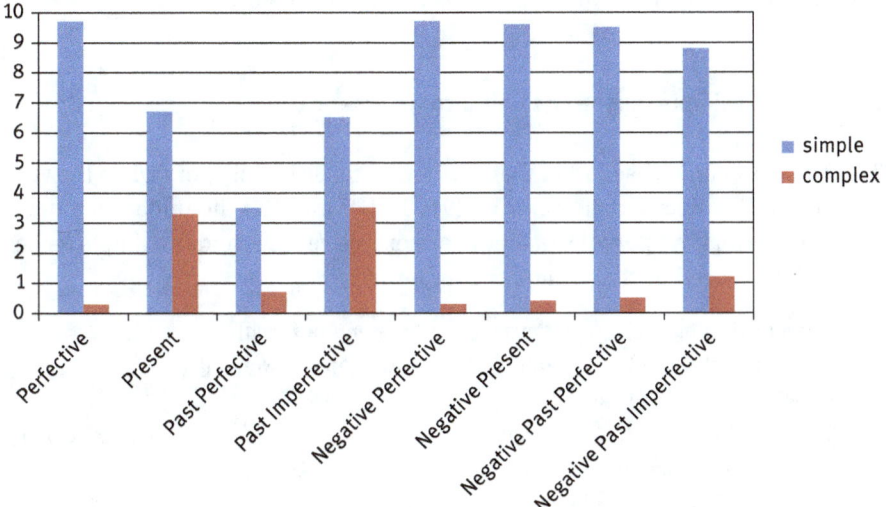

Figure 2: Relative frequency of simple and complex tenses.

The pairs of tenses display marked differences in frequency in the database.[5] Figure 1 represents the relative frequency of the 8 pairs of tenses and Figure 2 shows the relative frequency of each member of the pair.

---

5 The Shangaji database contains more or less 8,000 fully glossed sentences consisting of 30,400 running words. Of those 8,000 sentences 3,000 are isolated elicited sentences serving mainly as illustrative sentences for Shangaji verbs. The remaining 5,000 sentences are part of nineteen folk tales, twelve recipes, eighteen accounts of various activities and three short dialogues, all of which were collected during two fieldwork trips by the author, one in 2004 and the other in 2007. The database is not well balanced in terms of discourse type. Although also present in the stories and illustrative sentences, dialogues are particularly underrepresented.

A first observation is that simple tenses are far more frequent than complex ones and that the simple Perfective is omnipresent. Next, negative tenses, and especially the complex ones are very scarce. What is more, the complex Negative Perfective, Negative Past Perfective and Negative Past Imperfective are the only tenses that are exclusively found in elicited examples (i.e. examples explicitly elicited to obtain negative counterparts of complex Perfective, Past Perfective and Past Imperfective tenses). Notwithstanding the overall supremacy of simple tenses, there are two complex tenses that can compete with their simple counterparts: the complex Present and Past Imperfective.[6]

The following two subsections discuss the use and the formal characteristics of simple (Section 3.1) and complex tenses (Section 3.2) in more detail and compare them to conjoint and disjoint tenses in related languages.

3.1 Shangaji simple tenses and Bantu conjoint tenses

The use of a simple tense rather than a complex tense is obligatory when the verb is followed by a focused element (cf. (9)). In (11) and (12) the underlined noun and the interrogative particle =ni both have exclusive focus and the simple tenses cannot be replaced by their complex counterparts.[7]

(11) [mombé   z-aángu   z-oónxi   ti   z-ee-nttúwáakha]
     [10.cow   10-POSS1SG   10-all   COP   10-7.CONN-1A.woman]
     [All my cows are female.]
     ki-tti-sákh-á   n-ruruumbi   (cf. nrúrúumbi)
     1SG.SM-PRS-want-FV   3-bull
     'I want a bull [not another female]'

(12) o-tti-réntt-aá=<u>ni</u>?
     2SG.SM-PRS-want-FV=what
     'what are you doing?'

---

6 In recipes and other prescriptive discourse types the complex Present is almost as frequent as the neutral Present (45% vs 55% of the total hits for the Present pair). A possible explanation for this apparent break with the general pattern is that recipes often involve a fixed and limited set of ingredients that go through a series of different actions. Focus is on the different actions that need to be undertaken which could explain a preference for a complex tense.
7 The interrogative clitic =ni is interpreted as having exclusive focus because the speaker wants to know what, of all possible things the addressee might be up to. For a comparable explanation of exclusive focus with wh question words see Van der Wal (2009: 240).

This appears to imply that Shangaji simple tenses are term-focal. However, simple tenses are also attested in utterance-final position (cf. (13) and (15)), where the post-verbal element is as salient as the verb (cf. (16)) or when it has information focus but not exclusive focus (cf. (17)). The second and utterance-final verb in (13) gives new information but does not have exclusive focus as the act of swallowing is not exclusive to the act of chewing. If one wants to express that swallowing occurs instead or to the exclusion of chewing, the use of a complex tense is compulsory (cf. (14) and Section 3.2).

(13) si[8]-ńttó-rafun-áa-ru   ki-ttí-miínz-a
NEG.1SG.SM-PRS$_F$-chew-FV-FOC   1SG.SM-PRS-swallow-FV
'I am not only chewing, I am swallowing as well'

(14) zi-ńttó-minz-iíw-a   kha-zi-ńttó-rafun-iíw-a
10SM-PRS$_F$-swallow-PASS-FV   NEG-10SM-PRS$_F$-chew-PASS-FV
'they are being swallowed, they are not being chewed'

The three clauses in (15) all end in a simple tense of the verb -sola 'menstruate'. Again, the act expressed by the verb does not have exclusive focus. On the contrary, the use of the simple tense helps to express that all three cited women menstruate *as well* (not only the addressed girl, who is menstruating for the first time).

(15) pipyáa   oóntú   eékhál'   eepha   a-ttí-soól-a
1A.grandma.POSS2SG   1DEM$_I$ 1SM.sit.PFV.REL   16DEM$_I$ 1SM-PRS-menstruate-FV

na mamáa   oóntú   eékhál'   eepha   a-ttí-soól-a
and 1A.ma.POSS2SG   1DEM$_I$ 1SM.sit.PFV.REL   16DEM$_I$ 1SM-PRS-menstruate-FV

na n-ttwíi-ye   oóntú   aa-r'   ipháale
and 1-sister-9.POSS2SG   1DEM$_I$ 1SM-be.PFV.REL   16DEM$_{III}$

a-ttí-soól-a
1SM-PRS-menstruate-FV
'your grandmother who is sitting here also menstruates and your mother who is sitting here menstruates too and your sister over there menstruates as well'

In (16), a thetic utterance, a simple tense is followed by an equally salient subject.

(16) a-vir-i   siímba n-táriíkhi
1SM-pass-PFV   1A.lion 18-9.road
'[what happened?] a lion passed on the road'

---

8 *si* is a portmanteau morpheme expressing both negation and first person singular. Non-canonical mergers of a pre-initial negative marker and a first person singular subject marker are attested in many Bantu languages (Kamba Muzenga 1981: 182–191).

Finally, the underlined nouns in the short dialogue in (17) have information focus but they are not exclusively focused (which explains the absence of focus lowering) as it is implied that, next to the cassava and sorghum mentioned in the answer, several other plants were transplanted as well.

(17) n-khéy-eé=ni   námwáákha
     2PL.SM-transplant-PFV=what   1A.year.present
     'what have you transplanted this year?'

   si-thaw-éní   o-khéy-á   víí-tthu
   NEG.1SG.SM-lack-PFV 15-transplant-INF 8-thing
   'I have transplanted many things'

   o-nguúlu   ki-n-khéy-é   manttíóokha   n-tthááma
   17-9.hill 1SG.SM-1OM-transplant-PFV   1A.cassava   3-sorghum
   'on the hill I have transplanted cassava, sorghum, ...'

In sum, simple tenses are best considered focally neutral as they can be used in any context except when (exclusive) focus is on the verb (cf. also Section 3.2). The utterances in (13) and (15) make especially clear that simple tenses in Shangaji are not like canonical Bantu conjoint tenses whose unique common property is that they cannot occur in utterance-final position in a main clause. In closely related Makhuwa, for example, only the combinations in (11) and (12) are possible. However, Shangaji simple tenses do share an important property with Makhuwa conjoint tenses, namely, they are obligatorily selected when the post-verbal element has focus lowering applied to it. In (2b) the use of the Makhuwa disjoint alternative is prohibited, just as much as the use of the Shangaji complex counterpart is disallowed in (1b). Whereas in Makhuwa the restriction works both ways, in Shangaji focus lowering requires the use of a simple tense but a simple tense does not require focus lowering. In the following paragraphs I describe Shangaji focus lowering in more detail.

Focus lowering eliminates the first lexical or melodic H tone (and its double) of an element that immediately follows a simple tense and that has exclusive focus. A post-verbal element to which focus lowering applies may be a noun (including infinitives but not locative nouns), adjective, interrogative, a noun introduced by na 'with, by', and a phrase headed by a noun or an infinitive. In (18) the noun following the simple Present has focus lowering applied to it: it loses its first lexical H tone.[9]

---

[9] I have underlined the vowels with underlying grammatical and lexical high tone in this section in order to facilitate the understanding of the tonal processes involved.

(18) ki-tti-ń-sákh-a̱   na̱nkharariíwa̱   (cit. form: nańkhárariíwa̱)
      1SG.SM-PRS-1OM-want-FV   1A.dried.cassava
      'I want dried cassava [not something else]'

The same lowering process is attested in other contexts as well. Predicative lowering applies to non-verbal elements that are used as predicates (cf. (19) to (21)).[10] An important difference from focus lowering is that predicative lowering can apply to locative nouns, as seen in (21).

(19) oóntu   lata̱raawu
      1DEM₁   1A.thief
      'this is a thief'

(20) oómpu   o-zu̱ngulú̱w-éel-a
      15DEM₁   15-turn.around-APPL-INF
      'this is turning around (towards something)'

(21) aápha   va-ṉ-cuúwa̱
      16DEM₁   16-5-sun
      'here is in the sun'

Predicative lowering also applies in constructions expressing identification involving a verb 'to be'. An example with the verb -iya 'be' is given in (22).

(22) y-aa-s-íiy-eé=ru   naazi̱   (cit. form: naázi)
      9SM-COND-NEG-be-FV=FOC9.ripe.coconut
      'If it is not a ripe coconut ...'

Vocative lowering applies to nouns referring to the addressee, as illustrated in (23).[11]

(23) mwa̱namú̱uye 'girl!'

However, unlike the latter lowering processes, focus lowering in Shangaji is often accompanied by the assignment of an initial H tone to the focused noun. In (24)

---

10 The term 'predicative lowering' was first introduced by Schadeberg and Mucanheia (2000: 124) for Koti.
11 The use of the same strategy in (at least) three different contexts is remarkable. Van der Wal (2006), who describes the same phenomenon for Makhuwa-Enahara, convincingly argues that all three lowering processes are historically connected to the Proto Bantu H tone augment, or rather its absence. Although I find this diachronic explanation very convincing, I do think there might also be a more direct synchronic link between predicative lowering and focus lowering. As is shown by Creissels (2006: 357–359) non-verbal predicates and focused constituents are marked in the same way in many languages. A more literal translation of the utterance in (9a) would then be 'I beg it is money'.

the tonal pattern of the noun following the simple Present is lowered, i.e., its first lexical H tone is omitted, but an additional H tone appears on its first mora and doubles onto the next one.

(24) ki-tti-ń-sákh-a̱   álu̱gutaáwu̱   (cit. form: alu̱gútaáwu̱)
      1SG.SM-PRS-1SG.OM-want-FV 1A.cotton
      'I want cotton [not something else]'

The simple Present tense has two melodic high tones: one on the first mora of the macro-stem and another on the third mora of the stem.[12] It is therefore plausible that the final H tone has shifted onto the first mora of the immediately following noun in (24), whereas it has been omitted in (18). A similar phenomenon has been described for Koti (P311). When the Koti Present tense is followed by a focused noun (marked by focus lowering just as in Makhuwa and in Shangaji), its final H tone may 1) remain in situ and double onto the first mora of the focused noun, 2) shift onto the first mora of the focused noun and double, 3) be omitted. The first two possibilities are illustrated in (25) and (26), respectively (Schadeberg and Mucanheia 2000: 130).[13]

(25) ki-ni-n-khol-á̱   ń-si̱maana   (cit. form: nsímáana)
      1SG.SM-PRS-1SG.OM-hold-FV 1-child
      'I hold the child'

(26) ki-ni-n-khol-a̱   ń-si̱maana
      'I hold the child'

In Shangaji only the last two possibilities are attested (cf. (24) and (18), respectively). What is more, the proposed origin of a verb-final H tone is less straightforward for Shangaji as the initial H tone also appears after simple tenses that do not have a melodic H tone on a final mora. The simple Past Perfective in (27) and (28) has a pre-stem H tone on the second mora of its tense marker but does not have melodic H tones. One would thus not expect a following focused noun to have an initial H tone. The expected pattern can be seen in (27), but (28) shows that an initial H tone may co-occur with the simple Past Perfective.

(27) k-oó̱-t-él-e   w-u̱u-leé̱z-a   (cit. form: wuúleéza)
      1SG.SM-PST-come-APPL-PFV 15-2SG.OM-bid.farewell-INF
      'I came to bid you farewell [not for another reason]'

---

12 Note that melodic high tones are always assigned. An S3 tone is assigned to the final mora in the case of disyllabic stems.
13 An equivalent example of the third possibility is not given in Schadeberg and Mucanheia 2000.

(28) y-aw-ééntt-el-e   khúuni   (cit. form: khuúni)
      2SM-PST-go-APPL-PFV   9.firewood
      'they went after firewood [not after something else]'

It is my hypothesis that the pattern with the initial H tone has its origin in optional H tone shift (cf. (24)), but that it is now generalizing in Shangaji irrespective of the tonal specifications of the preceding verb. This generalization is most clearly attested with post-verbal phrases consisting of a single element. If the focused element is a phrase headed by a noun or an infinitive, two patterns arise. The first pattern involves focus lowering of the head (without assignment of an initial H tone) and absence of tonal modifications to the additional material. In this pattern head and modifier or argument typically (but not necessarily (cf. (31a)) occur in separate phonological phrases, as is the case in (29a) and (30a). The second pattern completely lowers the head noun or infinitive (all lexical / melodic H tones are omitted). Modifiers occur in their normal tonal pattern (cf. (29b), (30b)) but arguments of infinitives have focus lowering applied to them and an additional H tone is assigned to their first mora (cf. (31b)). In the second pattern the head always occurs in a single phonological phrase with the following element. The choice for one or the other pattern is dictated by the scope of focus. The first pattern implies even focus on the entire phrase. If (exclusive) focus is on the element following the head, the second pattern is used, as can be understood from the comments on the examples in (29b), (30b) and (31b).

(29) a) ki-tti-mw-éentt-el-a   n-gulukhaána   a   má-jíini
          1SG.SM-PRS-1OM-go-APPL-FV   1-doctor   1.CONN   6-ghost
          'I am going to the ghost doctor [not somewhere else]'

      b) ki-tti-mw-éentt-el-a   n-gulukhana   a   má-jíini
          1SG.SM-PRS-1OM-go-APPL-FV   1-doctor   1.CONN   6-ghost
          'I am going to the ghost doctor'

          [si-ní-mw-éentt-el-a   n-gulukhana   a   w-aánguúla]
          (NEG.1SG.SM-PRS-1OM-go-APPL-FV 1-doctor   1.CONN   15-extract.blood-INF]
          ['I am not going to the doctor who extracts blood']

(30) a) ki-tt-eéntt-él-a   vi-khalaángw' ipi
          1SG.SM-PRS-go-APPL-FV   8-pot   8DEM$_I$
          'I am going after these pots [not something else]'

      b) ki-tt-eéntt-él-a   vi-khalango   tthíimpi
          1SG.SM-PRS-go-APPL-FV   8-pot   8DEM$_{IE}$
          'I am going after these very pots'

[si-ń-sákh'   eépo]
(NEG.1SG.SM-PRS-want-FV 8DEM₍ᵢᵢ₎)
[I do not want those ones]'

(31) a) k-aw-éentt-el-e   o-tha̱zam-i̱w-á   na-n-gu̱lúkhaána̱
        1SG.SM-PST-go-APPL-PFV 15-look-PASS-INF with-1-doctor
        'I am going to be examined by the doctor [not somewhere else]'

    b) k-aw-e̱entt-el-e   o-tha̱zam-iw-a̱   ná-ń-gu̱lukhaána̱
        1SG.SM-PST-go-APPL-PFV 15-look-PASS-INF with-1-doctor
        'I am going to be examined by a doctor'

    [s-áw-éentt-el-e   o-thazam-iw-a   na-mú-tthú   puure
    [NEG.1SG.SM-PST-go-APPL-FV 15-look-PASS-INF with-1-person any]
    ['I am not going to be examined by just any person']

The pragmatic correlate of focus lowering in Shangaji is exclusive focus. The referent of the element to which focus lowering applies is selected to the exclusion of some alternative (Van der Wal 2009, 2011). The answer without focus lowering in (32a) implies that the speaker has eaten a green coconut amongst other things, whereas the application of focus lowering in (32b) makes clear that a green coconut was eaten, to the exclusion of all or at least some other possible edibles.

(32) a) o-rafun-eé=ni?   ki-rafun-u   li-kho̱lóoma
        2SG.SM-chew-PFV=what   1SG.SM-chew-PFV   5-green.coconut
        'what have you eaten?   I have eaten a green coconut [amongst other
        things]'

    b) o-rafun-eé=ni?   ki-rafun-u   lí-kho̱looma
        'what have you eaten? I have eaten a green coconut [not something else]'

The clearest examples are the ones with exhaustive focus, i.e. when one referent is selected to the exclusion of all possible alternatives, as is the case in (33).

(33) e-lúgúl-u   nyúumba̱   [kh-i-lugul-éní   y-itthu   ngíneénku]
     9SM-burn-PFV   9.house   [NEG-7SM-burn-PFV 7-thing   9.other]
     'a house has burnt down [nothing else]'

Exclusivity can also amount to an idea of unexpectedness or surprise (cf. 'of all possible alternatives s/he chooses to do X'), as is the case in (34) and (35).

(34) a-t-i   ná   má-u̱ulu
     1SM-come-PFV   with   6-leg
     'she came on foot! [of all possible ways]'

(35) n-táriikhi   n-vír-í   ńgúlu̱uwe
     18-9.road   18SM-pass-PFV   9.pig
     'on the road a pig passed!' [i.e., of all possible animals, it had to be a pig]

Although exclusive focus is conceivable with all types of post-verbal material, there are certain elements that block focus lowering; locative nouns, pronouns, most adverbs, proper nouns and (subordinated) verbs can never have focus lowering applied to them. In (36) focus lowering cannot apply to the locative noun, even if the answer implies that someone came by bicycle and not by car.

(36) a-t-i   teeí?   a-t-i   va-bisikale̱eta
     1SM-come-PFV   how   1SM-come-PFV   16-9.bike
     'how did he come? he came by bike'

In (37) the implication is that the speaker cooked on cooking stones and not on an alternative cooking device. In such a context one expects the pattern exemplified in (31b): an entirely low infinitive and an argument with focus lowering and an initial H tone. The infinitive in (37) is entirely low but focus lowering of the locative argument and the assignment of an initial H tone are blocked.

(37) k-aw-éentt-el-e   w-iiphey-a   va-ma̱-fiiya
     1SG.SM-PST-go-APPL-PFV   15-cook-FV   16-6-cooking.stone
     'I went to cook on the cooking stones'

     [s-áw-éentt-el-e   w-iiphey-a   va-fo̱gáawu]
     [NEG.1SG.SM-PST-go-APPL-FV   15-cook-INF   16-9.cooker]
     ['I did not go to cook on a cooker']

In sum, Shangaji simple tenses are unlike canonical Bantu conjoint tenses in that they can occur utterance-finally. However, they are like conjoint tenses in Makhuwa-Enaharra in that they need to be used when the post-verbal element has exclusive focus, which is in both languages marked by focus lowering. In Shangaji focus lowering may be accompanied by the assignment of an initial H tone to the focused noun. Although this H tone most probably has its origin in a verb-final H tone, it shows signs of becoming an independent property of term focus.

3.2 Shangaji complex tenses and Bantu disjoint tenses

The tenses in the right-hand column of Table 1 are referred to as complex tenses as they are probably all derived from a simple tense of the auxiliary -entta 'go to' followed by an infinitival main verb (see also Devos and Van der Wal 2010). This is most clearly the case with the complex affirmative and negative Present

Perfective which both (still) have an analytical structure, as seen in (38) and (39), respectively.

(38) entt'   o-xínj-á-xiínja
     1SM.go.PFV   15-cut-INF-RED
     khupé   miíyo   k-aa-ri   náá   khaázi
     EX   I   1SG.SM PST-be with-REL 9.work
     'he made cuts in it [the branch], while I was using it'

(39) s-eentt-én'   ó-ráfuún-a   k-entt'   ó-miínz-a
     NEG.1SG.SM-go.PFV 15-chew-INF   1SG.SM-go.PFV   15-swallow-INF
     'I did not chew, I swallowed'

In the other complex tenses, fusion of the auxiliary and the Infinitive has led to the creation of a new tense marker which is *-ntto-* in most tenses and *-tto(o)-* or *-ntto-* in the focal Present Imperfective. The latter allomorphy corresponds to the allomorphy between *-tti-* and *-n(i)-* in the simple Present Imperfective.

Complex tenses are considered verb-focal on the basis of two types of evidence (see also Devos and Van der Wal 2010). First, they cannot be followed by an element which has (exclusive) focus. As was seen in (7b), the combination of a verb-focal tense and a focally lowered noun is ungrammatical. Likewise, verb-focal tenses cannot be followed by the interrogative clitic =*ni* 'what?, why?, how?' (cf. (8b)). I do not have ungrammaticality judgments on the combination of verb-focal tenses with other interrogatives but the corpus findings are revealing. Verb-focal tenses are never followed by interrogatives except in one puzzling idiomatic expression containing a complex tense of an unidentified verb followed by the interrogative *teéi* 'how?' (cf. (40)) or its more emphatic variant *teíisa* (cf. (41)).[14]

(40) maá-ti   a-ńttó-raa   teeí?   a-ńttóo-vw-á
     6-water   6SM.PRS$_F$-??? how   6SM.PRS$_F$-ebb-FV
     'what is happening with the water? it is ebbing'

(41) a-ńttó-raá   teiisá?   entt'   o-xínj-á-xiínja
     1SM.PST-PFV$_F$-??? how   1SM.go.PFV   15-cut-INF-RED
     'what did she do [to it]? she made cuts [in it]'

---

14 The long final vowel of the verb in (40) and (41) is exceptional but as Shangaji intervocalic glides are often dropped in penultimate position, a stem *-raya* or *-rawa* could be hypothesized. However, there is no language-internal or comparative support for such a verb form. Another possibility is that it is an exceptional form of the verb *-ira* 'do' (for more on this verb see Devos and Bostoen 2012) or *-rowa* 'go'. The latter has a variant form *-rwaa* in some Makhuwa dialects (Charles Kisseberth, pers. comm.) but is not otherwise used in Shangaji.

The lowering of the interrogative in (40) and (41) is confusing. As focus lowering is prohibited after verb-focal forms (cf. (7b)), the lowering can only be predicative lowering (cf. (19) to (22)) in which case the expression, at least originally, contains two separate clauses (cf. 'The water is doing. How?'). Van der Wal (2009: 59) reaches a similar conclusion for utterances where the interrogative *esheeni* expressing 'why' is preceded by a disjoint form.

(42)   Makhuwa-Enaharra (Van der Wal 2009: 59)
       o-náá-rúp-a   esheení?
       2SG.SM-PRS.DJ-sleep-FV what
       'why are you sleeping?' (lit.: 'You are sleeping. Why?')

The utterances in (43) and (44) show that it is exclusive focus which is barred from occurring after a complex tense. In (43) a simple tense is followed by a post-verbal subject with exclusive focus. The same construction with a complex tense is grammatically correct (44), in which case the post-verbal subject cannot be interpreted as carrying exclusive focus, as indicated by the difference in translation.

(43)   a-ttíy-á   yeéne   a-ń-cúw-aá=yo
       1SM-PRS.be-FV   s/he   1SM-PRS-know-FV=REL
       'it is s/he who knows' [not someone else]

(44)   a-ttóowiy-á   yeéne   a-tthóng-ée=yo
       1SM-PRS$_F$.be-FV s/he   1SM-PRS-speak-PFV=REL
       'it could be her/him who has spoken'

The impossibility of complex forms co-occurring with post-verbal (exclusive) focus suggests that focus is on the event expressed by the verb. This brings us to the second type of evidence, namely the obligatory use of complex tenses when the verb carries exclusive focus. In (14), repeated here as (45), the use of a complex tense is required to contrast the actions expressed by the verbs. If one tense is replaced by a simple tense, as is the case in (13), repeated here as (46), the actions are no longer interpreted as being in contrast but rather as co-occurring.

(45)   zi-ńttó-minz-iíw-a   kha-zi-ńttó-rafun-iíw-a
       10SM-PRS$_F$-swallow-PASS-FV   NEG-10SM-PRS$_F$-chew-PASS-FV
       'they are being swallowed, they are not being chewed'

(46)   si-ńttó-rafun-áa-ru   ki-ttí-miínz-a
       NEG.1SG.SM-PRS$_F$-chew-FV-FOC   1SG.SM-PRS-swallow-FV
       'I am not only chewing, I am swallowing as well'

Moreover, when replacing the second verb in (46) by a complex tense, some additional context needs to be added to make clear that the actions are not taking place simultaneously, but rather alternatingly, as seen in (47).

(47) s-a-nttó-ráfun-áa-ru   k-aw-áax'   o-ráfuún-a
      NEG.1SG.SM-PST-IPFV$_F$-chew-FV-FOC 1SG.SM-PST-leave-PFV 15-chew-INF
      k-a-nttó-miínz-a
      1SG.SM-PST-IPFV$_F$-swallowing-FV
      'I was not only chewing, I left chewing and then started swallowing'

Similarly, when asking someone what s/he is doing (cf. (10)), the speaker expects a complete answer (cf. (10b)) and not an answer suggesting that you are doing something but might be doing something else as well, hence the ungrammaticality of (10b).

Exclusive focus on a post-verbal element or on the verb thus straightforwardly determines the choice between a simple and a complex tense. However, in other contexts both tenses are attested and it is less clear what determines the choice. Thetic utterances, for example, allow the use of either a simple (cf. (16)) or a complex tense (cf. (48)).

(48) n-oo-pátth-á   taámu   a-ttóo-lamuúw-a   mamáa-w-e
      and-15-get-INF 9.blood 1SM-PRS$_F$-get.up-FV 1A.mother-1-POSS1
      'and upon bleeding, her mother gets up'

Still, it can be concluded that the complex forms are derived from a construction containing the auxiliary -entta 'go' and a main verb in its infinitival form and that the auxiliary puts some kind of focus on the main verb. Support for these language-internal conclusions is found in nearby Bantu languages. Koti has pairs of tenses that are very similar to the ones found in Shangaji, as can be seen in Table 2.[15]

The tenses in the right-hand column all have an analytical structure and clearly involve the verb -etta 'go to'.[16] Following Schadeberg and Mucanheia (2000: 142–145) the auxiliary -etta adds a sense of progressivity. However, the authors also state that progressivity is not the most appropriate label for all the complex tenses. In the past tenses, for example, they indicate that "... the emphasis is not so much on the *ongoing action* but on the description of the activity" (Schadeberg and Mucanheia 2000: 142), which comes close to saying that the emphasis is on the verb itself, or that the auxiliary -etta puts some kind of focus on the infinitival main verb.

Even more interesting for this chapter is the resemblance between Shangaji complex tenses and disjoint tenses in two languages with a recognized CJ/DJ system:

---

15 Object markers are not included in the morphological structure of the tenses in Table 2 and the following ones as they are irrelevant to the present discussion.
16 One remarkable difference between Shangaji and neighboring Koti and Makhuwa is that it has prenasalization where Koti and Makhuwa lack it (see Devos and Schadeberg 2014).

Table 2: Koti paired tenses (Schadeberg and Mucanheia 2000).

	Simple	Complex
Present	SM-**ni**-VB-**a**	SM-**ni-tt-a** Infinitive
Recent past	SM-**a**-VB-**a**	SM-**a-ett-a** Infinitive
Remote past	SM-**aa**-VB-**iye**	SM-**aa-ett-iye** Infinitive
Situative durative	SM-VB-**aka**	SM-**ett-aka** Infinitive
Negative present	kha-SM-**ní**-VB-**a**	kha-SM-**ní-tt-a** Infinitive
		SM-**ni-tt-a** Neg. Infinitive
Negative recent past	kha-SM-VB-**eéni**	kha-SM-**ett-eéni** Infinitive
		SM-**a-ett-a** Neg. Infinitive
Negative remote past	kha-SM-**aa-iye**	kha-SM-**aa-ett-iye** Infinitive
		SM-**aa-ett-iye** Neg. Infinitive

Kimatuumbi and Ndengeleko. Kimatuumbi has pairs of tenses to which Odden (1996: 64–65) refers as verb-focal and noun-focal tenses rather than disjoint and conjoint tenses. The verb-focal tenses involve prefixes related to the verb *ti* 'say' or the verb *yeenda* 'go'. The pairs of tenses involving the latter verb are given in Table 3.

Odden (1996: 61) indicates that the verb-focal tenses put contrastive focus on the verb.

(49) Kimatuumbi (Odden 1996: 61)
 eendá-kaatá kaámba
 1SM.VFPRS-cut 9.rope
 'he is cutting rope (not doing something else to it)'

Ndengeleko has a CJ/DJ distinction in four tenses. As can be seen in Table 4, the disjoint tenses all contain a prefix that is most probably related to the verb *-yenda* 'go' (< PB *gènd).[17]

Ström (2013: 223) argues that the use of the disjoint form implies a certain level of focus on the verbal action, rather than on what follows.

---

[17] Ström (2013: 261) indicates that the prefix of the disjoint tenses could also be related to the verb *tenda 'act, make'. I find this a less likely source as we would still have to explain the exceptional loss of initial *t, whereas *g > 0 (except after nasal) is a regular sound change. The hypothesis of an auxiliary *-tenda* was probably put forward by the author because an auxiliary expressing 'to do' seems a more likely candidate for the expression of verb-focus than an auxiliary expressing 'to go' (but see Devos and Van der Wal 2014 for more examples of 'go' marking focus and Devos and Van der Wal 2010 for a discussion of this remarkable grammaticalization path) and because the auxiliary *-tenda* is used as an in-situ focus marker in related languages like Ngoni (N12), Ndendeule (N101) (see Güldemann 2003: 340–341; Morimoto 2013: 10–11) and Matengo (N13) (Yoneda 2009: 450) and less related languages like Digo (E73) (Nicolle 2013: 159–160).

Table 3: Kimatuumbi paired tenses (Odden 1996).

	Noun-focal	Verb-focal
Present progressive	SM-VB-a	SM-**enda**-VB-a
Past progressive	SM-VB-**a(g)e**	SM-**endee**-VB-a

Table 4: Ndengeleko paired tenses (Ström 2013).

	Conjoint	Disjoint
Present	SM-VB-a	SM-**endo/ando/ondo**-VB-a
Habitual	SM-VB-**aa**	SM-**andaa**-VB-a
Imperfective	SM-VB-**aga**	SM-**endaga/andaga**-VB-FV
Past imperfective	SM-VB-**age**	SM-**andage**-VB-a

In sum, comparative evidence not only supports the claim that complex tenses in Shangaji involve an auxiliary expressing 'to go' which puts focus on the main verb but it also shows that the complex tenses are reminiscent of disjoint tenses in at least two languages with a canonical conjoint-disjoint system.

4 A conjoint-disjoint system in the making or *in situ* verb- and NP-focus?

The preceding sections have made clear that the system of paired tenses in Shangaji displays many resemblances with the conjoint-disjoint alternation in related languages. The Shangaji complex tenses are formally and functionally comparable to disjoint forms in languages like Kimatuumbi and Ndengeleko and the simple forms resemble Makhuwa-Enaharra conjoint forms in that their use is obligatory whenever the post-verbal element is marked by focus lowering. However, simple tenses are also different from typical Bantu conjoint tenses as they are not barred from utterance-final position. Shangaji simple tenses can occur in four different contexts depending on whether there is a post-verbal element and whether the latter is subject to tonal modifications. To sum up, simple tenses can be (1) in utterance-final position (cf. (50)), (2) followed by an element which does not have focus lowering applied to it (cf. (51)), (3) followed by an element which has exclusive focus but blocks the application of focus lowering (cf. (52)) and (4) followed by an element which has focus lowering applied to it (cf. (53a) (and may have an additional initial H tone (cf. 53b)).

(50) ki-ttí-veénk-a   (#)
     1SG.SM-PRS-beg-FV
     'I beg / am begging [as well]'

(51) ki-ttí-vénk-á   n-zúrúukhu   (no FL)
     1SG.SM-PRS-beg-FV   3-money
     'I am begging for money [amongst other things]'

(52) ki-tt-étt-á   o-muú-ti   (FL blocked)
     1SG.SM-PRS-go-FV   17-3-town

     si-n-éntt-á   o-ń-líimpu
     NEG.1SG.SM-PRS-go-FV 17-3-well
     'I am going home, I am not going to the well'

(53) a) ki-tti-vénk-á   n-zuruukhu   (FL, no initial H)
        1SG.SM-PRS-beg-FV 3-money
        'I am begging for money [not for another thing]'

     b) a-tti-sákh-á   ḿbúukhu   (FL, initial H)
        1SM-PRS-want-FV   9.rat
        'I want a rat [not something else]'

Makhuwa-Enaharra allows the use of a conjoint tense in the last two contexts only. An interesting question now is whether Shangaji simple tenses show any signs of becoming grammaticalized for post-verbal focus, thus giving rise to a Makhuwa-like conjoint-disjoint system.

If the Shangaji alternating verb forms are indeed developing towards a conjoint-disjoint system one would expect at least some of the simple tenses to show a marked preference for occurring with an element to which focus lowering has applied (cf. (29)). Figure 3 shows the relative frequency of the simple Present Imperfective in the four positions illustrated in (27), (29), (30) and (28).[18]

It shows that, although the neutral Present Imperfective tense can occur utterance-finally, this is clearly not its preferred position. It also shows that there is some preference for the neutral Present Imperfective to combine with elements to which focus lowering has applied. However, the preference is not marked

---

18 I have chosen the Present Imperfective because it is one of the tenses where the alternation between the neutral and the verb-focal form appears to be well-established (cf. Figure 2).

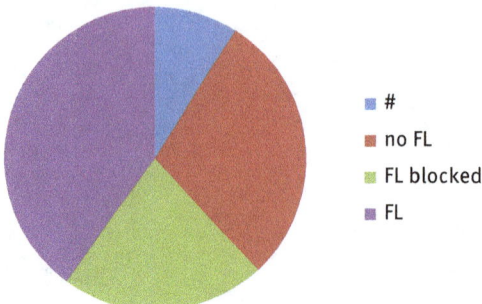

Figure 3: Relative frequencies of simple Present Imperfective in relation to what follows.

enough to suggest an imminent development towards a Makhuwa-like system, where focus lowering is either obligatory (FL) or blocked (FL blocked).

Another hypothesis comes to mind when comparing the Shangaji complex tenses to what Güldemann (2003: 340–341) refers to as dummy verb constructions. In languages like Ngoni (N12) and Ndendeule (N101) verb-focus is expressed by an English-like *do*-periphrasis. The following example is from closely related Matengo (N13) (see also Yoneda, this volume).

(54)　Matengo (Yoneda 2009: 450)
　　　Maria ju-a-tend-aje   ku-pomuleel-a
　　　Maria 1SM-PST-do-NPF 15-rest-INF
　　　'Maria rested / was resting'

Yoneda (2009: 450) indicates that the compound verb form in (53) involving the auxiliary *-tenda* 'do' is used when focus is on the action of the verb itself. In the cited languages the constructions involving the auxiliary 'do' are not disjoint tenses that alternate with conjoint tenses but they are simply used to put focus (either state of affairs focus or polarity focus) on the verb *in situ* (cf. Morimoto 2013). One might say that in Shangaji the auxiliary *-entta* 'go to' (which is described as a light verb in Devos and Van der Wal 2010) functions as an *in situ* marker of verb-focus.

An interesting question now is whether focus lowering (in combination with an initial H tone) might likewise be interpreted as an *in situ* marker of NP-focus. Until now we have seen that focus lowering is linked to the tense system in that it typically applies after simple tenses but cannot apply after the complex counterparts. In Section 3.1 it was shown that focus lowering eliminates the first high tone of the focused head of the noun phrase (typically a noun). The lowering can be supplemented by the assignment of a high tone to the noun-initial mora. Although the latter high tone can best be analyzed as originating from the preceding verb, the high tone may also appear when such an origin is not likely. This could be interpreted as a sign that focus lowering is becoming less closely linked to the simple tenses. A more telling sign is the fact that focus lowering in combination with a noun-initial high tone is sporadically attested after tenses that do not have a complex counterpart. The Durative Situative and the Negative Conditional in (55) and (56), respectively, are cases in point.

(55) ki-n-síngán-a   oozány-ánka   má-khólooma
     1SG.SM-PRS-meet-FV 1SM.buy-DSIT   6-green.coconut
     'I met her as she was buying green coconuts [although I told her to buy ripe ones]'

(56) aa-sí-síngan-e=ru   ń-xúuzi   a-tti-nánár-iíw-a
     1SM.COND-NEG-meet-FV=FOC[19] 3-sauce   1SM-PRS-annoy-PASS-FV
     'if he does not find sauce, he gets annoyed'

Both the Durative Situative and the Negative Conditional do not have a high tone in final position. It thus appears that the form of focus lowering that is detaching itself from the simple tenses is the one that includes an initial high tone. This is in line with a cross-linguistic tendency for focal variants to be more prominent than their non-focal counterparts. The more prominent variant of focus lowering (i.e., including the initial high tone), which could alternatively be described as the retraction of the first primary high tone to noun-initial position, is found in yet one other context. In the identificational construction in (57) the noun can occur with one out of three tonal patterns. When the noun occurs with its normal tonal pattern (cf. (57a)), it is interpreted as an afterthought. In (57b) predicative lowering is applied as is normally the case in identificational sentences. In (57c) the addition of a high tone to noun-initial position implies a focal interpretation.

(57) a) mweéyo   mw-a   a-símán-ġetthu
        you   2PLSM-COP 2-child-POSS1PL
        'you, that are our children, ...'

     b) mweéyo mwa asimanġetthu
        'you are our children'

     c) mweéyo mwa ásimanéethu
        'you are our children [we do not have any other children)]'

---

[19] The clitic-*ru* is conventionalized with conditional tenses and does not have a focus reading in this context (cf. (13) and (45) where it is translated as 'only').

Although examples like the ones in (55) to (57) are rare in my corpus, they do suggest that focus lowering in combination with an initial H tone might be on its way to become an autonomous feature of the noun phrase, i.e., no longer dependent on the presence of a simple tense and its prosodic characteristics.

To sum up, Shangaji simple tenses do not show signs of becoming grammaticalized for post-verbal focus and the language thus does not appear to be developing a conjoint-disjoint alternation. It might be more likely for Shangaji to further develop a system of *in situ* focus marking with verb-focus being marked by a dummy-verb construction and NP-focus being marked by tonal modifications of the focused noun. What might now be the effect of such an evolution on the Shangaji alternating verb forms in Table 1? My guess is that the alternation will be lost in most tenses with the verb-focal forms becoming less emphatic with time and eventually replacing the simple tenses. The most likely candidates for a consolidation of the alternation are the paired simple and complex Present (and maybe also Past) tenses (cf. their relative frequencies in Figures 1 and 2). However, rather than continuing to express a focal distinction, they are more likely to become associated with different tense / aspect semantics. In line with Güldemann (2003), it is not unlikely for the verb-focal tense to grammaticalize into a Present Progressive tense, whereas the simple tense might evolve into a General Present.

5 Conclusion

This chapter has shown that Shangaji has a series of paired tenses which display striking similarities with conjoint-disjoint tenses in other Bantu languages but cannot be identified as such because of the lack of an utterance-final restriction. Although Shangaji could be suggested to be on the verge of developing a Makhuwa-Enaharra-like conjoint-disjoint alternation, it has been argued that a system of *in situ* focus marking is a more likely development.

Abbreviations

APPL	applicative	DSIT	durative situative
CJ	conjoint	EX	exclamation
CONN	connective	FOC	focus
COP	copula	FV	final vowel
DEM$_I$, DEM$_{II}$, DEM$_{III}$	demonstrative (series 1, 2, 3)	INF	infinitive
		IPFV	simple Imperfective
DJ	disjoint	IPFV$_F$	complex Imperfective

LOC	locative	PRS_F	complex Present
NEG	negative	PST	Past
NPF	non-perfect final	PUL	penultimate lengthening
OM	object marker	RED	reduplication
PASS	passive	REL	relative
PFV	Perfective	SM	subject marker
POSS	possessive	VFPRS	verb-focal present
PRS	simple Present		

References

Creissels, Denis. 2006. *Syntaxe générale: une introduction typologique – Tome 2, La Phrase*. Paris: Lavoisier.

Devos, Maud. 2013. Vowel length in Shangaci: When lexical vowel length and penultimate lengthening co-occur. *Africana Linguistica* 19. 85–107.

Devos, Maud & Koen Bostoen. 2012. Bantu do/say polysemy and the grammaticalization of quotatives in Shangaci. *Africana Linguistica* 18. 97–133.

Devos, Maud & Thilo C. Schadeberg. 2014. How did Shangaji come to be a nasal language? In Iwona Kraska-Szlenk & Beata Wójtowicz (eds.), *Current research in African studies. Papers in honour of Mwalimu Dr. Eugeniusz Rzewuski*, 61–81. Warszawa: Elipsa.

Devos, Maud & Jenneke van der Wal. 2010. Go on a rare grammaticalisation path to focus. In Jacqueline van Kampen and Rick Nouwen (eds.), *Linguistics in the Netherlands* 27, 45–58. Amsterdam: John Benjamins.

Devos, Maud & Jenneke van der Wal. 2014. *'Come' and 'Go' of the beaten grammaticalization path*. Series Trends in Linguistics, vol. 272. Berlin, Boston: De Gruyter Mouton.

Güldemann, Tom. 2003. Present progressive vis-à-vis predication focus in Bantu: A verbal category between semantics and pragmatics. *Studies in Language* 27(2). 323–360.

Hyman, Larry M. & John Robert Watters. 1984. Auxiliary focus. *Studies in African Linguistics* 15. 233–273.

Kamba Muzenga, J. G. 1981. *Les formes verbales négatives dans les langues bantoues*. Tervuren: Musée Royal de l'Afrique Centrale.

Morimoto, Yukiko. 2013. Grammatical coding of PCF in Bantu. Paper presented at Workshop on Information Structure in Bantu languages, Berlin, 13 December.

Nicolle, Steve. 2013. *A grammar of Digo. A Bantu language of Kenya and Tanzania*. Dallas: SIL International.

Odden, David. 1996. *The phonology and morphology of Kimatuumbi*. Oxford: Clarendon Press.

Schadeberg, Thilo C. 2003. Historical linguistics. In Derek Nurse & Gérard Philippson (eds.), *The Bantu languages*, 143–163. London, New York: Routledge.

Schadeberg, Thilo C. & Francisco Ussene Mucanheia. 2000. *Ekoti. The Maka or Swahili Language of Angoche*. Köln: Rüdiger Köppe Verlag.

Ström, Eva-Marie. 2013. *The Ndengeleko language of Tanzania*. Gothenburg: University of Gothenburg PhD dissertation.

Van der Wal, Jenneke. 2006. Predicative tone lowering in Makhuwa. In Jeroen van de Weijer & Bettelou Los (eds.), *Linguistics in the Netherlands* 23, 224–236. Amsterdam: John Benjamins.

Van der Wal, Jenneke. 2009. *Word order and information structure in Makhuwa-Enahara.* Utrecht: LOT.

Van der Wal, Jenneke. 2011. Focus excluding alternatives: Conjoint/Disjoint marking in Makhuwa. *Lingua* 212 (11). 1734–1750.

Yoneda, Nobuko. 2009. Information structure and sentence formation in Matengo. In Manghyu Pak (ed.), *Current issues in unity and diversity of languages: collection of the papers selected from the CIL 18, held at Korea University in Seoul, on July 21–26, 2008,* 443–453. Seoul: The Linguistic Society of Korea.

Yukiko Morimoto
6 The Kikuyu focus marker *nĩ*: Formal and functional similarities to the conjoint/disjoint alternation

1 Introduction

This chapter investigates the formal and functional properties of focus constructions in Kikuyu (E51 in Guthrie's 1948 classification). I examine in particular the use of the focus marking proclitic *nĩ* that expresses both term focus and 'predicate-centered focus'. To the extent that the conjoint/disjoint alternation correlates with information structure (to varying degrees), the Kikuyu data bear crucial relevance to the conjoint/disjoint alternation. In order to provide a comprehensive picture of the formal and functional similarities observed between the Kikuyu focus system and the conjoint/disjoint alternation, this study extends the empirical domain beyond well-studied term focus to 'predicate-centered focus' – focus on verb lexemes and verb operators (Güldemann 2009).

Güldemann (2003) summarizes a set of recurrent properties that characterize the conjoint/disjoint morphology, as given in Table 1. The first property (a) is probably the most robust syntactic restriction shared by all languages that display the conjoint/disjoint opposition (cf. Van der Wal, this volume). Other properties have been further investigated in many more languages in subsequent work, and new findings and refinement to the generalizations have been put forward in recent literature (cf. Van der Wal, this volume, and references cited therein). These forms have been shown to correlate with different focus types: the disjoint form with predicate-centered focus, and the conjoint form with term focus.

The present work emerged out of research carried out in the project "Predicate-centered focus types in African languages", a project within Sonderforschungsbereich 632 "Information structure: the linguistic means for structuring utterances, sentences, and texts". I am grateful for the generous funding provided by the Deutsche Forschungsgemeinschaft (DFG). A version of this chapter was presented at the International Workshop on Bantu Languages at SOAS, London on 1 March 2014. I thank the audience for useful feedback. My thanks also go to my colleagues in the project, in particular Tom Güldemann and Ines Fiedler for their insights and inspiration. This study would not have been possible without the help of my informant, Anna Maria Nginah, and I thank her for her time and patience, and good linguistic insight. Lastly but not the least, valuable comments, suggestions, and insights from two anonymous reviewers and the editors of this volume greatly improved the content and presentation of this chapter. All errors and misrepresentations are my own.

Table 1: Recurrent properties of the CJ/DJ opposition (cf. Güldemann 2003: 328).

	Formally marked verb form (DJ)	Formally unmarked verb form (CJ)
a.	Verb can be clause-final	Verb can never be clause-final
b.	Postverbal material out-of-focus	Postverbal material in-focus
c.	Pronominal object possible	Pronominal object impossible
d.	Emphasis on positive truth value	Emphasis on postverbal constituent
e.	In polar questions and answers	In constituent question and answers
f.	Only in asserted main clause	Formal counterpart in non-asserted clause
g.	W/o formal negative counterpart	Formal negative counterpart
	Used for *Predicate-centered focus*	Used for *Term focus*

Taking these generalizations as a set of prototypical properties of the conjoint/disjoint opposition,[1] I argue that the Kikuyu focus system is strikingly comparable to the conjoint/disjoint alternation.

Focus constructions in Kikuyu have been reported to exist in two forms: (i) the fronted ex-situ structure with the proclitic *nĩ* (pronounced as [nɛ]), and (ii) the in-situ structure without *nĩ* (Bergvall 1987; Schwarz 2003, 2007). Wh-questions also come in these forms, and according to Schwarz (2003), there must be a structural parallel between wh-questions and answers. This chapter presents additional data on wh-questions and answers, which lead to generalizations diverging from previous studies: (i) wh-questions are generally prefered in the ex-situ structure, and for some cases not accepted in the in-situ structure; (ii) except for the subject, answers to wh-questions prefer the in-situ structure; (iii) thus there is no requirement that there be a structural parallel between wh-questions and answers, as previously argued (cf. Schwarz 2003). The new findings better elucidate (i) a subject/non-subject asymmetry in the expression of focus and (ii) more importantly, the parallelism between the preference of the unmarked (*nĩ*-less) verb form on the one hand, and the preference of the unmarked "conjoint" form in other Bantu languages on the other, for the expression of term focus.

---

[1] As vigorously argued by Yoneda (this volume), Matengo might be exceptional and/or more complex in a number of respects: the conjoint and disjoint forms are both morphologically marked; these forms do not exist in parallel, and the language therefore must fill in the "gaps" in the tense-aspect paradigm where one form does not exist by using the other form. For this reason, the mapping between form and information structural function is not as straightforward as might be observed in other conjoint/disjoint languages.

In addition, I present new data on 'predicate-centered focus' (Güldemann 2009) – focus on the lexical content of a verb and sentence operators such as TAM and polarity. Predicate-centered focus is expressed by the use of the proclitic *nĩ*, here scoping over the verb. I show that the data on predicate-centered focus enable us to bring out the formal and functional similarities between the *nĩ*-marked verb form and the disjoint verb form. The Kikuyu data on term focus (with the unmarked verb form) and predicate-centered focus (with the *nĩ*-marked verb form), therefore, together highlight the striking parallelism between the Kikuyu focus system and the conjoint/disjoint alternation.

In the present work I assume a functional definition of focus, which is represented by work of Chafe (1976), Dik (1997), Hyman and Watters (1984), Lambrecht (1994), to name but a few. According to Dik (1997: 326), the focal information is considered by the speaker to be the most important or salient information for the addressee to integrate into his pragmatic information in the given communicative setting. It is non-presupposed information – either a new/added piece of information, which we call 'assertive focus', or replacement of some piece of information X already assumed by the addressee, which we call 'contrastive focus'.

The rest of the chapter is organized as follows. In Section 2, I review previous findings on terms focus in Kikuyu reported by Schwarz (2003, 2007) and also point out diverging results in my data. Section 3 presents additional data and new findings on both assertive and contrastive term focus. Section 4 presents data on predicate-centered focus, and in the final section I summarize the findings and discuss some remaining issues for future research.

2 Nĩ marking in Kikuyu

The Kikuyu proclitic *nĩ*,[2] also an identificational marker in different context as illustrated in (1), is used to mark focus.

(1) a. *Peter nĩ́ mwarímṹ.*
 Peter ID teacher.
 'Peter is a teacher.'

 b. *Morothi nĩ́ nyámũ.*
 lion ID animal.
 'Lion is an animal.'

---

[2] Focus constructions involving an equivalent of the Kikuyu proclitic *nĩ* are reported in other languages of zone E, e.g., Vunjo (E62, Dalgish 1979; Moshi 1988), Kuria (E43, Cammenga 1994), Kamba (E55, Ndumbu and Whiteley 1962), Kĩĩtharaka (E54, Abels and Muriungi 2008).

As argued by Güldemann (2003), the focus use of *nĩ* is derived from the copular use in a cleft construction, a formal counterpart of the negative copula *ti*. In fact, as we will see in the following examples (e.g., (2), (5)), for subject focus, *nĩ* is still clearly a copula in the cleft construction where the verb is in the dependent form.

Although it will not be a central part of this chapter, it is worth discussing briefly the internal structure of phrases marked by *nĩ*. Bennett et al. (1985) assume that the *nĩ*-marked term focus appears in a cleft-like structure, whereby the particle *nĩ* functions as an identificational copula, followed by the dependent form of the predicate. Thus it resembles the cleft structure in English 'it is X that VERBs'. Indeed, in subject focus as in (2a), the subject marker on the predicate is the one used in a relative clause: the subject prefix in (2a) does not appear in its usual, main-clause form *a*- but rather as *ũ*- [ɔ] (Schwarz 2003: 58). Crucially, however, only in subject relatives does the verb have a different, 'dependent', subject marker. As such, the dependent form appears only when *nĩ* marks subject focus, as in [*nĩ* SUBJECT + dependent predicate]. The examples in (2) show a contrast between subject and object focus: the subject focus in (2a) has the dependent verb form *ũ-nyu-ir-e*, while the object focus in (2b) has the non-dependent form *a-nyu-ir-e*.[3]

(2) a. nĩ   Kamau   **ũ-nyu-ire**   njohi   nyingĩ.
     F   Kamau   1SM-drink-PFV   9.beer   9.lot
     '[Kamau]_F drank a lot of beer.'

    b. nĩ   njohi   nyingĩ   Kamau   **a-nyu-ire**.
     F   9.beer   9.lot   Kamau   1SM-drink-PFV
     'Kamau drank [a lot of beer]_F.'   (Mugane 1997: 148 (22))

A tonal difference is also reported depending on the presence/absence of *nĩ* in front of the verb (Bennett et al. 1985). This has been taken as an indication that the high tone that is present in the *nĩ*-marked focus structure marks the dependent predicate form (cf. also Güldemann 1996, 1999, 2003). This tonal difference exists,

---

[3] My informant, on the other hand, often produced the non-dependent verb form with the *a*-prefix for subject focus. Her intuition was that the use of the dependent form in (2a) is more prescriptive, and in everyday writing and speaking, she prefers to use the non-dependent verb form with a as in (14). It could be that in the speaker's grammar, *nĩ* is already analyzed as a focus clitic simply attaching to the focused element rather than the identificational copula taking a dependent clause.

however, only when the verb has the future tense marker *kaa*, as illustrated in (3). In other tenses, no tonal difference is observed (4).⁴

(3) a. nî́ á-kaa-re-ya mbóso
F 1SM-FUT-eat-IMPFV 6.bean
'She [will]_F eat the beans.'

b. a-kaa-re-ya mbóso
1SM-FUT-eat-IMPFV 6.bean
'She will eat the [beans]_F.' (based on Bennett et al. 1985: 168)

(4) a. nî́ á-rá:-re-ya mbóso
F 1SM-PROG-eat-IMPFV 6.bean
'She [is eating]_F the beans.'

b. á-rá:-re-ya mbóso
1SM-PROG-eat-IMPFV 6.bean
'She is eating the [beans]_F.'

In my data, the dependent verb form occurs, only optionally, with subject focus as in (2a); when the predicate is *nĩ*-marked, there is no tonal or morphological evidence that the predicate is in the dependent form. Therefore, based on just the subject focus, it is difficult to argue for a bipartite cleft structure of all *nĩ*-marked focus structures. Due to the absence of clear prosodic or morphological evidence, I analyze, following Schwarz (2007), both subject and non-subject term focus as well as 'predicate-centered focus' (where *nĩ* is placed immediately before the predicate) simply as focus-marking with no additional structure.

Regarding functions of the *nĩ*-particle, Armstrong (1940: 169–170) observes that utterances with the *nĩ*-particle are 'emphatic' – they express (i) certainty, (ii) determination, defiance, or challenge (to the hearer), and (iii) contradictions. Her observation will be elaborated in Section 4 under 'predicate-centered focus'. Schwarz (2003) observes that *nĩ* marks focus in general – both term focus and verum focus. Structurally, as already mentioned, there are ex-situ and in-situ focus constructions. Schwarz also shows in his data that structural parallels between questions and answers are preferred. Below, I review Schwarz's (2003) discussion on the ex-situ and in-situ structures.

---

4 The results were confirmed by a Praat analysis.

Generalizations about the use of ex-situ and in-situ structures (Schwarz 2003)
In the investigation of term focus that mainly involves wh-interrogatives and answers, Schwarz shows the following data and generalizations. First, there are ex-situ and in-situ structures for wh-questions and answers. The ex-situ structure involves a fronted constituent with the focus particle *nĩ*; and in the in-situ structure, focus appears in its canonical syntactic position without *nĩ*. For subject focus, only the ex-situ structure is available, as shown in (5). In (5a), the wh-subject is *noo*, a lexicalized form of *nĩ + oo* (Schwarz 2003: 56, fn 17). The appropriate answer also appears in the ex-situ structure, as in (5b). The unacceptability of the in-situ subject question and answer without *nĩ* is shown in (5c) and (5d) respectively.

(5) Subject wh-question (Schwarz 2003: 57 (29))
    a. ***n-oo***   *ũ-thom-ag-er-a*   *mwana ibuku?*   ex-situ Q w/ *nĩ*
        F -who   1SM-read-HAB-APPL-FV   1.child   5-book
        'Who (usually) reads a/the book to the child?'

    b. ***nĩ Abdul***   *ũ-thom-ag-er-a*   *mwana ibuku.*   ex-situ A w/ *nĩ*
        F -1.Abdul   1SM-read-HAB-APPL-FV   1.child   5-book
        Lit. 'It is Abdul who reads a/the book to the child.'

    c. **oo a-thom-ag-er-a mwana ibuku?*   *"in-situ" Q w/o *nĩ*

    d. *#[Abdul]$_F$ a-thom-ag-er-a mwana ibuku.*   #"in-situ" A w/o *nĩ*

Second, both ex-situ and in-situ structures are available for (both primary and secondary) objects (6)-(9) and locative and temporal adverbials (10)-(11). Examples (6) and (7) illustrate question-answer pairs of the sole object in the ex-situ and in-situ structures respectively.

(6) Ex-situ object question (Schwarz 2003: 54 (20))
    a. *nĩ-kee*   *Abdul*   *a-ra-nyu-ire?*   [AM: √]
        F -what   1.Abdul   1SM-PST-drink-PFV
        'What did Abdul drink?'

    b. *nĩ*   *ma-e*   *Abdul*   *a-ra-nyu-ire.*   [AM: √]
        F   6-water   1.Abdul   1SM-PST-drink-PFV
        Lit. 'It is water that Abdul drank.'

At the right of each example I have indicated the acceptability judgment given by my informant "AM". As we see in (7), there is also a difference in judgments between my informant and what is reported by Schwarz. My informant does not accept the in-situ structure in (7a) for an object question. In the next section I discuss the details of these new results obtained from my informant. Here I only note that new findings seem to more clearly elucidate the subject/non-subject asymmetry when we look at how subject and object wh-questions are most preferably answered. As it becomes clearer in Section 3 (see Table 2), my informant reports that in questions, only the ex-situ structure is available for both subject and object, but in answers to wh-questions, only the subject focus is allowed in the ex-situ structure while the non-subject answers prefer the in-situ structure.

(7) In-situ object question (Schwarz 2003: 55 (23)-(24))
    a. *Abdul*   *a-ra-nyu-ire*   *kee?*   [AM: *]
         1.Abdul   1SM-PST-drink-PFV   what

    b. *Abdul*   *a-ra-nyu-ire*   *ma-e.*   [AM: √]
         1.Abdul   1SM-PST-drink-PFV   water
         'Abdul drank water.'

Example (8) is a double object construction in which the primary (applied) object is in focus. Here again, Schwarz shows that both ex-situ and in-situ structures are available. The examples in (8a,b) are the ex-situ question and answer, and those in (8c,d) are the in-situ question and answer. The same generalization holds for the secondary object focus, as illustrated in (9). As in (6)-(7), here also, my informant consistently rejected the in-situ wh-question for these objects. The answer

Table 2: Speaker (AM's) judgment on ex-situ/in-situ structures.

Speaker AM	Exs	Ex-situ Q	Ex-situ A	In-situ Q	In-situ A
SUBJ	(2a), (5)	√	√	*	*
OBJ 1	(2b), (6)-(8)	√	√only contrastive⁺	*	√
OBJ 2	(9)	√	√only contrastive⁺	*	√
LOC	(10)	√	√only contrastive⁺	?√	√
TEMP	(11)	√	*	*	√
MAN	(12)	√	*	√	√
INSTR	(13)	*	*	√	√

⁺must be followed by at least the verb.

with *nĩ* is accepted, again, only when the focus constituent is followed by at least the verb, as in the b examples.⁵

(8) Question for the primary object (Schwarz 2003: 56, ex 25)

    a. *n-oo   Abdul a-thom-ag-er-a⁶   ibuku?* [AM: √]
       F-who1.Abdul 1SM-read-HAB-APPL-FV 5.book
       'Who does Abdul (usually) read a book to?'

    b. *ne mw-ana Abdul   a-thom-ag-er-a   ibuku.* [AM: √]
       F 1-child   1.Abdul 1SM-read-HAB-APPL-FV 5.book
       Lit. 'It is a child that Abdul (usually) reads a book to.'

    c. *Abdul a-thom-ag-er-a   oo   ibuku* [AM: *]
       1.Abdul 1SM-read-HAB-APPL-FV who 5.book

    d *Abdul a-thom-ag-er-a   mwana ibuku* [AM: √]
       1.Abdul 1SM-read-HAB-APPL-FV 1.child 5.book

(9) Question for the secondary object (Schwarz 2003: 56 (26))

    a. *nĩ-kee Abdul a-thom-ag-er-a   mwana?* [AM: √]
       F-what 1.Abdul 1SM-read-HAB-APPL-FV 1.child
       'What did Abdul read to the child?'

    b. *nĩ ibuku Abdul   a-thom-ag-er-a   mwana.* [AM: √]
       F 5.book 1.Abdul 1SM-read-HAB-APPL-FV 1-child

    c. *Adul athomagera mwana **kee**?* [AM: *]

    d. *Adul athomager-a mwana **ibuku**.* [AM: √]

Similarly, locatives and temporals are also reported to allow both ex-situ and in-situ structures. Again the a and b examples constitute a question-answer pair in the ex-situ structure, and the c and d examples, in the in-situ structure. As indicated at the right of these examples, for objects and locative/temporal adverbials, my informant consistently preferred the ex-situ structure for the wh-questions, and in-situ structure for the answers to these wh-questions.

---

5 That is to say that just [*nĩ* + object] as an answer is unacceptable for my informant.
6 Note that for non-subject focus in (8)–(11), the verb has the non-dependent form of the subject marker because, as mentioned earlier, the dependent form of the subject marker *ũ* is used only when the subject is in focus.

(10) Locative adverbial (Schwarz 2003: 56–57 (27))

    a. *nĩ-ko   Abdul   a-ra-edirie   gĩ-tonga   nyomba?*   [AM: √]
       F -where   1.Abdul   1SM-PST.sell.PFV   7-rich.man   9.house
       'Where did Abdul sell the house to the rich man?'

    b. *nĩ   Nairobi   Abdul   a-ra-edirie   gĩ-tonga   nyomba*   [AM: ??]
       F   Nairobi   1.Abdul   1SM-PST.sell.PFV   7-rich.man   9.house
       Lit. 'It's in Nairobi that Abdul sold the house to the rich man.'

    c. *Abdul   a-ra-edirie   gĩ-tonga   nyomba   **ko**?*   [AM: ?]
       1.Abdul   1SM-PST.sell.PFV   7-rich.man   9.house   where

    d. *Abdul a-ra-edirie gĩtonga nyomba **Nairobi**.*   [AM: √]

(11) Temporal adverbial (Schwarz 2003: 57 (28))

    a. *nĩ-re   Abdul   a-ra-edirie   gĩ-tonga   nyomba?*   [AM: √]
       F -when   1.Abdul   1SM-PST.sell.PFV   7-rich.man   9.house
       'When did Abdul sell the house to the rich man?'

    b. *nĩ   ira   Abdul   a-ra-edirie   gĩ-tonga   nyomba.*   [AM: *]
       F   y'day   1.Abdul   1SM-PST.sell.PFV   7-rich.man   9.house
       Lit. 'It was yesterday that Abdul sold the house to the rich man.'

    c. *Abdul a-ra-edirie gĩtonga nyomba **re**?*   [AM: *]

    d. *Abdul a-ra-edirie gĩtonga nyomba **ira**.*   [AM: √]

Manner and instrumental adverbials, on the other hand, only allow the in-situ structure in Schwarz's data. The ex-situ question-answer pair is unacceptable as shown in (12) for a manner adverbial, and in (13) for an instrumental adverbial. For my informant, however, the ex-situ structure in the question (12a) was perfectly acceptable.

(12) Manner adverbial (Schwarz 2003: 58 (31))

    a. **nĩ* atea   Abdul   a-ra-edirie   nyomba?*   [AM: √]
       F   how   1.Abdul   1SM-PST.sell.PFV   9.house
       'How did Abdul sell the house?'

    b. **nĩ* na-rua   Abdul   a-ra-edirie   nyomba.*   [AM: *]
       F   quickly   1.Abdul   1SM-PST.sell.PFV   9.house
       'Abdul sold the house QUICKLY.'

    c. *Abdul a-ra-edirie nyomba **atea**?*   [AM: √]

    d. *Abdul a-ra-edirie nyomba **na-rua**.*   [AM: √]

(13) Instrumental adverbial (Schwarz 2003: 58 (32))

a. *nĩ na kee Abdul a-ra-hor-a funda? [AM: *]
   F   with what 1.Abdul 1SM-PST-beat-FV 9.donkey
   'With what did Abdul beat the donkey?'

b. *nĩ na mo-te Abdul a-ra-hor-a funda. [AM: *]
   F   with 3-stick 1.Abdul 1SM-PST-beat-FV 9.donkey
   'With a/the stick Abdul beat the donkey.'

c Abdul arahora funda na kee? [AM: √]

d. Abdul arahora funda na mote. [AM: √]

3 New facts on term focus

In this section, I lay out some new facts mentioned only in passing in the previous section in comparison to the findings reported by Schwarz (2003). The new data for which there is no citation come from a Kikuyu mother-tongue speaker from the Murang'a region.[7] These data were provided during translation tasks that are designed to elicit utterances with various focal elements (Fiedler and Schwarz 2006). Especially where there was a discrepancy with previous studies, the grammaticality judgment was tested through further elicitation and questioning.

Table 2 shows a summary of the new findings, provided by my informant. The left-most column shows the different grammatical functions/semantic roles that are questioned/answered in the above examples. The corresponding example numbers are given in the next column, followed by the acceptability of the ex-situ structure for wh-questions and answers, and the in-situ structure for the same questions and answers.

The first striking finding is that, with the exception of the instrument, fronting (ex-situ with *nĩ*) is generally preferred or obligatory for all types of wh-questions. Second, except for subjects, the in-situ structure is preferred or obligatory for informational (non-contrastive) focus, such as answers to wh-questions. The subject, on the other hand, must be answered with *nĩ*. Thus we find a clear subject/non-subject asymmetry in the way focus is expressed (in answers to

---

[7] In a couple of sessions, I had two Kikuyu speakers. All the examples cited in the present work come from only one of them, "AM", and my conclusions are based on her grammatical judgment, although for all the relevant data for which the judgment was given from both speakers, their grammaticality judgments converged.

wh-questions). Thirdly, given the first two generalizations above, there is no free choice between the ex-situ and in-situ structures; nor is there a preference for the structural parallel between a question and answer, as previously reported.[8]

The last point worth mentioning is that, for objects and locatives, the *ni*-marked focus is acceptable only if it is contrastive and is followed by the verb as in [*nĩ* X(FOC) VERB]. The speaker's intuition was that without the verb, the utterance is somehow incomplete. At this point, I do not have a good explanation for why it is possible to say, for example *nĩ mutumia* 'the woman$_{FOC}$ (ate the beans)' for subject focus (cf. example (14)), but not *nĩ mboso* '(she ate) the beans$_{FOC}$' for object focus (cf. example (16)).

Examples (14) and (15) show subject wh-questions and answers. Answers like that in (14) with just [*nĩ* +the focused element] are indicated as the most natural answers to subject wh-questions.

(14) Subject question (animate subject)
 a. *nũ*[9]   *ũ-rá-re-iré*   *mbóso?*
    F .who   1SM.REL-PST-eat-PFV   6.bean
    'Who ate the beans?'

 b. *nĩ́   mútumía.*   √nĩ + SUBJ
    F   1.woman
    'A/the woman (ate them).'

 c. *nĩ́   mútumía   a-ra-sí-re-iré.*
    F   1.woman   1SM-PST-6OM-eat-PFV

(15) a. *nĩ́-ké   ke-getíni-a   ngúo   éno?*   (inanimate subject)
       F-what 3SG.SM-cut-FV 9.cloth 9.this
       'What can cut this cloth?'

   b. *nĩ́   káhiyo   gá:ká   (ka-gétini-a   ngúo   éno).*

---

8 One of the reviewers has questioned the validity and reliability of the differences between my findings and previous ones. It is possible that the discrepancy we find between previous studies like that of Schwarz (2003) and the present study is due to methodological differences. In my study, particularly for these diverging results, I asked the informant the same judgment questions over several interview sessions, elicited different examples of the same type, and ensured that her grammaticality judgment was consistent with the earlier one. Over several sessions, I have found that the judgments on the relevant points were quite robust, and I therefore believe that these new results are reasonably objective and unbiased. How the differences can be explained remains an open question for the moment.
9 The subject wh-word *nũ* in (14a) consists of *nĩ* + *ũ*.

F 12.knife 12.this 12SM-cut-FV 9.cloth 9.this
'This knife (can cut this cloth).'

Similarly, object wh-questions also occur only in the ex-situ structure, as exemplified in (16a). The answer to the question, however, appears in the canonical object position, as shown in (16b). The structure comparable to that in (14b) and (15b) is not acceptable, shown in (16c), as an answer to (16a).

(16) Object question

    a. *nĩ ké   mútumía   a-rá-ri-iré?*
       F.what   1.woman   1SM-PST-eat-PFV
       'What did the woman eat?'

    b. *(a-rá-ri-iré)   mbóso.*
       1SM-PST-eat-PFV   6.beans
       '(she ate) beans'

    c. **nĩ bóso.*   *nĩ + OBJ

For locative questions, the ex-situ structure seems to be preferred, but unlike the object wh-interrogatives as in (16), the in-situ structure is also acceptable, as shown in (17). The most appropriate answer is just the locative without *nĩ* since it is non-contrastive.

(17) Locative question

    a. *nĩ kó   mutumía   a-rá-thi-ire?*   ex-situ
       F.where   1.woman   1SM-PST-go-PFV
       'Where did the woman go?'

    b. *mutumía   a-rá-thi-íre   ko?*   in-situ
       1.woman   1SM-PST-go-PFV   where?

    c. (*nĩ) Europe.   *nĩ + LOC

Turning now to contrastive term focus, the generalizations are the same for the subject but different for non-subjects. Subject focus is always expressed with *nĩ*, whether it is assertive or contrastive, as shown in (18). The object and locative, on the other hand, can be marked by *nĩ* when they are contrastive (19). The locative, as with assertive focus, must be expressed in situ, without the *nĩ* marking, as shown in (20).

(18) Contrastive subject focus
    ní̵ mwaná ū-étóro,   tí   ngúi.   √nĩ + SUBJ contrastive
    F 1.baby 1SM.REL-be.asleep NEG 9.dog
    'It's the baby who's asleep, not the dog.'

(19) Contrastive object focus
  a. mutumía a-rá-re-y-a   mbóso, tí nyámá.
     1.woman 1SM-PROG-eat-FV 6.bean NEG 9.meat
     'The woman is eating beans, not the meat.'

  b. tí   nyámá mutumía a-rá-re-ya,   ní̵ mbóso.
     NEG meat 1.woman 1SM-PROG-eat-FV F beans
     'Not the meat, it's the beans the woman is eating.'   √nĩ + OBJ contrastive

(20) Contrastive locative focus
  a. a-ra-thi-ire   Europe, ti Asia.   in-situ
     1SM-PST-go-PFV   Europe NEG Asia

  b. nĩ Europe a-ra-thi-ire,   ti Asia.   ex-situ
     F Europe 1SM-PST-go-PFV   NEG Asia
     'She went to Europe, not to Asia.'

The facts are summarized as follows. First, subject focus is always marked by *nĩ*, regardless of whether it is assertive or contrastive. Second, object and locative appear without *nĩ* (in answers to wh-questions) and can be marked by *nĩ* only when they are contrastive. Third, adjuncts are not marked at all. Fourth, there is no structural parallel observed between wh-questions and answers.

Generalizations emerging from these facts are that, first, there is a subject/non-subject asymmetry for assertive focus on the one hand, and secondly, there is a hierarchy-based difference for contrastive focus on the other. We can think of these in terms of the hierarchies given in (21)-(22).

(21) Grammatical function hierarchies (e.g., Aissen 1999; Bresnan 2001)
  a. Subject > Non-subject
  b. Subject > Object > Oblique > Adjunct

(22) Markedness of focus types
    unmarked → non-contrastive focus > contrastive focus ← marked

Since the subject is prototypically a default topic cross-linguistically, subject focus is a relatively marked type of focus as opposed to non-subject focus. The relative markedness of subject focus is expressed by obligatory marking of *nĩ*. The fact that the object is marked by *nĩ* only when it is contrastive might be captured by associating the markedness of focus type, given in (22),[10] with the relational hierarchy in (21): subject focus is marked and hence marking is obligatory for both non-contrastive and contrastive focus; *nĩ* marking is only optional for object contrastive focus, and for elements lower in the relational hierarchy, *nĩ* marking is banned.

Furthermore, we might also include wh-focus in the markedness hierarchy of focus types. The fact that wh-focus is always marked by *nĩ* may lead one to place wh-focus as the most marked focus type:[11]

(23)		non-contrastive focus	>	contrastive focus >	wh-focus
Subject	nĩ			nĩ	nĩ
Object	Ø			nĩ	nĩ
Oblique	Ø			nĩ	nĩ
Adjunct	Ø			Ø	nĩ[12]

The markedness relation of the three focus types and morphological marking for the different grammatical functions in (23) are interpreted as implicational, in that when a given grammatical function is marked by *nĩ* for a given focus type, it is marked for any other focus type to the right (=more marked type) of the hierarchy. Some theoretical and empirical grounding remains to be established in the future for the hypothesis that wh-focus is more marked than assertive and contrastive focus, and/or whether these focus types should form a markedness hierarchy at all.

Lastly and most importantly for the purposes of this chapter, the use of the morphologically unmarked verb form to express all these types of term focus resembles the use of the conjoint verb form in other Bantu languages that display the conjoint/disjoint alternation. What is crucial here is not so much whether or not the focused (non-verbal) element is marked by *nĩ* in Kikuyu, but that the verb is unmarked, and the focused element follows it (without *nĩ*, except in subject focus). This is contrasted with the *nĩ*-marked verb, which typically indicates some type of focus on the predicate, to be made precise in the next section. This will

---

10 The opposition of non-contrastive vs. contrastive focus need not be binary, and can be taken as a continuum in which focus types such as wh-focus and selective focus may be placed.
11 This and the schema in (23) were suggested by one of the reviewers.
12 As shown in Table 2, the instrument, which can function as an oblique argument, seems to be an exception, as it is never marked by *nĩ*.

be then the second half of the whole picture showing an interesting parallelism between the use of *nĩ* in the Kikuyu focus system and the conjoint/disjoint alternation in other languages.

4 Predicate-centered focus

In this section, I present data on 'predicate-centered focus', focus on the non-nominal, predicative element of the clause (Güldemann 2009). Predicate-centered focus comes in two types, state-of-affairs focus and operator focus. State-of-affairs focus refers to narrow focus on the lexical content of the predicate and can be exemplified by a question-answer pair like that in (i). Operator focus refers to focus on sentence operators such as TAM and polarity. One subtype, TAM focus, takes narrow scope over the finite element of the predication and is exemplified in (ii)a. The second subtype of operator focus, polarity focus, has narrow scope over the truth-value of the utterance and is exemplified in (ii)b.

(i) State-of-affairs focus: narrow focus on the lexical content of the predicate
 Q: What did the princess do with the frog?
 A: She KISSED him.

(ii) Operator focus: focus on sentence operators such as TAM and polarity.
 a. TAM focus: narrow scope over the finite element of the predication
 Q: Is the princess kissing the frog (right now)?
 A: She HAS kissed him.

 b. Polarity focus: narrow scope over the truth-value of the utterance
 Q: I cannot believe the princess kissed the slippery frog.
 A: Yes, she DID kiss him.

Operator focus has been discussed for a number of African languages by Hyman and Watters (1984: 233) in terms of 'auxiliary focus', which they define as "the interaction between focus and the semantic features of tense, aspect, mood, and polarity". Polarity focus in particular has also been referred to as 'verum focus' (e.g. Höhle 1992). Predicate-centered focus is differentiated crucially from so-called predicate focus, which can have wide (VP) focus.

In the rest of this section, I present data showing how each of these types of predicate-centered focus is expressed in Kikuyu.

4.1 Operator focus

Polarity focus in Kikuyu is expressed by placing the proclitic *nĩ* in front of the canonical V(O) structure. Although *nĩ* always seems to have H tone, a phonetic analysis[13] indicates that *nĩ* has in fact no H tone but only has longer duration for truth-value focus (also noted by Armstrong 1940), and perhaps due to this, *nĩ* marking truth-value focus is perceived by native speakers to have a higher tone.

Example (24) illustrates a polarity question and answer. For predicate-centered focus, there is strong preference to have the *nĩ*-marking in questions, and likewise in the corresponding answers.

(24) Polarity question & answer
    a. *mutumía nĩ̂ a-rí-iré mbóso?*
       1.woman F 1SM-eat-PFV 6.bean
       'Did the woman eat the beans?'

    b. *ee, nĩ̂ a-rí-ire (mbóso).*
       yes F 1SM-eat-PFV 6.bean
       'Yes, she did (eat the beans).'

Similarly in corrective assertion, illustrated in (25), an answer to the polarity question in (25a) without the *nĩ*-marking would not have emphasis on the positive polarity and hence inappropriate as an answer, as (25b) indicates.

(25) Corrective assertion
    Q: 'They didn't steal it (did they?)'
    a. *Neguó, nĩ̂ m-aíire.*
       true F 2SM-steal.PFV
       'Yes, they did steal it.'

    b. #*neguó, máiire.* [not emphasizing the positive polarity]

TAM focus is also expressed by *nĩ* in front of the finite predicate. The focus particle *nĩ* is perceived as having a L tone. Again, according to our Praat analysis, this is not due to a lowered tone, but seems only due to a shorter duration – the point noted by Armstrong (1940) for truth-value focus (having a longer duration).

---

[13] Thanks to Siri Gjersøe for providing the Praat analysis.

(26) a. nĩ kũ-re-ya a-rá-re-ya mbóso
        F   INF-eat-IMPFV 1SM-PROG-eat-IMPFV 6.bean
      kana nĩ a-sí-re-ire?
      or   F   1SM-6OM-eat-PFV
      'Is she still eating the beans or has she eaten them already?'

    b. nĩ a-sí-re-íre.
      F   1SM-6OM-eat-PFV
      'She has eaten (them).'

A similar focus marking is reported in Mbala (K51) with a pre-initial marker *mu-* (discussed by Güldemann 2003: 341). The utterance without the pre-initial marker *mu-* (27a) expresses focus on the object, while the one with it (27b) is interpreted as truth-value focus.

(27) Mbala (K51, Ndolo 1972: 40)
    a. *gá-gòsuna ga-ga-loombulula gilùungu.*   OBJ = focus
      12-woman 12SM-FUT-demand.back calabash
      'The woman will ask for the calabash (to be) returned.'

    b. *gá-gòsuna **mu**-ga-ga-lóombulula gilùungu.*   truth-value focus
      12-woman FOC-12SM-FUT-demand.back calabash
      'The woman WILL ask for the calabash (to be) returned.'

We thus observe that the unmarked predicate expresses term focus and the marked predicate expresses predicate-centered focus. This resembles the conjoint/disjoint distinction in other Bantu languages, as partly shown in the discussion of term focus. In languages with the conjoint/disjoint distinction, term focus is generally expressed by the use of the unmarked (conjoint) verb form, and predicate-centered focus is expressed by the use of the marked (disjoint) form.

4.2 State-of-affairs focus

As mentioned earlier, state-of-affairs focus refers to narrow focus on the lexical content of the predicate. This is crucially distinguished from predicate focus, which often includes VP (wide) focus. Like operator focus, state-of-affairs focus in Kikuyu is expressed by the use of *nĩ* in front of the predicate.

Interestingly for state-of-affairs focus, there is a clear constructional difference between non-contrastive vs. contrastive state-of-affairs focus. Non-contrastive state-of-affairs focus is expressed by a canonical structure with *nĩ* in front of the predicate. As with TAM focus, *nĩ* is perceived as having a L tone, again due to a shorter duration. Contrastive state-of-affairs, on the other hand, is expressed by the verb doubling construction: [*nĩ* + non-finite V + finite V]. The subject, when present, can be positioned before the doubling.[14]

Example (28) illustrates non-contrastive state-of-affairs focus. Compare this with examples (29) and (30), which express, respectively, selective and corrective state-of-affairs focus. In examples (28) and (29), the utterance is identical, but due to the difference in the context (the preceding question), different constructions are used to make these utterances felicitous. As shown, for selective and corrective – which we might broadly call 'contrastive' – state-of-affairs focus, verb doubling is most felicitously used. The non-doubling counterpart in (29b) and (30b) is not felicitous as an answer to the preceding question/utterance.

(28) Non-contrastive state-of-affairs focus *nĩ* + verb
 {Kamau loves his car. Yesterday he took care of it. What exactly did he do with the car?}
 nĩ a-ra-mé-thodék-ire.
 F   1SM-PST-9OM-fix-PFV
 'He FIXED it.'

(29) Selective state-of-affairs focus *nĩ* + verb doubling
 {Kamau loves his car. Yesterday he took care of it. Did he wash or fix it?}

 a. *nĩ gū́-thodék-a a-ra-mé-thodék-ire.*
    F   INF-fix-FV   1SM-PST-9OM-fix-PFV
    'He FIXED it.'

 b. #*nĩ araméthodékire.* [not selective]

(30) Corrective state-of-affairs focus *nĩ* + verb doubling
 {The woman hit Peter.}

 a. *nĩ kū́-mu-igat-á a-mu-igát-íre.*
    F   INF-1OM-chase-FV   1SM-1OM-hit-PFV
    'She CHASED him away.'

 b. #*nĩ amuigátíre.*

---

14 Although this point is not discussed further in the present work, it is interesting that the *nĩ*-marked predicate can appear after the (topical) subject. Preliminary examination suggests that the subject preceding the *nĩ*-marked focus is internal to the clause, and the focus is therefore in

Interestingly, when asked for the Kikuyu translation of an utterance in the progressive, my speaker produced verb doubling:

(31) a. mwaná   nĩ   kū̆-re-ya   a-rá:-re-yá   mbó:so.
         1.child   F   INF-eat-FV   1SM-PROG-eat-IMPFV   6.bean
         'The child is eating beans.'

     b. Fafa   wanyú   nĩ   gŭ-kin-yá   a-rá:-kin-ya   (reu).
         Father your   F   INF-arrive-IMPFV 1SM-PROG-arrive-IMPFV now
         'Your father is arriving (now) [as we speak].'

Note that in Kikuyu, the progressive marker on the finite verb is obligatory, so we cannot exclude the possibility that it is the progressive marker and not the verb doubling that expresses progressivity. Indeed in (31a), the speaker reports that there is a focus reading of the progressive aspect of the action.[15] Nonetheless, it is curious that the speaker prefers the use of verb doubling to express progressivity outside focal context as is apparently the case in (31b). The use of verb doubling to express predicate-centered focus is also attested in languages of zones A, B, E, H, and K, and in some of these languages, we have data to show that the same construction is used to express progressivity without a progressive morpheme (De Kind et. al 2013, 2014; Güldemann et al. 2014 and references cited therein for individual languages in these zones).

Syntactic restriction parallel to that observed in the CJ/DJ alternation

As noted above, there is a striking parallelism between the *nĩ*-less, unmarked predicate and *nĩ*-marked predicate on the one hand, and the conjoint vs. disjoint forms on the other. First, a robust generalization of the conjoint/disjoint distinction is that the conjoint form can never be clause-final, while the disjoint form has no such restriction (cf. property a of Table 1). In Kikuyu, the unmarked predicate can never be clause-final, while the *nĩ* marked predicate can be (see also Güldemann 2008). Example (32) shows the unmarked verb, which is used to express term focus. The ungrammaticality of (32b) shows that this unmarked verb can never be clause-final. By contrast, example (33) is a *nĩ*-marked verb form,

---

so-called 'immediately before the verb' (IBV) position. Focus in IBV in VO languages has received increasing attention in recent work (e.g., Gibson et al., this volume; De Kind 2014; Muluwa and Bostoen 2014; Van der Wal and Namyalo 2014). Kikuyu *nĩ*-marked focus might also be on the way from (formerly) a more cleft-like structure to preverbal focus.

15 Strictly speaking with verbs of *come* and *go* as in (31), doubling indicates proximate future, namely "your father is just about to arrive".

which is used to express predicate-centered focus. Example (33b) shows that the *nî*-marked verb form can be clause-final.

(32) a. *mwaná á-rá-re-iré mbó:so.*   unmarked verb, term focus
        1.child 1SM-PST-eat-PFV 6.bean
        'The child ate the beans.'

    b. **mwaná árároíre.*   cannot be clause-final
        'The child ate.'

(33) a. *mwaná nî̂ á-rá-re-iré mbó:so.*   marked verb, truth-value focus
        1.child F 1SM-PST-eat-PFV 6.bean
        'The child did eat the beans.'

    b. *mwaná nî̂ árároíré.*   can be clause-final

Second, as indicated in examples (24)–(26), operator focus is expressed by the *nî*-marked predicate, just as it is expressed by the marked disjoint verb form (Güldemann 1996, 2003, properties d & e of Table 1; also Nshemezimana & Bostoen, this volume). Third, (non-subject) term focus is expressed by the unmarked structure – that is, in the canonical (non-subject) syntactic position – with the unmarked verb, just as it is expressed by the unmarked conjoint form (cf. Van der Wal, this volume, cf. property b of Table 1). Fourth, the grammatical context in which *nî* cannot appear is identical to the context where the disjoint form generally cannot appear, for example (Gecaga and Kirkaldy-Willis 1953: 19; cf. properties e, f & g of Table 1): (i) in all negative contexts; (ii) with consecutive tenses; (iii) in conditionals; (iv) in questions *how*, *when*, and *where*; and (v) in subordinate clauses.

These similarities point towards the need to recognize these sets of paradigms as one and the same phenomenon in terms of their pragmatic function, despite different formal manifestations.

An additional curious fact is that in a number of studies on the conjoint/disjoint alternation, the conjoint form in the present tense is often translated as habitual, while the disjoint form as progressive (cf. Van der Wal, this volume). In the examples from different languages in (34)-(37), the (a) examples in the CJ form are translated as habitual, and in the (b) examples in the DJ form, the progressive reading is preferred or at least easily available. In the Matengo examples in (37) and (38), we see that the disjoint form that is used to express progressivity also expresses predicate-centered (truth-value) focus.[16]

---

[16] Matengo as illustrated in (37) might be slightly difference case, because the verb *sleep* in Matengo is treated as a stative predicate, which normally disallows progressive (meaning more like to be *asleep*), and in order to express the present state, the DJ (=perfect) form must be used (Yoneda, this volume).

(34) Makhuwa (P31)
    a. *ni-n-thípá   nlittí.*   CJ*
       1PL.SM-PRS:CJ-dig   5.hole
       'We dig a hole.'

    b. *ni-náá-thípá.*   DJ
       1PL.SM-PRS:DJ-dig
       'We are digging.' (Van der Wal 2009: 218 (679))

(35) Swati (S43)
    a. *ngi-natsa…*   CJ
       1SG.SM-drink
       'I drink…'

    b. *ngi-ya-natsa.*   DJ
       1SG.SM-PRS.DJ-drink
       'I am drinking.' (Ziervogel and Mabuza 1976: 97, 98)

(36) Ha (JD66)
    a. *ba-rima   ibiharagi.*   CJ
       2SM-cultivate   beans
       'They cultivate beans.'

    b. *ba-ra-rima   (ibiharagi).*   DJ
       2SM-PRS.DJ-cultivate   beans
       'They cultivate/are cultivating (beans).' (Harjula 2004: 167)

(37) Matengo (N13)
    a. *Ju-gonel-aje   mu-súmba   ense.*   CJ
       1SM-sleep-CJ   18-7.room   7.this
       'He/she sleeps in this room.'

    b. *Ju-gonel-iti   mu-súmba   ense.*   DJ
       1SM-sleep-DJ   18-7.room   7.this
       'He/she is sleeping in this room.'
       (Q: "Where is he/she sleeping now?") (Yoneda 2009 (10))

(38) Matengo (N13)   DJ: truth-value focus
    {Did you go to the market?}
    n-a-jend-iti.
    1SG.SM-PST-go-DJ
    'I did. (Lit. I went).' Yoneda 2009)

In Haya (J22), the conjoint/disjoint distinction is mainly tonal. According to Hyman (1999), in the conjoint form, there is tonal reduction of the verb stem (the "out-of-focus" form), and in the disjoint form there is no tonal reduction (the "in-focus" form). Certain tenses never show tonal reduction and always appear in the 'in-focus' form. Progressive is one of such "marked" tenses.

(39) Haya (JE22, Hyman 1999: 160–161 exs (15), (17))
   a. Tonal reduction in unmarked tenses, aspects, and moods

	DJ: 'they tie' etc.	CJ: 'they tie Káto' etc.
Pres. hab.	ba-kóm-a	ba-kom-a káto
Past$_1$	bá-á-kôm-a	ba-a-kom-a káto
Past$_2$	ba-kom-íl-e	ba-kom-il-e káto
Past hab.	ba-a-kóm-ag-a	ba-a-kom-ag-a káto
Future$_1$	ba-laa-kôm-a	ba-laa-kom-a káto
Future$_2$	ba-li-kóm-a	ba-li-kom-a káto

   b. No tonal reduction in "marked" tenses, aspects, and moods

	'they are tying' etc.	'they are tying Káto' etc.
Progressive	ni-ba-kóm-a	ni-ba-kom-á káto
Perfect ("already")	bá-ákóm-il-e	bá-á-kóm-il-e káto
Experiential	ba-lá-kom-íl-e	ba-lá-kom-il-e káto
Persistive ("still")	ba-kyáá-kôm-a	ba-kyáá-kóm-a káto
Subjunctive	ba-kóm-a	kom-á káto
Imperative	kóm-a	kom-á káto
Past$_3$/Perf/Consec	bá-ka-kôm-a	bá-ka-kóm- káto

Note that in progressive (39b), the verb is prefixed by *ni*, derived from the identificational copula, and it is the form used in focus context in Haya (Hyman and Watters 1984; Hyman 1999; Güldemann 2003). Hyman (1999: 162) argues that it is indeed the focus marker in Haya. This further supports the idea that the expression of progressivity and focus are closely related (see also Nshemezimanana & Bostoen, this volume, and Ngoboka & Zeller, this volume, for a discussion on this point); the progressive reading of the "in-focus" form (e.g. *ní*-marked predicate in Kikuyu, the disjoint form in other Bantu languages) is not mere interpretational preference or coincidence, and is shared by the CJ/DJ alternation and the focus system of Kikuyu.[17]

---

[17] Ngoboka and Zeller (this volume) note that in Kinyarwanda, the marker for the disjoint verb form *-ra-* also appears in the progressive and persistive outside the context where the disjoint form is normally used in the language. Ngoboka and Zeller, however, leave the question open as to whether this *-ra* and the disjoint marker *-ra* are in any way (e.g. historically) related. See Nshemezimana and Bostoen (this volume) for another view on this point.

5 Summary and remarks

The main purpose of this chapter has been to present new data on both term focus and predicate-centered focus in Kikuyu and highlight the formal and functional similarities between the conjoint/disjoint alternation and the Kikuyu focus system. The results are summarized below on the following points: (i) the use of the focusing particle *nĩ* in Kikuyu, (ii) similarities between the unmarked predicate vs. *nĩ*-marked predicate on the one hand, and conjoint vs. disjoint verb forms in other Bantu languages on the other.

Use of nĩ in Kikuyu
The proclitic *nĩ*, which is also used as an identificational copula, figures centrally in the grammar of focus in Kikuyu and closely related languages. It is used in the following focal contexts and scope, as also summarized in Table 3:
- Term focus: subject focus is marked by *nĩ*; object and locative are marked by *nĩ* only when they are contrastive. Others appear without *nĩ*. The verb is unmarked.
- Truth-value focus is expressed by *nĩ* (perceived as H tone) directly preceding the predicate.
- TAM focused is expressed by *nĩ* (perceived as L tone) directly preceding the predicate.
- Non-contrastive state-of-affairs focus is expressed by *nĩ* directly preceding the predicate.
- Contrastive state-of-affairs focus is expressed by *nĩ*-marked predicate with verb doubling.
- The scope of *nĩ* is only the immediately following element.

Table 3: Summary of focus expressions.

	Assertive	Contrastive
Term focus		
Subject	nĩ + SBJ (14)–(15)	nĩ + SBJ (18)
Object	(V) OBJ (16)	(V) OBJ, nĩ + OBJ (19)
Locative	(V) LOC (17)	(V) LOC (17)
Operator focus	ní + PRED (24)/(26)	ní + PRED (25)
State-of-affairs focus	nĩ + PRED (28)	nĩ + INF.V + FIN.V (29)-(30)

Parallelism with the conjoint/disjoint morphology

From the Kikuyu data on both term focus and predicate-centered focus also emerged a striking parallelism between the focus marking strategy using *nĩ* in Kikuyu and the conjoint/disjoint alternation in other Bantu languages.

Distributionally, *nĩ* is a cross-categorial proclitic while the conjoint/disjoint morphology is a verbal affix. However, when one looks just at the verb form that expresses term focus vs. predicate-centered focus, the parallelism is rather obvious:

- Term focus is expressed by the unmarked verb form (without *nĩ* immediately preceding it), just as it is expressed by the unmarked conjoint form in the majority of relevant languages (cf. Van der Wal, this volume).
- Although the verb form is unmarked, the focused subject must always be marked by *nĩ* and expressed ex-situ in Kikuyu. This also parallels the CJ/DJ alternation, where the verb form is unmarked (=CJ form), but the focused subject must appear in the non-canonical postverbal position in many languages.
- Predicate-centered focus is expressed by the *nĩ*-marked predicate, just as it is expressed by the marked disjoint verb form (Güldemann 1996, 2003).
- The grammatical contexts in which the *nĩ*-marked verb cannot appear resemble the contexts where the disjoint form generally cannot appear – for instance, in subordinate clauses and conditionals, where there is no/little assertivity.
- The form that is used to express predicate-centered focus is also used to express progressivity both in the CJ/DJ alternation and the focus system with verb doubling.
- There is a robust syntactic requirement that the unmarked conjoint verb form must have a following element, while the marked disjoint form has no such restriction. The same holds for the unmarked (*nĩ*-less) verb and *nĩ*-marked verb.

On the last point above regarding the syntactic condition, a question might arise why it must be the formally marked form that can be independent/clause-final. The question seems to be two-fold: (i) why is the marked form the one that is used to express predicate-centered focus, and (ii) why can this form be independent/clause-final. As for (i), for Kikuyu, it is relatively clear that *nĩ* is formerly (and still is in other grammatical context) an identificational marker. One might therefore speculate that, for example, in the configuration expressing truth-value focus [(X) *nĩ VERB*] *nĩ* has been interpreted from a copula in a more cleft-like construction, "It-is (the case that) (X) VERBed" or "as for X it is (the case that) he/she-VERBed", to a focus marker. Pragmatically, when (any aspect of) the predicate is in focus, it is, in principle, all that is needed in an utterance, and any other constituents present in the utterance are non-focal, extra elements. I speculate, therefore, that (focally) marked verbs can be independent purely for pragmatic reasons.

The lexical source of the disjoint morphology is perhaps not as transparent as the Kikuyu focus marker, but for some languages, there is evidence that it was a former focus marker (cf. Güldemann 2003). This is also evident in the above data from Haya, in which the morpheme *ni* that marks the in-focus progressive aspect is also a focus marker (Hyman 1999: 162).

Another observation worth noting is that the verb doubling construction used to express predicate-centered focus (in particular, state-of-affairs focus) is attested in languages that apparently do not have the conjoint/disjoint verb alternation – i.e., languages of zones A, B, E, F, H, and K (also noted in Güldemann et al. 2014). To the extent that verb doubling and the disjoint form are used for the same pragmatic purposes (i.e. encoding predicate-centered focus), we might speculate that they exist complementarily across Bantu languages (see also Hyman, this volume). Further research comparing the CJ/DJ alternation and other focus-related systems across Bantu both from a synchronic and diachronic perspective may help us find an answer to why that might be, if that is indeed the correct generalization.

Abbreviations

1/2/3SG/PL	1st/2nd/3rd person singular/plural		
APPL	applicative	LOC	locative
CJ	conjoint	MAN	manner
DJ	disjoint	NEG	negative (marker)
F	focus (marker)	OBJ	object
FUT	future	OM	object marker
FV	final vowel	PFV	perfective
H	high tone	PROG	progressive
HAB	habitual	PRS	present
ID	identificational copula	PST	past
IMPFV	imperfective	SBJ	subject
INF	infinitive	SM	subject marker
INSTR	instrument	TEMP	temporal
L	low tone		

References

Abels, Klaus & Peter Muriungi. 2008. The focus marker in Kîîtharaka. *Lingua* 118. 687–731.
Aissen, Judith. 1999. Markedness and subject choice in optimality theory. *NLLT* 17. 673–711.
Armstrong, Lilias Eveline. 1940. *The phonetic and tonal structure in Kikuyu*. London: Oxford University Press.
Bennett, Patrick R., Ann Biersteker, Withira Gikonyo, Susan Hershberg, Joel Kamande, Caroyn Perez, & Martha Swearingen. 1985. *Gĩkũyũ nĩ Kioigire: Essays, texts and glossaries*. The African Studies Program, University of Wisconsin-Madison.
Bergvall, Victoria L. 1987. *Focus in Kikuyu and universal grammar*. Cambridge, MA: Harvard University PhD thesis.
Bresnan, Joan. 2001. *Lexical-functional syntax*. Oxford: Blackwell.
Cammenga, Jelle. 1994. *Kuria phonology and morphology*. Amsterdam: Vrije Universiteit Amsterdam PhD thesis.
Chafe, Wallace L. 1976. Givenness, contrastiveness, definiteness, subjects, topics, and point of view. In Charles N. Li (ed.), *Subject and topic*, 25–55. New York, San Francisco, London: Academic Press.
Dalgish, Gerard. M. 1979. Syntax and semantics of the morpheme *ni* in Kivunjo (Chaga). *Studies in African Linguistics* 10 (1). 47–64.
De Kind, Jasper. 2014. Pre-verbal focus in Kisikongo (H16a, Bantu). In Fatima Hamlaoui (ed.), 95–122. Berlin: *ZASPiL* 57.
De Kind, Jasper, Sebastian Dom, Gilles-Maurice de Schryver, & Koen Bostoen. 2013. Fronted-infinitive constructions in Kikongo (Bantu H16): Verb focus, progressive aspect and future tense. Paper presented at Societas Linguistica Europaea: 46th Annual Meeting. September 2013.
De Kind, Jasper, Sebastian Dom, Gilles-Maurice de Schryver & Koen Bostoen. 2014. Event-centrality and the pragmatics-semantics interface in Kikongo: From predication focus to progressive aspect and vice versa. Unpublished Ms. 13 March 2014.
Dik, Simon C. 1997. *The theory of functional grammar, part 1: The structure of the clause*. Berlin, New York: Mouton de Gruyter.
Fiedler, Ines & Anne Schwarz. 2006. Focus Translation. In Stavros Skopeteas, Ines Fiedler, Sam Hellmuth, Anne Schwarz, Ruben Stoel, Gisbert Fanselow, Caroline Féry & Manfred Krifka (eds.), *Questionnaire on Information Structure (QUIS)*. Interdisciplinary Studies on Information Structure 4. Working Papers of the SFB 632. Universität Potsdam.
Gecaga, B. Mareka & W. H. Kirkaldy-Willis. 1953. *A short Kikuyu grammar*. London: Macmillan and Co. Limited.
Guthrie, Malcolm. 1948. *The classification of the Bantu languages*. London: Oxford University Press for the International African Institute.
Güldemann, Tom. 1996. *Verbalmorphologie und Nebenprädikationen im Bantu: Eine Studie zur funktional motivierten Genese eines konjugationalen Subsystems*. Bochum-Essener Beiträge zur Sprachwandelforschung 27. Bochum: Universitätsverlag Dr. N. Brockmeyer.
Güldemann, Tom. 1999. The genesis of verbal negation in Bantu and its dependency on functional features of clause types. In Jean-Marie Hombert & Larry M. Hyman (eds.), *Bantu historical linguistics: Theoretical and empirical perspectives*, 545–587. Stanford, CA: CSLI Publications.

Güldemann, Tom. 2003. Present progressive vis-à-vis predication focus in Bantu: a verbal category between semantics and pragmatics. *Studies in Language* 27 (2). 323–360.

Güldemann, Tom. 2008. The relation between predicate operator focus and theticity: How preverbal clause operators in Bantu betray functional affinity. Paper presented at the Workshop on Predicate Focus, Verum Focus, Verb Focus: Similarities and Difference. University of Potsdam, November 2008.

Güldemann, Tom. 2009. Predicate-centered focus types: A sample-based typological study in African languages. Application for project B7 in the CRC 632 Information structure.

Güldemann, Tom, Ines Fiedler & Yukiko Morimoto. 2014. The verb in the preverbal domain across Bantu: infinitive "fronting" and predicate-centered focus. Paper presented at the *Workshop on Preverbal Domains*. ZAS, Berlin, November 2014.

Harjula, Lotta. 2004. *The Ha Language of Tanzania: Grammar, text and vocabulary*. Köln: Rüdiger Köppe Verlag.

Höhle, Tilman N. 1992. Über Verum-Fokus im Deutschen. *Informationstruktur und Grammatik*, 4:112–142.

Hyman, Larry M. 1999. The interaction between focus and tone in Bantu. In George Rebushi & Laurice Tuller (eds.), *The grammar of focus*. Amsterdam: John Benjamins.

Hyman, Larry M. This volume. Disentangling conjoint, disjoint, metatony, tone cases, augments, prosody, and focus in Bantu.

Hyman, Larry M. & John R. Watters. 1984. Auxiliary focus. *Studies in African Linguistics* 15 (3). 233–273.

Lambrecht, Knud. 1994. *Information structure and sentence form: Topic, focus and the mental representations of discourse referents*. Cambridge Studies in Linguistics 71. Cambridge: Cambridge University Press.

Ndumbu, J.M.G. & Wilfred Howell Whiteley. 1962. Some problems of stability and emphasis in Kamba one-word tenses. *Journal of African Languages* 1. 167–180.

Moshi, Lioba. 1988. A functional typology of "ni" in Kivunjo (Chaga). *Studies in the Linguistic Sciences* 18 (1). 105–134.

Mugane, John. 1997. *A paradigmatic grammar of Gĩkũyũ*. Stanford, CA: CSLI Publications.

Muluwa, Joseph K. & Koen Bostoen. 2014. The immediate before the verb focus position in Nsong (Bantu B85d, DR Congo): A corpus-based exploration. In Fatima Hamlaoui (ed.), *ZASPiL 57*, 123–135.

Ndolo, P. 1972. *Essai sur la tonalité et la flexion verbale du Gimbala*. Tervuren: Musée royal de l'afrique central.

Ngoboka, Jean Paul & Jochen Zeller. This volume. The conjoint/disjoint alternation in Kinyarwanda.

Nshemezimana, Ernest & Koen Bostoen. This volume. The conjoint/disjoint alternation in Kirundi (JD62): A case for its abolition.

Schwarz, Florian. 2003. Focus marking in Kikuyu. *ZAS Papers in Linguistics* 30. 41–118.

Schwarz, Florian. 2007. Ex-situ focus in Kikuyu. In Enoch O. Aboh, Katharina Hartmann & Malte Zimmermann (eds.), *Focus strategies in African languages. The interaction of focus and grammar in Niger-Congo and Afro-Asiatic*, 139–160. Berlin: De Gruyter.

Yoneda, Nobuko. 2009. Matengo-no doushi-katsuyoukei-to shouten (Verb inflection and focus in Matengo). *Swahili and Africa Research* 20. 148–164.

Yoneda, Nobuko. This volume. Conjoint/disjoint alternation and focus in Matengo (N13).

Van der Wal, Jenneke. This volume. What is the conjoint/disjoint alternation in Bantu languages? Parameters of crosslinguistic variation.

Van der Wal, Jenneke. 2009. *Word order and information structure in Makhuwa-Enahara*. Utrecht: LOT.
Van der Wal, Jenneke & Saudah Namyalo. 2014. On Luganda preverbal focus and morphological marking. Handout of the talk presented at the *Workshop on Preverbal Domains*. ZAS, Berlin, November 2014.
Ziervogel, Dirk and E. 1. Mabuza. 1976. *A Grammar of the Swati Language*. Pretoria: 1. L. van Schaik.

Ines Fiedler
7 Conjoint and disjoint verb forms in Gur? Evidence from Yom

The verbal system of Yom (Oti-Volta, Gur) differentiates between three distinct inflectional verb forms in the affirmative indicative main clause. By means of different suffixes on the verb, the syntactic status and pragmatic function of the verb and the element following it is indicated. Whereas the third verb form is used in the extra-focal part of *ex-situ* focus constructions and in narrative clauses, the distribution of the first two forms shows striking similarities to the conjoint/disjoint alternation in Bantu, as their use depends on the position in the clause and is sensitive to specific information-structural configurations. The paper seeks first to describe the basic morphological characteristics of the verbal system of Yom with respect to this alternation and secondly to discuss the role of pragmatic factors influencing the choice of the verb forms, before finally analyzing the syntactic restrictions and constraints for the use of either form. It shows that the distribution of the verb forms is mainly syntactically conditioned, as the disjoint and the background form occur only in final position in main clauses, and that this position is related to focus. In the conclusion, the findings of Yom are embedded within a wider context of West African languages.

1 Introduction

The verbal system of Yom (Oti-Volta, Gur) differentiates between three distinct inflectional verb forms with identical aspectual and temporal value employed in the affirmative indicative main clause. Their use depends on pragmatic and

---

I would like to express my gratitude to all people in Djougou who helped me during my research work carried out between 2005 and 2008, especially my language consultants Issifou Korogo, Abel Amos, Abraham Zoumarou as well as Ulrike Heyder and Dodi Forsberg from the Sudanese Interior Mission for their warm welcome. Thanks go also to Anne Schwarz, Stefan Elders, Tom Güldemann and Gudrun Miehe for lively discussions and helpful comments as well as to the participants of several conferences and to the anonymous reviewers for their questions and remarks. The present research was carried out within the framework of the project on "Focus in Gur and Kwa languages" as part of the Collaborative Research Centre (SFB) 632 "Information structure: The linguistic means for structuring utterances, sentences and texts", financed by the German Research Foundation. The present form of the article has much benefitted from ongoing work in the project "Predicate-centered focus types in African languages" which is also part of the SFB 632 and discussions with the project members, above all Tom Güldemann.

DOI 10.1515/9783110490831-007

syntactic conditions. The distribution and appearance of two of these aspectual verb forms is very similar to the conjoint/disjoint alternation found in Bantu languages (see inter alia Doke (1927) for Zulu; Meeussen (1959) for Kirundi; Creissels (1996) for Tswana; Güldemann (1996) for the first survey of this phenomenon across Savannah Bantu; and the chapters in this volume). Van der Wal (this volume) attempts to bundle the characteristics of this dichotomy as described for Bantu languages and provides the following definition: "The conjoint/disjoint alternation is an alternation between verb forms that are formally distinguishable, that are associated with an information-structural difference in the interpretation of verb and/or following element and of which one form is not allowed in [main clause] sentence-final position." (Van der Wal, this volume) The present paper will show that (part of) the distinct aspectual paradigms of Yom[1] can be analyzed alongside this definition[2] and represents therefore an instance of the conjoint/disjoint alternation outside the Bantu group, but still within Niger-Congo.

Yom is a tonal language with three tonemes, Low, High and Downstepped High (Beacham 1969, 1991).[3] Apart from these basic tones, there are two complex tones which represent combinations of tones: a falling and a rising tone. Tones serve to discriminate lexical items as well as grammatical categories, like verbal aspect.

Yom has a productive noun class system with a full-fledged concord system. The noun classes are indicated on the head noun by way of suffixes, but neglected in the glossing here.[4]

The language is characterized by a regular SVO word order in main as well as in subordinate clauses. This word order can be changed only in serial verb constructions, where the object of the second verb can take preverbal position (cf. Beacham 1991: 118) and in *ex-situ* object focus constructions. Any temporal, local or modal adjuncts normally occur in clause-final position; however, they can also be placed in clause-initial position in order to be focused. In a canonical main

---

[1] Yom is an Oti-Volta language of the Gur language family, spoken by about 300,000 people (Lewis et al. 2014, online version) in the department of Donga in Northern Benin.
[2] I am especially grateful to Stefan Elders (†2007) who was the first pointing me to the analogies between the Bantu conjoint/disjoint verb dichotomy and the one found in the Yom verb system, which he also found in Doyayo, an Adamawa language (cf. Elders 2005).
[3] The description of the tonal system follows Beacham (1991). It differs from his presentation in the marking of the tones: here, the low tone is indicated by a grave accent, the first non-low by an acute accent (= S[ame] tone in Beacham), and the second non-low (= D[rop]) by an acute accent plus following (↓) to indicate the downstep.
[4] Only for the agreement markers for subject and object, the class numbers are specified in the examples, following the conventions developed by Miehe et al. (2012: 7–10).

clause, the subject noun phrase can be realized either as a noun (with possible modifiers) or as a pronoun marked for noun class (cf. (1)). In the case of a nominal subject, no agreement marker is allowed on the verb.

(1) pɔ́yá / à   nyù-r   nyâm dà-déyŏ.
 woman / 1SM   drink-PFV   water wood-hut
 'The woman / she drank water in a bar.'[5]

The distinction between the three different inflectional verb forms in the affirmative indicative is exemplified below. Because of their similarity in syntactic behaviour and pragmatic distribution compared to the verb paradigms in some Bantu languages, two of these forms shall be called conjoint (CJ) and disjoint (DJ) verb forms following the convention in this volume; cf. examples (2a) and (2b). The third form is used in the extra-focal, background part of *ex-situ* focus constructions (2c) and in narrative clauses introduced by the conjunction *lèè* 'and then' (see 3.3). For now it will be called *background form* (BG), until a more convenient term is found.

(2) a. à   nyù-r   nyâm̀.   conjoint
 1SM   drink-PFV   water
 {What did the woman drink?} 'She drank WATER.'[6]

 b. à   nyù-r-wá.   disjoint
 1SM   drink-PFV-DJ
 {What did the woman do in the bar?} 'She DRANK.'[7]

 c. nyâm-nà   à   nyù-l-lá.   (<nyù-r-rá)[8]   background
 water-FOC   1SM   drink-PFV-BG
 {What did the woman drink?} 'She drank WATER.'
 (lit. It is water that she drank.)

---

5 If not otherwise stated, the data were gathered by the author during field research in Djougou (Benin) between 2005 and 2008.
6 Capital letters in the translation indicate which element of the clause is in focus.
7 One of the reviewers suggested that *-wa* might be analyzed as "antipassive", used when the direct object is suppressed. This is not exactly the case, as in a sentence where an adverbial phrase follows the disjoint form is normally also not used (cf. the discussion in Section 4.1).
8 Suffix *-rá* in (2c) is represented as *-lá* because of a general phonetic constraint which demands that in any case where two flapped [r] meet (here: the perfective *-r* plus the background *-rá*) they change into the double liquid *ll*. Note that the flap and the liquid are allophones of the one liquid phoneme in complementary distribution.

The three forms for the verb *nyù-r* 'to drink-PFV' differ with regard to the occurrence of a suffix and its form, thus indicating their respective syntactic and functional status within the functional domain of the perfective aspect. Whereas the conjoint form is simply the verb form, the other two forms show different suffixes: For the disjoint verb the suffix is *-wá* and for the background form it is *-rá*. The present paper will analyze the syntactic and pragmatic constraints which determine the use of the three different inflectional verb forms in Yom and relate them to the conjoint/disjoint dichotomy in Bantu languages.

The presentation is structured as follows: The basic structural characteristics of the conjoint and disjoint verb paradigms in Yom are described in Section 2. In Section 3, the possible pragmatic grounding for the regular conjoint/disjoint change is discussed. The syntactic conditions including restrictions and exceptions for the use of the disjoint form are analyzed in Section 4. In Section 5, the distribution of the verb paradigms in Yom are summarized and placed into a wider African context.

2 The formal expression of the three inflectional verb paradigms

Yom verbs can be divided into six subgroups according to the form of the suffix they display in the potential mood (Beacham 1969, 1991: 36).[9] All semantic subtypes of verbs are included in these morphologically determined classes, irrespective of their valency.

Besides these verb classes, the Yom verb system is characterized by an organization based on the aspectual domain. It differentiates two basic aspects, perfective and imperfective, by means of tonal changes and use of different verb suffixes. The third basic category was called potential aspect by Beacham (1991), and is basically a modal distinction. It is possible to further subcategorize these three central forms by preposing different auxiliaries to the verb or by using periphrastic constructions.

In addition, two other forms are of interest here which are built on the imperfective verb by means of special suffixes and, therefore, show the conjoint/disjoint dichotomy: the past progressive and the future progressive.

---

9 I follow here Beacham (1991: 31, 37) who states that the potential "may be considered the 'basic' form of the verb in that it is from it that the other forms may be described as to their differences or formation. It is the form which best serves to indicate the various verb classes ..." (1991: 31). Given this characterization, the glosses offered in Table 1 (column 4) are rather incorrect as they should also indicate the modal value of the verb forms.

Table 1: Overview of the verb classes in Yom (examples from Beacham 1991: 36).

Verb class		Form of the verb in potential	Example	Gloss
Class1: simplex verbs		root	da-	'buy'
Class 2: complex verbs	*i*-class	root + -*i* (if final)	cər-i	'receive'
		root + Ø (if non-final)	cər-	
	a-class	root + -*a*	dan-a	'come'
	na-class	root + -*na*	lənə-na	'take a walk'
	ii-class	root + -*ii*	fɛɣ-ii	'greet'
	aa-class	root + -*aa*	zan-aa	'take away there'

Note: For the sake of easier comprehension, only the morphological shape of the verb forms is given in the tables. The tone of the verbs is characterized by Beacham (1991: 36) as basically non-low (either with or without following downstep), but changes according to aspect. It is also conditioned by the tone of the subject agreement marker (in essence, there is a difference between 1st/2nd pronouns and class concords).

As indicated in the introduction, the Yom verb system differentiates between three inflectional verb forms: the so-called conjoint and disjoint forms, as well as a form used in background environments. On formal grounds, the conjoint verb can be analyzed as basic vis-à-vis the two other inflectional forms. It is represented by the verb stem (root +/− derivational morphemes) with distinct tonal patterns according to the aspect or mood expressed and also depending on the subject. By means of an additional suffix, aspect and mood can be further specified.

The disjoint and the background form are characterized by special morphemes suffixed to the verb stem. Whereas the shape of the suffix of the disjoint form differs according to the basic verb category, the background form is in all verbal environments characterized by one and the same suffix -*rá* (allomorphs -*lá*, -*ná*) which is segmentally identical to the focus marker but differs in tone. The focus marker has an underlying low tone, as in examples (2c) and (3); in the latter, it is used as an identificational marker which underlies its focus function; only in some environments it changes to high. The background marker, on the other hand, always shows a high tone. Furthermore, the background marker is identical to the form of the disjoint suffix for class 2 verbs in perfective (see Table 2). This apparent analogy in form, but not in function, will be considered in Section 3.3.

(3) má-ʊ́-rà
     1SG.SM-LNK[10]-FOC
     'It's me.' (Beacham 1991: 12)

---

10 -ʊ́- has mainly the function of linking personal pronouns and certain nouns with the focus marker -*rà* (cf. Beacham 1991: 13).

Table 2: Conjoint and disjoint verb forms in Yom.

	Class 1		Class 2	
	Conjoint	Disjoint	Conjoint	Disjoint
Perfective	stem[11] + -r	stem + -r + -wá	stem +-ń/-í/-ə́	stem + -ń/-í/-ə́ + -rá
Imperfective	stem + Ø	stem + Ø + -wá	stem + -á	
Past progressive	stem + -mə́	stem + -mə́ + -nì	stem + -mə́	stem + -á + -wá
Future progressive	ná/nà + stem + -mə́	ná/nà + stem + -má + -nì	ná/nà + stem + -má	stem + -mə́ + -nì ná/nà + stem + -má + -nì
Potential	stem (high tone)		stem (high tone) + -ná/v́	

Table 2 shows the basic forms of the conjoint and disjoint forms as displayed for the three basic categories and the two imperfective forms built with suffixes.[12] As all other tense or mood categories are formed either by additional auxiliaries or expressed by periphrastic constructions, the basic distinctions are found with them as well. Thus, the conjoint/disjoint dichotomy is only found in the two aspectual categories (across all tenses), but not in the potential mood. Furthermore, the distinction is basically not found in negative and subordinate clauses, with an exception for the two special forms of the imperfective. The six verb classes of Yom which were identified by suffix in Table 1 are reduced to two classes with the conjoint/disjoint marking shown in Table 2.[13]

The perfective aspect of simplex verbs (class 1) is characterized by the presence of the alveolar flap -r suffixed to the verb, whereas in complex verbs (class 2) a vowel (either the near-close near-front vowel ɪ or the mid central vowel ə) or the alveolar nasal is suffixed to the verb stem. In the imperfective, class 1 verbs are only represented by the verb stem, and class 2 verbs show suffix -á. In the past progressive, all verbs take the morpheme -mə́ to indicate this tense, and in future progressive, -má is suffixed to the imperfective verb and the future auxiliary precedes it.

The disjoint forms display the same tonal and segmental shape as the conjoint forms. The only difference is the occurrence of a special morpheme which is additionally suffixed to the verb. This morpheme has mostly the form -wá, but for

---

[11] For class 1 verbs, the stem is identical with the root, whereas for class 2 verbs (all other), the stem is composed of the root and a derivational morpheme.
[12] Cf. the discussion of the verbal system of Yom in Manessy (1975: 148–151) who already describes the existence of affirmative particles postposed to the verb when no complement follows and restricted to non-dependent clauses (Manessy 1975: 149).
[13] Cf. also Prost (1973: 953) who describes two main groups of verbs on the basis of their suffixes.

class 2 verbs in the perfective it is represented by -rá. In past as well as in future progressive, a third morpheme appears which has the form -nì. As is also evident from Table 2, the conjoint/disjoint dichotomy is neutralized in potential mood.

In the following section, the pragmatic constraints for the use of both forms are presented, before the structural conditions are analyzed in Section 4.

3 Focus structure and the inflectional paradigms

In dealing with Bantu languages, some authors link the conjoint/disjoint alternation directly to information structure, like Creissels (1996) who suggests that the conjoint form is used in Tswana when "a) syntactically, the verb form is not in final clause position and b) pragmatically, the constituent which follows the verb form provides some new information" (Creissels 1996: 111). Similarly, Güldemann (2003: 330f.) sees a direct relation between the conjoint/disjoint forms and the focal interpretation of a clause. He claims that in case of the disjoint form, the postverbal material represents discourse-old information, and it is a predication operator (truth value, tense/aspect) or the lexical meaning of the verb, which is in focus. When the conjoint form is used, on the other hand, it is the postverbal element which is supposed to correspond to new information and therefore is in focus.

In the following it will be shown on the basis of main assertive clauses that the distribution of the three inflectional verb forms is related to information structure, mainly following the same pragmatic requirements as is the case in Bantu languages (cf. Van der Wal, this volume). On the other hand, the distribution of the verb forms is also motivated by syntactic constraints (cf. Section 4).

3.1 The conjoint form and complement/adjunct focus

Previous treatments of the conjoint/disjoint dichotomy in Bantu and non-Bantu languages have shown that this distinction is primarily to be found in main affirmative clauses (cf. Hyman and Watters 1984; Güldemann 1996). Whereas the disjoint form is mainly restricted to non-dependent affirmative clauses, the conjoint form has a wider distribution and is less subject to pragmatic constraints. It occurs in main as well as subordinate, and in positive and negative clauses. The following observations reflect their occurrence in the canonical main clause, where no change of the linear order of constituents can be observed. These clauses represent the basic categorical structuring of topic-comment, with the focus being couched within the comment (cf. Lambrecht 1994: 15–18; Fiedler et al.

2010: 237). Thus, the focus in these clauses is either on the verb phrase including the object or on the object/adjunct alone, as exemplified in (4) which can represent the reply to the question either for the object or for the verb phrase.

(4) à   nyù-r   nyâm.
     1SM   drink-PFV   water
     {What did the woman drink? ~ What did the woman do?}
     'She drank WATER. ~ She DRANK WATER.'

A parallel example is shown in (5), with the postverbal modal adjunct being in focus. In addition to the verb form, the speaker decided to reinforce the adjunct. This is done by means of the focus marker -rá suffixed to it following the linking particle -ʊ́-.

(5) à   jì-r   yáɣʊ̀-yáɣʊ́-ʊ́-rà.
     1SM   eat-PFV   RED-greedily-LNK-FOC
     {How did the woman eat?} 'She ate GREEDILY.'

Apart from this very regular use of the conjoint form, where the syntactic construction seems to directly reflect the information-structural reading of the clause, there are other examples in which syntactic position and pragmatic reading are in conflict with each other, as in (6).

(6) pɔ́ɣá   wá   jì-r   jénéḿ,   àmá   à   nyù-r   jénéḿ.
     woman   NEG   eat-PFV   well   but   1SM   drink-PFV   well
     'The woman did not eat well, but she DRANK well.'

This example illustrates a contrast between two actions, namely eating and drinking. Even though in the second conjunct the focus lies unambiguously on the verb and not on the following adverb, the conjoint form can be used. That might be explained by a different interpretation of the speaker who rather interpreted the clause as having focus on the whole verb phrase, or by the syntactic ambiguity between verb-adverb expressions which may be either a core or non-core constituent within the clause (cf. Sections 3.2 and 4.1).

It follows from the examples that in most environments the canonical clause with conjoint verb form can be interpreted as displaying a topic-comment structure with the complement/adjunct or the whole verb phrase falling in the scope of focus. But this is not the only possible interpretation. As example (6) demonstrates, the conjoint form is even used in cases where the context determines that the verb, and not the postverbal material, provides the focal information.

3.2 The disjoint form and predicate-centered focus

The pragmatic interpretation of focus on the lexical meaning of the verb or some sentential operator (cf. the notion of predicate-centered focus in Güldemann 2009[14]) can be expressed by means of the disjoint form, as in (7a). This focus reading can even be strengthened by adding the focus marker -rà to the verb, as in example (7b). In fact, when eliciting focus on the lexical meaning of the verb, this was the form the language consultants preferred.

(7) a. pɔ́yá wá ǰi-r jénémˋ, àmá à nyù-r-wá jénémˋ.
    woman NEG eat-PFV well but 1SM drink-PFV-DJ well

 b. pɔ́yá wá ǰi-r jénémˋ, àmá à nyù-r-wá-rá jénémˋ.
    woman NEG eat-PFV well but 1SM drink-PFV-DJ-FOC well
    'The woman did not eat well, but she DRANK well.'

The pragmatic differences between the forms in (6), (7a) and (7b) are non-categorical and speaker-dependent, but the form with the focus marker indicates most clearly that the verb, and not the adverb, is in focus. So one could argue that the disjoint form alone allows only for a weaker focus interpretation, whereas the disjoint form plus focus marker represents a strong focus reading. Nevertheless, both structures can be found in contrastive as well as non-contrastive environments.[15]

The disjoint form is often used in cases of contrast. The negation of the first conjunct in (8) contrasts with the positive value of the second conjunct. This can be expressed with the conjoint form as in (8a), but the assertion and contrast can be intensified by the use of the disjoint form, as in (8b). The disjoint form thus excludes all doubts and the focus lies clearly on the verbal meaning. Here again, the assertion could be strengthened by using the focus marker after the disjoint verb.

(8) a. béyá wá sáŋ-ɔ́rɔ́ jénémˋ àmá kà wɔ́m-ɔ́r jénémˋ.
    child NEG dance-PFV well but 12SM hear-PFV well

 b. béyá wá sáŋ-ɔ́rɔ́ jénémˋ àmá kà wɔ́m-ɔ́r-wá jénémˋ.
    child NEG dance-PFV well but 12SM hear-PFV-DJ well
    'The child did not dance well, but s/he LISTENed well.'

---

14 The term "predicate-centered focus" was coined by Güldemann 2009. It subsumes different kinds of non-nominal foci, such as state-of-affairs focus (=verb focus) and focus on sentential operators (truth value focus, TAM focus).
15 There is no intonational cue observed so far for marking contrastiveness. The intonational characteristics of the constructions are a matter of future research.

The examples in (9) shows that the expression of predicate-centered focus is not a sufficient condition to trigger the use of the disjoint verb form. (9a) represents a polar question concerning the event which the woman has achieved with the water. The question is negated in the answers (9b, c), and at the same time corrected by stating that the woman did some other action concerning the water. Both answers can optionally end in the focus marker -rà. Neither in the question (9a) nor in the first answer (9b) can the disjoint form of the verb be used, because it is followed by the object as core constituent in nominal and pronominal form respectively. In (9c), which is also a felicitous reply to the question, the object as presupposed material is not overtly expressed and, accordingly, we find the disjoint form, directly indicating that the verb itself is in focus.

(9)   a. pɔ́yá   kpír-íí   nyâm ɔ̀ɔ́?
           woman pour_away-PFV water Q
           'Did the woman pour the water?'

      b. àá↓wó, à   nyù-r   mə̀   (-rà).
           no   1SM drink-PFV 3OM FOC
           'No, she DRANK it.'

      c. àá↓wó, à   nyù-r-wá (-rà).
           no   1SM drink-PFV-DJ FOC
           'No, she DRANK (it).'

Stative verbs also show the conjoint/disjoint dichotomy. In example (10) the verb occurs in its disjoint form, that is verb stem plus suffix -rá. The first-choice pragmatic interpretation, namely that the verb is in focus, is confirmed by the context.

(10) àáwó, kà   fùŋɔ́-rá.
       no,   12SM be_small.PFV-DJ
       {The child is tall.} 'No, s/he IS SMALL.'

All examples show focus on the lexical meaning of the verb signalled by use of the disjoint form. In some languages such as Bemba (Sharman 1956: 40, quoted in Hyman and Watters 1984: 266; cf. also Güldemann 2003: 339), the disjoint verb form also expresses truth value focus and focus on tense and aspect operators. This is not necessarily the case in Yom (Fiedler 2006: 115–117). Both of these focus types are mainly expressed by adding the focus marker -rà to the verb itself or to the verb phrase, as in (11) and (12a) indicating truth value focus, but the disjoint form alone can also fulfil this function, as in (12b).

(11) tà   yêl-↓lá-ʊ́-rá   ↓lée
     1PL.SM   see.PFV-DJ-LNK-FOC   like_this
     'We have really seen (something) here!' (Beacham 1991: 93)[16]

(12) a. àá↓wó, mà   séɣ-ər-wá-rà
        no,   1SG.SM wash-PFV-DJ-FOC
        {You haven't washed the clothes?} 'No, I HAVE.'

     b. àá↓wó, mà   séɣ-ər-wá
        no,   1SG.SM wash-PFV-DJ
        {You haven't washed the clothes?} 'No, I HAVE.'

To sum up, the examples presented here have revealed that the disjoint verb form in Yom triggers a state-of-affairs focus interpretation. In all cases where the disjoint form is used, the verb receives a focal interpretation, but the disjoint form does not have to occur for this to be the case, that is, the disjoint form does not appear in all verb focus environments where one would expect it to occur. Furthermore, other kinds of predicate-centered focus are only rarely, if at all, expressed by means of the disjoint verb alone. Thus, there is no one-to-one relation between the verb form used in a clause and the information-structural interpretation of it.

3.3 The background form in ex-situ focus constructions

In addition to the conjoint/disjoint forms, there is a third form that occurs in specific background and narrative environments. From a pragmatic point of view, it is not clear what joins these two conflicting contexts as the one clearly belongs to the background (in the background clause of *ex-situ* term focus constructions), and the other to the foregrounding of a narrative. A similar distribution is known from other West African languages (Hausa, Fula, and others; cf. Bearth 1993; Frajzyngier 2004; Fiedler and Schwarz 2005). Schwarz and Fiedler (2007: 280f.) tried to resolve this problem for some Gur and Kwa languages by hypothesizing that *ex-situ* focus constructions contain narrative clauses. Frajzyngier (2004) and Bearth (1993) explain this functional merge by assuming that both clause types are pragmatically dependent. The situation in Yom becomes further complicated as the suffix indicating the background form is identical to the disjoint form for class 2 verbs in the perfective, namely high-toned suffix -*rá*.

---

16 Beacham (1991) describes the context for this utterance as follows: "This expression is commonly used in connection with some unusual or special situation, perhaps something alarming or unpleasant, something that has taught them something." (1991: 97)

The following two examples are taken from a story about a blackman's and a whiteman's child who went out to play together. In the first clause (13a), the black child sees a yam hill, which is not mentioned in the clause, as it was already described in the sentence right before this one, hence the verb 'to see' gets the background particle. The sentence in (13b) represents an *ex-situ* focus construction with the same verb which again gets the same background marking because nothing follows.

(13) a. Lèè nɔ́r-sɔ́wrá ↓béyà yèl-lá, kà kpétɔ́ ká céér,
CNJ person-black child see.PFV-BG, CNJ stay.PFV CNJ regard.IPFV
kà wá wɔ̀r̃ ŋʊ̀ nyʊ̀ŋ.
CNJ NEG say.PFV 3OM IDEF
'Then Black-man's child saw (it), and kept on looking (at it), (but) he didn't say anything.'

b. Lèè sɔ́wrá ↓béyà ká Má-ʊ́-rá má yèl-lá, má-ʊ́ sè-rá.
CNJ black child that 1SG.SM-LNK-FOC 1SG.SM see.PFV-BG, 1SG.SM-LNK have.PFV-BG
'Then Black's child said, "It's I who saw (it), it's I who own (it).'" (Beacham 1991: 133)

As can be inferred from the overview on forms in Section 2, the verb *yèllá* in (13) is identical to the disjoint form, as shown in (11). This gives rise to the question why one and the same form may occur once in an environment with focal scope on the verb phrase, and once in narrative contexts and in the background clause of the *ex-situ* term focus construction. As the following examples show this is just a coincidence within this verb class. With verbs of class 1 and stative verbs, the forms are clearly distinct, as seen in (14).

(14) a. pɔ́yá-rá ↓á nyú-l-↓lá. background
woman-FOC 1SM drink-PFV-BG
{Who did drink the water?} 'The WOMAN drank (it).'

b. nyâm-nà à nyù-l-lá. background
water-FOC 1SM drink-PFV-BG
{What did the woman drink?} 'She drank WATER.'

c. à nyù-r-wá. disjoint
1SM drink-PFV-DJ
{What did the woman do in the bar?} 'She DRANK.'

The examples in (14a, b) are best analyzed as clefts. As in subject relative clauses (cf. example (27) below), (14a) shows that a change of tone occurs in subject clefts: the subject pronoun gets a high tone instead of a low tone, and the verb will have its basic tone pattern and not the tone it should have according to the aspectual value and person (Fiedler 2012: 559).

The following example illustrates the functional split between the different suffixes for a stative verb: in (15a), the verb 'want' provides the background for the focused argument, whereas in (15b) the argument of 'want' represents the clause-external topic in clause-initial position, and the verb is in the disjoint form. With this example, one could even argue that the disjoint form expresses an intensification of the verb semantic or something similar to truth value focus ('I love it so much' or 'I really love it!', cf. Jacob 2014).

(15) a. nyá-tārām-nà   mà   nɔ́-rá   background
       water-warm-FOC 1SG.SM want-BG
       {Do you want hot or cold water?} 'I want HOT WATER.'

    b. kà   àmìnàòŋ   jī-ʊ́,   mà   nɔ́-wá.   disjoint
       CNJ   banana   eat-VN   1SG.SM love-DJ
       {Do you like to eat bananas?} 'Eating bananas, I like (it) very much.'

    c. bám-pɔ́   ↓yēɛ̄?   mà   wá   ↓nɔ̄   bɔ̀.   conjoint
       swim-VN[17] EXCL, 1SG.SM NEG   want   14OM
       {Do you like to go swimming?} 'Swimming? I hate it.'

What becomes clear from these examples is that the morphological shape of the disjoint and the background suffixes is in most cases unambiguously discriminated; only in one case are the two forms identical. Given the fact that the form of the disjoint suffix for class 2 verbs in the perfective is an exception in the overall paradigm, one could argue that there was in former times a clear functional split between the marking of the background and the disjoint form: *-wá* was used as disjoint suffix, and *-rá* only as background marking element. For some unknown reason, maybe phonology, the function of *-rá* was then extended to the marking of the disjoint form for class 2 verbs. Another hypothesis would be that *-rá* represents the contracted form of the perfective marker *-r+-wa* where the glide was dropped.

---

[17] Class 1 verbs form their verbal nouns by suffixing the noun class marker for class 14 (examples 15 b and c). There is a phonological rule according to which verbs ending in a front vowel, alveolar flap or velar fricative get suffix *-ʊ* (15b), whereas all others take *-pə* (15c) (Fiedler 2012: 552).

4 Clause structure and the inflectional paradigms

4.1 The condition of clause-finality

The conjoint/disjoint alternation can be best observed in canonical affirmative main clauses with transitive verbs, as it is cancelled in negative and subordinate clauses. The conjoint form of the verb is either used when a direct object (16a), a locative adjunct (16b), a modal adverb like 'well' (16c), or a subordinate clause (16d) follows the verb. If nothing comes after the verb, as in (16e), the disjoint form has to be employed; the conjoint form instead would render this clause ungrammatical.

(16) a. à nyù-r nyâm. PFV/conjoint
 1SM drink-PFV water
 'He drank water.'

 b. à nyù-r dà-déyŏ.
 1SM drink-PFV wood-hut
 'He drank in a bar.'

 c. à nyù-r jénɛ́m̀.
 1SM drink-PFV well
 'He drank well.'

 d. à nyù-r bɔ́n dáná.
 1SM drink-PFV before 2SG:come_here.PFV
 'He drank before you arrived.'

 e. à nyù-r-wá. PFV/disjoint
 1SM drink-PFV-DJ
 'He drank.'

With a verb of motion in the imperfective aspect, which does not necessarily need a directional complement, the same distribution can be observed. When a locative adjunct is present, the conjoint form is used, as in (17a), whereas this form is excluded in clauses consisting only of subject and verb, as in (17b).

(17) a. à dé lòkòtórònŏ ɔ̀ɔ. IPVF/ conjoint
 1SM go.IPFV hospital Q
 'Does he go to the hospital?'

 b. à dé-wá. IPFV / disjoint
 1SM go.IPFV-DJ
 'He goes.' (lit.: He does go.) (Beacham 1991: 55)

Verbs of quality, which are normally intransitive, are subject to the same syntactic constraints (18).

(18) a. bɛ́yá wá fùŋɔ́, kà cèkɔ́-rá   stative / conjoint
       child NEG be_small.PFV, 12SM be_big.PFV-DJ
       'The child is not small, but big.' (lit. '..., it is big.')

    b. bɛ́yá fùŋɔ́-rá.   stative / disjoint
       child be_small.PFV-DJ
       'The child is small.'

To sum up, the division of the conjoint and disjoint verb forms has, as in Bantu languages, a syntactic basis in canonical affirmative main clauses. In all instances of the verb occupying clause-final position in the main clause, the disjoint form has to be used, whereas in all other instances the conjoint form appears. This distribution of the two verb forms can be seen as a general rule; some restrictions and exceptions for the use of the disjoint form will be presented in the following.

As was already pointed out by different authors for Bantu languages (Creissels and Robert 1998; Van der Wal, this volume), the disjoint form can also be exploited in contexts where some material comes after the verb, even though this happens rather rarely. This is also the case in Yom, as is shown by the next set of examples: (19a) demonstrates this with an adverb following the disjoint form and (19b) with a postpositional phrase; in (19c), which is an alternative to (16d), a subordinate clause and in (19d) an emphatic particle indicating a question follows the verb in its disjoint form.[18] With a polar question particle, the disjoint verb could be used as well (cf. example (28a) below). Furthermore, what joins the first three of the examples is that adverbial phrase and subordinate clause are separated from the verb by a pause, thus treated not as belonging to the core of the clause and giving the impression of an afterthought that was originally not planned to be added to the clause.

(19) a. àmá à nyù-r-wà jɛ́nɛ́m̀.
       but 1SM drink-PFV-DJ well
       {The woman did not eat well,} '... but she drank well.'

    b. ... àmá kà wɔ́m-ɔ́r̀-wá dà-déyù̀.
       but 12SM hear-PFV-DJ wood-hut
       {The child did not dance}, '... but heard (music) in the bar.'

---

[18] The emphatic particle at the end of the question is given as such in Beacham (1969: 110) who translates it as 'what about that', i.e. as question tag marker. It is quite possible that it is a bimorphemic element consisting of the particle bɛ́ 'of course' and the question particle áá.

c. *à   nyù-r-wá   bón   dáná.*
1SM drink-PFV-DJ before 2SG.SM:come_here.PFV
'He drank before you arrived.'

d. *máa   à   dəkùn-ɔ́-rá   béè.*
surely 1SM limp-PFV-DJ EMPH.Q
'He limped, didn't he?'

In fact, as (20) reveals, the disjoint verb form cannot appear in a sequence verb-direct complement. This is because the verb and complement form the core of a clause, proven by the fact that nothing can be inserted between the two, as indicated in (21). Thus, the nature of the relation of verb and following element (argument vs. non-argument) determines whether the verb can occur in non-final position in the disjoint form.

(20) *pɔ́yá   wá   jí-r   múrîi,   àmá   à   nyú-r/*nyù-r-wá   nyâm.*
woman NEG eat-PFV rice but 1SM drink-PFV / drink-PFV-DJ water
'The woman did not eat rice, but drank water.'

(21) *à   nyú-r   nyâm   yáyʊ̀.*   **à nyú-r̀ yáyʊ̀ nyâm̀.*
1SM drink-PFV water quickly
'She drank the water quickly.'

(22) demonstrates that in the potential mood the conjoint/disjoint alternation does not operate. Whether the verb is used transitively or intransitively, the same verb form shows up, without any additional suffix to mark the clause-final position of the verb.

(22) a. *à   nyú   nyâm.*
1SM drink.POT water
'He shall drink water.'

b. *à   nyú.*
1SM drink.POT
'He shall drink.'

c. **à   nyú-**wá**.*
1SM drink.POT-DJ

Even though the verb in potential mood does not illustrate the conjoint/disjoint alternation, there was one example in my data showing this pattern, as in (23).

(23) pɔ́ɣá   kàà   jī   jénɛ́m̀, àmá à nà nyú-wá jénɛ́m̀.
      woman NEG.POT eat.POT well   but 1SM FUT drink.POT-DJ well
      'The woman won't eat well, but she will DRINK well.'

The suffix added to the verb in potential mood in the second conjunct of the sentence can neither be interpreted as background form nor as focus marker, thus it can only be understood as signalling the disjoint form, and by this expressing that the state-of-affairs is in focus.

The condition of clause-finality is a common denominator of both the disjoint verb form and the background verb form whereas the conjoint form is excluded from that position. Furthermore, the background form is only allowed in clause-final position. This is shown in (24), and in (25), a narrative clause disposing a verb-complement phrase, a restriction that cannot be stated for the disjoint form.

(24) a. àá↓wó, Nyɔ́ɔ́-ʊ́-rá   à   dá-r   kà.
        no   PN-LNK-FOC 1SM buy-PFV 12OM
        {Did Bona buy a bicycle?} 'No, Nyoo bought it.'

     b. àá↓wó, Nyɔ́ɔ́ sēnā-rā   à   dá-l-lá.
        no   PN   only-FOC 1SM buy-PFV-BG
        {Did Bona and Nyoo buy a motorcycle?} 'No, only Nyoo bought one.'

(25) Lèè   né   cə̀r   pə́rʏʊ̀ kà   tə́míí   lí-rá-ŋà.
     CNJ   mother receive.PFV basket CNJ send_away.SER two-AG-12OM
     'Then the mother gave the basket to the second one and sent him off.'

The fact that the disjoint form can occur in SOME non-final environments in main clauses indicates that it is sensitive to the nature of the relation between verb and following element. When the latter belongs to the core of the predication, the disjoint is not allowed, but if it is not a core argument, the disjoint form has to occur.

4.2 The clause-type constraint

As already mentioned, the conjoint verb form has the least restrictions concerning its occurrence, whereas the disjoint form is excluded from contexts such as negative clauses, relative, conditional and other subordinate clauses, as well as potential mood. All these clause types are characterized by weak or no assertion (cf. Güldemann 2003: 331). The background form is totally restricted to narrative clauses and *ex-situ* term focus constructions and will not be considered here. I illustrate these facts in this section.

To begin, (26) shows the influence of polarity on the use of the disjoint form. Whereas in the second part of the sentence the disjoint form applies, in accordance with its main-clause-final position, it is not allowed in the first part because of the presence of the negation marker.

(26) nə́rá   wá   fùŋə́/ *fùŋə́-rá   àmá   bɛ́ɣá fùŋə́-rá.
      man   NEG   be_small.PFV / be_small.PFV-DJ   but   child be_small.PFV-DJ
      'The man is not small, but the child is small.'

The subject relative clause construction in (27a, b) serves as an example for the unacceptability of the disjoint form in a subordinate clause. The relative clause starts with an optional relative pronoun, followed by a resumptive pronoun co-referent to the subject, and ends obligatorily with a subordinating particle. The tonal structure of pronoun and verb changes to all high in subject relative clauses. If there is no overt object, the conjoint form has nevertheless to be used, as can be seen from the ungrammaticality of (27c). This behaviour in relative clauses cannot be explained solely by the fact that the verb is not in total clause-final position, as the subordinating particle is following. In other contexts, such as polar questions or exclamatives, a question marker or exclamative particle follows the verb and it may nevertheless occur in the disjoint form, as in (28).

(27) a. mà   yér   pɔ́ɣá   [(dé-ʊ́)   á   nyú-r   ↓nyám̀   nèɛ̀].
          1SG.SM see.PFV   woman   REL-1   1SM.REL   drink-PFV water   SUB
          'I saw the woman who drank water.'

      b. mà   yér   pɔ́ɣá   [(dé-ʊ́)   á   nyú-r   nèɛ̀].
          1SG.SM see.PFV   woman   REL-1   1SM.REL   drink-PFV   SUB
          'I saw the woman who drank.'

      c. *mà   yér   pɔ́ɣá   [(dé-ʊ́)   á   nyú-r-wá   nèɛ̀].
          1SG.SM see.PFV   woman   REL-1   1SM.REL   drink-PFV-DJ   SUB
          'I saw the woman who drank.'

(28) a. wə́m-ə́r-wá-áa?
          2SG.hear-PFV-DJ-Q
          'Did you hear it?' (Beacham 1991: 50)

      b. bà   nɔ̀-wá   lá tórà.
          3PL.SM want-DJ also
          'They want (it), also.' (Beacham 1991: 50)

Whereas the unacceptability of the disjoint form in relative clauses is absolutely strict, other subordinate clauses allow exceptions to that rule, as exemplified with conditional clauses in (29).

(29) a. {in the context of a contrast: the woman is ill and has to drink a lot but she refuses all the time – therefore, if she has drunk unexpectedly, the speaker wishes to be informed}

kà	pɔ́γá	nyú-r-wá,	bɔ́rɔ́-má	má.	conditional, positive
if	woman	drink-PFV-DJ	say-IMP	1SG.OM	

'If the woman HAS DRUNK, tell me.'

b.
kà	pɔ́γá	wá	nyú-r-wá,	bɔ́rɔ́-má	má.	conditional, negative
if	woman	NEG	drink-PFV-DJ	say-IMP	1SG.OM	

'If the woman has NOT drunk, tell me.'

but: c.
kà	à	dé-r, ...
if	1SM	go-PFV

'If he goes, ...' (Beacham 1991: 78)

Güldemann (1996: 180–187) discussed the occurrence of "predication focus" verb forms in certain kinds of subordinate clauses, such as concessive and conditional clauses, and explains this phenomenon with syntactic and functional properties of these clauses. First, he assumes that postponed dependent clauses rather do not constitute background information, following the iconic principle "old information first, focal information late in a clause", thus the possibility of predicate-centered (disjoint) verb forms in postponed clauses. Second, the distribution of information-salience in a clause-linkage construction is important. Whereas a prototypical foreground/background constellation shows an uneven distribution of salience between both parts, this asymmetry might be less severe in some clause-linkage types, thereby giving the subordinate clause more assertive value. Third, there is a relation between clause-linkage and the hierarchy in a text (Güldemann 1996: 328–329). The first property might be responsible for the non-neutralization of the conjoint/disjoint dichotomy in complement clauses, as these always follow the main clause verb. For the conditional clauses in (29a and b), which are preposed, the reason for the occurrence of the disjoint form might lie in the fact that there is no obvious asymmetry in the information value of both parts of the sentence. The construction in (29a) serves to focus on the action of drinking – in case the woman will unexpectedly drink, that is in contrast to the doubtful negative assumption, the speaker wishes to be informed. In general, when a doubt on the action to perform is presupposed, the disjoint form serves to express insistence of the counter-expectation. Even when the conditional is negated, the disjoint form is achievable, as in (29b) (but recall example (26), where it was not grammatical in a negated main clause).

Complement clauses show exactly the same distribution of the three inflectional verb forms as do main affirmative clauses:

(30) a. à wə̀rə́ ká pɔ́yá nyù-r nyám̀. conjoint
 1SM say.PFV that woman drink-PFV water
 'He said that the woman drunk WATER.'

b. à wə̀rə́ ká pɔ́yá nyù-r-wá. disjoint
 1SM say.PFV that woman drink-PFV-DJ
 'He said that the woman DRUNK.'

c. à wə̀rə́ ká yàyʊ̀-yàyʊ̀-rá pɔ́yá nyù-l-lá. background
 1SM say.PFV that RED-greedily-FOC woman drink-PFV-BG
 'He said that the woman drunk GREEDILY.'

In summary, the disjoint form is in general excluded from subordinate, negated, and potential mood clauses. Nevertheless, the examples have shown that it can still occur in specific, pragmatically determined environments, that is when the state-of-affairs is in focus, even if it does not stand in clause-final position in main clauses or if it occurs in subordinate clauses. This contradicts both the condition of clause-finality and the general restriction of disjoint forms to indicative main affirmative clauses.

5 Conjoint/disjoint in and outside Yom

5.1 The distribution of the conjoint/disjoint paradigms in Yom

Two of the three inflectional verb paradigms in Yom discussed above can be treated in analogy to Bantu as conjoint and disjoint verb forms. They behave alike with respect to nearly all criteria established for the respective Bantu verb forms (cf. the definition by Van der Wal, this volume). In particular, the Yom verb paradigms can be characterized by the following distributional properties: The occurrence of the conjoint form is largely syntactically conditioned, that is, it is only found in cases where some linguistic material follows the verb in main affirmative clauses; in other clause types, the conjoint/disjoint dichotomy is cancelled such that only the conjoint paradigm is found there. The disjoint form occurs primarily in clause-final position in affirmative main clauses and is mainly excluded from negative and subordinate clauses as well as from potential mood (but see the exceptions mentioned in Sections 4.1. and 4.2.). Both paradigms cannot occur with *ex-situ* term focus constructions and narrative clauses, where the third verb form, i.e. the background form, must apply, when the verb is clause-final. The distribution of the three forms is presented in Table 3.

Table 3: Distribution of the three inflected verb forms for transitive verbs.

Clause type	Position of verb	Conjoint	Disjoint -wá	Background -rá
Canonical transitive clause (non-subject focus, VP focus)	non-final	x	–	–
Term focus, ex-situ	final	–	–	x
	non-final	x	–	–
Narrative clause (lὲὲ)	final	–	–	x
	non-final	x	–	–
SoA focus	final	–	x	–
	non-final	x	(x)	–
Counter-expectation of action	final	–	x	–
	non-final	X	(x)	–
Negative clauses	final	x	–	–
	non-final	x	–	–
Subordinate clauses	final	x	(x)	–
	non-final	x	–	–

Beyond this clear picture of the distributional properties of the three verb forms, there are some peculiarities which can be accounted for by the following reasons:

i. It has been shown that the disjoint form can appear even though there is other linguistic material following the verb, as is also known from Bantu languages. This material may consist of question or emphatic particles, subordinate clauses, adverbs and postpositional phrases, but never of nominal complements. Adverbial and subordinate clauses following the verb seem to be set off from the rest of the clause by a pause, thus not belonging to the core of the clause. As far as particles are concerned, they have scope over the whole clause and therefore do not belong to the verb phrase, either. Consequently it is reasonable to conclude that the condition of clause-finality in terms of linearity is not a sufficient one. Whereas Elders (2005) argued in favour of an explanation in terms of syntactic linearity, implying that every clause-final position is really final, Buell (2006) discusses the condition of finality in terms of constituency. He concludes for Zulu that the disjoint form is found in all cases where the verb has final position in the surface constituencies which do not match directly to the linear order of the elements in the clause. In Yom, clause-finality is related to the question whether the postverbal element belongs to the core of the clause.

ii. Apart from the syntactic constraints mentioned, the use of one or the other form is strongly influenced by pragmatic considerations. In most cases, the conjoint form encodes that postverbal material is in focus. Nevertheless, some examples where the lexical meaning of the verb is pragmatically in focus and the conjoint form is still used because an adverb was following the verb, contradict this generalization. Depending on the speaker, the information-structural constraint can be served by using the disjoint form which unambiguously signals that the verb is in focus. Both strategies lead to a conflict between information-structural and syntactic condition: in order to recognize the syntactic constraints, the conjoint form has to be employed, whereas the information structure of the utterance demands the disjoint form.

Summing up, the use of all three forms is primarily syntactically conditioned: The conjoint form is used when something follows the verb in main clauses; in other clause types, the restriction of clause-finality is cancelled. In contrast, the background as well as the disjoint form have to occur at the end of the core of the clause, but are then restricted to only some clause types. Any postverbal material belonging to the core of the clause (i.e. the direct complement of the verb, some adverbial phrases, and complement clauses) is interpreted as focal, hence the postverbal position can be analyzed as default focus position. Any postverbal material not belonging to the core of the clause (i.e. some adverbial phrases, subordinate clauses) is non-focal, hence focus lies on the state-of-affairs expressed by the verb. Whether the transition between postverbal core and non-core constituents can be analyzed solely on pragmatic grounds, in accommodating these observations, is a matter of future research.

5.2 Conjoint/disjoint in a wider African perspective

The alternation of two distinct inflectional verb forms is not restricted to Bantu languages, as was shown by data from Yom, a Gur language. This language disposes of three distinct inflectional verb forms, marked by special suffixes, in order to answer information-structural and syntactic requirements.

This differentiation in the verb system – which shows an information-structural basis – can also be found in other languages of the Niger-Congo family (cf. for an overview Hyman and Watters 1984, Bearth 1993). Elders (2005) describes a similar situation for Doyayo, an Adamawa language, which has a tripartite verb paradigm. He claims that "With respect to Doyayo, several grammatical conditions are suggestive of a conjoint-disjoint distinction in the verb system: verb forms sensitive to their position in the clause/sentence; the presence vs. the absence of a constituent following the verb; the role of information structure: focus on the verb vs. focus elsewhere, or no focus; its marking by an inflectional verb suffix, accompanied by tonal alternations." (Elders 2005: 19). For the Oti-Volta subgroup of Gur, Manessy (1963, 1975) has shown that most of the languages of this group "disposent d'une particule affirmative [...], de sens accompli, qui apparaît exclusivement en fin d'énoncé après une base verbale [...] et qui est incompatible avec la négation." ['... dispose of affirmative particles [...] with perfective meaning which occur exclusively at the end of a clause after a verbal stem [...] and which are incompatible with negation.'] (1975: 146). He further explains for one of the languages treated, Moore, that this particle seems to have a "valeur d'insistance" (1975: 147). Schwarz (2010) has analyzed the syntactic distribution and pragmatic function of this and another particle more deeply for the four Oti-Volta languages Buli, Konni, Dagbani and Gurene. In these languages, the particles in question only occur in clause-final position in affirmative main clauses. From a pragmatic point of view they are used for the expression of predicate-centered focus. Outside Bantu, Gur and Adamawa, a more fine-grained differentiation of the verb system based on information-structural grounds is found in Atlantic languages, such as Wolof (cf. Robert 2000) and Fula (Apel 2012), to cite only some.

But this feature is not restricted to Niger-Congo languages, as was already discussed for groups of West African languages by Bearth (1993) and Frajzyngier (2004). Different Chadic languages, among them Hausa, as well as some Nilo-Saharan languages as Kanuri (Hutchison 1981) illustrate a similar kind of a tense/ aspect system based on information-structural grounds.

These remarks support the assumption of Creissels and Robert (1998) that such a relation between verbal inflection and information structure could be more widespread in Africa than available documentations suggest (1998: 175). It would therefore be highly advantageous in the future to compare the findings on the conjoint/disjoint dichotomy with the tense/aspect systems in other African languages.

Abbreviations

Arabic numerals indicate a noun class, or a person category when immediately followed by a gloss for gender and/or number.

AG	agentive suffix	IDEF	indefinite
BG	background marker	IMP	imperative
CJ	conjoint	IPFV	imperfective
CNJ	conjunction	LNK	linking morpheme
DJ	disjoint	NEG	negation marker
EMPH	emphatic particle	Q	question marker
EXCL	exclamative	OM	object marker
FOC	focus marker	PFV	perfective
FUT	future	PL	plural

PN	proper name	SG	singular
POT	potential	SM	subject marker
RED	reduplication	SUB	subordinating particle
REL	relative pronoun	VN	verbal noun
SER	serial verb		

References

Apel, Viktoria. 2012. Focalization in Fulfulde of Fuuta Jaloo (Guinea). Paper presented to the Workshop 'Mise en relief et mise en retrait: Le marquage morphologique de la hiérarchie discursive' (Fédération typologie et universaux linguistiques), Paris: CNRS, 19–20 October 2012.

Beacham, Charles Gordon. 1969. *The phonology and morphology of Yom*. Hartford Seminary Foundation. Ann Arbor, MI: University Microfilms, Inc.

Beacham, Charles Gordon. 1991. *Learning Yom: A voltaic language of the Atacora Province*. Charlotte, NC: SIM USA.

Bearth, Thomas. 1993. Satztyp und Situation in einigen Sprachen Westafrikas. In Wilhelm J. Möhlig, Siegmund Brauner & Hermann Jungraithmayr (eds.), *Beiträge zur afrikanischen Sprach- und Literaturwissenschaft*, 91–104. Köln: Köppe.

Buell, Leston. 2006. The Zulu conjoint/disjoint verb alternation: focus or constituency? *ZAS Papers in Linguistics* 43. 9–30.

Creissels, Denis. 1996. Conjunctive and disjunctive verb forms in Setswana. *South African Journal of African Languages* 16. 109–115.

Creissels, Denis & Stéphane Robert. 1998. Morphologie verbale et organisation discursive de l'énoncé: l'example du tswana et du wolof. *Faits de Langues*. 161–178.

Doke, Clement. 1992 [1927]. *Textbook of Zulu grammar*. Windhoek: Longman.

Elders, Stefan. 2005. Conjoint and disjoint in Doyayo: Bantu-like verb forms in an Adamawa language. Paper presented at the conference 'Focus in African Languages', Berlin: ZAS, 6–8 October 2005 (Ms.).

Fiedler, Ines. 2006. Focus expressions in Yom. *Gur Papers/Cahiers Voltaïques* 7. 112–121.

Fiedler, Ines. 2012. Yom. In Gudrun Miehe, Brigitte Reineke & Kerstin Winkelmann (eds.), *Noun class systems in Gur languages*. Vol. 2: Oti-Volta Languages, 533–565. Köln: Köppe.

Fiedler, Ines & Anne Schwarz. 2005. Out-of-focus encoding in Gur and Kwa. In Shinichiro Ishihara, Michaela Schmitz & Anne Schwarz (eds.), *Interdisciplinary studies on information structure* 3, 111–142. Potsdam: Universitätsverlag.

Fiedler, Ines, Katharina Hartmann, Brigitte Reineke, Anne Schwarz & Malte Zimmermann. 2010. Subject focus in West African languages. In Malte Zimmermann & Caroline Féry (eds.), *Information structure. Theoretical, typological and experimental perspectives*, 234–257. Oxford: Oxford University Press.

Frajzyngier, Zygmunt. 2004. Tense and aspect as coding means for information structure: A potential areal feature. *Journal of West African Languages* 30. 53–67.

Güldemann, Tom. 1996. *Verbalmorphologie und Nebenprädikationen im Bantu*. Bochum: Universitätsverlag Dr. N. Brockmeyer.

Güldemann, Tom 2003. Present progressive vis-à-vis predication focus in Bantu. *Studies in Language* 27. 323–360.

Güldemann, Tom. 2009. Predicate-centered focus types: A sample-based typological study in African languages. Application for project B7 in the CRC 632 'Information structure'.
Hutchison, John P. 1981. *A reference grammar of the Kanuri language*. African Studies Program at the University of Wisconsin, Madison.
Hyman, Larry M. & John Watters. 1984. Auxiliary focus. *Studies in African Linguistics* 15. 233–273.
Jacob, Peggy. 2014. The expression of intensification and its relation to predicate-centered focus. Paper presented at the Workshop 'Information structure in Africa', Kyoto University, 3 October, 2014.
Lambrecht, Knud. 1994. *Information structure and sentence form. Topic, focus, and the mental representations of discourse referents*. Cambridge: Cambridge University Press.
Lewis, M. Paul, Gary F. Simons & Charles D. Fennig (eds.). 2014. Ethnologue: Languages of the World, Seventeenth edition. Dallas, Texas: SIL International. Online version: http://www.ethnologue.com.
Manessy, Gabriel. 1963. Les particules affirmatives postverbales dans le groupe voltaïque. *Bulletin de l'I.F.A.N.* 25 (B) (1–2). 106–124.
Manessy, Gabriel. 1975. *Les langues Oti-Volta*. (Langues et civilisation à tradition orale 15). Paris: SELAF.
Meeussen, Achille E. 1959. *Essai de grammaire Rundi*. Annalen Wetenschappen van de Mens, Linguistik 24. Tervuren: Koninklijk Museum van Belgisch-Kongo.
Miehe, Gudrun, Ulrich Kleinewillinghöfer, Manfred von Roncador & Kerstin Winkelmann. 2012. Overview of noun classes in Gur (II) (revised and enlarged version). In Gudrun Miehe, Brigitte Reineke & Kerstin Winkelmann (eds.), *Noun class systems in Gur languages*. Vol. 2: Oti-Volta Languages, 5–37. Köln: Köppe.
Prost, André. 1973. Les langues de l'Atakora V: Le yom, langue des yoowa dits Pila-Pila. *Bulletin de l'IFAN* 35. 323–413.
Robert, Stéphane. 2000. Le verbe wolof ou la grammaticalisation du focus. In Bernard Caron (ed.), *Topicalisation et focalisation dans les langues africaines*, 229–267. Louvain, Paris: Peeters.
Schwarz, Anne. 2010. Verb-and-predication focus markers in Gur. In Ines Fiedler & Anne Schwarz (eds.), *The Expression of information structure in African languages. A documentation of its diversity across Africa*, 287–314. Typological Studies in Language (TSL) 91. Amsterdam and Philadelphia: John Benjamins.
Schwarz, Anne & Ines Fiedler. 2007. Narrative focus strategies in Gur and Kwa. In Enoch O. Aboh, Katharina Hartmann & Malte Zimmermann (eds), *Focus strategies in African languages. The interaction of focus and grammar in Niger-Congo and Afroasiatic*, 267–286. Berlin and New York: Mouton de Gruyter.
Sharman, J. C. 1956. The tabulation of tenses in a Bantu language (Bemba: Northern Rhodesia). *Africa* 16: 29–46.
Van der Wal, Jenneke. this volume. What is the conjoint/disjoint alternation in Bantu languages? Parameters of variation.

Denis Creissels
8 The conjoint/disjoint distinction in the tonal morphology of Tswana

1 Introduction

Some of the tenses that constitute the inflection of Tswana verbs have a distinction between a conjoint (henceforth: CJ) and a disjoint (henceforth: DJ) form. In the tenses that have this distinction, the CJ form cannot be found in clause final position, and cannot be separated from the following phrase by a pause, whereas the DJ form does not have this limitation, but is not excluded from non-final contexts either, and when in clause-internal position, is not necessarily separated from the following word by a perceptible pause.

As regards the function of the CJ/DJ distinction, Tswana (a.k.a. Setswana – Bantu S31) is among the languages that do not have an IAV focus position,[1] and in which the choice between CJ and DJ forms is determined by the distinction between post-verbal phrases that enrich or make more precise the comment expressed by the verb, and post-verbal phrases that do not contribute to the comment and fulfill the discourse function of afterthought (or antitopic).

The aim of this paper is to provide a precise description of the morphological distinction between CJ and DJ verb forms in Tswana.

Functionally, the CJ/DJ distinction in Tswana is straightforward, in the sense that in the tenses that have this distinction, there is not the slightest variation in the way it is conditioned, or in its function. But the distinction exists in some tenses only, and there is no feature (either morphological or semantic) common to the tenses that have this distinction, and only to them.

Moreover, the functional homogeneity of this distinction across the tenses that have it sharply contrasts with its extreme morphological heterogeneity. In Tswana, the existence of a CJ/DJ distinction is obvious in one tense only, the present positive, in which the distinction is made apparent by the presence vs. absence of the DJ marker *a* /a/ immediately after the subject marker. In all the other tenses in which a functionally identical distinction must be recognized, it has no segmental manifestation, and is manifested only in tone. In one tense (the perfect positive), the distinction affects the whole tonal contour of the verb stem,

---

[1] In Tswana assertive clauses, the only possible focalizing strategy is the use of a cleft construction in which the focalized phrase is the complement of *ke* [kɩ́] 'it is', and the verb is in the relative form.

and is therefore uncontroversial, but in the others, its manifestations are limited to the last syllable of verb forms, which raises the problem of a possible relationship with the tonal processes affecting the syllables that immediately precede a pause. It is particularly puzzling that the tonal melodies that in some tenses characterize the DJ form may be very similar to those characterizing the CJ form in other tenses, and vice-versa.

The paper is organized as follows. Section 2 gives the inventory of the synthetic forms of Tswana verbs and describes their morphological structure. Section 3 puts forward a system of rules accounting for their tonal contours. Section 4 compares the tonal behavior of Tswana verb forms in contexts selecting CJ forms with that of the corresponding forms in contexts selecting DJ forms. Section 5 discusses the possible correspondences between the tonal patterns of CJ and DJ forms. Section 6 summarizes the main conclusions.

The analysis is based on the pronunciation of a native speaker of the Ngwaketse dialect. The available documentation on other varieties as well as my own field notes on the Ngwato and Kgatla varieties suggest that the variation observed across Tswana varieties with respect to the details of the H tone spreading processes does not affect the overall organization of the system and the classification of the tenses according to the tonal behavior of verb forms in CJ and DJ contexts. Moreover, (Letšeng 1995) describes a system of tonal marking of the CJ/DJ distinction in Southern Sotho differing only in minor details from that analyzed here.

2 The inflected forms of Tswana verbs: inventory and structure

The list of the synthetic tenses of Tswana verbs with their precise morphological identification is given in Appendix 2.

A Tswana verb form consists of a *root* (irreducible lexical element) together with an obligatory suffix (the *final vowel*, or simply *final*) and a variable number of other affixes whose presence depends on a variety of factors, each affix having its position in the string. The root may be immediately followed by derivative suffixes that modify its meaning without altering its valency. The *extended* root is the part of the verb form constituted by the root and such derivative suffixes. The *stem* is the part of the verb form constituted by the root, the final, and all the formatives occupying a position between the root and the final. The formatives that precede the root constitute the *prefixal string*, and those that follow the final are designated as *postfinals*.

Starting from the extended root as the zero point, the order in which the affixes appear can be described as a sequence of positions numbered from –4 (the leftmost possible position) to +5 (the rightmost possible position).

Position −4 is occupied in the indicative present negative and indicative perfect negative by the negation marker *ga* /χa/, otherwise it remains empty.

Position −3 remains empty in the imperative. In the infinitive, which shows both morphologically and syntactically a mixture of nominal and verbal properties, it is filled by the prefix of noun class 15. In all the other tenses, it is obligatorily filled by a subject marker (henceforth SM). Four partially different sets of SMs must be recognized, depending on the individual tenses – see Appendix 1.

Position −2 can be filled by the following affixes or affix sequences: *a* /a/ (DJ form of the indicative present positive), *a* /a/ (indicative perfect negative), *tlaa* /tɬaa/ (future positive), *tlaa se* /tɬaa-sɪ/ (future negative), *ka* /ká/ (potential positive),[2] *ka se* /ká-sɪ/ ~ /ka-sɪ/ (potential negative),[3] *sa* /sa/ (circumstantial present negative, circumstantial perfect negative, infinitive present negative, and infinitive perfect negative), *se* /sɪ/ (subjunctive negative and imperative negative), or *sa* /sá/ (infinitive potential).

Position −1 can be occupied by OMs (see Appendix 1) and by the reflexive marker (or midvoice marker) /íⁿ/.[4] Up to three successive affixes can be found in this position.

Position +1 can be filled by one or more affixes encoding operations on verb valency: causative /(i)s/ or /J/,[5] applicative /ɛl/, anticausative /ɛχ/, /al/, /afal/, /aχal/, /ɛsɛχ/, or /Jɛχ/, reciprocal /an/.

Position +2 can only be occupied by a perfect marker /(i)l/ or /J/, used only in the perfect positive (in negative forms, 'perfect' is encoded by formatives occupying Slot −2).

Position +3 can only be filled by the passive marker /(i)w/.

Position +4 is the only one that can be left empty in no circumstances. The affix filling this position, traditionally called 'final (vowel)', is a vowel with four possible values: a, ɪ, ɛ, and e ~ ɪ (with an alternation that can be accounted for by a dissimilation rule). The final contributes to the identification of the individual

---

[2] An optional toneless variant /ka/ of this formative must be posited in the circumstantial and relative forms of the potential in order to account for the free variation observed in the tonal realization of these tenses.
[3] This formative must be analyzed as underlyingly /ká-sɪ/ when it follows a toneless SM, but a variant /ka-sɪ/ must be posited in order to account for its tonal properties when it follows a H-toned SM.
[4] The notation /íⁿ/ means that this formative triggers modifications of the onset of the following syllable identical to those triggered by the syllabic nasal, although no nasal is present in its surface form.
[5] /J/ is an abstract morphological element that can be posited in order to account for consonant alternations analyzable as originating from a phonological process of palatalization.

tenses, but does not carry any syntactic or semantic information of its own, since with the exception of e ~ ɪ (found in the perfect positive only), each final is shared by a set of forms impossible to define straightforwardly as sharing a particular set of syntactic or semantic features.[6]

Position +5 can be filled by one of the following three 'postfinals': /ŋ́/ (toneless syllabic nasal followed by a floating H tone) marking the plural of the imperative, the relative marker /ŋ́/, and /ŋ́/, clitic form of the interrogative pronoun *eng* [ɪŋ́] 'what'.[7]

3 Underlying tonal representations and tonal processes

3.1 Introductory remarks

In Tswana, the tonal behavior of verb prefixes cannot be accounted for by means of phonological rules applying to underlying H tones without positing invisible underlying elements or special boundaries. The introduction of floating L tones in the underlying representation of some prefixes would be a possible solution, but there is strong evidence that the L tone must be analyzed as the default tone, and the introduction of L tones in underlying representations would result in missing some important insights. The solution explored in (Creissels et al. 1997) was the introduction of 'empty syllables' doing more or less the same job as floating L tones in other frameworks. However, the discussion I had with Irina Monich about the paper she presented at the 5th International Conference on Bantu Languages in 2013 (see now Monich 2014) eventually convinced me of the theoretical shortcomings of resorting to empty syllables. Hence, another solution is explored here: the introduction, at some points in the prefixal sequence, of a special boundary (represented as =) whose properties with respect to tone spreading processes depart from those of the standard morpheme boundary and are more similar (although not identical) to those of the boundary between words (represented as #). An advantage of this solution is the plausibility of the diachronic interpretation it suggests. Many authors have observed that, in Bantu

---

[6] A limited number of verbs (such as *itse* [ìtsɪ́] 'know') invariably show the final ɪ in all tenses, except in the perfect positive. This irregularity does not affect the tonal behavior of these verbs, which is perfectly regular.

[7] In addition to these unproblematic postfinals, we will see in Section 4.2 that a postfinal consisting of a floating H tone provides a simple explanation of the tonal behavior of the final syllable of some verb forms.

languages, the formatives traditionally analyzed as verb prefixes often show a morphophonological behavior suggesting that verb forms synchronically analyzable as single words may result from the relatively recent univerbation of analytic verb forms. Consequently, the idiosyncrasies in the behavior of the verbal prefixes of Tswana are best viewed as the reflex of tonal processes that were active at word boundaries before the univerbation processes that converted former auxiliaries into prefixes took place.[8]

The general idea (which is by no means original in the Bantu context, since it is nothing more than a variant of the well-known Obligatory Contour Principle) is that most of the apparent complexity of the tonal morphology of Tswana results from conditions on repair rules motivated by a constraint on non-adjacency of H tone domains. A H tone domain is defined as a sequence of H-toned syllables that behaves as a single unit for tonal processes. Whenever two H tone domains are in contact, the violation of the non-adjacency constraint must be eliminated, but the possible repair strategies are not equally available, depending on the grammatical nature of the boundary. Five different repair strategies must be distinguished: (a) contraction of the second H tone domain, (b) contraction of the first H tone domain, (c) toneless vowel insertion, (d) downstep insertion, and (e) fusion. Fusion is always the last resort strategy, contraction can only affect non-monosyllabic H tone domains, a downstep can only be inserted before a non-monosyllabic H tone domain, and toneless vowel insertion can only operate if the inserted vowel takes the penultimate position in the verb form, but in other respects, the repair strategies are variously available and variously ranked, depending on the grammatical nature of the boundary:[9]

- special morpheme boundary: contraction of the second H tone domain > contraction of the first H tone domain > toneless vowel insertion > fusion
- special word boundary: contraction of the first H tone domain > downstep insertion > fusion
- standard word boundary: downstep insertion > fusion

---

8 For example, in Creissels et al. (1997), an empty syllable is posited in the underlying representation of H-toned OMs in order to account for their tonal behavior. However, historically, it is not necessary to assume an originally disyllabic form of object markers, since it can be assumed that, like other prefixes, OMs were originally autonomous units whose affixal status is the outcome of a historical process of cliticization. Consequently, the special limit posited to account for their tonal behavior has a natural interpretation as the reflex of the interaction between the verb and the OM at an early stage of the cliticization process.

9 No repair strategy has to be considered at standard morpheme boundaries, since in the account proposed in this paper, the delimitation of H tone domains and the formulation of tone spreading rules preclude H tone domain adjacency at standard morpheme boundaries.

3.2 The distribution of the special morpheme boundary =

Correct prediction of the surface tonal melodies by means of the rules proposed in the rest of this section requires positing the special boundary = in the following contexts:
- immediately after the SM in the DJ form of the indicative perfect positive, in the sequential 1, in the subjunctive positive, and in the circumstantial present positive before lexically H-toned stems (but not in the other tenses);
- immediately after the potential marker /ká/;
- immediately after the continuative marker /sá/;
- immediately after the underlyingly toneless OMs;
- immediately before the variant /ka/ of the potential marker;
- immediately before the negative marker /sa/;
- immediately before the underlyingly H-toned OMs.

3.3 Lexical and post-lexical tone rules

The rules analyzed in this section account for the tonal structure of verbal words, but the output of these rules may be further modified by the following post-lexical processes:
- if the last syllable of a word belongs to a H tone domain, and if the following word begins with at least two syllables that do not belong to a H tone domain, the first syllable of the second word is 'annexed' by the preceding H tone domain;
- if two H tone domains are in contact at a word boundary and the second one is monosyllabic, they merge into a single H tone domain;[10]
- if two H tone domains are in contact at a word boundary and the second one comprises two syllables or more, a downstep is inserted between them;
- if the right boundary of a non-monosyllabic H tone domain coincides with a pause, the last syllable in this domain is assigned a L tone, whereas the penultimate syllable is lengthened, and realized with a falling tone.

---

[10] A consequence of these two postlexical tonal processes is that the distinction between words beginning with two toneless syllables and words beginning with a H-toned syllable followed by a toneless syllable is neutralized when such words follow another word ending with a H-toned syllable. In both cases, the first two syllables of the second word are realized with a H L contour.

3.4 The H tone as the marked tone, and the notion of H tone domain

The tonal alternations affecting Tswana verb forms are at first sight fairly complex, but their description is facilitated by positing an underlying H vs. Ø rather than H vs. L contrast, and by describing tonal processes in terms of interaction between H tone domains rather than between the tones of individual syllables. L tones are accounted for as default tones assigned to syllables that are not included in a H tone domain after the limits of H tone domains have been established by means of rules (or constraints) formulated in terms of expansion of H tone domains and repair strategies eliminating the violations of the non-adjacency constraint.

Underlying H tone domains are defined as word-internal sequences of underlyingly H-toned syllables not interrupted by boundaries other than the standard morpheme boundary.

In the underlying tonal representations, the association of H tones to the syllables that constitute the stem is determined by morphological rules (see Sections 3.5 and 3.6), and each of the formatives that constitute the prefixal string is introduced as either associated to a H tone, or toneless. The first step in the derivation leading to the surface tonal contour is the merging of sequences of H-toned syllables not interrupted by special boundaries or word boundaries into H tone domains.

For example, the underlying structures of *ke ba bona* [kì-bá-bɔ́n-á] 'I see them' and *ke ka bona* [kì-ká-bɔ̀ná] 'I can see' equally include a H tone associated to the first syllable of the stem and a H tone associated to the preceding formative. However, in the case of *ke ka bona* [kì-ká-bɔ̀ná], the presence of the special boundary = after the potential marker prevents them from merging into a single H domain, which explains why, after annexing the second syllable of the stem, the H domain generated by the H tone of the root contracts in order to satisfy the non-adjacency constraint: [11]

#kɩ=bá-bɔ́n-a# → #kɩ=(bá-bɔ́)n-a#   (H tone domain constitution)
              → #kɩ=(bá-bɔ́n-á)#   (H tone domain expansion)

#kɩ-ká=bɔ́n-a# → #kɩ-(ká)=(bɔ́)n-a#   (H tone domain constitution)
              → #kɩ-(ká)=(bɔ́n-á)#   (H tone domain expansion)
              → #kɩ-(ká)=bɔ(n-á)#   (H tone domain contraction)

---

[11] The parentheses in the underlying representations make apparent the limits of H tone domains.

3.5 The lexical tone of verbs

Tswana has two tonal types of verbal lexemes (toneless and H-toned), irrespective of their length, syllabic structure, and morphological complexity. The perfect pre-final and the finals show no correlation with particular types of tonal contours, and are therefore best analyzed as underlyingly toneless too.[12]

3.6 Templates accounting for the tonal contour of verb stems

Ignoring tonal alternations resulting from the interaction between a prefix and the stem, or between the stem and a postfinal, four possible tonal structures must be recognized for verb stems, two for stems including a toneless root, and two for stems including a H-toned root. These are analyzed as resulting from the interaction between the inherent tonality of the root and the presence vs. absence of a grammatical H tone. The grammatical H tone contributes to the morphological identity of individual tenses, but does not carry a specific meaning by itself, since the tenses marked by this H tone do not share any syntactic or semantic feature. Consequently, any solution positing the grammatical H tone as underlyingly attached to a particular formative (as in Creissels et al. 1997) leads to needless complications. What I propose here is that the tonal processes resulting in the surface contour of verb forms operate on representations in which the lexical H and the grammatical H are not represented separately, and verb stems are directly represented with an underlying tonal contour determined by a morphological rule. The following chart summarizes the output of this rule:

		−lexH	+lexH
−grH	1 syll.	o	ó
	2 syll.	o o	ó o
	3 syll.	o o o	ó o o
	4 or more syll.	o o o … o	ó o o … o
+grH	1 syll.	ó	ó
	2 syll.	o ó	ó ó
	3 syll.	o ó ó	ó ó ó
	4 or more syll.	o ó ó … ó	ó ó ó … ó

---

[12] The subjunctive positive is the only tense with a systematic neutralization of the distinction between H-toned roots and toneless roots that requires positing a special set of morphological rules stipulating that, in the subjunctive positive, if no OM (or reflexive marker) is present: (a) if

In the simplest cases, if the grammatical H tone is not present and no particular interaction with a prefix or a postfinal occurs, the tonal contour of the stem represented in this chart is only modified by the expansion of the H domain generated by the underlying stem-initial H. For example, in non-prepausal position, the DJ form of the infinitive present positive shows the following tone pattern:

Lexically toneless verbs:

χʊ̀-tɬà	*go tla* 'to come'
χʊ̀-lìmà	*go lema* 'to cultivate'
χʊ̀-tswɛ̀lɛ̀là	*go tswelela* 'to continue'
χʊ̀-dùmèdìsà	*go dumedisa* 'to greet'
χʊ̀-dùmèdìsànà	*go dumedisana* 'to greet each other'
χʊ̀-dùmèdìsètsànà	*go dumedisetsana* 'to transmit greetings for each other'

Lexically H-toned verbs:

χʊ̀-dʒá	*go ja* 'to eat'
χʊ̀-réká	*go reka* 'to buy'
χʊ̀-rékísá	*go rekisa* 'to sell'
χʊ̀-símʊ́lʊ́là	*go simolola* 'to begin'
χʊ̀-tɬʰókómʊ́lòχà	*go tlhokomologa* 'to neglect'
χʊ̀-símʊ́lʊ́lɛ̀lànà	*go simololelana* 'to begin for each other'

If the grammatical H tone is present, and if the tone of the final syllable is not modified by the interaction with a postfinal or with the following word, the surface tone of the stem coincides with that indicated in the chart above, as illustrated by the CJ form of the present negative:

Lexically toneless verbs

χà-kí-tɬí	*ga ke tle* 'I do not come'
χà-kí-bàlí	*ga ke bale* 'I do not read'
χà-kí-tswèlélí	*ga ke tswelele* 'I do not progress'
χà-kí-tɬʰàlóχáɲí	*ga ke tlhaloganye* 'I do not understand'
χà-ŕì-dùmédísáŕì	*ga re dumedisane* 'we do not greet each other'
χà-ŕì-dùmédísétsáŕì	*ga re dumedisetsane* 'we do not greet people for each other'

---

the stem is lexically H-toned, the lexical H tone is deleted; (b) if the stem comprises three syllables or more, a H tone is assigned to the final; (c) the SM is followed by the special boundary =.

Lexically H-toned verbs

χà-kí-dʒí	*ga ke je* 'I do not eat'
χà-kí-rékí	*ga ke reke* 'I do not buy'
χà-kí-bérékí	*ga ke bereke* 'I do not work'
χà-kí-símʊ́lʊ́lí	*ga ke simolole* 'I do not begin'
χà-kí-sírélédíwí	*ga ke sirelediwe* 'I am not protected'
χà-ŕ-símʊ́lʊ́lɛ́láŕ	*ga re simololelane* 'we do not begin for each other'

3.7 First observations on word-internal H tone spreading

In the Tswana variety described in this paper, H tone spreading is limited in the number of syllables that can be affected. In verb forms, word-internal tone spreading affecting three successive toneless syllables can only be observed in the particular configuration dealt with in Section 3.9.5. In all the other configurations, the maximum range of word-internal H tone spreading is either one or two syllables. H tone spreading with a maximum range of two syllables occurs in syllable strings interrupted only by a standard morpheme boundary. In addition to the spreading of the lexical H tone within verb stems devoid of grammatical H tone, word-internal H tone spreading with a maximum range of two syllables can be observed with H tone domains generated by SMs or OMs. For example, the tonal contour of *ba a tlhaloganya* [bá-á-tɬʰálʊ̀χàɲ-à] 'they understand (DJ)' and *ke lo tlhaloganya* [kì-lʊ́-tɬʰálʊ́χàɲ-à] 'I understand you (CJ)' can be predicted as follows:

#bá-a-tɬʰalʊχaɲ-a# → #(bá)-a-tɬʰalʊχaɲ-a# (H tone domain constitution)
→ #(bá-á-tɬʰá)lʊχaɲ-a# (H tone domain expansion)

#kɪ=lʊ́-tɬʰalʊχaɲ-a# → #kɪ=(lʊ́)-tɬʰalʊχaɲ-a# (H tone domain constitution)
→ #kɪ=(lʊ́-tɬʰálʊ́)χaɲ-a# (H tone domain expansion)

However, toneless syllables immediately following a H-toned prefix, or separated from a H-toned prefix by a single toneless syllable, do not always undergo the spreading of this H tone. The explanation may be simply that, within sequences of syllables not interrupted by boundaries other than the standard morpheme boundary, the annexation of a toneless syllable is blocked by the presence of a H tone associated to the following syllable, as illustrated by the comparison of *ba a tlhaloganya* [bá-á-tɬʰálʊ̀χàɲ-à] 'they understand' and *ba a berekelana* [bá-à-bɛ́rɛ́k-ɛ́l-ànà] 'they work for each other'.

#bá-a-tɬʰaluχaɲ-a# → #(bá)-a-tɬʰaluχaɲ-a# (H tone domain constitution)
→ #(bá-á-tɬʰá)luχaɲ-a# (H tone domain expansion)

#bá-a-bɛrɛk-ɛl-an-a# → #(bá)-a-(bɛ́)rɛk-ɛl-an-a# (H tone domain constitution)
→ #(bá)-a-(bɛ́rɛ́k-ɛ́l)-an-a# (H tone domain expansion)

However, in cases such as *ke ka tlhaloganya* [kì-ká-tɬʰálʊ̀χà̰ɲà] 'I can understand (DJ)', there is no obvious explanation for the fact that the spreading of the H tone of the potential marker does not reach the second syllable of the stem. A crucial observation is that the tonal processes involving the prefixes showing such apparent exceptions to the rule of word-internal tone spreading are partially similar to those observed at word boundaries. In particular, word boundaries too allow for a spreading process limited to one syllable. This similarity justifies positing a special boundary = either to the left of to the right of the prefixes listed in Section 3.2, as in #kɪ-ká=tɬʰaluχaɲ-a#, underlying representation of *ke ka tlhaloganya* [kì-ká-tɬʰálʊ̀χà̰ɲà] 'I can understand'. The special boundary = blocks the application of the spreading rule allowing for the annexation of two successive toneless syllabes (henceforth designated as SPR2), but allows for the application of another spreading rule (SPR1) with a maximum range of one syllable.

3.8 H tone domain expansion/contraction within verb forms

Leaving aside for the moment processes whose effect is limited to the last syllable of verb stems, the interaction between H tone domains within verb forms can be analyzed as the result of the successive application of three rules or sets of rules:

(a) A first spreading rule (designated as SPR2 since it allows for the annexation of two syllables), already illustrated in Section 3.7, stipulates that, within syllable strings not interrupted by the special boundary =, H tone domains followed by one or more toneless syllables can annex the following syllable or the following two syllables, provided this does not result in adjacency with another H tone domain. The derivation of *ba a berekelana* [bá-à-bɛ́rɛ́k-ɛ́l-ànà] 'they work for each other' presented above illustrates a configuration in which SPR2 is blocked.

Note that the restriction to SPR2 holds only within the limits of syllable strings not interrupted by the special boundary =. The tonal behavior of the prefixes triggering the insertion of the special boundary = can only be predicted by positing that the expansion of a H-tone domain according to SPR2 can reach the special boundary = irrespective of what follows it. In this respect, the special boundary = behaves exactly like the word boundary #:

... ó) o = (ó ...   –SPR2→   ... ó ó) = (ó ...
... ó) o o = (ó ...   –SPR2→   ... ó ó ó) = (ó ...

(b) A second set of rules (REPAIR) deals with situations in which two H tone domains are adjacent through the special boundary = (either because the syllables on both sides of the boundary are underlyingly associated to H tones, or because a toneless syllable preceding the special boundary has been annexed by a H tone domain). In this configuration, four of the five repair strategies mentioned in Section 3.1 are available, and they are ranked as follows:
– the preferred strategy is the contraction of the second H tone domain, if it comprises two or more syllables (REPAIRa);
– if the second H tone domain is monosyllabic (and consequently cannot contract), and if the first H tone domain comprises two or more syllables, the non-adjacency constraint is satisfied by contracting the first H domain (REPAIRb);
– if the special boundary = is both immediately preceded and immediately followed by monosyllabic H domains, the non-adjacency constraint is satisfied by the insertion of a toneless vowel if and only if the inserted vowel takes the penultimate position in the verb form (REPAIRc);
– if two or more successive monosyllabic H domains are only separated from each other by the special boundary =, and the toneless vowel insertion strategy is not available, they merge (REPAIRe).[13]

(c) The repair rules presented in (b) can be followed by a second spreading rule (designated as SPR1 since it allows for the annexation of two syllables), applying to H tone domains whose right edge coincides with a special boundary =. This rule stipulates that, in this configuration, a toneless syllable immediately following the special boundary can be annexed by the H tone domain, provided this does not result in adjacency with another H tone domain included in the same word. This rule must be posited as applying step by step from left to right in order to account for the spreading of H tones in the following configuration :

... ó) = o = o ...   –SPR1→   ... ó = ó) = o ...   –SPR1→   ... ó = ó = ó) ...

---

[13] Alternatively, it could be posited that there is no repair, and that the violation surfaces.

3.9 Illustrations of the tonal processes involving the special boundary =

3.9.1 The behavior of the potential marker /ká/

The underlying tonal structure of *ke ka tlhaloganya* [kì-ká-tɬʰálʊ̀χàɲ-à] 'I can understand (DJ)' is #kɪ-(ká)=tɬʰalʊχaɲ-a#. Since the only H tone present in this representation immediately precedes the special boundary, it cannot spread according to SPR2 (which accounts for spreading with a possible range of two syllables), but only according to SPR1 (which accounts for spreading limited to one syllable):

#kɪ-ká=tɬʰalʊχaɲ-a# → #kɪ-(ká)=tɬʰalʊχaɲ-a# (H tone domain constitution)
→ #kɪ-(ká=tɬʰá)lʊχaɲ-a# (SPR1)

The special boundary also accounts for the L tone surfacing on the first syllable of underlyingly H-toned roots in *ò ka tshameka* [ʊ̀-ká-tshàmɪ́k-á] 'you(sg) can play'. The underlying structure is #ʊ-ká=tsʰámɪk-a#, where the special boundary = prevents the two underlying H tones from merging into a single H tone domain. In such cases, if the second H tone domain comprises two or more syllables (which is the case here after the application of SPR2), it contracts in order to eliminate the violation of the non-adjacency constraint:

#ʊ-ká=tsʰámɪk-a# → #ʊ-(ká)=(tsʰá)mɪk-a# (H tone domain constitution)
→ #ʊ-(ká)=(tsʰámɪ́k-á)# (SPR2)
→ #ʊ-(ká)=tsʰa(mɪ́k-á)# (REPAIRa)

In configurations in which two non-monosyllabic H domains are in contact through the special boundary =, the repair strategy is again the contraction of the second one, as illustrated by *ó ka tshameka* [ʊ́-ká-tshàmɪ́k-á] '(s)he can play':

#ʊ́-ká=tsʰámɪk-a# → #(ʊ́-ká)=(tsʰá)mɪk-a# (H tone domain constitution)
→ #(ʊ́-ká)=(tsʰámɪ́k-á)# (SPR2)
→ #(ʊ́-ká)=tsʰa(mɪ́k-á)# (REPAIRa)

In configurations in which the special boundary = is immediately followed by a H-toned syllable that cannot generate a non-monosyllabic domain, but preceded by a H tone domain comprising at least two syllables, as in *ó ka ja* [ʊ́-kà-dʒá] '(s)he can eat', contraction affects the only one of the two H domains that can contract, i.e., the first one:

#ʊ́-ká=dʒ-á# → #(ʊ́-ká)=(dʒ-á)# (H tone domain constitution)
→ #(ʊ́)-ka=(dʒ-á)# (REPAIRb)

A dissyllabic variant [káà] of the potential marker (as in ò *kaa ja* [ʊ̀-káà-dʒ-á] 'you (sg) can eat') appears if and only if the potential marker follows a toneless SM and immediately precedes a H-toned monosyllabic stem. In this configuration, none of the two H tone domains in contact can contract, since both are monosyllabic, but the insertion of a toneless copy of the preceding vowel ensures the respect of the non-adjacency constraint:

    #ʊ-ká=dʒ-á# → #ʊ-(ká)=(dʒ-á)#   (H tone domain constitution)
              → #ʊ-(ká)a=(dʒ-á)#   (REPAIRc)

Note that, in this configuration, monosyllabic toneless stems also surface with a H tone, but the difference in the underlying tone of the stem conditions a different treatment of the potential marker, since the only rule that applies in this case is SPR1, as illustrated by the tonal derivation of ò *ka tla* [ʊ̀-ká-tɬ-á] 'you (sg) can come':

    #ʊ-ká=tɬ-a# → #ʊ-(ká)=tɬ-a#   (H tone domain constitution)
             → #ʊ-(ká=tɬ-á)#   (SPR1)

3.9.2 The behavior of SMs in the circumstantial form of the present positive

In the circumstantial form of the present positive, when immediately preceded by the SM (which in this tense is invariably H-toned), lexically H-toned stems comprising two syllables or more surface with a L tone on their first syllable, as in *ke bina* [kí-bìn-á] 'while I dance'. Moreover, an additional syllable consisting of a L-toned vowel copy of the vowel of the SM appears when lexically H-toned monosyllabic stems are immediately preceded by the SM, as in *kee ja* [kíì-dʒ-á] 'while I eat'. This can be explained by positing that, in this tense, the SM is followed by the special boundary =, and consequently cannot merge with the first syllable of H-toned stems into a single H tone domain. If the H tone underlyingly attached to the first syllable of lexically H-toned stems generates a H tone domain comprising at least two syllables, the contraction of this H tone domain eliminates the violation of the non-adjacency constraint, but a toneless copy of the vowel of the SM is inserted if the contraction of the second H tone domain is not possible:

    #kí=bín-a# → #(kí)=(bí)n-a#   (H tone domain constitution)
             → #(kí)=(bín-á)#   (SPR2)
             → #(kí)=bi(n-á)#   (REPAIRa)

    #kí=dʒ-á# → #(kí)=(dʒ-á)#   (H tone domain constitution)
            → #(kí)ì=(dʒ-á)#   (REPAIRc)

3.9.3 The behavior of SMs in the DJ form of the perfect positive

In the DJ form of the perfect positive, if the stem is in contact with a H-toned SM, the H tone of the SM spreads to the first syllable of toneless stems only, though nothing seems to prevent it from spreading further, as in *ba dumedisetsanye* [bá-dúmèdìs-èts-àɲ-ì] 'they too have greeted people for each other (DJ)', whereas H-toned stems surface with a L tone on their first syllable, the following two syllables remaining H, as if a H tone went on spreading from the first syllable, as in *ba simololelanye* [bá-sìmʊ́lʊ́l-ɛ̀l-àɲ-ì] 'they have begun for each other'.

The explanation is that, in this tense, the special boundary = immediately after the SM blocks the application of SPR2 if the verb stem begins with two or more toneless syllables, and triggers the application of a repair rule if the verb stem begins with a H-toned syllable:[14]

#bá=dumedis-ets-aɲ-ι# → #(bá)=dumedis-ets-aɲ-ι# (H tone domain constitution)
→ #(bá=dú)medis-ets-aɲ-ι# (SPR1)

#bá=símʊlʊl-ɛl-aɲ-ι# → #(bá)=(sí)mʊlʊl-ɛl-aɲ-ι# (H tone domain constitution)
→ #(bá)=(símʊ́lʊ́)l-ɛl-aɲ-ι# (SPR2)
→ #(bá)=si(mʊ́lʊ́)l-ɛl-aɲ-ι# (REPAIRa)

3.9.4 The behavior of OMs in verb forms including a single OM (1)

Tswana has a distinction between underlyingly toneless OMs (1st person singular, 2nd person singular, and cl. 1) and H-toned OMs (all the others). The reflexive marker behaves in all respects like H-toned OMs.

However, when inserted between a H-toned SM and a H-toned root, an underlyingly H-toned OM surfaces with a L tone, as in *ó lo thusa* [ʊ́-lʊ̀-tʰús-á] '(s)he helps you(pl) (CJ)'. When inserted between a H-toned SM and a toneless root, an underlyingly H-toned OM also surfaces with a L tone, but the spreading of its H tone modifies the melody of the stem, as in *ó lo dumedisa* [ʊ́-lʊ̀-dúmédìs-à] '(s)he greets you(pl) (DJ)'. This can be predicted in a simple way by assuming that H-toned OMs are immediately preceded by the special boundary =:

#ʊ́=lʊ́-tʰús-a# → #(ʊ́)=(lʊ́-tʰú)s-a# (H tone domain constitution)
→ #(ʊ́)=(lʊ́-tʰús-á)# (SPR2)
→ #(ʊ́)=lʊ-(tʰús-á)# (REPAIRa)

---

[14] The difference with the cases analyzed in Sections 3.9.1 and 3.9.2 is that, in the perfect positive, the insertion of a toneless vowel (REPAIRc) never occurs, but the explanation is simply that, in the perfect positive, verb stems cannot be monosyllabic.

#ʊ́=lʊ́-dumedis-a# → #(ʊ́)=(lʊ́)-dumedis-a# (H tone domain constitution)
→ #(ʊ́)=(lʊ́-dúmé)dis-a# (SPR2)
→ #(ʊ́)=lʊ-(dúmé)dis-a# (REPAIRa)

In *ga ke lo dumedise* [χà-kí-lʊ́-dùmédís-î] 'I do not greet you (CJ)', the H-toned OM cannot generate a non-monosyllabic H tone domain, and consequently two monosyllabic H tone domains are in contact through the special boundary =. The violation of the non-adjacency constraint cannot be eliminated by inserting a toneless vowel or a downstep, since vowel insertion can only occur if the inserted vowel takes the penultimate position in the verb form, and downstep insertion is not available at word-internal boundaries. Consequently, the only possibility is the last resort strategy, namely fusion (REPAIRe).

#χa-kí=lʊ́-dumédís-î# → #χa-(kí)=(lʊ́)-du(médís-î)# (H tone domain constitution)
→ #χa-(kí=lʊ́)-du(médís-î)# (REPAIRe)

3.9.5 The behavior of OMs in verb forms including a single OM (2)

H tone spreading affecting three successive syllables inside a verb form is observed when the second underlyingly toneless syllable involved in this process represents an OM, as in *ba a go tlhaloganya le bone* [bá-á-χʊ́-tɬʰálòχàɲ-à] 'they understand you(sg) (DJ)'. This can easily be predicted without any additional ad hoc stipulation by inserting the special boundary = immediately after toneless OMs. In this configuration, the expansion of the H tone domain generated by the SM reaches the special boundary = as the result of the application of SPR2, and consequently the H tone domain can annex one more syllable by virtue of SPR1:

#bá-a-χʊ=tɬʰaloχaɲ-a# → #(bá)-a-χʊ=tɬʰaloχaɲ-a# (H tone domain constitution)
→ #(bá-á-χʊ́)=tɬʰaloχaɲ-a# (SPR2)
→ #(bá-á-χʊ́=tɬʰá)loχaɲ-a# (SPR1)

3.9.6 The behavior of OMs in verb forms including two or three OMs

In verb forms including two or three OMs (or one or two OMs plus the reflexive marker), the distinction between two tone classes of OMs disappears; the tone taken by each of the OMs depends exclusively on the context, not on the choice of a particular OM:
- when immediately followed by another OM, all the OMs invariably surface with a H tone;
- when preceded by another OM, an OM immediately preceding the verb stem surfaces with a H tone if the verb stem has the tonal pattern o ó ..., and with

a L tone in the other cases; if the melody of the verb stem when not influenced by a H-toned formative is entirely L, the L tones of its initial syllables give way to H tones.

These observations can be predicted by assuming that, in contact with another OM or with the reflexive marker, all OMs (including those which are toneless in forms including a single OM) are underlyingly H-toned, and preceded by the special boundary =. Sequences of two or three OMs are thus represented as =ó=ó- or =ó=ó=ó- at the beginning of the tonal derivation, which means that the first OM in a sequence of two OMs and the first two OMs in a sequence of three OMs generate adjacent monosyllabic H domains, a configuration that can only be regularized by the fusion of the monosyllabic H domains. The last OM in a sequence of two or three OMs is the only one which can surface with a L tone, due to the contraction of the H domain in which it is initially included, as illustrated by the derivations of *ga ke e ba lo rokisetse* [χà-kí-í-bá-lʊ́-rʊ́k-ís-éts-î] 'I do not make them sew them (the dresses) for you (CJ)' and *ga ke di ba lo apeisetse* [χà-kí-dí-bá-lʊ́-àpé-ís-éts-î] 'I do not make them cook it (the food) for you (DJ)'.

#χa-kí=í=bá=lʊ́-rʊ́k-ís-éts-î# → #χa-(kí)=(í)=(bá)=(lʊ́-rʊ́k-ís-éts-î)# (H tone domain constitution)
→ #χa-(kí)=(í)=(bá)=lʊ-(rʊ́k-ís-éts-î)# (REPAIRa)
→ #χa-(kí=í=bá)=lʊ-(rʊ́k-ís-éts-î)# (REPAIRe)

#χa-kí=dí=bá=lʊ́-apé-ís-éts-î# → #χa-(kí)=(dí)=(bá)=(lʊ́)-a(pé-ís-éts-î)# (H tone domain constitution)
→ #χa-(kí=dí=bá=lʊ́)-a(pé-ís-éts-î)# (REPAIRe)

3.10 The tonal behavior of postfinals

The postfinal of the imperative plural invariably surfaces with a L tone, and does not trigger any modification of the tonal contour of the stem to which it is suffixed, as illustrated by *lema* [lìmá] 'cultivate (imper.sg)/*lemang* [lìm-á-ŋ̀] 'cultivate (imper.pl). This can be predicted by positing that this postfinal is underlyingly a toneless syllabic nasal followed by a floating H tone that prevents the syllabic nasal from being annexed by a H tone domain.

The postfinal of relative verb forms and the interrogative clitic have exactly the same segmental form and tonal properties. Both are invariably realized as a H-toned syllabic nasal. The tonal contour of the stem to which they are suffixed differs from that predicted by the rules proposed in the previous sections by the deletion of the H tone of the last syllable of the stem, but only if it belongs to a non-monosyllabic H tone domain. This can be predicted by positing that these postfinals are separated from the stem by the special boundary =, which prevents the postfinal from merging with the last syllables of the stem into a single H domain and triggers the contraction of non-monosyllabic H tone domains including the last syllable of the stem. For example, the tonal contour of *ba tlhalogantseng* [bá-tɬʰàlʊ́χáń-ts-è-ŋ́] '(those who) have understood' can be explained as follows:

#bá-tɬʰalʊ́χáń-ts-é=ŋ́# → #(bá)-tɬʰa(lʊ́χáń-ts-é)=(ŋ́)# (H tone domain constitution)
→ #(bá)-tɬʰa(lʊ́χáń)-ts-e=(ŋ́)# (REPAIRb)

3.11 Tonal alternations affecting finals in the absence of any overt postfinal

In some tenses in which no overt postfinal is present, the verb stem shows tonal contours different from those predicted by the rule presented in Section 3.6. Crucially, in all cases, the deviation can be described as the contraction of a H tone domain including the last syllable of the stem. This is for example the case of the sequential 2, whose tone pattern is summarized in the following chart:

	lex. H-toned stem	lex. toneless stem
monosyllabic stem	ó	ó
2-syllable stem	ó ò̄	ò ó
3-syllable stem	ó ó ò̄	ò ó ò̄
4-syllable stem	ó ó ó ò̄	ò ó ó ò̄
5 syllables or more	ó ó ó ... ó ò̄	ò ó ó ... ó ò̄

the tonal contour of verb stems in the sequential 2

The crucial observation is that the L tones on the final syllables preceded by a H-toned penultimate syllable constitute the only difference with the pattern for stems including a grammatical H tone as defined in Section 3.6:

	lex. H-toned stem	lex. toneless stem
monosyllabic stem	ó	ó
2-syllable stem	ó ó̄	ò ó
3-syllable stem	ó ó ó̄	ò ó ó̄
4-syllable stem	ó ó ó ó̄	ò ó ó ó̄
5 syllables or more	ó ó ó ... ó ó̄	ò ó ó ... ó ó̄

the basic tonal contour of verb stems including a grammatical H tone

Within the framework adopted here, at least two relatively simple types of explanation can be considered: either the structure of such forms includes an underlying element not immediately apparent on the surface but responsible for the contraction of H tone domains including the last syllable of the stem (for example, a postfinal consisting of a floating H tone), or the boundary between such verb forms is not a standard word boundary, and allows for tonal interactions that do not occur at standard word boundaries.

The difficulty is that the analysis of the tone pattern illustrated by the sequential 2 interferes with the question of the tonal marking of the CJ/DJ distinction, which constitutes the topic of Section 4.

4 The tone of the final vowels of verb forms and the CJ/DJ distinction

4.1 DJ forms with stable final H tones in non-prepausal position

In the examples cited in this section, DJ forms in non-prepausal contexts are illustrated by sentences in which the verb is immediately followed by *le* /lí-/ 'too' plus a pronoun resuming the subject: in this context, conjunct forms are not allowed.

In some DJ forms, for example the DJ form of the infinitive present positive in (1), final H tones predicted by the rules posited in Section 3 are invariably maintained in non-prepausal contexts, and can only be modified by the postlexical rules that operate in prepausal position, according to which, (a) the penultimate syllable is lengthened, (b) if the tone of the penultimate syllable is H, it surfaces as a HL falling tone, and (c) a final H immediately preceded by another H (realized as HL) surfaces as L.

(1) a. *Ke batla go bereka.* / *Ke batla go bereka le nna.*
    b. 'I want to work.'   'I too want to work.'

kì-bàtɬ-à	χʊ̀-bɛ́rɛ̂ːk-à	kì-bàtɬ-à	χʊ̀-bɛ́rɛ́k-á	lí-ǹːná
1SG.SM-want-FV(CJ)	15-work-FV(DJ)	1SG.SM-want-FV(CJ)	15-work-FV(DJ)	ADD-1SG

Ke batla go go ya. / *Ke batla go go ya le nna.*
'I want to go there.'   'I too want to go there.'

kì-bàtɬ-à	χʊ̀-χûː-j-à	kì-bàtɬ-à	χʊ̀-χʊ́-j-á	lí-ǹːná
1SG.SM-want-FV(CJ)	15-17.OM-go-FV(DJ)	1SG.SM-want-FV(CJ)	15-17.OM-go-FV(DJ)	ADD-1SG

4.2 DJ forms that never end with two successive H-toned syllables

In other DJ forms, as illustrated in (2) by the DJ form of the present negative, in all contexts, the final H tones predicted by the rules posited in Section 3 are maintained if the final syllable constitutes a monosyllabic H tone domain, but give way to L tones whenever the rules posited in Section 3 delimit a H tone domain including the last two syllables of the verb form.

(2) a. *Ga ke lele.* / *Ga ke lele le nna.*
  'I do not cry.' 'I do not cry either.'

  χà-kí-lì:l-í   χà-kí-lìl-í   lí-ǹ:ná
  NEG-1 SG.SM-cry-FV(DJ)   NEG-1 SG.SM-cry-FV(DJ)   ADD-1SG

 b. *Ga ke tshabe.* / *Ga ke tshabe le nna.*
  'I am not afraid.' 'I am not afraid either.'

  χà-kí-tsʰâ:b-ì   χà-kí-tsʰáb-ì   lí-ǹ:ná
  NEG-1 SG.SM-be_afraid-FV(DJ)   NEG-1 SG.SM-be_afraid-FV(DJ)   ADD-1SG

In contrast to the DJ forms of the type presented in Section 4.1, which may have very different tonal melodies in prepausal and non-prepausal contexts, DJ forms of this type always show very similar melodies in prepausal and non-prepausal contexts.

If all verb forms in DJ contexts behaved in this way, one could consider positing that the boundary between verb forms and phrases in afterthought function triggers a post-lexical rule similar to that operating in prepausal contexts. This is however not the case. Historically, the tone pattern of such DJ form may have resulted from the morphologization of the post-lexical rule of prepausal lowering, but synchronically, we must posit something in their tonal structure distinguishing them from DJ forms occurring in the same contexts with a tonality that cannot be explained in the same way. More precisely, the underlying representation of DJ forms of this type must include an element triggering the contraction of H tone domains including the last syllable of the stem. This can be done very simply by positing a postfinal consisting of a floating H tone separated from the stem by the special boundary =. In such a configuration, if a non-monosyllabic H tone domain including the final is created, the postfinal triggers its contraction:

 #χa-kí-lıl-í=´# → #χa-(kí)-lı(l-í)=(´)# (H tone domain constitution)
    → #χa-(kí)-lı(l-í)# (floating tone deletion)

#χa-kí-tsʰáb-í=´# → #χa-(kí-tsʰáb-í)=(´)# (H tone domain constitution)
          → #χa-(kí-tsʰá)b-ɩ=(´)# (REPAIRb)
          → #χa-(kí-tsʰá)b-ɩ#   (floating tone deletion)

4.3 CJ forms with non-alternating finals

In some CJ forms (for example, the present positive circumstantial – Section 4.5.4, or the present negative – Section 4.5.5), final H tones are invariably maintained, irrespective of the grammatical nature and tone pattern of the following word. In contrast to disjunct forms, whose tonal structure may be blurred by the rules operating in prepausal position, the non-alternating nature of the CJ forms in question is obvious, since they cannot occur in contexts in which their tonal contour could undergo similar modifications.

4.4 CJ forms with alternating finals

Some other CJ forms show a tonal alternation if (and only if) the rules posited in Section 3 delimit a H tone domain including at least the last two syllables of the verb form. In this configuration, the last syllable surfaces with a L tone if and only if the following word begins with an underlyingly H-toned syllable and is neither a proper name nor a substantive. The explanation put forward here is that, depending on the nature of the following word, such CJ forms may be followed by a special word boundary.[15]

For example, *podi* [pódí] 'goat' and *ele* [élé] 'that one (cl. 9)', though having both a H-toned initial syllable, do not interact in the same way with a CJ verb form like *ke reka* [kʊ̀réká/à] 'I buy, I am buying (DJ)':

---

[15] Historically, it seems reasonable to assume that, originally, such CJ forms were followed by a special word boundary irrespective of the nature of the following word. In present-day Tswana, most substantives beginning with a H-toned syllable belong to class 9, whose original L-toned prefix has been maintained as a L-toned syllabic nasal with monosyllabic noun stems only (for example *ntša* [ɲ̀tʃá] 'dog'). What probably happened is that, when the L-toned prefix of class 9 was deleted, the tonal realization did not change, but the phonological conditioning was reanalyzed as a morphological conditioning involving not only nouns that originally had a L-toned prefix, but also proper names or common nouns of class 1a for which there is no evidence that a L-toned initial syllable was ever present. The result of this reanalysis was the partial re-establishment of an ordinary word boundary at the junction between this type of CJ forms and the following word, depending on the grammatical nature of the following word.

(3) a. *Ke reka podi.*
'I am buying a goat.'
kì-rék-|á| ↓pǔ:dì
1SG.SM-buy-FV(CJ) 9.goat

b. *Ke reka ele (podi).*
'I am buying that one (goat).'
kì-rék-|à| ê:lè
1SG.SM-buy-FV(CJ) 9.DEM

In these two sentences, *podi* [pǔdí] 'goat' and *ele* [élé] 'that one (cl. 9)' equally fulfill the object function in the construction of the same verb, and consequently argument structure plays no role in the tonal alternation. Since *podi* [pǔdí] 'goat' and *ele* [élé] 'that one (cl. 9)' show identical tonal behavior in all other contexts, the only possible relevant factor in a strictly synchronic account is the grammatical nature of the word in immediate postverbal position: *podi* is a substantive, whereas *ele* is a demonstrative used pronominally. Example (4) shows that the same change in the grammatical nature of the following word does not affect the tone of conjunct forms with non-alternating finals (in this example, the CJ form of the present negative).

(4) a. *Ga ke reke podi.*
'I am not buying a goat.'
χà-kí-rék-|î| ↓pǔ:dì
NEG-1SG.SM-buy-FV(CJ) 9.goat

b. *Ga ke reke ele (podi).*
'I am not buying that one (goat).'
χà-kí-rék-|î| ↓ê:lè
NEG-1SG.SM-buy-FV(CJ) 9.DEM

The following two examples provide additional illustrations of the contrast between CJ verb forms whose final shows no tonal alternation – see (5), and CJ verb forms with an alternating final – see (6).

(5) a. *Ga ke bereke nae.*
'I don't work with him/her.'
χà-kí-bérék-|î| nà:-ɛ́
NEG-1SG.SM-work-FV(CJ)   ADD-1

b. *Ga ke bereke nao.*
'I don't work with you(sg).'
χà-kí-bérék-|î| nâ:-ʊ̀
NEG-1SG.SM-work-FV(CJ)   ADD-2SG

c. *Ga re di bae mmogo.*
'We don't put them (cl.8) together.'
χà-ŕí-dì-bá-|î| m̀mɔ́:χɔ̀
NEG-1PL.SM-8.OM-put-FV(CJ) together

d. *Ga re di bae mo ntlong.*
'We don't put them (cl.8) in the house.'
χà-ŕí-dì-bá-|î| mó   ń-tɬʊ̀:-ŋ̀
NEG-1PL.SM-8.OM-   there   9-house-
put-FV(CJ)   LOC

(6) a. *Ke bereka nae.*
'I work with you(sg).'
kì-bérék-|á| nà:-ɛ́
1SG.SM-work-FV(CJ)   ADD-1

b. *Ke bereka nao.*
'I work with him/her.'
kì-bérék-|à| nâ:-ʊ̀
1SG.SM-work-FV(CJ)   ADD-2SG

c. *Re di baya mmogo.*
'We put them (cl.8) together.'

r̀-dí-báj-[á]　　　　　m̀mɔ́:χɔ́
1PL.SM-8.OM-put-FV(CJ)　together

d. *Re di baya mo ntlong.*
'We put them (cl.8) in the house.'

r̀-dí-báj-[á]　mó　ń-tɬʊ̀:-ŋ̀
1PL.SM-8.OM-put-FV(CJ)　there　9-house-LOC

The crucial observation is that, when followed by words beginning with a H-toned syllable, CJ forms with alternating finals show a tonal alternation that can be described as the contraction of a non-monosyllabic H tone domain including the last syllable of the verb form if and only if the following word is not a proper name or a substantive. This means that the boundary between such CJ forms and a word which is not a proper name or a substantive has in common with the special morpheme boundary = and the standard word boundary # that it triggers a process motivated by the constraint of non-adjacency of H domains, but apart from the general use of fusion as the last resort strategy, the details are different:

– when two H tone domains are in contact through the special morpheme boundary =, the available strategies are, in order of preference, (a) the contraction of the second H tone domain, (b) the contraction of the first H tone domain, and (c) the insertion of a toneless vowel;
– when two H tone domains are in contact through the standard word boundary #, the only available strategy is the insertion of a downstep;
– when two H tone domains are in contact at the boundary between a CJ form with an alternating final and a word which is neither a substantive nor a proper name, the available strategies are, in order of preference, (a) the contraction of the first H tone domain, and (b) the insertion of a downstep.

The only simple way to account for this alternation is to posit that, at the syntax-morphology interface, a special word boundary ≠ is inserted immediately after the CJ verb forms that have an alternating final if and only if the following word is not a proper name or a substantive. This special word boundary differs from the standard word boundary in that, if both immediately preceded and immediately followed by H tone domains, it allows for the contraction of the first H tone domain as a possible repair strategy.

#kɪ-rɛ́k-á#púdí#　→ #kɪ-(rɛ́k-á)#(púdí)#　(H tone domain constitution)
　　　　　　　　　→ #kɪ-(rɛ́k-á)#ꜜ(púdí)#　(REPAIRd)

#kɪ-rɛ́k-á≠é-lé#　→ #kɪ-(rɛ́k-á)≠(é-lé)#　(H tone domain constitution)
　　　　　　　　→ #kɪ-(rɛ́)k-a≠(púdí)#　(REPAIRb)

4.5 Possible tonal structures for verb forms in CJ and DJ contexts

Four tonal patterns are attested for the stems of verb forms in CJ contexts, and three for the stems of verb forms in DJ contexts.

4.5.1 Verb forms in CJ contexts with no grammatical H tone and a non-alternating final

In the absence of any tonal interaction with the prefixal sequence, the tonal contour of the stem in CJ verb forms belonging to this type would show the following pattern:

	lex. H-toned stem	lex. toneless stem
monosyllabic stem	ó	ò
2-syllable stem	ó ó	ò ò
3-syllable stem	ó ó ó	ò ò ò
4-syllable stem	ó ó ó ò	ò ò ò ò
5 syllables or more	ó ó ó ò … ò	ò ò ò ò … ò

However, in the only tense that has these characteristics in CJ contexts (the present positive circumstantial), all SMs are H-toned, the special boundary = is inserted between the SM and lexically H-toned stems, and the tonal contour of lexically toneless stems is always modified by the interaction with the prefixal H tones. For example, if a toneless OM is inserted between the SM and the stem, the first syllable of the stem is annexed by the H tone domain generated by the SM, and the tonal contour of the stem varies as follows:

	lex. H-toned stem	lex. toneless stem
monosyllabic stem	ó	ó
2-syllable stem	ó ó	ó ò
3-syllable stem	ó ó ó	ó ò ò
4-syllable stem	ó ó ó ò	ó ò ò ò
5 syllables or more	ó ó ó ò … ò	ó ò ò ò … ò

kí-mʊ̀-dʒá	ke mo ja 'while eating it (the ostrich, 1sg, CJ)'
kí-χʊ̀-tʰúsá	ke go thusa 'while helping you (1sg, CJ)'
kí-χʊ̀-tsʰámíkísà	ke go tshamekisa 'while playing with you (1sg, CJ)'
rí-χʊ̀-símʊ́lʊ́lèlà	re go simololela 'while beginning for you (1pl, CJ)'

	kí-mʊ́-ísà	*ke mo isa* 'while taking him/her away (1sg, CJ)'
	kí-mʊ́-dírèlà	*ke mo direla* 'while working for him/her (1sg, CJ)'
	kí-χʊ́-dúmèdìsà	*ke go dumedisa* 'while greeting for you (1sg, CJ)'

4.5.2 Verb forms in CJ contexts with a grammatical H tone and a non-alternating final

Whatever prefixes are added to them, and irrespective of the nature of the following word, the stem of CJ forms of this type varies in the following way:

	lex. H-toned stem	lex. toneless stem
monosyllabic stem	ó	ó
2-syllable stem	ó ó	ò ó
3-syllable stem	ó ó ó	ò ó ó
4-syllable stem	ó ó ó ó	ò ó ó ó
5 syllables or more	ó ó ó ó … ó	ò ó ó ó … ó

This type can be illustrated by the CJ form of the present negative:

χà-kí-dʒɪ́	*ga ke je* 'I do not eat (CJ)'
χà-kí-rékí	*ga ke reke* 'I do not buy (CJ)'
χà-kí-bérékí	*ga ke bereke* 'I do not work (CJ)'
χà-kí-símʊ́lʊ́lí	*ga ke simolole* 'I do not begin (CJ)'
χà-kí-sírélédíwí	*ga ke sirelediwe* 'I am not protected (CJ)'
χà-rí-símʊ́lʊ́lélání	*ga re simololelane* 'we do not begin (CJ)'

χà-kí-tɬí	*ga ke tle* 'I do not come (CJ)'
χà-kí-bàlí	*ga ke bale* 'I do not read (CJ)'
χà-kí-tswèlélí	*ga ke tswelele* 'I do not progress (CJ)'
χà-kí-tɬʰàlʊ́χáɲí	*ga ke tlhaloganye* 'I do not understand (CJ)'
χà-rí-dùmédísání	*ga re dumedisane* 'we do not greet each other (CJ)'
χà-rí-dùmédísétsání	*ga re dumedisetsane* 'we do not greet people for each other (CJ)'

4.5.3 Verb forms in CJ contexts with no grammatical H tone and an alternating final

When no prefixed formative influences it, the tonal melody of the stem of CJ forms of this type varies as indicated in the following chart. Note that, when no H-toned formative exerts an influence, the alternation is apparent only in the case of lexically H-toned stems comprising two or three syllables:

	lex. H-toned stem	lex. toneless stem
monosyllabic stem	ó	ò
2-syllable stem	ó ó/ò	ò ò
3-syllable stem	ó ó ó/ò	ò ò ò
4-syllable stem	ó ó ó ò	ò ò ò ò
5 syllables or more	ó ó ó ò ... ò	ò ò ò ò ... ò

This pattern can be illustrated by the CJ form of the present positive, when a toneless SM is immediately prefixed to the stem:

kì-dʒá	ke ja 'I eat (CJ)'
kì-rɛ́ká/à	ke reka 'I buy (CJ)'
kì-bɛ́rɛ́ká/à	ke bereka 'I work (CJ)'
kì-símʊ́lʊ́là	ke simolola 'I begin (CJ)'
kì-sírɛ́lɛ́dìwà	ke sirelediwa 'I am protected (CJ)'
r̀-símʊ́lʊ́lɛ̀lànà	re simololelana 'we begin for each other (CJ)'

kì-tɬà	ke tla 'I come (CJ)'
kì-bàlà	ke bala 'I read (CJ)'
kì-tswɛ̀lɛ̀là	ke tswelela 'I progress (CJ)'
kì-tɬʰàlòχaɲà	ke tlhaloganya 'I understand (CJ)'
r̀-dùmèdìsànà	re dumedisana 'we greet each other (CJ)'
r̀-dùmèdìsètsànà	re dumedisetsana 'we greet people for each other (CJ)'

H-toned prefixes may create conditions in which the alternation triggered by the special word boundary ≠ becomes apparent in a greater number of cases. For example, when the stem of the CJ form of the present positive immediately follows a H-toned SM, the alternations triggered by the special word boundary occur with H-toned stems comprising one, two or three syllables, and toneless stems comprising one or two syllables:

ʊ́-dʒá/à	ó ja '(s)he eats (CJ)'
ʊ́-rɛ́ká/à	ó reka '(s)he buys (CJ)'
ʊ́-bɛ́rɛ́ká/à	ó bereka '(s)he works (CJ)'
ʊ́-símʊ́lʊ́là	ó simolola '(s)he begins (CJ)'
ʊ́-sírɛ́lɛ́dìwà	ó sirelediwa '(s)he is protected (CJ)'
bá-símʊ́lʊ́lɛ̀lànà	ba simololelana 'they begin for each other (CJ)'

ʊ́-tɬá/à   ó tla '(s)he comes (CJ)'
ʊ́-bálá/à   ó bala '(s)he reads (CJ)'
ʊ́-tswɛ́lɛ́là   ó tswelela '(s)he progresses (CJ)'
ʊ́-tɬʰálʊ́χàɲà   ó tlhaloganya '(s)he understands (CJ)'
bá-dúmédìsànà   ba dumedisana 'they greet each other (CJ)'
bá-dúmédìsètsànà ba dumedisetsana 'they greet people for each other (CJ)'

However, the distinction between this type and that presented in Section 4.5.1 is always neutralized with H-toned stems of more than three syllables and with toneless stems of more than two syllables.

4.5.4 Verb forms in CJ contexts with a grammatical H tone and an alternating final

The tonal contour of the stem of CJ forms belonging to this type shows the following pattern:

	lex. H-toned stem	lex. toneless stem
monosyllabic stem	ó/ò	ó/ò
2-syllable stem	ó ó/ò	ò ó
3-syllable stem	ó ó ó/ò	ò ó ó/ò
4-syllable stem	ó ó ó ó/ò	ò ó ó ó/ò
5 syllables or more	ó ó ó ó ... ó/ò	ò ó ó ó ... ó/ò

This tonal type can be illustrated by the sequential 2:

à-dʒí   a je 'and (s)he will eat (CJ)'
à-bú-dʒí/ˬ   a bo je (bogobe) 'and (s)he will eat it (the porridge) (CJ)'
à-rékí/ˬ   a reke 'and (s)he will buy (CJ)'
à-bérékí/ˬ   a bereke 'and (s)he will work (CJ)'
à-símʊ́lʊ́lí/ˬ   a simolole 'and (s)he will begin (CJ)'
à-sírélédíwí/ˬ   a sirelediwe 'and (s)he will be protected (CJ)'
bà-símʊ́lʊ́lɛ́lání/ˬ   ba simololelane 'and they will begin for each other (CJ)'

à-jí   a ye 'and (s)he will go (CJ)'
à-χʊ́-jí/ˬ   a go ye 'and (s)he will go there (CJ)'
à-bàlí   a bale 'and (s)he will read (CJ)'
à-tswèlélí/ˬ   a tswelele 'and (s)he will progress (CJ)'
à-tɬʰàlʊ́χání/ˬ   a tlhaloganye 'and (s)he will understand (CJ)'
bà-dùmédísání/ˬ   ba dumedisane 'and they will greet each other (CJ)'
bà-dùmédísétsání/ˬ   ba dumedisetsane 'and they will greet people for each other (CJ)'

4.5.5 Verb forms in DJ contexts with neither a grammatical H tone nor a postfinal H tone

In non-prepausal position, if no H tone belonging to a prefixed formative exerts an influence, the tonal melody of the stem of DJ forms belonging to this type varies in the following way:[16]

	lex. H-toned stem	lex. toneless stem
monosyllabic stem	ó	ò
2-syllable stem	ó ó	ò ò
3-syllable stem	ó ó ó	ò ò ò
4-syllable stem	ó ó ó ò	ò ò ò ò
5 syllables or more	ó ó ó ò ... ò	ò ò ò ò ... ò

The DJ form of the present positive illustrates this tonal type:

kì-à-dʒá	ke a ja 'I eat (DJ)'
kì-à-rɛ́ká	ke a reka 'I buy (DJ)'
kì-à-bɛ́rɛ́ká	ke a bereka 'I work (DJ)'
kì-à-símʊ́lʊ́là	ke a simolola 'I begin (DJ)'
kì-à-sírélédìwà	ke a sirelediwa 'I am protected (DJ)'
ǹ-à-símʊ́lʊ́lɛ̀lànà	re a simololelana 'we begin for each other (DJ)'

kì-à-tɬà	ke a tla 'I come (DJ)'
kì-à-bàlà	ke a bala 'I read (DJ)'
kì-à-tswɛ̀lɛ̀là	ke a tswelela 'I progress (DJ)'
kì-à-tɬʰàlòχàɲà	ke a tlhaloganya 'I understand (DJ)'
ǹ-à-dùmèdìsànà	re a dumedisana 'we greet other (DJ)'
ǹ-à-dùmèdìsètsànà	re a dumedisetsana 'we greet people for each other (DJ)'

4.5.6 Verb forms in DJ contexts with a grammatical H tone and no postfinal H tone

In non-prepausal position, the stem of the DJ forms of this type shows the following pattern:

---

[16] This chart gives the tonal melody in non-prepausal position, but the reader must bear in mind that in prepausal position, H H sequences are automatically converted into HL L – see Section 4.1.

	lex. H-toned stem	lex. toneless stem
2-syllable stem	ó ó	ò ó
3-syllable stem	ó ó ó	ò ó ó
4-syllable stem	ó ó ó ó	ò ó ó ó
5 syllables or more	ó ó ó ó ... ó	ò ó ó ó ... ó

This pattern is only found in the DJ form of the perfect positive circumstantial (and this is why monosyllabic stems are not mentioned, since the perfect stem cannot be monosyllabic):

kí-dʒílé *ke jele* 'having eaten (1sg, DJ)'
kí-rékílé *ke rekile* 'having bought (1sg, DJ)'
kí-bérékílé *ke berekile* 'having worked (1sg, DJ)'
kí-síréléditswí *ke sireleditswe* 'having been protected (1sg, DJ)'
rí-símʊ́lʊ́lɛ́láɲí *re simololelanye* 'having begun for each other (1pl, DJ)'

kí-tsìlé *ke tsile* 'having come (1sg, DJ)'
kí-bàdílé *ke badile* 'having read (1sg, DJ)'
kí-tsàmáílé *ke tsamaile* 'having gone (1sg, DJ)'
kí-tɬʰàlʊ́χáńtsé *ke tlhalogantse* 'having understood (1sg, DJ)'
rí-dùmédísétsáɲí *re dumedisetsanye* 'having greeted people for each other (1pl, DJ)'

4.5.7 Verb forms in DJ contexts with a grammatical H tone and a postfinal H tone

With this tonal type of DJ forms (and only with this type), the only difference between prepausal and non-prepausal realizations is the falling realization of H-toned penultimate syllables in prepausal context.

	lex. H-toned stem	lex. toneless stem
monosyllabic stem	ó ~ ò	ó ~ ò
2-syllable stem	ó ò	ò ó
3-syllable stem	ó ó ò	ò ó ò
4-syllable stem	ó ó ó ò	ò ó ó ò
5 syllables or more	ó ó ó ... ó ò	ò ó ó ... ó ò

The indication of two possibilities with monosyllabic stems means that the L variant appears if and only if the stem is immediately preceded by a H-toned formative, as illustrated by the DJ form of the infinitive negative – see (7).

(7) a. *Go sa je go a bopamisa.*
'Not to eat makes one thin.'

χʊ̀-sà-dʒ-í   χʊ́-à-búpám-î:s-à
15-NEG-eat-FV(DJ)   15.SM-DJ-be_thin-CAUS-FV

b. *Go sa bo je (bogobe) go a bopamisa.*
'Not to eat it (porridge) makes one thin.'

χʊ̀-sà-bʊ́-dʒ-ì   χʊ́-à-búpám-î:s-à
15-NEG-14.OM-eat-FV(DJ)   15.SM-DJ-be_thin-CAUS-FV

This pattern can be illustrated by the DJ form of the sequential 2:

à-dʒí   *a je* 'and (s)he will eat (DJ)'
à-bʊ́-dʒì   *a bo je (bogobe)* 'and (s)he will eat it (class 14) (DJ)'
à-rékì   *a reke* 'and (s)he will buy (DJ)'
à-bérékì   *a bereke* 'and (s)he will work (DJ)'
à-símʊ́lʊ́ɲì   *a sirelediwe* 'and (s)he will be protected (DJ)'
à-sírélédíwì   *re a dumedisetsana* 'we greet people for each other (DJ)'
bà-símʊ́lʊ́lélánì   *ba simololelane* 'and they will begin for each other (DJ)'

à-jí   *a ye* 'and (s)he will go (DJ)'
à-χʊ́-jí   *a go ye* 'and (s)he will go there (DJ)'
à-bàlí   *a bale* 'and (s)he will read (DJ)'
à-tswèlélì   *a tswelele* 'and (s)he will progress (DJ)'
à-tɬʰàlʊ́χáɲì   *a tlhaloganye* 'and (s)he will understand (DJ)'
bà-dùmédísánì   *ba dumedisane* 'and they will greet each other (DJ)'
bà-dùmédísétsánì   *ba dumedisetsane* 'and they will greet people for each other (DJ)'

5 Correspondences between tone patterns in CJ and DJ contexts

Arithmetically, there are twelve possible combinations of the four tonal types of stems observed in CJ contexts and the three tonal types observed in DJ contexts, but six only are attested. Three of these combinations involve identical or similar tonal types in the contexts that make apparent a possible contrast between CJ and DJ forms, and therefore constitute the three possible tone patterns for the tenses with no tonal marking of the CJ/DJ distinction. The other three constitute the three possible tonal markings of the CJ/DJ distinction.

5.1 Tone patterns for the stem of tenses with similar contours in CJ and DJ contexts

The circumstantial form of the present positive is the only tense illustrating the pattern involving no grammatical H tone and the standard word boundary in all contexts.

The circumstantial form of the perfect positive is the only tense illustrating the pattern involving the grammatical H tone and the standard word boundary in all contexts.

The pattern with a grammatical H tone, the postfinal / ´ / in DJ contexts, and the special word boundary in CJ contexts if the following word is not a proper name nor a substantive, is by far the most common pattern for tenses that have similar tonal contours in CJ and DJ contexts. It is found in the following tenses:

    indicative future negative
    indicative potential negative
    infinitive present negative
    infinitive potential negative
    circumstantial present negative
    circumstantial perfect negative
    circumstantial future negative
    circumstantial potential negative
    imperative positive
    imperative negative
    subjunctive positive
    subjunctive negative
    sequential 2

5.2 Tone patterns for the stem of tenses with different contours in CJ and DJ contexts

The pattern with no grammatical H tone either in DJ or CJ contexts, no postfinal / ´ / in DJ contexts, and insertion of the special word boundary ≠ in CJ contexts, is relatively common. It is found in the following tenses:

    indicative present positive
    indicative future positive
    indicative potential positive
    circumstantial future positive
    circumstantial potential positive

infinitive present positive
infinitive future positive
infinitive potential positive
infinitive continuative
sequential 1

The pattern with the grammatical H tone both in CJ and DJ contexts, the postfinal / ˆ / in DJ contexts, and the standard word boundary in all contexts, is found in two tenses: the indicative present negative and the indicative perfect negative.

The pattern with no postfinal / ˆ / and no grammatical H tone in DJ contexts contrasting with the insertion of the special word boundary and the grammatical H tone in CJ contexts is found in one tense only, the indicative perfect positive.

6 Conclusion

Tswana tenses can be classified into three groups of tenses with tonal structures resulting in similar contours in CJ and DJ contexts, and three groups with tonal structures resulting in three possible types of contrasts between CJ and DJ verb forms. Unfortunately, no obvious generalization emerges from this classification correlating with any grammatical or semantic feature. The DJ marker that occupies Slot −2 in the structure of the indicative present positive is the only uncontroversial morphological element to which the function of marking the CJ/DJ distinction can be attributed. The tonal phenomena that contribute to this distinction (presence *vs.* absence of the grammatical H tone, presence vs. absence of the postfinal / ˆ / in DJ contexts, and possible insertion of the special word boundary ≠ in CJ contexts) have a distribution that does not make it possible to analyze them as carrying a specific information by themselves.

It must however be noted that, among the possible correspondences between the contours of verb forms in CJ and DJ contexts, only two are attested by more than two tenses:
- the type with similar tonal melodies in CJ and DJ contexts, and with specific tonal processes affecting the final both in CJ and DJ contexts;
- the type with no specific tonal process affecting the final in the DJ form, and tonal processes triggered by the presence of the special word boundary ≠ in the CJ form.

Consequently, in CJ contexts, the type of tonal behavior that requires positing the special word boundary ≠ between the verb form and the following word constitutes the rule, whereas the type of tonal behavior attributable to the invariable presence of the standard word boundary constitutes the exception. By contrast, in DJ contexts, there is no marked imbalance between tenses with tone patterns that require positing a postfinal / ˊ / in the DJ form, and tenses for which this postfinal must not be posited.

By way of a conclusion, I would like to briefly evoke the question of the existence of more or less similar systems in related languages. Unfortunately, apart from Southern Sotho, which according to (Letšeng 1995) has tonal contrasts between verb forms in CJ and DJ contexts that correspond almost exactly to those observed in Tswana, I have not been able to find a language with an involvement of tone in the CJ/DJ distinction whose comparison with Tswana could suggest a hypothesis about the emergence of such systems. For example, functionally, the CJ/DJ systems found in Nguni (S40) languages are to the best of my knowledge very similar to the Sotho/Tswana systems, but in Nguni languages, the CJ/DJ distinction seems to be limited to the tenses in which it is marked segmentally. No mention of tonal distinctions between DJ and CJ forms can be found in the literature, and my own field notes on Swati include no evidence of tonal distinctions comparable to those that mark the CJ/DJ distinction in Tswana or Southern Sotho. Tswana and its closest relatives seem to be unique in two respects. The first one is the imbalance between the very limited use of segmental marking (found in one tense only) and the proliferation of tonal marking of the CJ/DJ distinction. The second one is the remarkable heterogeneity of the tonal contrasts used to mark the CJ/DJ distinction, with two major types and four minor types that cannot be analyzed as the manifestations of underlying tonal morphemes that would be common to all the tenses that express the CJ/DJ distinction. Explaining the emergence of such a system will certainly constitute a major challenge for any attempt at elaborating a general hypothesis accounting for the development of CJ/DJ distinctions in Bantu languages.

Abbreviations

ADD = additive, CJ = conjoint, CL = noun class, CONT = continuative, CSTR = construct form marker, DJ = disjoint, FV = final vowel, H = high tone, IAV = immediate-after-verb, L = low tone, LOC = locative, NEG = negation, OM = object marker, PL = plural, SG = singular, SM = subject marker, SPR1 = H tone spreading of one syllable, SPR2 = H tone spreading of two syllables.

Appendix 1: Subject markers and object markers

Four different sets of SMs (conventionally labeled here A, B, C, and D) must be recognized in Tswana. Apart from the SM of class 1, the four sets differ from one another in tone only, since set D can be analyzed as a portmanteau resulting from the fusion of the SM itself with a formative whose underlying form is /a/. In contrast to the SMs, the OMs have the same underlying form in all tenses, but show complex tonal alternations conditioned by the context – see Sections 3.9.4 and 3.9.5.

The following chart presents the OMs as they appear when immediately preceded by a L-toned SM and immediately followed by the verb root:
The four sets of SMs have the following distribution:
- set A occurs in the indicative tenses, except those beginning with the negative marker *ga* [χà];
- set B occurs in the indicative tenses beginning with the negative formative *ga* [χà], in the subjunctive, in the circumstantial forms, and in the relative forms;
- set C occurs in the *sequential 2*;
- set D occurs in the *sequential 1*; its two tonal variants may well be dialectal variants, but for some speakers at least, they are in free variation.

		SM(A)	SM(B)	SM(C)	SM(D)	OM
1st person	singular	kì, ǹ	kí, ń	kì	kà	ń
	plural	ɾ̀	ɾ́	ɾ̀	rà, rá	ɾ́
2nd person	singular	ʋ̀	ʋ́	ʋ̀	wà	ʋ̀
	plural	lʋ̀	lʋ́	lʋ̀	lwà, lwá	lʋ́
3rd person	cl. 1[17]	ʋ́	á, ʋ́	à	à	mʋ̀
	cl. 2	bá	bá	bà	bà, bá	bá
	cl. 3	ʋ́	ʋ́	ʋ̀	wà, wá	ʋ́
	cl. 4	í	í	ì	jà, já	í
	cl. 5	lí	lí	ɾ̀	là, lá	lí
	cl. 6	á	á	à	à, á	á
	cl. 7	sí	sí	sì	sà, sá	sí
	cl. 8/10	dí	dí	dì	tsà, tsá	dí
	cl. 9	í	í	ì	jà, já	í
	cl. 11	lʋ́	lʋ́	lʋ̀	lwà, lwá	lʋ́
	cl. 14	bʋ́	bʋ́	bʋ̀	dʒwà, dʒwá	bʋ́
	cl. 15/17	χʋ́	χʋ́	χʋ̀	χà, χá	χʋ́

---

[17] In set B, the SM of cl. 1 shows a free variation between á and ʋ́ in the relative forms; in all the other forms using this set of SMs, the SM of cl. 1 can only be á.

Appendix 2: Morphological characterization of the tenses of Tswana verbs

(a) **Tenses in which the CJ/DJ distinction is not limited to tonal alternations affecting the last syllable of the verb form**

Indicative present positive: final vowel a; SM of set A; no grammatical H tone.
DJ: /a/ in Slot −2, no postfinal H tone
CJ: Slot −2 empty, alternating final

Indicative perfect positive: final vowel e~ɩ; SM of set A; /il~J/ (PRF) in Slot +2.
DJ: no grammatical H tone, special boundary = after the SM, no postfinal H tone
CJ: grammatical H tone, no special boundary after the SM, alternating final

(b) **Tenses with a CJ/DJ distinction limited to tonal alternations affecting the last syllable of the verb form**

A CJ/DJ distinction manifested in tonal alternations affecting the last syllable of the verb form may result from two distinct combinations: either a postfinal H tone in DJ contexts and a non-alternating final in CJ contexts, or no postfinal H tone in DJ contexts and an alternating final in CJ contexts.

Indicative present negative: final vowel ɩ; SM of set B; /χa/ (NEG) in Slot −4; grammatical high tone.
DJ: postfinal H tone
CJ: non-alternating final

Indicative perfect negative: final vowel a; SM of set B; /χa/ (NEG) in Slot −4; /a/ (PRF) in Slot −2; grammatical high tone.
DJ: postfinal H tone
CJ: non-alternating final

Indicative future positive: final vowel a; SM of set A; /tɬaa/ (FUT) in Slot −2; no grammatical H tone.
DJ: no postfinal H tone
CJ: alternating final

Indicative potential positive: final vowel a; SM of set A; /ká=/ (POT) in Slot −2; no grammatical H tone.
DJ: no postfinal H tone
CJ: alternating final

Circumstantial future positive: final vowel a; SM of set B; /tɬaa/ (FUT) in Slot −2; no grammatical H tone.
DJ: no postfinal H tone
CJ: alternating final

Circumstantial potential positive: final vowel a; SM of set B; /ká=/ (POT) in Slot −2; no grammatical H tone.
DJ: no postfinal H tone
CJ: alternating final

Infinitive present positive: final vowel a; /χʊ/ (CL15) in Slot −3; no grammatical H tone.
DJ: no postfinal H tone
CJ: alternating final

Infinitive future positive: final vowel a; /χʊ/ (CL15) in Slot −3; /tɬaa/ (FUT) in Slot −2; no grammatical H tone.
DJ: no postfinal H tone
CJ: alternating final

Infinitive potential positive: final vowel a; /χʊ/ (CL15) in Slot −3; /ká=/ (POT) in Slot −2; no grammatical H tone.
DJ: no postfinal H tone
CJ: alternating final

Infinitive continuative: final vowel a; /χʊ/ (CL15) in Slot −3; /sá=/ (CONT) in Slot −2; no grammatical H tone.
DJ: no postfinal H tone
CJ: alternating final

Sequential 1: final vowel a; SMs of set D; no grammatical H tone.
DJ: no postfinal H tone
CJ: alternating final

(c) **Tenses with similar contours in CJ and DJ contexts**
The lack of an apparent distinction between a DJ and a CJ form may result from two distinct combinations: either no postfinal H tone in DJ contexts and a non-alternating final in CJ contexts, or a postfinal H tone in DJ contexts and an alternating final in CJ contexts.

Circumstantial present positive: final vowel a; SM of set B followed by the special boundary = in contact with a H-toned stem; no grammatical H tone.
DJ: no postfinal H tone
CJ: non-alternating final

Circumstantial perfect positive: final vowel e~ɩ; SM of set B; /il~J/ (PRF) in Slot +2, grammatical high tone.
DJ: no postfinal H tone
CJ: non-alternating final

Indicative future negative: final vowel ɩ; SM of set A; /tɬaa-sɩ/ (FUT-NEG) in Slot −2; grammatical high tone.
DJ: postfinal H tone
CJ: alternating final

Indicative potential negative: final vowel ɩ; SM of set A; /ká-sɩ/ (POT-NEG) in Slot −2; grammatical high tone.
DJ: postfinal H tone
CJ: alternating final

Infinitive present negative: final vowel ɩ; /χʊ/ (CL15) in Slot −3; /=sa/ (NEG) in Slot −2; grammatical high tone.
DJ: postfinal H tone
CJ: alternating final

Infinitive perfect negative: final vowel a; /χʊ/ (CL15) in Slot −3; /=sa/ (NEG) in Slot −2; grammatical high tone.
DJ: postfinal H tone
CJ: alternating final

Infinitive future negative: final vowel ɩ; /χʊ/ (CL15) in Slot −3; /tɬaa-sɩ/ (FUT-NEG) in Slot −2; grammatical high tone.
DJ: postfinal H tone
CJ: alternating final

Infinitive potential negative: final vowel ɩ; /χʊ/ (CL15) in Slot −3; /ká-sɩ/ (POT-NEG) in Slot −2 ; grammatical high tone.
DJ: postfinal H tone
CJ: alternating final

Circumstantial present negative: final vowel ɩ, SM of set B, /=sa/ (NEG) in Slot −2, grammatical high tone.
DJ: postfinal H tone
CJ: alternating final

Circumstantial perfect negative: final vowel a; SM of set B; /=sa/ (NEG) in Slot −2; grammatical high tone.
DJ: postfinal H tone
CJ: alternating final

Circumstantial future negative: final vowel ɩ; SM of set B; /tɬaa-sɩ/ (FUT-NEG) in Slot −2; grammatical high tone.
DJ: postfinal H tone
CJ: alternating final

Circumstantial potential negative: final vowel ɩ; SM of set B; /ká-sɩ/ (POT-NEG) in Slot −2; grammatical high tone.
DJ: postfinal H tone
CJ: alternating final

Imperative positive: final vowel a or ɛ[18]; no SM; grammatical H tone.
DJ: postfinal H tone in the singular, postfinal /ŋ́/ in the plural
CJ: alternating final in the singular, postfinal /ŋ́/ in the plural

Imperative negative: final vowel ɩ; no SM; /sɩ/ (NEG) in Slot −2; grammatical H tone.
DJ: postfinal H tone in the singular, postfinal /ŋ́/ in the plural
CJ: alternating final in the singular, postfinal /ŋ́/ in the plural

Subjunctive positive: final vowel ɛ; SM of set B; no grammatical H tone.[19]
DJ: postfinal H tone
CJ: alternating final

---

18 In the imperative positive, the choice between the two possible finals depends on the presence of OMs.
19 In the subjunctive positive, if no OM or reflexive marker is inserted, stems including three syllables or more show a tonal contour contradicting the regularities observed in other tenses – see Section 3.5, Footnote 12.

Subjunctive negative: final vowel ɪ; SM of set B; /sɪ/ (NEG) in Slot −2; grammatical high tone.
DJ: postfinal H tone
CJ: alternating final

Sequential 2: final vowel ɪ; SMs of set C; grammatical high tone.
DJ: postfinal H tone
CJ: alternating final

Relative forms: in general, the only differences between the relative forms and the corresponding circumstantial forms are the presence of the postfinal /=ŋ́/ (REL) in Slot +5 and the free variation between SMs á and ʊ́ in class 1. The only particular case is the present positive, in which the SM is followed by the special boundary = in the circumstantial form, but not in the relative form. In all cases, there is no distinction between a CJ and a DJ form.

References

Creissels, Denis, Anderson M. Chebanne and Heather W. Nkhwa. 1997. *Tonal Morphology of the Setswana Verb*. München: LINCOM Europa.

Letšeng, Makhauta. 1995. *Les tiroirs verbaux du sotho du sud, formes simples et formes complexes*. University of Grenoble. MA thesis.

Monich, Irina. 2014. Tonal processes in the Setswana verb. *Journal of African Languages and Linguistics* 35. 141–204.

Sophie Manus
9 The conjoint/disjoint alternation in Símákonde

1 Introduction

The aim of this paper is to present a detailed analysis of the verbal conjoint/disjoint alternation in Símákonde. As in other Bantu languages, Símákonde has pairs of tenses that share TAM specifications but differ morphologically and in their relation to what follows. The conjoint/disjoint alternation displayed by Símákonde has been presented in Manus (2003, 2007 and 2010). The present paper offers an updated analysis of the phenomenon. The first-hand data presented here has been collected by the author between 1997 and 2010.

As will be demonstrated, three main criteria determine the CJ/DJ alternation in Símákonde: the segmental morphological marking, the syntactic context that influences the prosodic marking, and the pairing of alternating CJ and DJ forms. We will see in detail how these three criteria interact.

According to these criteria, Símákonde has four conjoint forms, four disjoint forms, two non-canonical pairs of forms and twenty-six unpaired forms, out of a total of thirty-six tense-aspect paradigms. As seen in Table 1, the four conjoint forms stand in contrast with corresponding disjoint forms, and the majority of the conjoint forms differ both morphologically (segmentally) and prosodically from their disjoint counterparts, while the remaining pair exhibits only prosodic differences.

The twenty-six remaining forms function prosodically the same as the four DJ forms but since they do not pair with corresponding CJ forms (third criterion), they are outside of the CJ/DJ alternation system and considered as neither conjoint nor disjoint. In my previous studies, I did not consider the pairing of CJ/DJ forms as a criterion for CJ/DJ and the twenty-six unpaired forms were seen as 'DJ only' because of their clear prosodic behaviour. Devos (2008) has a tripartite conjugational system for Makwe (a language closely related to Makonde), which contains one category of forms that only occur as DJ. As pointed out by Van der Wal in this volume, "Since the DJ verb form is in general less restricted in distribution than

---

I am very grateful to Larry Hyman and the anonymous reviewer of this paper for their comments and suggestions and to Leston Buell, Denis Creissels, Nancy Kula and Lutz Marten for all the lively discussions we had on the potential existence of CJ/DJ in relative clauses. I am of course solely responsible for the opinions expressed in this paper.

DOI 10.1515/9783110490831-009

Table 1: CJ/DJ pairs in the Símákonde verb system.

3 CJ/DJ pairs (morphologically[1] and prosodically different)	–Affirmative present –Affirmative resultative/recent past (P1) –Affirmative remote past (P2)
1 CJ/DJ pair (morphologically identical, prosodically different)	– Affirmative imperative
2 non-canonical pairs (morphologically identical, prosodically different)	– Affirmative subject relative present – Negative present/near future
26 unpaired tenses (prosodically DJ)	(See Manus 2003).

the CJ form and less specific in interpretation, it is easy to see how a tense can be 'DJ only'."

Not unlike what can be found in many other Bantu languages (cf. papers in this volume), the four pairs of tenses diplaying the CJ/DJ alternation are all affirmative tenses and occur in main clauses only. The three pairs which exhibit both a morphological and prosodic contrast between CJ and DJ are the present, the resultative/recent past (P1) and the remote past (P2); the one that exhibits only a syntactic phrasing difference (influencing the prosody) is the imperative.

In the following sections, we will look at the two[2] main criteria that define the CJ/DJ alternation in Símákonde: segmental morphological marking in Section 2, prosodic marking, syntactic context and information structure in Section 3. Finally in Section 4, we will look at two sets of verb forms that resemble CJ/DJ pairs in some aspects but are not (the subject relative present affirmative and the present/near future negative).

2 Segmental morphological marking

2.1 Segmentally distinct CJ/DJ pairs

In Símákonde, the distinction between CJ and DJ is marked on the verb by segmental morphology for most forms (three pairs out of the four identified in the

---

[1] segmentally.
[2] The third one (pairing) is already fulfilled for these forms as shown in Table 1.

verb system). Note that, as pointed out by Van der Wal (this volume), it often is impossible to segment one part as indicating DJ and another part as tense, since one morpheme will encode both affirmative present tense (in a main clause) and disjoint for example (1b).

In all three pairs, the disjoint form has a tense prefix, while its conjoint equivalent is not marked or has a zero morpheme as shown in the examples below. In (1), the affirmative present tense CJ has no tense prefix as shown in (1a), whereas the disjoint form has a tense prefix *-nku-* as shown in (1b).

(1)   a.   CJ   (*tú-Ø-súmá*   *sí-lóongo*)
                   1PL.SM-PRES-buy   7-pot
                   'We are buying (a) pot.'

        b.   DJ   (*tu-nku-súúma*)
                   1PL.SM-PRES-buy
                   'We are buying.'

In (1) and examples to follow, the parentheses indicate the edges of the phonological phrases. In Símákonde, the right boundaries of phonological phrases are marked by the systematic lengthening of the penultimate syllable and vowel length is not phonemic. CJ verb forms always phrase together with what follows, while DJ forms phrase separately. This will be described in details in Section 3. Note that penultimate lengthening (PUL) is not restricted to marking the conjoint/disjoint alternation in Símákonde (see Manus 2003, 2010 and *forthcoming*).

As seen in (2) and (3), the other two segmentally distinct pairs lack a tense prefix in the CJ but end in *-ile*. In the DJ, both take a distinct tense prefix *-ndi-* and end in *-a*.

(2)   a.   CJ   (*tú-Ø-súm-ílé*   *sí-lóongo*)
                   1PL.SM-P2-buy-SUFF   7-pot
                   'We bought (a) pot.'

        b.   DJ   (*tú-ndí-suûm-a*)
                   1PL.SM-P2-buy-SUFF
                   'We bought.'

(3)   a.   CJ   (*tu-Ø-sum-ile*   *sí-lóongo*)
                   1PL.SM-P1-buy-SUFF   7-pot
                   'We have bought (a) pot.'

        b.   DJ   (*tu-ndí-suúm-a*)
                   1PL.SM-P1-buy-SUFF
                   'We have bought.'

Table 2: Structure of the segmentally distinct pairs.

	CJ		DJ	
	-TAM-	-suff	-TAM-	-suff
PRES	-Ø-	-a	-nku-	-a
P1	-Ø-	-ile	-ndi-	-a
P2	-Ø-	-ile	-ndi-	-a

Contrary to the disjoint forms shown in (1b), (2b) and (3b), conjoint forms can never occur phrase-finally as shown in (4a) and (4b). We will discuss syntactic context, non-finality of CJ forms and phrasing in details below in Section 3.

(4) a. CJ *(tú-Ø-súmá)³
         1PL.SM-PRES-buy

     b. CJ *(tú-Ø-súm-ílé)
         1PL.SM-P2-buy-SUFF

We saw in (1), (2) and (3) the three CJ/DJ pairs that differ morphologically / segmentally. These differences are summarized in Table 2.

In Table 2, one can see that the CJ P1 and P2 tenses and the DJ P1 and P2 tenses are segmentally identical. There is, however, a tonal distinction, as shown in (5) and (6) below. Let us look at the CJ forms first. In (5a), the verb form bears a low tone pattern with a final (floating) high (that links to the first available syllable) and in (5b) the verb form bears a H plateau.

(5) a. CJ (ngu-Ø-sum-ilé   naângu)
             1SG.SM-P1-buy-SUFF   myself
             'I have bought myself (recently).'

     b. CJ (ngú-Ø-súm-ílé   naângu)
             1SG.SM-P2-buy-SUFF   myself
             'I bought myself (a long time ago).'

Likewise, the DJ P1 and the DJ P2 are segmentally identical, only their tone patterns differ as shown in (6a) and (6b). The first one has a LH penultimate melody

---

3 If these were pronounced, their penultimate vowel would have to lengthen due to penultimate lenghtening.

and a macrostem initial high; the second one has a LHL penultimate melody and a subject marker high on the pre-stem. See Manus (2015) for more information about the stem melodic patterns of disjoint verb forms in Símákonde.

(6). a. DJ (*ni-ndí-suúm-a*)
1SG.SM-P1-buy-SUFF
'I have bought (recently).'

b. DJ (*ní-ndí-suûm-a*)
1SG.SM-P2-buy-SUFF
'I bought (a long time ago).'

2.2 Segmentally identical CJ/DJ pair

The last CJ/DJ pair is identical segmentally: Both conjoint and disjoint forms of the imperative have no tense prefix, but they differ in terms of phrasing as shown in (7).

(7) a. CJ (*Ø-lol-a   sí-lóongo*)
IMP-look-SUFF   7-pot
'Look at (the) pot!'

b. DJ (*Ø-loól-a*)
IMP-look-SUFF
'Look!'

c. DJ (*Ø-loól-a*)   (*si-loôngo*[4])
IMP-look-SUFF   7-pot
'Look at (the) pot!'

d. (*si-loôngo*)
7-pot
'(a) pot'

In (7b) and (7c), the DJ verb undergoes penultimate lengthening and bears a high tone on its penult, while in (7a), the high tone of the penult has to shift in the phonological phrase and is realized on the following noun where it spreads up to the following high when there is one. The imperative is the only pair whose CJ and DJ tenses bear the same morphological tone patterns.

---

[4] This noun bears a LHL melody on its lengthened penult.

Table 3: Structure of the segmentally identical pair.

	CJ		DJ	
	-TAM-	-suff	-TAM-	-suff
IMP	-Ø-	-a	-Ø-	-a

2.3 Summary

All eight CJ/DJ paired tenses are exemplified in Table 4 below.

Table 4: Structure and examples of the eight paired tenses.

	TENSE	CJ FORM	DJ FORM
Segmentally distinct pairs			
Affirmative	Present	SMII[5]-Ø-VB-a	SMI-nku-VB-a
		(ngú-Ø-súm-á naângu)	(ni-nku-súúm-a)
		I buy/am buying myself	I buy/am buying
	P1		
	(result./recent past)		
	long form[6]	SMII-Ø-VB-ile	SMI-ndi-VB-a
	short form	SMII-Ø-VB-i	
	long form	(ngu-Ø-sum-ilé naângu)	(ni-ndí-suúm-a)
	short form	(ngu-Ø-sum-í naângu)	
		I have bought myself	I have bought
	P2		
	(remote past)		
	long form	SMII-Ø-VB-ile	SMI-ndi-VB-a
	short form	SMII-Ø-VB-i	
	long form	(ngú-Ø-súm-ílé naângu)	(ní-ndí-suûm-a)
	short form	(ngú-Ø-súm-í naângu)	
		I bought myself	I bought

---

5 There are two series of subject markers in Símákonde that differ only in 1sg : *ni* (SMI) and *ngu* (SMII) (cf. Manus 2003).

6 Some of the conjoint forms have both a long and a short form. This phenomenon is rare in Símákonde, since it is attested only for a few conjoint forms and some relatives. Both long and short forms are used very frequently. They are shown in Table 4.

Table 4: (continued)

TENSE		CJ FORM	DJ FORM
Segmentally identical pair			
	Imperative	VB-a	VB-a
	long form	(lol-a líjéémbe !)	(loól-á) (lijeémbe !)
	short form	(lo líjéémbe !)	
		Look at the hoe!	Look at the hoe!

As can be seen in Table 4, all conjoint verb forms do have one thing in common: They have no tense prefix. But the lack of tense prefix is not enough to make a conjoint form since conjoint forms are not the only ones in the Símákonde verb system that share this characteristic: 50% of the unpaired forms (that behave prosodically as DJ forms) also have no tense prefix (see Manus 2003 for an exhaustive list, structures and examples of all verb forms). Some conjoint forms also have a suffix *-ile*. Most disjoint forms have a tense prefix (as seen above, the disjoint imperative does not).

Having established the segmental morphological forms of the four CJ/DJ pairs, we now consider the second main criterion determining whether or not forms are CJ or DJ in Símákonde: prosodic marking (phonological phrases), which, as we shall see, is determined by the syntactic context and information structure.

3 Prosodic marking, syntactic context and information structure

As seen above, conjoint forms can never occur phrase-finally in a main clause in Símákonde (4). As pointed out by Van der Wal (this volume), this is the one property shared by conjoint verb forms in Bantu. Disjoint forms, on the contrary, can occur at the end of a phonological phrase (1b, 2b, 3b), though they do not have to (7c). In Símákonde, the right edge of a phonological phrase is always marked prosodically by penultimate lengthening, which has a direct influence on tonal patterns of verb forms and blurs the borders between phonological phrasing effects and potential tonal morphemes encoding the CJ/DJ alternation.

As described by Kraal (2005) for Chinnima (another Makonde language than the one discussed here), conjoint forms in Makonde "are post-verbal focus tenses, the focus being on the word following the verbal form in the same p-phrase. Their disjoint counterparts, being a p-phrase on their own, either have verbal focus, or simply are the unmarked forms."

We will first consider CJ forms, phonological phrases, tone and elements immediately after the verb (IAV), then DJ forms and IAV elements, and finally summarize in which syntactic contexts both CJ and DJ forms can or cannot occur.

3.1 Non-finality of conjoint forms, phonological phrases, tone and IAV elements

Since a conjoint form can never occur at the end of a phonological phrase in a main clause, it is always followed by an element with which it phrases and forms a single ph-phrase. It is then the penult of this element, in the position immediately after the verb, that is lengthened. The penult of the conjoint form is always short. The IAV element can bear different relationships to the verb: For example, it can be a pronoun reinforcing the subject (8)[7], an object noun (9a), an object interrogative (9b), an adverb (10), etc. In the following examples, the elements in focus are capitalized.

(8)   CJ   (á-Ø-tótá   náae)
              1SM-PRES-sew   herself/himself
              'She is sewing HERSELF.'

(9)   a.   CJ   (á-Ø-tótá   sí-júulu)
                  1SM-PRES-sew   7-hat
                  'She is sewing (the) HAT.'

      b.   CJ   (á-Ø-tótá   nyamaání)?
                  1SM-PRES-sew   what
                  'What is she sewing?'

(10)   CJ   (á-Ø-tótá   nameêne)
               1SM-PRES-sew   a lot
               'She is sewing A LOT.'

Since my aim in this paper is to discuss the CJ/DJ alternation system in Símákonde and not to describe and analyze the various tone patterns in CJ verb phrases, I will not address the tonal details here. However, it is important to note that the tone patterns of CJ forms and CJ verb phrases are conditioned by both 'grammar' and tone. In other words, the spreading or the shift of (high) tones from a CJ verb form to the IAV element in a CJ verb phrase is sensitive to the grammatical nature of the IAV element and also to its general tone pattern. For example, the (high) tones of CJ forms will spread or shift on following IAV nouns, but never on pronouns nor IAV

---

[7] As will be seen in (19), (20) and (21) below, the same IAV elements can occur with DJ forms.

adverbs, and never on nouns that are entirely low. Creissels (2012, revised in 2014) has observed similar tonal phenomena in Tswana (where he described sensitivity "to the grammatical nature of the following word and to the tone of its first syllable").

To illustrate this, let us look at a few examples. In (11b), the H of the CJ present plateaus from the first syllable of the CJ form until the next high tone (the H on the penult of the IAV object noun).

(11) a. (*li-jeémbe*)
 5-hoe
 '(a) hoe'

 b. CJ (*ngú-Ø-súmá   lí-jéémbe*)
 1SG.SM-PRES-buy 5-hoe
 'I am buying A HOE.'

If the object noun is entirely low as in (12a), there is no possible plateauing: The H of the CJ form can not spread on the IAV noun, as shown in (12b).

(12) a. (*si-pambeele*)
 7-rhinoceros
 '(a) rhinoceros'

 b. CJ (*ngú-Ø-lólá   si-pambeele*)
  1SG.SM-PRES-watch 7-rhinoceros
  'I am watching A RHINOCEROS.'

If the IAV element is a pronoun (13) or an adverb (14), the H on the conjoint form is blocked too, since it cannot spread and plateau onto pronouns[8] or adverbs.

(13) a. (*naângu*)
  'me/myself'

 b. CJ   (*ngú-Ø-tót-île   naângu*)
   1SG.SM-P2-sew-SUFF myself
   'I was sewing MYSELF.'

(14) a. (*nameêne*)
  'a lot'

 b. CJ (*ngú-Ø-tót-île   nameêne*)
  1SG.SM-P2-sew-SUFF   a.lot
  'I was sewing A LOT.'

---

[8] Except in the 3pl class 2 pronoun: vanaâo > vánááo.

The exact same tonal phenomena can be observed if the high of the CJ form is a final floating high instead of a H plateau, as in the resultative/ recent past (P1) for example. The final floating high of the CJ form spreads to the following (IAV) noun (until the next H) only if the noun bears at least one H tone (15); it links to the first available syllable (to the left: the last syllable of the CJ form) if the IAV noun is entirely low (16), or if the IAV element is a pronoun (17) or an adverb.

(15) a. (*li-guúŋu*)
 5-bread
 'bread.'

 b. CJ (*ngu-Ø-l-ile*   *lí-gúúŋu*)
 1SG.SM-P1-eat-SUFF   5-bread
 'I ate (the) BREAD!'

(16) a. (*vi-ndoolo*)
 8-lentil
 'lentils'

 b. CJ (*ngu-Ø-l-ilé*   *vi-ndoolo*)
 1SG.SM-P1-eat-SUFF   8-lentil
 'I ate LENTILS.'

(17) a. (*mweênu*)
 2PL
 'you, yourselves'

 b. CJ (*mu-Ø-takatuk-id-ilé*[9]   *mweênu*)
 2PL.SM-P1-stand.up-SUFF   2PL
 'You stood up, YOURSELVES.'

3.2 Disjoint forms and IAV elements

Contrary to conjoint forms, disjoint forms always constitute a single phonological phrase on their own and their penult is always lengthened (18). They can also be followed by a second element; in this case they do not phrase with it and constitute two distinct phonological phrases, whether this second element is a subject (19), an object noun (20a), an object interrogative (20b), an adverb (21), etc.

---

[9] -il-ile > id-ile. Cf. Manus 2003.

(18) DJ (*a-nku-tóóta*)
        1SM-PRES-sew
        'She is sewing.'

(19) DJ (*a-nku-tóóta*) (*náae*)
        1SM-PRES-sew   herself/himself
        'She is sewing herself.'

(20) a. DJ (*a-nku-tóóta*) (*sí-júulu*)
            1SM-PRES-sew   7-hat
            'She is sewing (a) hat.'

     b. DJ (*a-nku-tóóta*) (*nyamaání*)?[10]
            1SM-PRES-sew   what
            'What is she sewing?'

(21) DJ (*a-nku-tóóta*) (*nameêne*)
        1SM-PRES-sew   a.lot
        'She is sewing a lot.'

3.3 Inventory of CJ & DJ contexts and phrasing

Table 5 below summarizes both context and phrasing conditions for CJ and DJ. We will see in 4. that all of these conditions have to be satisfied for the second criterion for CJ/DJ to be fullfilled. When a form does not obey all of these conditions, it will not be considered CJ nor DJ.

Finally in Section 4 we will look at two sets of verb forms that resemble CJ/DJ pairs in some aspects but are not: The subject relative present affirmative and the present/near future negative.

Table 5: Phrasing & contexts for CJ & DJ forms.

CJ	DJ
(V _ IAV)	(V) _ (IAV)
*(V) _ #	(V) _ #

---

10 This is more of an echo question here. The regular WH-question occurs as expected with a CJ form as shown above in (9b).

4 Non-canonical pairs: The case of the subject relative present affirmative and of the present/near future negative

As shown in Hyman & Watters (1984), and as pointed out again by Van der Wal (this volume), though languages differ as far as the CJ/DJ distribution is concerned, one common trend is that the CJ/DJ alternation is often restricted "to the 'basic' or less marked tenses (affirmative, non-special mood)". Relative and negative tenses are thus generally not expected to display the CJ/DJ alternation (see Kavari, Marten & Van der Wal (2012) for a discussion about information structure and subordinate clauses and also Hyman (this volume) and Van der Wal (this volume) for discussions about the various reasons for the scarcity of CJ/DJ in relative and negative tenses).

Previous studies have identified very few CJ/DJ tenses in relative clauses in zone S: Buell (2006, Zulu, 1 tense), and in zone P: Devos (2008, Makwe, 1 tense), Kraal (2005, Chinnima, 2 tenses), Manus (2003, 2007, 2010, Símákonde, 1 tense).

We will explore below all three criteria applied in this study to define CJ/DJ pairs in Símákonde (pairing and morphological marking in 4.1. and prosodic marking, phonological phrases and syntactic context in 4.2.) and apply them to both pairs of non-canonical tenses. We will see how the two non-canonical pairs previously identified as CJ/DJ in Símákonde can actually be excluded from the CJ/DJ system, since they do not obey all three strict criteria used in this study, especially the second criterion: prosodic marking, phonological phrases and syntactic context. As far as phonological phrasing is concerned, both pairs show distributional properties that are completely non-canonical compared to those of the four CJ/DJ pairs presented above.

4.1 Pairing and morphological marking

For two of the three criteria used in this study, namely pairing and morphological marking, the subject relative present affirmative and the present/near future negative both seem to function like regular CJ/DJ pairs. They function in pairs and, morphologically, they resemble the imperative affirmative presented above since they have no tense prefix and are segmentally identical, as shown in Table 6 below.[11]

---

[11] Contrary to the imperative though, their tone patterns differ.

Table 6: Structure and examples of non-canonical pairs.

Non-canonical pairs			
Affirmative	Subject relative present	SMII-Ø-VB-a (muúnú) (á-Ø-sum-a lijeémbe) the man who is buying (the) hoe	SMII-Ø-VB-a (muúnú) (á-Ø-suûm-a) the man who is buying
Negative	Present/near future	NegPref-SMII-Ø-VB-a (á-ngú-Ø-súm-á lijeembe) I am not buying (the) hoe I will not buy (the) hoe	NegPref-SMII-Ø-VB-a (a-ngu-Ø-suum-a) I am not buying I will not buy

4.2 Prosodic marking, phonological phrases and syntactic context

4.2.1 The subject relative present affirmative

Let us first look at the subject relative present affirmative. At first sight, the pair might look like it displays a regular CJ/DJ alternation prosodically speaking, but a closer look shows a striking difference. The subject relative present affirmative can occur both with and without penultimate lengthening (PUL). In (22) below, the verb form seems to appear under a DJ form, since it constitutes a single phonological phrase and bears a lengthened penult. It is not followed by an IAV element. In (23) (with an object marker) and (24) (without), it seems to appear as a CJ form, since it has a short penult, phrases with the IAV element (an object noun here) and constitutes a single phonological phrase with it.

(22) DJ ? (ń-dyóóko)   (á-Ø-tukuûta)   (a-ndiî-gwa)
          1-child   1SM-PRES-run   1SM-P1-fall
          'The child who is running (just) fell.'

(23) CJ ? (ń-dyóóko)   (á-Ø-ń-nola   ń-néembo)   (a-ndiî-gwa)
          1-child   1SM-PRES-1OM-watch   1-elephant   1SM-P1-fall
          'The child who is watching an/the elephant (just) fell.'

(24) CJ ? (ń-dyóóko)   (á-Ø-lola   dí-mbúúdi)   (a-ndiî-gwa)
          1-child   1SM-PRES-watch   10-goat   1SM-P1-fall
          'The child who is watching (the) goats (just) fell.'

But the example in (25) illustrates that the relative verb followed by an IAV object noun can never take a lengthened penult and phrase separately as regular DJ forms should normally do.

(25) *(ń-dyóóko)   (á-Ø-loôla)   (dí-mbúúdi)   (a-ndiî-gwa)
    1-child   1SM-PRES-watch   10-goat   1SM-P1-fall
    'The child who is watching (the) goats (just) fell.'

This is a striking difference between all the DJ forms presented in this paper, and this relative form. When there is an IAV element, DJ forms must normally appear with PUL, followed by an element that also has PUL, as shown in (7c), (19), (20) and (21) above and (26) below.

(26) DJ (ni-nku-lóóla)   (dí-mbúúdi)
        1SG.SM-PRES-watch   10-goat
        'I am watching goats'

As shown in Table 5 summarizing phrasing & contexts for CJ & DJ forms, a regular DJ form should occur before an IAV element and before pause. The subject relative present affirmative with PUL (that resembles a DJ form) only occurs when the verb is final within its clause.

Let us compare:

- Main Clause:
(i) the child is watching goats   (DJ)   (ń-dyóóko)   (a-nku-lóóla)   (dí-mbúúdi)
(ii) the child is watching GOATS   (CJ)   (ń-dyóóko)   (á-Ø-lólá)   dí-mbúúdi)

- Relative Clause:
(iii) the child who is watching goats   (ń-dyóóko)   (á-Ø-lola)   dí-mbúúdi)
(iv) *the child (who is watching) (goats)   *(ń-dyóóko)   (á-Ø-loôla)   (dí-mbúúdi)

So it seems here that the subject relative present affirmative undergoes PUL for phrasing reasons that are independent from CJ/DJ issues: In this case, PUL is a mark of phrasing but not a mark of DJ.[12]

---

[12] Interestingly, Símákonde also has complex phrasing phenomena in noun-phrases that interact with the phrasing of the relative present tense described here. Phrasing phenomena in noun-phrases are CJ/DJ-like and have been observed in various Makonde languages by Kraal (Chinnima, 2005), Devos (Makwe, 2004, 2008) and Manus (Símákonde, 2003, 2010, *forthcoming*). In Símákonde for example, some modifiers trigger an obligatory phrasing with the head-noun (demonstratives), some modifiers can never phrase with the head noun (adjectives), and some can optionally phrase with the head noun (possessives). In the nominal domain, the CJ/DJ-like alternation is marked only prosodically (phonological phrases and tone), not segmentally. See Manus 2010 for a detailed inventory of all the complex phrasing options occuring in relatives between a verb form such as the subject relative present affirmative presented here, and a following object noun phrase made of a noun and one or more than one modifier in Símákonde.

Table 7: Phrasing & contexts in a main clause and in a relative clause.

Main clause (regular DJ)	Relative clause
(V) _ (IAV)	*(V) _ (IAV)
(V) _ #	(V) _ #

The unusual phrasing of CJ/DJ-like relative tenses seems to be a Makonde trend since the same kind of phenomenon has been observed in two other Makonde languages: Both Makwe (Devos 2004, 2008) and Makonde, Chinnima (Kraal 2005) attest a similar conjoint/disjoint-like distinction in at least one relative tense.

Chinnima (Makonde) attests a conjoint/disjoint-like distinction in two relative tenses: Direct relative present and direct relative present perfective (Kraal 2005). Kraal refers to these tenses as 'conjoint-disjoint' tenses[13], which are different from tenses that are conjoint and tenses that are disjoint. His system is tripartite like Devos's for Makwe. He has the following three categories of tenses: CJ, DJ and CJ-DJ. Just like the Símákonde subject relative present affirmative described above, the CJ-DJ tenses attested in Chinnima relatives have no tense prefix, the alternation is marked only by tone and phrasing (with PUL for the DJ-like forms, without PUL for the CJ-like forms). As mentioned above, according to his analysis, conjoint tenses are post-verbal focus tenses, whereas in the case of conjoint-disjoint tenses "the choice between the conjoint form and the disjoint form is not determined by focus, but by the syntactic environment": Whenever the mentioned relative tenses are followed by a post-verbal element, they form a single phonological phrase with it as shown in (27) and (28) below, exactly like the subject relative present affirmative in Símákonde.

Chinnima (Makonde, Kraal 2005: 210). Direct relative present (conjoint-disjoint).

(27) DJ *a-(vá-)yángaáta*
      's/he who helps (them)'

(28) CJ *a-(vá-)yángata váyééni*
      's/he who helps (the) guests'

The question here is whether the Chinnima conjoint-disjoint tenses can be considered paired tenses. They do not differ segmentally and one could argue that they are not different tonally either as the small tonal difference could be said to be an effect of the difference in phrasing. Is phrasing enough to identify them as tenses showing the conjoint/disjoint alternation? One thing for sure is that the choice between the conjoint and the disjoint form appears to be dictated only by

---

13 Conjoint tenses that are also disjoint or a tense that is both conjoint AND disjoint.

syntactic environment in Chinnima for all 'conjoint-disjoint' tenses, and in Símákonde for the non-canonical subject relative present affirmative.

Makwe (Devos 2004, 2008) also has one relative tense showing a so-called 'conjoint-disjoint' alternation (again marked only by tone): the relative past imperfective. In her tripartite system, some tenses are either conjoint or disjoint and work in pairs, some only occur as disjoint as shown in 1. above and some are 'conjoint-disjoint' or considered 'neutral'. The relative past imperfective is one of these 'neutral' tenses. But, contrary to what we just saw in Makonde Chinnima and in Símákonde, in Makwe, the relative past imperfective and all the other 'neutral' tenses can optionally phrase with the IAV element (CJ) or not (DJ), as shown in the following examples (29) to (32).

Makwe (Devos 2004: 217). Present progressive, conjoint-disjoint ('neutral').

(29)   DJ   (ankuyúúmá) (vitáabu)[14]
            'S/he is buying books.'

(30)   CJ   (ankuyúmá vítáabu)
            'S/he is buying books.'

Makwe (Devos 2004: 234). Subject relative past imperfective, conjoint-disjoint ('neutral')[15].

(31)   DJ   (á-cí-yákúúla)

(32)   CJ   (á-cí-yákúlá ...)[16]

In Símákonde, according to the three criteria used to determine whether tenses are CJ/DJ pairs or not, the subject relative present affirmative tenses are not considered like CJ/DJ tenses. They are non-canonical, since they do not behave like regular CJ/DJ pairs as far as phonological phrasing is concerned.

4.2.2. The present/near future negative

In Símákonde, the present negative is even more irregular prosodically than the subject relative present affirmative. What seems to be a DJ form can appear

---

[14] In Devos the end of a phonological phrase is marked by a vertical line. I used parentheses here for consistency.
[15] The only example of the Subject relative past imperfective appears in a table, out of context, and without glosses but it functions exactly like the present progressive shown in (29) and (30).
[16] The three dots (Devos 2004) indicate that this form is CJ and will have to be followed by something.

sentence-finally. It then has a lengthened penult, as shown in (33), and forms a single phonological phrase as a regular DJ form.

(33) (*a-ngu-Ø-suum-a*)
      NEG-1SG.SM-Ø-VB-buy-SUFF
      'I am not buying / I will not buy.'

But the problem is that it *has* to be utterance-final. It cannot be followed by another element with which it would not phrase, as shown in (34): In this, it differs from all other DJ verb forms of the system.

(34) *(*a-ngu-Ø-suum-a*)   (*si-juulu*)
      NEG-1SG.SM-Ø-buy-SUFF   7-hat

What seems to be the CJ form behaves like a regular CJ form though: It can never occur at the end of a phonological phrase (35). It is always followed by an IAV element with which it phrases and forms a single phonological phrase (36).

(35) *(*á-ngú-Ø-súm-á*)

(36) CJ ? (*á-ngú-Ø-súm-á   si-juulu*)
      NEGPREF-1SG.SM-Ø-buy-SUFF   7-hat
      'I am not buying / I will not buy (a) hat.'

If there was such a thing as a *defective* CJ/DJ pair, then the present/near future negative would be one. It has what looks like a regular CJ form as far as phonological phrases are concerned, but it has a defective / irregular DJ form that can only occur utterance-finally. The two forms are in complementary distribution: The form resembling the DJ form occurs utterance-finally and the one resembling a CJ form occurs in all other contexts.

The tone patterns of the present/near future negative are also unusual. The form with PUL that occurs sentence-finally is always entirely low, the form that occurs without PUL and phrases with an IAV element is always entirely high while the IAV element is always entirely low and this applies to all grammatical categories (nouns, pronouns, adverbs) and whatever the original tone patterns of the IAV noun.

5 Conclusion

Three main criteria have been used to determine the conjoint / disjoint alternation in Símákonde: segmental morphological marking; prosodic phrasing; and the pairing of alternating CJ and DJ forms. According to these criteria, Símákonde has four unambiguous pairs of CJ/DJ tenses (present affirmative, resultative/

recent past affirmative [P1], remote past affirmative [P2], imperative affirmative); twenty-six unpaired forms (disjoint-like prosodically) and two non-canonical pairs (subject relative present affirmative and present/near future negative) that resemble CJ/DJ but are too irregular to be considered as such. Devos (2004, 2008) and Kraal (2005) have also identified a category of irregular CJ/DJ-like tenses that they call "conjoint-disjoint" (Devos, Kraal) and "neutral" (Devos).

Three of the four CJ/DJ pairs (present, P1 and P2) have segmental morphological distinctions: The CJ forms having a zero tense prefix and sometimes an -ile suffix, and the DJ forms having tense prefixes (-*nku*-, -*ndi*-) and an -*a* suffix. The last pair (imperative) is identical segmentally (zero prefix and an -*a* suffix) and distinguished by tone only. The absence of tense prefix is not a clear mark of CJ forms though since half of the non-paired tenses (that are disjoint-like prosodically) do not have a tense prefix either.

Prosodically, as in other Bantu languages, disjoint forms can occur phrase-finally, though they do not have to, whereas conjoint forms can never occur phrase-finally. In Símákonde, the right edge of phonological phrases is systematically marked by the lengthening of the penult. Disjoint forms always constitute a single phonological phrase on their own and have a lengthened penult, whereas conjoint forms are always followed by an element with which they phrase, the penult of the conjoint form being short, when it is the penult of the IAV element that is lengthened. Disjoint forms can be followed by an IAV element, which then phrases separately. In Makonde, conjoint forms generally put the focus on the IAV element, whereas disjoint forms have verbal focus or are unmarked. The four pairs of tenses diplaying the CJ/DJ alternation in Símákonde are all affirmative tenses and occur in main clauses only.

Abbreviations

TAM	tense-aspect-mood	P2	remote past
CJ	conjoint form of the verb	P-PHRASE	phonological phrase
DJ	disjoint form of the verb	PRES	present tense
IAV	immediate after verb position	SM	subject marker
IMP	imperative	SMI	first series of subject markers
NEG	negative	SMII	second series of subject markers
PUL	penultimate lengthening	SUFF	suffix
P1	resultative/recent past	VB	verb base

References

Buell, Leston. 2006. The Zulu conjoint/disjoint verb alternation: Focus or constituency? *ZASPiL* 43. 9–30.
Creissels, Denis. 2012, revised in 2014. Conjoint and disjoint verb forms in Tswana and other Bantu languages. Fédération de Typologie et Universaux Linguistiques (FR 2559), Mise en relief et mise en retrait: le marquage morphologique de la hiérarchie discursive, Paris, 19–20 October 2012.
Devos, Maud. 2004. *A grammar of Makwe*. Leiden: Leiden University PhD dissertation.
Devos, Maud. 2008. *A grammar of Makwe*. München: Lincom Europa.
Hyman, Larry. This volume. Disentangling conjoint, disjoint, metatony, tone cases, augments, prosody, and focus in Bantu.
Hyman, Larry M. & John Watters. 1984. Auxiliary focus. *Studies in African Linguistics* 15. 233–273.
Kavari, Jekura U., Lutz Marten & Jenneke van der Wal. 2012. Tone cases in Otjiherero: head-complement relations, linear order, and information structure. *Africana Linguistica* 18. 315–353.
Kraal, Peter. 2005. *A grammar of Makonde (Chinnima, Tanzania)*. Leiden: Leiden University PhD dissertation.
Manus, Sophie. 2003. *Morphologie et tonologie du Símákonde, parlé par les communautés d'origine mozambicaine de Zanzibar et de Tanga (Tanzanie)*. Paris: Institut National des Langues et Civilisations Orientales (Langues'O) PhD dissertation.
Manus, Sophie. 2007. Phrasal Tone and the conjoint/disjoint distinction in Símákonde. Presentation at workshop *Focus prosody in Southern African languages*, Zentrum für Allgemeine Sprachwissenschaft (ZAS), Berlin, 22 November 2007.
Manus, Sophie. 2010. The prosody of Símákonde relative clauses. In Sophie Manus, Jean-Marc Beltzung, Laura Downing, Cedric Patin, Annie Rialland & Kristina Riedel (eds.), *Papers from the Workshop on Bantu Relative Clauses*, 159–186. ZASPiL 53 (1).
Manus, Sophie. 2015. Melodic patterns in Símákonde. In David Odden & Lee Bickmore (eds.), *Melodic tone patterns in Bantu*, 263–274. Special issue of *Africana Linguistica*. Tervuren: Royal Museum for Central Africa.
Manus, Sophie. Forthcoming. Penultimate shortening in NPs: The case of Símákonde. In Gene Buckley, Thera Crane & Jeff Good (eds.), *Revealing structure, finding patterns in grammars and using grammatical patterns to Elucidate Language: A festschrift to honor Larry M. Hyman*. Stanford: CSLI Publications.
Van der Wal, Jenneke. This volume. What is the conjoint/disjoint alternation in Bantu languages? Parameters of variation.

Nancy C. Kula
10 The conjoint/disjoint alternation and phonological phrasing in Bemba

1 Introduction

Starting with the pioneering work of Sharman and Meeussen (1955) and Sharman (1956), Bemba has long been known to have a conjoint/disjoint (CJ/DJ) alternation in its verb forms. The CJ/DJ alternation consists of complementary pairs of verb forms in particular tenses, distinguished by their morphological marking and distributional properties. Disjoint forms are generally able to occur finally in a main clause while conjoint forms are not. Associated with these distributional properties are interpretational properties which vary across different Bantu languages and reveal information structure.

The goal of this chapter is to present the properties of the CJ/DJ alternation in Bemba (Northern and Copperbelt dialects) and to specifically evaluate whether the alternation is encoded by tone in Bemba. Apart from segmental morphological marking of the CJ/DJ alternation in particular tenses, a significant number of other tenses show tone marking that distinguishes the context of occurrence of a verb form in the same way that the CJ/DJ alternation does. This raises the question whether such tone marking should be treated as encoding the alternation and if not, why the tonal distributions are so similar to the CJ/DJ alternation. The chapter argues that while differential tone marking may coincide with the CJ/DJ alternation, in indicating verb forms that can be final or not in main clauses, these tone differences are more aptly attributable to phonological phrasing. Thus, although phonological phrasing oft times matches the domains of the CJ/DJ alternation, the alternation itself is marked by segmental morphological morphemes in Bemba, rather than by tone. The interaction between the two comes from the fact that both the CJ/DJ alternation and phonological phrasing are used to express information structure.

The chapter is organised as follows: Section 2 provides background on Bemba tonology, which is relevant for the ensuing discussion; Section 3 presents

---

Thanks to Lee Bickmore for discussion on an earlier version of this chapter and to Lutz Marten for insights on the conjoint/disjoint alternation. Thanks also to two anonymous reviewers and the editors whose comments have significantly improved the clarity of the argument presented. Any errors and shortcomings are my own.

DOI 10.1515/9783110490831-010

the morphological segmental CJ/DJ alternation markers; Section 4 looks at prosodic marking with the goal of evaluating whether tone-marking independently encodes the CJ/DJ alternation; Section 5 looks at the interpretational properties of the CJ/DJ alternation and evaluates to what extent these also coincide with prosodic marking; Section 6 gives the final evaluation of prosodic marking of the CJ/DJ alternation in Bemba; Section 7 offers a short discussion of phrasal phonology in nominal forms; and Section 8 ends the chapter with some concluding remarks.

2 Background: Basic Bemba tonology

In order to understand both the CJ/DJ alternation and prosodic marking in Bemba it is necessary to present some background on the basic tonal structure of Bemba which is further detailed in Bickmore and Kula (2013), Guthrie (1945), Kula and Bickmore (2015), and Sharman and Meeussen (1955). These works should be consulted for more detailed discussion and additional examples.

The verbal tonology of Bemba distinguishes between lexically H-toned and toneless verb roots typically resulting in minimal pairs such as -lùk- 'weave' vs. -lúk- 'vomit'.[1] The tone-bearing unit (TBU) in Bemba is the mora with the following tonal structures attested: Cà, Càà, Cá, Cáá, Cáà, *Càá.

There are two main H tone spreading processes central to the tonology of Bemba: unbounded spreading and bounded spreading. Unbounded spreading spreads a H rightwards up to the end of the verb form, targeting all following toneless moras in a phrase-final word. The examples in (1) show unbounded spreading in a verb form where the initial mora of the 3rd plural subject marker is lexically H-toned (1a–b) and the following future marker -ka- and verb are toneless.[2] This contrasts with (1c) where the 1st plural subject marker is low-toned and the verb form therefore surfaces as all low.

---

[1] Unless otherwise stated all reference to 'Bemba' assumes that the point holds for both Northern and Copperbelt Bemba dialects, otherwise each dialect is referred to specifically. Copperbelt Bemba data are drawn from speakers mainly based in Ndola. The following consultants, whose input is graciously acknowledged, have provided data on either dialect: Honoria Mutale, Bupe Kula, Moses Nkandu, Fr. Kabiti, Oscar Mukabila and Mukanu Kapalanga.
[2] In all examples high tone is marked by an acute accent and low tone with a grave accent. Underlying lexical high tone is underscored. 1st and 2nd person plural subject markers are toneless while all other SMs are H. The class 1 singular object marker (OM) is toneless while all other OMs are H. TAMs have specific tones as will be presented in ensuing discussion and like in most Bantu languages derivational suffixes are all toneless. Examples show the standard Bantu verb structure: (NEG)-SM-TAM-(OM)-VERB STEM-(TAM)/FV.

(1) a. *bá̰-ká-lúk-á*
   2SM-FUT3-plait-FV
   'They will plait.'

   b. *bá̰-ká-lóóndólól-á*
   2SM-FUT3-explain-FV
   'They will explain.'

   c. *tù-kà-lòòndòlòl-à*
   1PL.SM-FUT3-explain-FV
   'We will explain.'

Unbounded spreading contrasts with bounded spreading, which does not spread a H to the end of the verb form. There are two contexts where bounded spreading applies. Examples in (2a–b) illustrate one of these – when the verb is followed by another constituent, here an adverb. Copperbelt Bemba (CB) and Northern Bemba (NB) differ with respect to the domain of bounded spreading which is ternary in CB and binary in NB. The examples in (2a–b) thus illustrate CB and only differ from (1a–b) in not having unbounded H spreading on the verb form. To show that this is not influenced by the tone of the following constituent both a low-toned adverb (2a) and one with an initial H (2b) are used. (2c) shows that there is no H spreading when the subject marker is low-toned.

(2) a. *bá̰-ká-lúk-à*   *bwììnò*
   2SM-FUT3-plait-FV   well
   'They will plait well.'

   b. *bá̰-ká-lóóndòlòl-à*   *sá̰àná*
   2SM-FUT3-explain-FV   a.lot
   'They will explain a lot.'

   c. *tù-kà-lòòndòlòl-à*   *bwììnò*
   1PL.SM-FUT3-explain-FV well
   'We will explain well.'

The other context where bounded spreading applies is when two Hs are separated by a number of toneless moras sufficient to allow bounded spreading. This is best illustrated by a preceding lexical H that is followed by a final H, for example as provided by the lexically H-toned post-verbal enclitic =*kó*.[3] Examples using the same toneless verbs and future marker as in (1) and (2) are given in (3).

---

[3] The enclitic =*kó̰* is a class 17 locative enclitic on the verb that can assume a number of other interpretations on which see Marten and Kula (2014) for discussion. In terms of prosodic structure the enclitic is part of the same prosodic word as its host.

(3) a. bá-ká-lóòndòlòl-à=kó
2SM-FUT3-explain-FV-17LOC
'They will also help to explain.'

b. bá-ká-lúk-ìl-à=kó
2SM-FUT3-plait-APPL-FV-17LOC
'They will plait in there.'

c. tù-kà-lòòndòlòl-à= kó
1PL.SM-FUT3-explain-FV-17LOC
'We will also help to explain.'

The lexical H of the subject marker in (3a–b) spreads in bounded fashion (ternary spread for CB) because of the following H on the final mora of the verb form, provided by the enclitic. As in the examples in (2) bounded spreading has a specified domain and does not continue to spread the H even when there are potential target toneless moras.

Bickmore and Kula (2013) propose that ternary spreading in CB is the result of two separate processes. The first is High Tone Doubling (HTD), which spreads a H to the following mora (whether that mora is in the same syllable or the next one). HTD is the only process that applies in bounded spreading in NB. By contrast in CB, HTD feeds a second process of Secondary HTD, which continues to spread the H to the first mora of the following syllable. The strongest evidence that these are separate processes is that the two processes are subject to different constraints. Of importance in the current discussion is that HTD applies even if it results in H adjacency with a following lexical H (an OCP violation), while Secondary HTD never allows such violations. Consider the CB examples below illustrating an OCP violation triggered by HTD and resulting in downstep (4a–b), in contrast to (4c) where Secondary High Doubling does not apply to avoid an OCP violation. (No downstep occurs between underlyingly adjacent Hs).

(4) a. bá-ká-ˈtú-lúk-á
2SM-FUT3-1PL.OM-plait-FV
'They will plait us (our hair)'

b. ú-kú-ˈléét-á
AUG-15-bring-FV
'to bring'

c. bá-ká-mù-lás-á
2SM-FUT3-1OM-hit-FV
'They will hit him/her.'

In (4a) the 3rd plural subject marker *bá-* and the 1st plural object marker -*tú-* are lexically H-toned. The H of the subject marker *bá-* undergoes HTD to the following toneless future marker -*ka-* despite the fact that there is a following lexical H which is therefore downstepped (indicated by superscript /!/). The same applies in the infinitive form in (4b) with a lexically H-toned verb. (4c) includes a lexically H-toned verb and toneless 2nd plural object marker -*mu-*, and shows only HTD of the initial H onto the following future marker but further spread by Secondary HTD is blocked as this would result in adjacency with the following lexical H of the H-toned verb. Thus, HTD and Secondary HTD contrast with respect to their applicability in OCP contexts. In contrast to this, HTD in NB is subject to the OCP and thus always avoids creating adjacent Hs. A second difference between the two processes is that HTD can spread a H onto a word-final TBU, but Secondary HTD cannot.

The final point to discuss in Bemba tonology is the range and use of Melodic Highs (MHs). As noted in Odden and Bickmore (2014) MHs are specific tones or tone patterns that are assigned to verb forms based on different morphological properties of the verb, especially TAMs. In Bemba TAMs introduce MHs which contrast in where they dock (Bickmore and Kula 2013): (i) on the final vowel (FV); (ii) on the second vowel of the stem (V2); or (iii) on the domain from V2 to the FV. A fourth set of TAMs have no MH. These tones are treated as MHs because they cannot be readily explained by tone spreading rules as discussed above and they occur similarly in stems with either underlying Hs or toneless verb roots as long as the TAM requirement is met. The crucial point for the current discussion is that these MHs interact with the tonal processes discussed above. Consider the MH patterns exemplified in (5) below. MHs like lexical Hs are underlined.

(5) MH patterns in Bemba

(i) TAMs with no MH:
Infinitive, Far Future (F3) (/ka-/), Habitual (/la-/), Progressive (/lée-/), Past Progressive (/a-lée-/), Desiderative 1 (/ka-lée/), Nearer Past (P2) (/á-cí-/), Immediate Future (F1) (/á-láa/), Continuous (/á-cí-láa/), Future Continuous (/ka-láa/), Imperative 2 (á-lii-), Hypothetical Continuous (preverbal /a-/, /láa-/), Desiderative 2 (/leé-/)

    a. *tù-kà-pàt-à*   'We will hate.'   (Future)
    b. *tù-là-pàt-à*   'We usually hate.'   (Habitual)
    c. *tù-lée-pát-á*   'We are hating.'   (Progressive)

In (5a–b) with no MH the verb forms surface as toneless. (5c) with a H on the progressive marker -*lée-* shows unbounded spreading to the end of the verb form. In this case surface Hs can be accounted for by rightward H spreading.

(ii) TAMs with a MH on the FV:
Imperative (with a H-toned Root and no OM), Subjunctive (without an OM), and the Negative Perfective.

    d. pàt-á̱　　　　　'Hate!'　　　　　(Imperative)
    e. tù-bé̱lééng-é̱　　'We should read.'　(Subjunctive)
    f. tà̱-tú-ꜝbé̱lééng-èlé̱　'We have not read.'　(Negative Perfective)

In (5d) the low-toned verb -pàt- surfaces with a final H without any local source and is as such accounted for as a final MH. In (5e) the presence of the final MH blocks unbounded spreading of the verb root H so that only HTD occurs. As a CB form Secondary HTD does not apply to avoid an OCP violation. In (5f) the negative prefix *ta-* is associated with a floating H that docks rightwards to the following subject marker resulting in downstep on the following lexical H of the verb root.[4] The verb root H shows bounded spreading involving Secondary HTD because of the following final MH. In both (5e–f) the final H cannot plausibly be derived from the preceding H and is therefore treated as a MH.

(iii) TAMs with a MH on V2 to the FV:
Perfective (/-ile/), Past4 Anterior/Perfect (/a-, -a/), Subjunctive (with OM), Imperative (with OM), Remote Past (P4) (/a-, ile/), Imperative 1 (pre-verbal /náa-/), Hypothetical (pre-verbal /a-/)

    g. tù-lòòndó̱lw-ée̱lé̱　　'We have introduced.'　　(Perfective)
    h. tù-mù-lòòndó̱ló̱l-é　　'We should introduce him.'　(Subjunctive w/OM)
    i. tw-àà-lòòndó̱lw-ée̱lé̱　'We introduced/explained.'　(Remote Past)

In all the forms in (5g–i) the verb, subject marker, object marker and TAM are lexically low-toned and thus cannot be the source of the MH that docks onto V2 to the FV.

(iv) TAMs with a MH on V2:
The Imperative with a toneless root and no OM.

    j. lòòndó̱lwèèl-à　　'Explain to x.'　　(Imperative w/o OM)

(5j) similarly involves a low-toned verb which surfaces with a MH on V2 in the imperative without any local source for the H.

---

[4] An alternative analysis would be to treat the negative *ta-* as lexically H-toned with the property of shifting its H to the following mora. In (5f) the vowel of *ta-* is underlined as the lexical bearer or trigger of the following H.

To sum up, we have seen that there are two productive H spreading processes in Bemba. Unbounded spreading spreads the rightmost H in a phrase-final word to any following toneless mora until the final mora. Bounded spreading, which can be either binary (NB) or ternary (CB), affects all other Hs, i.e. any H which is not the rightmost one in the word, and any H in a non phrase-final word. These processes are completely productive, applying to root Hs of both verbs and nouns, as well as to verbal or nominal prefixes. Nominals will be discussed in Section 7. Finally, we saw that these processes interact with MHs associated with particular TAMs and of which there are three docking patterns identified in Bemba.

With this background on Bemba tonology let us begin to consider the formal properties of the CJ/DJ alternation by looking at the TAM system of Bemba in order to identify which tenses contrast CJ/DJ forms in Bemba.

3 Segmental morphological markers of the CJ/DJ alternation

As in other Bantu languages, the CJ/DJ alternation in Bemba is encoded by segmental markers in at least some of the tenses where the contrast is expressed. Table 1 is a partial Bemba TAM system adapted from Nurse (2008) with some modifications based on fieldwork data in both NB and CB areas. Table 1 shows CJ/DJ forms only in those TAMs that mark the alternation segmentally. The table shows, in the vertical column, four pasts, a general present marked as 'zero' tense, and three future forms, which are contrasted in a horizontal row for perfective, imperfective (progressive), persistive and anterior (referred to as perfect in other works). Each cell indicates a prefix which occurs in the TAM position in the verb template and a final that occurs in the FV position. The anterior form of the general present ("zero") has a preverbal TAM marker in addition. In persistive forms a subject marker (SM) occurs between the persistive marker -cili- and the rest of the TAM marker. Persistives therefore have two SMs with -cili- 'still' acting as an auxiliary or deficient verb (Doke 1954).[5] The final line in each cell starting with ta- gives the negative form. When the ta- is underlined it reflects that it is associated with a H that shifts to the following mora.

---

5 See Nichols (2010) for some discussion of the persistive. The more complex TAMs in table 1 include further morphological breakdown which is not shown here for brevity.

Table 1: Bemba TAMs (adapted from Nurse 2008).

		PERFECTIVE		IMPERFECTIVE		PERSISTIVE		ANTERIOR	
Remote Past (P4) (timed)	CJ:	-a-	-ile	-alée-	-a	-ácíli-SM-alee-	-a	-a-	-a
	DJ:	-alí-	-ile					-alí-	-a
	ta-	-a-	-ile	ta- -alée	-a			ta- -a-	-a
Recent Past (P3)	CJ:	-á-	-ile	-álée-	-a	-ácíli-SM-álee-	-a		
	DJ:	-álii-	-a						
	ta-	-a-	-ile	ta- -álée	-a				
Earlier today Past (P2)		-ácí-	-a	-áciláa-	-a	-ácíli-SM-acílaa-	-a		
	ta-	-ácí-	-a	ta- -áciláa-	-a				
Immediate Past (P1)	CJ:	-á-	-a						
	DJ:	-áa-	-a						
Zero	CJ:	-Ø-	-a	-lée-	-a			-Ø- -ile	
	DJ:	-la-	-a			-cíli-SM-Ø-	-a	náa--Ø--a	
	ta-	-Ø-	-a	ta- -leé-	-a	-cíli-SM-la-	-a	ta- -a- -a	
								ta- -Ø- -ile	
Immediate Future (F1)	CJ:	-á-	-a	-ákuláa-	-a	-cíli-SM-akuláa-	-a		
	DJ:	-áa-	-a						
		-áláa-	-a						
	ta-	-aá-	-e	ta- -aá-	-e				
Later today Future (F2)		-lée-	-a						
	ta-	-aa-	-e						
After today Future (F3)		-ka-	-a	-kaláa-	-a	-cíli-SM-kaláa-	-a		
	ta-	-aka-	-e	ta- -akalée	-a				

The full set of segmental CJ/DJ markers which occur in affirmative tenses is given in Table 2.

The present/habitual, perfective and perfect (anterior) are tenses which frequently occur amongst tenses expressing the CJ/DJ alternation also in other Bantu languages (see e.g., Zulu, Doke 1947; Kirundi, Meeussen 1959; Tswana, Creissels

Table 2: Segmental markers of the CJ/DJ in Bemba.

	PRESENT / HABITUAL	P1/F1 (PERFECTIVE)		P3 (PERFECTIVE)		P4 (PERFECTIVE)		P4 (ANTERIOR)		ZERO (ANTERIOR)	
CONJOINT	-Ø-	-á-	-a	-á-	-a	-a-	-ile	-a-	-ile	-Ø	-ile
DISJOINT	-la	-áa-	-a	-álii-	-a	-alí-	-a	-alí-	-a	náa--Ø-	-a

1996; Ha, Harjula 2004; Makhuwa, Van der Wal 2009). In fact, Hyman and Watters (1984) point out that the CJ/DJ alternation arises in unmarked TAMs (that lack intrinsic focus), hence the occurrence in the habitual and past completive. In each case in Bemba the two forms can always be unambiguously distinguished (though see discussion of P1 below) with the disjoint form having more segments in the prefix than the conjoint form. Thus, for example, in the present/habitual the conjoint form has no overt marker (6a) while the disjoint form is marked by -*la*- (6b). In the perfective P4 the conjoint form is marked by the prefix -*a*- (6c) while the disjoint form is marked by -*alí*- (6d). These are illustrated in (6) using a low-toned verb. As noted earlier, conjoint forms are used when the verb is not final in a main clause while disjoint forms are used when the verb occurs main clause-finally. We refine the distributional properties involved in later discussion.

(6) a. *tù-lòòndòlòl-à*   *lyòònsé*   'We explain all the time.'   CJ
    b. *tù-là-lòòndòlòl-à*   'We (usually) explain.'   DJ
    c. *bá-á-lóòndólwéélé*   x   'They explained x.'   CJ   (MH$_{V2\text{-}FV}$)
    d. *bá-á¹lí-lóòndólwéélé*   'They explained.'   DJ   (MH$_{V2\text{-}FV}$)

Examples (6a–b) contrast the CJ/DJ alternation in the present/habitual with the disjoint form marked by -*la*-, with no tonal contrast in the verb form since the verb is low-toned. In (6c–d) the verb stem is identical between the conjoint and the disjoint forms with both having the V2-FV MH. The surface tone patterns follow from regular tone rules as discussed in Section 2. Thus in (6c–d), where both P4 forms are associated with the V2-FV MH, the preceding H cannot undergo unbounded spreading. It is ternary in (6c) and binary in (6d). The CJ/DJ marking is therefore carried by the segmentally different prefixes for the conjoint and disjoint forms.

Of the segmentally marked CJ/DJ forms given in Table 2 above the present/habitual, the P4 perfective and anterior, and the zero anterior forms all behave predictably with respect to their tone patterns which follow from the tonal patterns discussed in Section 2. The P1/F1 and the P3 forms, however, require some discussion.

For P1/F1 the difference between the conjoint and the disjoint forms is in the pre-radical prefix with the conjoint as /-á-/ and the disjoint as /-áa-/. This contrast is neutralized on the surface by vowel fusion of the CJ/DJ marker with the vowel of the preceding subject or tense markers. The result is that on the surface the CJ/DJ forms are segmentally identical as in (7) for the disjoint forms compared to (8) for the conjoint. They however show surface tonal differences which betray contrasting underlying representations (URs).

(7)   P1 Disjoint forms   UR   Gloss
   a.   bá-á-lúk-á   /bá-áa-luk-a/   'They have just woven.'
   b.   bá-á-ꜝléét-á   /bá-áa-léet-a/ 'They have just brought.'
   c.   bá-á-mù-lás-á   /bá-áa-mu-lás-a/ 'They have just hit him/her.'
   d.   tw-áá-ꜝlás-á   /tu-áa-lás-a/   'We have just hit.'

(8)   P1 Conjoint forms   UR   Gloss
   a.   bá-á-lúk-à...   /bá-á-luk-a/   'They have just woven x.'
   b.   bá-á-léét-à...   /bá-á-léet-a/   'They have just brought x.'
   c.   bá-á-mú-ꜝlás-á ...   /bá-á-mu-lás-a/ 'They have just hit him/her x.'
   d.   tw-àà-lás-á...   /tu-á-lás-a/   'We have just hit x.'

Although the above CJ/DJ forms are segmentally identical but tonally distinct, the differences in tone result directly from the indicated underlying vowel length contrast. This means that (7–8) do not provide examples of tonally marked CJ/DJ and are categorized as part of segmentally marked CJ/DJ. The difference in the stem tone pattern of the CJ and DJ forms is minimal and due entirely to unbounded H spreading in the DJ forms versus bounded spreading in the CJ forms.

In (7a–b) the rightmost H shows unbounded spreading that spreads the rightmost H to the end of the verb form. (7b) has a downstep on the root H because of spreading onto the second mora of the long disjoint prefix. In (7c) the H on the disjoint marker undergoes HTD (onto the second mora of the disjoint marker) but not Secondary HTD (onto the object marker) as this would result in an OCP violation. Finally in (7d), after the H on the disjoint prefix undergoes HTD, a tautosyllabic LHH contour is created on the initial syllable. This resolves to a level H, as rising tones are prohibited in Bemba. In the conjoint forms in (8a–b) we see bounded spreading due to a following constituent so that in this case the final TBU is low contra (7a–b). In (8b) we see no downstep, in contrast to (7b), because here the Hs are underlyingly adjacent and not derived. In (8c) HTD (onto the object marker) results in an OCP violation and downstep of the verb root H. Finally in (8d), the simple LH contour present on the first syllable is resolved to a level low tone, again to avoid a rising tone.

The final case of segmentally marked CJ/DJ to consider is P3. In this case the segmental contrast marking the CJ/DJ forms is being lost due to an ongoing loss of the P3 conjoint form in both Northern and Copperbelt Bemba (see Kula 2016 for discussion). Thus, current usage shows that only the (formerly) disjoint form is used to mark both forms of the CJ/DJ pair i.e. implying that there is no longer any segmental contrast in P3. There is however a contrast in tone with the disjoint form showing unbounded H spread, since it occurs at the end of a phrase, in contrast to the conjoint with bounded spreading. The question is whether such tonal marking can be considered to encode the CJ/DJ alternation. We pursue this question in the next section. On the loss of the segmental P3 conjoint marker: one of the motivations for the loss is tonal neutralization between the P3 and P4 conjoint forms which only differ in the tone of the initial (see Table 1). In terms of semantics the extended P3 disjoint form retains the recent past interpretation in contrast to the remote past. This implies that P3 must now be characterised with those TAMs that have no segmental encoding of the CJ/DJ alternation, discussed in Section 4 below. There are therefore 5 TAMs which express a segmental CJ/DJ alternation in Bemba, including P1 where the segmental contrast can only be seen underlying. The tonal patterns seen in these cases follow from regular tone rules and therefore do not provide motivation for considering the tone patterns as encoding the CJ/DJ alternation.

4 Prosodic marking: does tone encode the CJ/DJ alternation?

The preceding discussion has identified TAMs where the CJ/DJ alternation is encoded by segmental morphemes, differing according to the TAM involved. The question now is whether the alternation is encoded by tone in those TAMs where it is not segmentally marked in Bemba.[6] With respect to tonally encoded CJ/DJ alternation, Creissels (1996, 2012) demonstrates for Tswana that the tone marking involved in the CJ/DJ alternation in this language cannot be derived from regular tone rules and that a particular tone pattern may in fact alternate between marking the conjoint form in one case and the disjoint form in another. Thus, in Tswana, different morphological tone patterns are used to mark the alternation in different TAMs, just like different segmental morphemes are used. Creissels (1996) uses the inability to derive the tone of CJ/DJ forms from regular tone rules as indicative of the independence of the CJ/DJ alternation as a property of tense systems and not something that can be derived by phonological rules/constraints. To test Creissels' findings against Bemba, we now ask whether there are cases of tonally marked CJ/DJ in Bemba that are not predictable i.e. which do not follow from the rules presented in Section 2.

Following Kula and Bickmore (2015) the earlier established processes of bounded and unbounded spreading are adopted as diagnostics for phonological phrasing, with unbounded spreading indicating an immediately following right edge of a phonological phrase, and bounded spreading showing the absence of such a phonological phrase boundary after the verb. In Kula and Bickmore (2015)

---

[6] A similar question is investigated in Zeller et al. (this volume) evaluating whether prosodic characteristics of segmentally marked CJ/DJ in Zulu generalize to otherwise considered non-CJ/DJ tenses.

it is shown that in the phonology-syntax mapping, right edges of phonological phrases correspond to the right edges of syntactic maximal projections. Phonological phrasing therefore provides information on syntactic constituency. Thus, unbounded spreading is attested not only when a word is pre-pausal but also in a phrase-internal word, when a maximal projection immediately follows that word. Similarly, bounded spreading applies when there is no phonological phrase boundary between two words or the two words belong to the same maximal projection. Examples (9–11) show unbounded or bounded spreading on the verb in different syntactic contexts with parentheses indicating phonological phrase boundaries. Consider example (9) below, showing a subject-verb structure, where the subject is unambiguously in a separate maximal projection (NP) from the verb (VP).

(9) (Subject) (Verb)
    a. (ìmbálámínwé)   (shí-ká-sáláángán-á)
       9.ring   10SM-FUT3-unorder-FV
       'The rings will be unordered.'

    b. (àbálímí)   (bá-ká-lóóndólól-á)
       2.farmer   2SM-FUT3-explain-FV
       'The farmers will explain.'

In (9a–b) the subject and following verb belong to separate phonological phrases (p-phrases henceforth) indicated by unbounded H spreading both on the noun and the verb. In each case the initial H spreads in unbounded fashion to indicate that there is a p-phrase boundary immediately following. (10) below shows the phrasing between a verb and following objects when there is no object-marking on the verb.

(10) (Verb Object) (Object)
    a. (ùkú-shîik-il-à   ìmpéléémbé)   (ífíintú)
       15-bury-APPL-FV 9.antelope   8.thing
       'to bury the things for the antelope'

    b. (bá-ká-shîik-il-à   ùmúlímí)   (Búúpè)
       2SM-FUT3-bury-APPL-FV 1.farmer   1.Bupe
       'They will bury Bupe for the farmer.'

In (10a–b) the verb has bounded H spreading showing that the following object is part of the same p-phrase as the verb, with a p-phrase boundary following the first object indicated by unbounded H spreading on the object. The second object phrases separately and also shows unbounded spreading of its rightmost H. The examples in (11) show complementary data where a following object is object-marked on the verb.

(11) (Verb with OM) (Object)/(Adverb)
  a. (bá-ká-mú-shíík-íl-á)   (Chítúúndú)
     2SM-FUT3-1OM-bury-APPL-FV   1.Chitundu
     'They will bury for Chitundu.'

  b. (bá-ká-mú-shíík-íl-á)   (Chítúúndú)   (bwíínó)
     2SM-FUT3-1om-bury-APPL-FV   1.Chitundu   well
     'They will bury well for Chitundu.'

  c. (bá-ká-mú-shìik-il-à   bwììnò)   (Chítúúndú)
     2SM-FUT3-1OM-bury-APPL-FV   well   1.Chitundu
     'They will bury well for Chitundu'

(11a) shows that a co-referential object is phrased separately from the verb with the verb showing unbounded H spreading and therefore a following p-phrase boundary. (11b) illustrates an object-marked verb with a following object and adverb. With this order the verb phrases separately from the object as in (11a) and predictably shows unbounded H spreading. In (11c), by contrast, when the adverb precedes the object, it is phrased together with the verb and the verb shows bounded spreading. The object follows in a separate p-phrase. These examples thus illustrate that unbounded and bounded H spreading are completely productive and directly correlate with phonological phrasing which mirrors syntactic structure.

Based on the above distribution, the following sub-sections look first at phonological phrasing in segmentally marked CJ/DJ, followed by tenses without segmentally marked CJ/DJ to determine whether tonally encoded CJ/DJ can be motivated. If it turns out that the tone patterns found in these cases are not independent of the regular tone rules discussed, then we can conclude that tone does not encode the CJ/DJ alternation in Bemba. The discussion focuses more on CB but it is assumed that the analysis also holds for NB, adjusted for differences in bounded spreading. The choice of one dialect is here made simply for ease and clarity of exposition.

4.1 Phonological phrasing in segmentally marked CJ/DJ alternation

This section briefly looks at whether segmentally marked CJ/DJ forms are subject to the phonological phrasing rules discussed above. Examples of segmentally marked CJ/DJ forms were presented in Section 3. (12–13) present examples of p-phrasing in these contexts. Phonological phrase boundaries are marked by | throughout.

(12) a. bá-lóóndólòl-à lyòònsè | 'They explain all the time.' CJ
      b. bá-lá-lóóndólól-á | 'They explain.'   DJ
      c. bá-lá-lóóndólól-á | sáànà 'They explain a lot.'   DJ

The examples in (12) are from the present/habitual with (12a) showing the conjoint form which has no overt marker. In this case the verb form shows bounded spreading indicating that there is no immediate following phonological phrase boundary. (12b–c) are disjoint forms marked by -la- and in this case we see unbounded H spreading of the subject marker H to the end of the verb form, indicating a following phonological phrase boundary. Thus, both contexts show a following phonological phrase boundary, whether the disjoint form is final or not. The associated interpretational properties are discussed in Section 5. Since the tonal spreading patterns coincide exactly with the CJ/DJ alternation, this might suggest that tone also encodes the alternation, although in this case we would have to say that the alternation was doubly marked. Since the CJ/DJ alternation is only attested in main clauses, let us consider phonological phrasing in verb forms of embedded clauses. If the two tone patterns encode the CJ/DJ alternation then they should not occur in embedded clauses like relative clauses in (13). Only phonological phrasing following the verb is indicated.

(13) a. abáántú a̱bá-lóóndólól-á |
         '(I like) people who explain'

      b. abáántú a̱bá-lóóndòlòl-à lyòònsè |
         '(I like) people who always explain'

      c. útùbáántú tù-a̱-lóóndólól-á |
         '(These are) the people who have just explained (P1)'

      d. útùbáántú tù-a̱-lóóndólòl-à bwììnò |
         '(These are) the people who have just explained well (P1)'

(13a–b) are in the present/habitual and (13c–d) are P1 forms, both TAMs which otherwise contrast CJ/DJ forms (segmentally). In both pairs of examples unbounded H spreading applies when the verb form is phonological phrase final while bounded spreading applies when the verb form is non-phrase final. This aligns well with a treatment of the H spreading patterns as not encoding the CJ/DJ alternation but rather indicating phonological phrasing across the board. Note that the morphology in these non-contrasting forms is identical to the conjoint forms of these tenses. I assume that these do not indicate conjoint forms since there is no contrastive DJ form in these cases. In the next sub-section we consider TAMs without segmental marking of the CJ/DJ alternation to evaluate whether tone can be seen to encode the alternation there.

4.2 Tonal marking and phonological phrasing in non-contrasting TAMs

TAMs with no segmental contrast of the CJ/DJ alternation in Bemba nevertheless show surface tonal contrasts. These cases are examined to demonstrate that the attested tonal differences can in fact be explained by the regular tonal processes of the language and therefore further weaken the case for a tonally encoded CJ/DJ alternation in Bemba. Let us first consider forms without MHs and then consider those with MHs in order to establish how both types of forms follow from regular tone rules.

4.2.1 Forms without Melodic Highs

We first examine tenses without MHs and no underlying difference in TAM marking to evaluate whether their surface tones can be explained in a regular way. This includes all the futures, all progressive forms and the pasts P2 and P3 (see Table 1). Consider the case of the future F3 in the examples given in (14) below.[7]

(14) Future F3

	Phrase-final form	Non phrase-final form	Gloss
a.	tù-kà-lùk-à	tù-kà-lùk-à bwììnò	'We will weave'
b.	tù-kà-lás̱-á	tù-kà-lás̱-á bwíínó	'We will hit'
c.	tù-kà-lás̱h-íl-án-á	tù-kà-lás̱h-íl-án-à bwììnò	'We will hit for e.o.'
d.	bá̱-ká-lúk-íl-án-á	bá̱-ká-lúk-ìl-àn-à bwììnò	'They'll weave for e.o.'
e.	bá̱-ká-mú-pát-á	bá̱-ká-mú-pàt-à bwììnò	'They will hate him'
f.	bá̱-ká-ˈlás̱h-íl-á	bá̱-ká-ˈlás̱h-íl-à bwììnò	'They will hit for'

As can be seen, the pairs of verb forms are segmentally identical, but in most cases are tonally different. With a low-toned subject marker in (14a–c) the verb forms are identical in (14a) where there is no H in the whole verb form. The verb

---

7 The adverb *bwììnò* 'well', which follows all non phrase-final verb forms, is not given in the gloss. 'Phrase' in all examples and following discussion refers to phonological phrase.

forms are also identical in (14b) with a high-toned verb if the verb only has two moras because the H in the non phrase-final form spreads one to the right via HTD. This H undergoes Inter-word HTD spreading onto the initial mora of the following word followed by unbounded H spreading (see Kula and Bickmore 2015, for discussion). If suffixes are added in (14c) then the difference between the pair of verb forms emerges because bounded spreading can surface in the non phrase-final form. With a high-toned subject marker in (14d–f) we generally get a difference between the verb forms. In (14d) with a low-toned verb the unbounded-bounded H spreading contrast is easily expressed. The same holds for (14e) with an object marker. (14f) with a high-toned verb also retains the tonal contrast with downstep in both forms as long as there are sufficient morae after the verb root to express bounded spreading in the non phrase-final verb form. In all cases here, a rightmost H (where present) undergoes unbounded spreading in phrase-final forms. Conversely, non phrase-final forms show bounded spreading of the same H because another word follows in the same p-phrase.

The tone patterns seen in the future in (14) obtain in all TAMs without a MH as illustrated by some selected examples below from the infinitive, progressive, immediate future (F1), progressive recent past (P2), progressive far future (F3) and the intermediate past (P3). (X represents a following constituent like *bwìinò* 'well'.)

(15)   Phrase-final form   Non phrase-final form   Gloss
   a.   ù̱-kú-lóóndólól-á   ù̱-kú-lóòndòlòl-à X   'To explain'
   b.   tù-ḻéé-lóóndólól-á   tù-ḻéé-lóòndòlòl-à X   'We are explaining'
   c.   bá̱-áḻáá-lóóndólól-á   bá̱-áḻáá-lóòndòlòl-à X   'They will explain (F1)'
   d.   bá̱-ácíḻáá-lóóndólól-á   bá̱-ácíḻáá-lóòndòlòl-à X   'They were explaining (P2)'
   e.   tù-kàḻáá-lóóndólól-á   tù-kàḻáá-lóòndòlòl-à X   'We will be explaining (F3)'
   f.   tù-àḻíí-lóóndólól-á   tù-àḻíí-lóòndòlòl-à X   'We explained (P3)'

In these cases, as in (14), the pairs of forms are distinguished by patterns of unbounded versus bounded H spreading and pattern exactly as predicted by the tone rules. In the infinitive (15a) the H on the augment shifts to the next syllable and in (15f) a rise is avoided by shifting the initial H of the TAM to the next syllable. All patterns are explained by the foregoing discussion, namely that phrase-final forms show unbounded H spreading and non phrase-final forms show bounded spreading, serving to indicate phonological phrasing. The tone patterns are therefore not unique from, nor independent of p-phrasing tone patterns.

4.2.2 Forms with melodic highs

As noted in Section 2 above, certain TAMs have a MH tone associated with the verb stem of which 3 different MHs have been identified in Bemba; one that docks onto the FV; one that docks onto V2 to the final; and one that docks onto V2. The following discussion considers the role of MHs in the tonal patterns of segmentally non-contrasting TAMs. The question is whether verb forms with MHs show tonal differences in phrase-medial vs. phrase-final positions and if so, whether such differences cannot be explained by the regular tone rules discussed.

In (16) below, the MH docks onto the FV in the negative perfective (16a–b) and the subjunctive (without OM) in (16c–d). The negative marker *ta-* in (16a–b) is associated with a floating H that surfaces on the following syllable, as noted earlier.

(16) Forms with FV MH
   a. *ta̱-tú-lóóndólwèèlé* 'We haven't explained.'
   b. *ta̱-tú-lóóndólwèèlé Chítúúndú* 'We haven't introduced Chitundu.'
   c. *ba̱-lóóndólòl-é* 'They should explain.'
   d. *ba̱-lóóndólòl-é Chítúúndú* 'They should introduce Chitundu.'

As can be seen, the verb surfaces tonally (and segmentally) identically in the phrase-final and the non phrase-final pairs in (16a–b) and (16c–d). In this case, the phrase-final forms (16a,c) do not show the expected unbounded spreading because there is a H on the final and therefore bounded spreading must apply instead. Recall from earlier discussion that bounded spreading occurs in two contexts: when there is a following constituent that belongs to the same p-phrase as the verb, or when there is another H following within the verb. The latter is a purely phonological constraint on the occurrence of unbounded spreading. In this sense, the unexpected bounded spreading pattern of the phrase-final forms can be explained on phonological grounds, namely that unbounded spreading cannot occur because a H follows. Essentially, the MH on the final is now the rightmost H in the verb and being on the final mora of the verb form, cannot spread further in a phrase-final form with no following constituent. In the non phrase-final forms in (16b,d) the verb form final H can spread to the following word (inter-word HTD and unbounded spreading) if it is toneless, hence *Chìtùùndù* is realized all H in these examples.

There is thus no tonal contrast between the forms meaning that if tone was treated as encoding the CJ/DJ alternation then the contrast would not surface in all cases involving MHs. In this vein, Sharman (1956) treats TAMs with MHs as the only tenses showing no CJ/DJ alternation in Bemba. The preceding discussion provides an explanation for this observation: A contrast cannot surface because both forms have a MH that blocks unbounded H spreading in phrase-final forms so that they are identical to their counterpart non phrase-final forms.

(17) below shows examples where the MH docks onto V2 and all subsequent TBUs of the verb form. In this case, as in (16) above, there is no tonal distinction between the phrase-final and non phrase-final forms. (17a–b) illustrate the negative remote past (P4) and (17c–d) the present anterior.

(17)   Forms with V2-FV MH
   a. ta̱-tú-á̱-lóó'nd<u>ólwéélé</u>   'We did not explain.'
   b. ta̱-tú-á̱-lóó'nd<u>ólwéélé</u> fyòònse̱   'We did not explain everything.'
   c. ná̱á̱-tú-lòònd<u>ólól-á̱</u>   'We have explained.'
   d. ná̱á̱-tú-lòònd<u>ólól-á̱</u> fyòònse̱   'We explained everything.'

In the two TAMs in (17a–b) and (17c–d) above the MH docks onto V2 and all subsequent TBUs of the verb form. The phrase-final form tonally patterns with the non phrase-final form, because the MH blocks unbounded H spreading as discussed above.

From the foregoing discussion we can see that segmentally non-contrasting TAMs with MHs provide no support for a tonally encoded CJ/DJ alternation, because in these cases there is no overt difference between verb forms used in either phrase-final or non phrase-final contexts. We must conclude that in these cases the CJ/DJ alternation is not marked. This then leaves us with segmentally non-contrasting TAMs without MHs. In these cases the pairs of forms do surface as tonally different, although in contrast to tonally encoded CJ/DJ in other languages like Tswana, the tone patterns are highly predictable and consistent across different TAMs. In each case phrase-final forms show unbounded H spreading while non phrase-final forms show bounded H spreading. The questions that remain are whether these tone patterns play the dual role of both encoding the CJ/DJ alternation and phonological phrasing, or whether phonological phrasing itself encodes the CJ/DJ alternation. Before tackling these questions further let us consider the interpretational properties of the CJ/DJ alternation in Bemba as a second set of properties complementing the formal properties discussed thus far.

5 Interpretational properties of the CJ/DJ alternation in Bemba

As in a number of Bantu languages the CJ/DJ alternation correlates with information structure in Bemba. Conjoint forms are associated with term focus of the constituent following the verb which shows either new information or contrastive focus. I take contrastive focus to involve selection from a set of alternatives (following Lambrecht 1994) even in cases where the alternatives are not overtly specified but only understood by the interlocutors. Conjoint forms therefore involve focus on the constituent immediately after the verb (IAV) (see Watters 1979; Hyman and Watters 1984, Buell 2006; Van der Wal 2006, among others, for some discussion). Disjoint forms involve verb focus (new information, corrective or truth value). The main contrasting feature between the two forms is whether the verb is included in the focus or not, as Hyman and Watters (1984) point out and as following discussion will show: Disjoint forms always include the verb in the focus.[8]

In view of trying to evaluate whether p-phrasing via tone marking independently encodes the CJ/DJ alternation the information structure of non-contrasting TAMs will also be considered in comparison to (segmentally marked) CJ/DJ forms. Consider the examples below contrasting the information structure of conjoint versus disjoint forms drawn from Sharman (1956: 40). (Emphasis in original, morphological glosses added.)

(18) a. *Bushé mu-la-peep-a?*   DJ
    Q   3PL.SM-HAB.DJ-smoke-FV
    'Do you smoke?'

    b. *Ee tu-peep-a sekelééti*   CJ
    Yes   2PL.SM-smoke-FV   cigarettes
    'Yes, we smoke cigarettes.'
    (i.e. we smoke CIGARETTES, and not a pipe)

(19)
a.   *Nga mu-a-tǫ́b-á | úmutóndó bá-lɛ́ɛ́-is-a fúlw-á*   DJ
    COND   3PL.SM-F1-break-FV   3.pot   2SM-F2-come-FV   be.upset-FV
    'If you BREAK the pot they will be angry.'

b.   *Nga mu-a-tǫ́b-a úmutóndó | tu-ákuláá-tápíl-á*   CJ
    COND   3PL.SM-F1-break-FV   3.pot   2PL.SM-COMPL-draw-FV
    múnsupa
    18LOC.calabash
    'If you break the pot we shall (have to) use the calabash for drawing water.'

(18) is an example of segmentally marked CJ/DJ in the present/habitual. In the question in (18a), where the verb is final, the disjoint form marked by *-la-* is used.

---

8 Sharman (1956: 30) makes the same point if we treat his "emphasis" as focus: "All (…) [conjoint forms] throw emphasis (if any) on what follows the verb, or, more precisely are strongly linked to what follows (and formally therefore *cannot* stand at the end of a sentence). All (…) [disjoint forms] throw emphasis on the verb itself, or more precisely, have only a weak link with what follows (and formally therefore may stand in mid-sentence, or at sentence-end)." (Emphasis in original; parts in square brackets added).

In the answer (18b) the verb is in the conjoint form and the object following the verb is focused contrastively with the meaning 'Yes, and what we smoke is cigarettes, not anything else'. If the answer had been a simple affirmation then the disjoint form *ee, tu-la-peepa* 'yes we smoke' would be used.

(19) is an example of a non-contrasting TAM with differences in the tone of the verb form indicating p-phrasing. The verb in (19a) is identified as the phrase-final form, even though the verb has following constituents, because of unbounded H spreading on the root *tób-* 'break' where the lexical H spreads to the final vowel. What is important or in focus, in this case, is the breaking event about which the owner of the pot will be upset. There is also the possibility that the object following the verb is part of the focus but in either case the verb is part of the focus. The verb form of (19b) differs from (19a) in that the H of the verb root *tób-* does not spread to the final vowel i.e. it undergoes bounded H spreading because it is non phrase-final with a p-phrase boundary following the object. In this case the following constituent 'pot' is in focus and is interpreted as contrastively focused with the alternative water drawing utensil provided. (19) thus shows that phonological phrasing also correlates with information structure: Focus is borne by a constituent that is final in a phonological phrase.

Given the information structure of CJ/DJ forms as discussed above, we predict that a verb with object marking should appear in the disjoint form if a co-referential object NP follows, since the latter cannot be focused. Conversely, we expect question words which are inherently focused to occur following conjoint verb forms which signal a following constituent as focused. Both these predictions are borne out in the data in (20–21) below.

(20) a. *tù-là-mù-sààmbìlìsh-à* (Chisanga) DJ
2PL.SM-HAB.DJ-1OM-teach.CAUS-FV (Chisanga)
'We teach him (Chisanga).'

b. *bá-mú-sáàmbìlìsh-à* *pàcìbélúshì* (Chisanga) CJ
2SM-1OM-teach.CAUS-FV 16.saturday Chisanga
'They teach (him) Chisanga on Saturday.'

c. **bá-mú-sáàmbìlìsh-à*
2SM-1OM-teach.CAUS-FV

d. *bá-ká-mú-sáámbílísh-á |* (Chisanga)
2SM-FUT3-1OM-teach.CAUS-FV Chisanga
'They will teach him (Chisanga).'

e. **bá-ká-mú-sààmbìl-ìsh-à |* (Chisanga)
2SM-FUT3-1OM-teach-CAUS-FV Chisanga

In (20a–c) we have examples in the present/habitual where (20a) is the disjoint form (marked by -*la*-) with a following object marked constituent as non-focal. The corresponding conjoint form (20b) is only grammatical with a following focal constituent, here *Saturday*, and is otherwise ungrammatical in final position in (20c). Recall that in the present/habitual the disjoint form is marked by -*la*- and the conjoint form has no marking. Notice also that in the conjoint form (20b) we have bounded H spreading on the verb form, showing as discussed above that the tonal spreading patterns (and accompanying p-phrasing) also apply in segmentally marked CJ/DJ forms.

(20d–e) are examples where there is no CJ/DJ morpheme (in the future tense). In this case where only tone distinguishes phrase-final from non phrase-final verb forms the same focus interpretations also hold. When an object marker is present in (20d) and the co-referential object NP is not in focus then the verb shows unbounded H spreading and is phonological phrase final. The use of bounded H spreading in this case is ungrammatical as (20e) shows. Similar patterns are seen in questions as below.

(21)
a. Bùshé   bámàyó   bá̧-á-fík-íĺé   mwàkà   nshí?   (MH$_{v2\text{-}FV}$ CJ)
    Q   2.mother   2SM-P4.CJ-arrive-P4   3.year   what
    'What year did mother arrive?'

b. Bùshé   bámàyó   bá̧-á'lí̧-fík-'íĺé?   (MH$_{v2\text{-}FV}$ DJ)
    Q   2.mother   2SM-P4.DJ-arrive-P4
    'Did mother arrive?'

c. *Bùshé   bámàyó   bá̧-á'lí̧-fík-'íĺé   mwàkà   nshí?   (MH$_{v2\text{-}FV}$ DJ)
    Q   2.mother   2SM-P4.DJ-arrive-P4   3.year   what

d. Bùshé   bámàyó   bá̧-ká-fík-à   lììlálì |?
    Q   2.mother   2SM-FUT3-arrive-FV   when
    'When will mother arrive?'

e. Bùshé   bámàyó   bá̧-ká-fík-á | (lììlálì)?
    Q   2.mother   2SM-FUT3-arrive-FV   (when)
    'Will mother arrive? When?'

Examples (21a–c) involve a tense (P4) that has segmental markers for the CJ/DJ (see Table 1). (21a) with the conjoint marker -*a*- is grammatical with a following question word while use of the disjoint form -*alí*- in this context is ungrammatical as shown in (21c). When the disjoint form -*alí*- is used then the verb must be final, in a p-phrase with no following question word. In this case an initial question particle, marking a polar question, is used (21b). Note that the tone of all the forms in (21a–c) undergo bounded H spreading because of the presence of the MH.

(21d–e) illustrate the future which has no morpheme marking the CJ/DJ alternation. In this case we see that the question word *liilali* 'when' is grammatical in (21d) with bounded H spreading on the preceding verb, so that the verb and question word are in the same p-phrase, but would be ungrammatical if the verb showed unbounded H spreading as in (21e) which then indicates a phrase-final form. The question word in (21e) can only be licit if it is interpreted as an afterthought, in a different p-phrase, indicated here with parenthesis on *liilali* 'when'.

Another point to note on the interpretational properties of the CJ/DJ alternation is that constituents that follow the disjoint form may introduce new information. Thus, it appears that we cannot strictly define constituents following disjoint forms as always non-focal/topical or dislocated. Consider the examples below. (22) is a reformulation of (21b) with a following constituent showing a disjoint form with following new information.

(22) Bushe   bamayo   bá-á'lí-fík-'ílé   ulya   mwaka?   (MH$_{v2\text{-}FV}$ DJ)
     Q   2.mother 2SM-P4.DJ-arrive-P4   3DEM4   3.year
     'Did mother arrive the previous year?'

(23) and (24) are question-answer pairs demonstrating the range of use of the CJ/DJ alternation in particular contexts.

(23) a. Q: Bushe ba-Chocho   bá-'cít-à   inshi |?
            Q   2SM-Chocho   2SM-do-FV   what
            'What does Chocho do?'

    b. A1: Bá-lá-sáámbílíl-á.   DJ
            2SM-HAB.DJ-learn-FV
            'She studies/goes to school.'

    c. A2: Bá-lá-sáámbílíl-á   palicisano na   pacibelushi.   DJ
            2SM-HAB.DJ-learn-FV   16.Friday CONJ   16.Saturday
            'Yes she studies on Friday and Saturday.'   (VP focus)

The question in (23a) shows bounded H spreading on the verb implying no p-phrase boundary immediately following the verb with the question word in IAV position. Two answers are possible given in (23b–c). (23b) is in the disjoint form with no following constituents and the verb provides new information. (23c) is also in the disjoint form but also includes additional constituents following the verb which are in focus and is therefore a case of VP focus. Thus, disjoint forms indicate either Verb or VP focus. Both (23b–c) are marked by the disjoint marker -la- and in addition, also show unbounded H spreading on the verb form that has been shown to coincide with disjoint forms.

(24) a. Q: *Bushe   ba-Chocho   kanshi   na-bo   bá-lá-sáámbílíl-á?*   DJ
            Q   2SM-Chocho   so   CONJ-2RCD   2SM-HAB.DJ-learn-FV
            'So Chocho also studies/goes to school then?'

     b. A1: *Ee,   bá-sáámbìlìl-à   palicisano   na   pacibelushi*   CJ
            yes   2SM-learn-FV   16.Friday   CONJ   16.Saturday
            'Yes she studies/goes to school on Friday and Saturday.'   (IAV focus)

     c. A2: *Ee,   bá-lá-sáámbílíl-á,   nanguline   ni   palicisano*
            yes   2SM-HAB.DJ-learn-FV   although   COP   16.Friday
            na   pacibelushi   fye   (DJ, V focus)
            CONJ   16.Saturday   only
            'Yes she studies, although it is only on Friday and Saturday.'

     d. A3: **Ee, bá-lá-sáámbìlìl-à palicisano na pacibelushi*   (DJ, bounded spread)

In (24a) the verb occurs in final position and is in the disjoint form in this polar question. The possible answers to this question are given in (24b–d). (24b) is in the conjoint form and shifts the focus to the constituent following the verb. This can be interpreted as contrastive if we assume that specific days are selected out of the other days of the week. (24c) gives an answer where the verb is in focus and is treated as the most salient information with following information only providing further elaboration associated with the highlighted event. The verb is therefore in the disjoint form. As noted earlier, also in this case, the CJ/DJ forms are associated with contrasting tonal patterns that match up conjoint forms with bounded H spreading and disjoint forms with unbounded H spreading. (24d) shows that a segmentally marked disjoint form with bounded H spreading, which correlates with conjoint forms, is ungrammatical. This implies that CJ/DJ forms must match up with particular tone patterns correlating with the appropriate p-phrasing. If the focus is contrastive (or more precisely corrective) then only the conjoint form can be used as shown in (25) below where only the conjoint answer in (25b) is grammatical while the disjoint (25c) is unacceptable.

(25) a. Q: *Bushe   bamayo   bá-bóómbà/   bá-lá-bóómbá   palicisano?* (CJ or DJ)
            Q   2.mother 2SM-work/   2SM-HAB.DJ-work 16.Friday
            'Does mother work on Friday?'

b. A1: Iyoo,   bá-bóómb-à   palicitatu   CJ
        no   2SM-work-FV 16.Wednesday
        'No, she works on Wednesday.'

c. A2: *Iyoo, bá-lá-bóómb-á   palicitatu   DJ
        no   2SM-HAB.DJ-work-FV   16.Wednesday

Givón (1975) makes the same observation and distinguishes two types of focus structures in Bemba correlating with CJ/DJ forms: Complement focus (CJ forms) and VP focus (DJ forms). He treats the distribution as aspect focus and the CJ/DJ markers as focus scope markers. Details of terminology aside, the data he discusses firmly illustrate the VP vs. IAV focus discussed thus far. VP focus correlates with new information while IAV focus as noted earlier is either new or contrastive. Consider the examples below replicated from Givón (1975: 190) illustrating the use of P4 which has the V2-FV MH. The focus is in small caps in the gloss.[9]

(26) a. bá-àlí-bóòmbélé sáàná   'They WORKED HARD.'   DJ
     b. bá-à-bóòmbélé sáàná   'They worked HARD.'   CJ
     c. bá-àlí-bóòmbélé mùmúshí   'They WORKED IN THE VILLAGE.'   DJ
     d. bá-à-bóòmbélé mùmúshí   'They worked IN THE VILLAGE.'   CJ
     e. bá-àlí-bóòmbélé nèèmfúmù   'They WORKED WITH THE CHIEF.'   DJ
     f. bá-à-bóòmbélé nèèmfúmù   'They worked WITH THE CHIEF.'   CJ

In each disjoint case in (26) the VP is under the scope of focus so that each statement provides new information for a question like 'what did they do?'. In each conjoint case the constituent following the verb, i.e. the element in IAV, is in focus where the question asked includes the verb like 'how did they work?', 'where did they work?', 'with whom did they work?'. In addition, IAV focus tends to include contrastiveness so that the focus in each case offers a possible set of alternatives whether these are articulated or not. The distribution in (26), Givón argues, is supported by cleft focusing of the complement which obligatorily requires conjoint forms (Comp-focus in his terms) where the complement is in focus and the verb is presupposed, rather than disjoint forms where the verb is not presupposed. Thus clefting in a conjoint form in (27a) is grammatical while the same in not for the disjoint in (27b).

(27) a. mùùkáàté bá-à-líílé   'It's BREAD they ate.' (Comp focus)   CJ
     b. *mùùkáàté bá-àlí-líílé   (VP focus)   DJ

---

9 Tones are added as Givón only indicated tone on the TAMs.

Similarly, assuming the same presupposition argument, under the scope of negation only the conjoint form can be used (28a) vs. (28b), although note that the same distribution also holds when the verb is final (28c) vs. (28d).

(28) a. *ta-bá-à-lı̃lé umúkáàté*   'They didn't eat bread.'   CJ
    b. **ta-ba-àlí-lı̃lé umúkáàté*   'They didn't eat bread.'   DJ
    c. *ta-ba-à-lı̃lé*   'They didn't eat.'   CJ
    d. **ta-ba-àlì-lı̃lé*   'They didn't eat.'   DJ

Givón (1975: 191) argues that this can be explained if complement (conjoint) focus implies that the verb is not in focus, supporting the idea that in conjoint forms IAV focus is what is relevant. In the same vein, disjoint forms are excluded from (restrictive) relative clauses and other pre-suppositional clauses since the verb could not be new information in these cases.[10] Givón thus converges on the following distribution in Bemba aspect (CJ/DJ) focus:

| Verb not new information | = Comp focus | (CJ forms) |
| Verb new information | = VP focus | (DJ forms) |

This captures, as we have noted above, that disjoint forms involve either verb focus when the verb is final or VP focus when a disjoint form is used with a complement that is not an afterthought/presupposed. Conjoint forms involve focus on a following complement (IAV focus) excluding the verb in contexts where such a constituent is present, i.e. excluding examples like in (28).

A final case to consider is what form the verb takes in all new information contexts as in thetic sentences. Conjoint forms are generally used in answering questions like 'what happened?' (see Costa and Kula 2008) but disjoint forms can also be used to the exclusion of conjoint forms in some all new information contexts. Consider the examples in (29) as responses in a context discussing three former Zambian presidents.

(29) a. *Kaunda*   *à-àlí-ˈkúúlˈ-ílé*   *amasukulu ...*
        1.Kaunda   1SM-P4.DJ-build-PERF   6.school
        'President Kaunda built schools,...'

---

10 Note that given examples (27a) and (28c) it appears that conjoint forms can occur finally at least just in terms of surface linear sequence. (27a) might suggest that the CJ/DJ alternation is sensitive to underlying constituency since *bread* is a fronted object in this case, which can be treated as leaving a copy in some formalisations. Alternatively, the cleft structure in (27a) seems to include a relative clause 'its bread that they ate' which can be treated as falling outside the CJ/DJ alternation as in the examples in (13). For (28c) the expression of the CJ/DJ alternation in negative tenses still remains to be fully investigated but involves truth value/scope of assertion properties that must be incorporated. These issues are left to future research.

b. *Kaunda   à-à-kúúl'-ílé   amasukulu
   1Kaunda   1SM-P4.CJ-build-PERF 6.school

c. Kaunda   à-à-kúúl'-ílé   amasukulu
   1.Kaunda 1SM-P4.CJ-build-PERF 6.school
   aya-sha-i-ful-il-a
   6REL-NEG-REFLX-be.many-APPL-FV
   'President Kaunda built many schools.'

With all new information in (29a) the disjoint form is used and the conjoint form is ungrammatical (29b). If the conjoint form is used, as in (29c), then focus must be on the object which is in this case elaborated on as being extraordinary in some sense. From these examples it implies that we cannot conclude that all thetic sentences take the conjoint form. Indeed Hyman and Watters (1984) argue that such cases involve truth value focus so that some response is presupposed and thereby explaining the occurrence of disjoint forms in such contexts. It will be worth investigating whether conjoint forms in thetic sentences allow a possible contrastive interpretation which would then be deemed as licensing the conjoint form in those cases. I leave this matter to future research.

We can therefore conclude that in terms of the interpretational and the correlated distributional properties, the conjoint forms in Bemba show IAV focus which is either new information or contrastive focus, with the verb never included in the focus (pending further investigation of thetic sentences). The disjoint form, on the other hand, always includes the verb in the focus, and following constituents if they occur may consist of either back-grounded, additional, presupposed, non-focal information or new information when the whole VP is in focus. It should also be pointed out that it is much more natural and hence preferred to have no following constituent in the disjoint in cases where what follows is back-grounded/non-focal. A significant point to note is that these same properties also hold in non-contrasting TAMs where the verb form is distinguished by tone marking indicating phrase-final and non-phrase-final forms.

Having now discussed both the formal and the interpretational properties of the CJ/DJ alternation in Bemba, we can return to the question of whether the tonal patterns associated with the distinction (bounded and unbounded H spreading), or indeed the phonological phrasing which these tonal patterns signal, can be considered as encoding the CJ/DJ alternation.

6 Evaluating tone marking and p-phrasing in the Bemba CJ/DJ alternation

As has been demonstrated, the distribution and interpretation of verb forms from non-contrasting TAMs coincide with that of CJ/DJ forms by making reference to p-phrasing indicated by bounded and unbounded H spreading, i.e. disjoint verb forms require a following phonological phrase boundary. With respect to the mapping with syntactic structure and marking of syntactic constituency, the right edge of a p-phrase in non phrase-final forms always coincides with the right edge of the VP as in (30a) below. For phrase-final forms at least two structures are possible. In one structure the right edge of the p-phrase boundary coincides with the VP, in which case the following constituent is non-focal and outside the VP as in (30b). In the other structure, the following constituent is within the VP and must be part of the focus as in (30c). As noted earlier, the structure in (30a) indicates IAV focus, that in (30b) verb focus and that in (30c) indicates VP focus. The same phrasing also holds in (segmentally marked) CJ/DJ forms. (30) shows the non-contrasting future (F3).

(30) a. Conjoint (IAV focus)
    [bá-ka-luk-il-a Kabwe]$_{VP}$ Syntactic Structure
    (bá-ka-luk-il-a Kabwe)$_\varphi$ Prosodic Structure
    (bá-ká-lúk-il-a Kabwe)$_\varphi$ Bounded Spreading
    'They will weave for KABWE.'

  b. Disjoint (Verb focus, following constituent not part of focus)
    [bá-ka-luk-il-a]$_{VP}$ [Kabwe]$_{ADJT}$ Syntactic Structure
    (bá-ka-luk-il-a)$_\varphi$ (Kabwe)$_\varphi$ Prosodic Structure
    (bá-ká-lúk-íl-á)$_\varphi$ (Kabwe)$_\varphi$ Unbounded Spreading
    (bá-ká-lúk-íl-á)$_\varphi$ (Kábwé)$_\varphi$ Inter-word HTD & Unbounded Spreading
    'They will WEAVE (for Kabwe).'

  c. Disjoint (VP focus, following constituent part of focus)
    [bá-ka-luk-il-a Kabwe]$_{VP}$ Syntactic Structure
    (bá-ka-luk-il-a)$_\varphi$ (Kabwe)$_\varphi$ Prosodic Structure
    (bá-ká-lúk-íl-á)$_\varphi$ (Kabwe)$_\varphi$ Unbounded Spreading
    (bá-ká-lúk-íl-á)$_\varphi$ (Kábwé)$_\varphi$ Inter-word HTD & Unbounded Spreading
    'They will WEAVE FOR KABWE.'

In (30a–b) the prosodic structure matches the syntactic structure and can in this sense be argued to indicate constituency. The same holds for the (segmentally marked) CJ/DJ forms in which case we can claim that the CJ/DJ alternation marks syntactic constituency. However, the form in (30c) and the segmentally marked equivalent do not support this analysis, since there is a mismatch between the prosodic structure and the syntactic structure (see also Halpert, this volume, for similar mismatches in Zulu). Therefore at least the disjoint form cannot be relied upon to consistently indicate syntactic constituency.[11] What is interesting is that both the CJ/DJ alternation and p-phrasing coincide in producing exactly the same structure, i.e. we find no case where there is a mismatch between the CJ/DJ alternation and p-phrasing. In other words, the two systematically reinforce each other. Let us summarise the distributional properties of the CJ/DJ alternation and tone marking/p-phrasing to clarify whether they can be treated as different encoding strategies of the CJ/DJ alternation in Bemba. 5 pairs of distributional correlations are given in Table 3 below. ('tone marking' refers to tone in verb forms in non-contrasting TAMs).

In Table 3 below, (i&ii) compare the CJ/DJ alternation and tone marking with respect to whether they maintain a contrast when MHs are present. The segmentally marked CJ/DJ alternation retains the contrast (cf. 21a–b), but in tone marking cases the contrast between verb forms is lost (cf. 16–17). We saw earlier that this is because tone marking interacts with MHs which block unbounded H spreading in phrase-final forms. Thus, tonal marking is in this case a poor choice for encoding the distinction if the contrast cannot be expressed in some cases. A tonally marked CJ/DJ alternation needs to involve a tone pattern that

Table 3: Interaction between segmental CJ/DJ and tone/prosody.

	CJ/DJ and Tone-marking correlations	occur or not
(i)	CJ/DJ + MH	yes
(ii)	tone marking + MH	no
(iii)	CJ/DJ with no tone contrast	yes
(iv)	CJ/DJ with tone contrast	yes
(v)	tone marking with regular tone rules	yes
(vi)	tone marking independent of regular tone rules	no
(vii)	p-phrasing rules apply to CJ/DJ	yes
(viii)	p-phrasing rules apply to tone marking	yes
(ix)	no surface p-phrasing in some CJ/DJ	yes
(x)	no surface p-phrasing in some tone marking cases	no

---

11 This mismatch can be explained in various ways in different theories of the syntax-phonology mapping. In Kula and Bickmore (2015) we adopt an Optimality Theoretic approach formalizing mapping relations as violable constraints.

cannot be overridden i.e. one that is not derivable from the regular tone rules of the language as we see in Tswana. This means that tone marking does not distinctively mark CJ/DJ forms in Bemba. (iii&iv) evaluate whether segmentally marked CJ/DJ forms must occur with particular tone marking (unbounded and bounded H spreading) and show that, although they do in some cases (cf. 6a–b), this is not a requirement (cf. 20a–b). This shows that segmental CJ/DJ marking is independent of tonal marking and that the presence of tonal marking in these CJ/DJ forms is controlled by phonological rules outside of the CJ/DJ alternation, only specifically occurring when H-toned SMs, TAMs or roots are present. (v&vi) show that tone marking is never seen to be independent of regular tone rules (cf. 20d–e, 21d–e) and if this is a requirement in order to be an independent and distinct marker of the CJ/DJ alternation then tone marking falls short in this case. (vii&viii) show that phonological phrasing applies across the board in both CJ/DJ cases (cf. 12, 20b) as well as in non-contrasting TAMs (cf. 21d–e); this is as we would expect since tone marking is what indicates p-phrasing. But following (ix&x) there are cases where in segmentally marked CJ/DJ forms, if the tone conditions are not met, phonological phrasing cannot be read off the CJ/DJ forms (cf. 18a–b). To the contrary, this never happens in tonally marked cases showing that the tonal marking patterns and p-phrasing are one and the same thing, since the two H spreading patterns reflect p-phrasing. Thus, while we see evidence of independence between (segmentally marked) CJ/DJ and tone marking and the accompanying p-phrasing, we see a total dependence on tone marking and phonological phrasing. This implies that assuming tonally marked CJ/DJ forms is redundant since exactly the same information can be read off phonological phrasing. We must therefore conclude from the foregoing that tone does not encode the CJ/DJ alternation in Bemba.

This raises the question of which properties are central to the characterisation of the CJ/DJ alternation in Bemba. Although the general distributional facts above suggest that tone/phonological phrasing do not encode the CJ/DJ alternation in Bemba, CJ/DJ forms are seen to coincide with particular prosodic structure. Why should segmental marking be considered to encode the CJ/DJ alternation but p-phrasing not, if they are in fact seen to coincide? This issue is investigated by comparing in Table 4 how the (segmentally marked) CJ/DJ alternation and tone/p-phrasing relate to formal and interpretational properties of the CJ/DJ alternation as discussed in the foregoing. See Van der Wal (this volume) for a cross-Bantu comparison of these properties.

Reference to tone in Table 4 below implies phonological phrasing. There are only two points of contrast. The first is that while the CJ/DJ alternation is restricted to particular tenses, phonological phrasing (via tone) applies across the board,

Table 4: Correlation of general CJ/DJ properties with CJ/DJ and tone marking in Bemba.

Formal properties	CJ/DJ	TONE
Restriction in tenses	✓	✗
Relative clauses, pre-suppositional clauses, negative tenses	✗	✓
Object marking has effect	✓	✓
Interaction with dislocation	✓	✓
Applies to nominals	✗	✓
Interpretational properties		
Tense-aspect semantics	✗	✗
Information structure	✓	✓
– Verb focus	✓	✓
– IAV focus	✓	✓
– VP focus	✓	✓
Constituency		
Conjoint (IAV focus) – mark VP	✓ (✗)	✓
Disjoint (V focus) – mark V	✓ (✓)	✓
Disjoint (VP focus) – mark VP	✗ (✓)	✗

including in nominals as might be expected. This is also what we see of p-phrasing in other languages like Chichewa (Kanerva 1990) where it is marked by penultimate lengthening. The second is that while the CJ/DJ alternation does not occur in relative and presuppositional clauses, nor under the scope of negation, differences in phonological phrasing are still observed. As discussed earlier, there is no CJ/DJ alternation in relatives, pre-suppositional clauses, and negatives, because an information structure contrast requiring the verb to express new information focus cannot hold in these cases. This suggests that the CJ/DJ alternation, at least in Bemba, must indicate information structure. The parallelism we see between the CJ/DJ alternation and p-phrasing thus follows from the fact that p-phrasing is also used to express information structure (Costa and Kula 2008). Thus, as long as this can be read off the tone patterns, CJ/DJ forms show phonological phrasing that identifies the focus as occurring final in a p-phrase. We see this in the identical patterning of segmental CJ/DJ forms and p-phrasing on interpretational properties. There is no correlation with tense-aspect semantics so that the CJ/DJ alternation cannot be interpreted as marking particular aspectual contrasts, and since p-phrasing is not restricted only to TAMs we expect no interaction in this case either. With respect to constituent marking, there seems to be no particular restriction on the CJ/DJ alternation being the sole marker of syntactic constituency or indeed exclusively marking a particular constituent when either the conjoint or disjoint forms are used, since in each case it can equally be claimed to be marked by p-phrasing.[12]

Thus the conclusion is that the CJ/DJ alternation is marked segmentally in Bemba in the present/habitual; the P4 perfective; the P4 anterior; P1/F1; and the present anterior. The CJ/DJ alternation indicates information structure, highlighting constituents that are new information or contrastively focused. Phonological phrasing also signals information structure and for this reason the CJ/DJ alternation coincides with p-phrasing, identifying focus as p-phrase final.

A remaining question is whether there ever was a tonally marked CJ/DJ alternation in Bemba. This is difficult to evaluate but it is possible that the bounded and unbounded H spreading patterns may have initially been associated to only some tenses and then got extended over time to all tenses. I concur with Sharman (1956) in the evaluation that the fact that these patterns do not override MHs suggests that they came later than MHs, suggesting that they may have been an innovation in these instances.[13] This is supported by the fact that MHs (at least for the past tense) are reconstructed to PB (Meeussen 1967). Similarly, the extension to segmentally marked CJ/DJ forms is probably also an innovation. The extension of originally word level tone patterns to the phrasal level would aid such innovation processes.

Concluding that the CJ/DJ alternation is not tonally encoded in Bemba nicely expresses the fact that CJ/DJ marking is restricted to a limited number of tenses as attested in other Bantu languages. Although there is no a priori reason why a system that marks the CJ/DJ alternation in every tense would not exist, it is difficult to imagine a parallel system where its tonal marking was as unpredictable as it is in Tswana (Creissels 1996), for example, and that such marking is present in every TAM in a language. In this sense, Tswana fundamentally differs from Bemba in that the surface tonology of all verbs in Bemba can be predicted directly from the general tone rules of the language, whereas this is not the case in Tswana where an independent tone pattern must be specified to apply in particular TAMs and therefore be treated as encoding the CJ/DJ alternation. Similarly, Haya (Hyman, this volume) has specific focus marked TAMs that tonally contrast the CJ/DJ alternation only in those particular TAMs.

---

12 Disjoint forms can be treated as marking the right edge of a VP to account both for cases where only the verb is in the VP as well as those where the verb has a following complement. The problem is that the latter case also holds for conjoint forms. A solution would be to treat disjoint forms as the only part of the distinction that correlates with constituency (shown in brackets in Table 4). Needless to say a more elaborate syntax is needed to tease apart the possible differences that might exist here. I leave this to future research.

13 Sharman (1956) notes that the P2 form is older than the other past tense forms with an identifiable previously irregular conjoint form. Since the P2 disjoint form did not show unbounded spreading in the mid 1950s this provides further evidence that the unbounded H spreading pattern is a later innovation.

The final discussion in the next section briefly looks at p-phrasing in nominals where the patterns support the idea that p-phrasing is not restricted to verbal forms and is seen to apply identically to nominals in similar information structure contexts.

7 Phrasal tone patterns in nouns

The phrasal status of bounded and unbounded H spreading can also be seen in nominal forms as some of the examples in Section 3 (cf. 9–10) have already shown. Consider the following examples from Sharman and Meeussen (1955: 401) that illustrate the contrast. The tonal changes can be seen on the noun *ícisakuta* 'shelter' depending on whether the following constituent is within the same p-phrase or not. (Glosses have been added).

(31) Phonological phrasing in nominals
    a. *íci-sakuta*   *ci-i-koté*   →   *icísákútá | cííkoté*
        7-shelter   7SM-COP-old   'The shelter is old.'
    b. *íci-sakuta*   *ci-koté*   →   *icísakuta cikoté |*
        7-shelter   7SM-old   'an old shelter'
    c. *íci-sakuta*   *bá-kuul-ílé*   →   *icísakuta bá-kuul-ílé |*
        7-shelter   2SM-build-PERF   'The shelter they have built.'
    d. *ta-ku-li*   *íci-sakuta ...*   →   *takúli icísakuta ... |*
        NEG-17LOC-COP   7-shelter   'There is no shelter (there).'
    e. *ta-ku-li*   *íci-sakuta*   →   *takúli icísákútá |*
        NEG-17LOC-be   7-shelter   'There is no shelter.'
    f. *úku-kuul-a*   *íci-sakuta*   →   *ukúkuula icísákútá |*
        15-build-FV   7-shelter   'building a shelter'

(31a, e–f) show unbounded H spreading on the noun when it is final in its p-phrase, exactly parallel to verb forms. Similarly, (31b–d) show bounded spreading on the same noun when it is not final in its p-phrase. As these examples are from NB, the bounded H spreading is binary and therefore only involve spreading to the next mora to the right which in this case involves a shift from the augment, a process that occurs regularly to (VCV) noun class markers. The same patterns are also seen in CB illustrated in (32) with noun adjective pairs.

(32)   a. *icísákútá | cíí'kóté*   'The shelter is old.'
       b. *icísákútá | icí'kóté /...*   'an old shelter/ a/the shelter which is old'
       c. *icísákùtà cìkòté | /...*   'an old shelter/ a/the shelter which is old'
       d. *ùlú-táàndá lú-sùmá | /...*   'nice star/ a/the star which is nice'

(32a–b) show unbounded H spreading on the head noun implying that the following adjective/relative is not within the same phonological phrase as the head noun. In the relative in (32b) the augment is present in contrast to the adjectival and restrictive relative interpretations that have no augment.[14] (32c) shows bounded (ternary) H spreading on the head noun because the following constituent is within the same phonological phrase as the noun. In (32d) where the noun has a final lexical high we also see bounded spreading just as we saw in verb forms when a MH docks on the final.

In terms of information structure, in (31) the nominal is highlighted/more salient when it occurs p-phrase final and in (32) the phonological phrasing leads to different interpretations of the head noun as independent or part of the following constituent.[15] Thus, we notice that nominals pattern exactly the same as verb forms providing further evidence that bounded and unbounded H spreading are part of regular tone rules that are not restricted to verbs. Under this assumption the patterning of nominals can be easily explained by the same tone rules/p-phrasing without postulating that the CJ/DJ alternation is also encoded in nominals.

The overall picture that emerges is that we can distinguish the CJ/DJ alternation in forms where the distinction is segmentally marked. In these cases, in addition, conjoint forms correspond to bounded H spreading and disjoint forms to unbounded H spreading. As far as phonological phrasing is concerned, focus occurs on constituents that are final in a phonological phrase. This explains why VP focus in disjoint forms requires the verb and the following post-verbal constituent not to occur in the same p-phrase. In this sense phonological phrasing, independent of the CJ/DJ alternation, also plays a role in identifying which constituent is in focus. The interplay between the CJ/DJ alternation, phonological phrasing and focus interpretation is such that the CJ/DJ alternation is a subset of phonological phrasing (indicated by bounded and unbounded H spreading) and the two are both subsets of interpretation where constituents are identified as part of new information focus (V or VP focus),

---

14 Givón (1972) discusses similar noun-adjective examples which he treats on a par with relative clauses as indicating restrictive relatives in cases like (32c) and non-restrictive relatives in cases like (32b). See Kula (2007), Kula and Cheng (2007) for more recent discussion of this distinction.
15 Sharman and Meeussen (1955: 401) argued for a much tighter connection with CJ/DJ: "Nominals with low-toned radicals and suffixes also show (...) [unbounded H spreading] in stressed positions: thus ú-mu-lim-o → umúlímó ['work']. It serves exactly the same purpose as with verb tenses: i.e. it emphasizes the word carrying it: or, more properly, minimizes the grammatical link with the following word, if any, and is therefore the form which must be used at the end of a sentence: its absence implies a strong link with the word following, and is therefore the form used, for example, at the head of a relative clause, and before possessives." (Parts in square brackets added).

or new or contrastive focus (IAV focus). In this way we capture the fact that while phonological phrasing interacts with the identification of focused constituents it does not itself encode the CJ/DJ alternation which is left to specific morphemes in specific TAMs.

8 Conclusions

This chapter has argued that the Bemba CJ/DJ alternation is not as robust as has been assumed in previous literature. It is restricted only to those tenses that segmentally mark the contrast. Tenses without segmental marking of the CJ/DJ alternation have been shown to undergo regular tonal processes whose phrasal structure allows us to identify the different discourse functions of the constituents involved. Thus, phonological phrase boundaries, indicated by tone, coincide with different discourse functions depending on whether the verb is phrased with a following constituent or not. Quite consistently if the verb is phrased together with a following constituent then there is IAV focus, which is mainly contrastive and only occurs in the context of bounded H spreading. When there is a phonological phrase boundary immediately following the verb, then the verb must be in focus with both V and VP focus as options. These latter interpretations always coincide with unbounded H spreading on the verb. The parallelism between this phrasal pattern and the CJ/DJ alternation is that the two exhibit the same information structure leading us to conclude that the current phrasal patterns may have historically been restricted to particular tenses but has since been expanded to all tenses including those that are segmentally marked. It is probably due to this additional phrasal marking that the loss of the conjoint P3 form can easily be handled in the system since p-phrasing can be used to identify different information structure even if only one form (formally the disjoint form) is present. Under the line of argumentation presented here, this has led to the loss of the expression of the CJ/DJ alternation in P3, on a par with all other previously assumed tonal cases of the CJ/DJ alternation.

Thus, in terms of the morphology of the verb, in most TAMs there is a single TAM marker which is used regardless of whether the verb is phrase-final or non-phrase-final (contrasted by regular tonal processes). As shown above such TAM marking can often include a MH in addition to any segmental affix(es) which interacts with regular tone rules. In a few TAMs, however, there are two lexical allomorphs, the choice of which is dependent on whether the verb can occur phrase-finally or not, with accompanying focus interpretation. These are the TAMs that encode the CJ/DJ alternation. With respect to the distribution of CJ/DJ forms, the systematic observation in Bemba is that a conjoint form can never be final in a main clause while a disjoint form can be final or not. And in terms of interpretation the verb must be part of the focus in disjoint forms but must be excluded in conjoint forms.

This chapter has argued that the most insightful way of analyzing the Bemba CJ/DJ alternation is to treat the regularity seen in tone marking and the associated p-phrasing not as encoding the alternation but rather as the result of innovation of a possibly earlier restricted tonal process, thereby affording phonological phrasing a much greater role in the establishment of focus than previously assumed. It remains to be seen whether this pattern holds in other Bemba dialects in addition to NB and CB which are discussed here, and further, whether the diagnostics developed here can aid discussions on the interaction of the CJ/DJ alternation and phonological-phrasing in other Bantu languages.

Abbreviations

APPL	applicative	NB	Northern Bemba
CAUS	causative	NP	Noun Phrase
CB	Copperbelt Bemba	OCP	obligatory contour principle
COND	conditional	OM	object marker
CONJ	conjunction	P1/2/3/4	refer to different pasts
COMPL	complementizer	PL	plural
DEM	demonstrative	Q	question particle
F1/2/3	refer to different futures	SM	subject marker
FUT	future	V2	verb stem second vowel
FV	final vowel	VP	Verb Phrase
H	high tone	REFLX	reflexive
HAB	habitual	RCD	referential concord
HTD	high tone doubling	TAM	tense aspect mood
IAV	immediate after verb	TBU	tone bearing unit
LOC	locative		and numbers on nominals indicate noun class markers.
MH	melodic high tone		

References

Bickmore, Lee & Nancy C. Kula. 2013. Ternary spread and the OCP in Copperbelt Bemba. *Studies in African Languages and Linguistics* 42 (2). 101–132.

Buell, Leston. 2006. The Zulu conjoint/disjoint verb alternation: Focus or constituency? *ZAS Papers in Linguistics* 43: *Papers in Bantu Grammar and Description*. 8–30.

Costa, João & Nancy C. Kula. 2008. Focus at the interface: Evidence from Romance and Bantu. In Cecile de Cat & Katherine Demuth (eds.), *The Bantu-Romance connection: A comparative*

investigation of verbal agreement, DPs, and information structure, 293–322. Amsterdam: John Benjamins.
Creissels, Denis. 1996. Conjunctive and disjunctive verb forms in Setswana. *South African Journal of African Languages* 16 (6). 109–115.
Creissels, Denis. 2012. Conjoint and disjoint verb forms in Tswana and other Bantu languages. Ms., University of Lyon.
Doke, Clement, M. 1947. *Text-book of Zulu grammar*. Cape Town: Maskew Miller Longman.
Doke, Clement, M. 1954. *The Southern Bantu Languages*. Oxford: International African Institute, OUP.
Givón, Talmy. 1972. Studies in Cibemba and Bantu grammar. *Studies in African Linguistics, Supplement 3*.
Givón, Talmy. 1975. Focus and the scope of assertion: Some Bantu evidence. *Studies in African Linguistics* 6 (2). 185–205.
Guthrie, Malcolm. 1945. The tonal structure of Bemba. Unpublished PhD thesis, SOAS, University of London.
Halpert, Claire. This volume. Prosody/syntax mismatches in the Zulu conjoint/disjoint alternation.
Harjula, Lotta. 2004. *The Ha language of Tanzania: grammar, text and vocabulary*. Cologne: Rüdiger Köppe Verlag.
Hyman, Larry M. This volume. Disentangling conjoint, disjoint, metatony, tone cases, augments, prosody, and focus in Bantu.
Hyman, Larry, M. & John Watters. 1984. Auxiliary focus. *Studies in African Linguistics* 15 (3). 233–273.
Kanerva, Jonni. 1990. *Focus and phrasing in Chichewa phonology*. Stanford: Stanford University Ph.D. dissertation.
Kula, Nancy C. 2007. Effects of phonological phrasing on syntactic structure. *The Linguistic Review* 24. 201–231.
Kula, Nancy C. 2016. Reduction in remoteness distinctions and reconfiguration in the Bemba past tense. *Transactions of the Philological Society*.
Kula, Nancy C. & Lee Bickmore. 2015. Prosodic Phrasing in Copperbelt Bemba. *Phonology* 32 (1). 147–176.
Kula, Nancy C. & Lisa Cheng. 2007. Phonological and syntactic phrasing in Bemba relatives. *Journal of African Languages and Linguistics* 28. 123–148.
Lambrecht, Knud. 1994. *Information structure and sentence form*. Cambridge: Cambridge University Press.
Marten, Lutz & Nancy C. Kula. 2014. Benefactive and substitutive applicatives in Bemba. *Journal of African Languages and Linguistics* 34 (1). 1–44.
Meeussen, Achille E. 1959. *Essai de Grammaire Rundi*. Tervuren: Annales du Museé Royal, Série Sciences Humaines 24.
Meeussen, Achille E. 1967. Bantu grammatical reconstructions. *Africana Linguistica* 3. 81–121.
Nichols, Peter. 2010. A morpho-semantic analysis of the persistive, alterative and inceptive aspects in siSwati. SOAS, London: SOAS Phd dissertation.
Nurse, Derek. 2008. *Tense and aspect in Bantu*. Oxford: Oxford University Press.
Odden, David & Lee Bickmore 2014. Melodic tone in Bantu: Overview. *Africana Linguistica* 20. 3–13.
Sharman, John, C. 1956 The tabulation of tenses in a Bantu language (Bemba: Northern Rhodesia). *Africa* 26. 29–46.

Sharman, John, C. & Achille E. Meeussen. 1955. The representation of structural tones, with special reference to the tonal behavior of the verb in Bemba, Northern Rhodesia. *Africa: Journal of the international African Institute* 25 (4). 393–404.

Van der Wal, Jenneke. 2006 The disjoint verb form and an empty immediate after verb position in Makhuwa. *ZAS Papers in Linguistics* 43: *Papers in Bantu Grammar and Description*. 233–256.

Van der Wal, Jenneke. 2009. *Word order and information structure in Makhuwa-Enahara*. Leiden: University of Leiden Ph.D. dissertation.

Van der Wal, Jenneke. This volume. What is the conjoint/disjoint distinction alternation in Bantu languages? Parameters of variation.

Watters, John. 1979. Focus in Aghem. In Larry Hyman (ed.), *Aghem grammatical structure*, 157–189. Los Angeles: University of Southern California.

Zeller, Jochen, Sabine Zerbian & Toni Cook. This volume. Prosodic evidence for syntactic phrasing in Zulu.

Jochen Zeller, Sabine Zerbian and Toni Cook
11 Prosodic evidence for syntactic phrasing in Zulu

1 Introduction

The conjoint/disjoint (CJ/DJ) alternation in Zulu (Nguni; S42) is marked segmentally only in the present and the recent past tense, and most existing analyses of the alternation therefore focus on these tenses. Our paper differs from this work in that it is concerned with two tense forms that do not show segmental morphological marking of the CJ/DJ alternation, namely the future and remote past tense. We report the results of a study in which we examined the tonal and durational properties of these "non-alternating" tenses, which we then compared to the phonological properties of verbs in the CJ and DJ form in the present tense. A key question behind our study was whether any of the phonological properties we observed with the non-alternating tenses in different syntactic environments in Zulu should be interpreted as grammatical markers of the CJ/DJ alternation, or whether they simply follow from general phonological principles of the language (see Kula this volume, who investigates the same question for Bemba).

The CJ/DJ alternation in Zulu is generally analyzed as a reflex of syntactic constituency: the CJ form is licensed only when followed by overt vP-internal material; the DJ form signals that the verb is final in vP. In the present tense, these different syntactic contexts are associated with different phonological properties: the tonal and durational characteristics of verbs in phrase-medial position are different from those of verbs in phrase-final position. In this tense, the phrase-medial and phrase-final distinction is also marked by special CJ/DJ morphology. Our objective was to establish if, or to what extent, verbs in the future and remote past tense also exhibit the relevant phonological properties when they appear in phrase-medial and phrase-final positions, even though the verbs are not morphologically marked as either CJ or DJ.

As we discuss in the sections that follow, we find that with respect to their durational properties, phrase-medial and phrase-final verbs in the future and remote past tense behave like their counterparts in the present tense. To some extent, verbs in the non-alternating tenses also behave as expected with respect

---

We would like to thank our research participants for their time and their contribution to the study. We also thank the editors of this volume and three anonymous reviewers for helpful comments and suggestions. All errors remain our responsibility.

to H tone movement, but here our study also reveals some unexpected tonal patterns (particularly in the remote past) that do not follow straightforwardly from regular phonological principles. A particularly interesting finding is the sporadic occurrence of a H tone that some Zulu speakers associate with the final syllable of phrase-medial verbs in the remote past and future tense. A hypothesis that we put forward in this paper is that this final H tone is the realization of a tonal morpheme that (optionally) marks the CJ form in the relevant tenses in Zulu.

In Section 2, we present an overview of the CJ/DJ alternation in Zulu and motivate our research question. Section 3 describes our study, and Section 4 presents our results, which are discussed in Section 5. Section 6 offers a brief conclusion.

2 The conjoint/disjoint alternation and object marking in Zulu

In Zulu, the CJ/DJ alternation is marked by segmental morphology in two tenses. In the present tense affirmative, the DJ form is expressed by the prefix *ya-*, (1b); in the recent past tense affirmative, the DJ suffix *-ile* replaces the past tense marker *-e*, (2b):[1,2]

(1) a. *Ngi-fund-a   i-n-cwadi.*
       1SG.SM-read-FV   AUG-9-book
       'I'm reading a book.'

   b. *Ngi-ya-fund-a.*
       1SG.SM-DJ-read-FV
       'I'm reading.'

(2) a. *Ngi-fund-e   i-n-cwadi.*[3]
       1SG.SM-read-PST   AUG-9-book
       'I read a book.'

---

1 All examples in this paper are from Zulu, unless otherwise indicated. High tone is marked by an acute accent on the syllable; low tone is unmarked. In some examples, we have underlined the tone bearing units (TBU), i.e. the vowels to which H tones are underlyingly linked. Note that we have not marked tone on the examples provided in Section 2, since the tonal properties of the CJ/DJ alternation in Zulu are the topic of our empirical study, the results of which we report in Section 4. We have occasionally adjusted the glosses of examples that were adopted from the literature to this system.
2 These tenses can also be marked on the complements of certain auxiliary verbs, such as the so-called exclusive auxiliary *se-* (cf. *sengibuya naye*, 'I am now returning with him' vs. *sengiyabuya*, 'I am now already returning') or the continuous past tense auxiliary *be-* (cf. *bengihambe naye*, 'I had been walking with him' vs. *bengihambile*, 'I had been walking'). See Ziervogel, Louw and Taljaard (1985: 179, 182).
3 The recent past CJ suffix is slightly lengthened and pronounced with a high tone (see Section 5 for discussion).

b. *Ngi-fund-ile.*
   1SG.SM-read-PST.DJ
   'I read.'

It is by now firmly established that the CJ/DJ alternation in Zulu is an indicator of syntactic constituency. The CJ form is only possible if the verb is followed by overt material inside the vP; when no vP-internal material follows the verb, the DJ form must be used (Van der Spuy 1993; Buell 2005, 2006; Halpert 2012 a.o.). (3) contrasts with (1b), and (4) with (2b):

(3)   **Ngi-fund-a.*
      1SG.SM-read-FV
      Intended: 'I'm reading.'

(4)   **Ngi-fund-e.*
      1SG.SM-read-PST
      Intended: 'I read.'

The DJ form can be followed by postverbal material, but there is evidence that this material is always outside the vP (Van der Spuy 1993; Buell 2005, 2006; Cheng and Downing 2009; Adams 2010; Zeller 2012). For example, Buell (2006) shows that the question particle *na*, which only occurs outside the vP and which therefore cannot appear between the verb and a following constituent when the verb is in the CJ form, can intervene when the verb is in the DJ form (Buell 2006: 15):

(5)   a. *Ba-dlal-a   phandle   na?*
         2SM-play-FV   outside   Q
         'Are they playing outside?'

      b. **Ba-dlal-a   na   phandle?*
         2SM-play-FV   Q   outside

      c. *Ba-ya-dlal-a   na   phandle?*
         2SM-DJ-play-FV   Q   outside
         'Are they playing outside?'

Buell (2006) also shows that only elements following the CJ form of the verb can be focused in Zulu. (6a) can therefore function as a response to a question like "Where are the boys playing?", and the adverb can also be contrastively focused. In contrast, Buell (2006: 21) notes that *phandle* cannot be in focus when it follows the DJ form of the verb, as in (6b). Rather, (6b) would be an appropriate answer to a question such as "What are they doing outside?":

(6) a. *Ba-dlal-a phandle.*
    2SM-play-FV outside
    'They're playing OUTSIDE.'

 b. *Ba-ya-dlal-a phandle.*
    2SM-DJ-play-FV outside
    'They're playing outside.'

Based on Cheng and Downing (2009), we take the vP to be the domain of focus in Zulu; consequently, the unavailability of adverb focus in (6b) follows directly from *phandle* being outside the vP.

When the object-NP of a monotransitive verb agrees with the verb, and no other material is present in the vP, the DJ verb form is obligatory in Zulu. In this case, the object-marked NP cannot be focused and is therefore incompatible with a focus marker such as *kuphela*, 'only', as shown in (7c):

(7) a. *Ngi-bon-e i-kati (kuphela)*
    1SG.SM-see-PST AUG-5.cat only
    'I saw (only) the cat.'

 b. **Ngi-li-bon-e i-kati.*
    1SG.SM-5OM-see-PST AUG-5.cat

 c. *Ngi-li-bon-ile i-kati (*kuphela).*
    1SG.SM-5OM-see-PST.DJ AUG-5.cat only
    'I saw it, (*only) the cat.'

The implication is that object-marked NPs in Zulu are always dislocated to a vP-external position (see Van der Spuy 1993; Buell 2006; Cheng and Downing 2009; Adams 2010; Zeller 2012):

(8) *Ngi-li-bon-ile]$_{vP}$ i-kati.*
    1SG.SM-5OM-see-PST.DJ AUG-5.cat
    'I saw it, the cat.'

The claim that material following the DJ verb form in Zulu is dislocated is also supported by phonological evidence. In Zulu, the penultimate vowel of the last word within a prosodic phrase is lengthened (Khumalo 1987; Van der Spuy 1993). As shown by Cheng and Downing (2007, 2009), the right edge of a prosodic phrase always coincides with the right edge of a syntactic phrase (vP or CP) in Zulu. Therefore, the fact that the penultimate vowel of verbs in the DJ form is lengthened in Zulu shows that these verbs are final in their phrase. Material following the DJ form follows the right edge of the relevant phrase boundary and is therefore outside the vP:

(9)   ba-ya-dla:la ## pha:ndle   →   ba-ya-dlala]$_{vP}$ phandle

Penultimate lengthening in Zulu is correlated with high (H) tone movement (i.e. H tone shift or spread)[4]. In the present tense indicative, a lexical H tone originating on a prefix moves to the right as far as the penult when the verb is medial in its phrase. This is illustrated in (10) with the verb -*hlabelela*, 'sing', which is lexically toneless. If this verb appears in the CJ form and in phrase-medial position, as in (10a), the H tone originating on the subject prefix spreads to the penult, as shown in (10b).

(10)   Verb is phrase-medial – H tone spreads to penult:
    a.   *I-zin-gane*   *zi-hlabelel-a*   *i-n-goma*]$_{vP}$.
        AUG-10-child   10SM-sing-FV   AUG-9-song
        'The children are singing a song.'

    b.   *zíhlábéléla* ...]

However, when the verb is phrase-final and therefore appears in the DJ form, as in (11a), the H tone of the object marker spreads only as far as the antepenult, while the penult is lengthened, (11b) (Downing 1990; Cassimjee and Kisseberth 2001; Buell 2005):

(11)   Verb is phrase final – H tone spreads to antepenult:
    a.   *I-zin-gane*   *zi-ya-yi-hlabelel-a*]$_{vP}$ *i-n-goma.*
        AUG-10-child   10SM-DJ-9OM-sing-FV   AUG-9-song
        'The children are singing it, the song.'

    b.   *zíyáyíhlábéle:la*]

As noted in Cassimjee and Kisseberth (2001: 340), H tone movement to the antepenult is probably a consequence of the tendency to avoid the alignment of the right edge of an H tone domain with a metrically prominent syllable.[5] Since the lengthened penult is prominent, the H tone domain can only be extended to the antepenult (see Cassimjee 1998; Buell 2005: 67).

---

[4] Varieties of Zulu differ in showing either high tone shift or spread. The tone pattern in (10) and (11) reflects Durban Zulu, where prefix-induced H tone movement is typically realized as H tone spread, while stem-induced H tone movement is realized as shift (Cassimjee and Kisseberth 2001; Downing 2001a). In contrast, Zululand Zulu is reported to have tone shift in all environments (Cassimjee and Kisseberth 2001: 329). See also Section 4.2.1.

[5] However, Cassimjee and Kisseberth (2001: 341) discuss data from the Nguni language Phuthi, where H tone shift to the penult is blocked even in environments in which the penult is not lengthened. We return to this point in Section 5.

In this paper, we examine and compare the phonological properties of phrase-medial and phrase-final verbs in tense forms which do not mark the CJ/DJ distinction segmentally in Zulu (we henceforth refer to these forms as *non-alternating tenses*). The two non-alternating tenses we focus on are the future tense and the remote past tense:

(12) a. *I-zin-gane   zi-zo-hlabelel-a   i-n-goma]*$_{vP}$.
AUG-10-child   10SM-FUT-sing-FV   AUG-9-song
'The children will sing a song.'

b. *I-zin-gane   zi-zo-yi-hlabelel-a]*$_{vP}$ *i-n-goma.*
AUG-10-child   10SM-FUT-9OM-sing-FV   AUG-9-song
The children will sing it, the song.'

(13) a. *Ng-a-siz-a   u-Sipho]*$_{vP}$.
1SG.SM-RPST-help-FV   AUG-1a.Sipho
'I helped Sipho.'

b. *Ng-a-m-siz-a]*$_{vP}$ *u-Sipho.*
1SG.SM-RPST-1OM-help-FV   AUG-1a.Sipho
'I helped him, Sipho.'

The examples in (12) are in the future tense; (13) shows the remote past tense. The verb in each sentence is followed by an object-NP. The crucial difference between the (a)- and the (b)-examples is that the object agrees with the verb in the latter. Given the evidence discussed above, this means that the objects in (12b) and (13b) must be located outside the *v*P (as indicated by the bracketing). Note that the object-marked NPs in (12b) and (13b) can follow elements such as *na* and that they cannot be focused, which confirms that they are indeed dislocated:

(14) *U-zo-yi-hlabelel-a]*$_{vP}$ *na   i-n-goma?*
2SG.SM-FUT-9OM-sing-FV   Q   AUG-9-song
'Will you sing it, the song?'

(15) **Ng-a-m-siz-a]*$_{vP}$ *u-Sipho   kuphela.*
1SG.SM-RPST-1OM-help-FV   AUG-1a.Sipho   only
Intended: 'I helped him, Sipho only.'

Since the object-NPs in (12b) and (13b) are in *v*P-external positions, the verbs in these examples are phrase-final. In contrast, the objects of the non-agreeing verbs in the (a)-examples are inside *v*P, and the verbs are hence in phrase-medial position. Because the future and the remote past are non-alternating tenses, the difference between clauses with phrase-medial and phrase-final verbs is not marked by segmental CJ/DJ morphology. However, given the phonological processes associated with the CJ/DJ alternation that were discussed above, it is worth asking whether these processes can also be observed in constructions such as those in (12) and (13). If penultimate lengthening and H tone shift/spread to the antepenult are properties of verbs that are final in their (prosodic and syntactic) phrase, then the syntactic representations diagnosed in (12b) and (13b) above predict that these properties are also attested with verbs that agree with their objects in non-alternating tenses. In the following sections, we discuss the experiment in which we have tested these predictions, as well as our results.

3 Methodology

Data were collected by means of a read-production study. Based on the existing literature and the discussion in Section 2, we predict the following durational and tonal characteristics of the verb words in our target sentences:

Independent of morphological marking of the CJ/DJ distinction on the verb, penultimate lengthening is expected to occur on the verb word if it is immediately followed by an object-marked, right dislocated object, because in this case, the verb is in phrase-final position. If the following object is not object-marked/ right-dislocated, and the verb is therefore in phrase-medial position, no penultimate lengthening is expected to occur.

As for tonal characteristics, a H tone originating on the verb word is expected to shift (or spread) to the antepenultimate position if the verb is followed by an object-marked, right-dislocated object. If followed by an object inside the *v*P, shift (spread) to the penultimate syllable is expected to occur. Again, these expectations are independent of whether or not the CJ/DJ distinction is morphologically marked on the verb in the respective tense form.

3.1 Target sentences

A reading task was administered to the participants. Target sentences were constructed with transitive verbs in the present, the future and the remote past tense whose objects either occurred *v*P-internally (verb = phrase-medial) or in a right-dislocated position (verb = phrase-final), as indicated by the presence of an object marker.

As noted in Section 2, the present tense is one of the tense forms which has morphological marking of the CJ/DJ alternation and therefore serves as a control structure for which durational and tonal differences have firmly been established in the literature. The future tense and the remote past are two non-alternating tense forms, as exemplified in (12) and (13).

The future tense marker is *zo-*. Diachronically, it can be analyzed as a contracted form involving the auxiliary *za* (from the root *z-* 'to come'; Puhrsch 2005: 34), and an infinitive, e.g. *ngi-za-uku-thanda* > *ngi-zo-thanda*, 'I shall love' (Doke 1931: 162). It now represents the usual form of the future (Buell 2009: 74). The morpheme itself is toneless (Khumalo 1982: 43).

The marker of the Remote Past is *áa-*, which contracts with the subject marker. The vowel is long and realized with a HL tone pattern (Khumalo 1982: 37). Referring to Taljaard (1989: 36), Puhrsch (2005: 67) states that this morpheme does not have any tonal allomorphs, which means that it is always realized with a HL contour. Khumalo (1982: 44) also mentions a specific tone pattern HLL associated with the final vowel *-a* in the remote past (see Section 5).

An overview of one verb word in all six morphosyntactic contexts is given in Table 1.[6]

The morphosyntactic structures in Table 1 were repeated with seven different verbs, yielding 42 utterances per speaker. The target sentences were checked with the participants before recording took place. A list of sentences showing the seven different verbs is presented in Table 2 (present tense and phrase-medial verb only), with underlying H tones on verbs only. The verbs were chosen from the list provided by Buell (2004); the tone marking was checked against Rycroft (1981), given that Doke et al. (1990) provide the tonal forms of the imperative in which H- and low (L)-toned verbs converge on the same tone pattern. A full list of target sentences is provided in the appendix.

In order to bring out the tonal differences on the verb word as outlined in Section 2, the verb words had to comply with a number of phonological properties. First, due to an interdependence of the syllable count of the stem and the syllable targeted by tone movement, verb stems had to be longer than two syllables. Practically any work on Nguni tonology reports the alternating target for H tone shift/spread which was already mentioned in Section 2 and which depends on the position of the word in a phrase (Khumalo 1987; Downing 1990; Cassimjee 1998). In phrase-final position, H tone shift is to the antepenultimate syllable; in phrase-medial position, H tone shift targets the penultimate syllable, as shown in (16).

---

6 Table 1 shows the examples how they were presented to our speakers, i.e. in standard Zulu orthography (but note that vowels with underlying H tones are underlined in the verb words in the table). As mentioned above, the remote past marker in Zulu is *áa-*, which contracts with the subject marker *zí-* in the examples in Table 1. The resulting past tense subject marker is *záa-*, which is written as *za-* in Zulu.

Table 1: Morphosyntactic contexts of target sentences.

Tense	Phrase-medial verb	Phrase-final verb
Present	Izingane z<u>i</u>hlabelela ingoma.	Izingane z<u>i</u>yay<u>i</u>hlabelela ingoma.
Future	Izingane z<u>i</u>zohlabelela ingoma.	Izingane z<u>i</u>zoy<u>i</u>hlabelela ingoma.
Remote past	Izingane z<u>a</u>hlabelela ingoma.	Izingane z<u>a</u>y<u>i</u>hlabelela ingoma.

Table 2: Target sentences based on seven verbs.

	Zulu	English
1	I-zi-ngane z<u>i</u>-hlabelela i-ngoma.	The children sing a song.
2	U-mfundi <u>u</u>-namathiselisa i-phepa odongeni.	The student sticks paper to the wall.
3	U-John <u>u</u>-lekelela a-ba-zali ba-khe.	John assists his parents.
4	U-dokotela <u>u</u>-phefumulisa i-si-guli.	The doctor makes the patient breathe. [i.e. by means of a machine in a hospital]
5	U-dokotela <u>u</u>-fiphalisa i-si-guli.	The doctor causes the patient to lose hope.
6	B<u>a</u>-minyanisa a-ba-ntu.	They make the people squash together.
7	I-si-phepho s<u>i</u>-paqulukisa i-sakhiwo.	The storm causes the building to collapse.

(16) Zulu (Downing 1990: ex. [6], [7], [12])
    a. phrase-final; H tone from subject prefix
        b<u>a</u>-ya-límisa   'they help plow'
        <u>u</u>-ya-hlékisa   's/he amuses'
        <u>u</u>-ya-namathélisa   's/he makes stick'

    b. phrase-final; H tone from object prefix
        si-ya-<u>m</u>-límisa   'we help him plow'
        si-ya-w<u>a</u>-namathélisa 'we make them stick'

    c. phase-medial; H tone from subject prefix
        b<u>a</u>-limísa...   'they help plow'
        <u>u</u>-namathelísa...   's/he makes stick'

However, H tones which are sponsored by the antepenult syllable generally shift one syllable rightward to the penult, even when the verb is in phrase-final position:

(17) Zulu (Downing 1990: ex. [14]; slightly adapted)
    <u>u</u>-yá-lwa   's/he fights'
    u-ya-w<u>a</u>-bála   'you count them'
    si-ya-y<u>i</u>-líma   'we plow it'

Therefore, in order to avoid rightward tone shift of the kind illustrated in (17), the H tone must be contributed by a syllable earlier than the antepenultimate syllable. We ensured this by selecting only verbs for our study which were at least four syllables long.

A second phonological property of the verbs selected in our study is determined by the fact that the target of H tone spread/shift with phrase-final verbs has been reported to be influenced by the origin of the H tone. In Durban Zulu (Downing 2001a), a H originating on a verbal *prefix* of a phrase-final verb spreads to the antepenultimate syllable, as in (18) (see also [11b] above). However, a *verb stem-initial* H tone shifts to the penultimate syllable in this context, as shown in (19). Similar data exist from the Cele dialect of Zulu (Natal Coast Zulu in Khumalo 1981) and Ngoni (Cassimjee and Kisseberth 2001: ex. [14]).

(18)   Durban Zulu: pre-stem H tones target antepenultimate of phrase-final verbs
       (Downing 2001a: ex. [2])
       ụ́kú-kaka   'to surround'
       ụ́kú-kákisa   'to cause to surround'
       ụ́kú-kákisana   'to cause each other to surround'

(19)   Durban Zulu: verb stem-initial H tones target penultimate of phrase-final verbs
       (Downing 2001a: ex. [2])
       si-ya-thẹ́nga   'we buy'
       si-ya-thẹngísa   'we sell'
       si-ya-thẹngiséla   'we sell to'

Thus, in order for a H tone to spread to the antepenultimate syllable if the verb is final in a phrase, the H tone should originate on a verbal prefix, but not on the verb stem-initial syllable. As a consequence, only L-toned (toneless) verbs were selected for the study, and H tones were contributed by subject and object markers.

Finally, it is well-documented that in the Nguni languages, depressor consonants influence the realization of H tones in various ways (for a detailed phonetic study, see Traill et al. 1987). Given the various interactions of depressor consonants and tone, depressors have been avoided in the target sentences wherever possible,[7] but especially in the antepenultimate and penultimate syllables of verb words which serve as the target for H tone shift/spread.

3.2 Speakers

Three speakers were recorded, two female and one male. They were all students at the University of KwaZulu-Natal, and around 24 years of age at the time of recording. Speaker LM (female) is from the Tongaat-area, approximately 40 km

---

[7] Note that the future marker <zo> unavoidably contains a depressor consonant. However, as the future marker never occurs in the syllable that is the target of H tone shift, it is expected that it does not interfere with it. Furthermore, it should be noted that the bilabial implosive, represented by <b> in orthography is not a depressor, despite being voiced (Cassimjee and Kisseberth 2001: 331).

north of Durban, but lives in Durban now. She says, "back home" they speak "deep" Zulu. According to her, people from Durban can hear that she is not from Durban because of the way she speaks and the words she uses. However, another participant could not tell where LM was from just by listening to her recordings. Speaker RM (also female) is from Durban and grew up there. Speaker PB (male) is from KwaMashu, a former township of Durban. He has lived there all his life.

It is thus expected that speakers RM and PB show the tonal characteristics of Durban Zulu. LM's variety might be more mixed. However, due to the phonological and tonal make-up of the stimuli (see Section 3.1), the only tonal difference, if any, is predicted to be in the occurrence of H tone spread as opposed to H tone shift (with H tones originating from verbal prefixes). As this does not impede on the research questions concerning durational properties and the respective targets of H tone movement in the non-alternating tenses, the origin of the speaker did not lead to her exclusion.

3.3 Procedure

The recordings were done in a quiet office at the University of KwaZulu-Natal (Durban). The target sentences were given in Zulu orthography (which implies that tones are not indicated, and dislocated phrases are not separated by a comma, as would be necessary in English). They were presented in seven sets (corresponding to the seven different verbs used). Each set contained the six test sentences plus four additional filler sentences to provide some variation. Some of the fillers included the verb *phúmelela*, which is lexically H-toned.

There was a short break before each set so that the participant could familiarise him/herself with the data. Participants were instructed to read clearly but not unnaturally, e.g. like a newsreader or for teaching material.

It has been shown that speakers only disambiguate structures reliably if they are aware of differences between them (see Snedeker and Trueswell 2003; Breen et al. 2010 for English focus prosody). Taking this into account, we opted against randomization of the target sentences and directly contrasted the same verbs in different tenses and syntactic constructions in order to encourage prosodic disambiguation.

3.4 Data analysis

3.4.1 Length

For penultimate lengthening as an acoustic cue to phrase boundaries, the penultimate syllable of the verb word was delineated manually and saved in a Praat text grid, applying common acoustic cues to segment boundaries (see

Turk et al. 2006). The duration of the penultimate syllable was extracted automatically using a Praat Script. The descriptive and inferential statistics of the length measurements are provided in Section 4.

Khumalo (1987: 196) describes penultimate lengthening in Zulu (which he calls "prepausal lengthening") as a *vowel* being lengthened penultimately in a phrase. Some phonetic work on lengthening in Bantu languages also measures the duration of the penultimate vowel (see e.g. Downing and Pompino-Marschall 2013), while others have measured the duration of the penultimate *syllable* (Myers 1999, 2003). Both approaches find penultimate lengthening confirmed in the respective units measured. It thus remains an open empirical question if only the vowel or the entire syllable is lengthened when occurring in penultimate position. In the current study, the length of the penultimate syllable was measured. Compared to other acoustic studies that measure vowel length, we expect to find a longer absolute duration (given that two instead of one segments were measured). However, the relational aspect, i.e. lengthening in penultimate position, is not expected to be affected. (A non-systematic measure of the length of the penultimate vowel in a subset of our data confirmed the general pattern we found based on syllable length that we report in Section 4.1).

3.4.2 Tone annotation

Tone annotation was done for the verb words only and was based on auditory impression. Of central interest in tone annotation was the target of H tone movement. It was also noted if spread or shift occurred, although this question was not central to our research. Each author listened to the recordings (either alone or in groups of two), and transcribed the tone of the verb word. If necessary, pitch tracks were inspected in addition to the auditory impression. Agreement between the three annotators was reached concerning the tone pattern of nearly all verb words, at times including extensive discussion and re-listening.

4 Results

4.1 Length

As discussed in Section 2, a noted feature of the phrase-final verb form is prepausal lengthening of the penultimate syllable. Table 3 below gives the average length of the penultimate syllable in seconds (with its standard deviation) for each phrasal context, for each tense, and for each speaker. For each speaker, the relative penult length follows the exact same order, with the present medial

Table 3: Average length (in seconds) and standard deviation (in parentheses) of the penultimate syllable per tense, position and speaker.

		LM	PB	RM
Present Tense	medial	0.165 (0.028)	0.190 (0.026)	0.151 (0.018)
	final	0.233 (0.023)	0.217 (0.020)	0.175 (0.020)
Future Tense	medial	0.191 (0.039)	0.202 (0.022)	0.167 (0.022)
	final	0.242 (0.037)	0.232 (0.034)	0.185 (0.017)
Remote Past	medial	0.170 (0.026)	0.195 (0.024)	0.159 (0.028)
	final	0.235 (0.024)	0.227 (0.017)	0.185 (0.021)

being the shortest and the future final the longest. The data show that future and remote past verb forms behave similarly to the present, in that phrase-medial forms that are followed by a *v*P-internal object have shorter penults than the corresponding phrase-final forms which contain an object marker and co-occur with a right-dislocated object NP.

Figure 1 is a visual summary of the distribution. It shows the duration of the penultimate syllable of final (white boxes) versus medial forms (grey boxes) in morphologically marked (Present Tense) and unmarked tenses (Future and Remote Past) across all speakers. The bold-typed horizontal line in each box represents the median (i.e. a central tendency in the data, namely the breakdown point of 50% of the data). The boxes delineate the 75%- and 25%-quartiles. The whiskers (error bars) represent the largest and smallest values that are not more than 1.5 interquartile ranges away from the box. Individual dots represent data points outside this range.

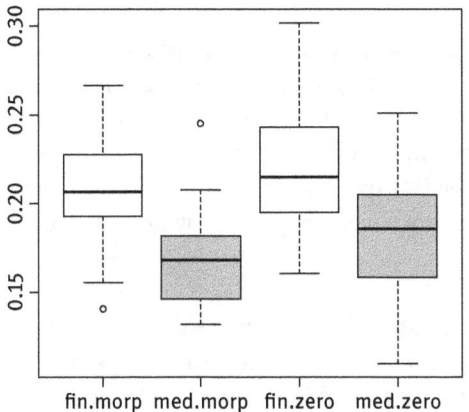

fin.morp = present tense final
med.morp = present tense medial
fin.zero = remote past and future final
med.zero = remote past and future medial

Figure 1: Boxplots showing the distribution by position and morphological marking.

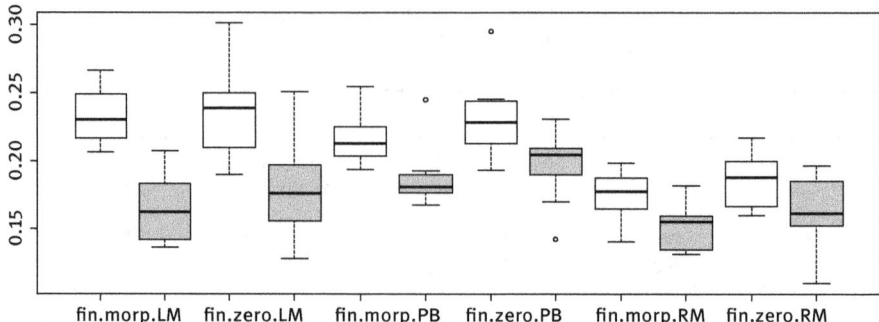

Figure 2: Boxplots showing the distribution by position, morphological marking, and speaker (white boxes represent final forms, grey boxes represent medial forms).

Visual inspection of the data shows that in general, in the morphologically marked present tense, medial and final forms differ more clearly in the length of the penultimate syllable, whereas there is a slightly larger overlap in morphologically unmarked forms.

Figure 2 shows the distribution per speaker. Visual inspection of the per-speaker distribution shows:

- for final versus medial forms: In morphologically marked present tense, the white and grey boxes for final and medial forms do not overlap for any speaker, thus suggesting a relevant difference between these conditions. For the morphologically unmarked forms, there is some overlap in the error bars (for LM and PB) and even in the boxes for speaker RM, being indicative of a somewhat closer distribution. Position and morphological marking are included in the statistical model as fixed factors.
- the medians and overall distribution of boxes differ across speakers, indicating individual differences in speech tempo. E.g. RM produces shorter syllables in nearly all conditions. Speaker is included as a random factor in the statistical model and random intercepts are calculated per speaker.
- the variance in duration differs, depending on speaker and tense, showing less variance e.g. for RM than for LM. Random slopes per speaker were added to the statistical model.

The visual inspection of the results suggests that the process of penultimate lengthening is directly associated with phrase-finality of a verb form, regardless of whether or not the CJ/DJ alternation is segmentally marked in the respective tense of the verb.

We also tested the results inferentially for significance. For the inferential analysis, R (R Development Core Team, 2010, version 2.12.0) and lme4

Table 4: Results of linear mixed model evaluating the ratings against the fixed factors "position", "morphological marking" and their interaction.

Coefficient	Estimate	Std. Error	t-value
Position	−0.0397	0.0132	−3.010
Morphological marking	0.0095	0.0066	1.442
Position x morph.marking	0.0025	0.0086	0.287

(Bates et al. 2011) were used to perform linear mixed effects analyses of the relationship between duration of penultimate syllable, position (final, medial) and morphological marking (marked, zero). As fixed effects, position and morphological marking (with interaction) were entered into the model. As random effects, intercepts for subjects and items, as well as by-subject and by-item random slopes for the effects of position and morphological marking were calculated (Cunnings 2012). Table 4 summarizes the results of the model.[8]

The mixed effects model with position, morphological marking and interaction of the two effects shows a statistically significant main effect for position (t = −3.01) but not for morphological marking nor for an interaction of position and marking.

We conclude that the process of penultimate lengthening is directly associated with phrase-finality of a verb form, regardless of whether or not the CJ/DJ alternation is segmentally marked in the respective tense of the verb.

4.2 Tone

In this section, we discuss our findings for the tone patterns for the present, future, and remote past, focusing specifically on the extent to which (ante) penultimate shift (Sections 2 and 3) characterizes the tenses that lack a segmental alternation between medial and final forms, i.e. future and remote past tense. Although our intention is to present our data largely descriptively, we adopt the domain-marking conventions of Optimal Domains Theory (ODT) as employed in Cassimjee (1998), Cassimjee and Kisseberth (2001), and articulated in Leben (2006). A H domain is defined as "a sequence of moras, the leftmost of which is H in underlying representation and the rightmost of which is H on the surface" (Leben 2006: 4). We use brackets to demarcate H domains, the underlying position of a H tone is underlined, and its surface position is marked with an acute accent.

---

[8] Since determining the precise degrees of freedom is non-trivial in linear mixed models, the t-values are approximations. An absolute t-value of 2 or greater indicates statistical significance at α = 0.05.

4.2.1 Present tense

In the present, the CJ form is distinguished from the DJ by the presence of the *ya*-morpheme in the latter. As laid out in the methodology section, our CJ stimuli consisted of toneless stems with a H-toned subject marker. It is well-established for Zulu phonology that in the CJ verb form, the H tone targets the penultimate syllable of the verb complex (Khumalo 1981, 1982; Downing 1990). This prediction was borne out for all of our speakers.

However, we encountered variation in whether the penult was the object of tone shift or spread. In Durban Zulu, H tones originating in the prefix domain are documented as spreading in Downing (2001a) and Cassimjee and Kisseberth (2001) (see footnote 4). Example (20) shows the more common pattern of H spread from the H tone of the subject marker, and (21) shows H shift. Two speakers (PB, RM) were categorical for H tone spread, and one (LM) varied between shift and spread.[9]

(20) a. *ú-phéfúmúlísa ...*   (LM, PB, RM)
     b. *ú-fíphálísa ...*   (PB, RM)

(21) a. *u-fiphalísa ...*   (LM)
     b. *si-paqulukísa ...*   (LM)

The patterns observed in the DJ form also largely confirmed our expectations. Due to prepausal lengthening of the penult, H tone movement targets the antepenult instead, and the penult is lengthened and realized with a falling tone. It is important to note that there are two H tone domains (HTDs) in DJ verb forms containing an object marker, the first encompassing prefixal material to the left of the object marker, and the second beginning with the object marker (Downing 1990; Cassimjee and Kisseberth 2001).[10]

---

9 Phonetically, the distinction between H tone shift and H tone spread may not always be quite as clear. Cassimjee and Kisseberth (2001: 333) note with respect to Zululand Zulu that "[i]n tone 'shift' from an initial syllable to a later position in the word, all the syllables up to the landing site are quite raised in pitch if none of the syllables from the point of origin to the landing site have a depressed onset." This formulation would also be compatible with spread. However, as a difference in the pattern between the speakers was clearly discernible, we transcribe it as a difference between spread and shift.

10 We have indicated the falling tone on the penultimate syllable in (22), but it should be kept in mind that this syllable is underlyingly toneless. Cassimjee and Kisseberth (2001: 331) describe different fall patterns that can be perceived on the penultimate syllable and which stem from an underlying H tone, L tone (= phonologically toneless) and a syllable containing a falling tone. They note that "[a] lengthened, non-depressed syllable which is toneless from a phonological point of view shows a very clear fall in pitch when immediately preceded by a H tone. [...] this falling pitch is predictable and is also quite distinct from the true falling-toned syllables (which have a somewhat greater duration of the H portion of the fall)".

(22) a. [sí-yá][lí-námáthísé]lî:sa   (LM, PB, RM)
     b. [ú-yá][bá-léké]lê:la   (LM, PB, RM)

Since the adjacent H tones on *ya-* and the following object markers (*lí*, *bá*) are created by spread onto *ya-* rather than underlyingly adjacent tone-bearing units (TBUs), it is not an environment for downstep, and the series of level H tones is expected (Cassimjee and Kisseberth 2001: 329). Interestingly, our speaker (LM), who varied between shift and spread in the CJ form, exhibited only H spread in the DJ.

4.2.2 Future tense

Our data confirm an analysis of the tone in the future tense in Zulu that was previously suggested for mutually intelligible Ndebele by Downing (2001b), and that is related to the diachronic status of the future morpheme as a formerly separate auxiliary verb. As noted in Section 3, the future tense is marked by the toneless future morpheme *zo-*, which is transparently derived from the verb *ukuza* 'come'. Notably, *zo-* behaves differently from other verbal prefixes in that it establishes its own prosodic domain, probably because it is historically derived from an auxiliary verb. In both the medial and final forms, *zo-* is final in this prosodic domain and therefore blocks rightward tone spreading from prefixal material to its left (as shown for Ndebele in Downing [2001b]). Due to the prosodic boundary established by *zo-*, the H from the subject marker cannot target any syllables within the stem, nor can it surface on the *zo-* itself. In the phrase-medial form of the verb, this means that the only syllable bearing a H tone is the subject marker, which is underlyingly H-toned.

(23) a. [sí-zo]namthiselisa ...   (LM, PB, RM)
     b. [ú-zo]lekelela ...   (LM, RM)

We also encountered an unexpected pattern in which the final syllable of the medial CJ verb bears a H tone.[11] This was common for speaker PB, and present in one example for RM:

---

11 One could perhaps argue that the H tone on the final syllable of the verb can somehow be linked to the tonal properties of the postverbal noun, which possibly influences the tones on the preceding verb word. Nouns in Zulu have both a pre-prefix and a prefix whose segmental shape is determined by the noun class to which the item belongs. The pre-prefix is underlyingly H-toned (cf. Buell 2009, citing Rycroft 1979), whereas the prefix is toneless. However, note that for nouns, the same rules of tone shift/spread apply as for verbs: shift/spread away from the point of origin towards the penult or antepenultimate. Thus, the H tone of a pre-prefix does not necessarily surface on the initial syllable. In addition, the postverbal context is comparable in all examples, but the final H tone on the verb surfaces only in some cases. We therefore assume that the final vowel in examples such as (24) is not in any way related to the presence of an (underlyingly H-toned) pre-prefix on the object.

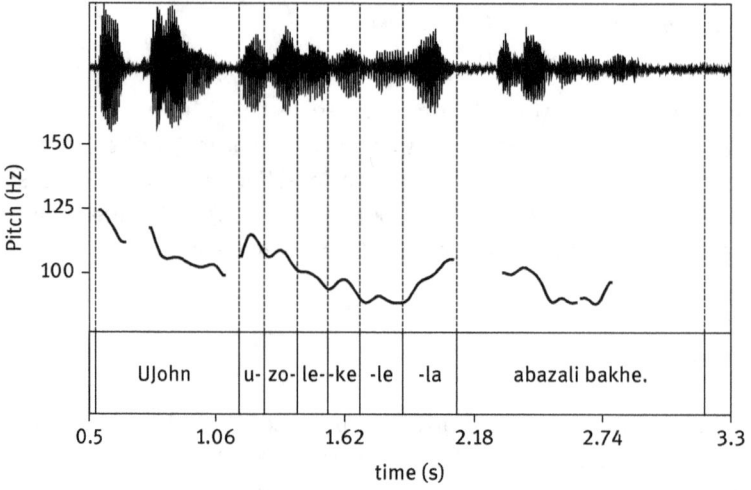

Figure 3: Pitch track for phrase-medial verb in the future tense (PB, male speaker).

(24) a. [ú-zo]lekelelá ...   (PB), see Figure 3
     b. [bá-zo]minyanisá ... (PB, RM)

Our stimuli also included the H-toned stem *phúmelela*. Due to the prosodic boundary established by *zo-*, the *phúmelela*-examples we recorded demonstrate that a stem H targets the penult of the phrase-medial verb in the future tense, as expected based on the data from the present tense.

(25)   [zí-zo][phu̱melé]la ...   (LM, PB, RM)

To some extent, the tonal facts from the phrase-final future agree with what was found for the present DJ. That is, the H from the object marker targets the antepenult of the verb complex and the penult is realized with a falling tone:

(26) a. [sí-zo][li̱-namathisé]lî:sa   (LM, PB, RM)
     b. [bá-zo][ba̱-minyá]nî:sa   (LM, PB, RM)

However, notice that the H of the subject marker is restricted to appear only on the subject marker itself, as attested in the future medial forms; it does not shift to the future tense marker. In this respect, the examples in (26) differ from the corresponding examples in the present DJ, where the H tone from the subject marker spreads to the DJ marker *ya-* (compare [22]). As noted above, we assume that this difference is due to the fact that *zo-* establishes its own prosodic domain and therefore blocks H tone movement from prefixal material to its left.

There are also a number of examples taken from the final future forms where the tonal patterns are considerably less clear. Recall that in the present DJ, all speakers uniformly had a H tone plateau (spread) from the subject marker through the antepenult, whereas the examples in (26) show shift rather than spread. Yet, this is not the case for all future DJ examples; in this tense, there is considerable variation between shift vs. spread from the H tone of the object marker to the antepenult. In certain constructions, we seem to find a little of both; that is, the H of the object marker does not surface where it is underlyingly linked, nor does it target only the antepenultimate syllable:

(27)   [ú-zo][si-phefúmú]li:sa   (LM, RM)

In others, antepenultimate shift does not seem to be at work at all, and we see a shift to the penult instead:

(28)   [sí-zo][si-paqulukí:]sa   (PB)

4.2.3 Remote past tense

In the remote past, the subject marker merges with the bimoraic remote past marker áa- (see Section 3.1). In this process, vocalic subject markers are replaced by glides and CV-shaped subject markers undergo vowel deletion; in all cases, the mora of the subject marker is lost:

(29)   sí + á: → sǎ: ú + á: → wǎ:

Our subjects realize the H of the resulting syllable either as a rising tone (as Cassimjee [1998: 229] reports for Xhosa), or as a H tone. Khumalo (1982: 39) analyzes the rising tone in this case as a result of a dissimilatory process.

We observed a good deal of variation regarding the tone pattern of phrase-medial verbs in the remote past, and some of the tonal properties we observed are unexpected. All together, we identified four distinct tonal patterns:

Pattern 1: The H tone associated with the remote past marker does not shift or spread to the stem; all syllables following the combined subject prefix/tense marker are L-toned. This option is only attested three times:

(30)   a.   [wǎ:]namathiselisa ...   (LM, RM)
       b.   [zǎ:]hlabelela ...   (LM)

Pattern 2: As in pattern 1, no H tone movement to the stem is observed, and all syllables following the tense marker are L-toned, except for the final vowel, to which a H tone is added. With LM, we observed the addition of the final H in more than half of all instances:

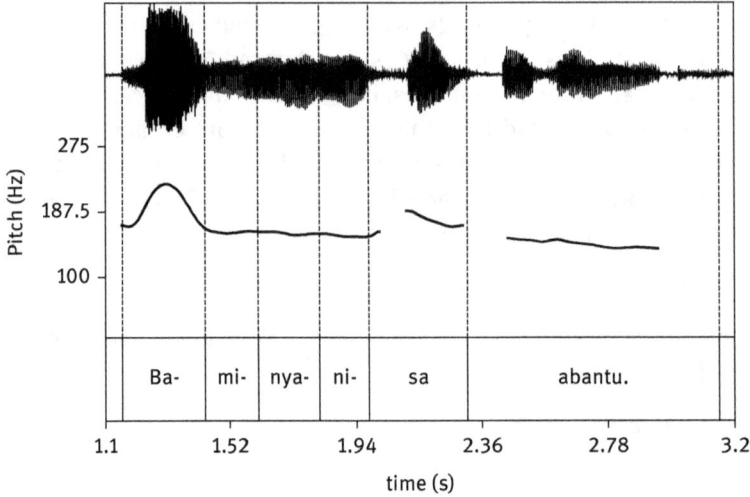

Figure 4: Pitch track of the phrase-medial verb in the remote past tense (LM; female speaker).

(31) a. [ză:]paquluki[sá] ... (LM)
     b. [bă:]minyani[sá] ... (LM), see Figure 4

Recall from Section 4.2.2 that a similar final H was found in some examples of phrase-medial verbs in the future tense.

Pattern 3: A third tonal pattern, attested with all three speakers, shows the H tone spreading from the remote past marker to the verb stem. However, contrary to what we expected in light of the tonal properties of phrase-medial verbs in the present and future tense, the H tone does not spread to the penult, but only as far as the antepenult:

(32) a. [wă:námáthísé]lisa ... (PB)
     b. [wă:phéfúmú]lisa ... (RM)

H tone spread to the antepenult does not seem to be restricted to lexically toneless verbs where the H tone originates on a prefix, but appears to be a general pattern of the remote past (where spread occurs at all): with the lexically H-toned verb *phúmelela*, the H tone that originates on the verb stem also surfaces only on the antepenult, and does not spread to the penult, as we would have expected:

(33)   [ză:][phúmé]lela ... (LM)

Compare (33) to the tone pattern in (34), with a present tense phrase-medial verb:

(34)   [zi-phúmélé]la ... (LM)

Pattern 4: The fourth pattern combines pattern 3 with the final H that was observed as part of pattern 2. The H tone of the tense marker spreads to the antepenult, the penult has a falling contour, but the final vowel is H again. This pattern was attested twice with speaker PB:

(35)   [bǎ:mínyá]nî[sá] ...   (PB)

In the phrase-final verb forms, we expected the H tone of the object marker to move only as far as the antepenult. Pre-stem H tones in (Durban) Zulu surface on the antepenult when the verb is phrase-final (Cassimjee and Kisseberth 2001; Downing 2001a), and this pattern is familiar from the present and future.[12] Our results confirmed this expectation: the H tone of the object marker spreads to the antepenult, and the tone on the lengthened penult is falling. Note that the pitch of the H tone on the object marker is slightly lower than the pitch of the adjacent remote past (subject) marker, which suggests that downstep has occurred. Unlike the examples in (22), the H tones that surface on adjacent syllables are sponsored on underlyingly adjacent TBUs, satisfying the environment for downstep (Cassimjee and Kisseberth 2001: 329).

(36)   a.   [zǎ:][!yí-hlábé]lê:la   (LM, PB, RM)
        b.   [wǎ:][!bá-léké]lê:la   (LM, PB, RM)

However, we also encounter a number of examples in this paradigm where no downstep is perceptible, despite its environment being met:

(37)   a.   [wǎ:][sí-fíphá]lî:sa   (LM, PB, RM)
        b.   [sá:][sí-páqúlú]kî:sa   (PB, RM)

5 Discussion

With respect to the tonal and durational characteristics of verb forms in the present tense, future tense and remote past in Zulu, our study confirms most of the predictions we derived from existing analyses in the literature (see Section 2). Regarding penultimate lengthening, we observed that the duration of the penultimate syllable of a verb followed by an object-marked object is consistently longer than the penult of a verb followed by an object complement. This is independent of a simultaneous morphological marking of these verb forms as CJ/DJ. Correspondingly, we observed that a H tone originating on a verbal prefix that

---

[12] Recall from Section 3.1 that stem-initiated H tones in Durban Zulu always shift to the penult, even with phrase-final verbs.

shifts/spreads into the stem targets the antepenultimate syllable of the verb when the following object is object-marked. These findings are consistent with the assumption (discussed in Section 2) that object-marked objects in Zulu are *v*P-external and that verbs immediately preceding an object-marked object are always phrase-final, even in tense forms in which phrase-finality of verbs is not marked by segmental DJ-morphology. With the exception of some tonal patterns in the remote past which we discuss below, the tonal and durational characteristics that we observed can be accounted for solely by phrasing, given that prosodic and syntactic phrasing coincide.

In the remainder of this section, we discuss some of our findings that we regard as particularly noteworthy.

5.1 Length

Our comparison of the length of the penultimate syllable between phrase-medial and phrase-final forms shows a difference which, depending on speaker, is around 50 ms (LM), 30 ms (PB) or 25 ms (RM). We have interpreted this stable difference as indicative of a phrase boundary between the verb and a right-dislocated object (cf. Cheng and Downing 2009 and Section 2). However, it is notable that the observed difference, although consistent, is rather small, considering that the length of the whole syllable is measured. This is evident when we compare our data with the results of another study on penultimate lengthening, that conducted by Downing and Pompino-Marschall (2013). The authors investigate penultimate lengthening as a cue to phrasing in the Bantu language Chichewa.[13] In their study, they measured the length of only the penultimate *vowel* on each constituent in a sentence like *mulimi wapatsa bambo tambaala* ("The farmer has given father a rooster"). According to their data, the difference in length between the penultimate vowel of the sentence-medial verb (*wa-patsa*; no object marking) and the penultimate vowel of the sentence-final noun (*tambaala*) is more than 85 ms.[14] The saliently lengthened penultimate vowel of the sentence-final word in Chichewa has been interpreted as culminative prominence at intonation

---

13 We are not aware of any comparable empirical study on length in Zulu which we could use as a basis for a comparison, and it is for this reason that we discuss the data from Chichewa here.
14 This value reflects the comparison of averages across all speakers and all focus conditions which are reported by Downing and Pompino-Marschall (2013) taken from the published results of the second set of the two sets of sentences that they investigated. In the first set of sentences no difference between the length of the penultimate vowels of verb and object emerges (cf. Downing and Pompino-Marschall 2013, [18]).

phrase (IP-) boundaries, which is conventionally transcribed by means of a colon or a doubled vowel. The length difference that we find in our study, however, is clearly not as salient, even though we measured syllables, and not vowels. This raises the question if a phrase-final verb and a right-dislocated object are indeed separated by an IP-boundary in Zulu or rather by another type of prosodic phrase, which induces a lengthening that is less salient than that found with sentence-final words (cf. Kanerva 1990, who suggests that two different levels of phrasing in Chichewa, namely IP and a Phonological Phrase [PP], can be distinguished by different degrees of length). In light of this question, it would be interesting to test whether the length differences increase when the durational properties of phrase-medial verbs in Zulu are compared to those of *sentence*-final verbs (i.e. phrase-final verbs that are not followed by right-dislocated material).[15] We intend to explore this issue further in future research.

Even though the length difference we observed in Zulu is perhaps less salient than expected, it nevertheless seems that a correlation between length and the target of H tone movement emerges: In the short penultimate syllables of the phrase-medial verbs, we find H tone movement to the penultimate position, whereas H tone movement to the penult seems to be blocked by the longer penultimate syllables of the phrase-final forms. As noted in section 2, Cassimjee and Kisseberth (2001: 334) propose that H tone movement to the antepenult results from the tendency to avoid the alignment of the right edge of a H tone domain with a metrically prominent syllable. It seems that the lengthening of the penult associated with phrase-final verbs is less salient when the verb is followed by right-dislocated material, but nevertheless salient enough to be regarded as metrically prominent and to block H tone movement.

5.2 Tone

Our study confirmed that a H tone sponsored by a subject marker moves to the right as far as the penult if the verb is in the present tense and phrase-medial in Zulu (Section 4.2.1). The fact that we did not observe this H tone spread or shift from the subject marker in the future tense (Section 4.2.2) follows from the status of *zo*-. As noted above, *zo*- is diachronically related to an auxiliary that has undergone

---

15 We thank a reviewer for raising this point. The reviewer also notes that right-dislocated objects can take scope under negation (Buell 2008; Zeller 2012), which can be interpreted as evidence that dislocated material is realized in a relatively "low" *v*P-external position, and is therefore presumably still located inside the constituent that corresponds to a major prosodic phrase (i.e. IP).

grammaticalization. The prosodic domain that blocks tone spread from the subject marker across *zo-* and into the stem can be regarded as evidence that this process, which would turn *zo-* into a prefixal tense morpheme, has not been fully completed. Otherwise, the non-alternating future tense shows the same phonological processes as the present tense, which marks the CJ/DJ alternation segmentally (the occurrence of a final H in some of our future tense examples is discussed below).

The tonal patterns in the remote past medial are somewhat involved. It was shown in Section 4.2.3 that we distinguished four patterns, which we repeat here for expository purposes:

(38)   Tone pattern of the remote past tense

Pattern 1: [wǎ:]namathiselisa ...
The remote past marker bears a rising tone, and the remainder of the syllables are toneless.

Pattern 2: [zǎ:]paquluki[sá] ...
As in Pattern 1, but with a H on the final syllable.

Pattern 3: [wǎ:námáthísé]lisa ...
Rising tone on tense marker, all stem syllables through the antepenult are H

Pattern 4: [bǎ:mínyá]nî[sá] ...
As in pattern 3, but with a falling tone on the penult and a final H.

With respect to the H tone of the remote past marker *áa-*, the four patterns in (38) show two options: one in which the H of the tense marker does not spread off the syllable to which it is underlyingly linked, and another in which it spreads through to the antepenult. These two options then independently co-occur with the final H, resulting in the four patterns in (38).

We therefore suggest that the difference between patterns 1 and 2 on the one hand and patterns 3 and 4 on the other is based on the optional spread of the H from the remote past tense marker *áa-*. In mutually intelligible Ndebele, this morpheme's H never spreads or shifts, and also suppresses the expression of any other H tones that may be underlyingly present in the verb complex, such as the H of an object marker or of a H-toned stem (Sibanda 2004: 278). Patterns 1 and 2 are then reminiscent of Ndebele, whereas patterns 3 and 4 show an instance of divergence from how the remote past tense behaves in Zulu's closely related cousin.

What is surprising about the patterns 3 and 4, though, is that the H should only spread to the antepenult. As discussed in previous sections, it is widely accepted that H tones target the penult phrase-medially, because the penultimate syllable of the verb is not lengthened. We would therefore expect the subject marker's H tone to spread all the way to the penult in the phrase-medial forms of the remote past. Herman (1996: 44) argues for the mutually intelligible Nguni language Swati that penultimate lengthening can be analyzed as the construction of a foot at the right edge of a verb complex. Following Herman, it is tempting to posit the existence of some sort of prosodic structure in this position in the remote past that would block the spread of the H to the penult. However, there is no penultimate lengthening in the remote past medial, so whatever is behind this pattern does not manifest itself beyond the blocking of H spread to the penult.

There also remain some lingering questions about the antepenultimate spread (as opposed to shift) shown in patterns 3 and 4. We hypothesize that the dominance of spread is due to the requirement that the remote past marker surfaces with its H, which necessarily creates an environment for spread and not shift because it creates a link between sponsor and target.

We turn next to the final H tone which was observed in patterns 2 and 4 of the remote past. Patterns 2 and 4 were only attested with two of the three speakers we recorded (LM and PB), and even these speakers did not systematically pronounce the final syllable of verbs in phrase-medial position with a H tone. The final H also appeared in some examples of phrase-medial forms of the future tense (see Section 4.2.2). In the following, we offer some speculations on the nature of this "occasional" final H, which are based on a comparison of different tonal analyses of the remote past that have been proposed for Zulu and related Bantu languages. The hypothesis that we will eventually put forward below is that this H tone may in fact be a grammatical marker of the CJ-form that speakers can optionally use in some tense forms in Zulu.

Khumalo (1982) claims that the remote past in Zulu is realised by the prefix *áa-* and a suffix *-a* that introduces a grammatical H tone. With verbs in phrase-final position, whose penult is lengthened, this H tone gives rise to the tone pattern HLL on the lengthened penult and the final vowel. This is shown in (39), adopted from Khumalo (1982: 49):

(39)   *wâ:thùkù'thê:là*

The grammatical H tone causes the lengthened penult to be pronounced with a falling tone, followed by a low final vowel.

Khumalo's analysis may indeed be able to explain some of the different tone patterns that we observed in the remote past. We found that with object-marked phrase-final verb forms, the H of the remote past is indeed realised as a falling tone on the penult, exactly as in (39). In contrast to (39), however, the H-toned object marker causes the intervening syllables to be H as well, due to the spread of the object marker's H to the antepenult. (40) repeats our example (36a) from Section 4.2.3:

(40)   [zǎ:][!yí-hlábé]lê:la

The final H tone we observed in patterns 2 and 4 with verbs in phrase-medial position can now be analysed as the realisation of Khumalo's grammatical H in contexts where there is no penultimate lengthening: With phrase-medial forms, the grammatical H would be realised on the final vowel. Since Khumalo does not include examples of remote past verbs phrase-medially, it is possible that his suffixal HLL is in fact simply a final H. Phrase-finally, the final syllable is extraprosodic, so it is inaccessible and the H is assigned instead to the penult. The penult in turn lengthens, and is realized as a falling tone. Although phonetically similar to the fall of final penults which are phonologically low (see footnote 10), the remote past penults are phonologically falling.

Such an analysis of the remote past also connects with other past tense morphologies in Bantu. A grammatical H associated with the final syllable of the remote past tense is also found in Umbundu (R11, spoken in Angola). Umbundu uses a general L-toned past tense marker -a-, and distinguishes between the near and the remote past through different suffixes: The remote past suffix in Umbundu is -á, the recent past is -éle:

(41)   a. *tw-a-land-éle*   'we (have) bought (near past)'
        b. *tw-a-land-á*   'we (have) bought (far past)'
                                [Umbundu; Nurse and Philippson 2006: 158]

A related, but slightly different, account of the tone pattern of the remote past tense in Zulu could incorporate the idea that the final H tone of patterns 2 and 4 does not originate on the final vowel, but on the verb stem. Cassimjee (1998) argues that in the closely related Nguni language Xhosa, a grammatical H tone is associated with the second mora of the verb stem in the remote past.[16] Although she does not provide examples of phrase-medial verbs, her discussion [p. 230] suggests that this H is expected to shift and to surface on the final syllable in these contexts. (Cassimjee [p. 230] argues that the constraint that prevents H tones on final syllables from being realised, which operates in the present tense medial, does not hold

---

16 This grammatical H seems to be related to a phenomenon briefly discussed in Kisseberth and Odden (2003: 61–2), Nurse and Philippson (2006: 165) and Nurse (2007: 173), which is referred to as a "melodic H". The melodic H is characterized as a grammatical tone attested in several Bantu languages which is preferably assigned to the second or final mora of the verb stem, "in contexts that are not well understood" (Nurse and Philippson 2006: 165). The examples discussed by Kisseberth and Odden (2003) include Yambasa, which marks the remote past by a H tone which spreads from the second to the final syllable of the stem, and Namwanga, which uses a grammatical H on the final vowel as a marker of the potential tense.

in the remote past.) Similarly, Donnelly (2007: 598, footnote 93) notes that in the Nguni language Phuthi, the remote past is formed by means of a grammatical H tone on the stem which spreads to the final syllable (presumably only with phrase-medial verbs). The segmental marker for the remote past in Xhosa and Phuthi is the prefix *áa-*, as in Zulu. One could therefore postulate that the remote past in Zulu is similar to Xhosa and Phuthi in that a grammatical H is associated with the stem in the remote past tense. According to this alternative, the final H of patterns 2 and 4 would be the realisation of this grammatical H tone, which has shifted to the right.[17]

We noted above that, according to Khumalo's (1982) analysis, the falling tone on the penultimate vowel of the phrase-final verb in our example (40) would be the result of the same grammatical H tone that is realised as an H on the final vowel with phrase-medial verbs. However, one problem for this analysis is raised by the fact that it does not account for the *absence* of the final H in patterns 1 and 3. In order to explain the variation we observed with respect to the remote past medial, we would have to stipulate that speakers can freely omit the grammatical H that is otherwise associated with the final vowel in patterns 2 and 4. But although one and the same speaker can sometimes shift between these different patterns in the remote past medial (e.g. PB alternates between patterns 3 and 4), all speakers consistently realise the phrase-final forms with a falling tone on the penult, including the speaker RM, who never produced a final H in any examples of the phrase-medial remote past. It is therefore not entirely clear that the tonal pattern of the remote past final forms really involves the same underlying H tone that is associated with the final vowel in the phrase-medial verb forms.

We therefore want to consider one more alternative analysis of the final H in patterns 2 and 4. This alternative is based on the assumption that the final H of the phrase-medial forms is not related to the falling tone on the penult in examples such as (40). According to this assumption, only the H of the object marker is present in the macrostem constituent when the verb is phrase-final in the remote past, and it is this H that spreads to the antepenult, producing a falling tone on the penult. This implies that the grammatical H tone observed in patterns 2 and 4 is only associated with phrase-medial, and never with phrase-final, verbs.[18]

This idea is interesting in the light of the tonal pattern of the recent past in Zulu, a tense form that we have not examined in our study. As noted in Section 2,

---

17 To explain pattern 4, one would have to assume that the spreading of the H of the subject prefix to the antepenult does not prevent the grammatical H from shifting to the final syllable.
18 Admittedly, this assumption does not explain the falling tone on the penult in Khumalo's example (39). Since we have not collected any original data with phrase-final verbs without object markers, we have to leave this point open.

the recent past distinguishes segmentally between a CJ and a DJ form. In the CJ form, the phrase-medial verb carries a H-toned suffix -é, while the DJ form is marked by the suffix -*ile*:

(42) a. *Ngi-fund-é   i-n-cwadi.*
       1SG.SM-read-PST   AUG-9-book
       'I read a book.'

  b. *Ngi-fund-ile.*
     1SG.SM-read-PST.DJ
     'I read.'

The final H tone in (42a) is commonly assumed to be associated directly with the tense suffix that marks the CJ form of the recent past (see e.g. Khumalo 1982). However, Cassimjee (1998: 202) provides evidence (for Xhosa) that the grammatical H associated with the CJ form of the recent past does not originate on the tense marker, but on the second syllable of the verb stem, from where it shifts to the end of the word (see also Donnelly 2007: 598, footnote 93, for Phuthi).[19] Importantly, this grammatical H is only associated with the CJ form of this tense in both Xhosa and Zulu. This means that the H tone should not be analysed as a part of the recent past tense morphology; rather, it seems to be *a marker of the CJ form*.

We therefore propose that the grammar of Zulu includes a grammatical H tone that marks the CJ form of the recent past. The occurrence of this grammatical H in Zulu is for the most part morphologically conditioned – it is systematically observed only in the recent past –, which is of course not uncommon in Bantu (cf. Creissels's [this volume] discussion of various tense forms in Tswana in which the CJ/DJ alternation is marked solely by tone). However, we consider it possible that the existence of a grammatical H tone that systematically marks the CJ form in one tense can lead to a situation in which speakers use the same grammatical H tone to mark the CJ form in other tenses, albeit not systematically. We therefore would like to put forward the hypothesis that the grammatical H that marks the CJ form of the recent past in Zulu is also used occasionally to mark the CJ form of tenses in which the CJ/DJ alternation is not marked by segmental morphology, i.e. the remote past and the future tense. According to this hypothesis, patterns 2 and 4 above combine the segmental remote past tense marker *áa-* with a grammatical H on the second mora of the verb stem which specifically marks the CJ form.

---

19 The final vowel in both the recent and the remote past tense is slightly lengthened and is realised as a falling tone. Cassimjee (1998) analyses this tone pattern in Xhosa by suggesting that the final suffix in the recent past is bisyllabic /ée/ (a contracted form of the long form suffix -*ile*), with the H realised on the penultimate syllable. Correspondingly, the final H that we observe in the remote past could be analysed as slightly lengthened with a falling tone (/áa/).

The H shifts to the right, and surfaces on the final vowel. This hypothesis, although perhaps not unproblematic, is consistent with the observation that the final H tone does not consistently appear in our remote past tense data, but also shows up in some instances of the future tense. We consider the idea that there may be a tonal morpheme in Zulu that is correlated exclusively with a verb in phrase-medial position a promising area for future research.[20]

6 Conclusion

Our study raises some interesting questions which deserve further research. Although the length data clearly suggest a boundary intervening between DJ-forms and postverbal material, it remains an open question as to which prosodic level this boundary belongs. In this article we only looked at two of the most well-known phonological correlates of phrasing in Nguni, namely tonal alternations and length. Further research could also take other segmental and tonal processes related to phrasing into consideration. Lanham (1960: 83), e.g., reports downstep to take place within a phrase. This means that in a sequence of high and low tones, a H tone following a low tone is lower in pitch than any earlier H tone (Lanham 1960: 83). However, after a phrase boundary, the pitch of H is "reset" (Lanham 1960: 90). Rycroft (1980: 6, footnote 20) also addresses this issue and suggests that downstep in Nguni occurs "irrespective of whether L tones intervene". Cross-linguistically, a further common cue to prosodic phrasing is preboundary lengthening (Vaissière 1983) in which a vowel preceding a word and/or phrase boundary is lengthened. Further research should take these further cues to phrasing into consideration.

As we noted in Section 3.3, the data for our phonetic analysis were elicited in a way that might make speakers aware of the relevant differences and thus might have prompted prosodic disambiguation. Therefore, another potential topic for future research would be to investigate to what extent our findings are representative of ordinary language use and whether speakers also realize the observed prosodic differences in more natural contexts.

The real challenge in understanding the relationship between lengthening on the one hand, and the target for H tone movement on the other, are the tone patterns from the remote past medial. Here, all accounts would predict tone

---

20 As a reviewer points out, it would be interesting to compare the tone movement patterns in the recent past to those that we observed in the remote past and future tenses, in order to see if these patterns provide further evidence for our idea that the final H observed in these different tenses is in fact the same morpheme.

movement to the penultimate syllable, but we find movement to the antepenultimate only, as if there was a phrase boundary intervening between verb and object. However, an intervening phrase boundary would not be predicted by syntax nor is it backed up by the length data. It therefore remains a puzzle.

As we noted in the introduction, a major question that motivated our study was whether any of the phonological differences that we observed between verbs in phrase-medial and phrase-final position can be interpreted as grammatical markers of the CJ/DJ alternation. In Section 5.2, we put forward the hypothesis that the final H tone that regularly appears on phrase-medial verbs in the recent past tense, but occasionally also in the remote past and future tense, may be considered a tonal morpheme marking the CJ form in Zulu. Apart from this final H, most of the regular durational and tonal patterns we observed can presumably be explained with reference to independent principles that operate at the interface between phonology and syntax (as Kula this volume also finds for Bemba). However, the variation we noted regarding the tonal properties of the remote past medial are again difficult to explain on the basis of regular phonological processes, and could be a symptom of a rather different scenario. For example, one alternative hypothesis (which was suggested to us by an anonymous reviewer) could be that at an earlier stage, the CJ/DJ alternation in Zulu was marked more systematically in various tenses, but by different tonal strategies (something which still seems to be the case in present-day Tswana; see Creissels [this volume]). According to this hypothesis, our findings, and in particular the lack of a uniform pattern in the remote past, could then be the result of this tonal system undergoing a change in Zulu, perhaps towards a strategy that employs a melodic H tone (see footnote 16). However, as the reviewer points out, before this hypothesis can be substantiated, more empirical work would be required that includes an extension of our study to other tense forms in Zulu. Since our research so far has only focused on the properties of the future and the remote past tense, our hypotheses and conclusions regarding the phonological regularities underlying the CJ/DJ alternation in Zulu can only be tentative. However, we hope that future research can shed more light on some of the ideas we have discussed here and answer some of the remaining questions that have arisen from our study.

Abbreviations and symbols

Following standard practice, we mark Bantu noun class prefixes and corresponding agreement markers through numbers. High tone is marked by an acute accent on the syllable; low tone is unmarked.

1SG, 2SG   first, second person singular

AUG	augment	OM	object marker
CJ	conjoint verb form	PST	recent past tense
DJ	disjoint verb form	Q	question particle
FUT	future tense	RPST	remote past tense
FV	final vowel	SM	subject marker

Appendix

Full list of target sentences

(1) Izingane zihlabelela ingoma.   'The children sing a song.'
Present Tense CJ: Izingane zi-hlabelela ingoma.
Present Tense DJ: Izingane zi-ya-yi-hlabelela ingoma.
Future Tense CJ: Izingane zi-zo-hlabelela ingoma.
Future Tense DJ: Izingane zi-zo-yi-hlabelela ingoma.
Remote Past CJ: Izingane z-a-hlabelela ingoma.
Remote Past DJ: Izingane z-a-yi-hlabelela ingoma.

(2) Umfundi unamathiselisa iphepa odongeni. 'The student sticks paper to the wall.'
Present Tense CJ: Umfundi u-namathiselisa iphepa odongeni.
Present Tense DJ: Umfundi u-ya-li-namathiselisa iphepa odongeni.
Future Tense CJ: Umfundi u-zo-namathiselisa iphepa odongeni.
Future Tense DJ: Umfundi u-zo-li-namathiselisa iphepa odongeni.
Remote Past CJ: Umfundi w-a-namathiselisa iphepa odongeni.
Remote Past DJ: Umfundi w-a-li-namathiselisa iphepa odongeni.

(3) UJohn ulekelela abazali bakhe. 'John assists his parents.'
Present Tense CJ: UJohn u-lekelela abazali bakhe.
Present Tense DJ: UJohn u-ya-ba-lekelela abazali bakhe.
Future Tense CJ: UJohn u-zo-lekelela abazali bakhe.
Future Tense DJ: UJohn u-zo-ba-lekelela abazali bakhe.
Remote Past CJ: UJohn w-a-lekelela abazali bakhe.
Remote Past DJ: UJohn w-a-ba-lekelela abazali bakhe.

(4) Udokotela uphefumulisa isiguli. 'The doctor makes the patient breathe.'
Present Tense CJ: Udokotela u-phefumulisa isiguli.
Present Tense DJ: Udokotela u-ya-si-phefumulisa isiguli.
Future Tense CJ: Udokotela u-zo-phefumulisa isiguli.
Future Tense DJ: Udokotela u-zo-si-phefumulisa isiguli.
Remote Past CJ: Udokotela w-a-phefumulisa isiguli.
Remote Past DJ: Udokotela w-a-si-phefumulisa isiguli.

(5) Udokotela ufiphalisa isiguli. 'The doctor causes the patient to lose hope.'
Present Tense CJ: Udokotela u-fiphalisa isiguli.
Present Tense DJ: Udokotela u-ya-si-fiphalisa isiguli.
Future Tense CJ: Udokotela u-zo-fiphalisa isiguli.
Future Tense DJ: Udokotela u-zo-si-fiphalisa isiguli.
Remote Past CJ: Udokotela w-a-fiphalisa isiguli.
Remote Past DJ: Udokotela w-a-si-fiphalisa isiguli.

(6) Baminyanisa abantu. 'They make the people squash together.'
Present Tense CJ: Ba-minyanisa abantu.
Present Tense DJ: Ba-ya-ba-minyanisa abantu.
Future Tense CJ: Ba-zo-minyanisa abantu.
Future Tense DJ: Ba-zo-ba-minyanisa abantu.
Remote Past CJ: B-a-minyanisa abantu.
Remote Past DJ: B-a-ba-minyanisa abantu.

(7) Isiphepho sipaqulukisa isakhiwo. 'The storm causes the building to collapse.'
Present Tense CJ: Isiphepho si-paqulukisa isakhiwo.
Present Tense DJ: Isiphepho si-ya-si-paqulukisa isakhiwo.
Future Tense CJ: Isiphepho si-zo-paqulukisa isakhiwo.
Future Tense DJ: Isiphepho si-zo-si-paqulukisa isakhiwo.
Remote Past CJ: Isiphepho s-a-paqulukisa isakhiwo.
Remote Past DJ: Isiphepho s-a-si-paqulukisa isakhiwo.

References

Adams, Nikki. 2010. *The Zulu ditransitive verb phrase*. Chicago: The University of Chicago Ph.D. thesis.

Bates, Douglas, Martin Maechler, & Ben Bolker. 2011. lme4: Linear mixed-effects models using S4 classes. R package version 0.999375-42. http://CRAN.R-project.org/package=lme4.

Breen, Mara, Evelina Fedorenko, Michael Wagner & Edward Gibson. 2010. Acoustic correlates of information structure. *Language and Cognitive Processes* 25 (7/8/9). 1044–1098.

Buell, Leston. 2004. Zulu verb list with tones. http://www.fizzylogic.com/users/bulbul/school/ZuluVerbList.html (accessed 5 December 2014).

Buell, Leston. 2005. *Issues in Zulu verbal morphosyntax*. Los Angeles: University of California Ph.D. thesis.

Buell, Leston. 2006. The Zulu conjoint/disjoint verb alternation: Focus or constituency? In Laura Downing, Lutz Marten & Sabine Zerbian (eds.), *Papers in Bantu Grammar and Description* (ZAS Papers in Linguistics 43), Berlin: ZAS, 9–30.

Buell, Leston. 2008. VP-internal DPs and right-dislocation in Zulu. In Marjo van Koppen and Bert Botma (eds.), *Linguistics in the Netherlands* 25, 37–49 Amsterdam: John Benjamins.

Buell, Leston. 2009. The distribution of the Nguni augment: A review. Talk presented at the Bantu Augment Workshop, Leiden University, 17, June 2009. Available online: http://www.fizzylogic.com/users/bulbul/school/buell-nguni-augment.pdf (accessed 14 May 2014).

Cassimjee, Farida. 1998. *Isixhosa tonology: An Optimal Domains Theory analysis*. Munich: Lincom Europe.

Cassimjee, Farida & Charles Kisseberth. 2001. Zulu tonology and its relationship to other Nguni languages. In Shigeru Kaji (ed.), *Proceedings of the Symposium Cross-Linguistic Studies of Tonal Phenomena*, 327–359.

Cheng, Lisa & Laura J. Downing. 2007. The prosody and syntax of Zulu relative clauses. In Nancy Kula and Lutz Marten (eds.), *SOAS WPL: Bantu in Bloomsbury* 15, 51–63.

Cheng, Lisa & Laura J. Downing. 2009. Where's the topic in Zulu? *The Linguistic Review* 26. 207–238.

Creissels, Denis. This volume. The conjoint/disjoint distinction in the tonal morphology of Tswana.

Cunnings, Ian. 2012. An overview of mixed-effects statistical models for second language researchers. *Second Language Research* 28 (3). 369–382.

Doke, Clement M. 1931. *Textbook of Zulu grammar*. London: Longmans.

Doke, Clement M., D. M. Malcolm, J. M. S. Sikanana, B. W. Vilakazi. 1990. *English-Zulu/Zulu-English Dictionary*. Johannesburg: Witwatersrand University Press.

Donnelly, Simon. 2007. *Aspects of tone and voice in Phuthi*. Urbana-Champaign: University of Illinois Ph.D. thesis.

Downing, Laura J. 1990. Local and metrical tone shift in Nguni. *Studies in African Linguistics* 21 (3). 261–317.

Downing, Laura J. 2001a. How ambiguity of analysis motivates stem tone change in Durban Zulu. UBC Working Papers in Linguistics 4. 39–55.

Downing, Laura J. 2001b. Ungeneralizable Minimality in Ndebele. *Studies in African Linguistics* 30 (1). 33–58.

Downing, Laura J. & Bernd Pompino-Marschall. 2013. The focus prosody of Chichewa and the Stress-Focus constraint: A response to Samek-Lodovici (2005). *Natural Language and Linguistic Theory* 31. 647–681.

Halpert, Claire. 2012. Argument licensing and agreement in Zulu. Cambridge, MA: Massachusetts Institute of Technology Ph.D. thesis.

Herman, Rebecca. 1996. Prosodic structure in SiSwati. *OSU Working Papers in Linguistics* 48. 31–55.

Kanerva, Jonni M. 1990. *Focus and phrasing in Chichewa Phonology*. New York & London: Garland.

Khumalo, J. S. Mzilikazi. 1981. Zulu tonology, part 1. *African Studies* 40 (2). 53–140.

Khumalo, J. S. Mzilikazi. 1982. Zulu tonology, part 2. *African Studies* 41 (1). 3–125.

Khumalo, J. S. Mzilikazi. 1987. *An autosegmental account of Zulu phonology*. Johannesburg: University of the Witwatersrand Ph.D. thesis.

Kisseberth, Charles & David Odden. 2003. Tone. In Derek Nurse & Gérard Philippson (eds.). *The Bantu languages*, 59–70. London & New York: Routledge.

Kula, Nancy. This volume. The conjoint-disjoint alternation and phonological phrasing in Bemba.

Lanham, L. W. 1960. The comparative phonology of Nguni. Grahamstown: Rhodes University Ph.D. dissertation.

Leben, William. 2006. Rethinking autosegmental phonology. In John Mugane, John P. Hutchison & Dee A. Worman (eds.), *Selected Proceedings of the 35th Annual Conference on African Linguistics*, 1–9. Somerville, MA: Cascadilla Proceedings Project.

Myers, Scott. 1999. Tone association and F0 timing in Chichewa. *Studies in African Linguistics* 28 (2). 215–239.
Myers, Scott. 2003. F0 timing in Kinyarwanda. *Phonetica* 60. 71–97.
Nurse, Derek. 2007. The emergence of tense in early Bantu. In Doris L. Payne and Jaime Peña (eds.), *Selected Proceedings of the 37th Annual Conference on African Linguistics*, 164–179. Somerville, MA: Cascadilla Proceedings Project.
Nurse, Derek & Gérard Philippson. 2006. Common tense-aspect markers in Bantu. *Journal of African Languages and Linguistics* 27. 155–196.
Puhrsch, Daniela. 2005. Die Darstellung der Tonologie des Verbalkomplexes im Zulu bei C. M. Doke, A. T. Cope, J. S. M. Khumalo und G. Poulos. Leipzig: University of Leipzig unpublished Master's thesis.
R Development Core Team. 2010. R: A language and environment for statistical computing. Vienna: R Foundation for Statistical Computing.
Rycroft, David K. 1980. The depression feature in Nguni languages and its interaction with tone. *Communication* 8. Grahamstown: Department of African Languages, Rhodes University.
Rycroft, David K. 1981. *Concise SiSwati dictionary*. Pretoria: J.L. van Schaik.
Rycroft, David K. 1979. Tonal formulae for Nguni. *Limi* 7. 5–44.
Sibanda, Galen. 2004. Verbal phonology and morphology of Ndebele. Berkeley: University of California Ph.D. thesis.
Snedeker, Jesse & John Trueswell. 2003. Using prosody to avoid ambiguity: Effects of speaker awareness and referential context. *Journal of Memory and Language* 48. 103–130.
Taljaard, P.C. 1989. Study Unit 6. Introduction to the prosodic features of Zulu. In Department of African Studies, University of South Africa (ed.), *Zulu. Study guide 2 for ZUA100-4, ZUB 100-9*, 31–42. Pretoria: University of South Africa.
Traill, Anthony, J.S. Mzilikazi Khumalo & Peter Fridjhon. 1987. Depressing facts about Zulu. *African Studies* 46 (2). 255–274.
Turk, Alice, Satzuki Nakai & Mariko Sugahara. 2006. Acoustic segment durations in prosodic research: a practical guide. In Stefan Sudhoff, Denisa Lenertová, Roland Meyer, Sandra Pappert, Petra Augurzky, Ina Mleinek, Nicole Richter & Johannes Schließer (eds.), *Methods in Empirical Prosody Research*, 1–28. Berlin & New York: Walter de Gruyter.
Vaissière, Jacqueline. 1983. Language-independent prosodic features. In Anne Cutler & Robert D. Ladd (eds.), *Prosody: Models and measurements*, 53–66. Berlin: Springer.
Van der Spuy, Andrew. 1993. Dislocated noun phrases in Nguni. *Lingua* 90. 335–355.
Zeller, Jochen. 2012. Object marking in isiZulu. *Southern African Linguistics and Applied Language Studies* 30 (2). 219–235.
Ziervogel, Dirk, Jacobus Abraham Louw & Petrus C. Taljaard. 1985. *A handbook of the Zulu language*. Pretoria: J.L. van Schaik (1st edition 1967).

Claire Halpert
12 Prosody/syntax mismatches in the Zulu conjoint/disjoint alternation

1 Introduction

The conjoint/disjoint alternation in Zulu has received several thorough treatments in the linguistic literature (e.g. Van der Spuy 1993; Voeltz 2004; Buell 2005, 2006). In particular, work by Van der Spuy (1993) and Buell (2005, 2006) has clearly established that the alternation in Zulu is sensitive to the right edge of a particular syntactic domain, which I identify here as vP. At the same time, this work on the alternation in Zulu, along with work on the Zulu prosody-syntax interface (e.g. Cheng & Downing 2009, 2012) has shown a tight correspondence between the right edge of the syntactic vP and the right edge of prosodic phrases in the language, a pattern also observed by Van der Spuy (1993), Buell (2005, 2006), and Zeller, Zerbian, and Cook (this volume), who examine prosodic evidence for the conjoint/disjoint in tenses without an overt morphological alternation. Given this correlation, we can ask whether the Zulu conjoint/disjoint alternation is at its heart a marker of prosodic or syntactic constituency – or whether there is in fact any distinction between the two in Zulu. In this chapter, I present new evidence about the relationship between the conjoint/disjoint alternation and prosody in the language. I discuss two phenomena that display a mismatch between prosodic boundaries and the disjoint form: (1) verbal clitic constructions and (2) shared object constructions. In both cases, prosodic boundaries are placed according to surface constituency while the choice of conjoint or disjoint form depends on non-surface syntactic structure.

These new insights on the relationship between the conjoint/disjoint alternation and prosodic phrase markers in Zulu have implications not just for the conjoint/disjoint alternation itself, but also for our broader understanding of the prosody-syntax interface. First, we learn that, contra Buell (2005)'s analysis, the conjoint/disjoint alternation is not sensitive to whether elements are

---

This research was supported in part by NSF Grant #1122426 Doctoral Dissertation Research: Argument Licensing and Agreement. I am grateful to all of my Zulu consultants in Umlazi Township, at the University of KwaZulu-Natal Howard College (Durban), and in Boston for their judgments and assistance with the Zulu data. In particular, I would like to thank Percival Buthelezi, Mpho Dlamini, Monwabisi Mhlophe, and the Katamzi family.

phonologically overt; this observation has consequences in turn for our understanding of the syntax of constructions with dislocated arguments. In addition, we gain valuable information about the relative timing of prosodic phrasing in the derivation. The tight correlation between prosodic and syntactic boundaries in Zulu led to recent proposals that its prosody is calculated early and can in fact influence the syntactic derivation (e.g. Cheng and Downing 2012). This new evidence on the conjoint/disjoint alternation shows that prosodic markers of phrase edges seem to be calculated after this process.

In addition to the prosody/syntax relationship, this chapter also addresses another piece of the conjoint/disjoint puzzle that has emerged in earlier work on the alternation in Zulu. As in many other Bantu languages, the conjoint/disjoint alternation in Zulu appears to intersect with focus interpretations in a predictable way (e.g. Hyman and Watters 1984; Creissels 1996; Güldemann 2003, Ndayiragije 1999; Güldemann 2003; Voeltz 2004, van der Wal 2011, and many others on Zulu and other Bantu languages). I follow Van der Spuy (1993) and Buell (2005, 2006) in concluding that the conjoint/disjoint alternation itself does not directly encode focus meanings. We can, however, combine these insights on the conjoint/disjoint alternation with the observations of Cheng & Downing (2012) to more precisely capture the indirect relationship between the conjoint/disjoint alternation and focus that results from a prosody/syntax interaction.

The remainder of this chapter is organized as follows: in Section 2, I provide an overview of prosodic phrasing and the conjoint/disjoint alternation in Zulu (Van der Spuy 1993; Buell 2005, 2006; Cheng and Downing 2012). In Section 3, I turn to evidence for a mismatch between conjoint/disjoint patterns and prosodic phrasing in Zulu. Section 4 discusses the implications of these findings and the interaction of the conjoint/disjoint alternation with focus interpretation. Section 5 concludes.

2 The conjoint/disjoint alternation and *v*P edge

In certain non-negative environments, Zulu verbal predicates display a morphological alternation. While the data in this chapter focuses on the alternation in the present tense, we also find a conjoint/disjoint distinction in 'near past' (perfective) and relative clauses (see Zeller, Zerbian, and Cook, this volume, for discussion of the conjoint/disjoint alternation in other tense environments in Zulu). The present tense forms alternate between the null conjoint and the disjoint *-ya-*. In the near past, the conjoint form is a suffixal *-é* while the disjoint is *-ile*. Relativized verbs alternate between a null conjoint and a suffixal *-yo* in the disjoint form.

(1) **Conjoint/disjoint: present tense alternation**
   a. *uMlungisi   u-pheka   iqa:nda   vP]*
      AUG.1.Mlungisi 1SM-cook   AUG.5.egg
      'Mlungisi is cooking an egg.'

   b. *uMlungisi   u-**ya**-phe:ka   vP]*
      AUG.1.Mlungisi 1SM-DJ-cook
      'Mlungisi is cooking.'

(2) **Conjoint/disjoint: near past alternation**
   a. *uMlungisi   u-phek-**e**   iqa:nda   vP]*
      AUG.1.Mlungisi 1SM-cook-PFV.CJ AUG.5.egg
      'Mlungisi cooked an egg.'

   b. *uMlungisi   u-phek-**i:le**   vP]*
      AUG.1.Mlungisi 1SM-cook-PFV.DJ
      'Mlungisi cooked.'

(3) **Conjoint/disjoint: relative clause alternation**
   a. *ngi-bona   umfana   o-pheka   iqa:nda   vP]*
      1SG.SM-see   AUG.1.boy 1REL-cook AUG.5.egg
      'I see a boy who's cooking an egg.'

   b. *ngi-bona   umfana   o-pheka-**yo**   vP]*
      1SG.SM-see   AUG.1.boy 1REL-cook-DJ
      'I see a boy who's cooking.'

As the examples above show, the disjoint form consistently appears when the verb is sentence-final, while the conjoint form appears on sentence-medial verbs. Van der Spuy (1993) and Buell (2005, 2006) demonstrate that the alternation is not merely sensitive to whether the verb is sentence-final, but rather to the syntactic structure of the verb and any following elements. In particular, the choice of conjoint or disjoint in Zulu is sensitive to a particular syntactic constituent, which Van der Spuy (1993) identifies as IP and Buell (2006) as AgrSP; in this chapter, I show that we can capture the facts in terms of whether vP is 'empty' or not, as stated in (4):

(4) **Conjoint-disjoint generalization in Zulu:**
   Conjoint (Ø): appears when vP contains material (after movement)
   Disjoint (ya): appears when vP does not contain material (after movement)

Van der Spuy (1993) and Buell (2005, 2006) rely on both syntactic and prosodic diagnostics to show the syntactic basis for the conjoint/disjoint alternation in Zulu. While the examples above merely show a difference between sentence-final (disjoint) and sentence-medial (conjoint) verbs, sentence medial verbs are sensitive to the syntactic position of following elements. Evidence for this sensitivity is outlined in the following subsections.

2.1 Syntactic evidence

When thematic arguments are present, the choice of conjoint or disjoint form depends on the syntactic position of the arguments. Non-agreeing subjects in Zulu are always in *v*P-internal positions, while agreeing subjects are outside *v*P (e.g. Halpert 2012). Objects follow a similar pattern: those that co-occur with object-marking are outside *v*P, while those that do not are typically inside *v*P.[1]

Here we can see evidence for the generalization in (4): the conjoint/disjoint alternation reflects a difference between *v*P-internal and *v*P-external arguments. Given the correlation between agreement and syntactic position of arguments, we find conjoint forms whenever there are non-agreeing arguments after the verb, as in (5) and (6), where the verb has undergone head-movement to a position above the base position of the subject (e.g. Buell 2005; Cheng and Downing 2012; Halpert 2015):

(5) **Non-agreeing subject: conjoint required**
    a. *ku-pheka*   *uSipho* $_v$P]
       17SM-cook   AUG.1.Sipho
       'Sipho's cooking.'

    b. **ku-**ya**-pheka* $_v$P] *uSipho*
       17SM-DJ-cook   AUG.1.Sipho

(6) **Non-agreeing object: conjoint required**
    a. *uSipho*   *u-pheka*   *iqanda* $_v$P]
       AUG.1.Sipho 1SM-cook   AUG.5.egg
       'Sipho is cooking an egg.'

    b. **uSipho*   *u-**ya**-pheka* $_v$P] *iqanda*
       AUG.1.Sipho 1SM-DJ-cook   AUG.5.egg

When all of the arguments co-occur with a corresponding agreement morpheme on the verb, the disjoint form is *always* required:

---

[1] Though so-called double-dislocation constructions are an exception, as will be discussed below (Voeltz 2004; Adams 2010; Zeller 2015).

(7) **Intransitive agreeing subject: disjoint required**
    a. (*uSipho*)   *u-**ya**-pheka*   *v*P]
        AUG.1Sipho   1SM-DJ-cook
        'Sipho is cooking.'

    b. **uSipho*   *u-pheka*   *v*P]
        AUG.1.Sipho   1SM-cook

    c. *u-**ya**-pheka*   *v*P]   *uSipho*
        1SM-DJ-cook   AUG.u.Sipho
        'Sipho is cooking.'

    d. **u-pheka*   *v*P]   *uSipho*
        1SM-cook   AUG.1.Sipho

(8) **Monotransitive agreeing object: disjoint required**
    a. *uSipho*   *u-**ya**-li-pheka*   *v*P]   *iqanda*
        AUG.1.Sipho   1SM-DJ-5OM-cook   AUG.5.egg
        'Sipho is cooking the egg.'

    b. **uSipho*   *u-li-pheka*   *v*P]   *iqanda*
        AUG.1.Sipho   1SM-5OM-cook   AUG.5.egg

In double object constructions, only one object may agree with the verb. In these constructions, the other object typically remains in situ in *v*P, yielding a conjoint form.

(9) **Double object construction: conjoint required**
    a. *uSipho*   *u-phek-ela*   *uMfundo*   *iqanda*   *v*P]
        AUG.1.Sipho   1SM-cook-APPL   AUG.1.Mfundo   AUG.5.egg
        'Sipho is cooking Mfundo an egg.'

    b. ***uMfundo***   *uSipho*   *u-**m**-phek-ela*   *iqanda*   *v*P]
        AUG.1.Mfundo   AUG.1.Sipho   1SM-1OM-cook-APPL   AUG.5.egg
        '(As for) Mfundo, Sipho is cooking an egg for him.'

    c. **uMfundo*   *uSipho*   *u-**ya**-m-phek-ela*   *iqanda*
        AUG.1.Mfundo   AUG.1.Sipho   1SM-DJ-1OM-cook-APPL   AUG.5.egg

    d. ***iqanda***   *uSipho*   *u-**li**-phek-ela*   *uMfundo*   *v*P]
        AUG.5.egg   AUG.1.Sipho   1SM-5OM-cook-APPL   AUG.1.Mfundo
        'As for the egg, Sipho is cooking it for Mfundo.'

    e. **iqanda*   *uSipho*   *u-**ya**-li-phek-ela*   *uMfundo*
        AUG.5.egg   AUG.1.Sipho   1SM-DJ-5OM-cook-APPL   AUG.1.Mfundo

In addition to these cases, Voeltz (2004), Adams (2010), and Zeller (2015) show that Zulu also allows 'double dislocation' constructions, where the non-agreeing object in a ditransitive appears to the right of the agreeing object. As Zeller demonstrates, in these constructions, both objects behave like right-dislocated elements. In terms of the conjoint/disjoint alternation, these constructions behave as expected, yielding a disjoint form:

(10) uSipho u-**ya-m**-phek-ela] uMfundo iqanda
AUG.1.Sipho 1SM-DJ-1OM-cook-APPL] AUG.1.Mfundo AUG.5.egg
'Sipho (did) cook Mfundo an egg.'

In addition to the evidence from arguments and agreement, Van der Spuy (1993) notes that vocative phrases that immediately follow a verb require the disjoint form:

(11) **Sentence-medial vocative: must follow disjoint form**
a. uSipho u-**ya**-gijima **Mama** phandle
AUG.1.Sipho 1SM-DJ-run 1.mother outside
'Sipho is running, Mom, outside.'

b. *uSipho u-gijima **Mama** phandle
AUG.1.Sipho 1SM-run 1.mother outside

The vocative *cannot* appear between a conjoint form of the verb and the object:

(12) **Sentence-medial vocative with object**
a. uSipho u-(*ya-)dlala ibhola **Mama** (phandle)
AUG.1.Sipho 1SM-(*DJ-)play AUG.5.soccer 1.mother (outside)
'Sipho is playing soccer, Mom, outside.'

b. uSipho u-**ya**-li-dlala **Mama** ibhola
AUG.1.Sipho 1SM-DJ-5OM-play 1.mother 5soccer
'Sipho is playing, Mom, soccer.'

c. *uSipho u-(li-)dlala **Mama** ibhola
AUG.1.Sipho 1SM-(5OM-)play 1.mother 5.soccer

Buell (2005) shows similar behavior with yes/no question particles *na/yini*.[2] These question particles cannot directly follow a conjoint form of the verb; instead, they must appear either immediately after a disjoint verb or after other postverbal material:

---

[2] While Buell (2005) only addresses the use of *na*, the speakers of Durban Zulu with whom I have worked prefer *yini* 'what' over *na* to mark yes/no questions. To my knowledge, the distribution of *yini* in this use mirrors the distribution of *na* described by Buell (2005). My original examples of question particle distribution will use *yini*.

(13) **Question particle: cannot immediately follow conjoint verb**
    a. *uSipho   u-**ya**-gijima **yini** (phandle)?*
       AUG.1.   1SM-DJ-run Q   outside
       'Is Sipho running (outside)?'

    b. **uSipho*   *u-gijima **yini** (phandle)?*
       AUG.1.Sipho 1SM-run Q   (outside)

    c. *uSipho   u-pheka   iqanda   **yini?***
       AUG.1.Sipho 1SM-cookr AUG.5.egg Q
       'Is Sipho cooking an egg?'

    d. *uSipho   u-**ya**-li-pheka   **yini** iqanda?*
       AUG.1.Sipho 1SM-DJ-5OM-cook Q   AUG.5.egg
       'Is Sipho cooking the egg?'

    e. **uSipho*   *u-pheka **yini** iqanda?*
       AUG.1.Sipho 1SM-cook Q   AUG.5.egg

Van der Spuy (1993) and Buell (2005, 2006) conclude that these particles must attach outside of the domain of the conjoint/disjoint alternation. Given our starting generalization, the requirement that the verb be in the disjoint form when immediately followed by one of these elements is expected: in such cases, *v*P itself is empty.

2.2 Prosodic evidence

Van der Spuy (1993) and Buell (2005, 2006) also identify prosodic diagnostics for determining syntactic boundaries. First, the process of *prepausal (penultimate) lengthening* in Zulu lengthens the penultimate syllable of a word (and inserts a subsequent pause) at the right edge of a syntactic phrase boundary. Since penultimate lengthening applies at the right edge of certain syntactic phrases (e.g. Cheng and Downing 2012), Van der Spuy (1993) uses it to demonstrate that conjoint forms in Zulu have a different syntactic constituency from disjoint forms.

In a sentence where the verb appears in the conjoint, Van der Spuy (1993) shows that the verb itself cannot bear penultimate lengthening, suggesting that there is no right edge of any syntactic phrase intervening between the verb and following material:

(14) **Conjoint verb: no penultimate lengthening**
    a. *uSipho   u-gijima **pha:ndle**)*
       AUG.1.Sipho 1SM-run outside
       'Sipho is running outside.' (✓goal reading, *location reading)

b. *uSipho   u-**giji:ma**)   phandle
AUG.1.Sipho   1SM-run   outside

By contrast, the disjoint form of the verb must receive penultimate lengthening:

(15) **Disjoint verb: penultimate lengthening required.**
    a. uSipho   u-ya-**giji:ma**)   phandle
       AUG.1.Sipho   1SM-DJ-run   outside
       'Sipho is running outside.' (* goal reading, ✓location reading)

    b. *uSipho   u-ya-gijima   phandle
       AUG.1.Sipho   1SM-DJ-run   outside

Van der Spuy (1993) takes this pattern as additional evidence that the disjoint verb does not form a syntactic constituent with following material. Note that in (14) and (15), *v*P-internal placement of the locative signaled by the conjoint form corresponds with a goal reading, while *v*P-external place yields a location reading.

Buell (2005) highlights a second prosodic process, *high tone shift*, that also targets the right edge of syntactic phrases. This process emerges on underlyingly toneless verbs that combine with a high-toned prefix. In these cases, the high tone of the pre-stem morpheme shifts to the right, surfacing either on the penult or the antepenult of the verb. When the verb is phrase-final, the high tone shifts only to the antepenult. When the verb is phrase-medial, the high tone shifts all the way to the penult. Again, this shift correlates with the conjoint/disjoint alternation: conjoint forms allow the shift to the penult, while disjoint forms require the high tone to surface on the antepenult. In the following examples, the noun class 2 subject agreement morpheme *bá-* has an underlying high tone, in contrast to the first person singular *ngi-*. With the low-tone verb *gijima* 'run', the high tone of *bá-* shifts to the antepenult of a disjoint verb, but all the way to the penult of a conjoint verb:

(16) **Disjoint form: high tone on antepenult**
    a. /ngi-ya-gijima/ → ngì-yà-gìjì:mà
       1SG.SM-DJ-run
       'I run.'

    b. /**bá**-ya-gijima/ → bà-yà-**gíji**:ma
       2SM-DJ-run
       'They run.'
       (Buell 2005, ex. 117)

(17) **Conjoint form: high tone on penult**
/bá-gijima nge-jubane/ → bà-gìjímà ngejuba:ne
2SM-run with.AUG-5.speed
'They run fast.'
(Buell 2005, ex. 119)

Taken together, this tonal evidence indicates that Zulu has a systematic means of marking the right edge of certain prosodic constituents (see also Cheng and Downing 2009, for discussion of this fact). When these prosodic boundaries fall on the verb itself, the disjoint morpheme typically appears; the conjoint form is used when the verb is not at the edge of a prosodic constituent.

2.3 Information structure

Finally, as Güldemann (2003), Voeltz (2004), and others have noted, the conjoint/disjoint alternation also appears to interact with information structure. We can see this type of interaction particularly clearly in the behavior of non-arguments. As we saw in the previous subsection, when locatives and adjuncts attach inside vP, they trigger the conjoint form; when they have a higher attachment site, they trigger the disjoint form (in the absence of any vP-internal elements):

(18) **Conjoint/disjoint optionality with adverb**
    a. uSipho   u-gijima **kakhulu**
       AUG.1.Sipho   1SM-run a.lot
       'Sipho runs a lot.'

    b. uSipho   u-**ya**-gijima **kakhulu**
       AUG.1.Sipho   1SM-DJ-run a.lot
       'Sipho runs a lot.'

For this class of adverb, there is a tendency to prefer conjoint forms when the adverb is focused or new information, but disjoint forms when the adverb is old information:

(19) Q: uNokukhanya   u-bhukuda kakhulu yini?
        AUG.1.Nokukhanya 1SM-swim a.lot   Q
        'Does Nokukhanya swim a lot?'

    A1: u-(ya)-bhukuda kakhulu uma   e-seThekwini
        1SM-(DJ)-swim a.lot   when 1PRT-be.at.AUG5.Durban
        'She swims a lot when she's in Durban.'

A2: *u-ya-bhukuda kakhulu uma e-seThekwini, kodwa hhayi uma*
1SM-DJ-swim a.lot when 1PRT-be.at.AUG5.Durban but not when
e-seMelika
1PRT-be.at.AUG5.America
'She does swim a lot when she's in Durban, but not when she's in America.'

This contrast mirrors the interpretation of *v*P-internal vs. right-dislocated (agreed-with) objects in Zulu (cf. Cheng and Downing 2009).

In addition to these adverbs, a small class of VP-level adverbs tends to have a default low attachment site, requiring the conjoint form:[3]

(20) **Low adverb: conjoint required**
    a. *uSipho   u-gijima **kahle***
        AUG.1.Sipho 1SM-run well
        'Sipho runs well.'

    b. * *uSipho   u-**ya**-gijima **kahle***
        AUG.1.Sipho 1SM-DJ-run well

We can find these adverbs co-occuring with disjoint verb forms in an even more limited set of circumstances: as with the other adverbs that appear with the disjoint, these adverbs must be old information. Beyond that requirement, speakers also prefer the predicate itself to be focused, as shown below:

(21) **Old information low adverb: disjoint permitted**
    Q: *uMfundo   a-ka-bhukud-i   kahle, a-ngi-thi?*
        AUG.1.Mfundo NEG-1SM-swim-NEG well NEG-1SG.SM-say
        'Mfundo doesn't swim well, does he?'

    A: *cha, u-ya-bhukuda kahle, kodwa uMthuli   u-ya-m-hlula*
        no 1SM-DJ-swim well but AUG.1.Mthuli 1SM-DJ-1OM-surpass
        'No, he does swim well, but Mthuli is better.'

If we follow Cheng & Downing (2009)'s claim that right-dislocation is associated with old information, these adverb cases show the same pattern as the arguments:

---

[3] I treat this class of adverbs as a purely descriptive category, following observations by Van der Spuy (1993), Buell (2005, 2006) and others on their predictable syntactic behavior. The class seems to mainly include manner adverbs, which cross-linguistically tend to have low attachment sites (e.g. Cinque 1999, and many others) and, as Buell (2005) points out, they also tend to have meanings that resist topicalization. For this discussion, I will set aside the question of how this distribution should be encoded in the grammar and simply treat it as another test for diagnosing-conjoint/disjoint behavior.

*v*P-internal elements trigger the conjoint, while the absence of any such element triggers the disjoint.

The behavior of locative elements also points to this conclusion. Goals in Zulu typically require a conjoint form (and typically co-occur with an applicative marker as well):

(22) **Goal reading: conjoint required**
    a. *uMfundo*   *u-gijim-ela*   ***esitolo***
       AUG.1.Mfundo   1SM-run-APPL   LOC.AUG.7.store
       'Mfundo is running to the store.'

    b. *uMfundo   *u-**ya**-gijim-ela*   ***esitolo***
       AUG.1.Mfundo   1SM-DJ-run-APPL   LOC.AUG.7.store

Locations, by contrast, can co-occur with either the conjoint or the disjoint form of the verb – and show the same context-sensitivity to old information and focus as the adverbs above:

(23) **Location reading: conjoint**
    Q: *uMfundo*   *w-enza=ni?*
       AUG.1.Mfundo   1SM-do=what?
       'What is Mfundo doing?'

    A: *uMfundo*   *u-gijima*   *esitolo*
       AUG.1.Mfundo   1SM-run   LOC AUG.7.store
       'Mfundo is running in the store.'

(24) **Location reading: disjoint**
    Q: *uMfundo*   *u-gijima*   *esitolo*   *yini?*
       AUG.1.Mfundo   1SM-run   LOC. AUG.7.store   Q
       'Is Mfundo running in the store?'

    A: *Yebo, u-ya-gijima esitolo!*
       yes   1SM-DJ-run   LOC.AUG.7.store
       'Yes, he is running in the store!'

To summarize what we've seen in this section, the conjoint/disjoint alternation distinguishes between different types of post-verbal elements: those inside *v*P trigger a conjoint form. When there is no *v*P-internal element present, either due to an absence of arguments/adjuncts or due to dislocation of any such elements, the disjoint form appears. This same syntactic boundary correlates with a prosodic one, resulting in disjoint verb forms that are marked as a prosodic phrase edge and conjoint verb forms that are not.

3 Against a prosodic account

The evidence in the previous section shows a strong correlation between the conjoint/disjoint alternation and prosodic markers of the *v*P edge. The disjoint form appears when a verb is at the right edge of a prosodic phrase, while the conjoint appears when the verb is medial in the prosodic phrase. In their work on prosodic boundaries in Zulu Cheng and Downing (2009) establish that prosodic phrase boundaries in Zulu occur at the right edges of *v*Ps and CPs. They connect this correlation between prosodic and syntactic phrases in Zulu to the cross-linguistic tendency for alignment of prosodic phrases with syntactic phases (Kahnemuyipour 2004; An 2007; Ishihara 2007; Kratzer and Selkirk 2007, a.o.).

Given this tight link between prosodic and syntactic boundaries, we must ask whether the conjoint/disjoint alternation is truly a syntactic process, or simply another marker of the prosodic phrase. This question becomes particularly relevant when we consider that in some respects, the conjoint/disjoint alternation appears to be a rather surface-oriented process. Buell (2005, 2006) notes this property in his analysis, encoding the alternation as a requirement on overt phonological content appearing within the relevant syntactic domain. In investigating this question, we might predict that if the disjoint form is merely another expression of the prosodic boundary associated with the right edge of *v*P, it should consistently pattern with prosodic processes. So far, the perfect match between prosodic and syntactic boundaries gives no way to rule out a prosodic/phonological account for the alternation. In this section, I present novel data that shows that we must distinguish the conjoint/disjoint alternation from purely prosodic processes. Two processes in particular allow us to separate the conjoint/disjoint alternation from the prosodic boundaries discussed above: the behavior of clitics and the behavior of shared objects in coordination.

3.1 Prosody mismatches

I'll turn first to the behavior of clitics with respect to the conjoint/disjoint alternation to show that different types of verbal enclitics in Zulu show identical behavior with respect to prosodic boundaries, yet differ in whether they trigger a conjoint or disjoint form when the verb is final in its clause.

Wh-enclitics form a single prosodic word with the verb. Prosodic phrase markers of the type we saw above typically fall on the final prosodic word in the prosodic phrase in Zulu (e.g. Buell 2005, Cheng and Downing 2012). If the disjoint morpheme were merely another marker of prosodic phrase-finality, we would expect it to appear in constructions where the verb and its *wh*-clitic are not followed by other material, since the verb is clearly phrase-final by other prosodic measures.

Buell (2005) shows that the *conjoint* is required in these cases:

(25) **wh-clitics: final prosody, conjoint verb**
    a. *ba-dlala:=phi?*
       2SM-play=where
       'Where are they playing?'

    b. * *ba-ya-dlala=phi?*
       2SM-DJ-play-where

    c. *u-fundisa:=ni?*
       2SG.SM-teach=what
       'What do you teach?'

    d. * *u-ya-fundisa=ni?*
       2SG.SM-DJ-teach=what
       Buell (2005, adapted from ex. 255)

The data in (25) show that the disjoint does not always appear on the verb when it is the final *prosodic* word in the phrase, as Buell notes. He concludes from this evidence that *wh*-clitics function as a separate lexical word/XP inside *v*P, which counts as independent material for the purpose of the conjoint/disjoint alternation.

Looking beyond *wh*-clitics, we find more striking evidence against a simple prosodic account. We can observe the relevant contrast if we compare the behavior of the *wh*- clitics to the behavior of another clitic, *=ke* 'so, then'.

Verbal clitics such as *=ke* also form a prosodic word with the verb, acting as a single unit for prosodic boundary placement. Unlike the *wh*-clitics, *=ke* requires a *disjoint* form of the verb – and not the conjoint:

(26) **non-*wh* clitics: final prosody, disjoint required**
    a. *bà-yà-gìjímà:=kè*
       2SM-DJ-run=KE
       'So they're running.'

    b. * *ba-gijima=ke*
       2SM-run=KE

These differences between *wh*-clitics and *=ke* show that the disjoint form is *not* always used when the verb is the final prosodic (or lexical) word. By contrast, prosodic boundaries such as penultimate lengthening or high tone shift *do* seem to simply mark the final prosodic word in the relevant domain. These prosodic markers are insensitive to the appearance and type of clitic that forms prosodic words with the verb.

A syntactic account can potentially distinguish between these two types of clitics. As Buell notes, *wh*-clitics plausibly originate inside *v*P, where he claims they can satisfy the conditions for the conjoint form. By contrast, since the =*ke* clitic does not require a conjoint form, we might wonder whether it originates in a *v*P-external position. Since =*ke* has a discourse-level function, apparently modifying the entire utterance, it is reasonable to assume that it has a higher syntactic attachment site. At the same time, however, it is clearly a verbal clitic – and, unlike the vocatives and question particles we saw earlier, its presence does not demarcate a syntactic boundary: in certain circumstances, it can attach to the verb even when followed by *v*P-internal material. In (27) below, the conjoint form of the near past is used when =*ke* attaches to a verb that is followed by a non-dislocated CP, while the parallel construction is ungrammatical with a question particle:

(27) a. *Si-bong-e=**ke**   ukuthi   abantu   ba-zi-phath-e   kahle*
      2PL.SM-thank-PFV=KE that   AUG.2.people 2SM-REFL-care-PFV   well
      'We are grateful that people took good care of themselves.'[4]

   b. * *u-bong-e*   ***yini*** *ukuthi*   *abantu*   *ba-zi-phath-e*   *kahle?*
      1SM-thank-PFV   Q   that   AUG.2.people 2SM-REFL-care-PFV   well
      intended: 'Was he thankful that people took good care of themselves?'

   c. *u-bong-**ile***   ***yini*** *ukuthi*   *abantu*   *ba-zi-phath-e*   *kahle?*
      1SM-thank-PFV   Q   that   AUG.2.people 2SM-REFL-care-PFV   well
      'Was he thankful that people took good care of themselves?'

Similarly, in (28), =*ke* may appear on the verb followed by a non-agreeing, non-dislocated object, while the question particle *yini* requires that the following object agree with the verb:[5]

(28) a. *a-ngi-thand-i=**ke***   *imifi:no*
      NEG-1SG.SM-like-NEG=KE   AUG.4.vegetables
      'Ok, so I don't like vegetables!'

   b. * *a-wu-thand-i*   ***yini***   *imifino?*
      NEG-2SG.SM-like-NEG   Q   AUG.4.vegetables
      intended: 'Don't you like vegetables?'

---

[4] http://mapholoba.blogspot.com, accessed April 10, 2012
[5] In these constructions, we cannot observe a contrast between conjoint and disjoint morphology because this contrast disappears in the presence of negation. Instead, the only cues for object placement come from object agreement and relative position.

c. *a-wu-yi-tha:nd-i*   *yini imifino?*
NEG-2SG.SM-4OM-like-NEG   Q   AUG.4.vegetables
'Don't you like vegetables?'

If =*ke* originates outside *v*P, then its cliticization to the verb is a fairly late process, following the calculation of the conjoint/disjoint distinction. At the same time, the cliticization feeds prosodic phrasing, giving us a clear way to distinguish between prosodic marking and the conjoint/disjoint alternation.[6]

We also find a mismatch between prosodic boundaries and the disjoint form in certain coordination constructions. The first member of a pair of coordinated verb phrases in Zulu has a prosodic boundary at its right edge:

(29) **Coordination: first member has prosodic boundary at right edge**

a. *ngi-ya-cu:la*   ) *futhi ngi-ya-da:nsa*   )
   1SG.SM-DJ-sing   and   1SG.SM-DJ-dance
   'I sing and I dance.'

b. * *ngi-cula   futhi   ngi-ya-dansa*
     1SG.SM-sing and   1SG.SM-DJ-dance

(30) *bà-yà-gíjì:mà*) *fùthì   bà-dlálà   íbhô:là*)
     2SM-DJ-run   and   2SM-play   AUG.5.ball
     'They run and they play soccer.'

The first verb in the coordination constructions in (29) and (30) behaves as though it were final in a prosodic constituent. It receives penultimate lengthening, consistent with the right edge of a prosodic boundary. In (30), high tone shift stops on the antepenult, as expected for a prosodic phrase-final verb. The verb also appears with disjoint morphology, as expected if it occupies a *v*P-final position.

The prosodic boundary in these constructions truly matches the edge of *v*P in the first conjunct: with a transitive verb in the first conjunct, the prosodic boundary goes on the *object*, which is the final prosodic word in the phrase. As expected, the conjoint form of the verb is required here:

(31) a. *ba-dlala   ibho:la*   ) *futhi ba-ya-gijima*
        2SM-play   AUG.5.ball   and   2SM-DJ-run
        'They play soccer and they run.'

---

[6] Another possible interpretation of the facts in (27) and (28) is that -*ke* can originate in *v*P-internal positions – but that it is invisible to the conjoint/disjoint alternation. As discussed in Halpert (2012), such an outcome would also be amenable to a syntactic analysis, but not a prosodic one.

b. * *ba-ya-dlala*   *ibhola*   *futhi*   *ba-ya-gijima*
    2SM-DJ-play   AUG.5.soccer   and   2SM-DJ-run

To summarize, the first conjunct in Zulu VP coordination has a prosodic boundary at its right edge. The final prosodic word in the conjunct receives a prosodic phrase boundary; the verb requires the conjoint form if it is not final in the first conjunct, but disjoint form if it is.

Zulu also allows coordinated verb phrases with a shared object realized inside the second conjunct.[7] In these constructions, the verb in the first conjunct still receives a prosodic phrase boundary, but appears in the *conjoint* form, despite being the final prosodic word in the phrase:

(32)   **Shared object: prosodic boundary in first conjunct, conjoint required**
       ngi-buk-e:la   )   *futhi*   (*ngi-phinde*)   *ngi-dlale*   *ibho:la*   )
       1SG.SM-watch-APPL)   and   1SG.SM-again   1SG.SM-play.SJC   AUG.5.soccer
       'I watch and I (also) play soccer.'

In (32), an applicative morpheme on the verb in the first conjunct requires an object. The shared object *ibhola* 'soccer' appears in the second conjunct, where it aligns with the prosodic phrase boundary. In the first conjunct, the verb still behaves as though it is at the edge of a prosodic phrase, receiving penultimate lengthening, but it must appear in the *conjoint* form, which otherwise corresponds to a verb followed by *v*P-internal material.

These two pieces of evidence – clitic behavior and coordination – both illustrate a mismatch between prosodic boundaries and the conjoint/disjoint. Given this split, it is not enough to simply say that the disjoint marker (and the conjoint/disjoint alternation more generally) is another indicator of prosodic constituency. In the next section, I discuss what implications this evidence has for our understanding of the alternation.

4 The conjoint/disjoint alternation and syntax

In section 2, we saw evidence that the conjoint/disjoint alternation in Zulu is sensitive to syntactic constituency and that the relevant syntactic domain also closely corresponded to the right edge of a prosodic boundary, which Cheng and Downing (2009, 2012) argue to be the right edge of *v*P. In the previous section, however, we saw that there is a difference in the distribution of

---

[7] Not all speakers of Durban Zulu with whom I worked accept these constructions. Those that do seem to prefer an auxiliary like *phinde* in the second conjunct to focus the second predicate.

prosodic boundaries and the conjoint/disjoint alternation, which means that the relationship between the conjoint/disjoint alternation and syntactic structure is not merely the same relationship that mediates syntax and prosodic phrasing.

Though Buell (2005, 2006) explicitly argues against a prosodic account of the conjoint/disjoint alternation, his analysis is ultimately phonological in nature: he proposes that the conjoint/disjoint alternation reflects *syntactic* structure – but depends on overt phonological content, as mentioned in the previous section. He proposes an EPP-like constraint that requires the constituent in which the verbal macrostem originates to contain "heavy (phrasal) overt material." The conjoint form appears when an argument or an adjunct remains in this domain, which allows the verb to raise to a higher head (Buell calls the phrase to which it raises *ya*P). If *v*P is devoid of arguments or adjuncts, the macrostem remains low to provide overt material in the relevant domain, causing the higher head to spell out as *ya*.

The new evidence presented in this chapter suggests that an account based on overt phonological content is untenable. First, the variable behavior of clitics suggests that there is no uniform way we can treat such elements. On Buell's analysis, the *wh*-clitic must count as independent heavy phonological content but also be part of the phonological word formed by the verb. By contrast, =*ke* does not count as independent phonological content, even though it is possible for =*ke* to surface on the verb and be followed by *v*P-internal material.

The coordination data in (32) is perhaps more problematic for such an approach. Recall that the conjoint form is used in the first conjunct of the two coordinated verb phrases, even though the shared object is overtly realized only in the second conjunct. We can therefore conclude that the conjoint/disjoint alternation cannot be tied to the phonological realization of a construction.

In short, this chapter presents a more nuanced understanding of what types of elements "count" for the conjoint/disjoint alternation. While clitics form a prosodic word with the verb, they "count" in their position of origin: the *v*P-internal *wh*-clitics yield a conjoint form while the discourse-level -*ke* counts as a *v*P-external element. Shared objects also "count" in their base (*v*P-internal) position, even if they are not pronounced in that position. The conjoint/disjoint alternation does not actually seem to care whether a particular element is overtly pronounced in the relevant domain, while the prosody, by contrast, does.

The fact that the conjoint/disjoint alternation in Zulu is sensitive to certain phonologically null elements gives us a way to investigate other aspects of *v*P syntax. In particular, while we saw earlier in this chapter that nearly all non-agreeing arguments are *v*P-internal in Zulu, the *v*P- external status of agreed-with arguments in Zulu (and Bantu more generally) is more controversial: are these elements *v*P-external by virtue of movement out of their base position (e.g. Carstens 2001, Buell 2005, Henderson 2006, Diercks 2010, on the status of agreeing subjects) or because they "double" a *v*P-internal null (*pro*) element in argument position (e.g. Givón 1976; Bresnan & Mchombo 1987; Van der Spuy 2001; Schneider-Zioga 2007; Zeller 2008)? If null elements like the elided object in the coordination constructions are visible to the conjoint/disjoint alternation, then it would perhaps be surprising if null elements like *pro* were not. We might expect these elements to pattern differently than traces of A-movement, though, which have been argued to be invisible for subsequent syntactic processes (e.g. Chomsky 1995, 2000, 2008).[8] If these conclusions are on the right track, the behavior of the conjoint/disjoint alternation may provide evidence for a movement account of agreeing arguments in Zulu, followed by the syntactic calculation of the conjoint/disjoint alternation, followed by calculation of prosodic boundaries.

Beyond the syntactic and prosodic elements, the final piece of the conjoint/disjoint puzzle in Zulu is the role of information structure. As we saw in Section 2.3, certain adjuncts can appear either with the conjoint or the disjoint form; the conjoint form tends to go with a new information reading on the adjunct, while the disjoint form requires the adjunct be old information and typically also correlates with focus on the predicate itself. Buell (2006) argues that this correlation is a side effect of the syntactic structure, a conclusion that this chapter supports. In particular, right-extraposition has both information structure consequences (the right-extraposed element is old/background, while elements inside *v*P can be focused) and consequences for the conjoint/disjoint alternation (if *v*P ends up empty, the disjoint will appear). In their work on double-object constructions and focus in Zulu Cheng and Downing (2012) argue that right-extraposition can be driven by the prosody itself: the need to align focused elements with prosodic boundaries (which predictably correspond to *v*P and CP edges) can force other elements to appear in *v*P-external positions. In this chapter, we've seen evidence that prosodic boundaries must be inserted fairly late, since they seem to follow syntactic processes involved in the conjoint/disjoint alternation, and therefore cannot be directly triggering information structure-related movement.

---

8 A reviewer points out that on a copy theory of movement, it's not clear that we would expect a distinction between unpronounced *pro* and unpronounced lower copies of A-moved elements within the narrow syntax. This issue of "trace invisibility" – why lower copies of A-movement do not behave as interveners in the syntax – is a general one in the syntactic literature (see e.g. Rezáč 2004; Ott 2015, for discussion and attempts to develop copy theory compliant instantiations of the principle).

5 Conclusion

In this chapter, I have built on existing work on on the Zulu conjoint/disjoint alternation to present new arguments for treating the phenomenon as a syntactic one and to shed light on the interaction between this morphosyntactic process and the placement of prosodic boundaries. While in most cases, the presence of a disjoint morpheme on the verb coincides with a prosodic boundary on the verb, I highlighted a few cases where these two processes do not line up. I argued instead that the conjoint/disjoint alternation is purely determined by whether there is material inside *v*P during the syntax: when *v*P contains a postverbal element, the conjoint verb form appears; when *v*P is empty, the disjoint appears. The cases of prosody/syntax mismatch result from the appearance of material inside *v*P that is not overtly pronounced. This type of evidence allows us to separate the two processes and to establish a relative ordering between syntactic operations and the insertion of prosodic boundaries in Zulu. It also gives us a new way to examine the question of how constructions with agreeing arguments are derived, suggesting that a movement analysis may be more in line with the behavior of the conjoint/disjoint alternation.

Abbreviations and symbols

In relevant examples, high tones are marked by acute accent; low tones by grave accent. Tones are otherwise not marked in example sentences. Square brackets] are used to mark syntactic boundaries, while parentheses) mark prosodic boundaries. Cardinal numbers (1, 2, 3. . .) are used to mark noun class; numbers followed by SG or PL mark local persons (1SG is first person singular).

AUG	augment vowel		PFV	perfective
APPL	applicative		PL	plural
CJ	conjoint		PRT	participial
DJ	disjoint		Q	question particle
KE	discourse clitic *ke*		REFL	reflexive
LOC	locative		REL	relative clause marker
NEG	negative		SG	singular
OM	object marker		SM	subject marker

References

Adams, Nikki. 2010. *The Zulu ditransitive verb phrase*. Chicago: University of Chicago dissertation.
An, Duk-Ho. 2007. Clauses in noncanonical positions at the syntax-phonology interface. *Syntax* 10 (1). 38–79.
Bresnan, Joan & Sam Mchombo. 1987. Topic, pronoun, and agreement in Chichewa. *Language* 63. 741–782.
Buell, Leston. 2005. *Issues in Zulu morphosyntax*. Los Angeles, CA: UCLA dissertation.
Buell, Leston. 2006. The Zulu conjoint/disjoint verb alternation: Focus or constituency? *ZAS Papers in Linguistics* 43. 9–30.
Carstens, Vicki. 2001. Multiple agreement and case deletion: Against *phi*-(in)completeness. *Syntax* 4 (3). 147–163.
Cheng, Lisa & Laura J. Downing. 2012. Against focusP: Arguments from Zulu. In Ivona Kucerova & Ad Neeleman (eds.), *Contrasts and positions in information structure*, 247–266. Cambridge: Cambridge University Press.
Cheng, Lisa Lai-Shen & Laura J. Downing. 2009. Where's the topic in Zulu? *The Linguistic Review* 26. 207–238.
Chomsky, Noam. 1995. *The minimalist program*. Cambridge, MA: MIT Press.
Chomsky, Noam. 2000. Minimalist inquiries: The framework. In Roger Martin, David Michaels & Juan Uriagereka (eds.), *Step by step: Essays on minimalist syntax in honor of Howard Lasnik*, 89–156. Cambridge, MA: MIT Press.
Chomsky, Noam. 2008. On phases. In Robert Freidin, Carlos Otero & Maria Luisa Zubizarreta (eds.), *Foundational issues in linguistic theory*, 133–166. Cambridge, MA: MIT Press.
Cinque, Guglielmo. 1999. *Adverbs and functional heads: A cross-linguistic perspective*. New York: Oxford University Press.
Creissels, Denis. 1996. Conjunctive and disjunctive verb forms in Tswana. *South African Journal of African Languages* 16. 109–115.
Diercks, Michael. 2010. *Agreement with subjects in Lubukusu*. Georgetown: University of George-town dissertation.
Givón, Talmy. 1976. Topic, pronoun and grammatical agreement. In Charles Li (ed.), *Subject and topic*, 149–188. New York: Academic Press.
Güldemann, Tom. 2003. Present progressive vis-à-bis predication focus in Bantu: A verbal category between semantics and pragmatics. *Studies in Language* 27 (2). 323–360.
Halpert, Claire. 2012. *Argument licensing and agreement in Zulu*: MIT dissertation.
Halpert, Claire. 2015. *Argument licensing and agreement*. New York: Oxford University Press.
Henderson, Brent. 2006. Multiple agreement and inversion in Bantu. *Syntax* 9 (3). 275–289.
Henderson, Brent. 2006. Multiple agreement and inversion in Bantu. *Syntax* 9 (3). 275–289.
Hyman, Larry M. & John Robert Watters. 1984. Auxiliary focus. *Studies in African Linguistics* 15. 233–273.
Ishihara, Shinichiro. 2007. Major phrase, focus intonation, multiple spell-out. *The Linguistic Review* 24. 137–167.
Kahnemuyipour, Arsalan. 2004. *The syntax of sentential stress*. Toronto: University of Toronto dissertation.

Kratzer, Angelika & Elisabeth Selkirk. 2007. Phase theory and prosodic spellout: The case of verbs. *The Linguistic Review* 24. 93–135.
Ndayiragije, Juvénal. 1999. Checking economy. *Linguistic Inquiry* 30 (3). 399–444.
Ott, Dennis. 2015. Symmetric Merge and local instability: Evidence from split topics. *Syntax* 18 (2). 157–200.
Rezáč, Milan. 2004. *Elements of cyclic syntax: Agree and Merge*. Toronto: University of Toronto dissertation.
Schneider-Zioga, Patricia. 2007. Anti-agreement, anti-locality and minimality. *Natural Language and Linguistic Theory* 25 (2). 403–446.
Van der Spuy, Andrew. 1993. Dislocated noun phrases in Nguni. *Lingua* 90 (4). 335–355.
Van der Spuy, Andrew. 2001. *Grammatical structure and Zulu morphology*. Johannesburg, South Africa: University of the Witwatersrand dissertation.
Voeltz, F.K. Erhard. 2004. Long and short verb forms in Zulu. Ms., University of Cologne.
van der Wal, Jenneke. 2011. Focus excluding alternatives: Conjoint/disjoint marking in Makhuwa. *Lingua* 212(11). 1734–1750.
Zeller, Jochen. 2008. The subject marker in Bantu as an antifocus marker. *Stellenbosch Papers in Linguistics* 38. 221–254.
Zeller, Jochen. 2015. Argument prominence and agreement: Explaining an unexpected object asymmetry in Zulu. *Lingua* 156. 17–39.
Zeller, Jochen, Sabine Zerbian & Toni Cook (this volume). Prosodic evidence for syntactic phrasing in Zulu. In Larry Hyman & Jenneke van der Wal (eds.), *The conjoint/disjoint alternation in Bantu* Trends in Linguistics, Mouton de Gruyter.

Jean Paul Ngoboka and Jochen Zeller
13 The conjoint/disjoint alternation in Kinyarwanda

1 Introduction

This chapter provides a comprehensive discussion of the conjoint/disjoint (CJ/DJ) alternation in Kinyarwanda (D61), the mother tongue of one of the authors of this chapter (JPN). In Section 2, we show in which tenses the alternation is realised through segmental morphology and which tonal processes are associated with the alternation. Section 3 examines the syntactic environments in which the CJ and the DJ forms of verbs are licensed in Kinyarwanda. We will contrast two prominent approaches that have been proposed to explain their distribution in various Bantu languages: the idea that the alternation is determined by information-structural properties of the clause, and the alternative view, according to which the alternation is a reflex of syntactic constituency. In Section 4, we briefly discuss the fact that the morpheme -*ra*-, which marks the DJ form of verbs in various tenses, also seems to have a variety of other grammatical functions. Section 5 presents our conclusion.

2 Grammatical marking of the conjoint/disjoint alternation

In this section, we demonstrate how the CJ/DJ alternation is grammatically marked in Kinyarwanda, by providing examples from all tenses in which the alternation is expressed through segmental morphology, grammatical tone, or both. In addition, we present data on certain tone shift phenomena in Kinyarwanda, which are not directly related to the CJ/DJ alternation, but which are necessary to understand why surface tone realisation may occasionally obscure the effects of the tonal patterns that are associated with the CJ/DJ alternation. Throughout this section, we illustrate the CJ form in Kinyarwanda with examples in which the verb is followed by overt material; in the examples showing the DJ form, the

---

We would like to thank the reviewers and the editors of this volume for helpful comments and suggestions. All errors remain our responsibility.

verb is clause-final (see Section 3 for a more detailed discussion of the syntactic environments that license the CJ and the DJ forms).[1]

2.1 Segmental marking and H tone deletion

2.1.1 Simple present and present perfective

In the simple present[2] and present perfective, the DJ form is marked segmentally by the morpheme -*ra*- in Kinyarwanda (see (2) and (4)). There is no segmental marking of the CJ verb form (see (1) and (3)). However, in the CJ form, the verb always has a low (L) tone, which means that lexical high (H) tones of verbs are deleted in the CJ form, (3). In the DJ form, L tone verbs remain low, (2); lexical H tones are retained, (4) (Sibomana 1974; Coupez 1980; Overdulve and Jacob 1998; Kimenyi 2002):

Toneless verb:

(1) a. *Abáana   basoma   ibitabo.*   [simple present CJ]
       a-ba-áana   ba-som-a   i-bi-tabo
       AUG-2-child 2SM-read-FV AUG-8-book
       'Children read books.'

   b. *Abáana   basomye   ibitabo.*   [present perfective CJ]
       a-ba-áana   ba-som-ye   i-bi-tabo
       AUG-2-child 2SM-read-PFV AUG-8-book
       'Children have just read books.'

(2) a. *Abáana   barasoma.*   [simple present DJ]
       a-ba-áana   ba-*ra*-som-a
       AUG-2-child 2SM-DJ-read-FV
       'Children read.'

   b. *Abáana   barasomye.*   [present perfective DJ]
       a-ba-áana   ba-*ra*-som-ye
       AUG-2-child 2SM-DJ-read-PFV
       'Children have just read.'

---

[1] We present each Kinyarwanda example by four lines. Line 1 represents vowel lengthening, surface tone, and phonologically conditioned sound changes. Line 2 presents the underlying morphemes and lexical tone; the interlinear glosses are in line 3; and line 4 provides a translation.

[2] The so-called narrative past in Kinyarwanda is morphologically identical to the simple present, but refers to past events. Since the CJ/DJ alternation is marked in the same way as in the simple present, we do not discuss the narrative past separately in this paper.

H-toned verb (H deleted in CJ form):

(3) a. *Abáarimú   bakora   akazi   keénshi.*   [simple present CJ]
    a-ba-áarimú   ba-kór-a   a-ka-zi   ka-iínshi
    AUG-2-teacher   2SM-work-FV   AUG-12-work   12-many
    'Teachers do a lot of work.'

  b. *Abáarimú   bakoze   akazi   keénshi.*   [present perfective CJ]
    a-ba-áarimú   ba-kór-ye   a-ka-zi   ka-iínshi
    AUG-2-teacher   2SM-work-PFV   AUG-12-work   12-many
    'Teachers have just done a lot of work.'

(4) a. *Abáarimú   barakóra.*   [simple present DJ]
    a-ba-áarimú   ba-*ra*-kór-a
    AUG-2-teacher   2SM-DJ-work-FV
    'Teachers work.'

  b. *Abáarimú   barakóze.*   [present perfective DJ]
    a-ba-áarimú   ba-*ra*-kór-ye
    AUG-2-teacher   2SM-DJ-work-PFV
    'Teachers have just worked.'

Although lexical H tones are retained in the DJ form, they may not always be realised on the verb radical. When an object marker is prefixed to the stem in Kinyarwanda, a lexical H tone of the verb shifts to the left and is realised on the object marker (see Goldsmith and Mpiranya 2010 for detailed discussion of leftward H tone shift in Kinyarwanda):

(5) a. *Abáarimú   baragákora.*   [simple present DJ]
    a-ba-áarimú   ba-ra-ka-kór-a
    AUG-2-teacher   2SM-DJ-12OM-work-FV
    'Teachers work (on) it.'

  b. *Abáarimú   baragákoze.*   [present perfective DJ]
    a-ba-áarimú   ba-ra-ka-kór-ye
    AUG-2-teacher   2SM-DJ-12OM-work-PFV
    'Teachers have just worked (on) it.'

That the source of the H tone in (5) is indeed the verb radical is demonstrated by comparing (5) with similar examples with a toneless verb, in which no H tone appears on the object marker:

(6) a. *Abáarimú barakareka.* [simple present DJ]
    a-ba-áarimú ba-ra-ka-rek-a
    AUG-2-teacher 2SM-DJ-12OM-leave-FV
    'Teachers leave it.'

   b. *Abáarimú barakaretse.* [present perfective DJ]
      a-ba-áarimu ba-ra-ka-rek-ye
      AUG-2-teacher 2SM-DJ-12OM-leave-PFV
      'Teachers have just left it.'

Lexical H tones are hence retained in the DJ form, although they may be realised on a different syllable as a result of leftward H tone shift.

2.1.2 Near past

The near past tense shows the same tone patterns with CJ and DJ forms as the simple present and the present perfective: The H tone of lexically H-toned verbs is deleted in the CJ verb form, but retained in the DJ form (Sibomana 1974; Kimenyi 2002). The difference between the near past and the tense/aspect forms discussed in Section 2.1.1 is that the DJ form is segmentally marked with the morpheme *-a-* in the near past (in the following, we provide examples of the near past both in the perfective aspect, marked with the suffix *-ye*, and the imperfective aspect, marked with the suffix *-aga*):

Toneless verb:

(7) a. *Umwáana yasomye ibitabo.* [near past CJ (perf.)]
    u-mu-áana a-a-som-ye i-bi-tabo
    AUG-1-child 1SM-PST-read-PFV AUG-8-book
    'The child read books.'

   b. *Umwáana yasomaga ibitabo.* [near past CJ (impf.)]
      u-mu-áana a-a-som-aga i-bi-tabo
      AUG-1-child 1SM-PST-read-IPFV AUG-8-book
      'The child was reading books.'

(8) a. *Umwáana yaasomye.* [near past DJ (perf.)]
    u-mu-áana a-a-a-som-ye
    AUG-1-child 1SM-PST-DJ-read-PFV
    'The child read/has read.'

b. *Umwáana   yaasomaga.*   [near past DJ (impf.)]
   u-mu-áana   a-a-a-som-aga
   AUG-1-child 1SM-PST-DJ-read-IPFV
   'The child was reading.'

H-toned verb (H deleted in CJ form):

(9) a. *Umwáarimú   yakoze   akazi   keénshi.*   [near past CJ (perf.)]
       u-mu-áarimú   a-a-kór-ye   a-ka-zi   ka-iínshi
       AUG-1-teacher 1SM-PST-work-PFV AUG-12-work 12-many
       'The teacher did a lot work.'

    b. *Umwáarimú   yakoraga   akazi   keénshi.*   [near past CJ (impf.)]
       u-mu-áarimú   a-a-kór-aga   a-ka-zi   ka-iínshi
       AUG-1-teacher 1SM-PST-work-IPFV AUG-12-work 12-many
       'The teacher was doing a lot of work.'

(10) a. *Umwáarimú   yaakóze.*   [near past DJ (perf.)]
        u-mu-áarimú   a-a-a-kór-ye
        AUG-1-teacher 1SM-PST-DJ-work-PFV
        'The teacher worked.'

     b. *Umwáarimú   yaakóraga.*   [near past DJ (impf.)]
        u-mu-áarimú   a-a-a-kór-aga
        AUG-1-teacher 1SM-PST-DJ-work-IPFV
        'The teacher was working.'

2.2 Segmental marking, H tone deletion and H tone addition: the remote past

As in the tense forms discussed in Section 2.1, the CJ form of the remote past tense (perfective and imperfective) is also marked through the deletion of lexical H tones (see (12)):

Toneless verb:

(11) a. *Abáana   baákinnye   umupiíra.*   [remote past (perf.) CJ]
        a-ba-áana   ba-á-kin-ye   u-mu-piíra
        AUG-2-child   2SM-REM-play-PFV AUG-3-ball
        'Children played (with) the ball.'

     b. *Abáana   baákinaga   umupiíra.*   [remote past (impf.) CJ]
        a-ba-áana   ba-á-kin-aga   u-mu-piíra
        AUG-2-child   2SM-REM-play-IPFV AUG-3-ball
        'Children were playing (with) the ball.'

H-toned verb (H deleted in CJ form):

(12) a. *Abakózi baámutemeye ibití.* [remote past (perf.) CJ]
a-ba-kózi ba-á-mu-tém-ir-ye i-bi-tí
AUG-2-worker 2SM-REM-1OM-cut-APPL-PFV AUG-8-tree
'Workers cut trees for him.'

b. *Abakózi baámutemeraga ibití.* [remote past (imperf.) CJ]
a-ba-kózi ba-á-mu-tém-ir-aga i-bi-tí
AUG-2-worker 2SM-REM-1OM-cut-APPL-IPFV AUG-8-tree
'Workers were cutting trees for him.'

As illustrated by (13) and (14), the DJ form of the remote past tense is marked segmentally with the morpheme -*ra*-. However, in contrast to the simple present and the present perfective, the DJ form of the remote past also has special tonal properties: While the lexical H tone of the verb is retained, a H tone is *added* to lexically toneless verbs in the DJ form of the remote past tense (see (13)) (Bizimana 1998; Overdulve and Jacob 1998; Goldsmith and Mpiranya 2010):

Toneless verb (H added in the DJ form):

(13) a. *Baáragúze.* [remote past (perf.) DJ]
ba-á-ra-gur-ye
2SM-REM-DJ-buy-PFV
'They bought.'

b. *Baáragúraga.* [remote past (impf.) DJ]
ba-á-ra-gur-aga
2SM-REM-DJ-buy-IPFV
'They were buying.'

H-toned verb:

(14) a. *Baáratémye.* [remote past (perf.) DJ]
ba-á-ra-tém-ye
2SM-REM-DJ-cut-PFV
'They cut.'

b. *Baáratémaga.* [remote past (impf.) DJ]
ba-á-ra-tém-aga
2SM-REM-DJ-cut-IPFV
'They were cutting.'

Examples (13) and (14) show that in the remote past, the tonal distinction between H-toned and toneless verbs is neutralised in both the CJ and the DJ form. However, the addition of a H tone to the first syllable of the verb stem is not only attested in the DJ form of the remote past, but also in other grammatical contexts (viz. in the participial remote past and in headless present relatives; Kimenyi 2002: 200ff.); it is also found with certain TAM markers in other Bantu languages of the same region (Larry Hyman p.c.). We therefore follow Jouannet (1985) and Kimenyi (2002) and analyse the H tone in examples such as (13) as a floating H tone that is associated with certain TAM forms, but that is not specific to the CJ/DJ alternation.

The examples in (11)–(14) illustrate the tonal pattern of the CJ and the DJ form in the remote past with verbs that are prefixed with biphonic subject markers, which have a CV shape. When the subject marker is monophonic (a glide or a nasal), the remote tense marker -á- merges with the subject marker, and as a result, the H tone of the tense morpheme shifts to the verb radical, obscuring the effects of H tone deletion with H-toned verbs in the CJ form (Sibomana 1974; Overdulve and Jacob 1998). This H tone shift can be observed in (15):

H-toned verb (H deleted in the CJ form, but H of tense marker shifts to radical):

(15) a. *Yakóze*   *akazi.*   [remote past (perf.) CJ]
   a-á-kór-ye   a-ka-zi
   1SM-REM-work-PFV   AUG-12-work
   'He did some work.'

b. *Yakóraga*   *akazi.*   [remote past (impf.) CJ]
   a-á-kór-aga   a-ka-zi
   1SM-REM-work-IPFV   AUG-12-work
   'He was doing some work.'

Because of the H tone shift demonstrated by (15), a lexically toneless verb also carries a H tone in the CJ form when the subject marker is monophonic (Sibomana 1974):

Toneless verb (H of tense marker shifts to radical):

(16) a. *Nasómye*   *igitabo.*   [remote past (perf.) CJ]
   n-á-som-ye   i-ki-tabo
   1SG.SM-REM-read-PFV   AUG-7-book
   'I read a book.'

b. *Nasómaga*   *igitabo.*   [remote past (impf.) CJ]
   n-á-som-aga   i-ki-tabo
   1SG.SM-REM-read-IPFV   AUG-7-book
   'I was reading a book.'

When an object marker intervenes between the remote past tense marker and the verb stem, the H tone of the tense morpheme shifts to the object marker. As a result, the verb radical remains low with H-toned and toneless verbs:

H-toned verb (H deleted in the CJ form, H of tense marker shifts to object marker):

(17) Nagúkoreye   akazi.   [remote past (perf.) CJ]
      n-á-ku-kór-ir-ye   a-ka-zi
      1SG.SM-REM-2SG.OM-work-APPL-PFV   AUG-12-work
      'I did the work for you.'

Toneless verb (H of tense marker has shifted to object marker):

(18) Nakúreebeye   amafoto.   [remote past (perf. CJ)]
      n-á-ku-reeb-ir-ye   a-ma-foto
      1SG.SM-REM-2SG.OM-look-APPL-PFV   AUG-6-picture
      'I looked at the pictures for you.'

In the same way, monophonic subject markers affect the realisation of tones in the DJ form of the remote past. It was shown above that a H tone is added to toneless verbs in the DJ form in this tense. However, when the subject marker is monophonic, the H tone of the remote past tense marker shifts to the next syllable, which in the remote past is the DJ-marker *-ra-*. In this case, the H tone associated with verbs in the DJ form of the remote past is deleted as a result of Meeussen's rule (see also Philippson 1998 for Kirundi; Kimenyi 2002):

H-toned verb (H of tense marker has shifted to *-ra-*; lexical H on radical is deleted):

(19) a. Yarákoze.   [remote past (perf.) DJ]
          a-á-ra-kór-ye
          1SM-REM-DJ-work-PFV
          'He worked.'

      b. Yarákoraga.   [remote past (impf.) DJ]
          a-á-ra-kór-aga
          1SM-REM-DJ-work-IPFV
          'He was working.'

Toneless verb (H of tense marker has shifted to -*ra*-; H is added in DJ form, but is deleted):

(20) a. *Yaráguze.* [remote past (perf.) DJ]
a-á-ra-gur-ye
1SM-REM-DJ-buy-PFV
'He bought.'

b. *Yaráguraga.* [remote past (impf.) DJ]
a-á-ra-gur-aga
1SM-REM-DJ-buy-IPFV
'He was buying.'

The H tone of the DJ form resurfaces when an object marker intervenes between -*ra*- and the verb stem, because in this case, the H of the DJ-marker and the H of the verb radical are no longer adjacent:

H-toned verb (H of tense marker has shifted to -*ra*-; lexical H of verb is retained):

(21) a. *Yarágakóze.* [remote past (perf) DJ]
a-á-ra-ka-kór-ye
1SM-REM-DJ-12OM-work-PFV
'He worked (on) it.'

b. *Yarágakóraga.* [remote past (impf.) DJ]
a-á-ra-ka-kór-aga
1SM-REM-DJ-12OM-work-IPFV
'He was working (on) it.'

Toneless verb (H of tense marker has shifted to -*ra*-, H added to radical in DJ form):

(22) a. *Yarábigúze.* [remote past (perf.) DJ]
a-á-ra-bi-gur-ye
1SM-REM-DJ-8OM-buy-PFV
'He bought them.'

b. *Yarábigúraga.* [remote past (impf.) DJ]
a-á-ra-bi-gur-aga
1SM-REM-DJ-8OM-buy-IPFV
'He was buying them.'

In sum, the data show that the CJ/DJ alternation in the remote past is formally marked as in the simple present: H tones are deleted in the CJ form; the morpheme -*ra*- is added in the DJ form. In addition, a grammatical H tone is added to the radical of toneless verbs, but as we noted above, we do not consider this H tone as a special marker of the DJ form.

2.3 No segmental marking, but H tone deletion: the subsecutive and conditional/hypothetical

In the subsecutive and conditional/hypothetical mood, there is no segmental marker of the DJ form. However, the CJ form is marked via H tone deletion, as in the tense forms discussed in Sections 2.1 and 2.2:

H-toned verb (H deleted in CJ form):

(23) a. *Araaza   akabaza   ikibázo.*   [subsec. mood CJ]
        a-ra-z-a   a-ka-báz-a   i-ki-bázo
        1SM-DJ-come-FV   1SM-SUBS-ask-FV AUG-7-question
        'He comes and asks a question.'

   b. *Ubíshaatse   waahiinga   isaámbu*
      u-bi-shaak-ye   u-aa-híing-a   i-saámbu
      2SG.SM-8OM-want-PFV   2SG.SM-COND-dig-FV AUG-9.farm
      yaawe.   [con./hypo.mood CJ]
      yaawe
      your
      'If you wanted it, you would dig your farm.'

(24) a. *Araaza   akabáza.*   [subsec. mood DJ]
        a-ra-z-a   a-ka-báz-a
        1SM-DJ-come-FV   1SM-SUBS-ask-FV
        'He comes and asks.'

   b. *Ubíshaatse   waahíinga.*   [con./hypo. mood DJ]
      u-bi-shaak-ye   u-aa-híing-a
      2SG.SM-8OM-want-PFV   2SG.SM-COND-dig-FV
      'If you wanted it, you would dig.'

Toneless verb (no grammatical difference between CJ and DJ form):

(25) a. *Araaza   akiicara   haasí.*   [subsec. mood CJ]
        a-ra-z-a   a-ka-iicar-a   haasí
        1SM-DJ-come-FV   1SM-SUBS-sit-FV   on.the.floor
        'He comes and sits on the floor.'

b. *Ubíshaatse   wareeba   uyu   mukino.*   [con./hypo.mood CJ]
   u-bi-shaak-ye   u-aa-reeb-a   uyu   mu-kino
   2SG.SM-8OM-want-PFV 2SG.SM-COND-look-FV 3.DEM 3-game
   'If you wanted it, you would watch this game.'

(26) a. *Araza   akiicara.*   [subsec. mood DJ]
        a-ra-z-a   a-ka-iicar-a
        1SM-DJ-come-FV   1SM-SUBS-sit-FV
        'He comes and sits down.'

   b. *Ubíshaatse   wareeba.*   [con./hypo. mood DJ]
      u-bi-shaak-ye   u-aa-reeb-a
      2SG.SM-8OM-want-PFV 2SG.SM-COND-look-FV
      'If you wanted it, you would watch.'

These examples demonstrate that in the subsecutive and conditional/hypothetical, CJ and DJ forms are only distinguished with verbs which are lexically H. With toneless verbs, the alternation is not grammatically marked.

2.4 No grammatical marking of the alternation: all other tenses

The remaining tenses or moods in Kinyarwanda do not show the CJ/DJ alternation (but see Note 3 below for a possible exception). For example, in the remote future, the morphophonological shape of all verbs in phrase-medial position is identical to the form of phrase-final verbs (the realisation of the present progressive and the near future will be discussed in Section 4):

Toneless verb:

(27) *Abáana   bazaakina   umupiíra.*   [remote future CJ]
      a-ba-áana   ba-zaa-kin-a   u-mu-piíra
      AUG-2-child   2SM-RFUT-play-FV   AUG-1-ball
      'The children will play (with) a ball.'

(28) *Abáana   bazaakina.*   [remote future DJ]
      a-ba-áana   ba-zaa-kin-a
      AUG-2-child   2SM-RFUT-play-FV
      'The children will play.'

H-toned verb:

(29) *Abáana   bazaakora   ikizaami.*   [remote future CJ]
    a-ba-áana ba-zaa-kór-a   i-ki-zaami
    AUG-2-child 1SM-RFUT-work-FV AUG-7-exam
    'The children will work (on) the exam.'

(30) *Abáana   bazaakora.*   [remote future DJ]
    a-ba-áana ba-zaa-kór-a
    AUG-2-child 1SM-RFUT-work-FV
    'The children will work.'

Notice that the remote future is marked segmentally by the tense morpheme -*zaa*-, and phonologically through deletion of lexical H tones in the affirmative indicative (H tones are retained in the negative) (Sibomana 1974; Overdulve and Jacob 1998; Kimenyi 2002).[3] The fact that the lexical H tone is deleted in both (29) and (30) shows that this process is not related to the CJ/DJ alternation.[4]

Table 1 summarises the results for the tenses discussed in Sections 2.1–2.4 (note that this summary applies only to the affirmative system; as we show below, the CJ/DJ alternation is not marked in the negative):

---

[3] As noted by a reviewer, Overdulve (1988: 37) lists examples of what he calls the "conjonctif futur", which appears in subordinate clauses and which, like the remote future, is formed with the morpheme -*zaa*-. Interestingly, it seems that in this tense, lexical H tones are retained when the verb is not followed by overt material (cf. *nzáakora cyaane*, 'I will work hard' vs. *nzáakóra*, 'I will work'). This contrast suggests that the "conjonctif futur", in contrast to the remote future, also shows the CJ/DJ alternation, by marking the CJ form through H tone deletion.

[4] This conclusion may be challenged by an alternative interpretation of the data. It could be argued that H tone deletion in the remote future tense and H tone deletion in the CJ form of the tenses discussed in the preceding sections are in fact the same process. From this perspective, (29) and (30) could be interpreted as showing that the remote future affirmative indicative obligatorily appears in the CJ form, regardless of whether or not the verb is followed by a complement. However, since neither of the two proposals about the function of the CJ/DJ alternation in Kinyarwanda that we discuss in Section 3 would explain this situation, we do not consider this possibility here and assume that the deletion of the H tone in the remote future is unrelated to the CJ/DJ alternation. Note that a similar issue arises with respect to the element -*ra*- in Kinyarwanda, which marks the DJ form in some tenses, but which can also express other grammatical functions, such as the progressive and the persistive. Again, this raises the question if, or to what extent, the grammatical role of -*ra*- in the progressive and the persistive is related to the grammatical function of -*ra*- in the CJ/DJ alternation. We return to this question in Section 4.

Table 1: Marking of the CJ/DJ alternation in Kinyarwanda.

Tense/mood	Segmental marking (DJ)	Tonal marking (CJ)
Simple present/narrative past	-ra-	H tone deletion
Present perfective	-ra-	H tone deletion
Near past	-a-	H tone deletion
Remote past	-ra-	H tone deletion
Subsecutive mood	none	H tone deletion
Conditional/hypothetical	none	H tone deletion
Other tenses/moods	none	none

3 The syntax and semantics of the conjoint/disjoint alternation

The CJ form in Kinyarwanda requires that the verb is followed by overt material in a main clause. If nothing follows the verb, the DJ form is obligatory:

(31) a. *Abagoré baáteetse inyama.* [remote past CJ]
 a-ba-goré ba-á-téek-ye i-nyama
 AUG-2-woman 2SM-REM-cook-PFV AUG-10.meat
 'Women cooked meat'

 b. **Abagoré baáteetse.* [remote past CJ]
 a-ba-goré ba-á-téek-ye
 AUG-2-woman 2SM-REM-cook-PFV

 c. *Abagoré baáratéetse.* [remote past DJ]
 a-ba-goré ba-á-ra-téek-ye
 AUG-2-woman 2SM-REM-DJ-cook-PFV
 'Women cooked.'

As is well-known, the CJ/DJ alternation in Bantu languages is often described in terms of information-structural packaging (see for example, Nshemezimana & Bostoen this volume, Ndayiragije 1999 for Kirundi; Creissels 1996, this volume for Tswana; Givón 1975 for Bemba, Kinyarwanda and Zulu; Güldemann 2003; Voeltz 2004 for Zulu; Hyman and Watters 1984 for Kirundi, Bemba and Aghem; Van der Wal 2009, 2011 for Makhuwa). For Kinyarwanda, a focus-analysis has been proposed by Givón (1975). Givón analyses the DJ-marker -*ra*- in Kinyarwanda as a "VP-focus particle" whose presence signals that the verb is focused, or included within the scope of focus (see also Kimenyi 1980; Botne 1983; Goldsmith and Mpiranya 2010). In contrast, the CJ form must be used when a complement of the verb is focused. The data in (31) are consistent with this approach: a possible reading of (31a) is with focus on the object; when the verbal predicate is in focus, as in (31c), the DJ form must be chosen.

However, the data in (31) are also compatible with an alternative account, which treats the CJ/DJ alternation as a reflex of constituency. For example, Van der Spuy (1993), Buell (2006) and Halpert (2015) argue that in the Bantu language Zulu, the CJ form must be used when the verb is followed by XP-internal material (with XP = vP or AgrSP/IP), while the DJ form is required in all other contexts. This type of analysis seems to underlie the description of the CJ/DJ alternation in Coupez (1980), who notes that in Kinyarwanda, "le disjoint s'emploie en fin de syntagme verbal et le conjoint [...] si le verbe est suivi d'au moins un mot appartenant à son syntagme" (p. 393) ["the disjoint is used at the end of the verb phrase and the conjoint when the verb is followed by at least one word in its phrase"; our translation, JPN & JZ].[5] Clearly, the distribution of the CJ and DJ forms in (31) also follows from this type of analysis.

In this section, we discuss in detail the syntactic contexts which license the CJ/DJ alternation in Kinyarwanda. In our discussion, we investigate to what extent the data follow from an analysis of the CJ/DJ alternation in terms of information structure, and whether data which are problematic for this view can be explained by the alternative analysis, according to which the alternation is determined by the constituent structure of the sentence.

3.1 Contexts in which the CJ/DJ alternation does not occur

In our discussion of the CJ/DJ alternation in Kinyarwanda in Section 2, we have provided examples from affirmative main clauses. However, as the following examples illustrate, verbs in relatives, negatives, and in most subordinate clauses in Kinyarwanda do not show the tonal or segmental distinctions that characterise the CJ/DJ alternation (Kimenyi 2002):[6]

---

[5] Kimenyi (2002) seems to be more ambivalent regarding the functional role of the CJ/DJ alternation. Although he occasionally refers to the element -ra- as a "focus marker" (e.g. Kimenyi 2002: 179), he also characterises the DJ-marker as a "morpheme which shows that the verb is complementless" (Kimenyi 2002: 173).
[6] Negated, relative and subordinate clauses in the simple present in Kinyarwanda are marked with a grammatical H tone which may appear on different syllables of the verb stem (see Kimenyi 2002).

Relative clauses: toneless verb

(32) a. *umwáana   usóma   ibitabo*
        u-mu-áana   u-som-a   -bi-tabo
        AUG-1-child 1SM.REL-read-FV AUG-2-book
        'a child who reads books'

   b. *umwáana   usóma*
        u-mu-áana   u-som-a
        AUG-1-child 1SM.REL-read-FV
        'a child who reads'

Relative clauses: H-toned verb

(33) a. *umwáana   ubáza   ibibázo*
        u-mu-áana   u-báz-a   i-bi-bázo
        AUG-1-child 1SM.REL-ask-FV AUG-8-question
        'a child who asks questions'

   b. *umwáana   ubáza*
        u-mu-áana   u-báz-a
        AUG-1-child 1SM.REL-ask-FV
        'a child who asks '

Negative clauses: toneless verb

(34) a. *Abaána   ntibakiná   amakaríta.*
        a-ba-áana   nti-ba-kin-a   a-ma-karíta
        AUG-2-child NEG-2SM-play-FV AUG-6-card
        'Children do not play cards.'

   b. *Abaána   ntibakiná.*
        a-ba-áana   nti-ba-kin-a
        AUG-2-child NEG-2SM-play-FV
        'Children do not play.'

Negative clauses: H-toned verb

(35) a. *Umwáana   ntaakorá   akazi.*
        u-mu-áana   nti-a-kór-a   a-ka-zi
        AUG-1-child NEG-1SM-work-FV AUG-12-work
        'A child does not do work.'

b. *Umwáana   ntaakorá.*
    u-mu-áana nti-a-kór-a
    AUG-1-child NEG-1SM-work-FV
    'A child does not work.'

Embedded clauses introduced by complementiser *kó*: toneless verb

(36) a. *Avuze   kó   asomá   ibitabo.*
         a-vúg-ye   kó   a-som-a i-bi-tabo
         1.SM-say-PFV that 1SM-read-FV AUG-8-book
         'He says that he reads books.'

   b. *Avuze   kó   asomá.*
       a-vúg-ye   kó   a-som-a
       1.SM-say-PFV that 1SM-read-FV
       'He says that he reads.'

Embedded clauses introduced by complementiser *kó*: H-toned verb

(37) a. *Avuze   kó   abazá   ibibázo.*
         a-vúg-ye   kó   a-báz-a i-bi-bázo
         1SM-say-PFV that 1SM-ask-FV AUG-8-question
         'He says he asks questions.'

   b. *Avuze   kó   abazá.*
       a-vúg-ye   kó   a-báz-a
       1SM-say-PFV that 1SM-ask-FV
       'He says he asks.'

The examples illustrate that the DJ-marker *-ra-*, which appears in the simple present in main clauses, does not appear in embedded, relative or negated clauses. There is also no tonal distinction between CJ and DJ forms in these morphosyntactic contexts.

In the literature, the fact that the CJ/DJ alternation in Kinyarwanda and other Bantu languages is not attested in the above contexts is generally explained on the basis of the assumption that the alternation is determined by information structure, and in particular that the DJ form expresses verb/VP or "auxiliary focus" (a notion introduced by Hyman and Watters 1984; see Section 3.2 below).[7]

---

[7] The analysis of the CJ/DJ alternation based on information structure can be stated in two different ways. As noted in the text, the DJ form could be interpreted as a marker of verb/auxiliary focus, but alternatively, it could instead be claimed that the CJ form marks focus on a post-verbal element (see Buell 2006 for a discussion of both views in relation to the CJ/DJ alternation in Zulu). Since the first interpretation seems to be the common analysis for Kinyarwanda and related Kirundi, we are mainly concerned with this alternative here, but see Van der Wal (2011) for an analysis of the CJ form in Makhuwa as a marker of post-verbal term focus.

For example, based on this view, Givón (1975) accounts for the absence of the CJ/DJ alternation from negatives by postulating that a negative statement presupposes its affirmative counterpart. The negation itself is therefore the focus of a negative statement, which means that the negated verb is outside the scope of the focus. Consequently, the DJ form is not licensed in negatives.

The absence of the alternation from subordinate clauses is taken to follow from the fact that only main clauses typically present foregrounded information and create what Hyman and Watters (1984: 254) call the "assertive environment" necessary for focus marking (focus being the asserted information presented against a presupposed background). In contrast, relatives and other types of embedded clauses usually present presupposed information and are non-, or only weakly, assertive (Hyman and Watters 1984; Güldemann 2003). Therefore, a grammatical marker for verb/VP or auxiliary focus is not expected to occur in these environments.[8]

The CJ/DJ alternation is not banned from all complementiser-introduced clauses in Kinyarwanda. In sentences following the quotative complementiser *ngo*, CJ and DJ verb forms are distinguished:

Clauses introduced by complementiser *ngo*: toneless verb

(38) a. *Aravúze   ngo   asoma   ibitabo.*
         a-ra-vúg-ye   ngo   a-som-a   i-bi-tabo
         1SM-DJ-say-PFV that   1SM-read-FV   AUG-8-book
         'He says that he reads books.'

   b. *Aravúze   ngo   arasoma.*
         a-ra-vúg-ye   ngo   a-ra-som-a
         1SM-DJ-say-PFV that   1SM-DJ-read-FV
         'He says that he reads.'

Clauses introduced by complementiser *ngo*: H-toned verb

(39) a. *Aravúze   ngo   abaza   ibibázo.*
         a-ra-vúg-ye   ngo   a-báz-a   i-bi-bázo
         1SM-DJ-say-PFV that   1SM-ask -FV   AUG-8-question
         'He says that he asks questions.'

---

8 According to the explanations described here, the CJ/DJ alternation is not attested in negatives, relatives, and certain subordinated clauses because the unmarked focus conditions of these constructions are pragmatically in conflict with the focus marking expressed by the DJ form. According to Hyman and Watters (1984), if a particular focus form is systematically excluded from certain environments, focus is "grammatically controlled" in these contexts, and no longer determined by the discourse. However, as Hyman and Watters (1984: 244, fn. 5) note, "the relationship between pragmatic and grammatical determinants of focus marking is a non-arbitrary one: what *tends* to be semantically in focus comes to be grammatically focused".

b. *Aravúze ngo arabáza.*
a-ra-vúg-ye ngo a-ra-báz-a
1SM-DJ-say-PFV that 1SM-DJ-ask-FV
'He says that he asks.'

It seems that, in contrast to the embedded clauses introduced by *kó*, *ngo*-clauses create the assertive environment necessary for the CJ/DJ alternation to be licensed.[9] We speculate that this is because a speaker does not commit him/herself to the truth of the proposition expressed by the *ngo*-clause, and directly reports somebody else's statement. Whereas *kó* is a genuine subordinating complementiser, *ngo* rather behaves like a clause-initial sentence-type particle that introduces root clauses. (We return to *ngo*-clauses in Section 3.4 below.)

An interesting contrast is illustrated by the following examples:[10]

(40) a. *Twaaboonye kó yasannyé inzu.*
Tu-a-bón-ye kó a-a-sán-ye i-n-zu
1PL.SM-PST-see-PFV that 1SM-PST-repair-PFV AUG-9-house
'We realized that he repaired a house.'

b. *Twaaboonye kó yasannyé.*
Tu-a-bón-ye kó a-a-sán-ye
1PL.SM-PST-see-PFV that 1SM-PST-repair-PFV
'We realized that he repaired.'

(41) a. *Twaaboonye yásannye inzu.*
Tu-a-bón-ye a-a-sán-ye i-n-zu
1PL.SM-PST-see-PFV 1SM-PST-repair-PFV AUG-9-house
'We realized he repaired a house.'

b. *Twaaboonye yáasánnye.*
Tu-a-bón-ye a-a-a-sán-ye
1PL.SM-PST-see-PFV 1SM-PST-DJ-repair-PFV
'We realized he repaired.'

In (40), the verb *bón-*, 'see', selects an embedded clause introduced by the complementiser *kó*, and as in (36) and (37), the CJ/DJ alternation is not realised in the

---

9 Note that the verb *vúg-*, 'say', in (38) and (39) appears in the DJ form, whereas the complement clauses in (36) and (37) trigger the CJ form. This suggests that the *ngo*-clauses in (38) and (39) may not be subordinated. We return to this point in Section 3.4. The same applies to direct quotes introduced by the complementiser *-ti*, which can also follow verbs in the DJ form in Kinyarwanda (see Coupez 1980).
10 We are indebted to an anonymous reviewer for making us aware of these data.

embedded clause (the segmental marker -*a*- does not appear in (40b)). However, the verb *bón*- in (40) and (41) (in contrast to the verb *vúg*-, 'say' in (36) and (37)) allows for the complementiser of a following clause to be dropped. Curiously, without the complementiser, the clause following *bón*- shows the CJ/DJ alternation. It is not clear to us at present why the omission of the complementiser produces the appropriate environment for the CJ/DJ alternation. We therefore have to leave the analysis of the contrast between (40) and (41) as a topic for further investigation.

3.2 The CJ/DJ alternation and information structure

As noted above, the CJ form in Kinyarwanda can only be used when the verb is followed by at least one postverbal constituent. No pause is allowed between the verb and the material immediately following it, which suggests that the postverbal material is located in a syntactically low, clause-internal position. The postverbal element that licenses the CJ form can be an object-NP, a sentential complement, a postverbal subject-NP, an adjunct, or a clitic:

NP-complement:

(42) a. *Abáana   baányooye   amatá.*   [monotransitive verb]
        a-ba-áana   ba-á-nyó-ye   a-ma-tá
        AUG-2-child   2SM-REM-drink-PFV AUG-6-milk
        'The children drank milk.'

     b. *Baáhaaye   Yohaáni   igitabo.*   [ditransitive verb]
        ba-á-há-ye   Yohaáni   i-ki-tabo
        2SM-REM-give-PFV 1.John AUG-7-book
        'They gave John a book.'

Clausal complement:

(43) a. *Baávuze   kó   mwaákoze.*   [finite clause]
        ba-á-vú-ye   kó   mu-á-kór-ye
        2SM-REM-say-PFV that   2PL.SM-REM-work-PFV
        'They said that you worked'

     b. *Aba   bagabo   baákuundaga   kudusuura.*   [infinitive]
        Aba   ba-gabo   ba-á-kúund-aga   ku-tu-suur-a
        2.DEM   2-man   2SM-REM-like-IPFV 15-1PL.OM-visit-FV
        'These men liked to visit us.'

Postverbal (VP-internal) subject NP:

(44) a. *Murí iyo miínsi híigaga abáana baké.* [expl const.]
muríiyo mi-nsi ha-á-íig-aga a-ba-áana ba-ké
18.LOC 4.DEM 4-day EXPL-REM-study-IPFV AUG-2-children 2-few
'In those days few children studied.'

b. *Mu Rwanda inkokó zaáryaga abakuúngu.* [subj-obj reversal]
mu Rwanda i-n-kokó zi-á-rí-aga a-ba-kuúngu
18.LOC 9.Rwanda AUG-10-chicken 10SM-REM-eat-FV AUG-2-rich people
'In Rwanda it is rich people who used to eat chicken.'

Adjunct:

(45) a. *Abáarimú baákoze néezá.* [manner adverb]
a-ba-áarimú ba-á-kór-ye néezá
AUG-2-teacher 2SM-REM-work-PFV well
'The teachers worked well.'

b. *Abáarimú baákoze vubá.* [manner adverb]
a-ba-áarimú ba-á-kór-ye vubá
AUG-2-teacher 2SM-REM-work-PFV quickly
'The teachers worked quickly.'

c. *Abáarimú baákoze ejó.* [temporal adverb]
a-ba-áarimú ba-á-kór-ye yesterday
AUG-2-teacher 2SM-REM-work-PFV yesterday
'The teachers worked yesterday.'

d. *Baábitooranyije n' íimáshiní.* [instrumental PP]
ba-á-bi-tóorany-ye n' i-máshiní
2SM-REM-8OM-sort-PFV with AUG-9.pen
'They sorted them with a machine.'

Clitic:

(46) *Twaányuzeyó.* [locative clitic]
Tu-á-nyúr-ye-yó
1PL.SM-REM-pass-PFV-LOC19
'We passed there.'

All examples in (42)–(46) are compatible with narrow term focus on the element following the verb.[11] For example, (42a) can be an appropriate answer to the question "What did the children drink?"; the object can also be modified by the focus marker *gusa*, 'only', (47a), and it can be a wh-phrase, (47b):

(47) a. *Abáana   baányooye   amatá   gusa.*
       a-ba-áana   ba-á-nyó-ye   a-ma-tá   gusa
       AUG-2-child 2SM-REM-drink-PFV AUG-6-milk only
       'The children drank only milk (not juice).'

   b. *Abáana   baányooye   ikí?*
       a-ba-áana   ba-á-nyó-ye   ikí
       AUG-2-child 2SM-REM-drink-PFV what
       'What did the children drink?'

The above data are therefore consistent with the idea that the CJ form in Kinyarwanda must be used when focus is on a complement.[12]

In contrast, in sentences where nothing follows the verb in Kinyarwanda, the DJ form must be used:

(48) a. *Abáana   baáranyóoye.*
       a-ba-áana   ba-á-ra-nyó-ye
       AUG-2-child 2SM- REM-DJ-drink-PFV
       'The children drank.'

   b. *Abáana   baárayanyóoye.*
       a-ba-áana   ba-á-ra-ya-nyó-ye
       AUG-2-child 2SM- REM-DJ-6OM-drink-PFV
       'The children drank it.'

   c. *Amatá   abáana   baárayanyóonye.*
       a-ma-tá   a-ba-áana   ba-á-ra-ya-nyó-ye
       AUG-6-milk AUG-2-child 2SM-REM-DJ-6OM-drink-PFV
       Lit: 'The milk, children drank it.'

---

11 Focusing the post-verbal element is even possible if this element is a locative clitic, as in example (46), which can be used as an answer to a question such as "Where did you pass?". Notice that locative clitics do not necessarily incorporate into the verb in the syntax, but can be analysed as (morphologically complex) heads of independent phrasal constituents inside the verb's complement which are linearly adjacent to the verb (see Ngoboka 2016).

12 Notice that strictly speaking, postverbal subjects, adverbials and clitics are not complements. However, we interpret Givón's notion of "complement" in a broad sense here, to refer to any postverbal, clause-internal element.

In (48a), the object of the verb *nyó-*, 'drink', has remained implicit. In this case, the new information is expressed by the verb, which according to Givón's (1975) analysis triggers the use of the DJ form marker *-ra-*, which signals that the verb is (part of) the focus. The verb focus-analysis also explains the use of *-ra-* in (48b), where the object of the verb *nyó-* is realised as a pronominal object marker (and therefore interpreted as given), and in (48c), where the object-NP is a left-dislocated topic. Since pre-verbal subjects in Kinyarwanda are obligatorily interpreted as given (cf. Givón 1975), the verb in (48b) and (48c) is the only constituent that can be interpreted as new information. Consequently, the DJ form must be used.

The meaning of the verb is not the only semantic aspect that can be focused in verbal constructions in the DJ form. Hyman and Watters (1984) introduce the notion of "auxiliary focus", which refers to constructions in which focus is placed on any of the semantic operators that are typically expressed by the auxiliary plus verb complex, namely tense, aspect, mood, and polarity. Güldemann (2003) uses the term "predication focus" to cover both auxiliary and narrow verb focus. It seems that all types of predication focus in Kinyarwanda can be expressed by means of the DJ form:[13]

Polarity:

(49) A: *Siinkeeká   kó   Yohaáni yakóze   ejó.*
          Si-n-kéek-a   kó   Yohaáni a-á-kór-ye   ejó
          NEG-1SG.SM-think-FV that 1.John   1SM-REM-work-PFV yesterday
          'I don't think John worked yesterday.'

      B: *Yarákoze.*
          a-á-ra-kór-ye
          1SM-REM-DJ-work-PFV
          'He *did* work.'

Tense:

(50) A: *Yohaáni yakóze   ejó*
          Yohaáni a-á-kór-ye   ejó
          1.John   1SM-REM-work-PFV yesterday
                   cyáangwá azaakora   ejó?
                   cyáangwá a-zaa-kór-a   ejó
                   or   1SM-RFUT-work-FV tomorrow.
          'Did John work yesterday, or will he work tomorrow?'

---

[13] In the remainder of this paper, we refrain from using the term "predication focus", in order to avoid confusion with the notion of "predicate focus", by which we mean focus on the verb plus VP-internal material.

B. *Yarákoze.*
   a-á-ra-kór-ye
   1SM-REM-DJ-work-PFV
   'He *worked*.'

Narrow verb focus:

(51) A. *Yohaáni yarákoze cyáangwá yaráryaamye?*
   Yohaáni a-á-ra-kór-ye cyáangwá a-á-ra-ryáam-ye?
   1.John 1SM-REM-DJ-work-PFV or 1SM-REM-sleep-PFV
   'Did John work or did he sleep?'

B. *Yarákoze.*
   a-á-ra-kór-ye
   1SM-REM-DJ-work-PFV
   'He *worked*.'

Sometimes an element can follow the DJ form of the verb in Kinyarwanda, but only if there is a clear intonational break after the verb, signaled by a pause ("comma intonation"). This suggests that postverbal material that follows the DJ verb form is not part of the core clause:

(52) *Abáarimú baárakóze *(,) ejó.*
   a-ba-áarimú ba-á-ra-kó-ye yesterday
   AUG-2-teacher 2SM-REM-DJ-work-PFV
   'Teachers worked, yesterday.'

As Givón (1975: 197) notes, an adverb separated from the main clause by a pause in Kinyarwanda is a right-dislocated afterthought topic, which represents given information. Since the preverbal subject-NP is also interpreted as given, the verb in (52) represents the new information, which according to Givón (1975) explains the use of the DJ marker *-ra-*.

When the extraposed element is an object-NP, comma intonation is required again, and in addition, an object marker corresponding to the postverbal NP is obligatory:

(53) *Abáana baára*(ya)nyóoye , amatá.*
   a-ba-áana ba-á-ra-*ya*-nyó-ye a-ma-tá
   AUG-2-child 2SM-REM-DJ-6OM-drink-PFV AUG-6-milk
   'The children drank it, the milk.'

The status of the postverbal NP in (53) as a clause-external afterthought is further confirmed by the fact that the NP cannot be followed by a temporal or manner adverb:

(54) *Abáana baárayanyóoye (,) amatá ejó.
a-ba-áana ba-á-ra-ya-nyó-ye a-ma-tá ejó
AUG-2-child 2SM- REM-DJ-6OM-drink-PFV AUG-6-milk yesterday
'The children drank it, the milk, yesterday.'

(55) *Yohaáni yarázoogeje (,) imódoká néezá.
Yohaáni a-á-ra-zi-óoz-ye i-módoká néezá
1.John 1SM-REM-DJ-1OOM-wash-PFV AUG-6-milk well
'John washed them, the cars, well.'

Examples (54) and (55) show that Kinyarwanda differs from Bantu languages such as Zulu, where object-marked NPs following the DJ form of the verb can be right-dislocated to a VP/vP-external, but clause-internal, position to the left of temporal and manner adverbs (see Cheng and Downing 2009; Zeller 2012, 2015).

3.3 Problems for a focus-based account

The Kinyarwanda data discussed in the preceding section are consistent with the idea that the CJ/DJ alternation is determined by the information-structural properties of the sentence. However, what does not follow straightforwardly from this idea is the observation that in most contexts, the CJ and the DJ form in Kinyarwanda are in complementary distribution (but see Section 3.4 below for exceptions). For example, all sentences in (42)–(46) become ungrammatical when the DJ instead of the CJ form is used:

(56) a. *Abáana baáranyóoye amatá.
a-ba-áana ba-á-ra-nyó-ye a-ma-tá
AUG-2-child 2SM-REM-DJ-drink-PFV AUG-6-milk
'The children drank milk.'

b. *Baáraháaye Yohaáni igitabo.
ba-á-ra-há-ye Yohaáni i-ki-tabo
2SM-REM-DJ-give-PFV 1.John AUG-7-book
'They gave John a book.'

(57) a. *Baáravúze kó mwaákoze.
ba-á-ra-vúg-ye kó mu-á-kór-ye
2SM-REM-DJ-say-PFV that 2PL.SM-REM-work-PFV
'They said that you worked'

b. *Aba   bagabo   baárakúundaga   kudusuura.
    Aba   ba-gabo   ba-á-ra-kúund-aga ku-tu-suur-a
    2.DEM   2-man   2SM-REM-DJ-like-IPFV 15-1PL.OM-visit-FV
    'These men liked to visit us.'

(58) a. *Murí   iyo   miínsi   háariigaga   abáana   baké.
         murí   iyo   mi-nsi   ha-á-ra-íig-aga   a-ba-áana   ba-ké
         18.LOC   4.DEM   4-day   EXPL-REM-DJ-study-IPFV AUG-2-children 2-few
         'In those days few children studied.'

     b. *Mu   Rwanda   inkokó   zararyaga   abakuúngu.
         mu   Rwanda   i-n-kokó   zi-ra-rí-aga   a-ba-kuúngu
         18.LOC   9.Rwanda AUG-10-chicken 10SM-DJ-eat-IPFV AUG-2-rich people
         'In Rwanda it is rich people who used to eat chicken.'

(59) a. *Abáarimú   baárakóze   néezá.
         a-ba-áarimú   ba-á-ra-kór-ye   néezá
         AUG-2-teacher   2SM-REM-DJ-work-PFV well
         'The teachers worked well.'

     b. *Abáarimú   baárakoze   vubá.
         a-ba-áarimú   ba-á-ra-kór-ye   vubá
         AUG-2-teacher   2SM-REM-DJ-work-PFV quickly
         'The teachers worked quickly.'

     c. *Abáarimú   baárakóze   ejó.
         a-ba-áarimú   ba-á-ra-kór-ye   yesterday
         AUG-2-teacher   2SM-REM-DJ-work-PFV yesterday
         'The teachers worked yesterday.'

     d. *Baárabitóoranyije   n'   îimáshiní.
         ba-á-ra-bi-tóorany-ye   n'   i-máshiní
         2SM-REM-DJ-8OM-sort-PFV   with   AUG-9.machine
         'They sorted them with a machine.'

(60) *Twaáranyúzeyó.
      tu-á-ra-nyúr-ye-yó
      1PL.SM-REM-DJ-pass-PFV-19.LOC
      'We passed there.'

The examples in (56)–(60) show that the DJ form is generally not possible when the verb is followed by postverbal clause-internal material. This is surprising under an account that attributes the choice of the verb to information structure: if the DJ form expresses that the verb is part of the focus, then we would expect the DJ form to be licensed with postverbal material whenever the whole VP-predicate is in the scope of focus, i.e. when the verb plus its complement present the new information. For example, (56a) would be expected to be grammatical as an answer to the question "What did the children do?". However, (56a) is not acceptable under this (or any other) reading.

The ungrammaticality of examples such as (56a), in which the DJ verb form is followed by an object, constitutes a major difference between Kinyarwanda and Kirundi, which is otherwise very similar to Kinyarwanda with respect to the CJ/DJ alternation. As noted in Meeussen (1959), Ndayiragije (1999), and Nshemezimana and Bostoen (this volume), verbs in the DJ form may be followed by object-NPs in Kirundi:

(61) a. *A-bâna   ba-á-ra-nyô-ye   amatá.*
       AUG-child   2SM-REM-DJ-drink-PFV   milk
       'Children drank milk.'

   b. *A-bâna   ba-á-(*ra)-nyô-ye   amatá.*
       AUG-2.child   2SM-REM-DJ-drink-PFV   milk
       'Children drank milk (not water).'

   c. *A-bâna   ba-á-(*ra)-nyô-ye   iki?*
       AUG-child   2SM-REM-DJ-drink-PFV   what
       'What did children drink?'
       (Kirundi; Ndayiragije 1999: 406; glosses adapted)

The absence of an object marker in (61a) suggests that the object is not dislocated, but has remained in complement position. This view is supported by the fact that objects following the DJ form in Kirundi can still appear to the left of manner adverbs, which shows that they are part of the core sentence:[14]

---

[14] If object right dislocation in Kirundi is possible without an object marker, then it could be that in (62), both the object and the adverb are dislocated. In this case, the word order of (62) would not constitute an argument for the assumption that the object is in complement position. However, note that according to the data in Ndayiragije (1999), the opposite word order Adv > Obj is ungrammatical in Kirundi:

(i)   **Yohani   a-á-ra-oógeje   néezá   imiduga.*
       1.John   1SM-REM-DJ-wash.PFV   well   cars
       'John washed cars well.'
       (Kirundi; Ndayiragije 1999: 410)

If Kirundi indeed allowed object dislocation without an object marker, then (i) should be grammatical (the adverb in (i) could either be right-dislocated, or in its base position). The ungrammaticality

(62) Yohani   a-á-ra-oógeje   imiduga néezá.
     1.John   1SM-REM-DJ-wash.PFV   cars   well
     'John washed cars well.'
     (Kirundi; Ndayiragije 1999: 410)

Ndayiragije notes that a sentence such as (61a) is incompatible with an interpretation of the object as new information (see (61b) and (61c)). According to Nshemezimana and Bostoen (this volume), a verb in the DJ form that is followed by an object (or other clause-internal material) is licensed in Kirundi in two possible contexts: (i) in thetic ('out-of-the-blue'; all new) sentences, and (ii) in predicate focus (topic-comment) constructions, in which the whole VP, including the verb and postverbal material, is focused. These facts are predicted by an analysis such as the one proposed by Givón (1975), according to which the DJ element *-ra-* marks the verb as being part of the focus. In contrast, in Kinyarwanda an object complement can *never* follow the DJ form of the verb clause-internally (see e.g. (56)), even if the information structure corresponds to the contexts identified by Nshemezimana and Bostoen (this volume). In order to express thetic sentences or predicate focus in Kinyarwanda, the CJ form is required; therefore, the sentences in (42)–(46) above with the verb in the CJ form can be used in "all new"-contexts (and can serve as answers to a question like "What happened?"), and they can also express predicate (VP-) focus (e.g. (42a) is appropriate as an answer to the question "What did the children do?" etc.).[15]

The fact that the DJ form in Kinyarwanda can never be used with an object complement suggests that the CJ/DJ alternation is not exclusively determined by the focus-properties of a sentence. Rather, it seems that the choice between the CJ and the DJ form is at least in part determined by the syntactic configuration (see Coupez 1980; Overdulve 1988; Kimenyi 2002). In fact, all examples discussed thus far are compatible with the view that the CJ form in Kinyarwanda is associated with the presence of overt postverbal material within VP (or some larger constituent, such as IP/AgrSP), while the DJ form appears when there is no overt material inside this constituent (either because the verb is the last word of the sentence, or because postverbal material is extraposed to a position outside the relevant constituent).

---

of (i) therefore supports the claim that the object in (62) is in its base position. However, it needs to be noted that according to a reviewer, (i) is actually grammatical in Kirundi, contrary to what is claimed by Ndayiragije. If this is the case, then the syntax of (61a) and (62) is more difficult to diagnose.

15 Givón (1975: 195) postulates a "discourse strategy", which stipulates that, whenever a complement is present in Kinyarwanda, it is obligatorily interpreted as focused and therefore automatically triggers the CJ verb form. However, this proposal does not seem compatible with our observation that transitive constructions with a CJ-verb form followed by a complement can express focus on the whole VP-predicate, and even contrastive focus on the verb (see (63) below).

A syntactic account of the CJ/DJ alternation that is based on these assumptions has been put forward for the Bantu language Zulu by Van der Spuy (1993) and Buell (2006). Buell (2006) argues against the view that the DJ form in Zulu expresses verb focus, and one of the arguments he puts forward can be replicated for Kinyarwanda. In a Zulu sentence in which the verb is followed by postverbal material that typically licenses the CJ form, the verb can nevertheless be contrastively focused. The same holds for Kinyarwanda:

(63) Siniigíisha   néezá aríko mvuga   néezá.
     si-n-íigiish-a   néezá aríko n-vúg-a   néezá
     NEG-1SG.SM-teach-FV well but   1SG.SM-speak-FV well
     'I don't teach well, but I speak well.'

The first conjunct in (63) determines that the verb in the second conjunct is contrastively focused. According to the focus account of the CJ/DJ alternation, this interpretation should trigger the DJ form. However, since the adverb *néezá* follows the verb, the CJ form must be chosen; in fact, the use of the DJ form would make (63) ungrammatical. This suggests that the form of the verb in (63) is not determined by the information structure, but by the syntax, of the sentence.

The hypothesis that the CJ/DJ alternation in Kinyarwanda is determined by constituency is also supported by the following discourse:

(64) Q: Uteekereza   ikí   kurí   Yohaáni?
         u-téekerez-a   ikí   kurí   Yohaáni
         2SG.SM-think-FV what 17.LOC 1.John
         'What do you think about John?'

    A1: Yohaáni? Ndamwáanga.
         Johaáni? n-ra-mu-áang-a
         1.John?   1SG.SM-DJ-1OM-hate-FV
         'John? I *hate* him.'

    A2: Yohaáni? Naanga   uriíya muhuúngu.
         Johaáni? n-áang-a   u-riíya mu-huúngu
         1.John?   1SG.SM-hate-FV 1-DEM 1-boy
         'John? I *hate* that guy.'

The pronominal object marker in (64A1) refers to the topic of the discourse, John, and is hence interpreted as given. Consequently, the new information is provided by the verb, and the use of the DJ form is hence expected under both a focus and a finality account (compare (48b) above). However, the information-structural properties of (64A2) are identical to those of (64A1). The only difference is that the discourse topic is not referenced by means of an object marker, but by means of a full NP (an epithet referring to John). If the choice of the DJ form in (64A1) was fully determined by the information structure, then we would expect the verb in (64A2) to be in the DJ form as well. However, the DJ form is impossible in this example. This suggests that it is the presence of an overt object complement that determines the use of the CJ in (64A2), while the DJ in (64A1) must be used because the verb is the final element of the clause.

3.4 Problems for a syntactic account

In the examples discussed in the preceding sections, postverbal, clause-internal material was shown not to be possible when the verb is in the DJ form. If this situation held as a general rule in Kinyarwanda, then it would provide support for an analysis of the CJ/DJ alternation based on constituency. However, as we show in this section, there are a number of exceptions to this generalisation that are problematic for the syntactic account. One exception is the focus marker *gusa*, 'only'. This focus marker can only appear after the DJ form in Kinyarwanda; the CJ form is not possible (see also Meeussen 1959 for Kirundi):

(65) a. *Arakóra   gusa.*
        a-ra-kór-a   gusa
        1SM-DJ-work-FV   only
        'He only works.'

    b. **Akora*   gusa.*
        a-kór-a   gusa
        1SM-work-FV   only
        Intended: 'He only works.'

There is no evidence that *gusa* in (65) is extraposed; in contrast to the examples with right-dislocated adverbs discussed in Section 3.2, there is no pause that separates the verb from the focus marker in (65a). A syntactic account of the CJ/DJ alternation therefore has trouble explaining (65): since *gusa* is not in a clause-external position, the verb should be in the CJ form. One could perhaps approach this problem by suggesting that the syntactic domain relevant for the CJ/DJ alternation is not established by the whole clause, but by a smaller constituent, which includes complements, clitics as well as temporal and manner adverbs, but excludes *gusa*. A potential candidate for this constituent could be the IP- (AgrS-) node, which arguably includes all arguments and most adjuncts, but the analysis would then require the assumption that *gusa* is base-generated in a *clause-internal* position *outside* IP. This assumption seems slightly ad hoc, as it is only supported by the data that are to be explained. In contrast, (65) follows straightforwardly and without stipulations from the focus-based account of the CJ/DJ alternation that was discussed in Sections 3.1 and 3.2: since the verb in (65) presents new information, we expect it to be marked by the DJ form, which according to the analysis in Givón (1975) marks the verb as focused.

Other elements that behave like *gusa* in that they must follow the DJ verb form in Kinyarwanda are adverbs such as *nyíne*, 'indeed', *kókó*, 'really', and *rwóose*, 'truly'. These adverbs contrast with manner adverbs such as *néezá*, 'well', and *vubá*, 'quickly' (which are verbal modifiers and require the CJ form; see (45) and (59) above) in that they emphasise the polarity of the sentence and hence mark auxiliary focus. Therefore, the focus account also predicts correctly that these adverbs can only combine with verbs in the DJ form.

Furthermore, some postverbal material is compatible with both the CJ and the DJ form of the verb in Kinyarwanda. As already noted in Section 3.1, clauses introduced by the complementiser *ngo* can combine with verbs in the DJ form, (66a), but they can also appear after CJ verb forms, (66b):[16]

(66) a. Aravúga   ngo ni mutó.
        a-ra-vúg-a   ngo ni mu-tó
        1SM-DJ-say-FV that be 2-young
        'He says that he is young.'

    b. Avuga   ngo ni mutó.
        a-vúg-a   ngo ni mu-tó
        1SM-say-FV that be 2-young
        'He says that he is young.'

Recall that clauses introduced by *ngo* express "reported speech". It is possible that this fact is reflected by the syntactic relation between the verb and the *ngo*-clause. Coupez (1980) analyses the relation between the *ngo*-clause and the preceding verb as parataxis, which means that *ngo*-clauses are not subordinated sentences, i.e. they are not represented as syntactic complements of the verb. Possibly, they are higher level adjuncts. The fact that *ngo*-clauses can follow the DJ form of the verb would be consistent with a syntactic approach if sentences introduced by *ngo* are indeed adjoined outside the phrasal category that is relevant for the CJ/DJ alternation. However, it is not quite clear why Kinyarwanda speakers also accept examples such as (66b), where the *ngo*-clause follows the CJ form of the verb. An

---

16 Notice that the CJ/DJ alternation is always attested in an *ngo*-clause (see Section 3.1), regardless of whether it follows the CJ or the DJ form of the verb.

account of the CJ/DJ alternation based on constituency would require the assumption that a clause introduced by *ngo* can appear in different syntactic positions, i.e. both outside and inside the phrasal category that determines the use of the CJ or the DJ form. (We return to this point briefly in Section 5).[17]

Certain adverbial elements in Kinyarwanda can also combine with both the CJ and the DJ form of the verb. One example already discussed in Givón (1975: 194) is the adverb *cyaane*, 'much, hard, a lot':

(67) a. *Arakóra   cyaane.*
        a-ra-kór-a   cyaane
        1SM-DJ-work-FV   hard
        'He works hard.'

     b. *Akora   cyaane.*
        a-kór-a   cyaane
        1SM-work-FV   hard
        'He works hard.'

According to Givón (1975), an example such as (67a) expresses predicate (VP-) focus; it can answer a yes-no question or can be used in "all new" contexts. In contrast, in (67b), focus is on the adverb; the example can hence be used as an answer to a question such as "How does he work?". This means that with respect to adverbs like *cyaane*, Kinyarwanda behaves exactly as predicted by an analysis which treats the DJ form as a marker of verb/VP focus.[18] In contrast, a syntactic account would have to stipulate that adverbs like *cyaane*, like *ngo*-clauses, can appear in different syntactic positions. However, this stipulation raises the question why this possibility does not exist with other manner adverbs such as *néezá*, 'well', and *vubá*, 'quickly', which seem to be restricted to one position in the syntax and always require the CJ form.

---

17 With respect to the alternation in (66), *ngo*-clauses in Kinyarwanda behave like argument clauses in Zulu and Makhuwa, which may also follow both the CJ and the DJ form of the matrix verb (see Halpert 2015 for Zulu; Van der Wal 2014 for Makhuwa). Buell (2006) and Halpert (2015) show that the CJ/DJ alternation in Zulu is determined by constituency. Zulu therefore provides independent support for the assumption that certain argument clauses can indeed appear in different positions in Bantu languages.

18 While the first author agrees with the meaning difference observed by Givón, he also notes that this contrast is very subtle. The (non-linguist) Kinyarwanda speakers we consulted could not detect any semantic or pragmatic difference between the use of the CJ or the DJ form before the adverb. However, most speakers preferred the DJ form when the examples were presented to them out of context. This presumably follows from the fact that the most neutral, or unmarked, interpretation that speakers assign to isolated sentences is a topic-comment structure, in which the subject-NP is interpreted as the topic and the VP-predicate as the focus (Lambrecht 1994). As discussed above, the focus account correctly predicts the choice of the DJ form in this case.

Other elements that can follow both the CJ and the DJ form of the verb in Kinyarwanda are adverbials that begin with the class 8 prefix *bi-*:[19]

(68) a. *Mariya   araseenga   bikábije.*
          Mariya   a-ra-seeng-a   bi-káby-ye
          1.Mary   1SM-DJ-pray-FV 8-exagerate-PFV
          'Mary prays too much.'

      b. *Mariya   aseenga   bikábije.*
          Mariya   a-seeng-a   bi-káby-ye
          1.Mary   1SM-pray-FV   8-exagerate-PFV
          'Mary prays too much.'

As in the examples in (67), the choice between (68a) and (68b) seems to be determined by the focus properties of the sentences: while (68a) expresses VP-focus, (68b) is most appropriate with a reading in which focus is on the adverb.

In sum, a purely syntactic account of the CJ/DJ alternation is also not without problems. While an analysis based on constituency seems suitable to account for the data discussed in the previous section, the examples in (65)–(68) are more difficult to explain from a purely syntactic perspective. In contrast, these data follow straightforwardly from an analysis according to which the CJ/DJ alternation is determined by the focus-properties of the sentence.

4 The morpheme *-ra-*

In the preceding section, we have compared two accounts of the CJ/DJ alternation, one which explains the alternation in terms of the information structure of the sentence, and one which regards it as a grammatical reflex of constituency. Before we turn to the conclusions that we draw from this comparison, we briefly address the fact that the morpheme *-ra-*, which marks the DJ verb form in the simple present, present perfective, and remote past tense, also seems to be associated with other grammatical functions in Kinyarwanda, such as tense and aspect (see Coupez 1980; Botne 1983; Shimamungu 1991; Bizimana 1998; Overdulve and Jacob 1998; Kimenyi 2002):

(69) *Abáana   barasoma   ikinyarwaanda.*
      a-ba-áana   ba-ra-som-a   ikinyarwaanda
      AUG-2-child   2SM-PROG/FUT-read-FV   7.Kinyarwanda
      'Children are reading Kinyarwanda (now).'   [present progressive]
      'Children will read Kinyarwanda (later today).' [near future]

---

19 We are indebted to a reviewer for making us aware of these examples.

As the translations show, the sentence in (69) can be interpreted as expressing the present progressive or the near future. Importantly, the use of -*ra*- in (69) does not seem to be governed by the same conditions that determine the use of -*ra*- as a DJ-marker: recall that object-NPs in complement position are never licensed with verbs in the DJ form in Kinyarwanda (see Section 3.3); in contrast, the verb in (69) can be followed by an object-NP. Moreover, this object-NP can even be narrowly focused: (69) is an appropriate answer to an object question ("What are the children reading?"; "What will the children read?"), the object can be modified with the focus marker *gusa*, 'only', (70), and it can be realised as a wh-phrase, (71):

(70) *Abáana   barasoma   ikinyarwaanda   gusa.*
      a-ba-áana   ba-ra-som-a   ikinyarwaanda   gusa
      AUG-2-child 2SM-PROG/FUT-read-FV 7.Kinyarwanda   gusa
      'Children are reading only Kinyarwanda.'   [present progressive]
      'Children will read only Kinyarwanda.'   [near future]

(71) *Abáana   barasoma   ikí?*
      a-ba-áana   ba-ra-som-a   ikí
      AUG-2-child 2SM-PROG/FUT-read-FV what
      'What are the children reading?'   [present progressive]
      'What will the children read?'   [near future]

Since the syntactic context in which -*ra*- is licensed in (69)–(71) is different from the contexts which license the DJ form in Kinyarwanda, authors such as Kimenyi (2002) and Ntwari (undated) assume that -*ra*- in examples such as (69)–(71) is not the DJ-marker, but instead has a temporal or aspectual function (a view that is reflected by our glosses in (69)–(71), which represent -*ra*- as a present progressive or future tense marker). According to this analysis, -*ra*- in Kinyarwanda is polysemous: it marks the DJ form when used in the simple present, the present perfective and the remote past, but it can also express progressive aspect or future tense.

However, the view that progressive aspect or future tense in Kinyarwanda are encoded by the morpheme -*ra*- is not entirely unproblematic. As (72) shows, embedded, negated or relative clauses can also be in the present progressive or near future, but crucially, the morpheme -*ra*- does not appear in these contexts:[20]

---

[20] Notice that, because of the omission of -*ra*-, the examples in (72) also have translations in the simple present, e.g. (72a) can mean 'He says that the children read books.'

(72) a. *Avuze   kó   abáana   basomá   ikinyarwaanda.*
       a-vúg-ye   kó   a-ba-áana   ba-som-a   ikinyarwaanda
       1SM-say-PFV that AUG-2-child   2SM-read-FV 7.Kinyarwanda
       'He says that children are reading Kinyarwada (now).'   [present progressive]
       'He says that children will read Kinyarwanda (later today).' [near future]

   b. *abáana   basomá   ikinyarwaanda*
      a-ba-áana   ba-som-a   ikinyarwaanda
      AUG-2-child 2SM-read-FV   7.Kinyarwanda
      'children who are reading Kinyarwanda (now)'   [present progressive]
      'children who will read Kinyarwanda (later today)' [near future]

   c. *Abáana   ntibasomá   ikinyarwaanda.*
      a-ba-áana   nti-ba-som-a   Ikinyarwaanda
      AUG-2-child NEG-2SM-read-FV 7.Kinyarwanda
      'Children are not reading Kinyarwanda (now).'   [present progressive]
      'Children will not read Kinyarwanda (later today).' [near future]

The examples in (72) demonstrate that a present progressive or near future reading does not require the presence of *-ra-* in Kinyarwanda. This casts doubt on the view that these functions are directly encoded by this morpheme in examples such as (69). Furthermore, recall from Section 3.1 that relative clauses, negatives and many embedded clauses in Kinyarwanda also block the use of the DJ-marker *-ra-*. This parallel is clearly not accidental, but rather suggests that *-ra-* in examples such as (69) and the DJ-marker *-ra-* are closely related, or even the same element. The latter position seems to be advocated by Overdulve (1988) and by Coupez (1980). For example, Coupez (1980: 384) states that "[l]e conjoint est exclu aux sens de présent et de future d'aujourd'hui, pour lesquels on emploie toujours le disjoint" ["the conjoint is excluded in the present and near future, in which the disjoint is always used"; our translation, JPN & JZ]. According to this view, the progressive and the near futur always require the DJ form and therefore are systematic exceptions to the rules that govern the distribution of the DJ-marker *-ra-* in Kinyarwanda in the simple present, the present perfective and the remote past tense. No matter whether the DJ form in the latter contexts is licensed by clause finality or by information structure, the examples in (69)–(71) suggest that there is a second, independent licensor of the DJ form, which is responsible for its occurrence in constructions such as (69)–(71).

It seems difficult to think of a way in which an analysis of the CJ/DJ alternation based on constituency could explain the obligatory occurrence of the DJ marker *-ra-* in the progressive and the near future. In contrast, a focus account of the alternation offers a possible explanation. Hyman and Watters (1984) and Güldemann (2003) discuss a number of African languages in which the marker of the progressive is formally identical to the marker of auxiliary focus (which according to the focus account of the CJ/DJ alternation is expressed by the DJ form in Kinyarwanda). Hyman and Watters (1984) explain this isomorphism through their assumption that the progressive is an "intrinsically focused" auxiliary category, which must therefore be marked by the relevant auxiliary focus marker.[21]

Following Hyman and Watters (1984), Güldemann (2003: 351) also analyses the progressive as "a category which combines aspect with focality" and proposes that the progressive developed as a result of a historical process in which an element with the pragmatic function of expressing verb or polarity focus gained the additional semantic property of imperfectivity. Moreover, Güldemann (2003: appendix) speculates about a further grammaticalisation path from the progressive to the near future (see also Nshemezimana and Bostoen (Chapter 14) on the relation between the progressive and the near future in Kirundi). According to these proposals, the analysis of the DJ form as a marker of auxiliary or verb focus ultimately also explains the occurrence of *-ra-* in examples such as (69).

It should be noted that the element *-ra-* in Kinyarwanda also appears obligatorily in other grammatical constructions, such as the persistive, the optative, and in various compound tenses (Sibomana 1974; Kimenyi 2002). In each of these constructions, a verb form marked by *-ra-* can co-occur with a focused object complement. While the persistive has also been analysed as an intrinsically focused category by Hyman and Watters (1984) and Güldemann (2003), it remains an open question if an account in terms of intrinsic focus can also be developed for the other contexts in which *-ra-* appears. We leave it as a topic for future research to establish whether *-ra-* in these constructions is identical, or historically related, to the DJ-marker *-ra-*, or if an entirely different function of *-ra-* has to be postulated to account for its occurrence in some of these contexts.

5 Conclusion

This chapter has provided a wide range of data that document phonological, morphological, syntactic and semantic/pragmatic aspects of the CJ/DJ alternation in Kinyarwanda. We have shown that the alternation is attested in the simple

---

[21] Güldemann (2003) notes the existence of languages in which the progressive is excluded from constructions in which narrow focus is on a complement. It seems that in these languages, the inherent focality of the progressive prevents the use of this aspect in constructions in which the verbal predicate is not part of the focus. In contrast, as shown in (70) and (71), the element *-ra-* in the present progressive and the near future in Kinyarwanda is possible even if a narrowly focused object complement is present. According to the analysis proposed by Hyman and Watters (1984), this means that its appearance is not pragmatically, but grammatically, controlled (see also note 8).

present, present perfective, near past and remote past tense, as well as in the subsecutive and conditional/hypothetical mood. While the CJ form is marked tonally through the deletion of lexical H tones, the DJ verb form is marked segmentally by the morpheme -*ra*- in the simple present, the present perfective, as well as the remote past, and by -*a*- in the near past tense.

Throughout our discussion, we have addressed the question of whether the CJ/DJ alternation is a reflex of syntactic constituency or information structure. Our description of the conditions which determine the choice between the CJ and the DJ verb form in Kinyarwanda has not yielded an entirely conclusive answer to this question. On the one hand, it is clear that at least some of the properties of the alternation are determined by the scope of focus. In constructions with a verbal complement in Kinyarwanda, the complement typically provides the new information, and the CJ form is obligatory. In contrast, sentences without a verbal complement are interpreted with verb/VP or auxiliary focus and require the DJ form (see Section 3.2). The strongest argument for a focus-based analysis comes from the data discussed in Section 3.4, which show that certain adverbial elements can follow both the CJ and the DJ form, with the choice being determined by whether focus is on the adverb only, or on the whole VP-predicate. In addition, we have shown that the CJ/DJ alternation is systematically excluded from weakly or non-assertive environments and that the DJ marker -*ra*- obligatorily appears in main clause affirmatives in the present progressive and the near future. As we discussed in Sections 3.1 and 4, it seems that only a focus-based analysis can offer plausible explanations for these latter observations.

On the other hand, we also discussed some aspects of the CJ/DJ alternation in Kinyarwanda that rather support an account based on constituency. As was shown in Section 3.3, it is not possible in Kinyarwanda to combine the DJ verb form with a genuine complement of the verb, even when the intended interpretation would be compatible with the scope of focus normally established by the DJ form (i.e. VP-focus). These data suggest that the alternation is at least in part determined by the syntax, in that the CJ verb form is required in Kinyarwanda when clause- or IP-internal material follows the verb in a sentence, while the DJ form is used in all other contexts.

These two approaches are not incompatible, and there are obvious ways in which the focus account and the syntactic account can be reconciled. As is probably true for many grammatical phenomena that show complex and sometimes contradictory properties, the hybrid status of the CJ/DJ alternation in Kinyarwanda could be viewed as the result of an ongoing historical development. It is possible that at an earlier stage, the CJ/DJ alternation in Kinyarwanda was systematically used as a focus-marking strategy; it was probably more like present-day Kirundi, which still allows verbs to appear in the DJ form before complements (see Section 3.3). Nshemezimana and Bostoen (this volume) show that in Kirundi, the DJ marker is optional in "neutral" topic-comment constructions: the DJ form can be used in these constructions, but as in Kinyarwanda, the CJ form is also possible in Kirundi when the whole VP-predicate (verb plus complement) is in the scope of focus. This means that in Kirundi, the neutral interpretation of a sentence in which the subject is the topic and the VP the focus can be expressed by two alternative verb forms. In contrast, other types of focus (complement focus; verb/auxiliary focus) are more restrictive and require either the CJ or the DJ form. It seems that in Kinyarwanda, the restrictiveness of the latter focus constructions was re-interpreted in syntactic terms; speakers re-analysed the choice between the CJ and the DJ form as being controlled by constituency. As a consequence, the optionality of the DJ form in verb-complement constructions was lost, and the CJ form became the compulsory form in all contexts where a complement is present, regardless of the discourse properties of the construction. According to this view, the CJ/DJ alternation in Kinyarwanda is first and foremost a marker of information structure, but it is grammatically controlled in environments with clause-/IP-internal postverbal material.[22]

Finally, we consider it noteworthy that those postverbal elements that can still follow both the CJ and the DJ form in present-day Kinyarwanda are certain types of clauses and adverbs, i.e. categories that can be realised in different syntactic positions: clauses can be complements as well as adjuncts; they tend to be extraposed and obligatorily appear in the right clausal periphery in many languages. Adverbs can appear in high and low positions and may or may not be selected by the verb (cf. Cheng and Downing 2014). It would be interesting to test whether the interpretation of a clause with an adverb such as *cyaane* in Kinyarwanda (which depends on whether the adverb follows the CJ or the DJ form of the verb) is also correlated with the adverb's syntactic position. The hypothesis would be that the adverb is in a IP-external position when it follows the DJ form (VP-focus), but inside the IP when the verb is in the CJ form (adverb focus) (see our brief discussion in Section 3.4). We have to leave the examination of this hypothesis, as well as the exploration of other issues raised by our description of the Kinyarwanda data, as objectives for future research.

---

22 See Güldemann (2003) who proposes an analysis along these lines for the use of the DJ form in Zulu.

Abbreviations and symbols

High tone is marked by an acute accent on the syllable; low tone is unmarked. Following the standard practice in the Bantu literature, we mark Bantu noun class prefixes and the corresponding agreement markers through numbers.

1,2 SG/PL first, second person singular/plural

APPL	applicative	LOC	locative
AUG	augment	NEG	negative
CJ	conjoint verb form	OM	object marker
COND	conditional	PFV	perfective aspect
DEM	demonstrative	PROG	present progressive
DJ	disjoint verb form	PST	near past tense
EXPL	expletive	REL	relative marker
FUT	near future tense	REM	remote past tense
FV	final vowel	RFUT	remote future tense
H	high tone	SM	subject marker
IPFV	imperfective aspect	SUBS	subsecutive
L	low tone		

References

Bizimana, Simon. 1998. *Imiteerere y'Ikinyarwaanda I* [The structure of Kinyarwanda I]. Kigali: Pallotti-Press.

Bostoen, Koen & Ernest Nshemezimana (this volume). The conjoint/disjoint alternation in Kirundi (JD62): A case for its abolition.

Botne, Robert D. 1983. The semantics of tense in Kinyarwanda. *Studies in African Linguistics* 14. 235–263.

Buell, Leston. 2006. The Zulu conjoint/disjoint verb alternation: Focus or constituency. *ZAS papers in Linguistics* 43. 9–30.

Cheng, Lisa Lai-Shen & Laura J. Downing. 2009. Where's the topic in Zulu? *The Linguistic Review* 26. 207–238.

Cheng, Lisa Lai-Shen & Laura Downing. 2014. The problem of adverbs in Zulu. In Johanneke Caspers, Yiya Chen, Willemijn Heeren, Jos Pacilly, Niels O. Schiller & Ellen van Zanten (eds.), *Above and beyond the segments: Experimental linguistics and phonetics*, 42–59. Amsterdam: John Benjamins.

Coupez, André. 1980. *Abrégé de grammaire rwanda*. Butare: Institut de Recherche Scientifique et Technologique.

Creissels, Denis. 1996. Conjunctive and disjunctive verb forms in Setswana. *South African Journal of African Languages* 16 (4). 109–115.

Creissels, Denis (this volume). Conjoint and disjoint verb forms in Tswana.

Givón, Talmy. 1975. Focus and the scope of assertion: some Bantu evidence. *Studies in African Linguistics* 6(2). 185–205.
Goldsmith, John A. & Fidèle Mpiranya. 2010. Rythm, quantity and tone in the Kinyarwanda verb. In John A. Goldsmith, Elizabeth Hume & Leo Wetzels (eds.), *Tones and features: phonetic and phonological perspectives*, 25–49. Berlin & Boston: Walter de Gruyter.
Güldemann, Tom. 2003. Present progressive vis-à-vis predication focus in Bantu: A verbal category between semantics and pragmatics. *Studies in Language* 27 (2). 323–360.
Halpert, Claire. 2015. *Argument licensing and agreement*. Oxford: Oxford University Press.
Hyman, Larry M. & John R. Watters. 1984. Auxiliary focus. *Studies in African Linguistics* 15(3). 233–273.
Jouannet, Francis. 1985. La variation tonale en Kinyarwanda. In Yves Cadiou (ed.). *Le Kinyarwanda: Etudes de morpho-syntaxe*, 105–139. Paris: Société pour l'information grammaticale.
Kimenyi, Alexandre. 1980. *A relational grammar of Kinyarwanda*. Berkeley: University of California Press.
Kimenyi, Alexandre. 2002. *A tonal grammar of Kinyarwanda: An autosegmental and metrical analysis*. Lewiston, N.Y: The Edwin Mellen Press.
Lambrecht, Knud. 1994. *Information structure and sentence form. Topic, focus and the mental representations of discourse referents*. Cambridge: Cambridge University Press.
Meeussen, Achiel E. 1959. *Essai de grammaire Rundi*. Tervuren: Annales du musée royal du Congo Belge, Série Sciences de l'Homme, Vol. 24.
Ndayiragije, Juvénal. 1999. Checking economy. *Linguistic Inquiry* 30(3). 399–444.
Ngoboka, Jean Paul. 2016. *Locatives in Kinyarwanda*. Durban: University of KwaZulu-Natal PhD thesis.
Ntwari, Gérard (undated). L'inversion du sujet en Kinyarwanda. Ms., Université Laval.
Overdulve, Cornelis-Marinus. 1988. *Précis de grammaire Kinyarwanda*. Kabgayi: Imprimerie de Kabgayi.
Overdulve, Cornelis-Marinus & Irénée Jacob. 1998. *Twige Ikinyarwaanda: Manuel d'apprentissage de la langue rwandaise*. Kigali: Pallotti Press.
Philippson, Gérard. 1998. Tone reduction vs. metrical attraction in the evolution of Eastern Bantu tone systems. In Larry Hyman & Charles W. Kisseberth (eds.), *Theoretical aspects of Bantu tone*, 315–329. Stanford: CSLI.
Shimamungu, Eugène-Marie. 1991. *Systématique verbo-temporelle du Kinyarwanda*. Lille: Ecole Nationale des Arts et Métiers.
Sibomana, Leonidas. 1974. *Deskriptive Tonologie des Kinyarwanda*. Hamburg: Helmut Buske Verlag.
Van der Spuy, Andrew. 1993. Dislocated noun phrases in Nguni. *Lingua* 90. 335–355.
Van der Wal, Jenneke. 2009. Word order and information structure in Makhuwa-Enahara. Utrecht: University of Leiden Ph.D. thesis (LOT dissertation series).
Van der Wal, Jenneke. 2011. Focus excluding alternatives: Conjoint/disjoint marking in Makhuwa. *Lingua* 121. 1734–1750.
Van der Wal, Jenneke. 2014. Subordinate clauses and exclusive focus in Makhuwa. In Rik van Gijn, Jeremy Hammond, Dejan Matić, Saskia van Putten & Ana Vilacy Galucio (eds.), *Information structure and reference tracking in complex sentences*, 45–70. Amsterdam: John Benjamins.
Voeltz, F.K.E. 2004. Long and short verb forms in Zulu. Ms., University of Cologne.

following word (*'forme mettant en évidence le mot suivant'*), while the disjoint has no special relation with the following word if any (*'forme sans rapport spécial avec un mot suivant éventuel'*) (Meeussen 1959: 109). He also observed that semantically speaking, the conjoint seems to signal a principal relation between different elements of a situation expressed by different clause constituents (verb, object, subject) and that it refers, for instance, to an action which a given agent normally and exclusively performs on a given object (*'Au point de vue du sens, le conjoint semble indiquer une relation de principe entre les divers éléments de situation indiqués par les formes qui figurent dans la proposition (verbe, objet, sujet); il indiquera donc par ex. une action que tel agent effectue normalement et exclusivement sur tel objet'*), while the disjoint rather signals a factual relation: an action, which if it is performed on an object, but could equally well be performed on any other constituent (*'Le disjoint indique une relation de fait: une action qui, si elle porte sur un objet, pourrait porter tout aussi bien sur un autre'*) (Meeussen 1959: 215–216). At the same time, he admitted that the use and the meaning of the conjoint and disjoint forms would need to be studied more closely, preferably by a grammarian from Burundi itself, given the delicate nature of this distinction (*'L'emploi et le sens des formes de conjoint et de disjoint devront être étudiés de plus près, de préférence par un grammairien du Burundi même, vu le caractère délicat de cette distinction'*) (Meeussen 1959: 216). Ever since, several Burundian linguists have shed their light on the conjoint/disjoint alternation in Kirundi (Sabimana 1986; Ndayiragije 1999; Bukuru 2003). Their accounts are partial, since they are part of more comprehensive studies devoted to other topics, and they also contradict each other in certain respects. Moreover, they are exclusively based on elicited data, which do not always excel in naturalness. Since several other authors have reused their evidence for comparative purposes, it might be beneficial to put a number of commonly reiterated assumptions regarding the conjoint/disjoint alternation in Kirundi to the test of a natural language corpus.

That is why in this chapter we intend to provide an in-depth description of the conjoint/disjoint alternation in Kirundi on the basis of a large text corpus that was compiled by Ferdinand Mberamihigo – with the help of his co-supervisor Gilles-Maurice de Schryver – as part of the joint UGent-ULB PhD research which he completed in 2014. This unannotated Kirundi corpus used for this study counts 1,918,292 tokens and covers a period of a bit more than 70 years, i.e. between 1940 and 2012. It comprises both written and oral texts pertaining to different topics, such as justice, law, education, literature, music, culture, history, etc. (Mberamihigo 2014: 54–66). The whole corpus is electronically perusable with dedicated corpus querying software, such as *WordSmith Tools*, which has been done for this chapter by the first author who is a native speaker.

In contrast to the PhD dissertation of Mberamihigo (2014) and related studies, such as de Schryver and Nabirye (2010) and Kawalya et al. (2014), the present chapter is not truly 'corpus-driven' in the sense that the corpus itself has not been considered to be the exclusive source of assumptions about Kirundi. Similar to earlier grammatical Bantu studies using corpora, for example de Schryver and Gauton (2002) and Bostoen et al. (2012), it is rather 'corpus-based' in that the corpus was combined with other methods, such as introspection and elicitation or consultation with native speakers. Along with introspection by the first author, a first elicitation of data was undertaken by means of the *Potsdam Questionnaire on Information Structure (QUIS)* (Skopeteas et al. 2006). All preliminary hypotheses emerging from this preparatory exercise were subsequently checked and further substantiated and refined on the basis of the Kirundi text corpus. Consequently, some exceptions notwithstanding, the evidence presented in this chapter is corpus data reflecting spontaneous language use. For each example it is indicated from which text it stems, to which genre it belongs and in which decade it was produced. The first line of each example represents a corpus extract in its original spelling, except for the surface phonemic tones, which we systematically added following the conventions used in the grammar of Meeussen (1959). The interlinear glossing is given below and is followed by a free English translation, which remains as closely as possible to the original. The tones noted in the morphological analysis on the second line are the underlying lexical or grammatical ones.

In Section 4 of this chapter, we make a case for the abolition of the conjoint/disjoint alternation in the analysis of Kirundi. We contest its empirical foundation in Kirundi on both morphological and functional grounds. However, because the conjoint/disjoint alternation has been recognized as part of Kirundi grammar ever since Meeussen (1959) and this chapter is part of a collective volume dedicated to this distinction in Bantu, we first describe it as thoroughly as possible assuming that it really exists. In Section 2, we first present an overview of the allomorphy's distribution in Kirundi's verb conjugation system and describe its segmental and supra-segmental features. In Section 3, we demonstrate that the conjoint/disjoint alternation is not directly conditioned by constituency and then examine how it correlates with different focus structures and word order types: object and adjunct focus after the verb (3.1), subject focus after the verb (3.2), predicate-centred focus (3.3), sentence focus (3.4), and topic-comment focus structure (3.5).

2 Distribution and formal marking of the conjoint/disjoint alternation

The conjoint/disjoint alternation has a limited distribution in the Kirundi verbal conjugational system. It can be morphologically signalled in only three conjugations, i.e. the present, the near past and the remote past, in both the indicative and conjunctive mood.[1] It is actually only the disjoint that is explicitly marked by means of a dedicated segmental morpheme, i.e. *-ra-* in the present (1) and the remote past (2) and *-a-* in the near past (3). This disjoint marker is added to the tense marker, which also occurs in the conjoint. Tense markers are *-ø-* for the present, *-a-* for the near past and *-á-* for the remote past. The following examples illustrate the morphological marking of the disjoint on the main verb of the main clause.

(1) Disjoint in the present indicative
Leeta irafásha mu gutáanga amafaráanga [...][2]
ø-leeta i-ø-ra-fásh-a mu ku-táang-a a-ma-faráanga
9-State 9SM-PRS-DJ-help-IPFV 18LOC 15-give-FV AUG-6-money
'The State helps by giving money [...].' (*Igitabu c'amatégeko*, law, 2000s)

(2) Disjoint in the remote past indicative
[...] yaráteeye akáamo abéenegíhugu bó mu Kiruundo [...]
a-á-ra-téer-ye[3] a-ka-áamo a-ba-éenegíhugu ba-ó mu Kirundo
1SM-REM.PST-DJ-launch-PFV AUG-12-call AUG-2-inhabitant 2-REF 18LOC Kirundo
'[...] he launched a call to the inhabitants of Kirundo [...].' (*Senate 1004–33*, politics, 2010s)

(3) Disjoint in the near past indicative
Ma, naabóonye Bikíra Mariyá [...]
ma N-a-a-bón-ye Bikíra Mariyá
mother 1SG.SM-N.PST-DJ-see-PFV virgin Mary
'Mother, I have seen the virgin Mary [...].' (*Ndongozi 5503*, religion, 1950s)

The next three examples show the corresponding conjoint forms. They bear the same tense and aspect markers as their equivalent disjoint form, but unlike the

---

[1] Verbs in the conjunctive mood designate an action associated with another in terms of conditionality, simultaneity, opposition, concession, etc. In Kirundi, this conjunction is marked by an initial high tone which is generally realized on the syllable following the subject prefix (Meeussen 1959: 109; Cristini 2000: 166–167).
[2] As shown in (1), the disjoint form is not incompatible with locative adverbials in Kirundi, unlike what Givón (1975: 194) claims for closely related Kinyarwanda.
[3] The high tone of the remote past marker is usually shifted one syllable to the right.

latter, they do not carry a dedicated conjoint morpheme. As for the near past conjoint form in (6), the vowel following the subject concord is short in contrast to the corresponding disjoint form in (3), where it is long due to the presence of the disjoint marker -a-.

(4) Conjoint in the present indicative
Nkomeza-magúfa ifasha umutíma waawe [...]
N-komer-i-a ma-gúfa i-ø-ø-fásh-a u-mu-tíma u-aawe
9-be.strong-CAUS-FV 6-bone 9SM-PRS-CJ-help-IPFV AUG-3-heart 3-your(SG)
'Carbohydrate helps your heart [...].' (*Vitamin D & Calcium*, health, 2000s)

(5) Conjoint in the remote past indicative
[...] yatéeye akáamo abanyeepolitiíke [...]
a-á-ø-téer-ye⁴ a-ka-áamo a-ba-nyeepolitiíke
1SM-REM.PST-CJ-launch-PFV AUG-12-call AUG-2-politician
[...] he launched a call to the politicians [...].' (*Senate 1004–33*, politics, 2010s)

(6) Conjoint in the near past indicative
[...] naboonye ikirúta ikiíndi.
N-a-ø-bón-ye i-ki-ø-rút-a^H i-ki-iíndi
1SG.SM-N.PST-CJ-see-PFV AUG-7-PRS-surpass-FV.REL AUG-7-other
'[...] I have seen what surpasses the other.' (*Agashitsi*, theatre, 1990s)

To mark the contrast with the disjoint and in line with Kirundi grammar conventions, we have glossed the conjoint in the examples (4) to (6) as -ø- for the time being. The conjoint forms above are tonally marked though. If one compares the conjoint verbs in (4) and (6) with their corresponding disjoint forms in (1) and (3), one observes that the lexical high tone of the verb is deleted in the conjoint forms. This high tone deletion signals a closer phonological link between the verb and its complement and has been reported in other Bantu languages (Hyman and Byarushengo 1984; Bickmore 1990; Zerbian 2004; Patin 2007). Although this needs further research, we assume that it is a prosodic effect that could be interpreted in terms of phonological phrasing rather than as a dedicated conjoint marker. It is only identifiable on lexically high verbs, in contrast to the disjoint affix, which marks all verbs irrespective of their lexical tone. Nevertheless, as we discuss below, this prosodic marker ties in perfectly well with the discursive function of the conjoint. It is well known that unlike the disjoint, the conjoint can

---

4 The high tone of the remote past marker is realized here on the first mora of the long vowel of the verb root whose inherently high tone has been deleted because of the high tone deletion rule associated with the conjoint.

neither be final in a main affirmative clause nor be separated from the following constituent by a pause (Meeussen 1959: 215).

Due to this high tone deletion, it is possible to observe an alternation which could be conceived as conjoint/disjoint in two verb conjugations actually not having an overt disjoint affix, i.e. the Potential marked by *-oo-* and the Subsecutive marked by *-ka-*. In these conjugations, a form maintaining the lexical high tone of the verb root can be opposed to a form in which this high tone is deleted, as shown in (7) vs. (8) for the Potential and (9) vs. (10) for the Subsecutive. In (8), the Potential verb *noomutoora* and the following question word *hé* 'where?' constitute a prosodic unit thanks to the deletion of the verb's lexical high tone which does surface in the potential verb *vyootóora* in (7).

(7) *Ibihúgu bishizé hamwé umweéte vyoot<u>ó</u>ora ivyó abanyágihúgu bakenéye.*
    i-bi-húgu   bi-shír-ye^H ha-mwé u-mu-eéte bi-oo-tóor-a
    AUG-8-country 8SM-put-PFV.REL[5] 16-one AUG-3-zeal 8SM-POT-find-IPFV
    i-bi-ó   a-ba-nyágihúgu   ba-kener-ye^H
    AUG-8-REF[6] AUG-2-population 2SM-need-PFV.REL
    'The countries which unite zeal may find what the population needs.' (*Inzira*, politics, 2000s)

(8) *Mbeéga uwoóza akúruta mu bwíizá nó mu bwíitoonzi noomut<u>o</u>ora hé?*
    mbeéga u-u-oo-əz-a^H a^H-ku-rut-a   mu   bu-íizá   nó
    QW   AUG-1-POT-come-IPFV.REL 1SM.CJC[7]-2SG.OM-surpass-IPFV 18LOC 14-beauty and
    mu   bu-íitoonzi   N-oo-mu-tóor-a   hé
    18LOC 14-sweetness 1SG.SM-POT-1OM-find-IPFV where
    'Where can I find the one who can beat you in beauty and in sweetness?' (*Rumarantimba*, theatre, 1980s)

The Subsecutive verb *bakabáana* in (9) maintains its lexical high tone and does not constitute a prosodic unit with the locative phrase by which it is followed.

---

[5] Some relative verb forms in Kirundi are characterized by what Meeussen (1959: 109) calls a "*ton postradical*", i.e. a high tone which is most often realized on a morpheme following the verb root, either on the extension or – in its absence – on the final vowel. We mark it as ^{H} in verb-final position independently of where it occurs on the surface.
[6] We label the morpheme -**o** as REF, since it is the common Bantu "-o of reference" (Ashton et al. 1954: 41; Dammann 1977; Van der Spuy 1993: 18). In Kirundi, it occurs, among others, in the anaphoric demonstrative, a.k.a. "*démonstratif II*", and in the so-called "*précessif*" which is homophonous except for the final high tone and actually is an independent demonstrative whose sole function is to serve as the antecedent to an object relative (Meeussen 1959: 91–92, 97–98).
[7] The conjunctive mood is characterized by a high tone which is realized either on the subject prefix or on the following syllable if the subject prefix consists of a single segment (Meeussen 1959: 125).

(9) Babwiirizwa gutaahuuka mu ngó záabo bakab*a*ana mu mahóro.
 ba-ø-ø-bwíirizw-a ku-tahuuk-a mu N-gó zi-áabo
 2SM-PRS-CJ-must-IPFV 15-return-FV 18LOC 10-homestead 10-their
 ba-ka-bá-an-a mu ma-hóro
 2SM-SUBS-live-ASSOC-IPFV 18LOC 6-peace
 'They must return to their homesteads and live together in peace.' (*GLO881*, politics, 1990s)

In (10) the same Subsecutive verb does form a prosodic unit with the locative phrase that follows, which is reflected in the deletion of its lexical high tone.

(10) *Náahó Abatuutsi babaandáanya kubá mu makaámbi, Abahutú biipfuuza kó bootaahá bakab*a*ana mu mihana iwaábo.*
 N'áahó a-ba-tuutsi ba-baandáany-a ku-bá-a mu ma-kaámbi
 even.if AUG-2-Tutsi 2SM-continue-IPFV 15-live-FV 18LOC 6-camp
 a-ba-hutú ba-ø-ø-íipfuuz-a kó ba-oo-taah-a[H]
 AUG-2-Hutu 2SM-PRS-CJ-wish-IPFV that 2SM-POT-return-IPFV.REL
 ba-ka-bá-an-a mu mi-hana i-aábo
 2SM-SUBS-live-ASSOC-IPFV 18LOC 4-household 4-their
 'Even if the Tutsi go on living in the (refugee) camps, the Hutu want them to be able to return and to live together in their households.' (*WTF_Kahise*, health, 2010s)

This tonal distinction is only identifiable with Potential and Subsecutive verbs having a lexical high tone. We therefore will not consider it as a true conjoint/disjoint alternation, even if this tonal pattern is also observed in the present, near past and remote past conjugations, which do have an overt disjoint marker. We still include both conjugations in Table 1 below, which presents an overview of formal conjoint/disjoint marking, especially because from a pragmatic point of view tonally distinct Potential and Subsecutive verbs behave similarly to those conjugations having a segmental conjoint/disjoint distinction (cf. infra).

In all other Kirundi verb conjugations, neither overt morphological disjoint marking nor distinctive prosodic effects are observed. Such is, for instance, the case with the subjunctive and the gerundive which are characterized by a distinctive tone pattern, i.e. the so-called "*ton postradical*", as well as with future verbs whose roots are automatically low (cf. Meeussen 1959: 106). Hence, whether the future verb is immediately followed by a constituent, as in (11), or is in sentence-final position, as in (12), no prosodic distinction can be made in terms of phonological phrasing. In both cases, the lexical high tone of -*bón*- 'see' is deleted. The phrase-final future verb in (12) does not carry a disjoint affix either, this in contrast to the present tense verb form *aragoowe* earlier in the phrase.

Table 1: Conjoint/disjoint marking in the conjugations where the alternation is observed.

Conjugation	TAM-marker	Disjoint	Conjoint
Present	-ø-	-ra- / +lexical H	-ø- / -lexical H
Near past	-a-	-a- / +lexical H	-ø- / -lexical H
Remote past	-á-	-ra- / +lexical H	-ø- / -lexical H
Potential	-oo-	-ø- / +lexical H	-ø- / -lexical H
Subsecutive	-ka-	-ø- / +lexical H	-ø- / -lexical H

(11) *Umuuntu weése azoobona ubukíriro bwa Muúngu.*
u-mu-ntu u-ése a-zoo-(*-ra/a-)-bón-a u-bu-kíriro bu-a Mungu
AUG-1-person 1-all 1SM-FUT-(*DJ)-see-IPFV AUG-14-salvation 14-CONN God
'Every person will receive God's salvation.' (*Yaga*, religion, 1960s)

(12) *Udáhiiríwe aragoowe utáraapfá azoobona.*
u-u-ta-híiriw-ye a-ø-ra-goorw-ye
AUG-1-NEG-be.happy-PFV 1SM-PRS-DJ-be.unhappy-PFV
u-u-ta-ráa-pfú-a a-zoo-(*-ra/a-)bón-a
AUG-1-NEG-INCP-die-IPFV 1SM-FUT-(*DJ)-see-IPFV
'The one who is not happy is unhappy; the one who is not dead yet will see.'
(*NiAgasaga*, theatre, 1960s)

The conjoint/disjoint alternation is also incompatible with negative verbs and relative clauses in Kirundi. Neither an overt disjoint marker nor tonal contrasts are observed in these conjugations that have their own distinctive tone pattern. The negative present also has a characteristic verb-final high tone (Meeussen 1959: 136), which surfaces on the final vowel of the negative present verb in (13). The lexical high tone of -*úumv*- 'to hear' is not present. Exactly the same verb form with the same tone pattern is observed when it is sentence-final, as in (14).

(13) *Ntimwumvá iyo mvúra iríko irasuuma?*
nti-mu-ø-(*-ra-)úumv-a^H i-o N-vúra i-ø-ri^H-kó
NEG-2PL.SM-PRS-(*DJ)-hear-IPFV 9-DEM$_b$ 9-rain 9SM-PRS-be.REL-17RM
i-ø-ra-suum-a
9SM-PRS-DJ-swhish-IPFV
'Don't you hear that swishing rain?' (*Kw'isoko_2011_13*, religion, 2010s)

(14)   Petero Nkurunziza arabábwira ntímwumvá.
       [...] a-ra-ø-(*-ra-)ba-bwír-a   ntí-mu-ø-(*-ra-)úumv-a^H
       [...] 1SM-DJ-PRS-(*DJ)-2PL.OM-say-IPFV   NEG-2PL.SM-PRS-(*DJ)-hear-IPFV
       'Peter Nkurunziza tells you, (but) you do not understand.' (*Itsitso_2011*, politics, 2010s)

Simple relative verbs also have a fixed tone pattern whether they are followed by a constituent, as in (15), or not, as in (16).

(15)   Hari abaryáama amasahá maké [...]
       ha-ri   a-ba-ø-(*-ra-)ryáam-a^H   a-ma-sahá   ma-ké
       16SM-be   AUG-2-PRS-(*DJ)-sleep-IPFV.REL AUG-6-hour   6-few
       'There are those who sleep few hours [...]' (*Imbonesha 119*, lifestyle, 2010s)

(16)   Mubarire agabúrire abáana níngoga kugíra babisé abaryáama.
       mu-bár-ir-e   a-gabúr-ir-e   a-ba-áana   níngoga
       1OM-say-APPL-IMP   1SM-feed-APPL-SUBJ   AUG-2-child rapidly
       kugíra   ba-bís-é   a-ba-ø-(*-ra-)ryáam-a^H
       so.that 2SM-give.place-SUBJ   AUG-2-PRS-(*DJ)-sleep-IPFV.REL
       'Tell him to feed the children rapidly so that they can give place to those who sleep.'

Simple relative clauses are not the only type of subordinate clauses not allowing for the conjoint/disjoint alternation. Most subordinate clauses have a verb that is formally identical to conjoint verbs in the main clause. Only subordinate verbs in the conjunctive mood can take a disjoint marker. Only direct speech clauses introduced by the quotative *ngo* allow disjoint-marking, as shown in (17). This indicates that these are rather to be considered as main clauses in contrast to indirect speech clauses introduced by the complementizer *ko* whose verb cannot be disjoint-marked, as *yabáaye* 'it has been' in (18).

(17)   Bamwé baravúga ngo turúumviikanye; abaándi ngo ntiharáagera.
       ba-mwé   ba-á-ra-vúg-a   ngo   tu-ø-ra-úumviik-an-ye
       2-one   2SM-REM.PST-DJ-say-IPFV   QUOT   1PL.SM-PRS-DJ-hear-ASSOC-IPFV
       a-ba-ndi   ngo   nti-ha-ráa-ger-a
       AUG-2-other   QUOT   NEG-16SM-INCP-arrive-IPFV
       'Some said 'we have just agreed with each other'; others said 'the moment has not yet come'.' (*Mushingantahe*, peace, 2000s)

(18) *Umuuntu yoovuga kó iyo Kómiíne yabáaye akarorero keezá mu vyeérekeye amagúme igihúgu gihitiyemwó.*

u-mu-ntu	a-oo-vúg-a	kó	i-o	kómiíne	i-á-(*-ra-)bá-ye
AUG-1-person	1SM-POT-say-IPFV	that	9-DEM$_b$	commune	9SM-REM.PST-(*DJ)-be-PFV
a-ka-rorero	ka-izá	mu	bi-éereker-ye		a-ma-gúme
AUG-12-example	12-good	18LOC	8SM-concern-PFV		AUG-6-crisis
i-ki-húgu	ki-ø-hítir-ye^H-mwó				
AUG-7-country	7SM-PRS-pass-PFV.REL-18RM				

'Someone would say that this municipality has been a good example concerning the crisis through which the country has just gone.' (*Mushingantahe*, peace, 2000s)

3 Functional conditioning of the conjoint/disjoint alternation

The conjoint has been characterized in Kirundi as a 'weak' form, which cannot express a complete thought on its own, but rather serves as an element introducing a constituent that follows. The *'infixe dynamiseur'* or disjoint, on the contrary, has been staged as a 'strong' form, which is capable of expressing a complete thought without being followed by an additional constituent (Ntahokaja 1994: 147). A conjoint verb cannot be clause-final in a main clause. A disjoint verb form can be clause-final, but does not need to be. Different types of clause constituents may follow it. As in closely related Kinyarwanda (Ngoboka and Zeller this volume), the adverb *caane* 'much, very, strongly, really' may occur after a disjoint verb, as in (19).

(19) *Unó muúsi ndanéezerewe caane n'úkó nashitse ngaáha i waányu.*

u-nó	mu-si	N-ø-ra-néezerw-ye	caane	na	u-ku-ó
3-DEM$_b$	3-day	1SG.SM-PRS-DJ-be.happy-PVF	really	with	AUG-15-REF
N-a-shik-ye	ngaáha	i	u-anyu		
1SG.SM-N.PST-arrive-PFV	here	19LOC	3-your(PL)		

'Today I am really happy with the fact that I have arrived here at your place.' (*Ijambo Bagaza*, politics, 1970s)

Nevertheless, unlike in Kinyarwanda (Ngoboka and Zeller this volume), not only adverbs, but also other constituents occur after disjoint verbs, as is clearly shown in the first three examples of this chapter. A disjoint verb form is followed there by a locative in (1) and an object in (2) and (3). Nothing indicates that these post-verbal constituents are extra-clausal. Prosodically, they are not preceded by a pause or marked by any other clear boundary, except that the lexical high tone of the preceding verb is not deleted as happens in conjoint verb forms (cf. supra).

Morphosyntactically, objects following a disjoint verb are not co-referenced by object prefixes on the verb, which would need to be the case if they were outside the clause. Object prefixes function as true pronouns in Kirundi in that they can only refer to aforementioned or dislocated objects. Object topicalization – both left and right topics – triggers obligatory object marking on the verb (Bukuru 1998, 2003: 244, 261). Hence, the presence of an object prefix requires a co-referential full object noun phrase to be extra-clausal, also if it follows the verb, as in (20). This example is grammatical, because the verb form is disjoint and can be clause-final. The extra-clausal interpellation *mwa mbwá mwe* 'you dogs', co-referential with the object prefix on the verb, occurs in the right periphery of clause and is preceded by a pause.

(20) *Ndabáshoboye, mwa mbwá mwe!*
   N-ø-ra-ba-shóbor-ye,   mwaa   N-bwá   mwe
   1SG.SM-PRS-DJ-2PL.OM-fool -PVF you 10-dog you.VOC
   'I have fooled you, you dogs!' (*Igiti*, theatre, 2010s)

In (21), both the subject *jeewé* 'me' and object *icáaboná* 'witness' are left-dislocated. They are co-referenced by respectively a subject prefix and an object prefix on the disjoint verb *naakizanye* 'I have come with' and the object once more on the final infinitive *kukiroondera* 'to look for one'.

(21) *Jeewé, icáaboná, naakizanye ni wé agisigáye kukiroondera.*
   jeewé i-ki-áabóna   N-a-a-ki-əz-an-ye   ni   wé
   me   AUG-7-witness   1SG.SM-N.PST-DJ-7OM-come-ASSOC-PFV   COP   him
   a-ki-sígar-ye[H]   ku-ki-roonder-a
   1SM-PERS-remain-PVF.REL   15-7OM-search-FV
   'As for me, a witness, I have brought one along, it is him [the opponent] who still has to look for one [i.e. a witness]'. (*Umusozi kivyeyi*, peace, 1990s)

In contrast, the sentence in (6), repeated below as (22), becomes ungrammatical, if one adds an object prefix to the conjoint verb form. The object prefix indicates that the post-verbal object must be outside the clause and the conjoint verb becomes clause-final, which is not allowed.

(22) ****nakiboonye, ikirúta ikiíndi.*
   N-a-ø-(*ki-)bón-ye   i-ki-ø-rút-a   i-ki-iíndi
   1SG.SM-N.PST-CJ-(*7OM-)see-PFV   AUG-7-PRS-surpass-FV   AUG-7-other
   '[…] I have seen what surpasses the other.' (adapted from *Agashitsi*, theatre, 1990s)

Examples such as (1)-(3), indicate that disjoint verb forms do not need to be clause-final. Like conjoint verbs forms, they can also occur in non-final position. The information structure of the sentence in (3), adapted here in (23), becomes totally different, if one adds an object prefix to the disjoint verb form. The post-verbal object *Bikíra Mariyá* is then placed outside the clause and can no longer be part of the focal information, as is the case in (3) (cf. infra). The disjoint would then receive a predicate-centred focus reading, for instance because its lexical meaning is contrasted with that of a previously mentioned verb.

(23)   *Ma, naamubóonye, Bikíra Mariyá [...]*
       ma   N-a-a-mu-bón-ye   Bikíra   Mariyá
       mother   1SG.SM-N.PST-DJ-1OM-see-PFV   virgin   Mary
       'Mother, I (really) have seen the virgin Mary [...].' (adapted from *Ndongozi 5503*, religion, 1950s)

The fact that both conjoint and disjoint verb forms may occur in non-final clause position in Kirundi seems to indicate that, unlike in the Nguni languages (Van der Spuy 1993; Buell 2006), the alternation is not a direct reflex of constituency, and also much less syntactically conditioned than in its closest relative Kinyarwanda (Ngoboka and Zeller this volume). It is therefore worthwhile examining more closely whether information structure is more fundamental in defining the alternation, as is for instance the case in Makhuwa (Van der Wal 2011). The first to account for the Kirundi conjoint/disjoint alternation within a proper information-structural framework were Edenmyr (2001) and Bukuru (2003). Bukuru described it as having to do with the encoding of focus as defined by Trask (1993: 105), i.e. 'a special prominence given to some element in a sentence which represents the most important new information in that sentence or which is explicitly contrasted with something else'. Bukuru (2003: 274) opposes conjoint verb forms as 'complement focus constructions' to disjoint verb forms which he typifies as 'verb phrase focus constructions' in accordance with Givón (1975) who analysed this alternation along similar lines in Chibemba, Kinyarwanda and Isizulu. In the following sub-sections, we will crosscheck Bukuru's analysis on the basis of our Kirundi corpus by examining the use of both conjoint and disjoint verb forms in relation to the 'focal information' in a linguistic expression, i.e. the most important or salient pragmatic information which the hearer has to seize according to the speaker (Dik 1997: 326). Focus can signal 'the presence of alternatives that are relevant for the interpretation of linguistic expressions' (Krifka 2007: 18 following Rooth 1985, 1992). The emphasized piece of information is either entirely new to the addressee or conflicts with an information which he/she previously presumed, i.e. informational or assertive focus versus identificational or contrastive focus (É. Kiss 1998). We do not treat each of these focus types separately, but we do refer to them in what follows.

3.1 Object and adjunct focus: conjoint

The conjoint is obligatory as soon as a post-verbal nominal or adverbial clause constituent conveys the focal information. Kirundi being a canonical SVO language, this constituent is most typically the object. Whether the object represents informational focus, as in (24), or identificational focus, as in (25), it can be focused in its canonical post-verbal position. In (24), the same conjoint verb is repeated in both the question and the answer. The object is both questioned and answered post-verbally. A disjoint verb form in the question would be ungrammatical here. In the answer it would be pragmatically infelicitous, because the scope of the focus would either be extended to the whole verb phrase or shifted to the verb itself (cf. infra).

(24) *Frida: Akora ikí? Carine: Akora utwíiwé.*
 a-ø-ø-kór-a [ikí]^{FOC}? a-ø-ø-kór-a [u-tu-íiwé]^{FOC}
 1SM-PRS-CJ-do-IPFV what 1SM-PRS-CJ-do-IPFV AUG-13-his
 'Frida: WHAT does he do? Carine: He does HIS BUSINESS.' (*Kirezi*, theatre, 1990s)

In (25), two post-verbal objects representing conflicting information are contrastively focused. Both in the question and in the answer a conjoint verb is used. A disjoint verb would also lead to pragmatic inappropriateness here.

(25) *Waménye umubiíndi w'ínzogá (...)? Oya, naménye icupá ry'íbiyéeri.*
 u-á-ø-mén-ye [u-mu-biíndi u-a i-N-yogá]^{FOC}
 2SG.SM-REM.PST-CJ-break-PFV AUG-3-JUG 3-CONN AUG-9-beer
 oya N-á-ø-mén-ye [i-ø-cupá ri-a i-bi-yéeri]^{FOC}
 no 1SG.SM-REM.PST-CJ-break-PFV AUG-5-bottle 5-CONN AUG-8-beer
 'Did you break A JUG OF (TRADITIONAL) BEER? No, I broke A BOTTLE OF (MODERN) BEER.' (*Subiza*, theatre, 1990s)

Other post-verbal constituents, such as the locative phrase *ku wuúndi mugabo* 'from another man' in (26), are also commonly focused in their canonical post-verbal position, in which case they equally require a conjoint verb. In the first clause, the possessive *rwaawé* 'yours' is contrastively focused in a cleft-like identification construction built around the negative copula *si*.

(26)　*Uryá mwáana dufisé si rwaawé. Namúvyaaye ku wuúndi mugabo.*
　　　u-ryá　　mu-áana　tu-ø-fít-ye　　　　si　　　[ru-aawé]^FOC
　　　1-DEM_c　1-child　　1PL.SM-PRS-have-PFV　NEG.COP　11[8]-your(SG)
　　　N-á-ø-mu-vyáar-ye　　　　　　[ku　　u-ú-ndi　　mu-gabo]^FOC
　　　1SG.SM-REM.PST-CJ-1OM-bear-PFV　　[17LOC　AUG-1-other　1-man]
　　　'That child we've got is not YOURS. I gave birth to him FROM ANOTHER MAN.'
　　　(*Kw'isoko_2012_07*, Religion, 2010s)

An intransitive verb is usually disjoint-marked, except when it is followed by a focused adjunct, as is the case for *tugeenda* 'we go' in (27). The constituent focused here is a manner clause in the conjunctive mood making clear how one can reach God. This example was taken from an initiation course for new converts preparing themselves to be baptized. The catechist explains them the ways to reach God.

(27)　*Tugeenda kwaa Dáawé wó mw'iijuru tújaanye n'úmukamá Yeézu.*
　　　tu-ø-ø-geend-a　　　　ku-a　　Dáawé　u-ó　　　mu-a　　i-ø-juru
　　　1PL.SM-PRS-CJ-go-IPFV　17-CONN　Father　1-REF　17-CONN　AUG-5-heaven
　　　[tu^H-ø-gi-an-ye　　　　　　　na　　u-mu-kamá　　Yeézu]^FOC
　　　1PL.SM.CJC-PRS-go-ASSOC-PFV　with　AUG-1-lord　　Jesus
　　　'We go to the Father who is in heaven BY GOING TOGETHER WITH THE LORD JESUS.'
　　　(*Yaga*, religion, 1960s)

If the focused object or adjunct is modified by *gusa* 'only', a conjoint verb form must precede it. Adding a disjoint marker to *yavyáara* 'she gave birth' in (28) would not only be pragmatically inappropriate, but simply ungrammatical. Similarly to what Van der Wal (2011: 1738) observed for Makhuwa, only the conjoint verb form is compatible with exclusive focus on a post-verbal constituent in Kirundi.

(28)　*Aríko yavyáara abakoóbwa gusa.*
　　　aríko　a-á-ø-vyáar-a　　　　　　　　[a-ba-koóbwa　gusa]^FOC
　　　but　　1SM-REM.PST-CJ-give.birth-IPFV　AUG-2-girl　　only
　　　'But she gave birth to GIRLS ONLY.' (*Bugaboburihabwa*, Nouvelles, 1990s)

3.2 Subject focus: conjoint

Kirundi subjects cannot be focused in their canonical pre-verbal position. They are focused either through a subject inversion or with a cleft. A subject

---

[8] All possessive pronouns in Kirundi can take the pronominal prefix of class 11 as default concord marker.

inversion construction is illustrated in (29). The focused logical subject occurs in post-verbal position and the verb takes a class 16 subject prefix. Whereas the *ha-* prefix is canonically a locative concord prefix, it is to be considered here as 'expletive' or 'impersonal'. Ndayiragije (1999) calls this construction the 'null expletive'. In (29), the subject noun phrase *bárya baáheekuuye abavyéeyi* 'those who deprived parents from their children', which follows the expletive verb *haáhemutse* 'betrayed', is contrastively focused. The focal information it conveys contrasts with the subject *bwóoko* 'ethnic group' of the preceding sentence. Such an impersonal verb preceding a focused subject is obligatorily conjoint.

(29) *Ntaa bwóoko bwágararije, ntaa bwóoko bwáahemutse. Haáhemutse bárya baáheekuuye abavyéeyi.*
ntaa [bu-óoko]^FOC bu-á-garariz-ye ntaa [bu-óoko]^FOC
NEG.COP 14-ethnic.group 14SM-REM.PST-revolt-PFV NEG.COP 14-ethnic.group
bu-á-hemuk-ye ha-á-ø-hemuk-ye
14SM-REM.PST-betray-PFV IMPRS-REM.PST-CJ-betray-PFV
[bá-rya ba-á-heekuur-ye^H] a-ba-vyéeyi]^FOC
2-DEM_c 2SM-REM.PST-deprive.from.child-PFV.REL AUG-2-parent
'There is no ETHNIC GROUP which revolted, there is no ETHNIC GROUP which committed treason. THOSE WHO DEPRIVED PARENTS FROM THEIR CHILDREN committed treason.' (*Ijambo.umwami*, politics, 1960s)

If *gusa* 'only' modifies the focused subject, as in (30), the expletive conjoint verb also correlates with exclusivity. Using a disjoint verb here would be ungrammatical. An interviewee stresses here that the aforementioned activity of collecting termites, i.e. *gukomanga*, is traditionally only practiced by men.[9]

(30) *Haákomaanga abagabo gusa.*
ha-á-ø-kómaang-a [a-ba-gabo gusa]^FOC
IMPRS-REM.PST-CJ-beat.the.ground-IPFV AUG-2-man only
'MEN ONLY beat the ground (to gather termites).'(*IragiNdanga*, traditional culture, 2000s)

The impersonal *ha-* construction is most natural in Kirundi with intransitive verbs, such as *-hemuk-* 'betray, commit treason' in (29), or with transitive verbs

---

[9] The verb *-kómaang-* refers here to the specific action of beating or stamping the ground to make termites surface (Rodegem 1970: 232). The verb can only be followed by the objects *ubunyabobo* '(group of) termites' *ikinyabobo* 'termite hill', which are not overt here.

whose object is not overt, as -*kómaang*- 'beat the ground' in (30). It has not been found in the corpus with transitive verbs having an overt object, in contrast to data presented in Sabimana (1986: 57), and copied by Morimoto (2000: 138), i.e. the sentence *hătanze inká Mudúga* 'it was Muduga who donated a cow'. Ndayiragije's (1999) so-called 'transitive expletive construction', which he illustrates with the often-cited example *ha-á-nyôye amatá abâna* 'children (not parents) drank milk' (e.g. Van der Wal 2009: 193; Hamlaoui and Makasso 2015: 56), is rather unnatural and sounds artificial to native speakers, such as the first author. If one wants to use a reversed word order to focus the subject of a transitive verb, OVS is more natural (Sabimana 1986; Ndayiragije 1999; Bukuru 2003). This common Bantu inversion construction, often discussed in the literature, is known as the 'subject-object reversal' (e.g. Kimenyi 1980; Kinyalolo 1991; Morimoto 2000). While it does occur in our Kirundi text corpus, it is – in contrast to the impersonal *ha-* construction – extremely rare. We were only able to retrieve a handful of examples in our text corpus, one of which is presented in (31), where exclusive focus is put on the post-verbal subject *abagabo* 'men' modified by the adverb *gusa* 'only'. Both the conjoint verb and the pre-posed object convey discourse-old information.

(31) *Ayo mazína yavúga abagabo gusa.*[10]
 a-a-o ma-zína a-á-ø-vúg-a [a-ba-gabo gusa]^{FOC}
 AUG-6-DEM$_b$ 6-self-praise.poem 6SM-REM.PST-CJ-speak-IPFV AUG-2-man only
 'MEN ONLY performed those self-praise poems.' (*IragiNdanga*, traditional culture, 2000s)

A much more frequent way to focus the subject of a transitive verb is by means of an identification construction, which can either stand on its own or be part of an encompassing (pseudo-)cleft. In (32), the subject is first questioned through a cleft introduced by the common Bantu copula *ni*. In the answer, the focused subject is preceded by the negative identification marker *atarí*, which signals a strong emphasis excluding all possible alternatives. In both sentences the thus focused subject is the head noun of a simple relative clause in which disjoint-marking is impossible.

---

10 The high tone which surfaces here on the root is not the lexical high tone, but the high tone of the remote past marker which is shifted one syllable to the right, because the subject prefix is a simple vowel cf. *yavúga* '(s)he spoke' vs. *baávuga* 'they spoke'.

(32) Q: *Ni ndé yabásaanze háriíya azá kubábwiira ati ni mugaruke?*
A: *Atari ikete Bulamatari yanyandikiye!*

ni   [ndé] ^{FOC}   a-á-ba-sáang-ye^H   ha-riíya   a^H-ø-əz-a
COP who   1SM-REM.PST-2PL.OM-join-PFV.REL   16-DEM_d 1SM.CJC-PRS-come-IPFV.REL
ku-ba-bwíir-a   a-ti   ni   mu^H-garuk-e^H
15-2PL.OM-say-FV   1SM-QUOT   COP   2PL.SM.CJC-return-SUBJ
atarí   [i-ø-keéte   Bulamataári   a-á-N-aandik-ir-ye^H] ^{FOC}
COP   AUG-5-letter governor   1SM-REM.PST-1SG.OM-wrote-APPL-PFV.REL

Q: 'WHO is it that has come to find you there telling you that you should go back?'
A: 'It is NOTHING BUT THE LETTER THAT THE GOVERNOR WROTE ME!' (*Mushingantahe*, peace, 2000s)

3.3 Predicate-centred focus: disjoint

If no specific nominal or adverbial clause constituent is targeted, but the predicate itself is narrowly focused, the use of a disjoint verb form is compulsory. 'Predicate' is understood here in the strict sense, namely as '[a] verb, or a complex structure consisting of a verb or auxiliary plus a closely bound meaningful element, when this is considered as a linguistic unit which can or must combine with specified arguments or participant roles to make up a clause' (Trask 1993: 213). The disjoint can either single out the verb lexeme itself or an operator expressing polarity, time, aspect, or modality that is associated with the verb. In (33), the disjoint verb *rirarima* 'it farms' conveys the new information given in answer to the preceding question. While the disjoint marker in the answer signals assertive focus exclusively on the verb lexeme, the conjoint verbs in the question and the preceding sentences are associated with focused objects.

(33) A: *Jeewé niitwa Ntezukwigira Imelda, nkaba ndí mw'iishírahámwe ry'ábahuuzaki- yaago.*
B: *Ryó rikora ikí?*
A: *Rirarima.*

jeewé   N-ø-ø-iít-u-a   [Ntezukwigira Imelda]^{FOC}   N-ka-bá-a
me   1SG.SM-PRS-CJ-call-PASS-IPFV   Ntezukwigira Imelda   1SG.SM-SUBS-be-IPFV
N-ø-rí   mu   i-ø-shírahámwe   ri-a   a-ba-huuzakiyaago.
1SG.SM-PRS-be   18LOC   AUG-5-association 5-CONN   AUG-2-equal.minded
ri-ó   ri-ø-ø-kór-a   [ikí]^{FOC}   [ri-ø-ra-rim-a]^{FOC}
5-REF   5SM-PRS-CJ-do-IPFV   what   5SM-PRS-DJ-cultivate-IPFV

A: 'Me, my name is Ntezukwigira Imelda and I am part of an association of equal-minded people.'
B: 'And what does it do?'
A: 'It farms.' (*Mushingantahe*, peace, 2000s)

In (34), the lexical meaning 'comb (the hair)' highlighted by the disjoint marker *-ra-* in *arawúsokoza* does not represent new information asserted against a neutral background, but rather a conflicting value realized against a non-neutral background (Hyman and Watters 1984: 240). It contrasts with the previously mentioned verb phrases *-hiinga imishatsi* 'plait hair' and *-tobora amatwí* 'pierce ears'. Identification focus on this disjoint verb serves here to exclude alternatives that matter for a correct interpretation of the utterance (Krifka 2007: 18; Van der Wal 2011: 1734). The idea of exclusion is reinforced by the clause-initial presence of the adverb *ahuúbwo* 'rather'. It contextually contrasts the unit that follows and is considered to be the most salient in the disclosure of information with earlier given alternatives now excluded from the focal domain.

(34) *Nta Muruúndikazi w'ukurí arí kumwé n'úmugeenzi wíiwé ahiinga imishatsi cáanké agatóbora amatwí ; ahuúbwo, arawúsokoza, akawúgira néezá.*

ntaa   mu-ruúndikazi   u-a   ukurí a-ri^H ku-mwé   na
NEG.COP 1-Burundian.woman 1-CONN truth 1SM-be.REL   17-one   with
u-mu-geenzi u-íiwe   a-ø-hiing-a^H i-mi-shatsi   cáanké
AUG-1-friend 1-her   1SM-PRS-plait-IPFV.REL AUG-4-hair   or
a-ka-tóbor-a   a-ma-twí
1SM-SUBS-pierce-IPFV   AUG-6-ear
[ahuúbwo   a-ø-ra-wú-sokoz-a]^{FOC} a-ka-wú-gir-a   néezá
rather   1SM-PRS-DJ-3OM[11]-comb-IPFV   1SM-SUBS-3OM-do-IPFV well

'There is no genuine Burundian woman who, while being with her friend, plaits hair or pierces ears; she will rather COMB IT and (subsequently) take care of it well.' (*Ndongozi5503 Usumbura*, information, 1950s)

In (35) alternatives are excluded by the adverb *gusa* 'only' modifying here the verb *turanyóoye* 'we drink', whose disjoint marker signals exclusive focus here.

---

[11] The 3OM *-wu-* refers here to *umushatsi*, the singular of the previously mentioned *imishatsi*. The singular and plural are interchangeably used in Kirundi to designate a person's hair.

(35) Ehe ntaa co turiiyé, turanyóoye gusa.
Ehe ntaa ki-ó tu-rí-ye^H tu-ø-ra-nyó-ye gusa
so NEG.COP 7-REF 1PL.SM-eat-PFV.REL 1PL.SM-PRS-DJ-drink-PFV only
'So, there is nothing that we eat, we DRINK ONLY.' (*Agashitsi*, drama, 1990s)

Also in (36), the lexical meaning of the disjoint verb *haratéze* 'it is very flat' displaying locative agreement is contrastively focused. This example is excerpted from a story on Burundian regions in which some of them are described as being hilly. Several regions share this landscape feature until you pass Mukinya and arrive in Bweru, which is rather flat. In the last sentence, the previously mentioned locative phrase *mu Bwéeru* is topicalized. This results in an (intransitive) locative inversion construction characterized by locative subject agreement, in this case on the focused disjoint verb. The class 18 locative phrase triggers concordance in class 16, because locative agreement has been levelled to this class in Kirundi. Locative inversion is a common Bantu inversion construction in which a locative phrase is preposed and the subject is postverbal. The preposed locative phrase triggers subject agreement on the verb, while the status of the inverted subject is typical of neither subjects nor objects (Bresnan and Kanerva 1989: 2).

(36) Ni kó hamezé kugeza uréenze ku Mukinyá, ugashika mu Bgeru. Mu Bgeru haratéze cane kand'imyonga yaho si myinshi.
ni ku-ó ha-mer-ye^H kugeza u-réeng-ye ku Mukinyá
COP 15-REF 16SM-be-PFV.REL until 2SG.SM-pass-PFV 17LOC Mukinyá
u-ka-shik-a mu Bwéeru mu Bwéeru [ha-ra-tég-ye
2SG.SM-SUBS-arrive-IPFV 18LOC Bweeru 18LOC Bweeru 16SM-DJ-be.flat-PFV
caane]^FOC kándi i-mi-óonga i-áaho si mi-ínshi
very and AUG-4-creek 4-its NEG.COP 4-many
'That is how it is until you pass Mukinya and arrive in Bweru. In Bweru IT IS VERY FLAT and the creeks are not plentiful.' (*Imigani*, stories, 1940s)

The disjoint can also express verbal 'truth focus' (Güldemann 2003: 330). Such is the case in (37), where the disjoint marker *-ra-* in *baárafáshije* 'they did help' highlights the positive truth-value of the assertion that traditional councillors or *Bashingantahe* had helped during a crisis. This had been questioned in the preceding interrogative sentence where the relative verb *baáfashije* is part of a presentative construction introduced by the locative copula *hari* 'there is'. The truth-value focus, signalled by the disjoint form, is reinforced here by the presence of the emphatic adverb *kóko* 'obviously'. The sentence in (19) is another example of truth focus marked by the disjoint and further strengthened by the adverb *caane* 'much, very, strongly, really'.

(37) Q: *Nooné murí aya magúme, abashíingaántahe hári icó baáfashije?*
A: *Abashíingantaáhe kóko baárafáshije.*

nooné mu-rí a-a ma-gúme a-ba-shíingantaáhe ha-ø-ri
QW 18LOC 6-DEM$_a$ 6-crisis AUG-2-traditional.councillor 16SM-PRS-be
i-ki-ó ba-á-fásh-ye^H
AUG-7-REF 2SM-REM.PST-help-PFV.REL
a-ba-shíingaántahe [kóko ba-á-ra-fásh-ye]^{FOC}
AUG-2-traditional.councillor obviously 2SM-REM.PST-DJ-help-PFV

Q: 'Was there anything during that crisis in which the traditional councillors helped?'
A: 'The traditional councillors DID OBVIOUSLY HELP.' (*Mushingantahe*, peace, 2000s)

Apart from truth-value, the disjoint may also signal focus bearing on other predication operators linked with the verb, such as tense, aspect and/or mood. In the corpus, no clear-cut examples of focus pertaining exclusively to tense or aspect were found, but such examples can be easily elicited, as illustrated in (38).

(38) A: *Da! Ndaháaye Kabuura ya maherá?*
B: *Reka, naráyamúhaaye.*

da [N-ø-ra-há-ye]^{FOC} Kabuura a-a ma-herá
father 1SG.SM-PRS-DJ-give-PFV Kabura 6-DEM$_a$ 6-money
rek-a [N-á-ra-ya-mu-há-ye]^{FOC}
leave-IMP 1SG.SM-REM.PST-DJ-6OM-give-PFV

A: 'Father! Do I give this money to Kabura?'
B: 'Leave it, I gave it to him.'

A corpus example conveying verb operator focus in a less straightforward way is the one in (39), where both predicates actually carry a disjoint marker. The alternatives contrasted here do not only pertain to the verbs' respective aspects, i.e. perfective vs. persistive, but also to their lexical meaning. The situation is one whereby a person called Nzorijana is lying on the ground. One of the bystanders wonders whether he is already dead using the verb *gushika* 'arrive' metaphorically. The disjoint marker *-a-* occurs, along with the tense and aspect marker, on the perfective auxiliary *-mar-* that conveys the notion of 'already'. The disjoint primarily indicates here that the focal information pertains to the accomplished status of the action designated by the verb rather than to the action itself, even if it is impossible to separate the two neatly. Another bystander opposes this while using the persistive aspect marker -cáa- conveying the notion of 'still'. Here too, the disjoint marker -ra- bears in the first place on this aspectual predication operator rather than on the verb lexeme. It is needs to be noted that the persistive is always disjoint-marked (Meeussen 1959: 134), which fits well with the fact that its aspectual semantics inherently convey predicate-centred focus.

(39) Q: Nooné yaamaze gushika?
      A: Oya aracáakúba igoónzi.
      nooné   [a-a-a-mar-ye   ku-shik-a]^FOC
      so   1SM-N.PST-DJ-finish-PFV   15-arrive-FV
      oya   [a-ra-cáa-kúb-a   i-ø-goónzi]^FOC
      no   1SM-DJ-PERS-tremble-IPFV   AUG-5-convulsion
      Q: 'So, HAS he ALREADY PASSED AWAY?'
      A: 'No, he IS STILL IN AGONY.' (Gikenye, theatre, 1970s)

The idiomatic expression gukúba igoónzi in (39) specifically refers to the last death spasms of someone in agony. The nominal constituent igoónzi 'convulsion', whose use tends to be restricted to this expression, is to be understood here as 'a closely bound meaningful element' in the sense of Trask (1993: 213) above. It is an inherent part of the focused predicate here rather than an external extra-focal argument combining with it to form a clause. Such idioms constitute an interesting test case for focus, since they bear interpretation only as a whole (Fanselow and Lenertová 2011: 178). The nominal constituent igoónzi 'convulsion' is obligatorily post-verbal and is never focused on its own. It cannot be preceded by a conjoint verb, which would mean that the post-verbal element is either specifically focused or more salient than the verb within the comment (cf. infra).

As evidenced by the examples presented so far in this subsection, disjoint verbs conveying predicate focus tend to be followed by an object or adjunct that is part of the focal information. The corpus contains very few examples of narrowly focused predicates that are not clause-final. This is not surprising, since an object representing given information tends to be pronominalized by a co-referential object prefix on the verb, while discourse-old adjuncts can simply be left out. The disjoint verb arawúsokoza 'she will comb it' in (34) above, for instance, includes the 3OM -wu- referring to the aforementioned umushatsi 'hair'. The removal of old information from after the focused predicate is also observed in the double noun phrase pre-posing construction in (21). Both the subject jeewé 'me' and object icáaboná 'witness' – both discourse-old – are left-dislocated there and co-referenced on the disjoint verb naakizanye conveying the focal information in the first part of the utterance.

In (40), the discourse-old object *abaantu baátiwe* 'invested people' is also right-dislocated and serves to disambiguate the pronominal reference on the disjoint verb *mwaárababóna* 'you saw them', i.e. the class 2 object prefix *-ba-*. The questioning pertains here to the predicate itself.

(40) *Ariko, mwaárababóna, abaantu baátiwe?*
ariko [mu-á-ra-ba-bón-a]^{FOC}   a-ba-ntu   ba-á-tir-u-ye^H
but   2PL.SM-REM.PST-DJ-2OM-see-PFV   AUG-2-person   2PL.SM-REM.PST-invest-PASS-
                                                       PFV.REL
'However, DID YOU SEE them, the people who were invested?' (*Mushingantahe*, peace, 2000s)

Nevertheless, although not commonly attested in the corpus, it is not ungrammatical to leave a discourse-old full object after a narrowly focused disjoint verb, as is shown in (41). This elicited example mimics a spontaneous speech context in which a full object just mentioned, as *inkeende* 'monkey', could be naturally repeated in the following sentence. In the answer, the lexical meaning of the predicate *nariíshe* 'I had killed' is narrowly focused and contrasted with that of *waráriiye* 'you had eaten'. The use of a conjoint verb form in this context would have been infelicitous.

(41) Q: *Nooné wewé ntiwiívugiye ngo waráriiye inkeende!*
      A: *Eka uraámbeesheye, jewe navúze nti nariíshe inkeende.*
nooné wewé nti-u-á-i-vúg-ir-ye   ngo   [u-á-ra-ri-ye
so   you   NEG-2SG.SM-REM.PST-REFL-say-APPL-PFV   QUOT   2SG.SM-REM.PST-DJ-
                                                                       eat-PFV
i-N-keende]^{FOC}   eka   [u-ø-ra-N-béesh-ir-ye]^{FOC}   jeewé
AUG-9-monkey   no   2SG.SM-PRS-DJ-1SG.OM-slander-APPL-PFV   I
N-á-ø-vúg-ye   n-ti   [N-á-ra-ic-ye]^{FOC}   i-N-keende
1SG.SM-REM.PST-DJ-say-PFV   1SG.SM-QUOT   1SG.SM-REM.PST-DJ-kill-PFV   AUG-9-monkey
Q: 'So did you not say yourself that you had eaten a monkey?'
A: 'No, you have slandered me, I said that I HAD KILLED a monkey.'

A narrowly focused disjoint verb can also be followed by a post-verbal constituent that cannot be dislocated, such as *na we* 'with you' in (42). The speaker expresses his amazement that Nuba is dating with – of all persons – Adelin, on whom he and his friends look down. For them, this implies that they have to break with her. In the question-like exclamation, *na Delino* is in exclusive focus, which accounts for the fact that the associative verb form *unywaana* 'you drink with' is conjoint. In the following sentence, the lexical content of the disjoint verb *turacáanye* 'we break' is narrowly focused. The prepositional phrase *na we* 'with you' representing given information is maintained, because the event structure of the preceding associative verb requires so. Pronominalization as a verbal object prefix would be ungrammatical here. As this example nicely illustrates, both conjoint and disjoint verb forms can be used before non-dislocated elements. The choice between both is clearly conditioned here by information structure. This indicates that although disjoint forms often occur clause-finally, especially when they are narrowly focused, they do not need to be final in their clause or constituent, even not when they are narrowly focused.

(42) *Ruba, unywaana na Delino? Kuva ubu turacáanye na we.*
 Ruba u-ø-ø-nyo-an-a [na Delino]ᶠᴼᶜ kuva.ubu
 Ruba 2SG.SM-PRS-CJ-drink-ASSOC-IPFV with Adelin henceforth
 [tu-ø-ra-ci-an-ye]ᶠᴼᶜ na we
 1PL.SM-PRS-DJ-cut-ASSOC-PFV with you
 'Ruba, you drink WITH ADELIN? Henceforth WE HAVE BROKEN with you.' (*NiAgasaga*, drama, 1960s)

In summary, from what precedes, it is clear that the disjoint marker is obligatory whenever the predicate or one of its operators is narrowly focused, be it informationally or contrastively. Güldemann (2003: 330–331) defines the narrow type of focus as 'predication focus', i.e. centred on the predicate but excluding objects and adjuncts. Disjoint verbs focused this way are very often clause-final, because canonically post-verbal constituents that represent discourse-old/given information tend to be dislocated or deleted from after such verbs. However, narrowly focused predicates do not need to be final in their constituent. They can be followed be non-dislocated elements, which indicates once more that constituency is not a decisive factor in the conditioning of the conjoint/disjoint alternation in Kirundi.

3.4 Sentence focus: disjoint

Disjoint verbs may not only be followed by elements conveying discourse-old/given information, but also by post-verbal elements that are part of the focal information. As we discuss in the present and the following sub-section, this happens in two distinct pragmatic contexts. One type of utterance in which a disjoint verb can precede an object or another post-verbal constituent are 'out-of-the blue' declarations whose propositional content is 'all new' and thus 'all focus'. Lambrecht (1994: 233) uses the term 'sentence focus' to refer to such expressions in which no pragmatic presupposition is formally evoked. Sasse (1987) calls them 'thetic statements' in opposition to 'categorical statements', which most typically have a clause-internal topic-comment structure. He further lists a number of typical domains for thetic expressions in the world's languages: (a) existential statements (in a wider sense: presence, appearance, continuation, etc., positively and negatively); (b) explanations (with or without preceding questions such as 'what happened?', 'why did it happen?', etc.), (c) surprising or unexpected events; (d) general statements (aphorisms, etc.); (e) background descriptions (local, temporal, etc., setting); (f) weather expressions; and (g) statements relating to body parts (Sasse 1987: 566–567). Example (1) above is the first sentence of an article of law and could thus be seen as an instance of a general statement, while (3) is rather an expression of surprise. Someone reports the exclamation by a young boy to his mother after he had seen the Virgin Mary appear while he was herding his cattle. The announcement by a journalist in a radio news broadcast in (43) is a thetic statement that could be seen as the explanatory answer to the implicit question 'What happened?'. Using the conjoint in such an out-of-the-blue announcement would be discursively inappropriate, because it would signal that the statement's most salient information is the entity following the predicate, which is not the case. The focal information pertains here to the event as a whole, which is centred on the disjoint-marked predicate.

(43) *Abapóoliísi baárafáshe umugwi w'ábaantu.*
   [a-ba-póoliísi ba-á-ra-fát-ye   u-mu-gwi   u-a   a-ba-ntu]^FOC
   AUG-2-police 2SM-REM.PST-DJ-arrest-PFV AUG-3-group 3-CONN AUG-2-person
   'THE POLICE ARRESTED A GROUP OF PEOPLE.' (*Imigwi*, information, 2010s)

The example in (43) is thus an instance of what Sasse (1987: 526) calls 'event-central theticity' as opposed to 'entity-central theticity': "[b]oth share the property of 'positing' something ..., but they differ crucially as to what is posited: an entity-central thetic statement is a type of utterance stating the existence of an entity, while an event-central thetic statement is one which states the existence of an event" (as cited in Güldemann 2010: 87). Especially event-central thetic expressions share with disjoint-marked, narrowly focused predicates the fact that the focal information does not pertain to one specific entity or argument, but rather bears on the event as a whole to which the utterance refers and which is anchored on the predicate. In a sentence with predicate focus, the predicate is specifically highlighted vis-à-vis other clause constituents. In a thetic statement, this clause-internal structure is levelled. The scope of focus is extended to the entire proposition presenting the whole event as the most salient information (cf. Güldemann 2013 with reference to Güldemann 1996). Due to this focus on the event, predicates in event-central thetic statements also tend to be disjoint-marked, at least in those tenses which allow for such overt marking.

This does not mean that the disjoint does not occur in entity-central thetic statements. Such statements usually involve an existential construction centred around a non-verbal predication marker that cannot be disjoint-marked. But even then an event can still be attributed to the central entity. Just like in argument focus constructions, this is done through a cleft. However, instead of (re-)stating discourse-old/given information, as is normally done in a relative clause following a focused argument, the relative clause following the central entity in a thetic expression also conveys new information. The auxiliary *-rikó* is commonly used to introduce the relative clause in an entity-central thetic cleft. While simple relative verbs cannot be disjoint, a complex relative clause introduced by the auxiliary *-rikó* does allow disjoint-marking on the main verb. This auxiliary is composed of the copula *-ri* 'be' and the locative class 17 referential marker *-ko* and thus literally means 'be there'. It has grammaticalized, however, into an auxiliary conveying progressive aspect, i.e. *'une action qui est en cours'* (Meeussen 1959: 200). The explanation in (44) is such a cleft construction, which could be interpreted as entity-central in the sense that one first introduces the presence of a rat, to which an action is subsequently attributed. Given that this event is also discourse-new information, it is conveyed through a disjoint-marked verb, which is possible thanks to the use of the *-rikó* auxiliary.

(44) *Ico gikomyé urugi co n'igiki? Ngirango ni imbeba iríko iriyangarira.*
 i-ki-o ki-kóm-ye[H] u-ru-ugi ki-ó ni [i-ki-kí][FOC]
 AUG-7-DEM_b 7SM-hit-PFV.REL AUG-11-door 7-REF COP AUG-7-what
 [ngirango ni i-N-beba i-ø-ri[H]-kó i-ra-i-angaar-ir-a][FOC]
 maybe COP AUG-9-rat 9SM-PRS-be.REL-17RM 9SM-DJ-REFL-wander-APPL-IPFV
 'WHAT IS IT THAT JUST HIT THE DOOR? MAYBE IT IS A RAT WHICH IS WANDERING.'
 (*Abuzukuru*, theatre, 1970s)

Meeussen (1959: 200) wonders whether *-rikó* systematically triggers disjoint-marking on the main verb, as is the case in (44), but also in (13). This interconnection between the progressive aspect of *-rikó* and the disjoint would be in line with a more general polysemy between progressivity and predicate-centred focus which has been reported in several Bantu languages (Hyman and Watters 1984; Wald 1997; Güldemann 2003; De Kind et al. 2015). As part of a cleft construction, *-rikó* is indeed predominantly followed by a disjoint verb in the corpus. It seems to be a common means of attributing a discourse-new event to the central entity in a thetic construction, even if this needs to be examined more closely. In (45), *-rikó* is also part of a cleft, but followed by a conjoint verb. This is not an entity-central thetic statement, but an argument focus cleft construction whose relative clause represents discourse-old information with regard to the head noun, i.e. the focused subject.

(45)   Ni wé nyéne ubwíiwe azóoba aríko abábwiira amajaambo yahóra abwíira abakúunzi bíiwe.

ni	[wé	nyéne	u-bu-íiwe]^FOC	a-zóo-bá-a^H	a-ø-ri^H-kó
COP	him	self	AUG-14-his	1SM-FUT-be-IPFV.REL	1SM-PRS-be.REL-17RM

a^H-ba-bwíir-a   a-ma-jaambo a-á-hór-a^H   a^H-bwíir-a
1SM.CJC-2OM-tell-IPFV AUG-6-WORD 1SM-REM.PST-remain-IPFV.REL 1SM.CJC-tell-IPFV
a-ba-kúunzi   ba-íiwe
AUG-2-beloved   2-his

'It is he himself who will be telling you the stories he was often telling to his beloved ones.' (*Yaga*, religion, 1960s)

3.5 Topic-comment structure: disjoint/conjoint

So far we have discussed pragmatic contexts where conjoint or disjoint verb forms are mutually exclusive. There is one discourse setting where this choice is less clearly conditioned. When the verb phrase as a whole – the predicate together with post-verbal constituents – is focused, both conjoint and disjoint verb forms are observed without a very straightforward determination. This is what Lambrecht (1994) calls 'predicate focus'. Predicate is understood here in the broad sense, i.e. as '[t]hat constituent of a sentence, most typically a verb phrase, which combines with the subject NP to make up a complete sentence' (Trask 1993: 213). This focus-structure type fulfils the basic communicative function of predicating a property of a given topic (Lambrecht 1994: 336). It corresponds to the typical 'topic-comment articulation' (Andrews 2007: 149), which is 'the universally unmarked type of focus structure' (Van Valin and LaPolla 1997: 206). When focus is neither on a specific constituent (either argument/adjunct focus or predicate-centred focus), nor on the whole sentence (sentence focus/theticity), conjoint and disjoint forms are both pragmatically appropriate. In the conversation in (46), the traditional councillors are questioned on what they have done during a crisis. Because the answer is not satisfying, the question is repeated after a while and answered again. In the question itself, a conjoint verb is used which is associated with the narrow argument focus on the question word *ikí*. In the first answer, the whole verb phrase represents new information, but a conjoint form is used, as would be the case if only the object were focused. The post-verbal element is considered here to be the most salient information. Using a disjoint verb form would not be pragmatically inappropriate here. It would put more emphasis on the contrast between the verb -kóra 'do' used in the question and -hísha 'hide' in the answer. In the second answer, a disjoint form is used, which is in line with the fact that the comment on the topic is restricted here to the predicate itself. This corresponds to narrow assertive focus on the verb lexeme. Verbs not followed by a narrowly focused object or adjunct are always disjoint-marked.

(46) Q: Abashíingantaáhe mwaákoze ikí?
A: [...] Umwé weése yahísha umutwé wíiwé.
[...]
Q: Abashíingantaáhe mwaákoze ikí?
A: [...] bamwé baárahúunze.

a-ba-shíingantaáhe   mu-á-ø-kór-ye   [ikí]^{FOC}
AUG-2-traditional.councillor   2PL.SM-REM.PST-CJ-do-PFV   what
u-mwé   u-eése   [a-á-ø-hísh-a   u-mu-twé   u-íiwé]^{FOC}
1-one   1-all   1SM-REM.PST-CJ-hide-IPFV AUG-3-head   3-his
ba-mwé   [ba-á-ra-huung-ye] ^{FOC}
2-one   2SM-REM.PST-DJ-flee-PFV

Q: 'Traditional councillors, WHAT have you done?'
A: '[...] everyone HAS HIDDEN HIS HEAD.'
Q: 'Traditional councillors, WHAT have you done?'
A: 'Some HAVE FLED.' (Mushingantahe, peace, 2000s)

Even if the discourse-new comment consists of a transitive predicate and its object, the verb can be disjoint-marked, as in (47). This example originates from the same text as (46). A similar kind of object question is asked and once more the whole verb phrase in the answer represents new information. This time the verb in the answer is disjoint-marked, as would be the case if only the predicate were narrowly focused. Using a conjoint verb form here would also be pragmatically appropriate. It would have marked information conveyed by the verb itself as less salient than that conveyed by the post-verbal element.

(47) Q: Mbeéga abarezi baákoze ikí [...]?
A: Abarezi bó mw'iiseminaári y'í BUTA baárihweeje ikibázo c'ámacáakubíri mu Buruúndi, [...]

Mbeéga a-ba-rezi   ba-á-ø-kór-ye   [ikí]^{FOC}
QW   AUG-2-educator 2SM-REM.PST-CJ-do-PFV   what
a-ba-rezi   ba-ó   mu   i-ø-seminaári   i-a   í   Buta
AUG-2-educator   2-REF   18LOC   AUG-9-seminary   9-CONN   19LOC   Buta

[ba-á-ra-íihweez-ye   i-ki-bázo   ki-a   a-ma-cáakubíri
2SM-REM.PST-DJ-analyze-PFV AUG-7-issue 7-CONN   AUG-6-discrimination
mu   Buruúndi]^FOC
18LOC   Burundi
Q: 'WHAT did the educators do?'
A: 'The educators of Buta seminary ANALYSED THE ISSUE OF (ETHNIC)
DISCRIMINATION IN BURUNDI.' (*Mushingantahe*, peace, 2000s)

In a topic-comment structure, Kirundi speakers seem to have a choice between the conjoint and the disjoint verb form. If they use the conjoint, this signals that the most salient new information is the constituent following the predicate, even if the whole verb phrase conveys discourse-new information. If they uses the disjoint, this rather indicates that the event as a whole – centred on the predicate – is the most important pragmatic information.

3.6 Summary

Table 2 below summarizes the correlations between focus structure, word order and disjoint/conjoint marking as extensively discussed in the preceding subsections.

Syntactic constituency does not directly condition the conjoint/disjoint alternation in Kirundi, as shown at the beginning of this section. As summarized in Table 2, it correlates more strongly with information structure. The choice between conjoint and disjoint verb forms is to a great extent predictable on the basis of a sentence's focus structure, especially if it concerns marked focus. Only in sentences with a topic-comment structure does the choice between conjoint and disjoint verb forms seem to be free. The new information is not added here as the answer to an explicit question. The comment can therefore be considered as a less marked focal domain, but inside of which one element can be more highlighted than another. When a disjoint verb form is used in the comment the information conveyed by the verb or one of its operators is presented as the most salient information. Our impression is that morphologically unmarked conjoint verb forms are much more frequently used in this pragmatic context, but this needs to be tested through a distributional analysis of the corpus. As soon as a sentence has a marked focus structure, conjoint and disjoint verb forms are in perfect complementary distribution. Conjoint verb forms are obligatory in the case of focus on a post-verbal constituent, while disjoint verb forms are obligatory in the case of predicate-centred focus and all-focus sentences.

Table 2: Correlation between focus structure, word order and conjoint/disjoint marking.

Focus structure	Word order and focused constituents	Verb marking
Object/adjunct focus	SV**O/ADJ**	CJ
Subject focus	OV**S** / ha-V**S**	CJ
Predicate-centred focus	(O/ADJ ,) S**V** (O/ADJ)	DJ
Sentence focus	**SVO/ADJ**/**ha-VS**	DJ
Topic-comment	S**VO/ADJ**	CJ/DJ

4 Conclusion: a case for the abolition of the conjoint/disjoint dichotomy

So far we have attempted to describe the conjoint/disjoint alternation under the assumption that it really exists in Kirundi, as has been assumed ever since Meeussen (1959). On the basis of that description, we could maintain that hypothesis and argue that the conjoint and the disjoint are different types of focus markers. Nevertheless, by way of conclusion, we would rather like to rely on our account of the conjoint/disjoint alternation to make a case for its abolition in Kirundi grammar. Even if for tradition's sake it would no doubt be easier to sustain the dichotomy, we think that it is closer to empirical reality to only preserve the so-called 'disjoint' as a true focus marker, both from a formal and functional point of view.

Formally speaking, only three conjugations in both the indicative and conjunctive mood allow the presence of an extra affix in the morphological verb slot that is normally reserved for TAM markers. This is -*ra*- for the present and the remote past and -*a*- for the near past. Instead of adding grammatical meaning to the verb form, as the proper tense markers of these conjugations do, it signals pragmatic information.

Functionally speaking, the -*ra*-/-*a*- allomorph following the tense marker signals that the verb to which it is added hosts the most important or salient pragmatic information in a given communicative setting (Dik 1997: 326). In its narrowest use, it indicates that the verb itself or one of its operators conveys the focal information. The scope of the disjoint-marked focus is then analogous to 'argument focus' (Lambrecht 1994: 228ff) or 'term focus' (Güldemann 2003: 330), except that it does not target specific nominal or adverbial clause constituents, but the verb itself. The -*ra*-/-*a*- focus marker highlights the event expressed by the predicate or an operator intimately linked with it. In its widest use, the disjoint extends the scope of pragmatic salience to the whole discourse-new utterance of which the event referred to by the predicate is the central element; hence the correlation between disjoint-marking and theticity, especially event-central thetic utterances. The *-ra-/-a-* allomorph is only obligatorily marked on the verb in these two communicative settings that are rather extraordinary in terms of referentiality of information. Entities are more common topics and foci than states of affairs are, and the default progression of information flow is one whereby a new piece of information is projected against a discourse-old/given background (Güldemann 2013). Pragmatic markedness thus correlates with morphological markedness.

In the more default topic-comment articulation, the *-ra-/-a-* focus marker is not disallowed, but it is optional. A speaker may morphologically mark that the information conveyed by the predicate is also pragmatically salient, but he does not have to. The unmarkedness of this focus structure does not require specific morphological focus marking on the verb. The verb can remain morphologically unmarked.

As soon as a non-verbal clause constituent is narrowly focused – be it the subject, an object or an adjunct – the predicate can no longer be focus-marked. This morphologically unmarked verb form has traditionally been interpreted as the 'conjoint'. However, rather than being an empirical reality, this 'conjoint' seems to be a theoretical construct purely created to signal the absence of the 'disjoint' marker. It does not have a dedicated morpheme. Moreover, the high tone deletion associated with so-called 'conjoint' verbs is a phonological phrasing effect that is also observed in conjugations that do not allow for 'disjoint'-marking, such as the Potential and the Subsecutive. Rather than being a tone pattern specifically marking the conjoint, it could be interpreted as the unmarked sentential intonation pattern that is realized whenever it is not countered by the disjoint or by a verb conjugation-specific tone pattern, such as the one observed for the future tense.

The 'conjoint' form itself is also not a focus marker, contrary to what Ndayiragije (1999) seems to assume, when he calls the disjoint morphology an 'antifocus' marker. Disjoint markers do more than simply indicating that there is no post-verbal focus. Unlike Bukuru (2003: 274), we would also not consider a 'conjoint' verb as a 'complement focus construction'. Focus on a specific non-verbal constituent is not signalled by a morpheme on the predicate but rather by the position of an argument vis-à-vis the predicate. Linearly speaking, arguments are commonly focused in the post-verbal domain, often in clause-final position but not always. In the case of arguments, such as the subject, which canonically occur pre-verbally, this entails word order inversion, combined with expletive subject marking on the verb in the case of intransitive predicates. Syntactic configuration suffices to account for focus on a non-verbal constituent.

It is not necessary to posit a 'conjoint' null-morpheme. Hence, instead of maintaining the conjoint/disjoint distinction in Kirundi and the consistent null-marking of the 'conjoint' it entails, it would be closer to empirical reality to get rid of it altogether. Without claiming anything about the empirical basis of the conjoint/disjoint alternation in other Bantu languages, we propose to abolish it in Kirundi and to give the 'disjoint' its rightful recognition as a dedicated marker of 'event focus'.

If we do so, it also becomes easier to understand why this focus marker is disallowed in certain clause types. The fact that it is predicate-centred explains first of all why it is incompatible with verbal negation marking or as Ndayiragije (1999: 407) observes: "The marker -ra- is in complementary distribution with the negation marker, even though the two markers show up in different structural positions on the inflected verb". It is without a formal negative counterpart, because negation fulfils exactly the same function as the -ra-/-a- morpheme, only negatively: it contradicts either the lexical contents conveyed by the predicate or an operator linked with it. It also accounts for the fact that it is incompatible with most types of subordinate clauses, such as simple relative clauses or complement clauses introduced by the complementizer *ko*. The most salient pragmatic information signalled by this focus marker tends to be hosted in the asserted main clause rather than in subordinate clauses which tend to contain non-asserted information. Clauses introduced by the quotative *ngo*, on the other hand, do allow the -ra-/-a- focus marker, because they report direct speech. In this regard, complex relative clauses introduced by the auxiliary -*rikó* also seem to have more asserted force than simple relative clauses, but this could be historically motivated, as we discuss below. Finally, the restriction of the -ra-/-a- allomorph to the present and past tense conjugations can be explained by the fact that the highlighted asserted information needs to have a sufficiently high degree of factivity. Events that happened in the past or occur in the present are usually more factual and have a stronger assertive force than events that will take place in the future or are wished or supposed to (have) occur(ed).

We end with a historical note concerning the possible origin of the focus marker formerly called 'disjoint'. The fact that it occurs in the verb's TAM slot is in all likelihood due to the fact that it used to be proper TAM-marker. In this regard, it is interesting to note that the focus marker -ra- is not only homophonous with the so-called 'adhortative' marker in Kirundi (Meeussen 1959: 112–113), but also with the progressive marker in Kinyarwanda (Kimenyi 1980). Rather than being homonyms, these morphemes are no doubt cognates manifesting different meanings. The 'adhortative' affix occurs in verbs used to give instructions, recommendations or orders which do not need to be carried out immediately. Meeussen (1959: 113) considers it as a kind of future imperative and it indeed has a near future meaning. This is interesting, since present progressives, and presents more generally, often become (near) futures in Bantu languages (and elsewhere) (Bastin 1989; Nurse 2008: 118). Moreover, it is well known that progressive aspect and predicate-centred focus are semantically closely connected and often expressed by the same markers in Bantu (Hyman and Watters 1984; Güldemann 2003; De Kind et al. 2015). The progressive is an "inherently focused verb category" (Güldemann 2003: 346ff) in which the on-going nature of the event described by the verb is the most important information and thus forms the focal domain of the expression. Hence, it would be easily conceivable how the -*ra*- marker underwent a split evolution in Kirundi from a progressive affix – as it still is in Kinyarwanda – to an 'event focus' marker on the one hand and an 'adhortative' near future marker on the other hand. In its function as a dedicated progressive marker, -*ra*- was replaced in Kirundi by the auxiliary -*rikó*. The latter remained closely linked with the -*ra*- marker, since the auxiliary usually combines with a main verb marked by -*ra*-. Progressivity and predicate-centred focus strongly overlap in complex verb constructions introduced by -*rikó*. That is why they are so frequently used instead of simple relative clauses in order to convey discourse-new information, for instance in entity-central thetic clefts. In such a construction, the -*ra*- focus marker remains closely connected to its original progressive meaning, a phenomenon known as 'persistence' (Hopper 1991: 28–30) in grammaticalization studies. If the Kirundi focus marker -*ra*- did indeed develop from a progressive affix, a remaining question is why its allomorph is -*a*- in the recent past. This needs to be examined more closely to see whether the same allomorphy was originally involved in the expression of progressive aspect.

Alternatively, it is not inconceivable that the event focus meaning of -*ra*- is primary to its progressive focus meaning, which is still attested in Kinyarwanda but further evolved to an adhortative near future meaning in Kirundi. The fact that a marker -*ra*- expressing 'verbal focus' and/or 'progressivity' is attested in other Great Lakes Bantu languages, especially in Kirundi's close relatives of the West Highlands group (Nurse and Muzale 1999: 536–537), suggests that a more systematic historical-comparative study is required to solve that question. Such a study would logically start with a systematic comparison between Kirundi and its closest relative Kinyarwanda, where the use of 'disjoint' markers appears to be more conditioned by constituency (Ngoboka and Zeller this volume). Based on the widespread progressive/event focus polysemy of -*ra*- in West Highlands Great Lakes Bantu, our hypothesis would be that Kinyarwanda syntactically reanalysed the formerly more pragmatic function of -*ra*-, as it is still observed in Kirundi, which turns out to be more conservative in this respect.

Abbreviations

APPL	applicative	NEG	negative
ASSOC	associative	OM	object marker
AUG	augment	PASS	passive
AUX	auxiliary	PERS	persistive
CAUS	causative	PFV	perfective
CJ	conjoint	PL	plural
CJC	conjunctive mood	POT	potential
CONN	connective	PRN	pronoun
COP	copula	PRS	present
DEM$_x$	demonstrative of type/degree x	PST	past
DJ	disjoint	QUOT	quotative
[...]^{FOC}	focal domain	QW	question word
FUT	future	RM	referential marker
FV	final vowel	REF	reference
[...]^H	floating high tone	REFL	reflexive
IMP	imperative	REL	relative
IMPRS	impersonal	REM.PST	remote past
INCP	inceptive	SM	subject marker
IPFV	imperfective	SG	singular
LOC	locative prefix	SUBJ	subjunctive
N	homorganic nasal	SUBS	subsecutive
N.PST	near past		

Acknowledgements

We wish to thank Jenneke van der Wal, Gilles-Maurice de Schryver, Sebastian Dom and Jasper De Kind as well as the two anonymous reviewers for their useful comments on an earlier version of this article. The usual disclaimers apply. We are also grateful to Ferdinand Mberamihigo for the innumerable hours of hard work, which he carried out to compile the Kirundi text corpus, on which this article is based.

References

Andrews, Avery D. 2007. The major functions of the noun phrase. In Timothy Shopen (ed.), *Clause structure, language typology and syntactic description, Vol. 1: Clause structure*, 132–223. Cambridge: Cambridge University Press.

Ashton, Ethel O., Enoch M. K. Mulira, E. G. M. Ndawula & Archibald Norman Tucker. 1954. *A Luganda grammar*. London, New York & Toronto: Longmans, Green.

Bastin, Yvonne. 1989. El prefijo locativo de la clase 18 y la expresión del progresivo presente en Bantu. *Estudios africanos* 4. 35–55, 61–86.

Bickmore, Lee Stephen. 1990. Branching nodes and prosodic categories: Evidence from Kinyambo. In Sharon Inkelas & Draga Zec (eds.), *The phonology-syntax connection*, 1–17. Chicago: University of Chicago Press.

Bostoen, Koen, Ferdinand Mberamihigo & Gilles-Maurice de Schryver. 2012. Grammaticalization and subjectification in the semantic domain of possibility in Kirundi. *Africana Linguistica* 18. 6–40.

Bresnan, Joan & J. M. Kanerva. 1989. Locative inversion in Chichewa – a case-study of factorization in grammar. *Linguistic Inquiry* 20 (1). 1–50.

Buell, Leston. 2006. The Zulu conjoint/disjoint verb alternation: focus or constituency? *ZAS Papers in Linguistics* 43. 9–30.

Bukuru, Denis. 1998. *Object marking in Kirundi and Kiswahili*. Dar es Salaam: University of Dar es Salaam MA thesis.

Bukuru, Denis. 2003. *Phrase structure and functional categories in the Kirundi sentence*. Dar es Salaam: University of Dar es Salaam Ph.D. thesis.

Creissels, Denis. 1996. Conjunctive and disjunctive verb forms in Setswana. *South African Journal of African Languages* 16 (4). 109–115.

Cristini, Giovanni. 2000. *Nouvelle grammaire kirundi/Indimburo y'ikirundi*. Bujumbura: Presses Lavigerie.

Dammann, Ernst. 1977. Das '-o of reference' in Bantusprachen. In B. Benzing, O. Böcher & G. Meyer (eds.), *Wort und Wirklichkeit: Studien zur Afrikanistik und Orientalistik, Eugen Ludwig Rapp zum 70. Geburtstag. Teil II: Linguistik und Kulturwissenschaft*, 31–43. Meisenheim-am-Glan: Anton Hain.

De Kind, Jasper, Sebastian Dom, Gilles-Maurice de Schryver & Koen Bostoen. 2015. Event-centrality and the pragmatics-semantics interface in Kikongo: From predication focus to progressive aspect and vice versa. *Folia Linguistica Historica* 36. 113–163.

de Schryver, Gilles-Maurice and Rachélle Gauton. 2002. The Zulu locative prefix ku-revisited: A corpus-based approach. *Southern African Linguistics and Applied Language Studies* 20 (4). 201–220.

de Schryver, Gilles-Maurice & Minah Nabirye. 2010. A quantitative analysis of the morphology, morphophonology and semantic import of the Lusoga noun. *Africana Linguistica* 16. 97–153.

Dik, Simon C. 1997. *The theory of functional grammar, Part 1: The structure of the clause*. Berlin & New York: Mouton de Gruyter.

É. Kiss, Katalin. 1998. Identificational focus versus information focus. *Language* 74 (2). 245–273.

Edenmyr, Niklas. 2001. *Focus control in Kirundi*. Stockholm: Stockholm University MA thesis.

Fanselow, Gisbert & Denisa Lenertová. 2011. Left peripheral focus: Mismatches between syntax and information structure. *Natural Language and Linguistic Theory* 29. 169–209.

Givón, Talmy. 1975. Focus and the scope of assertion: Some Bantu evidence. *Studies in African Linguistics* 6 (2). 185–205.

Güldemann, Tom. 1996. *Verbalmorphologie and Nebenprädikationen im Bantu. Eine Studie zur funktional motivierten Genese eines konjugationalen Subsystem*. Bochum: Universitätsverlag Dr. N. Brockmeyer.

Güldemann, Tom. 2003. Present progressive vis-à-vis predication focus in Bantu. A verbal category between semantics and pragmatics. *Studies in Language* 27 (2). 323–360.

Güldemann, Tom. 2010. The relation between focus and theticity in the Tuu family. In Ines Fiedler & Anne Schwarz (eds.), *The expression of information structure: A documentation of its diversity across Africa*, 69–94. Amsterdam & Philadelphia: John Benjamins.

Güldemann, Tom. 2013. The relation between predicate operator focus and theticity in Bantu. Paper presented at the Ghent-Berlin Workshop 'Information Structure in Bantu', December 10–11, Humboldt University Berlin.

Hamlaoui, Fatima & Emmanuel-Moselly Makasso. 2015. Focus marking and the unavailability of inversion structures in the Bantu language Bàsàá (A43). *Lingua* 154. 35–64.

Hopper, Paul J. 1991. On some principles of grammaticalization. In Elizabeth Closs Traugott & Bernd Heine (eds.), *Approaches to grammaticalization* (Typological Studies in Language 19), 17–35. Amsterdam: Benjamins.

Hyman, Larry Michael & Ernest Rugwa Byarushengo. 1984. A model of Haya tonology. In George N. Clements & John Anton Goldsmith (eds.), *Autosegmental studies in Bantu tone*, 53–104. Dordrecht: Mouton de Gruyter; Foris Publications.

Hyman, Larry & John Robert Watters. 1984. Auxiliary focus. *Studies in African Linguistics* 15 (3). 233–273.

Kawalya, Deo , Koen Bostoen & Gilles-Maurice de Schryver. 2014. Diachronic semantics of the modal verb -sóból- in Luganda: A corpus-driven approach. *International Journal of Corpus Linguistics* 19 (1). 60–93.

Kimenyi, Alexandre. 1980. *A relational grammar of Kinyarwanda*. Berkeley: University of California Press.

Kinyalolo, Kasangati Kikuni Wabongambilu. 1991. *Syntactic dependencies and the spec-head agreement hypothesis in Kilega*. Los Angeles: University of California (UCLA) Ph.D. thesis.

Krifka, Manfred. 2007. Basic notions of information structure. In Caroline Féry, Gisbert Fanselow & Manfred Krifka (eds.), *Working Papers of the SFB 632, Interdisciplinary Studies on Information Structure (ISIS) 6*, 13–56. Potsdam: Universitatsverlag Potsdam.

Lambrecht, Knud. 1994. *Information structure and sentence form*. Cambridge: Cambridge University Press.

Mberamihigo, Ferdinand. 2014. *L'expression de la modalité en kirundi. Exploitation d'un corpus électronique*. Bruxelles/Gand: Université libre de Bruxelles (ULB), Université de Gand (UGent) PhD thesis.

Meeussen, Achiel Emiel. 1959. *Essai de grammaire rundi*. Tervuren: Musée royal de l'Afrique centrale.

Morimoto, Yukiko. 2000. *Discourse configurationality in Bantu morphosyntax*. Stanford: Stanford University Ph.D. thesis.

Ndayiragije, Juvénal. 1999. Checking economy. *Linguistic Inquiry* 30 (3). 399–444.

Ngoboka, Jean Paul & Jochen Zeller. this volume. The conjoint/disjoint alternation in Kinyarwanda.

Ntahokaja, Jean Baptiste. 1994. *Grammaire structurale du kirundi*. Bujumbura: Université du Burundi.

Nurse, Derek. 2008. *Tense and aspect in Bantu*. Oxford: Oxford University Press.

Nurse, Derek & Henry R. T. Muzale. 1999. Tense and aspect in Great Lakes Bantu languages. In Jean Marie Hombert & Larry M. Hyman (eds.), *Bantu historical linguistics: Theoretical and empirical perspectives*, 517–544. Stanford: CSLI Publications.

Patin, Cédric. 2007. Shingazidja focus hierarchy. *Nouveaux cahiers de linguistique française* 28. 147–154.

Rodegem, F. M. 1970. *Dictionnaire rundi-français*. Tervuren: Musée royal de l'Afrique centrale.

Rooth, Mats. 1985. *Association with Focus*. Amherst: University of Massachusetts Ph.D. thesis.

Rooth, Mats. 1992. A theory of focus interpretation. *Natural Language Semantics* 1. 75–116.

Sabimana, Firmard. 1986. *The relational structure of the Kirundi verb*. Bloomington: Indiana University PhD thesis.

Sasse, Hans-Jürgen. 1987. The thetic/categorical distinction revisited. *Linguistics* 25. 511–580.
Skopeteas, Stavros, Ines Fiedler, Samantha Hellmuth, Anne Schwarz, Ruben Stoel, Gisbert Fanselow, Caroline Féry & Manfred Krifka. 2006. *Questionnaire on information structure (QUIS): Reference manual*. Potsdam: Universitätsverlag Potsdam.
Trask, Robert Lawrence. 1993. *A dictionary of grammatical terms in linguistics*. London & New York: Routledge.
Van der Spuy, Andrew. 1993. Dislocated noun phrases in Nguni. *Lingua* 90. 335–355.
Van der Wal, Jenneke. 2009. *Word order and information structure in Makhuwa-Enahara*. Utrecht: LOT.
Van der Wal, Jenneke. 2011. Focus excluding alternatives: Conjoint/disjoint marking in Makhuwa. *Lingua* 121 (11). 1734–1750.
Van Valin, Robert D. & Randy J. LaPolla. 1997. *Syntax: Structure, meaning, and function*. Cambridge: Cambridge University Press.
Wald, Benji. 1997. Grammar and pragmatics in the Swahili auxiliary focus system. *The Annual Proceedings of the Berkeley Linguistics Society* 32 (2). 128–139.
Zerbian, Sabine. 2004. Phonological phrases in Xhosa (Southern Bantu). *ZAS Papers in Linguistics* 37. 71–99.

Nobuko Yoneda
15 Conjoint/disjoint distinction and focus in Matengo (N13)

1 Introduction

Matengo is a Bantu language spoken in the southwest part of Tanzania, N13 according to Guthrie's classification (Guthrie 1948). Matengo verbs can appear in two forms, one of which cannot appear at the end of a main clause. This verb form ends with a final suffix -*aje*[1], and it always requires a following element.

(1) a. *ju-a-butuk-aje*[2] *Samuél.*
       1SM-PST-run-CJF 1.Samuel
       'Samuel ran.'

    b. **Samuél ju-a-butuk-aje.*
       1.Samuel 1SM-PST-run-CJF

This same restriction can be observed in several Southern and Eastern Bantu languages, and this verb form is called the 'conjoint (CJ) form'. The counterpart is called the 'disjoint (DJ) form' (Meeussen 1959). As a basic rule, the CJ form in Matengo is used when the focus is on the element following the verb (Yoneda 2006, 2009a, 2009b, 2011)[3]. The CJ final -*aje* also has a 'non-perfect' aspectual

---

This chapter is based on my presentation at the 3rd International Conference on Bantu Languages held in March 2009 in Tervuren, and the International Workshop on Bantu Languages held in March 2014 in London. I would like to thank all those who gave me helpful comments during that conference and workshop. Of course any mistakes are my own responsibility. All the data on Matengo were collected through fieldwork in Tanzania by the author, with the financial support of Grants-in-Aid for Scientific Research (No.15251004/ 19520343/ 20320059). My biggest thanks goes to John Kasuku B. Mapunda, my language consultant in Litembo, Tanzania.

1 Matengo has no official orthography. In this chapter, I use the same orthography as in Yoneda (2006), which is based on Swahili orthography. The biggest differences are the vowels. Matengo has a 7-vowel system unlike Swahili: each vowel is referred as i = [i], $\underline{e}$ = [e], e = [ɛ], a = [a], $\underline{o}$ = [o], o = [ɔ], u = [u]. Each vowel contrasts between long and short. Long vowels are written as double letters — e.g. ee = [e:].

2 *ju-a-butuk-aje* is pronounced as *jwabutuka* as a result of morpho-phonological rules. However, when the example is hyphenated, each morpheme is shown in the underlying form. See also footnote 5.

3 Because of this function, Odden (1984) calls this verb form in Kimatuumbi 'noun-focal tense'.

DOI 10.1515/9783110490831-015

function (Yoneda 2000, 2009a, 2009b). The formal and functional properties of the CJ form with -*aje* can thus be summarized as follows:

a) syntactic restriction   - does not appear at clause final
b) informational function - focus on the following element
c) aspectual function   - non-perfect

However, these restrictions and functions cannot always be present at the same time. The purpose of this chapter is to examine in detail the behaviour of the CJ and DJ forms, and the relation between focus and these verb forms in Matengo. In this chapter, I will discuss (i) how focus is expressed in Matengo, (ii) how the CJ and DJ forms in Matengo deal with or compromise the restrictions and functions, and (iii) whether or not the CJ form really has the function of encoding focus. The main argument will be the following: despite the strong tendency and preference to use the CJ form of the verb when the verb is followed by a focal element, the functional distribution of these forms is not categorical. This is due to the fact that, as will be explicated, the Matengo CJ/DJ system is too "defective". As a compromise, the functional requirement is sometimes not respected, and the distribution is determined solely by the syntactic requirement.

2 Verb forms in Matengo

2.1 Structure of the verb and TA system in Matengo

The structure of the Matengo verb is as shown in (2).

(2) SM- **TM-** (OM-) BASE (-PreF)[4] **-F**
    tu-   a-   gu-   lapul -ø   -iti   > twagúlapwíle[5]
    1PL.SM- PST- 2SG.OM- beat   -PF
    'We beat you.'   **perfect past**

The subject marker (SM) and the object marker (OM) agree with the subject noun and object noun respectively. The verb base (BASE), which can be divided into

---

[4] The prefinal slot (PreF) only appears when TM is ø and F is -*aje* (simple near past) with a CVC verb base. It is only to adjust the length of the verb and has neither grammatical nor semantic function.
[5] When morphological and morpho-phonological rules apply to the combination of these morphemes, the surface form of the verb may look quite different from the underlying form. In this chapter, the underlying forms are shown in the examples.

the verb root and derivational suffixes, contains the basic meaning of the verb. The combination of the tense marker (TM) and the final suffix (F) determines the tense, aspect, and mood of the verb, and the final suffix alternates between the CJ form and the DJ form.

As mentioned, the CJ form cannot appear at the clause final position,[6] as shown in (3), and the DJ form does not have such a restriction, as shown in (4).

(3) the CJ form
    a. *tu-a-hemel-aje*   *sukáli.*   **simple far past (CJ)**
       1PL.SM-PST-buy-CJF 9.sugar
       'We bought sugar.'

    b. **tu-a-hemel-aje.*
       1PL.SM-PST-buy-CJF

(4) the DJ form
    a. *tu-a-hemel-iti*   *sukáli.*   **perfect past (DJ)**
       1PL.SM-PST-buy-PF 9.sugar
       'We bought sugar.'

    b. *tu-a-hemel-iti.*
       1PL.SM-PST-buy-PF
       'We bought (it).'

(4) is an example of the DJ form, allowed in both the clause final and non-clause final position. There is another type of DJ form, which cannot take any following element and must be clause-final.

(5) the DJ form
    a. *tu-í-hemel-a.*   **confirming future (DJ)**
       1PL.SM-FUT-buy-BF
       'We will (surely) buy (it).'
    b. **tu-í-hemel-a*   *sukáli.*
       1PL.SM-FUT-buy-BF 9.sugar

---

6 There is an exception, namely in relative clauses (cf. Hyman in this volume), where the verb is formally equal to the CJ form in non-relative clauses.
    i) a. *ng'ombi jee*   *tu-hemel-áje* > *tuhémála*   'the cows which we bought this morning'
       10.cows 10.RM   1PL.SM-buy-CJF
      b. *ng'ombi jee*   *tu-hemel-a* > *tuhéme*   'the cows which we buy'
       10.cows 10.RM   1PL.SM-buy-BF

Table 1: Tense/aspect/mood in Matengo.

1. Simple (non-perfect) form	conjoint final: -aje[7] basic final: -a				
simple far past	SM-	a-	BASE	-aje	CJ: − clause final
simple near past	SM-	ø-	BASE (-it)	-áje	
simple present	SM-	ø-	BASE	-a	
simple future	SM-	í-	BASE	-aje	
simple go-future	SM-	aká-	BASE	-aje	
2. Perfect form	perfect final: -iti				
perfect past	SM-	a-	BASE	-iti	DJ: ± clause final
perfect present	SM-	ø-	BASE	-ití	
3. Confirming form	basic final: -a				
confirming future	SM-	í-	BASE	-a	DJ: + clause final
confirming go-future	SM-	aká-	BASE	-a	
4. Subjunctive conjoint form	conjoint final: -ajé				
present	SM-	ø-	BASE	-aje	CJ: − clause final
future	SM-	i-	BASE	-ajé	
go-future	SM-	aka-	BASE	-ajé	
5. Subjunctive disjoint form	subjunctive final: -í				
present	SM-	ø-	BASE	-í	DJ: ± clause final
future	SM-	i-	BASE	-í	
go-future	SM-	aka-	BASE	-í	

(5) is an example of the DJ form in the confirming future tense. The confirming future is used only as a positive polarity answer for the question of whether the event in question takes place, or to confirm that the event will surely take place. The verb in the confirming future tense can only appear clause-finally without any following element. Verb forms in Matengo can thus be divided into three types according to clause position: the CJ form, which cannot appear clause-finally, the DJ form of the perfect type, which can appear both in the clause-final and non-clause-final position, and the DJ form of the confirming type, which can only appear in the clause-final position.

Table 1 shows the verb forms and tense/aspect/mood paradigm in Matengo. The forms which cannot appear clause finally are indicated by '− clause final', the form which can appear both in the clause final and non-clause final position is indicated as '± clause final', and the form which can only appear at the clause final position is indicated by '+ clause final' in Table 1.

---

[7] The tone markings of TMs and finals here are in underlying forms. Notice that they appear in different tones due to phonological rules. In particular, finals -aje, -ajé, -iti, -í appear in a different tone when they co-occur with TM.

As Table 1 shows, the simple (= non-perfect) verb forms have only the CJ form, and the perfect verb forms have only the DJ form. According to this distribution, the CJ/DJ distinction in Matengo is obviously related to aspect, in addition to (or rather than) focus. Moving down the CJ/DJ paradigm in Table 1, we see that only in the subjunctive mood (4 and 5 in Table 1) do the CJ/DJ forms exist in pairs for each tense in Matengo. We will discuss this imbalance in the distribution of the indicative mood in Section 4.

2.2 Deletion of the final syllable of the verb

Before starting the main discussion, I will briefly explain the morpho-phonemics of verb endings. When the basic final -*a* is added to a verb base ending in /l/, the final syllable of the verb becomes *la*. When followed by a word, the verb final syllable *la* is deleted, as shown in (6). This occurs only when the verb stem (BASE+F) has three syllables or more, and does not occur when the verb stem has less than three syllables, such as *pala*, as shown in (7), (Yoneda 2000: 173). This only happens for a verb whose base final is /l/, and not for other consonants.

(6) *jubambali*　　　　　　　　*íng'oma*.　　　　　　　　**simple present (CJ)**
　　 ju-bambal-il-a　　　　　　　íng'oma
　　 1SM-stretch.skin-APPL-BF　9.drum
　　 'He stretches a skin on the drum.'

(7) *jupala*　　　*íng'oma*. cf. **jupa íng'oma*　　　　　**simple present (CJ)**
　　 ju-pal-a　　　íng'oma
　　 1SM-want-BF　9.drum
　　 'He wants a drum.'

When a verb ending with -*aje* is not clause-final, the final syllable of the verb, *je*, is deleted, and appears as -*a*. This means that -*aje* never appears as -*aje*, because the verb ending with -*aje* (= CJ form) always requires an element after it. Although it appears always as -*a*, I still consider the underlying form of this suffix to be -*aje* and distinguish it from the basic final -*a*, because verb forms ending with the basic final suffix -*a* behave differently, as shown in (8).

(8)　a.　*tuhemala*　　　*ng'ómbe*.　　　　　　　　**simple near past (CJ)**
　　　　 tu-hemel-áje　　ng'ómbi
　　　　 1PL.SM-buy-CJF　10.cows
　　　　 'We bought cows (this morning).'

b. *tuheme*   *ng'ómbe*.   **simple present (CJ)**
   tu-hemel-a *ng'ómbi*
   1PL.SM-buy-BF 10.cow
   'We buy cows.'

As (8a) shows, the CJF *-aje* causes a change in the vowel quality of the final syllable of the verb base when it is suffixed to disyllabic or polysyllabic verb roots (Yoneda 2000: 170), and *tu-hemel-aje* becomes *tuhemalaje*. In addition, the final syllable is deleted due to the presence of the following element, and therefore the resultant form of the verb is *tuhemala*. In (8b), on the other hand, the basic final *-a* does not change the vowel of the final syllable of the verb base. The basic final *-a* is suffixed, and it becomes *tu-hemel-a,* and the final syllable *-la* is deleted due to the presence of the following element, and the stem *hemela* has three syllables. The resulting form of the verb is *tuheme*.

3 Focus strategies

Focus is defined here as the core new information, the element which the speaker considers to be the most prominent in the utterance (Yoneda 2008, 2010). This section discusses how different kinds of foci are marked in Matengo.

3.1 Term focus

For the expression of term focus—that is, when the focus is on subjects, objects, or adverbs—the CJ form is used.

3.1.1 Focus on subjects, objects or adverbs
The CJ form, such as simple far past, simple near past, simple present, and simple future, is used to express term focus, and the focused elements appear immediately after the verb (IAV) in these CJ forms[8]. One of the typical examples of term focus is when the focus is on the contrastive element, as shown in examples (9) to (11).

---

8 It is possible to use a cleft sentence to put an element in focus .
   ii) *ju-a-bí*   *María,* *joo* *a-n-jángátja*   *Tóm.*
       1SM-PST-BE.PF 1.Maria   1.RM   1SM-1.OM-help.CJF 1.Tom
       'It was Maria who helped Tom.'

(9) *ju-jemb-a Tóm, ngaa María.* **simple present (CJ)**
 1SM-sing-BF 1.Tom NEG 1.Maria
 'Not Maria but TOM will sing.'

(10) *María ju-i-hemel-aje ílasí, ngaa ílombi.* **simple future (CJ)**
 1.Maria 1SM-PST-buy-CJF 8.potatoes NEG 8.maizes
 'Maria will buy POTATOES not maizes.'

(11) *i-bi ílasí na íjabujabu.*
 8SM-BE.PF 8.potatoes and 8.yam
 ílasí ju-a-hemel-aje Tóm, íjabújabú ju-a-hemel-aje Sámuel.
 8.potatoes 1SM-PST-buy-CJF 1.Tom 8.yams 1SM-PST-buy-CJF 1.Samuel
 'There are potatoes and yams. TOM bought potatoes and SAMUEL bought yams.'
 simple far past (CJ)

Subject term focus and non-subject focus behave the same. Another typical example of term focus is new information, such as the answer to a wh-question, as shown in (12) to (16). Wh-interrogative words also appear IAV in the CJ form.

(12) *ju-lel-a nyane*[9]? **simple present (CJ)**
 1SM-cry-BF who
 'Who is crying?'
 ju-lel-a María.
 1SM-cry-BF 1.Maria
 'MARIA is crying.'

(13) *Kinúnda ju- telek-aje kike?* **simple near past (CJ)**
 1.Kinunda 1SM-cook-CJF what
 'What did Kinunda cook?'
 ju-telek-aje ínyama.
 1SM-cook-CJF 9.meat
 'He cooked MEAT.'

(14) *ju-í-kelabuk-aje lile?* **simple future (CJ)**
 1SM-FUT-return-CJF when
 'When will he return?'

---

[9] The last syllable of *wh*-interrogative words is usually deleted in a sentence, and *nyane* appears as *nya*. The same applies to *kike* in (13), *lile* in (14), and *kwako* in (15). They appear as *ki*, *li*, and *kwa* respectively.

ju-í-kelabuk-aje   kilábu.
1SM-FUT-return-CJF tomorrow
'He will return TOMORROW.'

(15) kitábu senzé gu-a-hemel-aje   kwako?   **simple far past (CJ)**
     7.book 7.this 2SG.SM-PST-buy-CJF where
     'Where did you buy this book?'
     n-a-hemel-aje   kú-soko.
     1SG.SM-PST-buy-CJF 17LOC-5.market
     'I bought (it) at the MARKET.'

(16) a. tu-som-a   na   amábu   mu-súmba   senzé.[10] **simple present (CJ)**
        1PL.SM-read-BF   with 1.mother 18LOC-7.room 7.this
        '{With whom do you read (in this room?)}We read WITH MOTHER in this room.'

     b. tu-som-a   mu-súmba   senzé na   amábu.   **simple present (CJ)**
        1PL.SM-read-BF   18LOC-7.room 7.this with 1.mother
        '{Where do you read (it) with your mother?}We read with mother IN THIS ROOM.'

(17) is an example with an indefinite noun *múndu* 'someone'. When the indefinite noun follows the verb, usually the DJ form is preferred and the use of the CJ form would be a little odd, because the element IAV in the CJ form is typically focused, and indefinite nouns usually cannot be focused.[11] This shows that the CJ form triggers an (exclusive) focus interpretation on the following element.

(17) a. ?ju-a-jemb-aje   múndu.   **simple far past (CJ)**
        1SM-PST-sing-CJF 1.person/someone
     b. ju-a-jemb-iti   múndu.   **perfect past (DJ)**
        1SM-PST-sing-PF   1.person/someone [thetic]
        'Someone sang.'

3.1.2 Relation among term focus, word order, and verb form
As we have seen, the CJ form is used to express term focus, and the elements placed IAV in the CJ form are focused. Two conditions are involved here: word

---

10 The examples in (16) show that IAV in the CJ form is the focus position. In colloquial speech, however, it is natural to put only the focused element without any following element. See Yoneda (2011) for more details of the relation between focus and postverbal elements.
11 Sentence (17a) would be appropriate when saying '(not an animal but) a human being sang' (Yoneda 2008).

order (IAV) and verb form (CJ form). The examples in (18) and (19) below show more clearly that information structure affects both word order and the choice of verb form.

'Samuel ran.'
(18) Simple far past (CJ)   (= (1))
    a.   *ju-a-butuk-aje   Samuél.*   [*Samuel* = focus]
        1SM-PST-run-CJF 1.Samuel
    b. **Samuél   ju-a-butuk-aje.*
        1.Samuel 1SM-PST-run-CJF

(19) Perfect (DJ)
    a.   *ju-a-butuk-iti   Samuél.*   [*Samuel* = not topic, not focus, thetic sentence]
        1SM-PST-run-PF 1.Samuel
    b.   *Samuél   ju-a-butuk-iti.*   [*Samuel* = topic]
        1.Samuel   1SM-PST-run-PF

The principle of information-structurally motivated sentence formation in Matengo is that 'Topical elements occur preverbally, and non-topical elements occur postverbally' (Yoneda 2008, 2010, 2011). This principle allows two types of non-topical elements to occur after the verb,[12] more specifically, in the IAV position (see Watters 1979; Buell 2006; Van der Wal 2009, 2011). The first type is a focused element like *Samuél* in (18a), which appears with the CJ form and is an appropriate answer to a question like 'Who ran?' The other type is an element which is neither focus nor topic like *Samuél* in (19a), i.e. a thetic utterance, which appears with the DJ form. This is appropriate, for example in an out-of-the-blue context or as an answer to 'What happened?'. When the DJ form is used and the subject is placed sentence initial as shown in (19b), *Samuél* is topical. The example (18b), in which the verb in the CJ form appears at the clause-final position, is ungrammatical.

These examples show how word order and the verb form relate to information structure in Matengo. Therefore, information structure is relevant in (at least) two areas in Matengo grammar: one is word order, and the other is the verb form. These points are summarized as follows:

Word order (Yoneda 2011: 755)
    Topical elements occur before the verb, and non-topical elements occur postverbally.
    The focused element, if there is any, occurs IAV.

---

12 See footnote 13.

Verb form (Yoneda 2009b, 2009c)
> When the element IAV is focused, the CJ form is used; when the element IAV is not focused, there is a strong preference to use the DJ form.

In summary, the occurrence of the CJ form involves both syntactic as well as information structural conditions: The CJ form cannot appear in the clause-final position, and the element which follows it is in focus. On the other hand, the DJ form has no such syntactic constraints or requirements on the informational value of a possible following element.

However, we have also seen that the CJ form is restricted to a certain TAM semantics, and hence in some cases, these requirements clash. What happens, for example, if object focus needs to be expressed in a DJ tense? Or vice versa if an intransitive verb is conjugated in a CJ tense? We will see how such cases happen and how these cases are solved in Section 4.

3.2 VP focus

When the focus is on VP, the CJ form is used, just like term focus, as shown in (20a) and (21a).

(20) 'Maria FRIED SWEET POTATOES, she didn't boil potatoes.'
    a. *María   ju-a-kalang-aje mbátata,   ngaa kú-tutu-a ílasí.*
       1.Maria 1SM-PST-fry-CJF 10.sweet potatoes NEG INF-boil-BF 8.potatoes
                                                                                                                simple far past (CJ)
    b. *María ju-a-tend-aje   kú-kalang-a mbátata,   ngaa kú-tutu-a ílasí.*
       1.Maria 1SM-PST-do-CJF INF-fry-BF   10.sweet potatoes NEG INF-boil-BF 8.potatoes
                                                                                                                  simple far past LVC

(21) '{What are they doing?} They are SELLING SWEET POTATOES.'
    a. *a-hemales-a   mbátata.*   **simple present (CJ)**
       2PL.SM-sell-BF 10.sweet potatoes
    b. *a-tend-a   kú-hemales-a mbátata.*   **simple present LVC**
       2PL.SM-do-BF   INF-sell-BF   10.sweet potatoes

It is also possible to use the light verb construction (LVC). The light verb *-tend-* 'to do' is followed by the infinitive content verb, as in (20b) and (21b). However, examples where the infinitive of the LVC is followed by yet another element, such as (20b) and (21b), are provided only when I ask my consultant if that is possible. The LVC with a following element seems to be not very natural although it is not ungrammatical, and using the CJ form, such as in (20a) and (21a), is a more natural utterance and preferable for VP focus.

The CJ form is used to express not only term focus but also VP focus, that is, (20a) could be used as an answer to both 'What are they buying?' and 'What are they doing?' However, again there are some exceptions for using the CJ form to express VP focus. We will examine this issue in Section 4.

3.3 Predicate-centred focus

Predicate-centred focus involves focus on the non-nominal, predicative element of a clause, such as the verb lexeme, TAM, and the truth-value of the utterance (Güldemann 2009; Morimoto in this volume).

3.3.1 Narrow focus on the verb lexeme

When the verb lexeme is focused, the LVC is used. Focus is on the verb lexeme in examples (22), (23a), and (24a). In (22), the light verb *-tend-* 'to do' is followed by *kúkalanga*, the infinitive content verb *-kalang-* 'to fry', as in the equivalent of 'Maria will do frying'. The light verb *-tend-* 'to do' is followed by *kúkina*, the infinitive content verb *-kin-* 'to dance' in (23a), and by *kúsoma*, the infinitive content verb *-som-* 'to read' in (24a) .

(22) María ju-í-tend-aje   kú-kalang-a, ngaa kú-tutu-a.   **simple future LVC**
      1.Maria 1SM-FUT-do-CJF INF-fry-BF   NEG INF-boil-BF
      'Maria will FRY (it), not boil (it).'

(23) a. ju-a-tend-aje   kú-kin-a.   **simple far past LVC**
         1SM-PST-do-CJF INF-dance-BF
         '{What did he do?} He DANCED.'
      b. #ju-a-kin-iti.   **perfect past (DJ)**
         1SM-PST-dance-PF

(24) a. n-tend-a   kú-som-a   péna (ngaa kú-handik-a). **simple present LVC**
         1SG.SM-do-BF   INF-read-BF only (NEG INF-write-BF)
      b. *n-som-a   péna.   **simple present (CJ)**
         1SG.SM -read-BF only
         'I am only READING (not writing).'

As shown in (23b), the DJ form is grammatical, but it puts emphasis on completion (see 3.3.2), and is not appropriate for showing focus on the verb lexeme. Example

(24b) shows that just a focus particle like 'only' is not sufficient to satisfy either the syntactic or the focus condition.

The examples in (25) show how different verb forms are used depending on where the focus is.

(25) a. *ju-a-tend-aje*   *kú-som-a.*   [verb lexeme focus]   **simple far past LVC**
1SM-PST-do-CJF   INF-read-BF
'He STUDIED.'

b. *ju-a-som-aje*   *mwikindamba.*   [term focus / VP focus]   **simple far past (CJ)**
1SM-PST-read-CJF   18LOC.7.hut
'He studied in a HUT. / He STUDIED IN A HUT.'

c. *ju-a-som-iti*   *mwikindamba.*   [idiomatic expression]   **perfect past (DJ)**
1SM-PST-read-PF   18LOC.7.hut
'He studied in a hut. (= He didn't have formal education)'

The focus is on the verb lexeme in (25a), on the element IAV in (25b). This is term focus, and it can be VP focus as well. 'To study in a hut' in (25c) is an idiomatic expression, which means 'to have only informal education'. It is interesting that this has an idiomatic reading. This could indicate that the following element cannot be focused (Fanselow and Lenertova 2011), and therefore the DJ form is used.

In examples (22) to (25), the light verb *-tend-* 'to do' is in the CJ form in all the a. examples, and focused verb lexemes *kúkina*, *kúkalanga*, and *kúsoma* are placed immediately after it. Thus, it seems that focus is on the element following the CJ verb form, as with term focus. However, the light verb appears in the DJ form when the following content verb is stative, as shown in (26a).

(26) a. *losí*   *lu-tend-iti*   *kú-nyolek-a.*   **perfect present LVC (DJ)**
11.river   11SM-do-PF   INF-be.deep-BF
'{What is the problem of the river, is it deep or rapid?} The river is DEEP'

b. **losí*   *lu-tend-a*   *kú-nyolek-a.*   **simple present LVC (CJ)**
11.river   11SM-do-BF   INF-be.deep-BF

In (26), *kúnyoleka* 'to be deep' is focused. The stative verbs always occur in the perfective present to express the present situation. When the focus is on such a verb lexeme, the content verb itself appears in infinitive form and the preceding light verb *-tend-* 'to do' appears in perfect present, the DJ form. Therefore, the LVC shows focus on the verb lexeme, regardless of the CJ/DJ alternation of the light verb.

3.3.2 Truth-value focus

To express focus on positive polarity or truth-value focus, the DJ form is used, as shown in (27) to (30).

(27) n-a-som-iti. **perfect past (DJ)**
1SG.SM-PST-read-PF
'{Did you read this book?} (Yes,) I did read (it).'

(28) a. María ju-a-telek-iti, ngaapa ju-a-jegw-iti **perfect past (DJ)**
1.Maria 1SM-PST-cook-PF NEG.PST 1SM-PST-forget-PF
'{Did Maria cook?/ Didn't Maria forget to cook?} Maria cooked, she didn't forget (it).'
b. María ju-a-telek-iti ínyama, ngaapa ju-a-jegw-iti.
1.Maria 1SM-PST-cook-PF 9.meat NEG.PST 1SM-PST-forget-PF
'Maria cooked meat, she didn't forget (it).'

(29) n-som-iti. **perfect present (DJ)**
1SG.SM-read-PF
'{Have you read this book?} (Yes,) I have read (it).'

(30) n-í-som-a. **confirming future (DJ)**
1SG.SM-FUT-read-PF
'{Will you surely read this book?) (Yes,) I will (surely) read (it).'

Of course, the answer *ee* 'yes' is most naturally used as an affirmative answer for polar questions. However, perfect forms put focus on the fact that it (has) happened, as shown in (27), (28), and (29). The verbs in perfect form usually appear clause-finally in this usage; nevertheless, some words may follow the verb, as shown in (28b).

(30) is in the 'confirming future'. As explained earlier in Section 2.1, it is a form used to confirm a future event,[13] and can be used only as a confirmation to questions like 'Will you do?' The verb in this form cannot take any following element, and it must always appear in the clause-final position.

3.3.3 TAM focus

TAM focus is the case where the focus is on the aspect of the verb, such as the completion of an action or being in progress.

---

[13] It is grammatically differentiated from the so-called definite future, which takes the form [*mwiti/ ngiti* + subjunctive] in Matengo (Yoneda 2006).

When the focus is on the completion, the perfect form is used, that is, the DJ form. In this case, as well, usually it appears without any following word.

(31) n-som-ití.   **perfect present (DJ)**
      1SG.SM-read-PF
      '{When will you read this book?} I HAVE ALREADY read (it).'

As shown in the translation, the utterance in (31) is appropriate as an answer to a question like 'Are you going to read?' or 'When are you reading?' and stresses the fact that the reading has already been completed. Focus is not on the action itself, but on the completive aspect of the action.

When the focus is on the fact that the action is in progress, the copular expression with a *be*-verb is used.

(32) tu-bí   mu-kú-lj-a.
      1PL.SM-be.PF   18LOC-INF-eat-BF
      'We ARE (IN THE MIDDLE OF) eating.'

(33) ju-a-bi   pu-kú-pomulel-a.
      1SM-PST-be.PF 16LOC-INF-rest-BF
      'He WAS (IN THE MIDDLE OF) resting.'

(34) n-i-bja   pu-kú-som-a.
      1SG.SM-FUT-be.CJF 16LOC-INF-rest-BF
      'I will BE (IN THE MIDDLE OF) reading.'

The expression in (32) is the equivalent of 'we are/have been in eating'; the *be*-verb in present perfect is followed by the locative prefix *mu-* 'in' and *kúlja*, the infinitive content verb *-lj-* 'to eat'. The expression in (33) is in the past tense, and in the equivalent of 'he was at resting,' the *be*-verb in the far past perfect is followed by the locative prefix *pu-* 'at' and the infinitive content verb *kúpomulela* 'to rest'. The locatives *mu-* 'in' and *pu-* 'at/on' are interchangeable. In both (32) and (33), that is, perfect aspect, the DJ form is used. However, in the future tense, as in (34), the *be*-verb appears in the CJ form; hence, here, the CJ/DJ alternation does not seem to be involved in the focus.

3.4 Summary of focus strategies

Our discussion up to this point can be summarized as follows:

- Term focus is expressed in the IAV position with the CJ form.
- VP focus is expressed with the CJ form.
- Narrow focus on the verb lexeme is expressed by the LVC.
    (-*tend*- 'to do' + infinitive of a content verb).
- Truth-value focus is expressed by the DJ form.
- TAM focus:
    Focus on perfect aspect is expressed by the perfect form, that is, the DJ form.
    Focus on progressive aspect is expressed by the copular expression.
    (*be*-verb + LOC-infinitive of a content verb)

These are the basic rules. They show that the CJ/DJ forms have different functions and are used appropriately depending on the information structure, specifically focus. However, as I have already mentioned, there are cases that do not follow these basic rules. As we have seen in Table 1, it is only in the subjunctive mood in Matengo that the CJ/DJ forms exist in pairs, but in the indicative this is not the case. The CJ form exists only in non-perfect (=simple) form, while the DJ form exists only in non-simple (perfect or confirmed) form in the indicative. As a result, sentences in a non-perfect aspect are associated with term focus or VP focus, while sentences in a perfect aspect would not be able to express term focus or VP focus. However, this ideal matching of course does not conform to the actual usage.

Table 2 shows how the CJ/DJ forms are distributed across the paradigm and used to express different focus types. The cells indicated by * are unacceptable forms since they do not satisfy the syntactic condition of clause-finality. The open cells without any marks are not ungrammatical, but do not satisfy the information structural condition shown above each cell. Cases that satisfy both the syntactic and information structural conditions are shown by the cells with √. We can see from this table how limited the cases with √ are in Matengo that respect both the syntactic and information structural conditions.

Now the question is, what would happen when aspectual, syntactic, and information structural requirements do not match in one way or another: If we want to express, for example, an utterance in simple near past, where the IAV element is non-focal, there is no available form because of aspectual problems. In the following section, we will see how these gaps and ungrammatical cases are treated.

4 Cases when the requirements conflict

Section 3 has shown examples of the case where the choice of the CJ/DJ forms is determined by information-structural conditions. However, facts are more

Table 2: Distribution of the CJ/DJ forms in the indicative mood.

					Informational condition			Syntactic condition
					Term /VP focus	Truth-value / TAM focus	Non-focus IAV	Clause-final
Past tense: a-	Simple past	SM- a- BASE	-aje	(CJ)	✓			*
	Perfect past	SM- a- BASE	-iti	(DJ)		✓	✓	✓
Present tense: ø-	Simple near past[14]	SM- ø- BASE(-it)	-áje	(CJ)	✓			*
	Perfect present	SM- ø- BASE	-iti	(DJ)		✓	✓	✓
	Simple present	SM- ø- BASE	-a	(CJ)	✓			*
Future tense: í-	Simple future	SM- í- BASE	-aje	(CJ)	✓	✓		*
	Confirming future	SM- í- BASE	-a	(DJ)	*	✓	*	✓

---

14 I place the simple near past in 'present' tense because the present tense marker ø- is used. In Matengo, the present tense marker ø- is used for simple near past and it is used to refer to the event in past (before the time of utterance) but as occurring on the same day. This seems to be related to the time recognition of Matengo people that the same day is 'present' (see Yoneda 2006 for more details).

complex, because three requirements, namely, informational, syntactic, and aspectual requirements, are interacting for the choice of the CJ/DJ forms, and sometimes they clash in a sentence since the CJ form and the DJ form do not exist in pairs. That is, the CJ form exists only with non-perfect, while the DJ form can only be perfect. This section discusses how gaps in Table 2 are filled.

4.1 Perfect vs. non-perfect in past tense

The conjoint final -*aje* also has the function of the 'non-perfect' aspect, and the perfect final -*iti* is the 'perfect' aspect. Therefore, there must be an aspectual difference between (35a) and (35b) in addition to whether or not *ínyama* 'meat' is in focus.

(35) 'My friend bought meat.'
    a. *nkósi gwa ju-a-hemel-aje ínyama.*   **simple far past (CJ)**
        1.friend 1.my 1SM-PST-buy-CJF 9.meat
    b. *nkósi gwa ju-a-hemel-iti ínyama.*   **perfect past (DJ)**
        1.friend 1.my 1SM-PST-buy-PF 9.meat

Native speakers of Matengo with whom I consulted explained the difference between (35a) and (35b) as follows: Example (35a) can be used not only as an answer to the question 'What did your friend buy?' but also to the question 'What was your friend buying at that time?' as an answer 'My friend was buying meat'. Or, it can be used to answer a question like 'Why were you there at that time?' as an answer '(I was here), because my friend was buying the meat.' Therefore, (35a) can be used both after the action of buying is completed and when the action was not finished. On the other hand, (35b) can refer only to the situation after the action is completed. Thus, according to this explanation, strictly speaking there is indeed an aspectual difference. Nevertheless, the distinction between perfect and non-perfect often becomes unclear in past tense, especially in cases where the presence/absence of term focus is in question, and the CJ form (non-perfect = simple) is used to show term focus. In other words, the informational requirement has priority over the aspectual requirement. A similar example is given in (36). Although, strictly speaking, there is an aspectual distinction between (36a) and

(36b), in the case when *kundza* 'outside' is in focus, (36a) is used regardless the aspectual difference.

(36) 'Children danced outside.'
    a. *báná*   *a-a-kín-aje*   *kundza.*   **simple far past (CJ)**
       2.children 2SM-PST-dance-CJF LOC17.outside

    b. *báná*   *a-a-kín-iti*   *kundza.*   **perfect past (DJ)**
       2.children 2SM-PST-dance-PF LOC17.outside

However, it is only in the case of past tense that the aspectual difference becomes insignificant and the verb forms can distinguish focus and non-focus. In other tenses, this is not possible.

4.2 The disjoint form with focus

The CJ/DJ forms exist almost in pairs in the past tense, because the aspectual difference denoted by each form is so minimal that it can be 'deprioritized', and information structure takes priority in the choice of these forms. Unlike past tense, however, the aspectual difference is too significant to be simply ignored for the sake of respecting the information structural conditions in present tense. Some verbs, especially inchoative or stative verbs, appear with perfect present to indicate the present (on going) situation, and with simple present to indicate habitual actions. Therefore, the perfect form, that is the DJ form, must be used to express the present situation regardless of focus or non-focus.

    When a predicate like *-gonel-* 'to fall asleep' expresses the present state or ongoing action, the DJ (perfect) form must be used regardless of what is in focus, as the CJ form would render the habitual reading. That means, term focus with such predicates must be expressed by the information structurally inappropriate DJ form. The use of the information structurally appropriate CJ simple form would give a different temporal semantics than intended.

(37) a. *ju-gonel-ití*   *mu-súmba*   *senzé.*   **perfect present (DJ)**
       1SM-fall.asleep-PF 18LOC-7.room 7.this
       '{Where is she sleeping?} She is (now) sleeping IN THIS ROOM.'
  cf. b. *ju-gonel-a*   *mu-súmba*   *senzé.*   **simple present (CJ)**
       1SM-fall.asleep-BF 18LOC-7.room 7.this
       '{Where does she usually sleep?} She (usually) sleeps IN THIS ROOM.'

(38) *jóó ju- gonel-ití   nyane ?*   **perfect present (DJ)**
      1RM 1SM-fall.asleep-PF who
      'Who is sleeping?'
      ju- gonel-ití   María.   **perfect present (DJ)**
      1SM-fall.asleep-PF Maria
      'MARIA is sleeping.'

(39) *ju-hwa-ití nyane?*   **perfect present (DJ)**
      1SM-die-PF who
      'Who has died?'
      ju-hwa-ití María.   **perfect present (DJ)**
      1SM-die-PF 1.Maria
      'MARIA has died.'

The verb *-gonel-* 'to fall asleep' occurs in the perfect present to express the state of being asleep. Even if we want to put focus on the element IAV, perfect present, the DJ form must be used, as shown in (37a) and (38). The CJ form would give the habitual meaning as shown in (37b), not in the state of being asleep. In (39), although the element IAV is clearly focused, the DJ form, the same form in the case of thetic meaning, is used, because again there is no alternative available. Here, aspect has priority over information structure.

The same solution is seen for a conditional clash in VP focus. (40a) is the example of using the DJ form for VP focus.

(40)   *ju-tend-a kike?*   **simple present (CJ)**
          1SM-do-BF what
          'What is he doing?'
     a.   *ju-gonel-iti   mu-sumba   sangu*   **perfect present (DJ)**
          1SM-fall.asleep-PF 18LOC-7.room 7.my
          'He is SLEEPING IN MY ROOM.'
    cf. b. *ju-som-a   mu-sumba   sangu*   **simple present (CJ)**
          1SM -read-BF 18LOC-room 7.my
          'He is STUDYING IN MY ROOM.'

Both (40a) and (40b) are the answers for the same question 'What is he doing (now)?' When the answer is 'he is sleeping in my room', and the focus is on VP, perfect present has to be used, as in (40a). Even the question itself is in the simple present, because the verb *-gonel-* 'to fall asleep' is inchoative, compared with (40b), the case of a dynamic verb.

The CJ form is the one that is used to express term focus and VP focus. However, in the case of inchoative and stative verbs in the present tense, in which the perfect aspect must be clearly maintained, the DJ form is substituted, because there is no appropriate CJ form to indicate perfect aspect. In the present tense, the syntactic requirement and the aspectual requirement are strictly obeyed, but the informational requirement is violated.

4.3 The conjoint form without focus

The opposite clash also occurs, that is, the case of a sentence without term focus in non-perfect aspect. As we have seen in Section 4.2, aspectual difference is strict in the present tense. This means that when non-perfect aspect is indicated, there is no other choice than using the simple form (the CJ form) to keep the appropriate aspect, even in a case where the sentence does not have term focus or VP focus. Moreover, when the CJ form is used, the syntactic restriction of non-finality must be observed.

4.3.1 "Dummy" focus

In order to satisfy the syntactic condition that the CJ form cannot be clause-final, a cognate object is used whenever possible as illustrated in (41).

(41) a. *ju-heng-a líhengu.* **simple present (CJ)**
 1SM-work-BF 5.work
 'He works/is working.' literal meaning: 'He is working work.'
 b. **ju-heng-a.* **simple present (CJ)**
 1SM-work-BF
 cf. c. *ju-heng-ití.* **perfect present (DJ)**
 1SM-work-PF
 'He has already worked.'

In order to express 'he works' in (41a), the simple present, the CJ form must be used even though there is no focus element in the IAV position, because here the DJ form is not available due to the aspectual requirement. The verb *-heng-* in (41) means 'to work'; therefore, the noun *líhengu* 'work' does not contain any informational value as focus. However, it needs to be there because of the syntactic restriction. Without this, the sentence is ungrammatical, as shown in (41b), and the perfect present (which is DJ and can appear clause-finally) leads to a different meaning, as shown in (41c). I call the elements that are placed IAV only to satisfy the syntactic condition "dummy" focus.

Likewise, the noun *mási* 'water' in (42a) does not have any informational value because the verb *-hog-* itself already has the meaning 'bathe', which naturally involves water. Nevertheless, it appears IAV in the CJ form as dummy focus just to satisfy the syntactic requirement.

(42) a. *mwana ju-hog-a mási.* [thetic] **simple present (CJ)**
       1.child 1SM-bathe-BF 6.water
       'A child is bathing water/a child bathes water.'
    b. **mwana ju-hog-a.* **simple present (CJ)**
       1.child 1SM-bathe-BF

Matengo has only a handful of cognate objects, so a more general way to satisfy the syntactic condition of the CJ form is just placing arguments at the IAV position even though they are not in narrow focus.

(43) *ji-kun-a   íhyula.* [thetic] **simple present (CJ)**
      9SM-rain-BF 9.rain
      'It is raining.'
(44) *ki-golok-a kijongu.* [thetic] **simple present (CJ)**
      7SM-fly-BF 7.bird
      'A bird is flying.'
(45) *mbomba ju-telek-a ngondi.* [thetic] **simple present (CJ)**
      1.woman 1SM-cook-BF 10.beans
      'A woman is cooking beans.'

(43) to (45) are examples of thetic sentences, neutral description, thus lacking term focus and VP focus, but the simple present (the CJ form) is used. The subject nouns in (43) and (44) and the object noun in (45) are in the IAV position. These nouns have to be there due to the syntactic restriction of the CJ form, although none of them is in narrow term focus and it is information-structurally suboptimal. The same sentence as (45) can be also used for term focus, such as the answer to the question 'What is the woman cooking?' or for VP focus, such as the answer to the question 'What is the woman doing?' Therefore, the exact information-structural interpretation of the sentence depends on the context. Only syntactic and aspectual, but not informational, requirements are respected here.

4.3.2 Light verb construction

There is another common way to satisfy the syntactic requirement of the CJ form, namely using the LVC, with *-tend-* 'do' and the infinitive verb, as we saw in Section 3.3.1 in the discussion of verb lexeme focus.

(46)　　mwana ju-tend-a　　kú-butuk-a.　　　　[thetic]　　**simple present LVC (CJ)**
　　　　1.child　1SM-do-BF　INF-run-BF
　　　　'A child is running.'

In (46) it seems that the verb lexeme *kúbutuka* 'to run' is focused, and it *is* used for that purpose. However, in this case, it is a thetic sentence and the infinitive verb *kúbutuka* 'to run' is not focused, it is only there for syntactic reasons. This happens often, for example, with intransitive verbs such as (47), or when the verb has only one internal argument and this is topicalized as shown in (48).

(47)　a.　*tu-í-tend-aje*　　　*ku-pomulel-a.*　　　　　　　**simple future LVC (CJ)**
　　　　　1PL.SM-FUT-do-CJF　INF-rest-BF
　　　　　'We will rest.'
　　　b.　* *tu-í-pomulel-aje.*　　　　　　　　　　　　　　**simple future (CJ)**
　　　　　1PL.SM-FUT-rest-CJF
(48)　　*kibę́ga*　　*n-tend-a*　　*kú-bom-a.*　　[*kibęga* is topic]　**simple present LVC (CJ)**
　　　　7.clay pot　1SG.SM-do-BF　INF-make-BF
　　　　'Clay pot, I make (it).'

4.4 Summary

According to what we have seen in this section, it seems that the morphology and syntactic position work together for the expression of focus, with some compromise, while respecting the "inviolable" syntactic constraint. This compromise is obviously due to the deficient CJ/DJ distribution in Matengo. It is a contrast to languages such as Makhuwa, which has a more complete CJ/DJ distribution.

Example (49) is an example of Makhuwa (Van der Wal 2006). The verb in (49a) has the CJ form, and *maláshi* 'grass' is focused. On the other hand, the verb in (49c) has the DJ form, so *maláshi* 'grass' is not in focus in (49c).

(49)　　Makhuwa (Van der Wal 2006: 235)
　　　a.　*enyómpé tsi-n-khúúrá malashí.*　　'The cows eat GRASS.'　　(CJ)
　　　　　cows　　　SM-PRS-eat　　grass
　　　b　**enyómpé tsi-n-khúúrá.*　　　　　　(The cows are eating.)　　(CJ)
　　　　　cows　　　SM-PRS-eat
　　　c.　*enyómpé tsi-náá-khúura maláshi.*　'The cows eat grass.'　　(DJ)
　　　　　cows　　　SM-PRS.DJ-eat　grass
　　　d.　*enyómpé tsi-náá-khúura.*　　　　　'The cows are eating.'　　(DJ)
　　　　　cows　　　SM-PRS.DJ-eat

Similar examples can be found in the subjunctive in Matengo. The verb in (50a) has the CJ form, and *míhambu minyáhi* 'new songs' is focused in (50a). On the other hand, the verb in (50c) has the DJ form, so *míhambu minyáhi* 'new songs' is not in focus in (50c). When there is no element after the verb, the DJ form is used as shown in (50d).

(50) Matengo
    a. *tu-jemb-aje   míhambu minyáhi.*   'Let's sing NEW SONGS.'   (CJ)
       1PL.SM-sing-CJF 4.songs   4.new
    b. **tu-jemb-aje.*   (Let's sing.)   (CJ)
       1PL.SM-sing-CJF
    c. *tu-jemb-i   míhambu minyáhi.*   'Let's sing new songs.'   (DJ)
       1PL.SM-sing-SF 4.songs   4.new
    d. *tu-jemb-i.*   'Let's sing.'   (DJ)
       1PL.SM-sing-SF

However, it is only in the subjunctive where the informational function of the CJ/DJ form is as clear as in Makhuwa. In the indicative, the mapping between the information structural function and the choice of the CJ/DJ forms is not always one-to-one, and, as we have seen, the treatment of focus cannot be as rigidly controlled compared to Makhuwa.

Table 3 shows a comparison of the CJ/DJ system in Makhuwa and Matengo, focusing on the present tense, where the aspectual difference between simple and perfect is significant.

The situation in Matengo is thus as follows: In the past tense, both the CJ and DJ forms exist, so that focus and non-focus can be distinguished by verb form, ignoring or "deprioritizing" the minimal aspectual difference. In the present tense, however, regardless of whether or not the IAV element is in focus, the DJ form must express the perfect aspect, since there is no CJ form that expresses the same aspect. Conversely, if the verb does not have a focused element, and

Table 3: Comparison of the conjoint/disjoint forms in Makhuwa and Matengo (Yoneda 2008).

	CJ (+ focus)		DJ (−focus)	
	Makhuwa	Matengo	Makhuwa	Matengo
Simple (non-perfect) present	Yes	Yes	Yes	No
Perfect present	Yes	No	Yes	Yes

                    use the DJ form   use the LVC or
                                            the CJ form +dummy focus

the perfect aspect does not convey the intended tense-aspectual meaning, then a "dummy" focus is placed after the CJ form, or the LVC is used in order to respect the syntactic requirement, as Table 3 shows.

5 Conclusion

In this chapter, I have discussed the syntactic, tense-aspectual and information-structural requirements on the CJ/DJ forms and the problematic cases. As a general rule, the CJ form is used to express term focus and VP focus, and the DJ form, predicate-centred focus. When there is no focused element after the verb (when there is no element after the verb and when there is a non-focused element), the DJ form is used. However, this choice of the verb form based on the presence or absence of focus sometimes becomes obscured. Requirements of information structure, syntax, and aspect interact, and sometimes conflict on the use of CJ/DJ forms. The deficient CJ/DJ distribution with aspectual imbalance makes the verb form choice intricate.

In the interaction of these requirements, they are not equally respected. According to what we have seen, information structure has priority over aspect in the past tense, where the aspectual difference is not significant. In the present tense, however, the aspectual requirement becomes essential and must be observed. The syntactic requirement is always strictly respected. Therefore, we can see the following hierarchy among requirements in the present tense:

(51)   syntactic condition > semantic (aspectual) condition > information structural condition

Here, the question might even be whether the CJ form indeed encodes focus. Clearly, there are strong tendencies that the element in IAV appears with the CJ form (Yoneda 2006, 2009b). In addition, there are unquestionable cases where the CJ form expresses focus, namely in the subjunctive, in which the CJ/DJ forms exist in pairs. However, as shown, IAV elements occurring with the CJ form are not always focused, and can sometimes express their focality with the DJ form in the indicative. If there is no appropriate verb form, another verb form can be used to compensate, thereby neglecting the informational value of the focus. There seem to be too many exceptions to say that encoding the presence/absence of focus is the function of the CJ/DJ verb form, and the CJ/DJ system in Matengo seems too incomplete to distinguish focus and non-focus. The only restriction for the use of these forms is the syntactic one. In order to satisfy this restriction, it becomes necessary to accept compromise and exceptions. As a result, the function of the CJ form as "marking focus" seems to become unclear. Concerning the positional focus marking, namely, IAV, if there is a focused element, it will be placed IAV and no other position in a clause. However, this does not mean that every element in IAV position has to be necessarily focused.[15] Matengo is a language that grammatically distinguishes topical elements from non-topical ones (Yoneda 2004, 2008, 2009a, 2009c, 2010, 2011). Focus, on the other hand, does not seem to be strictly under such grammatical control.

The relation between focus and the CJ/DJ forms or the position of IAV is summarized as follows: In the indicative, where the CJ/DJ forms do not exist in pairs, the morphology, namely the CJ form, is neither necessary nor a sufficient condition for the correct interpretation of focus, and word order, namely immediately after the verb position, is a necessary but not sufficient condition for the expression of focus. Therefore, neither of them is a sufficient condition and the CJ/DJ forms are not even a necessary condition for focus interpretation in Matengo.

In Matengo, word order has the function of expressing information structure. Therefore, topics and non-topics are expressed by their position in the sentence (Yoneda 2008, 2011). Thus, term focus, or at least the possibility of being the term focus is already indicated by IAV position; so what the verb form should express seems to be not what is focused, but rather what is NOT focused. Further investigation into the possibilities regarding the function of the DJ form, such as defocusing, is clearly needed. Other questions that arise include why Matengo keeps the CJ/DJ distinction in spite of such defectivity, whether this system is diachronically on its way out, and whether it is unique for Matengo, or what the situation of neighbouring languages is like. These questions will be worth investigating in future research.

---

15 Yoneda (2011) claims that there are different kinds of slots after the verb, namely, the focus slot IAV and non-topic/non-focus slot after the focus slots. When a sentence has an focused element, it is assigned to the focus slot, while when a sentence has non-focused element, the focus slot is kept empty and the non-focused element in the next slot is expressed IAV. This means that a focused element and a non-focused element are assigned to different slots, even though they both appear IAV. See Yoneda (2011) for more details.

iii) V   [focus] [non focus]
  ju-í-lomb-aje   *ngʼombe* ø.
  1SM-FUT-buy-CJF   9.cow
  "{Answer for "What will he buy?"} He will buy a cow."

iv) V   [focus] [non focus]
  ju-hik-iti   ø   *mundo.*
  1SM-arrive-SF   1.someone
  "{Hearing someone's knocking}Someone has come."

Abbreviations

1sg, 2sg: 1st person singular, 2nd person singular
1pl, 2pl: 1st person plural, 2nd person plural

APL	applicative	PF	perfect final
BE	*be*-(copular) verb	PreF	Prefinal
BF	basic final	PST	past
CJ	conjoint	REF	reflexive
DJ	disjoint	RM	relative marker
FUT	future	SF	subjunctive final
IAV	immediately after the verb	SM	subject marker
INF	Infinitive prefix	TM	tense marker.
LOC	locative marker		
NEG	negative		
CJF	conjoint final (=non-perfect final)		
OM	object marker		

Matengo has a noun class system. The number after each noun shows its noun class and the number after affixes show the noun class with which the affix agrees.

References

Buell, L. 2006. The Zulu conjoint/disjoint verb alternation: Focus or constituency? *ZAS Papers in Linguistics* 43. 9–30.

Fanselow, Gisbert & Denisa Lenertová. 2011. Left peripheral focus. Mismatches between syntax and information structure. *Natural Language & Linguistic Theory* 29. 169–209.

Güldemann, Tom. 2009. Predicate-centered focus types: A sample-based typological study in African languages. Application for Project B7 in the CRC 632 Information structure.

Guthrie, M., 1948. *The classification of the Bantu languages*. London: Oxford University Press.

Hyman, Larry. This volume. Disentangling Conjoint, Disjoint, Metatony, Tone Cases, Augments, Prosody, and Focus in Bantu.

Meeussen, A. E. 1959. *Essai de grammaire Rundi*. Tervuren: Musée Royale de l'Afrique Central.

Morimoto, Yukiko. This volume. The Kikuyu focus marker *nĩ*: formal and functional similarities to the conjoint/disjoint system.

Odden, David 1984. Formal correlates of focusing in Kimatuumbi. *Studies in African Linguistics* 15. 275–299.

Van der Wal, Jenneke. 2006. The disjoint verb form and an empty immediate after verb position in Makhuwa. *ZAS Papers in Linguistics* 43, 233–256.

Van der Wal, Jenneke. 2009. *Word order and information structure in Makhuwa-Enahara*. Utrecht: LOT.

Van der Wal, Jenneke. This volume. What is the conjoint/disjoint alternation in Bantu languages?

Yoneda, Nobuko. 2000. *A descriptive study of Matengo, a Bantu language of Tanzania*. Ph.D. dissertation, Tokyo University of Foreign Studies.

Yoneda, Nobuko. 2004. Matengo-go no shudai: ta no Bantu-shogo tono hikaku kara. In T. Masuoka(ed.), *Shudai no Taisho*, 171–190. Tokyo: Kuroshio-Shuppan.

Yoneda, Nobuko. 2005. Matengo-go no "hokan-go" to jouhou-kouzou. In S. Kato & H. Yoshida (eds.), *Gengo-Kenkyu no Shatei*, 189–211. Tokyo: Hitsuji-Shobo.

Yoneda, Nobuko. 2006. Matengo-go ni okeru "mirai" to "genzai": 2-shurui no jikan-kyokai. In M. Nakagawa & T. Sadanobu (eds.), *Gengoni Arawareru "Seken" to "Sekai"*, 129–151. Tokyo: Kuroshio- Shuppan.

Yoneda, Nobuko. 2008. Matengo-go no jouhou-kouzou to gojun. *Gengo-Kenkyu* 133. 107–132.

Yoneda, Nobuko. 2009a. Information structure and sentence formation in Matengo. In Manghyu Pak (ed.), *Current issues in unity and diversity of languages* (Selected papers from CIL 18), 443–453. Seoul: Linguistic Society of Korea.

Yoneda, Nobuko. 2009b. Matengo-go no dousi-katsuyoukei to shouten. *Journal of Swahili & African Studies* 20. 148–164.

Yoneda, Nobuko. 2010. Topical hierarchy and grammatical agreement in Matengo (N13). In K. Legère & C. Thornell (eds.), *Bantu Languages: Analysis, Description and Theory*, 315–323. Köln: Rüdiger Köppe Verlag.

Yoneda, Nobuko. 2011. Word order in Matengo (N13): Topicality and informational roles. *Lingua*. 121 (5). 754–771.

Language index

(Whole chapter pages are in bold)

Abo 109, 111, 112, 116, 118, 120
Adamawa 58, 62n, 96, 176n, 196, 197, 198
Aghem 48, 55, 58, 60, 62n, 63, 65, 65n, 66, 66n, 79, 79n, 83, 84, 85–8, 92, 97, 99, 102, 104, 119, 120, 294, 362
Armenian, Eastern 76, 95, 98, 99
Atlantic (Niger-Congo) 59, 80, 92, 98, 197
Austronesian 81

Bafia 111
Bakweri 111
Bantoid 62n, 79, 79n, 88, 92
Bantu (see individual languages)
Basaa 108, 109, 109n, 111, 120, 424
Baynunk 66n
Bemba (Cibemba) 4, 7, 15, 16, 19, 20, 24, 28, 30, 31, 33, 39, 47, 48, 51, 52, 55, 60, 61, 62n, 79, 83, 84, 88, 92, 99, 100, 102, 103, 111, 117, 119, 121, 184, 199, **258–294**, 295, 324, 327, 362, 401
Bembe 111
Benue-Congo 56, 62n, 119
Benue-Kwa 55, 59, 62, 98
Binja-Sud 111
Binza 111
Bodo 111
Bukusu (see Lubukusu)
Buli (Bantu) 197
Buli (Gur) 197

Chadic 65, 82, 97, 99
Chichewa (Chewa) 57, 70, 96, 287, 293, 316, 316n, 317, 327, 328, 348, 423
Chope 16
Chuwabo 16

Dagbani 197
Doyayo 55, 58, 62n, 96, 176n, 196, 198
Duala 108, 109, 111

Efik 56, 57, 62n
Ejagham 62n
Enya 111

Eton 111
Ewondo 111

Fula 79, 80, 92, 185

Giphende 113, 114, 118
Grassfields Bantu 65, 79n, 85, 102, 103
Gungbe 74, 75, 79, 80, 92, 93
Gur 4, 62n, 96, **175–199**
Gurene 197
Gwari 56, 62n

Hausa 64, 66, 185, 197
Haya 16, 19, 20, 28, 30, 31, 32, 33, 39, 51, 52, 58, 79, 83, 84, 88, 92, 104, 111, 112, 116, 117, 120, 168, 171, 288, 424
Herero (see Otjiherero)
Hindi 79, 80, 81, 82, 92, 93

Igbo 55, 62n

Jamaican Creole 79, 80, 92, 96

Kanuri 197, 199

Karitiâna 79, 80, 81, 92, 96, 99
Kikongo (Kongo) 78, 79, 83, 84, 88, 92, 95, 99, 113, 119, 172, 199, 423
Kikuyu (Gikuyu) 5, 10, 11, 55, 77, 79, 83, 84, 92, 98, **147–174**, 451
Kimatuumbi 16, 23, 26, 34, 42, 43, 59, 123, 139, 140, 145, 426n, 451
Kinyarwanda (Rwanda) 4, 8, 11, 16, 19, 20, 24, 27, 28, 29, 33, 39, 40, 45, 49, 51, 51n, 52, 54, 58, 62, 79, 83, 84, 89, 92, 111, 168n, 173, 328, **350–389**, 393n, 399, 401, 420, 421, 424
Kirundi (Rundi) 1, 2, 4, 6, 8, 9, 13, 15, 16, 19, 20, 26, 28, 33, 39, 41, 43, 44, 44n, 45, 46, 49, 51, 52, 54, 59, 62n, 73, 74, 79, 83, 84, 89, 90, 92, 98, 102, 111, 120, 173, 176, 265, 293, 357, 362, 365n, 375, 375–6n, 376, 378, 384, 385, 387, 388, **390–425**, 451

Kituba (Kikongo ya leta, Monokutuba) 79, 83, 84, 92
Konni 197
Kwa 55, 59, 62, 80, 95, 98, 175n, 185, 198, 199

Lamba 111
Lega 111
Lingala 79, 83, 84, 92, 99
Lozi 111
Lubukusu (Bukusu) 76, 96, 114, 348
Luganda 1, 11, 13, 104, 105, 106, 107, 112, 114, 115, 116, 117, 120, 174, 422, 424

Makhuwa (Emakhuwa) 5, 11, 13, 14, 15, 16, 19, 20, 23, 24, 26, 27, 28, 33, 34, 35, 39, 40, 44, 45, 47, 48, 50, 51, 52, 53, 60, 72, 72n, 73, 74, 75, 79, 83, 84, 88, 92, 99, 103, 106, 107, 109, 111, 115, 116, 121, 122, 123, 124, 130, 131n, 132, 135, 136n, 137, 138n, 140, 141, 142, 144, 146, 167, 174, 266, 294, 349, 362, 365n, 380n, 388, 401, 403, 425, 447, 448, 451 (see also Shangaji)
Makonde 2, 3, 4, 7, 16, 19, 20, 22, 28, 32, 33, 34, 37, 39, 51, 52, 54, 59, 111, **239–257**
Malay, Sri Lankan 66, 67
Matengo 4, 9, 16, 19, 20, 28, 33, 37, 38, 39, 40, 42, 44, 48, 51, 52, 60, 79, 83, 84, 88, 92, 139, 142, 146, 148n, 166, 166n, 167, 173, **426–452**
Mbole-Tooli 111
Mboshi 111
Mbuun 78, 79, 83, 84, 85, 88, 92, 95
Mituku 111
Moore 197

Naki 79, 79n, 83, 84, 88, 88n, 89, 92, 96
Ndebele 16, 39, 40, 60, 311, 318, 327, 328
Ndengeleko 10, 16, 36n, 60, 139, 140, 145
Ngizim 79, 80, 82, 83, 92, 93, 96
Niger-Congo 62, 98, 102, 173, 176, 196, 197, 199
Nyanga 111
Noni 79, 79n, 83, 84, 85, 88, 92, 97

Ostyak 64, 65, 66
Oti-Volta 175, 175n, 196, 197, 198, 199
Otjiherero (Herero)

Phuthi 299n, 321, 322, 327
Podoko 79, 80, 82, 83, 88, 92, 97
Pove 111

Quechua, Southern 92, 98

Ronga 16

Sambaa (Shambala) 16, 19, 20, 22, 24, 28, 33, 39, 51, 52, 59, 111
Sango 111
Selayar 79, 80, 81, 92, 96
Sereer 79, 80, 92
Shangaji (Shangaci) 4, 5, 10, 11, 36n, 43, 55, **122–146**
Símákonde (see Makonde)
Sinhala, Colloquial 55, 60, 66n, 67, 99
Songye 108, 111, 121
Sotho (Sesotho) 15, 16, 19, 20, 26, 28, 30, 33, 34, 39, 41, 46, 49, 51, 52, 58, 59, 60, 99, 111, 117, 201, 232, 238
Swati 16, 29, 42, 50, 60, 111, 167, 174, 232, 293, 319, 327, 328

Tangale 65, 66, 97
Teke 111
Tonga 16, 106, 107, 111, 115, 117, 119
Tshwa 16
Tsonga 16, 111
Tswana (Setswana) 4, 5, 15, 19, 20, 24, 26, 28, 30, 31, 33, 34, 39, 49, 51, 52, 54, 57, 58, 61, 62n, 95, 111, 117, 119, 176, 181, 198, **200–238**, 247, 257, 265, 268, 275, 286, 288, 293, 322, 324, 327, 348, 362, 387, 423
Tunen 79, 83, 84, 85, 88, 92, 98
Tupi 80
Turkish 75, 76, 96

Umbundu 114, 115, 116, 120, 320
Uralic 64

Venda 15, 16, 34, 34n, 59, 111

Xhosa 16, 22, 58, 111, 313, 320, 321, 322, 322n, 327, 425

Yom 4, 5, 10, 55, 62n, 66, 96, **175–199**
Yoruba 92, 95
Yucatec Maya 77, 78, 95, 96, 99

Zulu (Isizulu) 4, 9, 11, 12, 15, 16, 19, 20, 23, 24, 25, 28, 31, 33, 34, 39, 41, 43, 44, 45, 48, 49, 50, 51, 52, 53, 57, 58, 59, 60, 70, 71, 79, 83, 84, 88, 92, 93, 95, 99, 111, 119, 176, 195, 198, 250, 257, 265, 268n, 285, 292, 293, 294, **295–328, 329–349**, 362, 363, 365n, 373, 377, 380n, 386n, 387, 388, 389, 401, 423, 451

Subject index

affirmative particles 180n, 197
argument focus 84, 414, 415, 418
augment 4, 11, 62n, 100, 105–8, 109, 111, 112, 114, 114n, 115, 116, 118, 131n, 273, 289, 290, 347
auxiliary focus 103, 161, 365, 366, 371, 379, 384, 385, 386

background marking 5, 66, 102, 103, 104, 175, 177, 177n, 178, 179, 185–7, 191, 193, 194–5, 346, 366, 407, 413, 419

clause-finality 23n, 48, 63, 65, 70, 89, 111, 148, 165, 166, 170, 176, 188–197, 266, 351, 399–401, 410, 412, 419, 428–430, 434, 435, 438, 440, 441, 445
clitic 18, 19, 27, 45, 50, 66, 76, 113, 113n, 118, 128n, 136, 143n, 147–9, 149n, 150n, 162, 169, 170, 203, 204n, 216, 260, 260n, 261, 329, 340–5, 368, 369, 370, 378
constituency v, 4–5, 8–10, 14, 27, 33, 42, 45–8, 50–2, 56, 62–3, 112, 195, 269, 282n, 284–5, 287, 288n, 295, 297, 329, 335, 344, 350, 363, 377–81, 383, 385–6, 390, 392, 401, 412, 417, 421
coordinated verb phrases 343, 344, 345

dislocation 26, 27, 50, 100n, 113, 115, 287, 332n, 334, 338, 339, 375n

focus markers/particles 5, 8, 42, 56, 57, 64, 64n, 66, 72, 74, 77, 80, 81, 83, 93, 94, 102, 105n, 110, 118, 139n, 147, 152, 162, 168, 170, 171, 179, 179n, 182–4, 191, 197, 298, 362, 363n, 370, 378, 382, 384, 390, 418–21, 437
focus-based 8, 10, 25, 27, 42, 46, 47, 50–1, 56, 373, 379, 385

Immediately After the Noun (IAN) 117
Immediately After the Verb (IAV) v, 5, 6, 11, 20, 40, 48, 49, 52, 62–5, 68, 70, 72–5, 79, 80, 82–8, 91–4, 105–7, 109, 115–9, 124, 130, 200, 221, 232, 246–9, 251–6, 276, 279–84, 287, 291, 292, 431–4, 440, 441, 444–6 448–51
Immediately Before the Verb (IBV) 62, 64–6, 68, 75–6, 78–81, 83, 84, 86, 88, 91–3, 164n
imperfective 36, 37, 127, 128, 136, 140, 141, 141n, 178, 180, 188, 254, 254n, 264, 265, 353, 354
inflection 1, 7, 102, 102n, 112, 116, 125, 125n, 175, 177, 178–194, 196, 200
interfaces 3, 5, 8, 9, 12, 37, 48, 56, 222, 324, 329
intonation phrase 70

marked/unmarked 10, 11, 18, 34, 35, 43, 103, 104, 118, 148, 148n, 149, 159–60, 163, 164n, 165–6, 168, 169–70, 206, 245, 250, 256, 266, 288, 307, 366n, 380n, 384, 390, 415–7, 419
metatony 4, 5, 11, 62n, 100, 108–12, 116, 117, 117n, 118
morphosyntactic focus marking 4, 64–8

nominal 1, 17, 23, 52–5, 76, 78, 80, 86, 104–7, 107n, 109, 112–7, 177, 184, 195, 202, 252n, 259, 264, 287, 289–91, 402, 406, 410, 418
noun phrase 7, 55, 85–6, 117, 124, 142–4, 176–7, 252n, 400, 404, 410

object marker/marking 9, 18, 25, 25n, 26–7, 49, 50, 70, 115, 125, 125n, 138n, 204n, 233, 251, 259n, 262, 263, 267, 269, 270, 273, 277, 278, 287, 296–301, 304, 307, 310–3, 315, 316, 318, 319, 321n, 332, 352, 357, 358, 371–3, 375, 375n, 377–8, 400, 427

parameters 14–56, 62–68, 78, 79, 83, 84, 91
penultimate lengthening 3, 6, 7, 32, 54, 70, 123–4, 205, 218, 241, 242n, 243, 243n, 245–6, 248, 251, 255, 256, 287, 296n, 298, 299, 299n, 301, 305–9, 310, 310n,

Subject index — **457**

315, 316–7, 319, 320, 320n, 323–6, 341, 343, 344, 351n
perfect(ive) 29, 30, 31, 34, 37, 38, 84, 93, 104, 109, 111, 125n, 126, 126n, 127–8, 132, 136, 166n, 168, 177n, 178, 179, 180, 181, 185, 187, 197, 200, 202, 203, 203n, 205, 207, 214, 214n, 228, 230, 231, 234, 253, 263, 264, 265, 266, 274, 288, 330, 347, 351–5, 362, 381–5, 409, 429, 430, 437–45, 448, 449
phonological phrase/prosodic phrase 6, 8, 32, 33, 36, 54, 123, 123n, 124, 133, 241, 243, 245, 246, 248, 250, 251, 252n, 253, 254n, 255, 256, 268–72, 272n, 277, 278, 284, 290, 291, 298, 317, 317n, 329, 339, 340, 343, 344
predicate-centred focus 6, 8, 9, 10, 18, 41, 42, 68, 69, 91, 147, 148, 149, 151, 161–71, 183, 183n, 197, 390, 392, 401, 406–12, 414, 415, 417, 418, 420, 421, 436–9, 449
predicative lowering 4–5, 107, 109, 116, 131, 131n, 137, 143
progressive 11, 16, 29, 35, 36, 37, 40, 56, 101, 103, 104, 108, 115, 140, 144, 165, 166, 166n, 168, 168n, 171, 178, 180–1, 254, 254n, 262, 264, 272, 273, 360, 361n, 381, 382–5, 414, 420, 421, 440
pronominal 148, 184, 221, 371, 377, 403n, 410–2
pronoun 26, 45, 50, 82, 110, 117, 135, 177, 179, 179n, 187, 192, 202, 218, 246–8, 255, 400, 403n

relative clause 3, 18, 19, 29, 33–35, 37, 39, 76, 77, 87, 102–3, 104, 110, 112, 113, 116, 118, 124, 126, 150, 187, 191–3, 200n, 203, 216, 233, 238, 239n, 240, 244n, 249, 250–4, 254n, 256, 271, 282, 282n, 287, 290, 290n, 330, 356, 363, 363n, 364, 365, 366, 366n, 382, 383, 390, 395n, 397, 398, 405, 408, 414–5, 420, 421, 428n

segmental marking 28, 29, 31, 232, 264, 265, 272, 278, 286, 291, 321, 351–9, 362, 368
shared object 329, 340, 344, 345

tense, future 29, 30, 32, 38, 40, 93, 101, 103, 104, 109, 110, 111, 113, 151, 165n, 168, 178, 180, 181, 202, 230, 234, 235, 236, 237, 240, 249, 251, 255, 256, 259, 260, 262, 264, 265, 272–3, 278, 279, 284, 295, 296, 300, 301, 302, 303, 304n, 307, 309, 311–4, 315, 317–9, 323, 323n, 324, 325, 360, 361, 361n, 382, 383, 384, 384n, 385, 396, 419, 421, 428, 429, 431, 438, 438n, 439, 441
tense, past 2, 29, 31, 32, 36, 37, 38, 84, 101, 102, 104, 105, 109, 110, 111, 113, 126–8, 132, 138–40, 144, 168, 178, 180, 181, 240, 244, 254, 254n, 255–6, 262, 263, 265, 266, 268, 272–3, 275, 288, 288n, 295–6, 296n, 300–3, 307, 309, 313–323, 323n, 324, 325, 330, 331, 342, 351n, 353–362, 383, 385, 390, 393–394, 396, 397, 405n, 418, 420, 421, 427n, 429, 431, 434, 440, 441, 442–3, 449
tense, present 10, 16, 18, 19, 29, 30, 32, 33, 34, 35, 36, 37, 38, 39, 40, 56, 93, 100, 101, 104, 109, 110, 111, 113, 125n, 126, 127, 128, 128n, 130, 132, 136, 139, 140, 141, 144, 166, 202, 205, 208, 213, 219, 220, 221, 223, 224–5, 227, 230–1, 234, 240–1, 244, 247, 249, 250–5, 256, 264, 265, 266, 271, 276, 278, 288, 295, 296, 299, 301, 302, 303, 307–9, 310–2, 314, 315, 317, 318, 320, 325–6, 330–1, 351–3, 362, 363n, 365, 381–5, 390, 393, 396–7, 418, 420, 429, 430–7, 441, 443, 444–9
term focus 6, 9, 41, 42, 62, 63, 67–9, 71, 76, 77, 83, 91, 92, 94, 135, 147–52, 156, 158, 160, 163, 165, 166, 169, 170, 185, 186, 191, 194, 195, 275, 365, 370, 418, 431–3, 435–7, 440, 442, 443–6, 449, 450
tone cases 4, 5, 11, 62n, 100, 112–6, 118
tone, floating H tone 203, 203n, 216, 218, 219, 220, 242, 248, 263, 274, 356
tone, H tone deletion 351, 354, 356, 359, 361n, 362, 394, 394n, 395
tone, H tone domains 204, 204n, 205, 206–23, 299, 309, 310, 317
tone, H tone doubling 261ff
tone, H tone reduction 32, 116, 117, 168

tone, H tone shift 132, 133, 243, 246, 263, 264, 273, 289, 299, 299n, 301, 302, 303, 304, 304n, 305, 306, 309, 310, 310n, 311n, 312, 313, 315n, 317–21, 321n, 322, 323, 336, 341, 343, 350, 352, 353, 356, 357–8, 393n, 402, 405n

tone, H tone spreading 101, 113n, 114, 201, 203, 204n, 209–12, 214, 215, 243, 246–8, 259–64, 266–80, 283, 284–6, 288–291, 299, 301, 302, 304, 305, 306, 310, 310n, 311, 311n, 312–21, 321n

tone, melodic H tone 125, 125n, 126, 130, 132, 132n, 133, 272, 274, 320n, 324

topology 62, 63, 64–6, 68, 72, 75, 79–80, 84, 88, 92

truth focus 408, 409

verb focus 41, 69, 93, 109, 139n, 142, 144, 183n, 185, 276, 282, 284, 287, 371–2, 377, 384, 386

vP-internal position 295, 297, 301, 307, 332, 336–9, 342, 343n, 344, 345, 346, 369

wh-questions/interrogatives 64–5, 72, 73, 128n, 130, 136–7, 148, 152–9, 203, 216, 246, 248, 249n, 408, 432

www.ingramcontent.com/pod-product-compliance
Lightning Source LLC
Chambersburg PA
CBHW052009290426
44112CB00014B/2179